Bosnian, Croatian, Serbian,
a Textbook

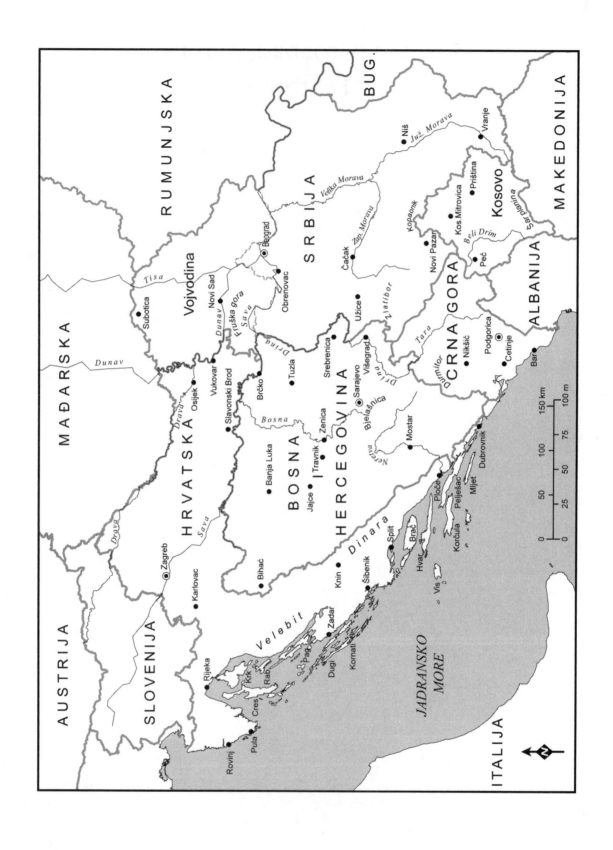

Bosnian, Croatian, Serbian, a Textbook

With Exercises and Basic Grammar

Second Edition

Ronelle Alexander
Ellen Elias-Bursać

The University of Wisconsin Press

The University of Wisconsin Press
1930 Monroe Street, 3rd Floor
Madison, Wisconsin 53711-2059
uwpress.wisc.edu

3 Henrietta Street
London WC2E 8LU England
eurospanbookstore.com

1 3 5 4 2

Printed in the United States of America

The Library of Congress has cataloged the first edition as follows:
Alexander, Ronelle.
Bosnian, Croatian, Serbian, a textbook: with exercises and
basic grammar / Ronelle Alexander and Ellen Elias-Bursać.
p.   cm.
Includes index.
ISBN 0-299-21204-1 (pbk.: alk. paper)
1. Bosnian Language—Grammar, Comparative—Croatian. 2. Bosnian
Language—Grammar, Comparative—Serbian. 3. Croatian Language—
Grammar, Comparative—Bosnian. 4. Croatian Language—Grammar,
Comparative—Serbian. 5. Serbian Language—Grammar, Comparative—
Bosnian. 6. Serbian Language—Grammar, Comparative—Croatian.
I. Elias-Bursać, Ellen. II. Title.
PG1229.A444   2006
491.8'282421—dc22
2006046201

Second edition ISBNs: 978-0-299-23654-0 (pbk.: alk. paper) — 978-0-299-23653-3 (e-book)

Publication of this book has been made possible in part by a grant
from the Peter N. Kujachich Endowment in Serbian and Montenegrin Studies
at the University of California, Berkeley.

✎ Contents

---

* The symbols B, C and S identify words or phrases which are used predominantly in the corresponding country or countries. The symbols E and J identify words that belong to the *ekavian* and *ijekavian* pronunciation areas, respectively.

❧ Preface to the Second Edition

The second edition of *Bosnian, Croatian, Serbian, A Textbook with Exercises and Basic Grammar* contains several new features. These include

- specific assignments and guidelines for self-study students
- commentary on Montenegrin culture and the status of the Montenegrin language (see p. 87)
- updated maps reflecting border changes in Serbia and Montenegro
- a new Appendix 9, listing all verbs introduced in *Textbook* by verb and accentual type
- expanded glossaries, including new vocabulary and more extensive referencing
- revisions and additions both in the grammar and exercise sections

Despite these changes the A exercises have remained unchanged, allowing one to continue to use the existing audio recordings (the only change is in the ordering of Lessons 16-19). Two sets of answer keys, one for the first edition and one for the second edition, are available at

www.bcsgrammarandtextbook.org.

Students: please read the *Guide for Students* on p. xiii ! Self-study learners should also read the *Guide for Teachers* p. xiv.

❧ Preface to the First Edition

When Yugoslavia broke up into smaller successor states, the language called Serbo-Croatian was replaced by Bosnian, Croatian, and Serbian. Accordingly, those who used to study Serbo-Croatian must now choose which of the three successor languages they wish to learn. Often they have no choice, and must simply study whichever of the three is being taught where they happen to be studying, and trust in the assurance that learning one will allow them to "get by" in either of the others. This book solves the problem by presenting all three together in a way that gives equal weight to each one. It demonstrates by example that although the three languages are very similar they are not identical: each has its own characteristic features. In particular, each expresses a unique historical and cultural identity. At the same time they are similar enough in grammar and vocabulary that they can be taught together in a single classroom.

The advantages of this method are numerous. Students are able to choose which of the three languages they want to focus on, and are able at the same time to learn as much (or as little) as they wish about each of the other two. Teachers are able to work in a single class with students who choose to learn one or more than one of the three languages. Universities in a quandary about which of the three languages to offer may rest assured that all are covered. In short, this book restores a sense of balance to the study of the region. It is dedicated both to the practicality of learning that which is similar as a unit, and to teaching the recognition of that which is unique and separate in the cultures of Bosnia and Herzegovina, Croatia, Serbia, and Montenegro. Among the reading selections are three short stories written especially for this book, one each from Bosnia and Herzegovina, Croatia, and Serbia. Reading selections also include letters composed by natives of the three languages, and poems by poets representing the several cultural traditions throughout the region covered by BCS.

We give basic dialogues in three versions, one each for Bosnian, Croatian and Serbian. Reading selections and illustrations also represent the three different languages and cultures. As the title of the book suggests, the ordering is always alphabetical: all three are given equal weight. In the construction of the dialogues and the choice of readings selections, we have attempted to strike a balance between that which is common to the three and that which is characteristic of each one's unique identity. Whenever we speak of grammar or vocabulary common to all three we use the acronym BCS, and whenever we speak of one of the three separate languages we use the initials B, C, or S. In the lesson vocabularies and in both glossaries, we have indicated words which are markedly B, C, or S by means of these abbreviations. It has not always been possible to make these identifications unambiguously, since the degree to which certain words are shared varies from word to word and speaker to speaker. In each instance we have made the most reasoned judgment on the basis of reference manuals and the advice of native language professionals.

This book has been designed to complement *Bosnian, Croatian, Serbian: A Grammar with Sociolinguistic Commentary*, and should if possible be used in conjunction with it. The *Grammar* provides more thorough grammar explanations than does the *Textbook*; it also contains a detailed outline of the social, political and historical circumstances which allow BCS to be viewed as one system utilized by three different languages. All language material in both books is accented according to a simpler marking system than found in native manuals, a system developed specifically for these books. We took as authoritative in assigning accents the following manuals: Vladimir Anić, *Veliki rječnik hrvatskoga jezika* (Zagreb, 2003); Lana Hudeček, Milica Mihaljević, Luka Vukojević, *Hrvatski jezični savjetnik* (Zagreb, 1999); Morton Benson (with the collaboration of Biljana Šljivić-Šimšić), *Serbocroatian-English Dictionary* (Belgrade and Philadelphia, 1971), and the six-volume *Rečnik srpskohrvatskog književnog jezika* (published by Matica srpska between 1967 and 1976).

Our intent in producing this book has been to bring some measure of unification to the fragmentation of language teaching which came about as a result of the wars accompanying the breakup of Yugoslavia. On a more personal level, we also both wish to give back (or forward) to students of generations to come something of what each of us has gained through many years of interaction with wonderful people, their cultures and their languages. The dialogues and exercises are an outgrowth of those developed by Ellen Elias-Bursać over a ten-year period teaching at Harvard University, and the underlying principle of the book (that of combining the unity of BCS and the separateness of B, C and S in a single volume) was devised by Ronelle Alexander, who also wrote all the grammar sections and devised the system of accentual marking.

We realize that not everyone will agree with all the choices we have made in our attempt to find a balance among the many different facets of usage, both official and colloquial, in the three languages. Our intent has been to give as true a picture as possible of existing usage within a framework that is accessible to students and usable in the classroom. We welcome reactions, comments, and errata via: http://www.bcsgrammarandtextbook.org.

ᔖ Acknowledgments

This book could never have been written without the help of many people. There were the language teachers whose creative work on language instruction shaped the thinking behind the exercises, in particular E. Wayles Browne, Marijana Cesarec, Patricia Chaput and Thomas F. Magner. There were ten years of students who asked good questions and taught the teachers as they learned. Funding from the Consortium for Language Teaching and Learning, and the opportunity to rely on the expertise of the Media Production Services and Harvard's Language Resource Center, made developing the materials possible. Undergraduate and graduate students, native speakers of Bosnian, Croatian or Serbian, contributed to the discussion and recording of the exercises, now available as the *Bosnian, Croatian, Serbian Audio Supplement*. Bruce Molay helped to develop a website for the draft version of the textbook, and the website made it possible for several teachers to teach from draft versions of the *Textbook* for two years. Both Steve Salemson and Gwen Walker of the University of Wisconsin Press gave encouragement and guidance, and Zagreb Film has allowed us to bring Professor Baltazar to America.

We extend special thanks to David Albahari and Muharem Bazdulj for writing stories especially for the *Textbook*, to Ferida Duraković for the use of her poem and to Miro Gavran for the use of his story. Thanks are also due to Dušan Radović's son, Desanka Maksimović's heirs, and the Vasko Popa Archive, for allowing the use of their poems and other writings; to the Milman Parry Collection of Oral Literature at Harvard University for the use of the transcribed excerpt from Stanko Pižurica's oral epic; and to Zrinka Babić-Jelaska for her delightful review exercises which inspired parts of Lesson 8.

To Nijaz Alić, Sue Brown, Svetlana Broz, Karen Chemel, Maša Čulumović, Mima Dedaić, David Elmer, Mirza Fehimović, Ana Galjanić, Rajka Gorup, Giga Graćan, Robert Greenberg, Nora Hampl, Vlada Ignjatović,Ređija Ikanović, Milan Ječmenica, Nada Ječmenica, Ivona Josipović, Marina Jovanović, Emir Kamenica, Jasmin Mehović, Mia Midenjak, Liba Mikić, Nataša Milas, David Mladinov, Kevin Moss, Zoran Mutić, Svetlana Nikolić, Đurđa Otržan, Vlado Pavlinić, Emina Peljto, Haso Peljto, Nada Petković, Azra Pravdić, Slobodan Radoman, Jasmina Riđanović, Midhat Riđanović, Jeff Spurr, Obrad Šćepanović, Catherine Škarica, Jasna Šojer, Toma Tasovac, Mary Thompson-Popović, Charles Ward and Milka Zečević we express heartfelt thanks in the name of the students who will benefit from the many ways they have given of their time and expertise. Special thanks are due to Natalija Novta and Aida Vidan for their unstinting dedication to the project, to Traci Lindsey for her fine editing, and to Dragan Momirović, Darko Poslek and Srđan Vujica for their help with the letters in Lesson 16. Acknowledgments for photographs, maps and fonts can be found on p. 497.

✎ Guide for students

Welcome to the study of BCS. You will find that the cultures of Bosnia and Herzegovina, Croatia, Montenegro, and Serbia have a great deal to offer. There are movies, music, poetry and fiction, a compelling history, and political issues that have shaped not only the Balkans but also the world. This book will help you gain access to them.

Students, whether enrolled in a course or working on their own, who choose to study these languages generally have a clear sense of why they are doing so – whether for reasons of intellectual curiosity, employment, family, scholarship or research – and often they know in advance which of the three languages they are interested in learning. Other students may be intrigued by the general area, and wish to acquire an overall knowledge of its languages. This textbook furnishes the tools students need to master any one of the three (Bosnian, Croatian, or Serbian) while at the same time allowing them familiarity with the other two.

The first eight lessons introduce the cases and the past and present tenses, and the next two give full treatment of the future and the past tenses. Lessons 11-15 deal with more advanced grammatical issues such as comparatives, numbers, conditional and participial usage, and aspect, while Lessons 16-20 provide practice in reading. Brief grammar explanations accompany most lessons; more detailed explanations on all topics are available in the book's companion volume, *Bosnian, Croatian, Serbian: A Grammar with Sociolinguistic Commentary*. Recordings of the exercises in Lessons 1-14 and of the poems and the stories are available on CD as a separate unit called *Bosnian, Croatian, Serbian Audio Supplement*. Poetry is the focus of Lessons 17-19 because poems by their nature exploit the mechanics of language and will help reinforce your mastery of the grammar. There are photographs all through the *Textbook*: use these both as examples of the language in action and as material for discussion. And, of course, enjoy *Profesor Baltazar*!

The Appendices provide many useful resources. In them you will find a 24-page section of paradigms, a guide to conjugation listing all the verbs which are used in the *Textbook*, a list of the recordings in the audio supplement, a BCS-English glossary with about 5000 entries and an English-BCS glossary with 3700 entries.

Surround yourself with the language as much as you can while you study it. If you can find a subtitled film, watch it at least twice. Get a recording of the kind of music you like from the BCS region and listen to a song until you can sing it. Visit www.bcsgrammarandtextbook.org for useful internet links, reading lists and information about films and music.

ᕲ Guide for teachers

In courses designed for the study of Bosnian, Croatian, Serbian (referred to throughout this book as BCS), there are bound to be some students intent on the study of Bosnian, some on the study of Croatian and some on the study of Serbian. This course is designed to meet the needs of all these students. Most students will decide during the first week of class which of the three [B, C, or S] to focus on in spoken and written work. If they stay with that choice for at least one semester, they can not only gain a coherent spoken and written mastery of their chosen language, but also learn about the other two from their classmates.

Although the in-class exercises and drills may be used by the class as a group, they are best suited for work in smaller groups of two or three students each. You will find that a student speaking Croatian can easily go through an exercise paired with a student speaking Bosnian, each of them using their version as a guide; the same is true of Serbian / Bosnian or Serbian / Croatian pairs. Each student should choose a name from among those listed in the Appendix on page 317 and use it throughout the semester as his or her in-class name, substituting this name for the numbers 1 or 2 which identify the speakers in each exercise.

Optimum use of the exercises and drills

The teacher should first introduce a new exercise or drill by reading it aloud and then having the students repeat it as a group. After this the teacher should assign each student a partner. Even in a class of only four or five, students benefit from working in pairs or threes, as this gives them the chance to speak more, and to try things they might be reluctant to try in front of a larger group. Once each student has tried all the roles, they should then go through the exercises again, replacing the italicized words and expressions with the suggestions listed in the section marked with the symbol ☞.

The early lessons refer to props to be used in the classroom. These are listed under the heading called *rekviziti*. For instance, the props for Lesson 1 are: *pas* (dog), *mačka* (cat), *bilježnica* [C] *sveska* [S] *teka* [B] (notebook), *knjiga* (book), *papir* (paper), *cipela* (shoe), *auto* (car). The more of the *rekviziti* the teacher can supply in the classroom for each lesson, either as real objects or as paper cut-outs, the easier it will be for students to master vocabulary and grammar. While students are working in pairs or threes, the instructor should circulate around the classroom, visiting each pair of students to respond to questions that may arise and to make corrections and suggestions. Whenever possible, students should use props, and go through exercises on their feet, with their partner or partners. Ideally, class time should be punctuated by several sessions in partner pairs, interspersed with grammar and other explanations addressed to the class as a whole.

Organization of the lessons

Each lesson has three sections of material. The "**A**" section includes demonstration exercises. If a course meets three or more times a week for an hour, an **A** section exercise might be used to start a class, while courses organized in one or two longer sessions can use the **A** sections to punctuate segments of the session. After the class works through an **A** section, students may be assigned to perform it as a skit, or to use it as a model on which they base an exchange of their own design.

The "**B**" section includes drills for further in-class practice on the grammar set forth in the A section exercises, and the "**C**" section includes homework assignments. Vocabulary lists give words new to that lesson in alphabetical order; the Glossaries at the back of the book list all words from the lessons plus some additional vocabulary. Grammar explanations in this textbook are brief, since much fuller information is given in the companion volume *Bosnian, Croatian, Serbian: A Grammar with Sociolinguistic Commentary*, whose first fifteen chapters are designed to complement Lessons 1-15 of this *Textbook*. Boldfaced numbers in brackets direct the student to the section in *Grammar* which contains a more extensive discussion of any one grammar point.

Designation of differing forms

The symbols B, C, and S identify words which are used predominantly (or exclusively) in the corresponding country or countries and less so (or not at all) in the others. The symbols E and J identify words that belong to the *ekavian* and *ijekavian* pronunciation areas, respectively. The B, C, S symbols are used throughout the book, while the E, J symbols appear in the prompts below exercises and in the glossary (but not in vocabulary boxes, since the words in question usually occur next to one another and the differences are easy to spot). Croatian and Bosnian use *ijekavian* pronunciation exclusively, while Serbian usage includes speakers of both *ekavian* and *ijekavian*. For the most part the Serbian exercises use *ekavian* examples but there are a few examples of Serbian *ijekavian* usage; these are identified as such.

Titles and exercises throughout the book are given in Bosnian, Croatian and Serbian versions when there are differences. The order in which these are given always corresponds to the order "B,C,S". Thus, *ijekavian* forms (marked [J]) precede *ekavian* ones (marked [E]), and B forms are always listed first. For example: *Vježbe* [J] *Vežbe* [E] and *Domaći zadatak* [B,S] *Domaća zadaća* [C]. The only exception concerns titles of published works which are given in the original form only, for example: *Pingvin Charlie* or *Ljepotica i zvijer*.

If a word in the vocabulary lists is NOT followed by one of these bracketed designations, this means that it is used in the same way by all speakers of Bosnian, Croatian and Serbian. If a word is used with the same meaning in both Bosnian and Croatian, it is marked [B,C], and if it is used with the same meaning in both Bosnian and Serbian it is marked [B,S]. In the few instances when a word is marked [B,C,S], this means that the word in question is used in all three, but that one of the three also uses another word in this meaning. For example: *avion* [B,C,S] *zrakoplov* [C] "airplane"; or *stric* [B,C,S] *amidža* [B] "[paternal] uncle."

When the prompts listed in the instructions below exercises include replacement vocabulary options, these are given in alphabetical order. If any one replacement option has differing forms, the set of forms is given as a single unit comprising the B, C, and S words, also in alphabetical order. Here is an example, taken from Lesson 4, exercise A3. Note the sequencing for "orange," "bread," "cheese" within the larger list.

☞**For other snacks use**: jabuka, naranča [C] narandža [B] pomorandža [S], komad hljeba [B,S] komad kruha [C] parče hleba [S], komad sira [B,C] parče sira [B,S], kreker, kruška, orah, slatkiš, šljiva, voće.

Organization of vocabulary boxes within lessons

In the vocabulary lists of all lessons, **nouns** are given in the nominative singular form; when the form of the stem is different in other cases, the genitive singular is given as well. Up through Lesson 7, **adjectives** are given in masculine, neuter and feminine forms, and both the infinitive and 1st person singular are given for every **verb**. Starting from Lesson 8, only the dictionary form (masculine singular short form) is given for adjectives, except in those instances where the stem of the masculine form is different from that of other forms: for these adjectives the feminine singular is also given. After this point, the 1st singular form of verbs is given only when it is not directly predictable from the infinitive form. Since the form of an **adverb** is equivalent to the neuter singular adjective form, it is assumed by Lesson 3 that students will be able to derive adverbs from the corresponding adjective.

Accent

In BCS, as in most other languages, only one syllable per word is accented. All vowels are either *long* or *short*, and accented vowels carry either *falling* or *rising* tone. It is not necessary to teach all elements of this complex accentual system, either at the outset or at all, since one can communicate perfectly well by simply knowing the place of accent and a few important instances of vowel length. It is recommended that students mark the accent-bearing syllable in each word in their written work. It is not necessary for them to specifically learn other components of the accent markings unless they or their teachers desire it. For those who do want (now or eventually) to learn the full system, all examples in this book are marked for all components of the accent.

Most books which mark BCS accent use a system of five marks. This book uses a simpler system while still managing to convey the same information. Only two marks are used. The underscore *(a)* means that a vowel is long, and the grave accent *(à)*, means that a vowel bears rising accent. A long rising vowel, therefore, is one which has both these marks, as in the word *(glàva)*, and a short rising vowel is one which has only the grave accent, as in *(vòda)*. If no grave mark is present, then the assumption is that the word has falling accent on the first (or only) syllable, either long, as in *(jā)*, or short, as in *(mačka)*.

The "accent" of each word, therefore, is a complex of several factors. These include place of accent, presence or absence of length, and rising or falling tone. In certain instances, the form of the accent will change in different grammatical forms of the word; these changes follow recognizable patterns and are identified in vocabulary lists. For more on the nature of rising and falling accent, and on accentual shifts conditioned by grammatical form, see Chapter 19 of *Bosnian, Croatian, Serbian: A Grammar with Sociolinguistic Commentary*.

Unaccented words and clitics

A small number of words are *unaccented*. This means that they do not carry any accent at all, but rather are pronounced together with a neighboring word, sharing its accent. This group of words includes all prepositions, the negative particle *(ne)* when used before a verb form, and a set of words called clitics. Clitics are object pronouns *(ju, je, ga, ih, joj, mu, im, nas, vas, nam, vam)*, auxiliary verbs *(sam, si, je, smo, ste, su; ću, ćeš, će, ćete, će)*, the question particle *li*, and the particle *se*. Clitics are never accented, although two of them do contain long vowels (the object pronoun *joj* and the 3rd person plural clitic *će*).

When a present tense verb form has falling accent (necessarily on the first syllable) and is preceded by the negative particle, this particle will always draw the accent to itself, as short rising (for instance, *kāžem* vs. *nè kāžem*). Similarly, the accent can shift to the preposition from a pronoun or noun object; this occurs most frequently in Bosnian. When the grave mark appears on the negative particle or the preposition, the word following does *not* have an accent, but is rather pronounced together with the preceding preposition or negative particle, as a single unit.

1st	first person	Gsg	genitive singular
2nd	second person	(I)	imperfective aspect
3rd	third person	*indecl.*	indeclinable
abbr.	abbreviation	inf.	infinitive
adj.	adjective	Instr	instrumental case
adj. form	word has meaning of a noun but form of an adjective	(I/P)	both imperfective and perfective aspect
adv.	adverb	*Isg*	instrumental singular
Acc	accusative case	[J]	ijekavian word or words
Apl	accusative plural	[J] [B/S]	ijekavian words specific to
Asg	accusative singular		Bosnian and Serbian
aux	auxiliary form		ijekavian usage
[B]	Bosnian usage	Loc	locative case
[B,C]	Bosnian and Croatian usage	Lsg	locative singular
[B,C,S]	Bosnian, Croatian and Serbian usage (where there also exists another word or phrase which is used in only one or two of the others)	*m, masc.*	masculine
		n, neut.	neuter
		Nom	nominative
		Npl	nominative plural
		Nsg	nominative singular
[B,S]	Bosnian and Serbian usage	(P)	perfective aspect
[C]	Croatian usage	pl	plural
coll.	collective	*(pl form)*	word exists only in plural form
colloq.	colloquial	*prep.*	preposition
cons.	consonant	pres.	present tense
Dat-Loc	dative-locative case	*pron.*	pronoun
DLsg	dative-locative singular	*pron.adj.*	pronominal adjective
DLIpl	dative-locative-instrumental plural	*quest.*	question
		[S]	Serbian usage
[E]	ekavian word or words	sg	singular
e.g.	for example	Voc	vocative case
f	feminine		
fem.	feminine		
(f sg form)	word takes endings of a feminine singular noun		
Gen	genitive case		
Gpl	genitive plural		

* see p. 313 for abbreviations used in the appendices and p. 389 for abbreviations used in the glossaries.

Sarajevo

Zagreb

Belgrade

Bosnian, Croatian, Serbian,
a Textbook

Prva lekcija • Lesson One

Rekviziti [**Props**]: àuto, bìlježnica [C] sveska [S] tȅka [B], cìpela, ključ, knjiga, mačka, òlovka, pàpir, pas, pìsmo, udžbenik.

A1   ⊙1,2 [See p. 383]

VOCABULARY

a	and, but	prvi, prvo, prva	first
biti	to be	sam	[I] am
bok! [C]	hi! bye!	si	*(familiar)* [you] are
ćao! [B,S]	hi! bye!	stùdent	student
ciao [C]	hi! bye!	ti	*(familiar)* you
i	and	tko [C]	who
ja	I	zdravo! [B,S]	hi! bye!
kàko	how	zòvem se	my name is [= I am called]
ko [B,S]	who	zòveš se	your name is [= you are called]
lèkcija	lesson	zvati se	to be called

KAKO SE ZOVEŠ?

Bosnian	Croatian	Serbian Latin	Serbian Cyrillic
1. Zdravo!	1. Bok!	1. Ćao!	1. Ћао!
2. Zdravo! Ko si ti?	2. Bok! Tko si ti?	2. Ćao! Ko si ti?	2. Ћао! Ко си ти?
1. Ja sam stùdent i zòvem se .... A kàko se ti zòveš?	1. Ja sam stùdent i zòvem se .... A kàko se ti zòveš?	1. Ja sam stùdent i zòvem se .... A kàko se ti zòveš?	1. Ja сам студент, и зовем се. .... А кàко се ти зовеш?
2. Zòvem se	2. Zòvem se	2. Zòvem se	2. Зòвем се ....

✍ **Insert** your own name in the appropriate blank. [For translations of A exercises see Appendix 10.]

The words **bok**, **ciao**, **ćao** and **zdravo** are used both as 'hello' and 'goodbye' among colleagues, acquaintances, or people of the same age. [For more information on vocabulary see Glossaries in the Appendix.]

**GRAMMAR**

* Alphabets and sounds *

Two alphabets are in use in the region where B, C, and S are spoken, called "Latin" and "Cyrillic." S uses both alphabets while B and C use the Latin alphabet. [1] Learning to pronounce B, C, or S is easy, because each alphabet letter corresponds to only one sound. [2] See p. 315 for more on pronunciation and alphabet, and p. xvi for explanation of the accentuation system. Numbers in brackets in the grammar sections refer to more detailed explanations in *Bosnian, Croatian, Serbian: A Grammar with Sociolinguistic Commentary*.

* Verb conjugation *

Every verb has six forms in the present tense. [7a] Here is the verb *zvati se,* used to identify a person's name. The particle *se* accompanies the verb but does not always follow the verb directly. Rather,

zòvem se	I am called	*zòvemo se*	we are called
zòveš se	you are called	*zòvete se*	you are called
zòve se	s/he is called	*zòvu se*	they are called

the particle *se* is required to be in the second position of the sentence, no matter where the verb occurs. This is true for any verb that occurs with the particle *se*, such as *kàže se* "one says." [12a-b]

* Singular and plural *you* *

Use the singular form *ti* (and the verb form ending in *-š*) to refer to a single person you know well. Use the plural form *vi* (and the verb ending in *-te*) to refer either to a group of people or to a single person you are on more distant, polite terms with. [6]

* The verb *to be* *

The usual forms of the verb *biti* "to be" are short, and cannot occur alone at the beginning of a sentence. They are always placed in the second position of the word or clause. [7b] The chart to the right gives the forms.

sam	[I] am	*smo*	[we] are
si	[you] are	*ste*	[you] are
je	[s/he] is	*su*	[they] are

* Vocabulary differences *

A number of words have different forms in Bosnian, Croatian and Serbian. For instance, the word meaning "who" is *ko* in B and S, and *tko* in C, while the word for "what" is *šta* in B and S, and *što* in C.

 A2   ⊙3,4,5,6,7,8

VOCABULARY

auto	car	olovka	pencil
bilježnica [C]	notebook	on	he, it
cipela	shoe	ona	she, it
da	yes	ono	it
da li [B,S]	[in questions]	ovaj, ovo, ova	this
ime	name	ovo je	this is
je	is	papir	paper
ključ	key	pas	dog
knjiga	book	pismo	letter, envelope
li [B,C]	[in questions]	pitanje	question
mačka	cat	sveska [S]	notebook
moj, moje, moja	my, mine	šta [B,S]	what?
na engleskom	in English	što [C]	what?
naš, naše, naša	our, ours	taj, to, ta	this, that
ne	no	tamo	there
nije	is not	teka [B]	notebook
njegov, njegovo, njegova	his	tvoj, tvoje, tvoja	(familiar) your, yours
njen, njeno, njena [B,C,S]	her, hers	to	this, that
njezin, njezino, njezina [C]	her, hers	udžbenik	textbook
njihov, njihovo, njihova	their, theirs	vaš, vaše, vaša	(polite) your, yours

ŠTA JE OVO? [B,S] ŠTO JE OVO? [C]

Bosnian	Croatian	Serbian Latin	Serbian Cyrillic
1. Šta je ovo?	1. Što je ovo?	1. Šta je ovo?	1. Шта је ово?
2. To je *olovka*.	2. To je *olovka*.	2. To je *olovka*.	2. То је *оловка*.
1. Je li *tvoja*?	1. Je li *tvoja*?	1. Da li je *tvoja*?	1. Да ли је *твоја*?
2. Da, *moja* je.	2. Da, *moja* je.	2. Da, *moja* je.	2. Да, *моја* је.
1. Ne, ne! Nije *tvoja*!	1. Ne, ne! Nije *tvoja*!	1. Ne, ne! Nije *tvoja*!	1. Не, не! Није *твоја*!
Njena je!	*Njezina* je!	*Njena* je!	*Њена* је!

✍ **Replace** *olovka* with bilježnica [C] sveska [S] teka [B], cipela, mačka. **Replace the possessives** *tvoj*, *moj* **and** *njen* [B,S] *njezin* [C] **with** naš, njegov, njihov, vaš.

Bosnian	Croatian	Serbian Latin	Serbian Cyrillic
1. Šta je ovo?	1. Što je ovo?	1. Šta je ovo?	1. Шта је ово?
2. To je *udžbenik.*	2. To je *udžbenik.*	2. To je *udžbenik.*	2. То је *уџбеник.*
1. Je li *tvoj?*	1. Je li *tvoj?*	1. Da li je *tvoj?*	1. Да ли је *твој?*
2. Da, *moj* je.	2. Da, *moj* je.	2. Da, *moj* je.	2. Да, *мој* је.
1. Ne, ne! Nije *tvoj!* *Njen* je!	1. Ne, ne! Nije *tvoj!* *Njezin* je!	1. Ne, ne! Nije *tvoj!* *Njen* je!	1. Не, не! Није *твој!* Њен је!

☞ **Replace** *udžbenik* **with** auto, papir, pas, ključ **and use possessives** njegov, naš, vaš, njihov.

Bosnian	Croatian	Serbian Latin	Serbian Cyrillic
1. Šta je ovo?	1. Što je ovo?	1. Šta je ovo?	1. Шта је ово?
2. To je *pismo.*	2. To je *pismo.*	2. To je *pismo.*	2. То је *писмо.*
1. Je li *tvoje?*	1. Je li *tvoje?*	1. Da li je *tvoje?*	1. Да ли је *твоје?*
2. Da, *moje* je.	2. Da, *moje* je.	2. Da, *moje* je.	2. Да, *моје* је.
1. Ne! Nije *tvoje! Moje* je!	1. Ne! Nije *tvoje! Moje* je!	1. Ne! Nije *tvoje!* *Moje* je!	1. Не! Није *твоје!* *Moje* је!

☞ **Replace** *pismo* **with** ime or pitanje **(write a name or a question out on a piece of paper and use that as the object of the exchange) and use possessives** njen [B,S] njezin [C] njegov, naš, vaš, njihov.

⚙ GRAMMAR

* Nouns and gender *

Nouns in BCS can be masculine, feminine or neuter. Masculine nouns, like *pas*, usually end in a consonant. Feminine nouns, like *mačka*, usually end in -a. Neuter nouns, like *pitanje*, end in -e or -o. [5a] Possessive pronominal adjectives, like *moj, tvoj* or *njihov*, have endings similar to the nouns they agree with. For example: *moj pas* (masculine), *moje pitanje* (neuter), *moja mačka* (feminine). [11a]

* Pronouns *

Subject pronouns are used for emphasis, or when the person or thing is mentioned for the first time. They are omitted otherwise, since the verb form alone gives the necessary information. In the 3rd person, the choice of pronoun is determined by the gender of the noun referred to. The plural

	singular		plural	
masculine	*on*	he, it	*oni*	they
neuter	*ono*	it	*ona*	they
feminine	*ona*	she, it	*one*	they

forms *one* and *ona* are used only to refer to exclusively feminine or neuter groups, respectively, while the masculine *oni* refers to masculine only, a mixed group, or the general idea "they." [6]

* Questions *

Questions which expect the answer "yes" or "no" are formed in different ways. The most frequent way in S is to place *da li* before the verb, and the most frequent way in B and C is to place *li* after the verb. [8b] Other questions begin with a question word such as "what," "who," or the like, as in English. The question marker (question word, *da li* or the sequence "verb + *li*") always stands at the beginning of a sentence. [8a]

* Adjectives *

Adjectives usually precede a noun. Many adjectives, and all possessive pronominal adjectives, can also occur after a form of the verb "to be," as in *pas je moj, mačka je tvoja*. In both instances the ending of the adjective must agree with the noun to which it refers. Neuter adjectives end in either *-o* or *-e* depending on the preceding consonant (for instance, *njihovo* but *naše*). **[11, 11a]** Adjectives in glossary listings are given in the order "masculine - neuter – feminine," as in *moj, moje, moja*. After Lesson 8, only the masculine form is given unless there is an otherwise unpredictable change, in which case the feminine is also given.

 A3   ⊙ 9,10

VOCABULARY

dan	day	na hrvatskom	in Croatian
dobar, dobro, dobra	good	na srpskom	in Serbian
dobar dan	hello	sladak, slatko, slatka	sweet
ili	or	vi	you *(plural)*
kaže se	is said, one says	zove se	his/its/her name is
kako se kaže (....)	how do you say (....)	zovemo se	our name is
mi	we	zovete se	your name is
na bosanskom	in Bosnian	žena	woman, wife

DOBAR DAN

[#1 and #2 are students. They meet a couple named George and Mary, who are walking with **#3**, another student. They strike up a conversation as they stroll.]

Bosnian
1. Dobar dan!
2. Dobar dan! Kako je sladak ovaj pas!
1. To je njihov pas [*points to Mary and George*], nije moj. Je li to tvoja mačka?
2. Da, moja je.
1. Kako se zove?
2. Mačka se zove Maca. A kako se zove taj slatki pas?
3. Zove se Freddy.
2. A kako se ti zoveš?
1. Ja se zovem .... , a vi?
2. Mi se zovemo .... i .... A vi, kako se zovete?
George: Moje ime je George, ovo je moja žena Mary, a Freddy je naš. Moje pitanje je: Kako se kaže George na hrvatskom i srpskom?
1. George se kaže Juraj na hrvatskom.
2. A Đorđe na srpskom.
Mary: A na bosanskom?
3. Ili Juraj ili Đorđe.

Croatian
1. Dobar dan!
2. Dobar dan! Kako je sladak ovaj pas!
1. To je njihov pas [*points to Mary and George*], nije moj. Je li to tvoja mačka?
2. Da, moja je.
1. Kako se zove?
2. Mačka se zove Maca. A kako se zove taj slatki pas?
3. Zove se Freddy.
2. A kako se ti zoveš?
1. Ja se zovem .... , a vi?
2. Mi se zovemo .... i .... A vi, kako se zovete?
George: Moje je ime George, ovo je moja žena Mary, a Freddy je naš. Moje je pitanje: Kako se kaže George na hrvatskom i srpskom?
1. George se kaže Juraj na hrvatskom.
2. A Đorđe na srpskom.
Mary: A na bosanskom?
3. Ili Juraj ili Đorđe.

Serbian Latin

1. Dobar dan!
2. Dobar dan! Kako je sladak ovaj pas!
1. To je njihov pas [*points to Mary and George*], nije moj. A da li je to tvoja mačka?
2. Da, moja je.
1. Kako se zove?
2. Mačka se zove Maca. A kako se zove taj slatki pas?
3. Zove se Fredi.
2. A kako se ti zoveš?
1. Ja se zovem .... , a vi?
2. Mi se zovemo .... i .... A vi, kako se zovete?
Džordž: Moje ime je Džordž, ovo je moja žena Meri, a Fredi je naš. Moje pitanje je: Kako se kaže Džordž na hrvatskom i srpskom?
1. Džordž se kaže Juraj na hrvatskom.
2. A Đorđe na srpskom.
Meri: A na bosanskom?
3. Ili Juraj ili Đorđe.

Serbian Cyrillic

1. Добар дан!
2. Добар дан! Како је сладак овај пас!
1. То је њихов пас [*points to Mary and George*], није мој. А да ли је то твоја мачка?
2. Да, моја је.
1. Како се зове?
2. Мачка се зове Маца. А како се зове тај слатки пас?
3. Зове се Фреди.
2. А како се ти зовеш?
1. Ја се зовем .... , а ви?
2. Ми се зовемо .... и .... А ви, како се зовете?
Џорџ: Моје име је Џорџ, ово је моја жена Мери, а Фреди је наш. Моје питање је: Како се каже Џорџ на хрватском и српском?
1. Џорџ се каже Јурај на хрватском.
2. А Ђорђе на српском.
Мери: А на босанском?
3. Или Јурај или Ђорђе.

🖎 **Students** should speak this and other conversations aloud. Each student should assume one of the numbered roles. When names are to be inserted in blanks, students can either use their own names or choose a B, C, or S name from the list on p. 317.

Self-study learners (those who are working on their own rather than in a classsroom setting): Read through each exercise several times. Then repeat after the recording until you are familiar with the exchange. Finally, study the grammar sections after each A exercise and use this information to analyze the grammar in the exercises.

⚙️GRAMMAR

* Adjectives, continued *

The masculine form of adjectives can end in a consonant or *-i*. Most masculine adjectives have both forms. [17] The form sometimes changes before the ending *-i* (for instance, *sladak* but *slatki;* for more, see p. 25). [16b] The demonstrative pronoun *ovaj* "this" must also agree with its noun when it functions as an adjective (for instance, *ovaj pas, ovo pitanje, ova mačka*). [11b] When the words *ovo* or *to* are used to present something or someone, they do not change form. For instance: *ovo je moj pas, to je moja mačka*). [9]

* Spelling of proper names *

Proper names often have different forms (or spellings) in B, C, or S. In addition, C spells foreign names as in the original language (thus *George, Catherine, Mary*), while S spells them as they are pronounced in the original language (thus *Džordž, Ketrin, Meri*). While B can use either means of spelling, there is a greater tendency toward the C usage. [1c]

VOCABULARY

ali	but	jèsam	[I] am (emphatic)
Amerikànac	American person, man	jèsi	[you] are (emphatic)
Amerìkanka	American woman	jest [C]	[he, it, she] is (emphatic)
Austràlac [C]	Australian person, man	jeste [B,S]	[you] are (emphatic)
Australijànac [B,S]	Australian person, man	jeste [B,S]	[he, it, she] is (emphatic)
Australìjanka [B,S]	Australian woman	jèsu	[they] are (emphatic)
Aùstralka [C]	Australian woman	Kanàđanin	Canadian person, man
Bosànac	Bosnian person, man	Kanàđanka	Canadian woman
Bòsanka	Bosnian woman	nìsu	[they] are not
čòvek	man, person	oni	they
čòvjek	man, person	prijatelj [B,C]	friend
Crnogòrac	Montenegrin man/person	prijatelji [B,C]	friends
Crnogòrka	Montenegrin woman	profesor	professor, teacher
dòmaća zàdaća [B,C]	homework	profesòrica [B,C]	professor, teacher (f)
dòmaći zadàtak [S]	homework	profèsorka [B,S]	professor, teacher (f)
drȕg [B,S]	friend, companion	Srbin	Serbian man/person
drugovi [B,S]	friends, companions	Srpkinja	Serbian woman
Èngleskinja	Englishwoman	studèntica [B,C]	student (f)
Ènglez	Englishman	stùdentkinja [B,S]	student (f)
Francùskinja	Frenchwoman	su	[they] are
Fràncuz	Frenchman	vèžba	exercise
Hrvȁt	Croatian man/person	vjèžba	exercise
Hrvàtica	Croatian woman		

PAS I MAČKA

Bosnian
1. Jèsi li tȋ stùdent?
2. Da, jȃ sam stùdent. Da li si tȋ stùdentica?
1. Jèsam.
3. I jȃ sam stùdentica. A George i Mary, šta su oni?
2. George je profesor, a Mary je profesòrica.
3. A njihov pas?
2. Njihov pas nìje profesor. Pas nìje čòvjek! Ali on jeste naš prijatelj.
3. Jèsu li pas i mačka prijatelji?
2. I jèsu i nìsu.
1. Je li George *Fràncuz*?
2. Ne, on je *Ènglez*.
1. A šta je Mary?
2. Òna je *Èngleskinja*.

Croatian
1. Jèsi li tȋ stùdent?
2. Da, jȃ sam stùdent. Jèsi li tȋ stùdentica?
1. Jèsam.
3. I jȃ sam stùdentica. A George i Mary, što su oni?
2. George je profesor, a Mary je profesòrica.
3. A njihov pas?
2. Njihov pas nìje profesor. Pas nìje čòvjek! Ali on jest naš prijatelj.
3. Jèsu li pas i mačka prijatelji?
2. I jèsu i nìsu.
1. Je li George *Fràncuz*?
2. Ne, on je *Ènglez*.
1. A što je Mary?
2. Òna je *Èngleskinja*.

Serbian Latin

1. Da li si tī stùdent?
2. Da, jā sam stùdent. Da li si tī stùdentkinja?
1. Jèsam.
3. I jā sam stùdentkinja. A Džordž i Meri, šta su òni?
2. Džordž je pròfesor, a Meri je pròfesōrka.
3. A njihov pas?
2. Njihov pas nìje pròfesor. Pas nìje čòvek! Ali òn jeste naš drȗg.
3. Da li su pas i mȁčka prijatelji?
2. I jèsu i nìsu.
1. Da li je Džordž *Francùz?*
2. Ne, òn je *Ènglēz.*
1. A šta je Meri?
2. Òna je *Ènglèskinja.*

Serbian Cyrillic

1. Да ли си тӣ стỳдент?
2. Да, јā сам стỳдент. Да ли си тӣ стỳденткиња?
1. Јèсам.
3. И јā сам стỳденткиња. А Џорџ и Мери, шта су òни?
2. Џорџ је прòфесор, а Мери је прòфесōрка.
3. А њихов пас?
2. Њихов пас нѝје прòфесор. Пас нѝје чòвек! Али òн јесте наш дрȳг.
3. Да ли су пас и мȁчка пријатељи?
2. И јèсу и нѝсу.
1. Да ли је Џорџ *Францȳз?*
2. Не, òн је *Ènглēз.*
1. А шта је Мери?
2. Òна је *Ènглèскиња.*

☞ **Replace** *Francùz* **with** Bòsanac, Crnògorac, Hr̀vāt, Sr̀bin. **Replace** *Ènglēz* **with** Amerìkanac, Austràlac [C] Australìjanac [B,S], Kanàđanin; **replace** *Ènglèskinja* **with** Amerìkanka, Australìjanka [B,S] Austràlka [C], Kanàđanka.

☞ **In the lines referring to George's and Mary's nationalities, switch 'George' with 'Mary,' and use as replacements** Francùskinja, **and** Bòsanka **or** Crnògorka **or** Hr̀vatica **or** Sr̀pkinja.

> The exercise above uses the terms *Bòsanac* and *Bòsanka* rather than *Bòšnjāk* and *Bòšnjakinja*. In current usage the terms *Bòšnjāk* and *Bòšnjakinja* refer specifically to members of the Muslim community, while the terms *Bòsanac* and *Bòsanka* refer to any resident of Bosnia and Herzegovina.

⚙ GRAMMAR

* Nouns denoting professions and nationalities *

Nouns denoting nationalities have two forms, one referring to females alone (such as *Amerìkanka*) and one referring both to males and to the general idea (such as *Amerìkanac*). Many nouns denoting professions function in a similar manner: for instance, *stùdentica* and *stùdentkinja* mean only "female student" while *stùdent* means either "male student" or just "student." **[5b]**

* The verb *to be*, continued *

There are two sets of longer forms for this verb, which are given in the chart to the right. One set is used to express negation and the other is used in questions and for emphasis. In this second meaning, C uses *jest* in 3rd singular while B and S use *jeste*. **[7b]**

long (negation)		long (emphasis)	
nìsam	nìsmo	jèsam	jèsmo
nìsi	nìste	jèsi	jèste
nìje	nìsu	jeste, jest	jèsu

* Plural of masculine nouns *

The plural of masculine nouns ends in *-i*. **[32a]** Masculine nouns containing a single syllable frequently add the syllable *-ov-* or *-ev-* before the ending *-i*. **[32e]** For instance, the plural of *prijatelj* is *prijatelji* while the plurals of *drȗg* and *brȏj* are *drugovi*, and *brojevi*. Long vowels frequently shorten in these plurals. **[166b]**

* Vocabulary differences, continued *

The suffixes denoting female humans often vary between B, C, and S. In addition, certain words referring to basic concepts are used with different frequencies and sometimes with different meanings in B, C, and S. For instance the word *drȗg* is used more frequently in S in the meaning, "friend, companion," while *prijatelj* is used in this meaning in B, C (and all three use *prijatelj* in the meaning "life-long friend").

🏃 VJEŽBE [J] VEŽBE [E] [Exercises]

Self-study learners: For the solutions to exercises in sections B and C of each lesson, consult the answer keys available for download at www.bcsgrammarandtextbook.org

B1

Bosnian	Croatian	Serbian	Serbian Cyrillic
1. Ko je student?	1. Tko je student?	1. Ko je student?	1. Ко је студент?
2. *On je.*	2. *On je.*	2. *On je.*	2. *Он je.*
1. Ko?	1. Tko?	1. Ko?	1. Ко?
2. *On!*	2. *On!*	2. *On!*	2. *Он!*

Replace *on* **with** òna, jȃ, tȋ, **and replace** *je* **with** sȁm, sȉ. **As you are saying each sentence, point to the person you are speaking about.**
Self-study learners (those who are working on their own): Write some names from p. 317 on pieces of paper and point to them as you do this exercise.
All students: For an overview of conjugation forms, see Appendix 6, pp. 333-339.

B2

Ask each other these questions (using information from A3 and A4):

Bosnian, Croatian and Serbian Latin	Serbian Cyrillic
Kàko se zòve òvaj student?	Кàко се зòве òвaj студент?
[B,C] Kàko se zòve òva studentica?	
[S] Kàko se zòve òva studentkinja?	Кàко се зòве òва студенткиња?
[B,C] Kàko se zòvu profesor i profesòrica?	
[S] Kàko se zòvu profesor i profesòrka?	Кàко се зòву професор и професòрка?
Kàko se zòvemo mȋ?	Кàко се зòвемо мȋ?
Kàko se zòve njihov pas?	Кàко се зòве њихов пас?
Kàko se zòve njègova mačka?	Кàко се зòве њègова мачка?
Kàko se zòve tvȏj prijatelj?	Кàко се зòве твȏj друг?

B3

In this exercise, use the name you have chosen from the list on p. 317 to be your B, C, or S name.

Bosnian	Croatian
1. Kàko se zòveš na èngleskom?	1. Kàko se zòveš na èngleskom?
2. Zòvem se *Caitlin.*	2. Zòvem se *Caitlin.*
1. A kàko je tvòje bòsansko ime?	1. A kàko je tvòje hrvàtsko ime?
2. *Dželìla.*	2. *Ìva.*

Serbian Latin	Serbian Cyrillic
1. Kàko se zòveš na èngleskom?	1. Кàко се зòвеш на èнглеском?
2. Zòvem se *Kejtlin.*	2. Зòвем се *Кејтлин.*
1. A kàko je tvòje srpsko ime?	1. А кàко је твòje српско име?
2. *Gordana.*	2. *Гордана.*

B4

<table>
<tr><td>Bosnian, Croatian and Serbian Latin</td><td>Serbian Cyrillic</td></tr>
</table>

Bosnian, Croatian and Serbian Latin
1. Kàko se kȁže *pencil*?
2. *Pencil* se kȁže ȍlȍvka.

Serbian Cyrillic
1. Како се каже *pencil*?
2. *Pencil* се каже ȍловка.

☞ **Replace** *pencil* **with** question, dog, cat, man, notebook, car, shoe.

B5

Ask each other these questions:

Bosnian, Croatian and Serbian Latin
1. Kàko se kȁže "studentica" na srpskȍm?
2. Kàko se kȁže "profesȍrka" na bȍsanskȍm i hr̀vatskȍm?
3. Kàko se kȁže "tko" na srpskȍm i bȍsanskȍm?
4. Kàko se kȁže "sveska" na hr̀vatskȍm ili bȍsanskȍm?

Serbian Cyrillic
1. Како се каже "студентица" на српскȍм?
2. Како се каже "професȍрка" на бȍсанскȍм и хр̀ватскȍм?
3. Како се каже "тко" на српскȍм и бȍсанскȍм?
4. Како се каже "свеска" на хр̀ватскȍм и бȍсанскȍм?

B6

Bosnian	Croatian	Serbian Latin	Serbian Cyrillic
1. Ko je òva žèna?	1. Tko je òva žèna?	1. Ko je òva žèna?	1. Ко је ȍва жèна?
2. Òna se zòve	2. Òna se zòve	2. Òna se zòve	2. Òна се зȍве ....
1. A šta je òna?	1. A što je òna?	1. A šta je òna?	1. А шта је òна?
2. *Profesòrica* je.	2. *Profesòrica* je.	2. *Profesȍrka* je.	2. *Професȍрка* је.

Bosnian	Croatian	Serbian Latin	Serbian Cyrillic
1. Ko je òvaj čòvjek?	1. Tko je òvaj čòvjek?	1. Ko je òvaj čòvek?	1. Ко је òвај чòвек?
2. Ȍn se zòve	2. Ȍn se zòve	2. Ȍn se zòve	2. Ȍн се зòве ....
1. A šta je on?	1. A što je on?	1. A šta je on?	1. А шта је ȍн?
2. *Profesor* je.	2. *Profesor* je.	2. *Profesor* je.	2. *Професор* је.

☞ **Pick a different name (than the one used in B3) from the list of names given on p. 317. Replace** *profesòrica* [B, C] *profesȍrka* [S] **with** studèntica [B,C] stùdentkinja [S] **and then replace** *profesor* **with** student. **Also** try some of the nationalities given in A4.

B7

Analysis and Discussion:

1. Pick three examples of feminine, neuter and masculine nouns used in this lesson.
2. Give three examples of possessive pronominal adjectives used in this lesson.
3. What are the pronouns used in this lesson?
4. Fully conjugate the present tense of the verbs *biti* and *zvati se*.

✍ DOMAĆA ZADAĆA [B,C] DOMAĆI ZADATAK [S]
[Homework]

Recommendation for written exercises throughout the book: While simply filling in the blank with the word or words requested will help you learn, you will learn much more if you write each sentence out in full.

C1

Fill in the blanks with the appropriate form of *zvati se*

Example: Kȁko .... (ona)?   .... (Sanja) **becomes**   Kȁko se zòve?   Zòve se Sanja.

Bosnian, Croatian, Serbian Latin
1. Kȁko .... (ti)?
   Zòvem se .... (your name)

2. Kȁko .... (oni)?
   ....George i Mary.

3. Kȁko .... (mi)?
   .... (your names).

4. Kȁko .... (on)?
   .... George.

5. Kȁko .... (vi)?
   .... (your name[s]).

Serbian Cyrillic
1. Кȁко .... (ти)?
   Зȍвем се .... (your name)

2. Кȁко .... (они)?
   .... Џорџ и Мери.

3. Кȁко .... (ми)?
   .... (your names).

4. Кȁко .... (он)?
   .... Џорџ.

5. Кȁко .... (ви)?
   .... (your name[s]).

C2

Bosnian
1. Ko je tȁ žèna?
   Òna ....

2. Ko je tȁj čòvjek?
   Ȍn ....

3. Šta sam jȁ?
   Vȋ ....

4. Šta sam jȁ?
   Tȋ ....

5. Ko ste vȋ?
   Jȁ ....

6. Ko ste vȋ?
   Mȋ ....

Croatian
1. Tko je tȁ žèna?
   Òna ....

2. Tko je tȁj čòvjek?
   Ȍn ....

3. Što sam jȁ?
   Vȋ ....

4. Što sam jȁ?
   Tȋ ....

5. Tko ste vȋ?
   Jȁ ....

6. Tko ste vȋ?
   Mȋ ....

Serbian Latin	Serbian Cyrillic
1. Ko je ta žena?	1. Ко је та жена?
Ȍna	Ȍна ....
2. Ko je taj čovjek?	2. Ко је тај човек?
Ȍn	Ȍн ....
3. Šta sam ja?	3. Шта сам ја?
Vi	Ви ....
4. Šta sam ja?	4. Шта сам ја?
Ti	Ти ....
5. Ko ste vi?	5. Ко сте ви?
Ja	Ja ....
6. Ko ste vi?	6. Ко сте ви?
Mi	Ми ....

☞ **Insert the required form of the verb** biti **and your choice of:** prijatelj [B,C] drug [S], profesor, profesorica [B,C] profesorka [S], student, studentica [B,C] studentkinja [S] **combined with** moj, tvoj, njegov, njen [B,S] njezin [C], naš, vaš, njihov. **Write out** each question and answer in full.

C3

If this is the answer, what is the question?

Bosnian	Croatian	Serbian Latin	Serbian Cyrillic
1. Zovem se Dubravka.	1. Zovem se Dubravka.	1. Zovem se Dubravka.	1. Зовем се Дубравка.
2. Pas je moj.	2. Pas je moj.	2. Pas je moj.	2. Пас је мој.
3. Mačka se zove Maca.	3. Mačka se zove Maca.	3. Mačka se zove Maca.	3. Мачка се зове Маца.
4. Moje ime je George.	4. Moje je ime George.	4. Moje ime je Džordž.	4. Моје име је Џорџ.
5. Na hrvatskom se kaže Juraj.	5. Na hrvatskom se kaže Juraj.	5. Na hrvatskom se kaže Juraj.	5. На хрватском се каже Јурај.
6. Na srpskom se kaže Đorđe.	6. Na srpskom se kaže Đorđe.	6. Na srpskom se kaže Đorđe.	6. На српском се каже Ђорђе.
7. I Juraj i Đorđe.	7. I Juraj i Đorđe.	7. I Juraj i Đorđe.	7. И Јурај и Ђорђе.
8. Jesam.	8. Jesam.	8. Jesam.	8. Јесам.

C4

Consult the Cyrillic penmanship guide on p. 319 and work through the practice sheets on pp. 14-17. Then write the following words out in Cyrillic. Designate the words as B, C, or S where appropriate. Circle the accent-bearing syllable in each word.

pas	prijatelj	on	profesorica	Đorđe	to	ste
mačka	ovaj	tvoje	bilježnica	sveska	Juraj	moj
profesor	zovu se	njihova	je	drug	profesorka	teka
tko	ime	ključ	papir	cipela	naše	

C5

Translate into B, C, or S:

1. I am a student.
2. The American man is a professor.
3. His name is George, and her name is Mary.
4. The dog is her friend.
5. The cat is theirs.
6. The American woman is a professor.
7. Who is that man?

C6

Rehearse A3 outside of class for an in-class performance.

Geografska pitanja [B,C,S] Zemljopisna pitanja [C]

VOCABULARY

Albànija	Albania	Mađarska	Hungary
Àustrija	Austria	Makedònija	Macedonia
Bosna i Hèrcegovina	Bosnia and Herzegovina	more	sea
Bùgarska	Bulgaria	pìtanja	issues
Crna Gòra	Montenegro	Rùmunija [B,S]	Romania
geògrafski, geògrafsko, geografska [B,C,S]	geographical	Rùmunjska [C]	Romania
		Slovènija	Slovenia
Hrvàtska	Croatia	Srbija	Serbia
Itàlija	Italy	Vojvodina	Vojvodina
Jàdransko more	Adriatic Sea	zemljopisni, zemljopisno, zemljopisna [C]	geographical
Kosovo	Kosovo		

☞ **Enter** the name of each country or region where it belongs on the blank map on p. 13. Consult the map at the beginning of the book.

Albànija, Àustrija, Bosna i Hèrcegovina, Bùgarska, Crna Gòra, Hrvàtska, Itàlija, Jàdransko more, Kosovo, Mađarska, Makedònija, Rùmunija [B,S] Rùmunjska [C], Slovènija, Srbija, Vojvodina.

Албàнија, Àустрија, Босна и Хèрцеговина, Бỳгарска, Вòјводина, Итàлија, Јàдранско мòре, Косово, Мàђарска, Македòнија, Румỳнија, Словènија, Србија, Хрвàтска, Црна Гòра.

The solid line demarcating the boundaries of Kosovo—on both the map on the next page and the map on the inside cover—represents Kosovo as an independent state. Although this is generally accepted at the international level, not all countries have recognized this status for Kosovo.

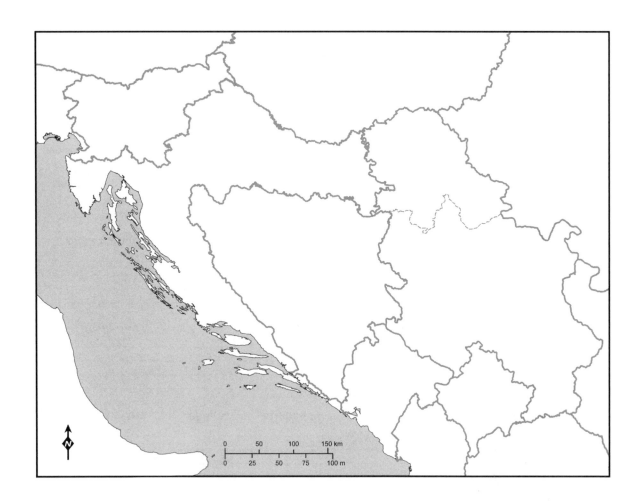

Prva lekcija   Lesson One

Cyrillic practice

Below are examples of Cyrillic letters in upper and lower case, with the latter given both in initial and non-initial position in the word. Each word is given in italics as well. While most letters are similar in italics, there are a few that are quite different, particularly **g**: г and *г*, **d**: д and *д*, **i**: и and *и*, **t**: т and *т*. See p. 319 for handwriting guides.

А [A] Африка *Африка*   април *април*   дан *дан*

Б [B] Босна *Босна*   босански *босански*   добар *добар*

В [V] Војводина *Војводина*   висок *висок*   твој *твој*

Г [G] Грета *Грета*   географија *географија*   август *август*

Д [D] Дубровник *Дубровник*   децембар *децембар*   среда *среда*

Ђ [Đ] Ђорђе *Ђорђе*   ђак *ђак*   мађарски *мађарски*

Е [E] Европа *Европа*   енглески *енглески*   један *један*

Ж [Ž] Жаклина *Жаклина*   жена *жена*   може *може*

З [Z] Загреб *Загреб*	за *за*	кроз *кроз*
И [I] Италија *Италија*	имати *имати*	молим *молим*
Ј [J] Југославија *Југославија*	јануар *јануар*	моје *моје*
К [K] Косово *Косово*	ко *ко*	српски *српски*
Л [L] Лондон *Лондон*	леп *леп*	али *али*
Љ [Lj] Љубљана *Љубљана*	љубав *љубав*	недеља *недеља*
М [M] Македонија *Македонија*	март *март*	нема *нема*
Н [N] Нови Сад *Нови Сад*	новембар *новембар*	речник *речник*
Њ [Nj] Њујорк *Њујорк*	његов *његов*	питање *питање*
О [O] Орегон *Орегон*	октобар *октобар*	лош *лош*

П [P]	Подгорица *Подгорица*	петак *петак*	ципела *ципела*
Р [R]	Румунија *Румунија*	руски *руски*	црн *црн*
С [C]	Србија *Србија*	септембар *септембар*	писмо *писмо*
Т [T]	Тексас *Тексас*	тата *тата*	четвртак *четвртак*
Ћ [Ć]	Ћуприја *Ћуприја*	ћирилица *ћирилица*	кућа *кућа*
У [U]	Уганда *Уганда*	уторак *уторак*	јун *јун*
Ф [F]	Француска *Француска*	фебруар *фебруар*	кафа *кафа*
Х [H]	Хрватска *Хрватска*	хлеб *хлеб*	њихова *њихова*
Ц [C]	Црна Гора *Црна Гора*	црвен *црвен*	француски *француски*

Ч [Č]   Чикаго *Чикаго*   човек *човек*   мачка *мачка*

Џ [Dž] Џули *Џули*   џез *џез*   уџбеник *уџбеник*

Ш [Š]   Шарлота *Шарлота*   шта *шта*   ваше *ваше*

Druga lekcija • Lesson Two

Novi rekviziti: avionsko p̀ismo, časopis, h̀emijskà òlovka [B,S] k̀emijskà òlovka [C], m̀ajmun, marka, m̀edved [E] m̀edvjed [J], p̀ero, r̀azglednica, rèčnik [E] rjèčnik [J].

A1   ⊙13,14

VOCABULARY

četvr̀tak	Thursday	p̀isati, p̀išem	to write
č̀itati, č̀itam	to read	p̀onedeljak	Monday
da	*(clause connector)*	p̀onedjeljak	Monday
dr̀ugi, dr̀ugo, dr̀uga	second	r̀aditi, r̀adim	to work
ga	it *(m,n)*, him	rèčnik	dictionary
ìmati, ìmam	to have	rjèčnik	dictionary
izv̀ini; izv̀inite [B,S]	sorry!	roman	novel
je	it *(f)*, her	srèda	Wednesday
m̀olim?	yes? what?	srijèda	Wednesday
m̀orati, m̀oram	must, to have to	subota	Saturday
m̀ože	sure! O.K.	sutra	tomorrow
ne	not	u + *Acc*	on [a day of the week]
ǹedelja	Sunday	ùčiti, ùčim	to study
ǹedjelja	Sunday	utorak	Tuesday
nego	but, rather	vèžbati, vèžbam	to practice
ǹemati, ǹemam	not to have	v̀idimo se!	see you!
òdgovor	answer	vjèžbati, vjèžbam	to practice
opr̀osti; opr̀ostite [C]	sorry!	zajedno	together
pero	pen	žèleti, žèlim	to wish, to want
p̀etak	Friday	žèljeti, žèlim	to wish, to want

UČITI ZAJEDNO

Bosnian
1. *Mehmede!*
2. Molim?
1. Ìmaš li *tȅku?*
2. Ìmam *je,* ali ǹemam *rjèčnik.* Ìmaš li ga ti?
1. *Rjèčnik* ìmam, ali *tȅku* ǹemam. Žèliš li da *ùčimo* zajedno sutra?
2. Sutra, to jest *četvr̀tak?* Izv̀ini, ne u *četvr̀tak* nego u *p̀etak.*
1. Mòže! V̀idimo se u *p̀etak.*

Croatian
1. *Tomislave!*
2. Molim?
1. Ìmaš li *b̀ilježnicu?*
2. Ìmam *je,* ali ǹemam *rjèčnik.* Ìmaš li ga ti?
1. *Rjèčnik* ìmam, ali *b̀ilježnicu* ǹemam. Žèliš li da *ùčimo* zajedno sutra?
2. Sutra, to jest *četvr̀tak?* Opr̀osti, ne u *četvr̀tak* nego u *p̀etak.*
1. Mòže! V̀idimo se u *p̀etak.*

Serbian Cyrillic
1. *Надо!*
2. Молим?
1. Да ли имаш *свеску?*
2. Ѝмам *je,* али н̀емам *речник.* Да ли га ти имаш?
1. *Речник* имам, али *свеску* н̀емам. Да ли жѐлиш да *ỳчимо* заједно сутра?
2. Сутра, то јест *четвр̀так?* Извини, не у *четвр̀так* него у *пȅтак.*
1. Мòже! Видимо се у *пȅтак.*

Serbian Latin

1. Nȁdo!
2. Molȋm?
1. Da li ȉmaš *svesku*?
2. Ȉmam je, ali nȅmam *rečnȋk*. Da li ga tȋ ȉmaš?
1. *Rečnȋk* ȉmam, ali *svesku* nȅmam.
   Da li žȅlȋš da *učȋmo* zajedno sutra?
2. Sutra, tȍ jest *četvȑtak*? Ȉzvȋni, ne u *četvȑtak* nego u pȅtak.
1. Mȍže! Vȉdȋmo se u pȅtak.

☞ **Replace** *učiti* **with**: čȉtati, rȁditi, pȉsati, vežbati [E] vjȅžbati [J], **and** *četvȑtak* **and** *pȅtak* **with** ponȅdeljak [E] ponȅdjeljak [J], ȕtorak, srȅda [E] srijȅda [J], sȕbota, nȅdelja [E] nȅdjelja [J].

☞ **Replace** *ȉmati bȉlježnicu* [C] *svesku* [S] *tȅku* **with** pȉsati pȉsmo; *ȉmati rečnȋk* [E] *rječnȋk* [J] **with** pȉsati knjigu.

☞ **Replace the italicized pair of words** *rečnȋk* [E] *rječnȋk* [J] **and** *bȉlježnica** [C] *sveska** [S] *tȅka** [B] **above with the following pairs:** ȍlovka, pȅro; pȉsmo, pȁpȋr; pȉtanje, ȍdgovor; rȍman, udžbenȋk.

☞ **Replace** 1st and 2nd person address with 3rd person singular or plural, using verbs and nouns from the previous replacement exercises.

---

* Some words which are italicized in the exercise, such as *bȉlježnicu, svesku* or *tȅku* – are spelled differently than they are in the replacement cues given beneath the exercise, which in this instance are *bȉlježnica* [C] *sveska* [S] *tȅka* [B]. This is because the replacement clues generally give the word in the nominative case. In the context of the exercise, however, the words are often in a different case. For instance *bȉlježnicu, svesku* or *tȅku* are here in the accusative case. The same applies to the pair *vȉsokog / vȉsoki* given in A2. The former, in the accusative case, appears in the exercise, while the latter, in the nominative, is given in the clues below the exercise and in the vocabulary box. See pp. 323-329 for an overview of case endings.

⚙ GRAMMAR

* Addressing people: the vocative case *

Nouns take different endings to indicate different functions. When a person is being addressed, the ending -*e* is often added to a masculine name (for instance, *Mehmede!*), and the ending -*a* on a feminine name is sometimes replaced by -*o* (for instance, *Nȁdo!*). [19]

* Accusative case *

The cases of a noun (other than the vocative) express grammatical relations in a sentence. [18] The subject case is called the "nominative," and its singular form is here abbreviated [Nsg]. [20] The case called "accusative" expresses, among other things, direct object meaning; its singular form is here abbreviated [Asg]. [22] To form the accusative of feminine nouns and adjectives, replace the ending -*a* with -*u* (Nom. *moja mačka*, Acc. *moju mačku*). Neuter nouns and many masculine nouns have the same endings in both cases. For instance, the phrases *tvoj udžbenik* and *njegovo pismo* could be either Nsg or Asg. [21a]

* Time expressions: days of the week *

To specify that something happens on a particular day of the week, use the preposition *u* plus the accusative form of the day in question, as in *u četvrtak* "on Thursday," *u subotu* "on Saturday." [23c]

* Negation *

A verb is negated by placing the particle *ne* in front of the verb form. It is pronounced together with the verb as if the two were a single word; in certain instances the accent shifts onto the particle *ne*. Only a few verbs have separate negative forms, in which the negative particle fuses with the verb. One of these is *nȅmati* "not have" (conjugated *nȅmam, nȅmaš*, etc.), and another is the negative present tense of *biti* (*nȉsam, nȉsi*, etc.). [25a]

* Present tense of verbs *

The infinitive of a verb usually ends in -ti. There are three present tense conjugations, named after the 3rd singular ending, which can be -a, -i or -e. The 1st and 2nd person forms simply add -m, -š, -mo or -te to this ending, but the 3d plural ending in each case is different. [13] Here are sample conjugations:

a-conjugation				i-conjugation				e-conjugation	
ìmati	to have			ùčiti	to study			pìsati	to write
ìmām	ìmāmo	1st		ùčīm	ùčīmo	1st		pìšēm	pìšēmo
ìmāš	ìmāte	2nd		ùčīš	ùčīte	2nd		pìšēš	pìšēte
ìmā	ìmajū	3rd		ùčī	ùčē	3rd		pìšē	pìšū
singular	plural			singular	plural			singular	plural

When the present tense is directly predictable from an infinitive in -iti or -ati, as in the above examples, there is no need to learn it specifically. But in those verbs where the present tense stem is not predictable from the infinitive, it must be learned specifically. For example: infinitive pìsati, present tense pìšēm; or infinitive zvati but present tense zòvēm. [14] Vocabulary entries for verbs give infinitive and 1st sg pres. For an overview of conjugation forms, see Appendix 6, pp. 333-339.

* The conjunction *da* *

When two verbs are used in succession, English frequently expresses the second by an infinitive, as in "We want TO STUDY" or "I want us TO STUDY." In B, C, and S the way such infinitives are expressed depends on several factors. When the two verbs have the same subject, as in the first example, C and S differ. C almost always uses an infinitive for the second verb (žèlīmo ùčiti) while S usually uses a sequence of da plus present tense (žèlīmo da ùčīmo), though it can also use the infinitive. B uses both more or less equally. [26c] When the two verbs have different subjects, however, the second verb can only be expressed by a phrase containing the conjunction da and the present tense, as in žèlīm da ùčīmo "I want us to study." [26b]

* Variant forms: ijekavian and ekavian *

A number of words can occur either with the vowel -e- or with the sequence -je- (sometimes -ije-). Any one speaker will use either the former type (called "ekavian") or the latter (called "ijekavian"). Both are given in vocabulary lists without marks; elsewhere they are identified [E] (ekavian) and [J] (ijekavian). B and C use only ijekavian, while S uses both ekavian and ijekavian depending on the region (ekavian throughout most of Serbia, and ijekavian in Bosnia, southwestern Serbia and Montenegro). There is no difference in meaning. It is important to realize that not all instances of -e- or -ije- are affected; for instance, the words meso "meat" and pìjēm "I drink" are the same throughout B, C, and S. The relevant instances must be learned individually. [3]

* Object pronouns, clitic forms *

There are two types of accusative case object pronouns – "clitic" (short form) and "full" (long form). The clitics, which are used in most instances, are unaccented and come in second position in the sentence. In 3rd singular the same form is used for masculine and neuter. In 3rd plural the same form is used in all three genders. [24a]

	singular		plural	
	nominative	accusative	nominative	accusative
1st	jā	me	mî	nas
2nd	tî	te	vî	vas
3rd masc.	ȍn	ga	òni	ih
3rd neut.	òno	ga	òna	ih
3rd fem.	òna	je, ju	òne	ih

There are two forms for the feminine singular accusative, je and ju. Croatian uses both, more or less interchangeably. [64] Bosnian and Serbian, however, use ju only in certain past tense constructions (see p. 143). For now, those focusing on B and S should learn je as the feminine accusative singular.

VOCABULARY

a!	aha!	njega	him, it
br̲z, br̲zo, br̲za	speedy, fast	nju̲	her, it
drag, drago, draga	dear	ȍnaj, ȍno, ȍna	that
gledati, gledam	to watch	r̍đav, r̍đavo, r̍đava [S]	bad
glup, glupo, glupa	stupid	ru̲žan, ru̲žno, ru̲žna	ugly
gospȍdin	gentleman, man	srećan, srećno, srećna [S]	happy, lucky
gospȍđa	lady, madam	sretan, sretno, sretna [B,C]	happy, lucky
kȍga	whom	stvarno	really
lahak, la̍hko, la̍hka [B]	light [not heavy], easy	te̲žak, te̲ško, te̲ška	heavy, difficult
lak, la̍ko, la̍ka [B,C,S]	light [not heavy], easy	tu̲žan, tu̲žno, tu̲žna	sad
lep, le̍po, le̍pa	beautiful, nice	velik, veliko, velika	big, large
lijep, lijȅpo, lijȅpa	beautiful, nice	videti, vidim	to see
loš, loše, loša [B,C,S]	bad	vidjeti, vidim	to see
ma̲li, ma̲lo, ma̲la	small	visok, visoko, visoka	tall
nizak, nȉsko, nȉska	short, low	zaista	indeed, really

KOGA VIDIŠ?

Bosnian and Croatian
1. .... ! Ȍnaj čovjek je stva̲rno visok!
2. Molim? Kȍga vidiš?
1. Vidim ȍnog visokȍg čȍvjeka.
2. A, njega! Zaista je visok!

Serbian Latin
1. .... ! Ȍnaj čovek je stva̲rno visok!
2. Molim? Kȍga vidiš?
1. Vidim ȍnog visokȍg čoveka.
2. A, njega! Zaista je visok!

Serbian Cyrillic
1. .... ! Ȍнaj чове̄к je стварно висо̄к!
2. Молим? Кȍга видиш?
1. Видим ȍног високȍг чове̄ка.
2. А, њега! Заиста je висо̄к!

☞ **Replace** čovek [E] čovjek [J] **with** gospȍdin, gospȍđa, profesor, student; visoki* **with** br̲zi, dobri, dragi, glupi, lahki [B] laki [B,C,S], le̲pi [E] lijȅpi [J], loši [B,C,S] r̍đavi [B,S], ma̲li, niski, ru̲žni, slatki, srećni [S] sretni [B,C], te̲ški, tu̲žni, veliki. **Replace** videti [E] vidjeti [J] **with** gledati. **Replace** njega **with** nju̲ **where appropriate.**

[* See boxed explanation on p. 20]

⚙ GRAMMAR

* Accusative case of animate nouns *

Masculine nouns denoting animate beings have a different ending in the accusative case. The noun ending is -a and the adjective ending is -og; for instance Nom visoki student, Acc visokog studenta. [21a] The accusative case of both ko and tko "who" is kȍga. [21c]

* Object pronouns, full forms *

Full form object pronouns are accented and can occur in any sentence position. Use them as the object of a preposition or to indicate emphasis. [24] Like the clitic pronouns, the same form is used for 3rd singular masculine/neuter, and a single form is used for all three genders in 3rd plural.

	singular		plural	
	nominative	accusative	nominative	accusative
1st	ja	mene	mi	nas
2nd	ti	tebe	vi	vas
3rd masc.	on	njega	oni	njih
3rd neut.	ono	njega	ona	njih
3rd fem.	ona	nju	one	njih

* Demonstrative pronominal adjectives *

The English words "this" and "that" correspond to three different pronominal adjectives in BCS. One, ovaj, means "this [close by]"; another, onaj, means "that [far away]"; and the third, taj, covers the neutral ground in between. It is translated either "this" or "that" depending on the context. Like all adjectives, these pronominal adjectives must change forms to agree with the noun to which they refer. [11b]

* Fleeting vowels in adjectives *

The masculine nominative singular form of many adjectives ends in a consonant preceded by -a. This -a- is called a "fleeting vowel" because it disappears in all other forms of the adjective; for instance pametan, pametno, pametna. If this vowel appears in the suffix -ak, its loss will sometimes cause the preceding consonant to shift to another consonant; for instance nizak, nisko, niska. [16b]

The Neretva River, Bosnia and Herzegovina

The town of Rab on the island of Rab, Croatia

VOCABULARY

beo, belo, bela	white	medved	bear
bijel, bijelo, bijela	white	medvjed	bear
boja	color	plav, plavo, plava	blue
brat	brother	otac, oca	father
crn, crno, crna	black	ovde	here
crven, crveno, crvena	red	ovdje	here
crvena boja	the color red	pas, psa	dog
dobro	good, O.K.	sestra	sister
ej!	hey!	sve	all, everything
film	movie	voleti, volim	to love; to like (I)
fin, fino, fina	fine	voljeti, volim	to love; to like (I)
kupiti, kupim	to buy (P)	za + Acc	for
kupovati, kupujem	to buy (I)	zašto	why
majka	mother	zato što	because
majmun	monkey	žut, žuto, žuta	yellow

KUPUJEM PSA

Bosnian
1. Ej, šta radiš?
2. Kupujem *psa* za *mog brata*.
1. *Ovog žutog* ovdje?
2. Ne, *onog crvenog* tamo.
1. Zašto ne želiš da kupiš *žutog psa*?
2. Zato što *moj brat* voli *crvenu* boju!
1. Dobro, i *crveni* je fin!

Croatian
1. Ej, što radiš?
2. Kupujem *psa* za *moga brata*.
1. *Ovoga žutog* ovdje?
2. Ne, *onoga crvenog* tamo.
1. Zašto ne želiš kupiti *žutoga psa*?
2. Zato što *moj brat* voli *crvenu* boju!
1. Dobro, i *crveni* je fin!

Serbian Latin
1. Ej, šta radiš?
2. Kupujem *psa* za *mog brata*.
1. *Ovog žutog* ovde?
2. Ne, *onog crvenog* tamo.
1. Zašto ne želiš da kupiš *žutog psa*?
2. Zato što *moj brat* voli *crvenu* boju!
1. Dobro, i *crveni* je fin!

Serbian Cyrillic
1. Еј, шта радиш?
2. Купујем *пса* за *мог брата*.
1. *Овог жутог* овде?
2. Не, *оног црвеног* тамо.
1. Зашто не желиш да купиш *жутог пса*?
2. Зато што *мој брат* воли *црвену* боју!
1. Добро, и *црвени* је фин!

☞ **Replace** *crveni* and *žuti* **with** beli [E] bijeli [J], crni, dobri, lepi [E] lijepi [J], plavi; **replace** *pas* **with** auto, cipela, mačka, majmun, medved [E] medvjed [J]. **Replace** *pas* **with** film, **using adjectives listed in A2**. **Replace** *brat* **with** ti, ona, oni, vi, sestra, majka, otac.

⚙ GRAMMAR

* Accusative of animate masculines and fleeting vowels *

As seen in the previous lesson, masculine nouns referring to animate beings take the ending -*a* in the accusative case. Some such nouns also have a fleeting vowel in the final syllable. This vowel is lost before the ending -*a*, for instance Nom *pas*, Acc *psa*. Sometimes, as in the case of *otac* (Acc *oca*) "father," the stem changes further when this vowel is lost. **[21b]** When fleeting vowels are present, the Acc sg of a masculine noun is given in vocabulary listings.

* Verbal aspect, introduction *

There are two BCS verbs for most verbal ideas, a concept known as "verbal aspect." One of these two verbs refers to a single action in terms of actual or envisioned completion, and is called the "perfective aspect." The other refers to repeated action, a single action in progress, or the general idea of an action, and is called the "imperfective aspect." The two verbs have the same basic dictionary meaning, and almost always share the same root, as in *kùpiti* "buy" [perfective] vs. *kupòvati* "buy" [imperfective]. Henceforth these two categories are noted (P) and (I), respectively, in vocabulary listings. **[28]**

* Prepositions *

Prepositions require that a specific case follow them. Among the prepositions which require the accusative case are *za*, which nearly always corresponds to English "for," **[23b]** and *u*, which when followed by the name of a weekday means "on" that day of the week. **[23c]** The names of weekdays are not capitalized.

* Long and short adjectives *

Most adjectives have both short and long forms. Some adjectives, such as *m̲a̲l̲i̲* "little," adjectives in *-ski̲*, and certain others, have only the long form; others, including pronominal adjectives such as *njegov* "his," have only short forms. Most, however have both long and short forms. The difference is most clearly seen in masculine nominative singular, as in *b̲r̲z* (short) vs. *b̲r̲z̲i̲* (long). Feminine and neuter distinguish short from long only in the final vowel, as in *b̲r̲za* (short) vs. *b̲r̲za* (long); sometimes there is an accentual difference as well, as in *crvèna* (short) vs. *crvena̲* (long). **[17]** Only the short form is given in vocabulary lists, but the long form is also given in the BCS-English glossary if there is an accentual difference between the two. Long forms are given in replacement cues beneath exercises. There is relatively little difference in meaning between long and short forms (for more discussion, see p. 37). Although one should always use the short forms after the verb "to be," as in *ònaj pas je c̲r̲n* "that dog is black," the long forms are used in most other instances. **[17b]** There is also a "longer" form, made by adding an extra *-a* to the long adjective ending *-og*, used more commonly in C. For more about this "longer" form, see the grammar section, **Long and "longer" adjectives**, on p. 54.

* Adjectives ending in *-o* *

The masculine short form of some adjectives ends in *-o*, but the stem of all other forms ends in *-l*; for instance, *dèbeo, dèbelo, dèbela* "fat." The word for "white" also belongs to this group in ekavian; for instance, *beo, b̲e̲lo, b̲e̲la*. In ijekavian, however, the masculine form ends in *-l*: *bij̲e̲l, bij̲è̲lo, bij̲è̲la*. **[16c]**

* Verbs in -ovati *

Verbs whose infinitive ends in *-ovati* replace the sequence *-ova-* of the infinitive by the sequence *-uj-* in the present tense. **[14e]** There are a number of relatively common verbs with this conjugation. Among them is the verb *kupovati* "to buy," whose conjugation is given to the right. Students must pay particular attention to this difference between infinitive and present tense!

kupòvati	buy
kùpuj̲e̲m	*kùpujemo*
kùpuj̲e̲š	*kùpujete*
kùpuj̲e̲	*kùpuj̲u̲*

The countryside in the Šumadija region near Aranđelovac, Serbia

VOCABULARY

abecedna bilježnica [C]	wordlist notebook	jutro	morning
abecedna teka [B]	wordlist notebook	kasa [S]	cash register
abecedni [B,C,S]	alphabetical	kemijska olovka [C]	ballpoint pen
američki, američko, američka	American	lepo	nicely
avionsko pismo	airmail letter	lijepo	nicely
azbučna sveska [S]	wordlist notebook	odlično	excellent
azbučni [S]	alphabetical	marka	stamp
blagajna [B,C]	cash register	moći, mogu, možete	to be able, can (I)
časopis	magazine	molim vas	please
dobro jutro	good morning	molim lepo	you're welcome
doviđenja	goodbye	molim lijepo	you're welcome
francuski, francusko, francuska	French	nemački, nemačko, nemačka	German
gramatika	grammar	njemački, njemačko, njemačka	German
hemijska olovka [B,S]	ballpoint pen	običan, obično, obična	ordinary
hvala	thank you	ovakav, ovakvo, ovakva	this kind
hvala lijepa [C]	thanks so much	papirnica	stationery store
hvala lepo [S]	thanks so much	platiti, platim	to pay
hvala lijepo [B,C,S]	thanks so much	pogledati, pogledam	to take a look (I)
izvolite!	may I help you?	razglednica	picture postcard
izvolite!	here you are!	svakako	certainly

PAPIRNICA

Bosnian
1. *Dobar dan!*
2. *Dobar dan,* izvolite!
1. Molim vas, imate li *novi njemački udžbenik?*
2. Imamo *ga.* Želite li *ga?*
1. Hvala, svakako, i želim kupiti *običnu olovku.*
2. Želite li ovakvu *žutu?* Lijepo piše.
1. Odlično! A mogu li kupiti *abecednu teku za rječnik* ovdje?
2. Imamo *je.* Želite li pogledati? Izvolite.
1. Hvala lijepo! To je sve. Mogu li platiti?
2. Molim lijepo. Ovdje je blagajna.
1. [*#1 pays*] Doviđenja!
2. Doviđenja!

Croatian
1. *Dobar dan!*
2. *Dobar dan,* izvolite!
1. Molim vas, imate li *novi njemački udžbenik?*
2. Imamo *ga.* Želite li *ga?*
1. Hvala, svakako, i želim kupiti *običnu olovku.*
2. Želite li ovakvu *žutu?* Lijepo piše.
1. Odlično! A mogu li kupiti *abecednu bilježnicu za rječnik* ovdje?
2. Imamo *je.* Želite li pogledati? Izvolite.
1. Hvala lijepa! To je sve. Mogu li platiti?
2. Molim lijepo. Ovdje je blagajna.
1. [*#1 pays*] Doviđenja!
2. Doviđenja!

Serbian Latin	Serbian Cyrillic
1. *Dobar dan!*	1. *Добар дан!*
2. *Dobar dan,* izvolite!	2. *Добар дан,* изволите!
1. Molim vas, da li imate *novi nemački udžbenik?*	1. Молим вас, да ли имате *нови немачки уџбеник?*
2. Imamo *ga.* Da li *ga* želite?	2. Имамо *га.* Да ли *га* желите?
1. Hvala, svakako, i želim da kupim *običnu olovku.*	1. Хвала, свакако, и желим да купим *обичну оловку.*
2. Da li želite ovakvu *žutu?* Lepo piše.	2. Да ли желите овакву *жуту?* Лепо пише.
1. Odlično! A da li mogu da kupim *azbučnu svesku za rečnik* ovde?	1. Одлично! А да ли могу да купим *азбучну свеску за речник* овде?
2. Imamo *je.* Da li je želite pogledati? Izvolite.	2. Имамо *je.* Да ли je желите погледати? Изволите.
1. Hvala lepo! To je sve. Da li mogu da platim?	1. Хвала лепо! То je све. Да ли могу да платим?
2. Molim lepo. Ovde je kasa.	2. Молим лепо. Овде je каса.
1. [*#1 pays*] Doviđenja!	1. [*#1 pays*] Довиђења!
2. Doviđenja!	2. Довиђења!

☞ **Replace** *dobar dan* with dobro jutro, *nemački* [E] *njemački* [J] *udžbenik* with američki časopis, francuska gramatika; **replace** *obična olovka* with fino pero, hemijska [B,S] kemijska [C] olovka; **replace** *abecedna* [B,C,S] *azbučna* [S] *bilježnica* [C] *sveska* [S] *teka* [B] **with** jedna avionska marka, jedno avionsko pismo, razglednica.

☞ **Practice** this as a skit, using some of the words above as replacements. Note that the end of the recorded version is slightly different than the textbook version. There will be several such minor discrepancies in the recordings of other lessons.

☞ **Self-study learners:** Pay attention both to the verb *želeti* [E] *željeti* [J], and to the endings of nouns and adjectives that specifically mark them as masculine, neuter, and feminine. Look at the verbs you have used so far and mark them as to whether they belong to the a-, i-, or e- conjugation, using as a guide the verb table on p. 21.

Daytime greetings: People greet each other with "*Dobro jutro*" from early morning to 10:00 a.m. After that "*Dobar dan*" is used, until just before 6:00 p.m. when evening is considered to begin.

⚙ GRAMMAR

* Addressing people: politeness formulas *

Various politeness formulas take different endings depending on how one normally addresses the person in question. In the meaning "excuse me," one says *oprosti* or *izvini* to a person one addresses as *ti*, and *oprostite* or *izvinite* to a person (or people) one addresses as *vi*. Another word in this category, which means either "May I help you?" or "Here you are" (depending on the context) is *izvoli / izvolite.* [15]

* The verb *moći* *

The verb meaning "can, be able" is slightly irregular. The 1st singular and 3rd plural forms differ only in accent and vowel length. [14f] The 3rd singular form of this verb has two meanings: "s/he can" and the more impersonal "OK, fine, possible." Here is the conjugation:

moći	can, be able
mogu	*možemo*
možeš	*možete*
može	*mogu*

⚐ VJEŽBE [J] VEŽBE [E]

B1

Bosnian	Croatian	Serbian Latin	Serbian Cyrillic
1. Jasna!	1. Jasna!	1. Jasna!	1. Jasna!
2. Molim?	2. Molim?	2. Molim?	2. Молим?
1. Je li ta *mačka moja*? Želim da imam *crnu mačku*.	1. Je li ta *mačka moja*? Želim imati *crnu mačku*.	1. Da li je ta *mačka moja*? Želim da imam *crnu mačku*.	1. Да ли је та *мачка моја*? Желим да имам *црну мачку*.
2. Ne, *moja* je, nije *tvoja*!	2. Ne, *moja* je, nije *tvoja*!	2. Ne, *moja* je, nije *tvoja*!	2. Не, *моја* је, није *твоја*!
1. Jesmo li prijatelji? Šta je *tvoje*, to je i *moje*! Ovo je naša *crna mačka*.	1. Jesmo li prijatelji? Što je *tvoje*, to je i *moje*! Ovo je naša *crna mačka*.	1. Da li smo drugovi? Šta je *tvoje*, to je i *moje*! Ovo je naša *crna mačka*.	1. Да ли смо другови? Шта је *твоје*, то је и *моје*! Ово је наша *црна мачка*.

☞ **Instead of** *mačka* and *crna mačka* use dobra knjiga, mala olovka, lepi [E] lijepi [J] udžbenik.

☞ **Replace** *moja* and *tvoja* with njena [B,C,S] njezina [C], njegova, njihova.

B2

Bosnian	Croatian	Serbian Latin	Serbian Cyrillic
1. Vidiš li *onog niskog gospodina*?	1. Vidiš li *onog niskog gospodina*?	1. Da li vidiš *onog niskog gospodina*?	1. Да ли видиш *оног ниског господина*?
2. Da, vidim i *niskog gospodina* i *nisku gospođu*.	2. Da, vidim i *niskog gospodina* i *nisku gospođu*.	2. Da, vidim i *niskog gospodina* i *nisku gospođu*.	2. Да, видим и *ниског господина* и *ниску госпођу*.

☞ **Instead of** *niski gospodin* and *niska gospođa* use slatka mačka, slatki pas; ružni profesor, ružna profesorica [B,C] profesorka [S]; tužni Kanađanin, tužna Kanađanka; dragi Bosanac, draga Bosanka **or** dragi Hrvat, draga Hrvatica **or** dragi Srbin, draga Srpkinja; brzi Amerikanac, brza Amerikanka.

B3

Bosnian	Croatian	Serbian Latin	Serbian Cyrillic
1. Je li *ovaj mali pas* za mene?	1. Je li *ovaj mali pas* za mene?	1. Da li je *ovaj mali pas* za mene?	1. Да ли је *овај мали пас* за мене?
2. Nije. *Mali pas* je za *onog studenta* tamo.	2. Nije. *Mali pas* je za *onog studenta* tamo.	2. Nije. *Mali pas* je za *onog studenta* tamo.	2. Није. *Мали пас* је за *оног студента* тамо.
1. Izvinite, želim vašeg *velikog psa*.	1. Oprostite, želim vašeg *velikog psa*.	1. Izvinite, želim vašeg *velikog psa*.	1. Извините, желим вашег *великог пса*.
2. Ne može. *Veliki pas* je moj.	2. Ne može. *Veliki pas* je moj.	2. Ne može. *Veliki pas* je moj.	2. Не може. *Велики пас* је мој.

☞ **Instead of** *mali* and *veliki pas*, use a) plavi and crveni rečnik [E] rječnik [J], b) teško and lahko [B] lako [B,C,S] pitanje. **Replace** *onaj student* with loši profesor, ružni čovek [E] čovjek [J], visoka žena.

B4

Fill in the blanks with words for the weekdays. For the remaining blanks in the even-numbered sentences, choose one verb from column A and one noun from column B to complete the sentence.

A
kupiti
pisati
čitati
vežbati [E] vježbati [J]
učiti
gledati

B
pas, mačka, majmun, medved [E] medvjed [J],
domaća zadaća [B,C] domaći zadatak [S]
knjiga, časopis, novine,
bosanska **or** hrvatska vježba **or** srpska vežba,
ruski **or** nemački [E] njemački [J] jezik,
film

Bosnian
1. Šta želite raditi u .... ?
    (ponedjeljak)
2. U .... želimo ....
  (ponedjeljak)
3. Šta želiš da radimo u .... ?
    (utorak)
4. U .... želim ....
   (utorak)
5. Šta želiš da studenti rade u .... ?
    (srijeda)
6. U .... želim ....
  (srijeda)
7. Šta želiš da Sanja radi u .... ?
    (četvrtak)
8. U .... želim ....
  (četvrtak)
9. Šta želiš raditi u ....?
    (petak)
10. U .... želim ....
  (petak)
11. A šta želiš da radim u .... ?
    (subota)
12. U .... želim ....
  (subota)

Croatian
1. Što želite raditi u .... ?
    (ponedjeljak)
2. U .... želimo ....
  (ponedjeljak)
3. Što želiš da radimo u ....
    (utorak)
4. U .... želim ....
  (utorak)
5. Što želiš da studenti rade u .... ?
    (srijeda)
6. U .... želim ....
  (srijeda)
7. Što želiš da Sanja radi u .... ?
    (četvrtak)
8. U .... želim ....
  (četvrtak)
9. Što želiš raditi u .... ?
    (petak)
10. U .... želim ....
  (petak)
11. A što želiš da radim u .... ?
    (subota)
12. U .... želim ....
  (subota)

Serbian Latin
1. Šta želite da radite u .... ?
    (ponedeljak)
2. U .... želimo ....
  (ponedeljak)
3. Šta želiš da radimo u .... ?
    (utorak)
4. U .... želim ....
  (utorak)
5. Šta želiš da studenti rade u .... ?
    (sreda)
6. U .... želim ....
  (sreda)

Serbian Cyrillic
1. Шта желите да радите у .... ?
    (понедељак)
2. У .... желимо ....
  (понедељак)
3. Шта желиш да радимо у .... ?
    (уторак)
4. У .... желим ....
  (уторак)
5. Шта желиш да студенти раде у .... ?
    (среда)
6. У .... желим ....
  (среда)

7. Šta želiš da Sanja radi u .... ?
           (četvrtak)

8. U .... želim ....
   (četvrtak)

9. Šta želiš da radiš u .... ?
           (petak)

10. U .... želim ....
    (petak)

11. A šta želiš da radim u .... ?
            (subota)

12. U .... želim ....
    (subota)

7. Шта желиш да Сања ради у ....?
           (четвртак)

8. У........ желим ....
   (четвртак)

9. Шта желиш да радиш у .... ?
           (петак)

10. У .... желим ....
   (петак)

11. А шта желиш да радим у .... ?
           (субота)

12. У .... желим ....
   (субота)

ponedjeljak ponedeljak	utorak	srijeda sreda	četvrtak	petak	subota	nedjelja nedelja

☞ **Construct** a chart like this, filling in the activities described for each day above. Then make a calendar describing your own week.

B5

Bosnian and Croatian	Serbian Latin	Serbian Cyrillic
1. Možeš li *gledati film* u utorak?	1. Da li možeš da *gledaš film* u utorak?	1. Да ли можеш да *гледаш филм* у уторак?
2. Ne mogu. Moram *učiti*.	2. Ne mogu. Moram *da učim*.	2. Не могу. Морам *да учим*.
1. Možeš li u petak?	1. Da li možeš u petak?	1. Да ли можеш у петак?
2. Mogu u *srijedu*.	2. Mogu u *sredu*.	2. Могу у *среду*.
1. Odlično! Onda se vidimo u *srijedu*.	1. Odlično! Onda se vidimo u *sredu*.	1. Одлично! Онда се видимо у *среду*.

☞ **Replace** *gledati* and *film* with a) čitati and velika knjiga; b) kupiti and pas; c) pisati and teško pismo; d) učiti and bosanski jezik, hrvatski jezik or srpski jezik. **Replace** *učiti* with a) čitati and nemački [E] njemački [J] časopis; b) pisati and roman; c) vežbati [E] vježbati [J] and bosanski jezik, hrvatski jezik or srpski jezik. **Replace** the italicized days of the week with other weekdays.

B6

Questions to ask each other, using phrases and vocabulary from 2A1, 2A3 and 2A4:

A1   [B,C] Zašto studenti žele učiti zajedno?
        [S] Zašto studenti žele da uče zajedno?

A3   [B,S] Zašto #2 kupuje crvenog psa za brata?
        [C] Zašto #2 kupuje crvenoga psa za brata?

A4   [B] Zašto #1 želi kupiti njemački udžbenik, običnu olovku i abecednu teku?
        [C] Zašto #1 želi kupiti njemački udžbenik, običnu olovku i abecednu bilježnicu?
        [S] Zašto #1 želi da kupi nemački udžbenik, običnu olovku i azbučnu svesku?

👉 **Read** this paragraph to one another out loud in class, alternating sentences. Then read it again, having changed it so that the subjects are plural: two women and two men.

Bosnian

Emìna ne žèli da ùči u nèdjelju. Òna žèli gledati film. Ali mòra ùčiti! Čìta udžbenik, pìše domàću zadàću i vjèžbu. Njèn prijatelj Mèhmed je zòve. On žèli gledati jèdan dobar bòsanski film. Da li ga mogu gledati zajedno? Òna žèli, ali ne mòže. Mòra ùčiti. Òna mòra ùčiti i u ùtorak i u srijèdu, ali mòže gledati film u pètak. Mèhmed mòra ràditi u pètak. On mòže gledati film u sùbotu. I òna mòže u subotu.

Croatian

Jasna ne žèli ùčiti u nèdjelju. Òna žèli gledati film. Ali mòra ùčiti! Òna čìta udžbenik, pìše domàću zadàću i vjèžbu. Njèzin prijatelj Gòran ju zòve. On žèli gledati jèdan dobar hrvàtski film. Mogu li ga gledati zajedno? Òna žèli, ali ne mòže. Mòra ùčiti. Òna mòra ùčiti i u ùtorak i u srijèdu, ali mòže gledati film u pètak. Gòran mòra ràditi u pètak. On mòže gledati film u sùbotu. I òna mòže u subotu.

Serbian Latin

Nàda ne žèli da ùči u nèdelju. Òna žèli da glèda film. Ali mòra da ùči! Òna čìta udžbenik, pìše domàći zadatak i vèžbu. Njèn prijatelj Tòmislav je zòve. On žèli da glèda jèdan dobar srpski film. Da li mogu da ga glèdaju zajedno? Òna žèli, ali ne mòže. Mòra da ùči. Òna mòra da ùči i u ùtorak i u srèdu, ali mòže da glèda film u pètak. Tòmislav mòra da ràdi u pètak. On mòže da glèda film u sùbotu. I òna mòže u subotu.

Serbian Cyrillic

Нàда не жèлѝ да ỳчѝ у нèдељу. Òна жèли да глèда филм. Али мòра да ỳчи! Òна чѝта уџбенѝк, пѝше домàћѝ задатак и вежбу. Њèн прѝјатељ Тòмислав је зòве. Он жèли да глèда добар српскѝ филм. Да ли могу̣ да га глèдају заједно? Òна жèли, али не мòже. Мòра да ỳчи. Òна мòра да ỳчи и у ỳторак и у срèду, али мòже да глèда филм у пèтак. Тòмислав мòра да рàдѝ у пèтак. Он мòже да глèда филм у сùботу. И òна мòже у сùботу.

The Montenegrin coast near Boka Kotorska

✍ DOMAĆA ZADAĆA [B,C] DOMAĆI ZADATAK [S]

C1

Form questions and answers according to the following example:
a. Šta *imam* i šta *nemam*? [B,S]   Što *imam* i što *nemam*? [C]
        b. Ìmam *pàpir* ali nèmam *òlovku.*

Write out six other versions of this question and answer pair. Replace the italicized forms in the question with other forms of *imati* and *nèmati* (using "you," "he," "they," etc.), and replace the nouns *papir* and *òlovka* in the answer with words from the following list.

rječnik [J]	tèka [B]	pìtanje	ključ
rèčnik [E]	ròman	òdgovor	cipela
bìlježnica [C]	udžbenik	pìsmo	vježba [J]
sveska [S]	pèro	pàpir	vežba [E]

C2

Each set of parentheses contains a noun plus the masculine singular form of various adjectives.
1) **Put** each noun into the accusative form, and change the adjectives to match the noun both in case and gender. **Example:**
        Kòga vidiš?   Vidim .... (onàj, vìsoki, stùdentica)
        Vidim ònu vìsoku stùdenticu.

2) **Then** rewrite the sentences replacing each noun (or adjective + noun) with the appropriate clitic pronoun. **Example:**
        Vidim ònog stùdenta   **becomes**   Vidim ga

a. Kòga vidiš?
Vidim .... (naš, vìsoki, profesor).
Vidim .... (tvoj, dobar, prijateljica).

a. Кòга видиш?
Видим .... (наш, вѝсокѝ, професор).
Видим .... (твòј, добар, другарица).

b. [B,S] Šta vidiš? [C] Što vidiš?
Vidim .... (vaš, crveni, auto).
Vidim .... (njegov, crni, mačka).
Vidim .... (naš, mali, pas).
Vidim .... (moj, bosanski, knjiga).
Vidim .... (tvoj, veliki, rječnik).
Vidim .... (taj, plavi, blagajna).

b. Шта видиш?
Видим .... (ваш, црвени, ауто).
Видим .... (његов, црни, мачка).
Видим .... (наш, мали, пас).
Видим .... (мòј, босанскѝ, књига).
Видим .... (твòј, велики, речник).
Видим .... (тàј, плави, каса).

c. [B,S] Šta òni pìšu? [C] Što òni pìšu?
Òni pìšu .... (jèdan, pìsmo).

c. Шта они пишу?
Они пишу .... (један, пѝсмо).

d. [B,S] Šta čìtaš? [C] Što čìtaš?
Čìtam .... (òvaj, tužni, knjiga).
Čìtam .... (naš, bosanski, časopis).

d. Шта читаш?
Читам .... (овàј, тужни, књига).
Читам .... (наш, босанскѝ, часопис).

C3

Fill in each blank with the correct form of the pronoun given in parentheses.

1. Ovo pismo je za .... (vi).
2. Ona crna mačka je za .... (ja).
3. Taj pas je za .... (on).
4. Bijela knjiga je za .... (ona).
5. Veliki udžbenik je za .... (oni)
6. Crvena olovka je za .... (mi).

1. Ово писмо је за .... (ви).
2. Она црна мачка је за .... (ја).
3. Тај пас је за .... (он).
4. Бела књига је за .... (она).
5. Велики уџбеник је за .... (они).
6. Црвена оловка је за .... (ми).

C4

Identify the subject of each of the sentences below, and then translate the sentences into English.

1. Njega vidim, ali nju ne vidim.
2. Psa gledaju mali majmun i velika mačka.
3. Imamo li je?
4. Kako se kaže teka na srpskom?
5. Gledamo ga, ali on nas ne vidi.
6. Vidiš li onog dobrog čovjeka?

1. Њега видим, али њу не видим.
2. Пса гледају мали мајмун и велика мачка.
3. Да ли је имамо?
4. Како се каже тека на српском?
5. Гледамо га, али он нас не види.
6. Да ли видиш оног доброг човека?

C5

Read these words aloud. After each word write its meaning, and then give the appropriate grammatical information for the form of the word: if it is a noun or adjective, state case and gender; and if a verb, state person and number.

његову	другарица	пса	оловка
мачка	можемо	друга	речник
видим	црвену	га	виде
госпођу	књига	гледамо	Француз
уџбеник	нашег	медведа	часопис
бела	срећну	каже се	граматика
каса	папир	добру	лоша
брз	драгог	сутра	господин
њихова	кључ	низак	петак

VOCABULARY

bòsanski, bòsansko, bòsanska crnògorski, crnògorsko, crnògorska glȁvni grȁd	Bosnian Montenegrin capital [city]	hȑvatski, hȑvatsko, hȑvatska sȑpski, sȑpsko, sȑpska	Croatian Serbian

Consult the map at the beginning of the book and fill in the blanks with the appropriate city names.

1. Хрва̀тски гла̀вни гра̏д је ....

2. Сро̀пски гла̀вни гра̏д је ....

3. Цр̀ногорски гла̀вни гра̏д је ....

4. Бо̀сански гла̀вни гра̏д је ....

1. Hȑvatski glȁvni grȁd je ....

2. Sȑpski glȁvni grȁd je ....

3. Crnògorski glȁvni grȁd je ....

4. Bòsanski glȁvni grȁd je ....

Treća lekcija • Lesson Three

VOCABULARY

broj; brojevi	number	na + *Acc*	on, onto
danas	today	osoba	person
fino	fine	pitati, pitam	to ask (I)
grozno	awful	poznavati, poznajem	to be acquainted with (I)
jako	very, strongly	strašno	terribly
jedan, jedno, jedna	one	super	great, terrific
jedni	some	tako	so, thus
jutros	this morning	tako-tako	so-so
loše	badly	tražiti, tražim	to seek, to search for (I)
ljudi	people	treći, treće, treća	third
misliti, mislim	to think (I)	večeras	this evening
misliti na	to think of (I)	vrlo	very
muškarac, muškarca	man		

KAKO STE?

Bosnian

1. .... !
2. Molim?
1. Kako si?
2. *Dobro*, a ti?
1. *Odlično*.
2. Ko su ti ljudi?
1. Oni tamo? Oni su naši prijatelji. Zovu se Jasmin i Jasna.
2. Ne. Ne mislim na Jasmina i Jasnu. Njih poznajem. Nego ko su oni *muškarci* tamo?
1. Ah! Njih ne poznajem. Zašto pitaš?
2. Pitam zato što tražim jednu osobu.
1. Kako se zove?
2. Zove se *Emir Begović*.
1. Poznajem *Emira Begovića*. *On* nije *danas* ovdje, ali imam *njegov* broj.
2. Vrlo dobro! Hvala!
1. Molim!

Croatian

1. .... !
2. Molim?
1. Kako si?
2. *Dobro*, a ti?
1. *Odlično*.
2. Tko su ti ljudi?
1. Oni tamo? Oni su naši prijatelji. Zovu se Darko i Anka.
2. Ne. Ne mislim na Darka i Anku. Njih poznajem. Nego tko su oni *muškarci* tamo?
1. Ah! Njih ne poznajem. Zašto pitaš?
2. Pitam zato što tražim jednu osobu.
1. Kako se zove?
2. Zove se *Ivan Božić*.
1. Poznajem *Ivana Božića*. *On* nije *danas* ovdje, ali imam *njegov* broj.
2. Vrlo dobro! Hvala!
1. Molim!

Serbian Cyrillic

1. .... !
2. Молим?
1. Како си?
2. *Добро*, а ти?
1. *Одлично*.
2. Ко су ти људи?
1. Они тамо? Они су наши другови. Зову се Мирко и Јован.
2. Не. Не мислим на Мирка и Јована. Њих познајем. Него ко су они *мушкарци* тамо?
1. Ах! Њих не познајем. Зашто питаш?
2. Питам зато што тражим једну особу.
1. Како се зове?
2. Зове се *Милорад Јовановић*.
1. Познајем *Милорада Јовановића*. *Он* није *данас* овде, али имам његов број.
1. Врло добро! Хвала!
2. Молим!

Serbian Latin

1. .... ?

2. Molim?

1. Kako si?

2. *Dobro*, a ti?

1. *Odlično.*

2. Ko su ti ljudi?

1. Oni tamo? Oni su naši drugovi. Zovu se Mirko i Jovan.

2. Ne. Ne mislim na Mirka i Jovana. Njih poznajem. Nego ko su oni *muškarci* tamo?

1. Ah! Njih ne poznajem. Zašto pitaš?

2. Pitam zato što tražim jednu osobu.

1. Kako se zove?

2. Zove se *Milorad Jovanović.*

1. Poznajem *Milorada Jovanovića. On* nije *danas* ovde, ali imam *njegov* broj.

2. Vrlo dobro! Hvala!

1. Molim!

☞ **Replace** *dobro* **and** *odlično* **with** fino, grozno, loše, strašno, super, tako-tako.

☞ **Replace** *muškarac* **with** žena. **Replace the man's name** *Emir Begović* [B] *Ivan Božić* [C] *Milorad Jovanović* [S] **with a woman's name:** Amila Begović [B] Ankica Radić [C] Mirjana Jovanović [S], **and along with the change of name, change** *njegov* **to** njen [B,C,S] njezin [C].

☞ **Replace** *danas* **with** večeras, jutros.

☞ **Make this into a plural version: use a woman's and man's name, and replace** *njegov* **with** njihov.

☞ **Play** this conversation as a performance.

Self-study learners: Find all the instances in the above conversation of subject pronouns (*ja, ti, on,* etc.) and find all the instances where such pronouns could have been used but were not. Finally, find the object pronouns and determine whether they are long or short forms.

⚙ GRAMMAR

* Nominative plural of nouns *

The nominative plural ending is -*i* for most masculine nouns and -*e* for most feminine nouns. It is -*a* for all neuter nouns. **[32a]** Masculine monosyllabic nouns usually add -*ov*- before the plural ending. **[32e]** If the final consonant is one of a group called "soft," **[32f]** such a noun will add -*ev*-. Masculine nouns which have "fleeting -*a*-" in their stem lose it before the Nom.pl. ending. **[32c]** Here are examples:

	masculine				neuter	feminine
Nominative singular	*student*	*grad*	*broj*	*Amerikanac*	*pitanje*	*sestra*
Nominative plural	*studenti*	*gradovi*	*brojevi*	*Amerikanci*	*pitanja*	*sestre*

* Nominative plural of adjectives *

All adjectives, including descriptive adjectives such as *visoki* "tall," possessive pronominal adjectives such as *njihov* "theirs," and demonstratives such as *taj* "this / that," have the same endings in the nominative plural as the nouns they refer to. **[32a]**

masculine sg	*visok*	*njihov*	*taj*
masculine pl	*visoki*	*njihovi*	*ti*
neuter pl	*visoka*	*njihova*	*ta*
feminine pl	*visoke*	*njihove*	*te*

* The words meaning *person, people* *

The plural of *čovek* [E] *čovjek* [J] is *ljudi* Put differently, the word *čovek* [E] *čovjek* [J] "person" occurs only in the singular, and the word *ljudi* "people" only in the plural. **[37c]** There is another word meaning "person," which is *osoba* (plural *osobe*)

* Conjugation of *poznavati* *

As seen in the conjugation given to the right, verbs with infinitives ending in *-znavati* replace the sequence *-ava-* of the infinitive by the sequence *-aj-* in the present tense. This type of conjugation is also found in the verb *davati* "give," as well as in many verbs ending in *-davati*. Thus, the present tense of *davati* is *dajem, daješ, daje, dajemo, dajete, daju*. [30a]

poznavati	know, be acquainted with
poznajem	*poznajemo*
poznaješ	*poznajete*
poznaje	*poznaju*

* Long-form pronouns used for emphasis *

Long form pronouns occur primarily as objects of prepositions. But they are also used to convey emphasis. Used in the latter meaning, they most frequently occur at the beginning of a sentence. [24b]

* Case forms of personal names *

Most men's names end in a consonant or *-o*, and most women's names end in *-a*. In the accusative case, names take the same endings as masculine and feminine nouns, respectively. Family names, both men's and women's, usually end in a consonant. Men's family names take masculine case ending but women's family names do not change. One says, therefore, *poznajem Marka Ilića*, but *poznajem Anu Ilić*. [37a]

* Adverbs *

Adverbs describe a state (as in *dobro sam* "I'm fine") or an action (as in *dobro piše* "s/he writes well"). BCS adverbs are almost always identical in form to Nom.sg. neuter adjectives. Thus if one knows that the adjective *loš* means "bad," one can derive the adverb *loše* "badly" (and vice versa). One can predict that *fino*, the adverbial form meaning "fine!" is equivalent to the Nom.sg. neuter form of the adjective *fin* "fine." Henceforth adverbs will not be given separately in vocabulary lists. [35]

* The word for *one* *

The word *jedan* "one" is an adjective and must agree with its noun. It can mean either the number "one" (as in *imam samo jednu olovku* "I have only one pencil") or the indefinite article (as in *tražim jednu osobu* "I'm looking for a [specific] person"). When used in the plural, *jedni* means "some." Note that whereas English can use the word "one" to replace a noun (as in "that long ONE is mine"), BCS uses only the long form of the adjective (thus, *onaj dugi je moj*). [36c] In a few instances, the distinction between long and short adjectives in BCS is parallel to that between English "the" and "a/an," as seen in sentences like *imam nov udžbenik* "I have A new textbook" vs. *novi udžbenik je dobar* "THE new textbook is good." Students should avoid this parallel, however, as it fails to hold in the majority of cases. Long adjectives are used in many instances where English would use "a/an" (even in phrases after *jedan* such as *jedan veliki grad* "one/a big city"); furthermore there are quite a few BCS adjectives which have only long forms. The safest rule is to use short forms after "to be," and long forms everywhere else.

Textbooks

Paints and varnishes

VOCABULARY

divan, divno, divna	marvelous	pravi, pravo, prava	real
jesen (f)	autumn, fall	prozor	window
kroz + Acc	through	radost (f)	joy
laku noć	good night	reč (f)	word
ljubav (f)	love	riječ (f)	word
matematika	mathematics	trenutak [B,C,S]	moment
momenat [B,S]	moment	veče [B,S]	evening
noć (f)	night	večer [C] (f)	evening
onda	then	već	but, rather
poezija	poetry	velik, veliko, velika	great

LAKU NOĆ!

Bosnian
1. Dobro veče, šta radite?
2. Gledam kroz prozor. Kako je divna *noć*!
1. Zaista jeste. Pravi je momenat za veliku *ljubav!*
2. Ne mislim na *ljubav*, već na *poeziju.*
1. Na *poeziju?* Zašto ne na *ljubav?*
2. Zato što volim *riječi*, a ne ljude.
1. Onda, lahku noć!

Croatian
1. Dobra večer, što radite?
2. Gledam kroz prozor. Kako je divna *noć*!
1. Zaista jest. Pravi je trenutak za veliku *ljubav!*
2. Ne mislim na *ljubav*, već na *poeziju.*
1. Na *poeziju?* Zašto ne na *ljubav?*
2. Zato što volim *riječi*, a ne ljude.
1. Onda, laku noć!

The expression *Dobro veče* [B,S] *Dobra večer* [C] "Good evening" is used as a greeting after about 6 p.m. Note that the word may be either neuter (*veče*), or feminine (*večer*).

Laku noć "Good night" often stands alone as a phrase. Grammatically, however, it is the object of the unspoken sentence *Želim ti/vam laku noć* "I wish you a good night." This is why the word for "night" is in the accusative in this phrase. For an explanation of the forms *ti* and *vam*, see the grammar sections on p. 85.

Serbian Latin
1. Dobro veče, šta radite?
2. Gledam kroz prozor. Kako je divna *noć*!
1. Zaista jeste. Pravi je momenat za veliku *ljubav!*
2. Ne mislim na *ljubav*, već na *poeziju.*
1. Na *poeziju?* Zašto ne na *ljubav?*
2. Zato što volim *reči*, a ne ljude.
1. Onda, laku noć!

Serbian Cyrillic
1. Добро вече, шта радите?
2. Гледам кроз прозор. Како је дивна *ноћ*!
1. Заиста јесте. Прави је моменат за велику *љубав!*
2. Не мислим на *љубав*, већ на *поезију.*
1. На *поезију?* Зашто не на *љубав?*
2. Зато што волим *речи*, а не људе.
1. Онда, лаку ноћ!

꙰☞ **Replace** *noć* with jesen, *ljubav* with radost, *poezija* with matematika, *reči* [E] *riječi* [J] **with** brojevi.

 **GRAMMAR**

* Feminine nouns ending in a consonant *

Most feminine nouns end in -*a*, but several end in a consonant. The nominative and accusative singular of these nouns have the same form. Adjectives, however, keep the "feminine" endings that match nouns in -*a*. The result is that whereas noun and adjective endings

	fem. in -*a*	fem. in cons.
Nsg	vèlika poèzija	vèlika ljùbav
Asg	vèliku poèziju	vèliku ljùbav

match in most feminine nouns, they are different in this group of feminine nouns. To help remember this, the student is advised to learn these (and all) nouns together with an adjective. [31]

* Accusative plural *

The accusative plural is the same as the nominative plural for neuter nouns and for both types of feminine nouns. Masculine nouns, however, have a separate accusative plural ending, which is -*e*. [33]

	masculine	neuter	feminine -*a*	feminine in cons.
Nominative plural	dòbri ljùdi	dòbra pìtanja	dòbre žène	dòbre stvàri
Accusative plural	dòbre ljùde	dòbra pìtanja	dòbre žène	dòbre stvàri

* Added syllables in the plural *

Many masculine monosyllabic nouns add the syllable -*ov*- (or -*ev*-, after a soft consonant) before all plural endings. Some, however, do not; these must be learned. [32e] Plurals of monosyllabic nouns are given in vocabulary lists. Most neuter nouns ending in -*me* add the syllable -*en*- before plural endings. [32h]

	masculine (with added syllable)			(no added syllable)		neuter
Nominative singular	drȗg	brȏj	òtac	pȁs	dȃn	ȉme
Nominative plural	drùgovi	bròjevi	òčevi	psȉ	dȁni	imèna
Accusative plural	drùgove	bròjeve	òčeve	psȅ	dȁne	imèna

* Negation, continued *

The particle *ne* placed before the verb (and pronounced together with the verb) negates the entire sentence. The same particle placed before another word class has its own accent, and means "not X but Y." [25b]

* Long and short adjectives in this book *

The majority of adjectives have both long and short forms; although the short forms most frequently occur in the nominative (when they occur at all), they can in principle occur in other cases as well. Since it is impossible to give long and short versions for all adjectives anytime they are mentioned, this book will utilize the following conventions. Vocabulary lists give the short form (as do all dictionaries). Replacement cues under exercises give the long form (for practical reasons, as the long forms are used in most instances). Grammar charts make a compromise, giving short form adjectives in the nominative and long form adjectives in all other cases. Students interested in the accentual distinctions between long and short forms may see them in these charts; others may ignore these accentual differences.

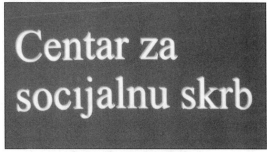

Center for Social Welfare

VOCABULARY for A3, A4

alèrgičan, alèrgično, alèrgična	allergic (to)	òtac; òčevi	father, fathers
čìji, čìje, čìja	whose	ozbȉljan, ozbȉljno, ozbȉljna	serious
dèbeo, dèbelo, dèbela	fat, thick	samo	only
dug, dȕgo, dúga	long	sav, sve, sva	all
grȁd; gradovi	city	sèlo	village
gradić	small town	sìgurno	certainly
idèja	idea	stvar (f)	thing
kàkav, kàkvo, kàkva	what kind (of)	tanak, tanko, tanka	thin, slender
kòji, kòje, kòja	which	televízija	television
kratak, krátko, krátka	short	vȉše	more
nèki, nèko, nèka	some	vȉše vòleti, vȉše volím	to prefer (I)
neozbȉljan, neozbȉljno, neozbȉljna	silly, not serious	vȉše vòljeti, vȉše volím	to prefer (I)
novine (pl form)	newspaper		

ŠTA VIŠE VOLIŠ? [B,S]   ŠTO VIŠE VOLIŠ? [C]

Bosnian and Serbian Latin
1. Šta vȉše volíš? *Pse ili mačke?*
2. Vȉše volím *pse.* Alèrgičan sam na *mačke.*
1. Jȃ volím *mačke* ali samo *nekȇ.*
2. *Kàkve mačke? Velikȇ ili malȇ?*
1. Volím *velikȇ mačke,* a tȋ? Kàkve *pse* volíš?
2. Jȃ volím samo *malȇ pse.*

Croatian
1. Što vȉše volíš? *Pse ili mačke?*
2. Vȉše volím *pse.* Alèrgičan sam na *mačke.*
1. Jȃ volím *mačke* ali samo *nekȇ.*
2. *Kàkve mačke? Velikȇ ili malȇ?*
1. Volím *velikȇ mačke,* a tȋ? Kakve *pse* volíš?
2. Jȃ volím samo *malȇ pse.*

Serbian Cyrillic
1. Шта вȉше волȉш? *Псе или мачке?*
2. Вȉше волȉм *псе.* Алèргичан сам на *мачке.*
1. Јȃ волȉм *мачке* али само *некȇ.*
2. *Какве мачке? Великȇ или малȇ?*
1. Волȉм *великȇ мачке,* а тȋ? Кȁкве *псе* волȉш?
2. Јȃ волȉм само *малȇ псе.*

Hairdresser
for women and
men

✍ **Replace** *psi* and *mačke* **with a)** gradovi, gradići, sela; **b)** knjige, filmovi; **c)** novine, televízija; **d)** rȅči [E] rijèči [J], brojevi; **e)** stvȃri, idèje;. **Instead of** *veliki* and *mali* **use   a)** kratak, dug; **b)** dèbeo, tanak; **c)** ozbȉljan, neozbȉljan, **or other adjectives from earlier exercises.**

✍ **Retell** the exercise as a conversation between two people using formal address (using *vȋ* forms instead of *tȋ* forms).

Tricky translation of prepositions: Phrases such as *misliti na* and *alèrgičan na* do not translate into English the same way. For instance, in these phrases English has "think OF," but "allergic TO."

ČIJE SU OVE OLOVKE?

Bosnian, Croatian and Serbian Latin
1. Čìje su òve olo̱vke?
2. Mòje.
1. Kòje su tvòje?
2. Sve su mòje.
1. I duge̱ i kratke̱? Sigu̱rno su òve duge̱ tvòje, a kratke̱ mòje.
2. Ne, sve su mòje.

Serbian Cyrillic
1. Чѝје су òве оло̱вке?
2. Мòје.
1. Кòје су твòје?
2. Све су мòје.
1. И дуге̱ и кратке̱? Сигу̱рно су òве дуге̱ твòје, а кратке̱ мòје.
2. Не, све су мòје.

☞ **Replace** olo̱vka **with** cìpela, časopis, knjiga, pìtanje, rečni̱k [E], rječni̱k [J], stva̱r, udžbeni̱k, **and replace** dugi̱ **and** kratki̱ **with a)** be̱li [E] bije̱li [J] **and** crni̱; **b)** debeli̱ **and** tanki̱; **c)** dobri̱ **and** loši̱; **d)** ružni̱ **and** le̱pi [E] lije̱pi [J]; **e)** te̱ški̱ **and** lahki̱ [B] laki̱ [B,C,S]; **f)** veliki̱ **and** mali̱, **and adjectives from earlier exercises.**

☞ **Retell** the exercise using formal address (using vi̱ forms instead of ti̱ forms).

⚙ GRAMMAR

* Interrogative pronominal adjectives *

Here are the nominative forms of interrogative adjectives **[36a]** and the word "all." **[36b]** Since they are adjectives, they must agree with the noun they modify.

For full declensions of these and similar pronominal adjectives, consult the charts on pp. 326-327.

	singular			plural			
	masc.	neut.	fem.	masc.	neut.	fem.	
	kòji	kòje	kòja	kòji	kòja	kòje	which
	čìji	čìje̱	čìja	čìji	čìja	čìje̱	whose
	kàkav	kàkvo	kàkva	kàkvi	kàkva	kàkve	what [kind]
	sav	sve	sva	svi	sva	sve	all

* Sound shifts in nominative plural *

Masculine nouns ending in -k, -g or -h replace these consonants with -c, -z, or -s, respectively, before the Nom. plural ending -i. **[32b]** Here are examples:

Nsg	udžbeni̱k	bùbreg	òrah
Npl	udžbeni̱ci	bùbrezi	òrasi

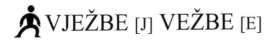 VJEŽBE [J] VEŽBE [E]

B1

Bosnian	Croatian	Serbian Latin	Serbian Cyrillic
1. Mislim na prijatelja.	1. Mislim na prijatelja.	1. Mislim na druga.	1. Мислим на друга.
2. Na koga?	2. Na koga?	2. Na koga?	2. На кога?
1. Na *Jasmina!*	1. Na *Ivana!*	1. Na *Mirka!*	1. На *Мирка!*
2. Ali zašto ne misliš na *Jasnu?*	2. Ali zašto ne misliš na *Anku?*	2. Ali zašto ne misliš na *Tomislava?*	2. Али зашто не мислиш на *Томислава?*
1. Zato što na *nju* ne volim da mislim.	1. Zato što na *nju* ne volim misliti.	1. Zato što na *njega* ne volim da mislim.	1. Зато што на *њега* не волим да мислим.

☞ **Replace the names used here with other personal names** (see p. 317 for list of names), **and then with the following pairs: a)** ova žena, onaj muškarac; **b)** naš profesor, onaj profesor; **c)** ta osoba, ti ljudi.

B2

Bosnian	Croatian	Serbian Latin	Serbian Cyrillic
1. Koga vidiš?	1. Koga vidiš?	1. Koga vidiš?	1. Кога видиш?
2. Vidim i *njega* i *nju* i *njih.*	2. Vidim i *njega* i *nju* i *njih.*	2. Vidim i *njega* i *nju* i *njih.*	2. Видим и *њега* и *њу* и *њих.*
1. Molim?	1. Molim?	1. Molim?	1. Молим?
2. *Jasmina* i *Mersihu* i neke *studente.*	2. *Darka* i *Anku* i neke *studente.*	2. *Mirka* i *Mariju* i neke *studente.*	2. *Мирка* и *Марију* и неке *студенте.*

☞ **Replace the names given above with names that you choose from the list on p. 317. Replace** *student* **with** Amerikanac, Amerikanka, Englez, Engleskinja, Francuz, Francuskinja.

B3

Bosnian and Serbian Latin	Croatian	Serbian Cyrillic
1. Mislim na *ideje.*	1. Mislim na *ideje.*	1. Мислим на *идеје.*
2. Na šta?	2. Na što?	2. На шта?
1. Na *ideje!*	1. Na *ideje!*	1. На *идеје!*
2. Ali zašto ne misliš na *stvari?*	2. Ali zašto ne misliš na *stvari?*	2. Али зашто не мислиш на *ствари?*
1. Zato što su *ideje* prave, a *stvari* su neozbiljne.	1. Zato što su *ideje* prave, a *stvari* su neozbiljne.	1. Зато што су *идеје* праве, а *ствари* су неозбиљне.

☞ **Replace** *ideje* **and** *stvari* **with: a)** časopisi, novine; **b)** gradovi, gradići; **c)** noći, dani; **d)** pitanja, odgovori.

B4

Redo these sentences as negatives:

Bosnian, Croatian	Serbian Latin	Serbian Cyrillic
1. Čȉtam ròman i mislȋm na tebe.	1. Čȉtam ròman i mislȋm na tebe.	1. Читам роман и мислим на тебе.
2. Pòznajem tȅ ljude.	2. Pòznajem tȅ ljude.	2. Познајем те људе.
3. Ȉmamo novine.	3. Ȉmamo novine.	3. Имамо новине.
4. Pas je prijatelj.	4. Pas je drȗg.	4. Пас је друг.
5. Volȋm misliti na velikȇ gradove.	5. Volȋm da mislȋm na velikȇ gradove.	5. Волим да мислим на велике градове.

B5

Bosnian	Croatian	Serbian Latin	Serbian Cyrillic
1. Šta vidiš kroz pròzor?	1. Što vidiš kroz pròzor?	1. Šta vidiš kroz pròzor?	1. Шта видиш кроз прозор?
2. Vidȋm *i velikȇ i malȇ pse*.	2. Vidȋm *i velikȇ i malȇ pse*.	2. Vidȋm *i velikȇ i malȇ pse*.	2. Видим *и велике и мале псе*.
1. Dobro, vidȋm *jèdnog velikog psa*, ali gdje su *mali*?	1. Dobro, vidȋm *jèdnoga velikog psa*, ali gdje su *mali*?	1. Dobro, vidȋm *jednog velikog psa*, ali gde su *mali*?	1. Добро, видим *једног великог пса*, али где су *мали*?
2. Tamo su i *mali* i *velikȋ psi*.	2. Tamo su i *mali* i *velikȋ psi*.	2. Tamo su i *mali* i *velikȋ psi*.	2. Тамо су и *мали* и *велики пси*.
1. A, sad ih vidȋm!	1. A, sad ih vidȋm!	1. A, sad ih vidȋm!	1. А, сад их видим!

☞ **Replace italicized words in the second line with: a)** plȃvȇ i žútȇ cȉpele; **b)** vȉsoki i niski profèsori, **and make appropriate adjustments in following lines.**

B6

Ask each other these questions (based on material in the dialogues in 3A1, 3A2, 3A3 and 3A4). Insert in the blank the B, C, or S name of a student playing the numbered part.

Bosnian, Croatian and Serbian Latin	Serbian Cyrillic
A1 Kòga trȃžȋ .... (brȏj 2)?	A1 Кога тражи .... (број 2)?
A2 Zašto .... (brȏj 1) mislȋ na ljȕbav?	A2 Зашто .... (број 1) мисли на љубав?
Zašto .... (brȏj 2) mislȋ na poèziju?	Зашто .... (број 2) мисли на поезију?
A3 Zašto .... (brȏj 2) vȉšē volȋ pse?	A3 Зашто .... (број 2) више воли псе?
A4 Čȉjē su kràtkȇ òlovke, mòje ili tvòje?	A4 Чије су кратке оловке, моје или твоје?

B7

Bosnian and Serbian Latin	Croatian	Serbian Cyrillic
1. Na šta si alèrgičan?	1. Na što si alèrgičan?	1. На шта си алергичан?
2. Jȃ sam alèrgičan na .... (ona).	2. Jȃ sam alèrgičan na .... (ona).	2. Ја сам алергичан на .... (она)
1. A jȃ sam alèrgična na .... (on).	1. A jȃ sam alèrgična na .... (on).	1. А ја сам алергична на .... (он).

☞ **Fill the blanks with the correct form of the word in parentheses, and then with the correct form of** idèje, knjige, novine, òni, profèsori, rečnȋci [E] rječnȋci [J], stvȃri, udžbenȋci.

✍ DOMAĆA ZADAĆA [B,C] DOMAĆI ZADATAK [S]

C1

Give the singular form for each of these nominative plural forms. Circle the accented syllable.

bròjevi	бро̀јеви
òlovke	о̀ло̲вке
lju̲di	љу̲ди
knji̲ge	књи̲ге
pi̲sma	пи̏сма
òčevi	о̀чеви
pȉtanja	пи̏та̲ња
ključevi	кључеви
udžbeni̲ci	уџбени̲ци
stva̲ri	ства̲ри
mačke	мачке

C2

Give the nominative and accusative plural forms of each of the following. Circle the accented syllable.

žèna	udžbeni̲k	жѐна	уџбени̲к
gra̲d	prijatelj	гра̲д	пријатељ
lju̲bav	pèro	љу̲бав	перо
rjèčni̲k	dru̲g	речни̲к	дру̲г
tèka	jèzik	свеска	јѐзик
pas	film	пас	филм
òlovka	pȉtanje	о̀ло̲вка	пи̏тање
stva̲r	časopi̲s	ства̲р	часопи̲с
kàsa	blaga̲jna	каса	блага̲јна

C3

Make pairs consisting of a preposition from column A and a noun or phrase from column B.
Remember that each of these prepositions requires the accusative case.

A	**B**	**A**	**B**
za	mòji dra̲gi prijatelji	за	мо̀ји дра̲ги другови
kroz	o̲n	кроз	о̲н
misliti na	dòbra pȉtanja	мислити на	до̀бра пи̏та̲ња
alèrgičan na	mi̲	алѐргичан на	ми̲
	di̲vna no̲ć		дивна но̲ħ
	òni		они
	loš časopi̲s		лош часопис

C4

Note: the following two exercises are intended to give the student practice in the Cyrillic alphabet, in addition to practice in grammar.

Read the following words aloud. For each of the noun + adjective combinations, identify (a) case, (b) number, and (c) gender. That is, say whether it is (a) nominative or accusative, (b) singular or plural, and (c) masculine, neuter or feminine.
For each of the verb forms identify (a) person, and (b) number. That is, say whether it is (a) 1st, 2nd or 3rd person and (b) singular or plural.

adjectives and nouns	**verbs**
дивне ноћи	виде
црвеног пса	имају
једно питање	волимо
	желим да купим
брзи ауто	желе да видиш
лепе жене	смо
велике људе	
добри другови	
тешку реч	
праве идеје	

C5

Combine the nouns, adjectives and verbs given in C4 to make four sentences. Write the sentences out in Cyrillic.

Sentences
1.
2.
3.
4.

C6

Analysis
1. What ways to make questions have you learned in the first three lessons?
2. Find five examples of expressing negation in the material you have seen until now.
3. Provide full present tense conjugation for three verbs from Lesson 2 (other than *imati, učiti, kupiti* or *pisati*).
4. Which masculine nouns seen so far have the nominative plural ending in -*ovi* and -*evi*?
5. Which feminine nouns seen so far are of the type that end in a consonant?
6. How would you describe the differences between Bosnian, Croatian and Serbian based on what you have learned so far?
7. Give five examples of adjectives and five examples of adverbs used in the first three lessons.

VOCABULARY

granica	border	teći, tečem (3rd pl. teku)	to flow
reka	river	ušće	river mouth, confluence
rijeka	river	uz	along, along with
stvarati, stvaram	to create		

For help in answering these questions consult the map at the beginning of the book.

<u>Bosnian and Croatian</u>
1. Koja rijeka teče kroz Zagreb?
2. Koje rijeke teku kroz Beograd i stvaraju ušće?
3. Koje su velike bosanske rijeke?
4. Koje su velike crnogorske rijeke?
5. Koja rijeka teče uz bosanskohrvatsku granicu?
6. Koja rijeka teče uz bosanskosrpsku granicu?
7. Koja rijeka teče uz hrvatskosrpsku granicu?

<u>Serbian Latin</u>
1. Koja reka teče kroz Zagreb?
2. Koje reke teku kroz Beograd i stvaraju ušće?
3. Koje su velike bosanske reke?
4. Koje su velike crnogorske reke?
5. Koja reka teče uz bosanskohrvatsku granicu?
6. Koja reka teče uz bosanskosrpsku granicu?
7. Koja reka teče uz hrvatskosrpsku granicu?

<u>Serbian Cyrillic</u>
1. Која река тече кроз Загреб?
2. Које реке теку кроз Београд и стварају ушће?
3. Које су велике босанске реке?
4. Које су велике црногорске реке?
5. Која река тече уз босанскохрватску границу?
6. Која река тече уз босанскосрпску границу?
7. Која река тече уз хрватскосрпску границу?

Confluence (in Belgrade) of the Sava and Danube rivers

Četvrta lekcija • Lesson Four

Novi rekviziti: jabuka, keks, kreker, kruška, orah, slatkiš, sok od naranče [C] sok od narandže [B] sok od pomorandže [S], stolica, šljiva.

ꙮA1   ⊙ 29,30

Beč, Beča	Vienna	Njemačka	Germany
četvrti, četvrto, četvrta	fourth	nov, novo, nova	new
devojka	girl, young woman	Novi Beograd	New Belgrade
djevojka	girl, young woman	Novi Zagreb	New Zagreb
Engleska	England	odakle	from where
Europa [C]	Europe	Pariz, Pariza	Paris
Evropa [B,S]	Europe	roditelj	parent
Francuska	France	SAD	USA
Grčka	Greece	Severna Amerika	North America
iz + *Gen*	from	Sjeverna Amerika	North America
Južna Amerika	South America	Španija [B,S]	Spain
Kalifornija	California	Španjolska [B,C]	Spain
London, Londona	London	Stari Grad	part of Sarajevo
momak, momka	boy, young man	takođe [B,S]	also
Moskva	Moscow	također [B,C]	also
Nemačka	Germany		

On the use of Cyrillic. From now on all S material is given alternately in Serbian Latin and Serbian Cyrillic. Students who choose to focus on Serbian should use the opportunity to write homework only in Cyrillic.

ODAKLE STE?

Bosnian
1. Odakle su tvoji roditelji?
2. Moji roditelji su iz .... A tvoji?
1. Moji roditelji su iz .... A jesi li i ti iz .... ?
2. Ja sam također iz .... A ti? Jesi li i ti iz .... kao što su tvoji roditelji?
1. Nisam. Ja sam iz ....
2. A ona djevojka tamo? Odakle su njeni roditelji?
1. Njeni roditelji su iz ....
2. A onaj momak? Odakle su njegovi roditelji?
1. Njegovi roditelji su iz ....

Croatian
1. Odakle su tvoji roditelji?
2. Moji su roditelji iz .... A tvoji?
1. Moji su roditelji iz .... A jesi li i ti iz .... ?
2. Ja sam također iz .... A ti? Jesi li i ti iz .... kao što su tvoji roditelji?
1. Nisam. Ja sam iz ....
2. A ona djevojka tamo? Odakle su njezini roditelji?
1. Njezini su roditelji iz ....
2. A onaj momak? Odakle su njegovi roditelji?
1. Njegovi su roditelji iz ....

Serbian
1. Odakle su tvoji roditelji?
2. Moji roditelji su iz .... A tvoji?
1. Moji roditelji su iz .... A da li si i ti iz .... ?
2. Ja sam takođe iz .... A ti? Da li si i ti iz .... kao što su tvoji roditelji?
1. Nisam. Ja sam iz ....
2. A ona devojka tamo? Odakle su njeni roditelji?
1. Njeni roditelji su iz ....
2. A onaj momak? Odakle su njegovi roditelji?
1. Njegovi roditelji su iz ....

ꙮ **Fill in the blanks using the following**: Beč, Čikago [S] Chicago [B,C], Engleska, Europa [C] Evropa [B,S], Francuska, Grčka, Južna Amerika, Kalifornija*, London, Mađarska, Moskva, New York [B,C] Njujork[S]*, Nemačka [E] Njemačka [J], Novi Beograd, Novi Zagreb, Pariz*, SAD, Severna Amerika [E] Sjeverna Amerika [J], Stari Grad, Španija [B,S] Španjolska [B,C], Washington [B,C] Vašington[S]*.

---

* **Note**. B,C often, but not always, spell foreign place names as in the original; S spells them phonetically.

 **GRAMMAR**

* Forms of the genitive case *

One of the most important BCS cases is the genitive case. The endings for masculine and neuter nouns are the same as those for masculine animate accusative nouns. The endings for the two kinds of feminine nouns are -*e* and -*i*, respectively, and the ending for all feminine adjectives is -*e*. **[42a]**

	masculine	neuter	feminine -a	feminine -cons
Nominative singular	*nov grad*	*novo selo*	*nova knjiga*	*nova ljubav*
Genitive singular	*novog grada*	*novog sela*	*nove knjige*	*nove ljubavi*

* Fleeting vowels and consonant softening *

As in the animate accusative masculine, nouns with fleeting -*a*- in Nominative singular [Nsg] lose this vowel in Genitive singular [Gsg]. The stem to which the Gsg ending is added is the base stem for all other endings. **[42b]** If it is different from the Nsg it is given in vocabulary listings. The masculine-neuter adjective ending -*og* appears as -*eg* after "soft" consonants. These are: *š, ž, dž, č, ć, đ, nj, lj, j, c*. **[32f]**

* Possible accent shifts *

Several masculine nouns have a long final syllable in Nsg, and a short rising accent on the prefinal syllable. When endings are added, the long syllable becomes the prefinal syllable, with a long rising accent. **[42b]** Certain verbs also shift the accent between the infinitive and the present tense. The shift can be from rising to falling, or to rising one syllable closer to the beginning of the word. In verbs of the *a*-conjugation, the shift occurs in all forms but 3rd plural (thus: *nemati, nemam* but *nemaju*). **[14a]** All these shifts are quite noticeable in speech.

Nsg	London	fakultet
Gsg	Londona	fakulteta
infinitive	kazati	govoriti
1sg.pres.	kažem	govorim

* Question words and conjunctions *

To ask about a person's place of origin, English speakers must use the phrase "where ... from" (as in "where are you from?"). Speakers of BCS use the single question word *odakle*. Like other question words, it comes at the beginning of the sentence. **[49]** The conjunction *kao* "like, as" may be followed directly by a noun or pronoun, but if it is followed by a clause containing a verb it takes the form *kao što*. **[50]**

* Pronunciation of alphabet letters *

Alphabet letters are pronounced as follows; *ah, beh, tse, chuh, chyuh, deh, juh, jyuh, eh, ef, geh, hah, eee, yuh, kah, el, lyuh, muh, nuh, nyuh, o, peh, ruh* (or *ehr*), *suh* (or *ess*), *shuh, teh, oo, vuh, zuh, zhuh*. Note that the order of letters in Cyrillic is different. The abbreviation SAD (USA) is pronounced "ess-ah-deh." The English letters **q, w, x** and **y** are pronounced: *koo* [S] *kveh* [B,C], *duplo-veh, eeks,* and *eepsalon*.

Street names

VOCABULARY

čak	even	nema	there is no (.....)
dakle	therefore	prijateljica [B,C,S]	friend (f)
drugarica [B,S]	friend (f)	tako je	that's right!
gde	where	tri	three
gdje	where	tu	here
jer	because	znati, znam	to know (I)
kod + Gen	at, by		

KOD KOGA SU NAŠE KNJIGE?

Bosnian
1. *Hasane*, gdje je moja *knjiga*?
2. Tu kod mene je.
1. A *Zlatanova knjiga*?
2. I njegova *knjiga* je kod mene.
1. A *Mirjanina knjiga*?
2. Čak je i njena *knjiga* kod mene.
1. Zašto su sve naše *knjige* kod tebe?
2. Jer ih čitam.
1. A kod koga je ona knjiga naše prijateljice *Hane?*
2. Čija?
1. *Hanina!*
2. Eh, te *knjige* nema. Ne znam kod koga je.
1. Dakle tri *knjige* su kod tebe, a jedne *knjige* nema?
2. Tako je!

Croatian
1. *Ante,* gdje je moja *knjiga*?
2. Tu kod mene je.
1. A *Brankova knjiga*?
2. I njegova *knjiga* je kod mene.
1. A *Mirjanina knjiga*?
2. Čak je i njezina *knjiga* kod mene.
1. Zašto su sve naše *knjige* kod tebe?
2. Jer ih čitam.
1. A kod koga je ona knjiga naše prijateljice *Dijane?*
2. Čija?
1. *Dijanina!*
2. Eh, te *knjige* nema. Ne znam kod koga je.
1. Dakle tri *knjige* su kod tebe, a jedne *knjige* nema?
2. Tako je!

Serbian
1. *Мирко*, где је моја *књига*?
2. Ту код мене је.
1. А *Слободанова књига*?
2. И његова *књига* је код мене.
1. А *Мирјанина књига*?
2. Чак је и њена *књига* код мене.
1. Зашто су све наше *књиге* код тебе?
2. Јер их читам.
1. А код кога је она књига наше другарице *Гроздане?*
2. Чија?
1. *Грозданина!*
2. Ех, те *књиге* нема. Не знам код кога је.
1. Дакле три *књиге* су код тебе, а једне *књиге* нема?
2. Тако је!

☞ **Replace the names above with**: Ana, Andreja, Dobrilo, Hrvoje, Hajrudin, Jelena, Juraj, Saša, Zehra.

☞ **Replace** *knjiga* **with** bilježnica [C] sveska [S] teka [B], časopis, knjiga poezije, pismo, roman, udžbenik.

Street names

⚙ GRAMMAR

* Possessive pronominal adjectives *

An adjective formed from a person's name specifies that the person is the possessor of something indicated by a particular noun. To form this adjective, subtract the ending from the genitive form of the person's name (see box below), and then add the possessive suffix, which is *–in-* if the possessor is feminine, and *-ov-* or *-ev-* if the possessor is masculine. To that, then add the regular adjective endings. Such adjectives have only short forms, and only single words can express possession in this way. [41b] Here are examples:

name	name (Gsg)	sex	possessive adjective	adjective + noun (m)	adjective + noun (f)
Mìrjana	*Mìrjan-e*	female	*Mìrjan-in*	*Mìrjanin rječnik*	*Mìrjanina knjiga*
Pètar	*Pètr-a*	male	*Pètr-ov*	*Pètrov rječnik*	*Pètrova knjiga*

* Short form adjectives in the genitive case *

Most adjectives which have both short and long forms use the short forms in the nominative case only, and the long forms elsewhere. But the possessive pronominal adjectives (including those such as *njègov* "his," *njihov* "theirs, their," *njèzin* [C] *njen* [B,C,S] "her, hers") have short form endings in Gsg masculine. These endings are like those of the nouns: *od njihova grada* "from their city," *brat njèzina učitelja* "her teacher's brother." The long endings are also possible, as in *do njègovog auta* "by his auto," *kod njènog oca* "at her father's." The short endings are officially required in C, though the long endings can sometimes be heard. The long endings are much more frequent in B and S. [42c]

* Uses of the genitive case *

The genitive is used with a number of prepositions, among which are *iz* "out of, from" [43a] and *kod*, which means "by, with, at." When a person's name follows *kod*, the meaning ranges from temporary possession to physical location (this location is usually, but not always, one's own house). [43b] The genitive case is also used with the unchanging word *nema*, which signifies the absence of something or someone. [44c, 59b] When two nouns are adjacent and the second is in the genitive case, the meaning is similar to that of English "of." For instance, *čaša hladne vode* means "a glass OF cold water." [44a]

* Pronouns in the genitive case *

The genitive forms of *ko* [B,S] *tko* [C] "who," and of all personal pronouns except for fem. sg. full form [42d] are identical to the accusative forms. Here are the genitive case forms of *šta* [B,S] *što* [C], and of the full form feminine personal pronouns:

Nom	*šta* or *što*	*òna*
Acc	*šta* or *što*	*nju* [full]
Gen	*čega*	*nje* [full]

* Turning questions into statements*

To make a question part of a statement, simply treat the question word as a conjunction. Contrary to English, the word order does not change. Thus, a question such as *gde* [E] *gdje* [J] *je moja knjiga?* "where is my book?" is inserted directly after the main verb, creating the statement *ne znam gde* [E] *gdje* [J] *je moja knjiga* "I don't know where my book is." [51]

VOCABULARY

bez + *Gen*	without	mlȅko	milk
čaj	tea	mlijȅko	milk
čȁša	glass	nàranča [C]	orange
dvȃ	two *(m, n)*	nàrandža [B]	orange
dvȇ	two *(f)*	nešto, nečega	something
dvȉje	two *(f)*	nȉšta, nȉčega	nothing
glȃdan, glȃdno, glȃdna	hungry	od + *Gen*	of, from
hlȁdan, hlȁdno, hlȁdna	cold	ȍrah	walnut
hlȅb [S]	bread	pȁrče, pȁrčeta [B,S]	piece
hljȅb [B,S]	bread	pȉvo	beer
jȁbuka	apple	pomòrandža [S]	orange
jȍš	more, still	pun, puno, puna	full
kȁfa [B,S]	coffee	sȉr	cheese
kȁva [C]	coffee	slȁtkiš, slȁtkiša	candy, sweets
kȅks	cookie	sȍk, sȍka	juice
kòmad, komàda [B,C,S]	piece	šljȉva	plum
krȅker	cracker	tȍpao, tȍplo, tòpla	warm
kruh [B,C]	bread	vȉno	wine
krȕška	pear	vȍće	fruit
lȇd	ice	vȍda	water
limunàda	lemonade	žȅdan, žȅdno, žȅdna	thirsty
minerȃlnȃ vòda	mineral water		

I JOŠ NEŠTO ...

Bosnian	Croatian	Serbian
1. .... ! Jeste li žȅdni? Žèlite li čašu *sòka*?	1. .... ! Jeste li žȅdni? Žèlite li čašu *sòka*?	1. .... ! Da li ste žȅdni? Žèlite li čašu *sòka*?
2. Ne, hvàla, ìmam *sòka od nàrandže,* ali žèlim *hlȁdnē vòdē* bez leda.	2. Ne, hvàla, ìmam *sòka od nàranče,* ali žèlim *hlȁdnē vòdē* bez leda.	2. Ne, hvàla, ìmam *sòka od pomòrandže,* ali žèlim *hlȁdnē vòdē* bez leda.
1. Izvòlite punȗ čašu *hlȁdnē vòdē.* Šta još žèlite?	1. Izvòlite punȗ čašu *hlȁdnē vòdē.* Što još žèlite?	1. Izvòlite punȗ čašu *hlȁdnē vòdē.* Šta još žèlite?
2. Molȉm *dvȃ keksa.*	2. Molȉm *dvȃ keksa.*	2. Molȉm *dvȃ keksa.*
1. Ìmamo ȍva *dvȃ fȋna keksa.* Mȍže?	1. Ìmamo ȍva *dvȃ fȋna keksa.* Mȍže?	1. Ìmamo ȍva *dvȃ fȋna keksa.* Mȍže?
2. Mȍže, hvàla!	2. Mȍže, hvàla!	2. Mȍže, hvàla!
1. I još nešto?	1. I još nešto?	1. I još nešto?
2. Hvȁla, ništa vȉše!	2. Hvȁla, ništa vȉše!	2. Hvȁla, ništa vȉše!

🖙 **Fill in the blank** with the vocative of a classmate's Bosnian, Croatian, or Serbian name.

🖙 **Replace the beverages with**: čaj, kȁfa [B,S] kȁva [C], limunàda, minerȃlnȃ vòda, mlȅko [E] mlijȅko [J], pȉvo, vȉno.

🖙**Replace** *žȅdan* **with** glȁdan, **and the nouns with words for foods instead of beverages.**

🖙**For other snacks use**: jȁbuka, nàranča [C] nàrandža [B] pomòrandža [S], kòmad hljeba [B,S] kòmad kruha [C] pàrče hleba [S], kòmad sira [B,C] pàrče sira [B,S], krȅker, krȕška, ȍrah, slȁtkiš, šljȉva, vȍće.

🖙**Add the adjectives** sladak **and/or** topao. **Replace** *dvȃ* **with** trȉ, čètiri.

**GRAMMAR**

* Numbers *

The word for 1 is an adjective and agrees with its noun. **[36c]** The forms of the words for 2 and "both" depend on the gender of what is counted: if it is masculine the words are *dva* and *oba*, respectively but if it is feminine they are *dve* [E] *dvije* [J] and *obe* [E] *obje* [J], respectively. The forms for 3 and 4 do not change. **[46]** After the numbers 2, 3, and 4, masculine and neuter nouns and modifiers all take the ending -*a*. Feminine nouns and modifiers take endings which look like the regular Gsg endings, but are not long. **[46a]**

	masculine	neuter	feminine
1: *jèdan / jèdno / jèdna*	*jèdan veliki grad*	*jèdno veliko selo*	*jèdna velika knjiga* (*stvar*)
2: *dva / dve* or *dvije*	*ova dva velika grada* (*sela*)		*ove dve* or *dvije knjige* (*stvari*)
both *oba / obe* or *obje*	*oba velika grada* (*sela*)		*obe* or *obje knjige* (*stvari*)
3 [4] *tri [četiri]*	*ova tri [četiri] velika grada* (*sela*)		*ove tri [četiri] knjige* (*stvari*)

* Partitive genitive *

The genitive direct object conveys the idea "some [of]" or a "part of" something as in, for instance, *želiš li soka?* "would you like some juice?" This meaning is called the "partitive genitive." By contrast, the accusative direct object denotes a general idea or any one thing in its entirety; for instance *volim sok* "I like juice" (general) or *želim jedan sok* "I want [a glass / can / bottle] of juice" (entire unit). **[45]**

* Names, continued *

Masculine names ending in -*a* take the case endings of feminine nouns in -*a*. Certain masculine names ending in -*o*, the most common of which is *Ìvo*, also take these case endings. Their gender is masculine, however, requiring masculine adjectives, as in *poznajem samo jednog Nìkolu, i jednog Ìvu* "I know only one Nikola, and one Ivo." Names ending in -*ski* or -*ska* are declined as adjectives. Feminine surnames take case endings only if they end in -*a*. **[89d]**

Street names

VOCABULARY

blizu + *Gen*	near	obe	both *(f)*
čega	what *(genitive)*	obje	both *(f)*
daleko	far	ploča [C]	blackboard
do + *Gen*	next to, up to	pored + *Gen*	next to
drugo	second, secondly	prvo	first, firstly
eno	there is	ruski [jezik]	Russian [language]
evo	here is	s + *Gen*	from, off of
između + *Gen*	between, among	sa +*Gen*	from, off of
na + *Acc*	into	stolica	chair
nemački [jezik]	German [language]	tabla [B,S]	blackboard
njemački [jezik]	German [language]	zelen, zeleno, zelena	green
oba	both *(m)*	zid	wall

TRAŽIM NEKE STVARI

Bosnian

1. .... ! Tražim neke stvari.
2. Koje stvari?
1. Prvo, *rječnik*. Imaš li ga?
2. Koji *rječnik*? S *engleskog* na *bosanski*, ili sa *bosanskog* na *engleski*?
1. Sa *bosanskog* na *engleski*, onaj *plave* boje.
2. Ah, evo *ga* ovdje, blizu tebe! Još nešto?
1. Da, drugo, nema *mog udžbenika*. Znaš li gdje je?
2. Znam. Eno *ga* daleko od tebe, tamo do *teke* pored *table*.
1. Pored čega?
2. Pored *table*!
1. A onda gdje su moje *dvije lijepe olovke*?
2. Obje olovke su između *bosanskog rječnika* i tvog *udžbenika*.

Croatian

1. .... ! Tražim neke stvari.
2. Koje stvari?
1. Prvo, *rječnik*. Imaš li ga?
2. Koji *rječnik*? S *engleskoga* na *hrvatski* ili s *hrvatskoga* na *engleski*?
1. S *hrvatskoga* na *engleski*, onaj *plave* boje.
2. Ah, evo *ga* ovdje, blizu tebe! Još nešto?
1. Da, drugo, nema *moga udžbenika*. Znaš li gdje je?
2. Znam. Eno *ga* daleko od tebe, tamo do *bilježnice* pored *ploče*.
1. Pored čega?
2. Pored *ploče*!
1. A onda gdje su moje *dvije lijepe olovke*?
2. Obje olovke su između *hrvatskog rječnika* i tvog *udžbenika*.

Serbian

1. .... ! Тражим неке ствари.
2. Које ствари?
1. Прво, *речник*. Да ли га имаш?
2. Који *речник*? Са *енглеског* на *српски*, или са *српског* на *енглески*?
1. Са *српског* на *енглески*, онај *плаве* боје.
2. Ах, ево *га* овде, близу тебе! Још нешто?
1. Да, друго, нема мог *уџбеника*. Да ли знаш где је?
2. Знам. Ено *га* далеко од тебе, тамо до *свеске* поред *табле*.
1. Поред чега?
2. Поред *табле!*
1. А онда где су моје *две лепе оловке*?
2. Обе оловке су између *српског речника* и тво*г уџбеника*.

☞ **Fill** in the blank with the vocative of a classmate's Bosnian, Croatian, or Serbian name.

☞ **Replace** *engleski* **and** *bosanski, hrvatski, srpski* **with a)** engleski, ruski; **b)** francuski, nemački [E] njemački [J].

☞ **Replace** *udžbenik, rečnik* [E] *rječnik* [J] **and** *olovka* **with** bilježnica [C] sveska [S] teka [B], cipela, čaša, knjiga poezije, papir, pero, pismo.

☞ **Replace** *tabla* [B,S] *ploča* [C] **with** stolica, zid, prozor, **and** *plavi* **with** crni, crveni, zeleni, žuti.

GRAMMAR

* Prepositions with the genitive, continued *

The preposition *od* "from" can sometimes be used in expressions of possession; it is also used together with the preposition *do* "to / up to / next to" to define the limits of something (as in "from X to Y"). The preposition *s* means "from / down from." It is often used together with the preposition *na* [+ Acc] in expressions meaning "from ... to." The preposition *s* takes the form *sa* when the following word begins with a similar sounding consonant, although in S it usually takes the form *sa* elsewhere as well. [43a]

* "Pointer" words *

The words *evo* and *eno* are used to point something out to someone. The person or thing being identified is usually marked by genitive case endings. To identify something close by, use *evo*, and to identify something further away, use *eno*. [44c]

* English *It is*... sentences *

Many English sentences which begin with "It is..." do not have an identifiable subject; the English word "it" simply holds the place of a subject. But BCS sentences of this sort have no subject at all, and the verb is always 3rd singular. For example, there is no grammatical subject in *koliko je od X do Y?* "how far is it from X to Y?" or *nije daleko* "it isn't far." [48]

* Verb conjugation *

Among the verbs whose present tense is not predictable from the infinitive are *jesti*, [40c] *piti*, [14d] and *uzeti*. [52f] Their conjugations are:

jesti	eat		*piti*	drink		*uzeti*	take
jedem	*jedemo*		*pijem*	*pijemo*		*uzmem*	*uzmemo*
jedeš	*jedete*		*piješ*	*pijete*		*uzmeš*	*uzmete*
jede	*jedu*		*pije*	*piju*		*uzme*	*uzmu*

* Long and "longer" adjectives *

The Gsg ending for masc-neut long form adjectives is *-og*. There is also a "longer" form, ending in *-oga*. There is no difference in meaning: both *velikog* and *velikoga* are possible. Longer forms are frequent in high style, and more frequent in C than they are in B or S. If an adjective is used alone, standing for a noun, then the longer form is required. However if another modifier is present the long form is sufficient. Thus, one says *želim crvenoga* "I want the red one," but may say *želim onog crvenog* "I want that red one." If two long forms are in sequence, the first is frequently longer, as in *jednoga finog dana* "one fine day." [42c]

Names of city squares

🏃 VJEŽBE [J] VEŽBE [E]

B1

Hold a conversation in the classroom about where each of the students is from, using A1 as the model. Include in the conversation an exchange where you spell your name out for your interlocutor.

Self-study learners: Memorize the alphabet and practice spelling various words out loud. If you are focusing on Serbian, memorize the order of letters in the Cyrillic alphabet.

B2

Bosnian	Croatian	Serbian
1. *Čija* je ȍvo *olovka*?	1. *Čija* je ȍvo *olovka*?	1. *Čija* je ȍvo *olovka*?
2. Ȍvo je *olovka moje prijateljice.*	2. Ȍvo je *olovka moje prijateljice.*	2. Ȍvo je *olovka moje prijateljice.*
1. A *pas Freddy*? *Čiji* je *on*?	1. A *pas Freddy*? *Čiji* je *on*?	1. A *pas Fredi*? *Čiji* je *on*?
2. *Freddy* je *pas* ȍnog Ȅngleza Georgea.	2. *Freddy* je *pas* ȍnoga Ȅngleza Georgea.	2. *Fredi* je *pas* ȍnog Ȅngleza Džordža.
1. Ah, *Freddy* je *njȅgov pas*!	1. Ah, *Freddy* je *njȅgov pas*!	1. Ah, *Fredi* je *njȅgov pas*!
2. Da! *Freddy* je *Georgeov pas.*	2. Da! *Freddy* je *Georgeov pas.*	2. Da! *Fredi* je *Džordžov pas.*
1. A *čija* je *mačka Mȁca*?	1. A *čija* je *mačka Mȁca*?	1. A *čija* je *mačka Mȁca*?
2. *Mȁca* je *mačka* ȍne djevȍjke Zlȁte.	2. *Mȁca* je *mačka* ȍne djevȍjke Dubravke.	2. *Mȁca* je *mačka* ȍne devȍjke Dubravke.
1. Daklȅ, *Mȁca* je *njȅna* a nȉje *Azrina*?	1. Daklȅ, *Mȁca* je *njȅzina* a nȉje *Ankičina*?	1. Daklȅ, *Mȁca* je *njȅna* a nȉje *Mȉrjanina*?
2. Da, *Mȁca* je *Zlȁtina.*	2. Da, *Mȁca* je *Dubravkina.*	2. Da, *Mȁca* je *Dubravkina.*

👉 **Replace** *olovka, moja prijateljica, pas Freddy* [B,C] *Fredi* [S], *mačka Mȁca* **with other names and nouns.**

B3

Bosnian	Croatian	Serbian
1. Ȍvo je *auto* mȍg prijatelja *Hasana*.	1. Ȍvo je *auto* mȍga prijatelja *Branka*.	1. Ȍво је *ауто* мог пријатеља *Слободана*.
2. Daklȅ, ȍvo nȉje *auto* ȍne *studentice Azre*? I ona ȉma *auto zelȅne* bȍje.	2. Daklȅ, ovȍ nȉje *auto* ȍne *studentice Ankice*? I ona ima *auto zelȅne* bȍje.	2. Даклȅ, ово нȉје *ауто* онȅ *студенткиње Мирјанȅ*? И она има *ауто зелȅне* бȍје.
1. Ne, *auto* nȉje *Azrin*, vȅć *Hasanov*.	1. Ne, *auto* nȉje *Ankičin*, vȅć *Brankov*.	1. Не, *ауто* нȉје *Мирјанин*, већ *Слободанов*.

👉 **Replace** *auto* with jabuka, kruška, novine, ȍrah, pȉvo, sȍk, **and the above personal names with others. Replace** *zelȅni* **with** crvȅni, crȉni, plȁvi, žȕti.

B4

Bosnian and Serbian
1. Šta želiš?
2. *Vode.*
1. Evo, izvoli čašu *vode.* A šta želiš još?
2. Molim *jednu jabuku.*
1. Nema problema! Imamo *ih.*

Croatian
1. Što želiš?
2. *Vode.*
1. Evo, izvoli čašu *vode.* A što želiš još?
2. Molim *jednu jabuku.*
1. Nema problema! Imamo *ih.*

🖝 **Replace** *voda* **with other beverages, such as**: čaj, kafa [B,S] kava [C], limunada, pivo, sok, vino, **and** *jabuka* **with other fruits such as**: kruška, naranča [C] narandža [B] pomorandža [S], orah, šljiva.

🖝 **Replace** the number 1 with 2, 3 or 4.

B5

Bosnian
1. Koliko je od (New York) do (Chicago)?
2. Daleko.
1. A koliko je od (Sjeverna Amerika) do (Evropa)?
2. Vrlo daleko.
1. A je li vrlo daleko od (Oakland) do (San Francisco)?
2. Ne, nije. Blizu je.
1. A od (Stari Grad) do (Marijin Dvor)?
2. Možeš ići čak i bez (auto)!
1. Stvarno!

Croatian
1. Koliko je od (New York) do (Chicago)?
2. Daleko.
1. A koliko je od (Sjeverna Amerika) do (Europa)?
2. Jako daleko.
1. A je li vrlo daleko od (Oakland) do (San Francisco)?
2. Ne, nije. Blizu je.
1. A od (Zagreb) do (Novi Zagreb)?
2. Možeš ići čak i bez (auto)!
1. Stvarno!

Serbian Cyrillic
1. Колико је од (Њујорк) до (Чикаго)?
2. Далеко.
1. А колико је од (Северна Америка) до (Европа)?
2. Врло далеко.
1. А да ли је врло далеко од (Окланд) до (Сан Франциско)?
2. Не, није. Близу је.
1. А од (Београд) до (Нови Београд)?
2. Можеш да идеш чак и без (ауто)!
2. Стварно!

🖝 **Insert** the correct forms of the words in parentheses. See A1 for other possible place names.

B6

Bosnian
1. Pored koga si?
2. Do *Zlatana.*
1. Do *Zlate?*
2. Ne! Do *njega!*

Croatian
1. Pored koga si?
2. Do *Branka.*
1. Do *Branke?*
2. Ne! Do *njega!*

Serbian
1. Pored koga si?
2. Do *Slobodana.*
1. Do *Svetlane?*
2. Ne! Do *njega!*

🖝 **Replace** these names with the names your classmates have chosen or choose one from p. 317.

Bosnian	Croatian	Serbian
1. Pored čega si?	1. Pored čega si?	1. Поред чега си?
2. Do *table*.	2. Do *ploče*.	2. До *табле*.
1. Do *prozora*?	1. Do *prozora*?	1. До *прозора*?
2. Ne! Ovdje!	2. Ne! Ovdje!	2. Не! Овде!

☞ **Replace** *tabla* [B,S] *ploča* [C] **and** *prozor* **with other words for objects in the classroom, such as:** bilježnica [C] sveska [S] teka [B], knjiga, mačka, majmun, medved [E] medvjed [J], pas, stolica, zid.

B7

Bosnian	Croatian	Serbian
1. Je li *rječnik* ovdje?	1. Je li *rječnik* ovdje?	1. Da li je *rečnik* ovde?
2. Evo ga.	2. Evo ga.	2. Evo ga.
1. Ali vidim da nema *olovke*.	1. Ali vidim da nema *olovke*.	1. Ali vidim da nema *olovke*.
2. Tačno. Nema *je*.	2. Točno. Nema *je*.	2. Tačno. Nema *je*.
1. Onda gdje je?	1. Onda gdje je?	1. Onda gde je?
2. Ne znam, ali nema problema. Tu je *moja*.	2. Ne znam, ali nema problema. Tu je *moja*.	2. Ne znam, ali nema problema. Tu je *moja*.
1. Hvala!	1. Hvala!	1. Hvala!

☞ **Replace** *rečnik* [E] *rječnik* [J] **and** *olovka* **with two of these nouns:** avionsko pismo, časopis, ključ, knjiga, majmun, papir, pas, razglednica, udžbenik.

B8

Questions to ask each other based on the materials in dialogues 4A1, 4A2, 4A3 and 4A4:

A1 Odakle su roditelji vašeg profesora?
A2 Čije su knjige kod vas, a kod koga su vaše knjige?
A3 Zašto broj 2 nije žedan?
A4 Koje stvari traži broj 1?

☞ **Make up** a question of your own based on material from the A dialogues to ask a classmate using the question words *zašto, čiji* or *kod koga*.

Street names

57
Četvrta lekcija   Lesson Four

✍ DOMAĆA ZADAĆA [B,C] DOMAĆI ZADATAK [S]

C1

Insert the genitive form of the phrase in parentheses into the blank.

> **Note**: in this and other exercises it is frequently the case that the only difference between B and C on the one hand, and S on the other, is that the S sentences appear in Cyrillic. This has been done to give students learning Serbian sufficient practice in reading and writing the Cyrillic alphabet.

Note:

1. [B,C] Ovo je problem .... (veliki grad).

   [S] Ово је проблем .... (велики град).

2. [B,C] Rijeke .... (naša zemlja) teku kroz mnoge gradove.

   [S] Реке .... (наша земља) теку кроз многе градове.

3. [B,C] Oni nemaju naše brojeve .... (telefon).

   [S] Они немају наше бројеве .... (телефон).

4. [B,C] Ne želim da kupiš psa .... (crvena boja), već .... (zelena boja).

   [S] Не желим да купиш пса .... (црвена боја), већ .... (зелена боја).

5. [B,C] Traže li ti ljudi kuću .... (naš dragi prijatelj)?

   [S] Да ли ти људи траже кућу .... (наш драги друг)?

6. [B,C] Glavni grad .... (Crna Gora) je Podgorica, a glavni grad .... (Srbija) je Beograd. Glavni grad .... (Hrvatska) je Zagreb, a glavni grad .... (Bosna i Hercegovina) je Sarajevo.

   [S] Главни град .... (Црна Гора) је Подгорица, а главни град .... (Србија) је Београд. Главни град .... (Хрватска) је Загреб, а главни град .... (Босна и Херцеговина) је Сарајево.

C2

Translate into B, C, or S:

1. My mother is from South America.

2. Her father is from Sarajevo.

3. Their parents are from Italy.

4. The (female) student is from Greece.

5. His (male) friends are from France.

6. Your professors are from Washington.

7. Our dear (female) professors are from Hungary.

C3

Complete these number phrases, writing the number out as a word and adding the appropriate endings to the adjective and noun. Replace the word 'both' with *oba, obe* [E] *obje* [J] as appropriate.

     Example: 4 (dobr<u>i</u> pas) **becomes** četiri dobra psa

3 (lȅpa stv<u>a</u>r) [E] (lijȅpa stv<u>a</u>r) [J]

2 (cȑvena mačka)

4 (glȁvan gr<u>a</u>d)

1 (dr<u>a</u>g čòvek) [E] (dr<u>a</u>g čòvjek) [J]

both (zelèna bȉlježnica) [C] (zelèna sveska) [S]

     (zelèna tȅka) [B]

3 (dùga rȅka) [E] (dùga rijȅka) [J]

4 (vèlika knjiga)

2 (slȁdak keks)

both (dòbra drug<u>a</u>rica) [S] (dòbra prijatèljica) [B,C]

1 (m<u>a</u>la čaša)

3 (m<u>a</u>l<u>i</u> mȅdved) [E] (m<u>a</u>l<u>i</u> mȅdvjed) [J]

both (rùžan stùdent)

4 (dòbro pȉtanje)

2 (plȁva šljiva)

3 (ozbȉljan muškàrac)

both (dȅbeo udžben<u>i</u>k)

2 (tȅžak klj<u>u</u>č)

3 (vȉsok gospòdin)

C4

If these are the answers, what are the questions?

<u>Bosnian and Croatian</u>

1. Mòji ròditelji su iz Mađarsk<u>e</u>.

2. Iz Kalifòrnij<u>e</u> sam.

3. Dalèko.

4. Freddy je Georgeov pas.

5. Evo udžben<u>i</u>ka.

6. J<u>a</u> sam do pr<u>o</u>zora.

7. Ne, hv<u>a</u>la, ȉm<u>a</u>m sòka.

8. Da, ȉmam oba rječn<u>i</u>ka.

9. Sve su òl<u>o</u>vke mòje!

<u>Serbian</u>

1. Мòји ròдитељи су из Мађарск<u>е</u>.

2. Из Калифòрниј<u>е</u> сам.

3. Далèко.

4. Фрȅди је Џорџов пас.

5. Ево уџбен<u>и</u>ка.

6. J<u>a</u> сам до пр<u>о</u>зора.

7. Не, хв<u>а</u>ла, ȉм<u>a</u>м сòка.

8. Да, ȉмам оба речн<u>и</u>ка.

9. Све су òл<u>о</u>вке мòје!

C5

Translate each preposition below and use it in a short sentence which you also translate into English.
    Example: na   **becomes**   "to"   Alergična sam na slatkiše. "I'm allergic to sweets."

1. od	8. iz
2. na	9. do
3. blizu	10. kroz
4. za	11. između
5. s	12. u
6. uz	13. kod
7. pored	14. bez

C6

Combine each preposition with the adjective + noun phrase given to its right, making the grammatical changes in the adjective + noun phrase that the preposition requires.
    Example: kod   tvoja prijateljica   **becomes**   kod tvoje prijateljice

	Bosnian	Croatian	Serbian
od	malo parče sira	mali komad sira	мало парче сира
pored	crna tabla	crna ploča	црна табла
za	dobra riječ	dobra riječ	добра реч
s, sa	bosanskohrvatska granica	bosanskohrvatska granica	босанскосрпска граница
uz	jedna kafa	jedna kava	једна кафа
iz	kratka noć	kratka noć	кратка ноћ
između	ovaj i onaj zid	ovaj i onaj zid	овај и онај зид
do	mala kruška	mala kruška	мала крушка
kroz	hladna voda	hladna voda	хладна вода
kod	dragi čovjek	dragi čovjek	драги човек
bez	crno vino	crno vino	црно вино

Then rewrite each noun-adjective phrase replacing the noun-adjective phrase by a pronoun.
    For example: kod velikog prozora   >   kod njega

C7

Write out the street and square names in the photographs on pp. 48, 50, 52, 54 and 57 and mark which are the names of women and which the names of men. Then derive the actual name (i.e. nominative form) for each person. For more information on the declension of personal names, see p. 325.

VOCABULARY

deo, dȅla; delovi	part, section	putòvnica [C]	passport
dio, dijȅla; djelovi	part, section	Republika Srpska	Republic of Srpska
dok	while	sȁstojati se [od], sȁstojīm se [od]	to consist [of] (I)
Federàcija	Federation	slobodno	freely
pȁsoš [B,S]	passport	te	and
putòvati, putujēm	to travel (I)	uključìvati, uključujēm	to include (I)

<u>Bosnian.</u> Bosna i Hèrcegovina se sȁstojī od dvȃ dijȅla. Jèdan dio se zovȇ Federàcija Bosnē i Hèrcegovine, i uključujē gradove Mòstar, Sàrajevo, Tuzlu, Zenicu, Bȉhać, te Gòražde, dok se drugȋ dio zovȇ Repùblika Srpskā i uključujē gradove Prijȅdor, Banjā Lȕku, te Bòsanski Brȍd. Mòže se slobodno putòvati od jèdnog do drugȏg dijȅla bez pȁsoša.

<u>Croatian.</u> Bosna i Hèrcegovina se sȁstojī od dvȃ dijȅla. Jèdan se dio zovȇ Federàcija Bosnē i Hèrcegovine, i uključujē gradove Mòstar, Sàrajevo, Tuzlu, Zenicu, Bȉhać, te Gòražde, dok se drugȋ dio zovȇ Repùblika Srpskā i uključujē gradove Prijȅdor, Banjā Lȕku, te Bòsanski Brȍd. Mòže se slobodno putòvati od jèdnog do drugȏg dijȅla bez putòvnice.

<u>Serbian.</u> Bosna i Hèrcegovina se sȁstojī od dvȃ dȅla. Jèdan deo se zovȇ Federàcija Bosnē i Hèrcegovine, i uključujē gradove Mòstar, Sàrajevo, Tuzlu, Zenicu, Bȉhać, te Gòražde, dok se drugȋ deo zovȇ Repùblika Srpskā i uključujē gradove Prijȅdor, Banjā Lȕku, te Bòsanski Brȍd. Mòže slobodno da se putujē od jèdnog do drugȏg dȅla bez pȁsoša.

> The spellings *Banja Luka* and *Banjaluka* are both used. In the accusative case, one encounters three different possibilities: *Banja Luku*, *Banjaluku* and *Banju Luku*.

📖 Story: Albahari

Read Part I of the story "Osam malih priča o mojoj ženi" by David Albahari (p. 341).

Two stories of eight episodes each are provided in the appendices, and are given as reading assignments for Lessons 4-19. A third, also in eight episodes, comprises Lesson 20. The author of the first, *Osam malih priča o mojoj ženi* [Eight Small Stories about My Wife], is David Albahari; the author of the second, *Ljubav na španjolski način* [Love in the Spanish Style], is Muharem Bazdulj; and the author of the third, *U zagrljaju rijeke* [In the River's Embrace], is Miro Gavran.

David Albahari (b. 1949) has published a number of novels and collections of short stories; he writes in Serbian. Muharem Bazdulj (b. 1977) is the author of novels and stories, and writes in Bosnian. Miro Gavran (b. 1961) is best known for his plays, but he has also published novels and stories; he writes in Croatian.

For references, and information on these and other writers whose work has been translated into English, consult www.bcsgrammarandtextbook.org .

Peta lekcija • Lesson Five

〜A1   ⊙37,38

dosadan, dosadno, dosadna	boring	pecivo	bread roll
drugi, drugo, druga	other, another	pet	fifth
đak	pupil	peti, peto, peta	five
ići, idem	to go (I)	piti, pijem	to drink (I)
jagoda	strawberry	po	each
jesti, jedem	to eat (I)	pomorandža; Gpl -i [S]	orange
kamo [C]	[to] where	priča	story
kazati, kažem	to say (I/P)	ptica	bird
koliko	how much, how many	puno	a lot
kuća	house	slab	weak
kuda [B,S]	[to] where	smokva	fig
malo	a little	šaren, šareno, šarena	colorful
mnogo	a lot	učitelj	schoolteacher
naranča; Gpl -i [C]	orange	uzimati, uzimam	to take (I)
narandža; Gpl -i [B]	orange	zao, zlo, zla	evil
odgovarati, odgovaram	to answer (I)	zmija	snake

PET MAČAKA I PET PASA

Bosnian

Kratka priča:

Pet *velikih mačaka* i pet *debelih pasa* ide u grad.

- Gdje idete, *mačke*? - pitaju *psi*.
- Idemo od jedne kuće do druge - kažu *mačke*.
- Koliko imate kuća? - pitaju *psi*.
- Imamo pet malih kuća za pet *velikih mačaka* -
  kažu *mačke*.
- Zašto idete od kuće do kuće? - pitaju *psi*.
- Da *jedemo kruške. Gladne* smo - odgovaraju
  mačke.
- Malo *krušaka* ili puno *krušaka*? - pitaju *psi*.
- Svaka uzima po *dvije kruške* - kažu *mačke*.

Croatian

Kratka priča:

Pet *velikih mačaka* i pet *debelih pasa* ide u grad.

- Kamo idete, *mačke*? - pitaju *psi*.
- Idemo od jedne kuće do druge - kažu *mačke*.
- Koliko imate kuća? - pitaju *psi*.
- Imamo pet malih kuća za pet *velikih mačaka* -
  kažu *mačke*.
- Zašto idete od kuće do kuće? - pitaju *psi*.
- Da *jedemo kruške. Gladne* smo - odgovaraju
  mačke.
- Malo *krušaka* ili puno *krušaka*? - pitaju *psi*.
- Svaka uzima po *dvije kruške* - kažu *mačke*.

Serbian

Кратка прича:

Пет *великих мачака* и пет *дебелих паса* иде у град.

- Куда идете, *мачке*? - питају *пси*.
- Идемо од једне куће до друге - кажу *мачке*.
- Колико имате кућа? - питају *пси*.
- Имамо пет малих кућа за пет *великих мачака* - кажу *мачке*.
- Зашто идете од куће до куће? - питају *пси*.
- Да једемо *крушке. Гладне* смо - одговарају *мачке*.
- Мало *крушака* или пуно *крушака*? - питају *пси*.
- Свака узима по *две крушке* - кажу *мачке*.

✍ **Replace** *mačka* **and** *pas* **with these pairs:** momak **and** devojka [E] djevojka [J]; ptica **and** zmija; student **and** studentica [B,C] studentkinja [S]; učitelj **and** đak.

☞ **Replace** *kruška* **with:** jabuka, jagoda, naranča [C] narandža [B] pomorandža [S], pecivo, orah, smokva, šljiva.

☞ **Replace** *jesti* **with** piti, *gladan* **with** *žedan*, **and use the names of beverages introduced in exercise 4A3. Leave off the last line in this version.**

☞ **Replace** *veliki* **and** *debeli* **with** dosadni, slabi, srećni [S] sretni [B,C], šareni, tanki, zli.

When counting on your fingers in BCS your palm is horizontal and turned toward you. Start with your thumb pointing upward for *one* 👍, then extend your index finger, *two*, the middle finger, *three*, the ring finger, *four* and the little finger, *five*.

⚙ GRAMMAR

* Genitive plural *

There are two different endings for the Genitive plural [Gpl], *-a* and *-i*. The ending *-a* is required by all neuter nouns, nearly all masculine nouns, and most feminine nouns in *-a*. **[57a]** The ending *-i* is required by all feminine nouns in a consonant and three masculine nouns (*mesec* [E] *mjesec* [J], *ljudi*, and *sat* in the meaning "hour"); it is also found in a sizeable number of feminine nouns in *-a*. **[57b]** The vowels in both endings are distinctively long, and the vowel preceding the genitive plural [Gpl] ending *-a* is also lengthened. If the Gpl ending *-a* follows two consonants other than *st, zd, št, žd, šć, šč* or *ždž*, another *-a-* must be inserted between them. **[57a]** The ending for all adjectives in Gpl is *-ih*. **[57c]** Below are examples.

	Nominative singular	Genitive singular	Genitive plural
masculine	dobar momak	dobrog momka	dobrih momaka
	velik grad	velikog grada	velikih gradova
	jedan sat	dva sata	pet sati
neuter	kratko pismo	kratkog pisma	kratkih pisama
	veliko gnijezdo	velikog gnijezda	velikih gnijezda
feminine -a	mlada sestra	mlade sestre	mladih sestara
	dobra majka	dobre majke	dobrih majki
feminine -cons	velika stvar	velike stvari	velikih stvari

* Uses of the genitive plural *

The Gpl is used after adverbs of measure such as *malo* "a little" *mnogo* "much, many," *puno* "a lot," *koliko* "how much, how many." The Gsg is used only when the noun following refers to something that cannot be counted; for instance *puno kiše* "a lot of rain," *malo vode* "a little water." **[59a]** The Gpl is also used after all numbers other than 1-4 (or compound numbers ending in them, such as 21-24, 31-34, etc.). If such a phrase is the subject of a sentence, the verb is 3rd singular; for instance: *Pet mačaka ide u grad* "Five cats are going to town." Below are the numbers from 5-19 and the multiples of 10 up to 100. **[58]**

5	pet	9	devet	13	trinaest	17	sedamnaest	30	trideset	70	sedamdeset
6	šest	10	deset	14	četrnaest	18	osamnaest	40	četrdeset	80	osamdeset
7	sedam	11	jedanaest	15	petnaest	19	devetnaest	50	pedeset	90	devedeset
8	osam	12	dvanaest	16	šesnaest	20	dvadeset	60	šezdeset	100	sto

* Adverbs of direction *

To ask "where" in the sense of "whither" (= where to), Croatian uses *kamo*. Bosnian and Serbian use either *kuda* or *gde / gdje* to ask this question; there is no difference in meaning. **[55c]**

* Distributive *po*"

The preposition *po* expresses the idea of distribution, and is best translated "each" or "apiece." The case following it is determined by the particular sentence, although it is almost always the accusative. [59c]

A2   ⊙39,40

VOCABULARY

ako	if	pare (pl form)	money
banka	bank	peške [S]	on foot
benzin, benzina	gasoline	pješice [B,C]	on foot
bioskop [S]	movie theater	pješke [B,S]	on foot
čekati, čekam	to wait (I)	posle + *Gen*	after
četiri	four	poslije + *Gen*	after
dati, dam	to give (P)	pozorište [B,S]	theater
devet	nine	pre + *Gen*	before
doći, dođem	to come (P)	prije + *Gen*	before
dolaziti, dolazim	to come (I)	problem, problema	problem
fakultet, fakulteta	academic dept.	ručak, ručka	lunch, dinner
hteti, hoću, hoćeš	to want (I)	sat; *Gpl* sati	hour, o'clock
htjeti, hoću, hoćeš	to want (I)	šest	six
ima	there is, there are	što se mene tiče	as far as I'm concerned
jedanaest	eleven	ticati se, tiče se + *Gen*	to concern (I)
kazalište [C]	theater	uzeti, uzmem	to take (P)
kino [B,C]	movie theater	večera	supper
novac, novca	money	vreme, vremena	time
odmah	immediately	vrijeme, vremena	time

NEMA NOVCA!

Bosnian and Croatian

1. Ako ima vremena prije *ručka*, idem *na fakultet*.
2. Ima vremena, ali nema para.
1. Nema novca?! Idem odmah u banku, ako daš auto!
2. Ne možeš uzeti auto, jer nema benzina.
1. Nema problema. Idem pješice do banke, a poslije banke idem *na fakultet*.
2. A poslije *fakulteta*?
1. Evo me! Dolazim na *ručak* u *četiri sata*!
2. Što se mene tiče, možeš doći i u šest. *Ručak* te čeka, ako ga hoćeš jesti.

Serbian

1. Ako ima vremena pre *ručka*, idem *na fakultet*.
2. Ima vremena, ali nema para.
1. Nema novca?! Idem odmah u banku, ako daš auto!
2. Ne možeš da uzmeš auto, jer nema benzina.
1. Nema problema. Idem peške do banke, a posle banke idem *na fakultet*.
2. A posle *fakulteta*?
1. Evo me! Dolazim na *ručak* u *četiri sata*!
2. Što se mene tiče, možeš da dođeš i u *šest*. *Ručak* te čeka, ako hoćeš da ga jedeš.

☞ **Replace** *ručak* **with** večera **and** *(na) fakultet* **with** (u) bioskop [S] (u) kino [B,C], (u) kazalište [C] (u) pozorište [B,S], **and** *4:00 p.m.* **with** 9:00 p.m., *6:00 p.m.* **with** 11:00 p.m.

Mealtimes: Breakfast is between 6:00 and 7:00 a.m. Most jobs start at 8:00. At work people have a late-morning snack, and then they have dinner, or lunch *(ručak)*, the main meal of the day, with their family when everyone gets home from work and school in the late afternoon, around 4:00 or 5:00 p.m. Supper *(večera)* follows between 7:00 and 8:00 p.m. and is usually more of a snack than a full meal.

The universities in Bosnia and Herzegovina, Croatia, Montenegro, and Serbia are loosely knit institutions linking a number of separately run departments or schools called *fakulteti*, each dedicated to a range of subjects (the humanities, engineering, architecture, political science, etc.) similar to US medical, law or business schools. Most of the universities in Bosnia and Herzegovina, Croatia, Montenegro, and Serbia have no central campus, so a student would be more likely to say that s/he is going "to the faculty" (*na fakultet*) to take a class or to study, rather than "to the university" (*na sveučilište* or *na univerzitet*).

⚙ GRAMMAR

* Uses of the genitive case, continued *

The unchanging word *nema*, signifying the non-existence or absence of something or someone, always requires the genitive. The unchanging word *ima*, signifiying existence or presence, uses the nominative for a single unit which can be counted, but requires the genitive if the meaning is partitive. **[59b]** Certain verbs also require a genitive object. One is *bojati se* "fear," and another is *ticati se* "concern," which usually appears in the phrase *što se tiče* + Gen "as concerns ... ." **[60]** Certain other fixed phrases can take a genitive object, for instance *igrati lopte* "play ball."

* Prepositions with the accusative case *

When used with the accusative case, both *u* and *na* denote "motion toward." Some nouns take *u* in this meaning and others take *na*; the identity of nouns as "*u*-words" or "*na*-words" must be learned. "*U*-words" tend to be those which denote enclosed, three-dimensional spaces, and "*na*-words" tend to be those which denote surfaces or more abstractly conceived concepts. **[55a]**

* Telling time *

The time of day is identified by the number plus the correct case form of the word for "hour" (*sat*); the preposition *u* specifies the time something happens. Thus: *u četiri sata* "at 4:00," *u pet sati* "at 5:00." Time after the hour is expressed by the conjunction *i* and time before the hour by the preposition *do*. Thus: *u pet i deset* "at 5:10 (at ten past five)," *u pet do deset* "at 9:55 (at five to ten)." **[61c]**

* Motion verbs and aspect *

The imperfective verb *ići* means "go." Perfective verbs are made from it by adding prefixes, e.g. *doći* "come." Imperfective verbs are then made from each of these perfectives by adding the same prefix to the relatively rare verb *laziti*; thus *dolaziti* is the imperfective verb meaning "come" **[54]**

* The verb "want" *

The present tense of "want" (infinitive *hteti* [E] *htjeti* [J]) is the only BCS verb other than *moći* whose 1st singular ends in -*u*. Both 3rd singular and 3rd plural end in -*e*, but 3rd plural has a long vowel. The negated form has its own separate conjugation, in which the segment *ne-* replaces the syllable *ho-* of the affirmative form. **[52d]**. See p. 130 for more information on these forms.

hteti or *htjeti* want		not want	
hoću	*hoćemo*	*neću*	*nećemo*
hoćeš	*hoćete*	*nećeš*	*nećete*
hoće	*hoće*	*neće*	*neće*

The Bank of Vojvodina, Belgrade

Pedestrians

VOCABULARY

advòkat, advokáta [B,S]	attorney	prevòditelj [C]	translator
àmidža [B]	paternal uncle	sèdmica [B,S]	week
amidžìnica [B]	pat. uncle's wife	stànica	station
bùdem	am (P)	strìc [B,C,S]	paternal uncle
dàidža [B]	maternal uncle	strìna [B,C,S]	pat. uncle's wife
daidžìnica [B]	mat. uncle's wife	sùdac, sùca [C]	judge *(m)*
dòčekati, dòčekam	to greet arrival (P)	sudìja [B,S]	judge *(m)*
ìdūći, ìdūće, ìdūća	next, coming	svòj, svòje, svòja	one's own
kàko za kòga	a matter of taste	tèča [S]	aunt's husband
kòlodvor [C]	railway station	tètak, tètka [B,C,S]	aunt's husband
lèkarka [S]	doctor *(f)*	tetka	aunt
lijèčnica [C]	doctor *(f)*	tjèdan, tjèdna [C]	week
ljèkarka [B,S]	doctor *(f)*	ùjak [B,C,S]	maternal uncle
nèdelja [S]	week	ùjna [B,C,S]	mat. uncle's wife
nèdjelja [B,S]	week	zanìmljiv, zanìmljivo, zanìmljiva	interesting
òdvjetnīk [C]	attorney	žèleznička stànica [S]	railway station
pak	and, but rather	žèljeznička stanica [B,S]	railway station
pìsac, pìsca	writer	žíveti, žívim	to live (I)
posao, posla	job	žívjeti, žívim	to live (I)
prevòdilac, prevòdioca [B,S]	translator		

KO DOLAZI? [B,S]   TKO DOLAZI? [C]

Bosnian
1. Ìdūće sèdmice u srijèdu, u pêt sáti, idēm na stànicu nekoga dòčekati.
2. Ko dòlazi?
1. *Brat* mog *òca.*
2. Znâm da je dàidža majčin *brat.* Da li se kàže "*àmidža*" za òčevog bràta?
1. Da! Tàko je. Tȯ je mòj *àmidža.*
2. Šta rȁdi i gdje žìvi?
1. *On* je *sudìja* i žìvi u Bihàću.
2. *Sudìja!* Da li je *amidžin* pòsao zanìmljiv?
1. Kàko za kòga. On svòj pòsao vòlī.
2. Jâ žèlim da bùdem *advòkat.*

Croatian
1. Ìdūćeg tjèdna u srijèdu, u pêt sáti, idēm na kòlodvor nekoga dòčekati.
2. Tko dòlazi?
1. *Brat* mòga *òca.*
2. Znâm da je ùjak majčin *brat.* Kàže li se "*strìc*" za òčeva bràta?
1. Da! Tàko je. Tȯ je mòj *strìc.*
2. Što rȁdi i gdje žìvi?
1. *On* je *sùdac* i žìvi u Rijèci.
2. *Sùdac!* Da li je *stričev* pòsao zanìmljiv?
1. Kàko za kòga. On svòj pòsao vòlī.
2. Jâ pak žèlim bìti *òdvjetnīk.*

Serbian
1. Идỳће нèдеље у срèду, у пêт сáти, идēм на жèлезничку стàницу да некога дòчекам.
2. Ко дòлази?
1. *Брат* мòг *òца.*
2. Знâм да је ỳјак мàјчин *брат.* Да ли се кàже "*стрùц*" за òчевог бра̏та?
1. Да! Тàко је. Тȯ је мòј *стрùц.*
2. Шта ра̏ди и где жѝви?
1. *Он* је *судùја* и жѝви у Нȍвом Са̏ду.
2. *Судùја!* Да ли је *стрùчев* посао занùмљив?
1. Кàко за кòга. Он свȏј посао во̑лū.
2. Jâ жèлим да бу̏дем *адвòкат.*

KINSHIP CHART
Uncles and Aunts

BLOOD RELATIVES	THEIR SPOUSES
maternal uncle	**maternal uncle's wife**
ujak [B,C,S]..*ujna* [B,C,S]	
daidža [B]..*daidžinica* [B]	
maternal or paternal aunt	**maternal or paternal aunt's husband**
tetka ....*tetak* [B,C,S], *teča* [S]	
paternal uncle	**paternal uncle's wife**
stric [B,C,S]..*strina* [B,C,S]	
amidža [B]..*amidžinica* [B]	

☞ **Replace** *brat* **with** sestra, *otac* **with** majka, *amidža* [B] *stric* [B,C,S] **with** amidžinica [B] strina [B,C,S] **and make further versions inserting** daidža [B] ujak [B,C,S], daidžinica [B] ujna [B,C,S], teča [S] tetak [B,C,S], tetka **wherever relevant.**

☞ **Replace** *sudac* [C] *sudija* [B,S] **and** *advokat* [B,S] *odvjetnik* [C] **with** lekarka [S] liječnica [C] ljekarka [B,S] **and** medicinska sestra **or** pisac **and** prevodilac [B,S] prevoditelj [C].

☞ **Make** a list of the differences among B, C, and S found in this exercise.

Self-study learners: Extend this list to include material from the preceding four lessons as well.

⚙ GRAMMAR

* Genitive phrases of time *

When an "adjective + noun" phrase specifies a point in time, it takes Gsg without a preposition. For instance: *iduće subote* "next Saturday," *ovog vikenda* "this weekend." **[61b]**

* Verbs and aspect *

Perfective verbs are usually made by adding a prefix to a basic imperfective verb. Sometimes this changes the meaning, essentially creating a new (but related) verb. For instance, adding *do-* to the imperfective verb *čekati* "wait" creates the perfective verb *dočekati* "meet someone [on arrival]." **[53b]**

* The possessive adjective *svoj* *

The possessive pronominal adjective *svoj* "one's own" is declined exactly like *moj* and *tvoj*. It is used if the possessor is the subject of the sentence. It is optional in 1st and 2d persons (thus "I like my work" can be *volim moj posao* or *volim svoj posao*). However, it is required in the 3rd person in the meaning "one's own," and impossible in the meaning "another's." Thus, *on voli svoj posao* means "he likes his [= his own] work" while *on ne voli njegov posao* means "he doesn't like his [= another's] work." **[72a]**

* The verb *budem, budeš* etc *

The verb *biti* has a second present tense, used in contexts requiring a perfective verb. It is a regular *e*-conjugation present tense formed from the stem *bud-* . **[52c]** These forms are used in perfective meanings of the verb "to be," such as after the conjunction *da* (as in *želim da budem advokat* "I want to be a lawyer"). This is also the stem for the imperative (see Lesson 7).

	singular	plural
1st	*budem*	*budemo*
2nd	*budeš*	*budete*
3rd	*bude*	*budu*

* Bosnian vocabulary *

Bosnian has a number of Turkish-derived words which reflect its Islamic cultural heritage. Among these are names for family relations. Thus, the word for "mother's brother" is *ujak* in S and C but *daidža* in B, and the word for "father's brother" is *stric* in S and C but *amidža* in Bosnian. Similarly, "grandmother" is *baba* or *baka* in S and C, but *nena* in B. **[176a]**

VOCABULARY

deset	ten	ne dolazi u obzir	out of the question
dvanaest	twelve	pojesti, pojedem	to have something to eat (P)
izlazak	going out	popiti, popijem	to have something to drink (P)
kada	when	popodne	afternoon
kafana [B,S]	café	predstava	performance
kako da ne	of course, definitely	uveče [S]	in the evening
kavana [C]	café	vani [C]	outside
muzej, muzeja	museum	vikend	weekend
napolju [B,S]	outside	zar	really?
naveče [B]	in the evening	zar ne	isn't that so?
navečer [C]	in the evening	zar ne možemo?	can't we?

IZLAZAK U GRAD

Bosnian and Croatian

1. Kada možeš doći sutra?
2. U četiri sata *popodne*.
1. A u koliko sati onda možemo ići u *kino* da gledamo *film*?
2. U pet sati.
1. Želiš li da idemo poslije nešto pojesti i popiti?
2. Kako da ne!
1. Mama, do kada on i ja možemo biti vani?
3. Do deset sati.
1. Zar ne možemo do dvanaest?
2. Ne dolazi u obzir! Sutra nije vikend. Dobro, možete biti vani do jedanaest sati.

Serbian

1. Kada možeš da dođeš sutra?
2. U četiri sata *popodne*.
1. A u koliko sati onda možemo da idemo u *bioskop* da gledamo *film*?
2. U pet sati.
1. Da li želiš da idemo posle nešto da popijemo i pojedemo?
2. Kako da ne!
1. Mama, do kada on i ja možemo da budemo napolju?
3. Do deset sati.
1. Zar ne možemo do dvanaest?
2. Ne dolazi u obzir! Sutra nije vikend. Dobro, možete biti napolju do jedanaest sati.

🖎 **Replace** *kino* [B,C] *bioskop* [S] **with** grad, kafana [B,S] kavana [C], kazalište [C] pozorište [B,S], muzej **and replace** *film* **with** ljudi, predstava. **Replace** 4:00 with 7:00 or 11:00.

> **Note.** Both expressions of the infinitive (želim BITI and želim DA BUDEM) are used throughout B, C, S, but the frequency varies significantly. The first is vastly more common in C, so C as presented here uses only that form. The second is more frequent in S, so S as presented here uses that form predominantly but not exclusively. Since in this matter B tends more to the C usage, in this book B is usually (though not always) presented with the infinitive form. Students will learn the subtleties of usage via exposure to the language.

Dubrovnik cafe

National Museum, Belgrade

 **GRAMMAR**

* Negation *

Questions which expect a negative answer or which express surprise begin with the particle *zar*, followed by a negated verb, as in, for instance, *zar ne možete doći danas?* "can't you come today?" **[56d]** The BCS prefix *ni-* turns the question words *ko, tko* and *šta* into negative pronouns. Thus, *niko* [B,S] *nitko* [C] (Acc-Gen *nikoga*) means "nobody, and *ništa* means "nothing." Whenever these words appear in a sentence the verb must also be negated, as in, for instance, *ne vidim nikoga* "I don't see anyone." **[56a]** The compound conjunction *ni... ni* means "neither... nor." If that which is contrasted is a verb, this conjunction takes the form *niti... niti.* **[56c]**

* Aspect and prefixation *

Adding a prefix to a verb makes it perfective, and usually changes to meaning to a certain extent. For some verbs, however, adding a prefix simply indicates a single completed instance of an action. Thus the imperfective verbs *jesti* and *piti* mean "eat" and "drink" in general terms, while the perfectives *pojesti* and *popiti* mean "finish eating" or "drink up" (referring in each case to a particular item of food or particular drink on a particular occasion). **[53b]**

* More on vocabulary differences *

The vast majority of words in B, C, and S are used by all speakers of B, C, and S with the same meaning. A number of words, however, are clearly recognized as either Croatian or Serbian, and these words are marked [C] and [S], respectively, in vocabulary lists. Thus, pairs like *vani* and *napolju* "outside," *kazalište* and *pozorište* "theater," *kino* and *bioskop* "cinema," *vlak* and *voz* "train," and *tjedan* and *nedelja* "week," are markedly C vs. S words. **[172a]** Sometimes B will use both (as in the case of "outside"), sometimes it will prefer the Serbian word (as in the case of "theater" and "train"), sometimes it will prefer the Croatian word (as in the case of "cinema"), and in a few instances it will have its own word altogether, as in the case of family terms But there are also a number of words which, although they are not used with equal frequency throughout the entire region, are not limited to one area. Thus, for instance, *abeceda* [B,C,S] "alphabet" is used everywhere, while *azbuka* [S] "alphabet" is used only in Serbian. In similar fashion, *paradajz* [B,C,S] "tomato" is used everywhere, while *rajčica* [C] is used only in Croatian; and *trenutak* [B,C,S] "instant, moment" is also used everywhere, while *momenat* [B,S] is used in the same meaning only in Bosnian and Serbian. In these cases, the markings [S] or [C] do not carry the same meaning as they do in the first group of words. **[172b]**

Croatian National Theater

✦ VJEŽBE [J] VEŽBE [E]

B1

Bosnian	Croatian	Serbian
1. Šta to nosiš?	1. Što to nosiš?	1. Šta to nosiš?
2. Nosim dvanaest *jabuka*.	2. Nosim dvanaest *jabuka*.	2. Nosim dvanaest *jabuka*.
1. A koliko je *studenata* ovdje?	1. A koliko je *studenata* ovdje?	1. A koliko je *studenata* ovde?
2. Ima nas *deset studenata*.	2. Ima nas *deset studenata*.	2. Ima nas *deset studenata*.
1. Onda svaki *student* može uzeti po jednu, a ti i ja po dvije *jabuke*.	1. Onda svaki *student* može uzeti po jednu, a ti i ja po dvije *jabuke*.	1. Onda svaki *student* može da uzme po jednu, a ti i ja po dve *jabuke*.
2. Kako da ne!	2. Kako da ne!	2. Kako da ne!

☞ **Replace** *jabuka* **with** čaša vina, komad [B,C] parče [B,S] sira, kruška, olovka, orah, pecivo, slatkiš, šljiva.

☞ **Replace** *student* **with** devojka [E] djevojka [J], đak, momak, prijatelj [B,C] drug [S].

B2

Bosnian	Croatian	Serbian
1. Šta to imaš?	1. Što to imaš?	1. Шта то имаш?
2. Imam voća.	2. Imam voća.	2. Имам воћа.
1. Puno ili malo voća?	1. Puno ili malo voća?	1. Много или мало воћа?
2. Puno!	2. Puno!	2. Много!
1. Kakvog voća ima?	1. Kakvog voća ima?	1. Какво воћа има?
2. Imam *krušaka, narandži* i *jabuka*.	2. Imam *krušaka, naranči* i *jabuka*.	2. Имам *крушака, поморанџи* и *јабука*.
1. Koliko imaš *krušaka, narandži* i *jabuka*?	1. Koliko imaš *krušaka, naranči* i *jabuka*?	1. Колико имаш *крушака, поморанџи* и *јабука*?
2. Ima pet *krušaka*, tri *narandže* i sedam *jabuka*.	2. Ima pet *krušaka*, tri *naranče* i sedam *jabuka*.	2. Има пет *крушака*, три *поморанце* и седам *јабука*.

☞ **Replace italicized words with:** jagoda, orah, smokva, šljiva.

B3

Bosnian and Serbian	Croatian
1. Čega ima mnogo, a čega malo?	1. Čega ima puno, a čega malo?
2. Ima mnogo *vremena*, a malo *novca*.	2. Ima puno *vremena*, a malo *novca*.

☞ **Replace** *vrème* [E] *vrijème* [J] **and** *novac* **with the pairs:**

a) bela [E] bijela [J] mačka, crni pas; **b)** srećni [S] sretni [B,C] student, tužni student; **c)** teški posao, lahki [B] laki [B,C,S] odmor; **d)** žuta kruška, crvena jabuka.

B4

Bosnian	Croatian	Serbian Cyrillic
1. Šta želiš da radiš *idućeg vikenda?*	1. Što želiš raditi *idućeg vikenda?*	1. Шта желиш да радиш *идућег викенда?*
2. *Idućeg vikenda* hoću da idem u *London.*	2. *Idućeg vikenda* hoću ići u *London.*	2. *Идућег викенда* хоћу да идем у *Лондон.*

☞ **Replace** *vikend* **with:** nedelja [S] sedmica [B] tjedan [C].

☞ **Replace** *London* **with** Bosna i Hercegovina, Crna Gora, Grčka, Hrvatska, Mađarska, Pariz, Srbija.

B5

1. Imam *deset slatkih sokova.*
2. Kada uzmem *šest*, koliko ih onda imaš?
1. Onda imam *četiri slatka soka.*

☞ **Replace the numbers 10 and 6 with others, and replace** *slatki sok* **with:** dobro pitanje, dugo pismo, slobodna nedelja [S] sedmica [B] slobodni tjedan [C], tužni film, važna stvar.

B6

Bosnian	Croatian	Serbian
1. Idem do *amidže!* Nema me do 9 sati naveče! Idemo zajedno u *grad.*	1. Idem do *strica!* Nema me do 9 sati navečer! Idemo zajedno u *grad.*	1. Idem do *strica!* Nema me do 9 sati uveče! Idemo zajedno u *grad.*
2. Ne tiče *me* se šta radiš kod *amidže*, ali moraš doći do 8:00.	2. Ne tiče *me* se što radiš kod *strica*, ali moraš doći do 8:00.	2. Ne tiče *me* se šta radiš kod *strica*, ali moraš da dođeš do 8:00.
1. Kako mogu doći u 8:00 ako smo vani do 9:00?	1. Kako mogu doći u 8:00 ako smo vani do 9:00?	1. Kako mogu da dođem u 8:00 ako smo napolju do 9:00?
2. Moraš. Ove sedmice ideš u školu *ujutro.*	2. Moraš. Ovog tjedna ideš u školu *ujutro.*	2. Moraš. Ove nedelje ideš u školu *ujutro.*

☞ **Replace** *grad* **with:** bioskop [S] kino [B,C], kafana [B,S] kavana [C], kazalište [C] pozorište [B,S].

☞ **Replace** *amidža* [B] *stric* [B,C,S] **with** amidžinica [B] strina [B,C,S], daidža [B] ujak [B,C,S], daidžinica [B] ujna [B,C,S], tetka.

☞ **Replace** *ujutro* **with** popodne.

☞ **Redo** B6 to read as if there are two parents speaking instead of one.

Elementary and secondary schools in the cities of Bosnia and Herzegovina, Croatia, Montenegro, and Serbia generally work in two shifts. Students alternate, attending morning classes one week, and afternoon classes the next.

B7

Answer the following questions, which make reference to the dialogues in 5A1, 5A2, 5A3 and 5A4:

A1.   a. [B,S] Kuda idu mačke i zašto?

        [C] Kamo idu mačke i zašto?

        b. Zar mačke jedu kruške?

        c. Koliko krušaka uzima svaka mačka?

A2   a. Zašto ide broj 1 u banku i kako?

        b. U koliko sati dolazi broj 1 na ručak i zašto?

A3   a. [B,S] Ko dolazi na stanicu, majčin ili očev brat?

        [C] Tko dolazi na kolodvor, majčin ili očev brat?

        b. [B,S] Šta on radi i zašto?

        [C] Što on radi i zašto?

A4   a. [B,C] U koliko sati idu broj 1 i broj 2 u kino?

        [S] U koliko sati idu broj 1 i broj 2 u bioskop?

        b. [B,C] Žele li nešto pojesti i popiti poslije kina? Ako žele, zašto žele? Ako ne žele, zašto ne žele?

        b. [S] Da li žele nešto da pojedu i popiju posle bioskopa? Ako žele, zašto žele? Ako ne žele, zašto ne žele?

        c. [B,C] Zašto oni ne mogu biti vani do dvanaest sati?

        c. [S] Zašto oni ne mogu biti napolju do dvanaest sati?

☞ **Prepare** two questions of your own, based on the dialogues in the A sections, to ask another student in class. Use the question words *zar, koliko, odakle* or *zašto*.

Lock & Key
Production and sale of
secure locks, safes and cylinders
Founded in 1970

✍ DOMAĆA ZADAĆA [B,C] DOMAĆI ZADATAK [S]

C1

Mala Mara i njene životinje

čuti, čujem	to hear (I/P)	pevati, pevam	to sing (I)
igrati, igram	to play (I)	pjesma	song
kod kuće	at home	pjevati, pjevam	to sing (I)
lopta	ball	ptičiji, ptičije, ptičija [B,S]	bird (*adj*)
najbolje	the best	ptičji, ptičje, ptičja [C]	bird (*adj*)
najzad	finally	razred	class, grade (year in school)
ne voli da čuje	won't hear of it	škola	school
niti	neither	voditi, vodim	to take, lead (I)
niti ... niti	neither ... nor	za vreme	during
nositi, nosim	to take, carry (I)	za vrijeme	during
odmor	recess, rest period	zviždati, zviždim	to whistle (I)
pesma	song	životinja	animal

Mala Mara ima (veliki žuti pas). Njen pas se zove "Žućko." Ona ima i (mala mačka) (crna boja). Mara i Žućko često igraju lopte zajedno. Mačka ne igra lopte. Ona to ne voli. Mara ima i (ptica) (plava boja). Marina ptica vrlo lijepo pjeva kad je Mara kod (kuća). Najzad, Mara ima i (jedna šarena zmija). Šarena zmija je tanka i duga. Ona niti igra lopte, niti pjeva.

Mara ide svaki dan u (škola). Ona je đak prvog razreda. U (ponedjeljak) vodi (žuti pas) u (škola). Marin učitelj voli (Žućko). Za vrijeme (odmor) svi đaci igraju lopte zajedno. U (utorak) Mara vodi (crna mačka) u (škola). Ni mačka ni učitelj to ne vole. Niko ne igra lopte. Mačka gleda (učitelj), i učitelj gleda (mačka).

U (srijeda) Mara nosi (ptica) (plava boja) u (škola). Svi vole (ptica), jer tako lijepo pjeva. Ne mogu da pjevaju kao ptica, ali mogu da zvižde uz (ptičja pjesma). Svi to rade svaki put kad ona pjeva. U (četvrtak) Mara nosi (zmija) u (škola). Niko to ne voli – ni učitelj, ni zmija, ni drugi đaci. Niko ne zna šta da radi.

U (petak) Mara ništa ne vodi niti šta nosi u (škola). Sve njene životinje su kod kuće. Učitelj kaže da je to najbolje. Ali Mara ne voli to da čuje.

☞ **Write** this story out, giving the words in parentheses the endings they require.

☞ **Try** to figure out whether this story is written in Bosnian, Serbian or Croatian. Which are the words that might help you decide? Try to make this decision on your own before looking at the answer at the bottom of p. 78. Then list all the words which prove this to be the right answer.

C2

Provide opposites for the following words.

Bosnian and Croatian	Serbian	Bosnian and Croatian	Serbian
adjectives	**adjectives**	**adverbs**	**adverbs**
zao	зао	mnogo	много
lak [lahak]	лак	daleko	далеко
dosadan	досадан		
dug	дуг	**pronouns**	**pronouns**
mali	мали	neko **or** netko	неко
topao	топао	nešto	нешто
crn	црн		
ružan	ружан		
debeo	дебео		
nizak	низак		
ozbiljan	озбиљан		

C3

Translate into B, C, or S:

1. I have ten colorful cats.

2. They go to the theater, we go to a cafe.

3. Alexander is hungry. First, he eats ten oranges, five figs, three apples, and seven pieces of cheese, and then he is not hungry.

4. Three heavy dictionaries and three light books are near the window.

5. Two happy (female) students see six sad (male) students.

6. There are no fat birds.

7. Next week I am going to South America!

8. Students watch professors and teachers every day.

9. His maternal uncle's wife and her maternal uncle's wife are friends, and they are arriving at the station on Saturday at 10 o'clock.

C4

Here are verbs from the first five lessons. For each infinitive, provide its English meaning, and the 1st person singular (j<u>a</u>) and 3rd person plural (òni) forms.

-a- conjugation	-e- conjugation	-i- conjugation	special conjugation
ìgrati	k<u>a</u>zati	vòditi	biti
pevati	teći	nòsiti	htjeti, hteti
pjevati	mòći	dòlaziti	
p<u>i</u>tati	ìći	mòliti	бити
gledati	dòći	tr<u>a</u>žiti	хтети, хтјети
ìmati	čuti	r<u>a</u>diti	
odgov<u>a</u>rati	piti	mìsliti	
stv<u>a</u>rati	jesti	žèleti, žèljeti	
	zvàti se	vìdeti, vìdjeti	
	ùz<u>e</u>ti	vòleti, vòljeti	
ѝграти	pozn<u>a</u>vati		
певати		вòдити	
п<u>и</u>тати	k<u>à</u>зати	нòсити	
гледати	тèћи	дòлазити	
ѝмати	мòћи	мòлити	
одгов<u>à</u>рати	ѝћи	тр<u>à</u>жити	
ств<u>à</u>рати	дòћи	р<u>à</u>дити	
	чути	мѝслити	
	пити	жèлети, жèљети	
	jести	вѝдети, вѝдјети	
	звати се	вòлети, вòљети	
	ýз<u>е</u>ти		
	позн<u>à</u>вати		

C5

Životinje

Connect word to animal:

pas

majmun

mačka

mèdved, mèdvjed

zmìja

ptica

C6

Place the word in column B into the sentence in column A where it belongs.

Column A	Column B
a. Zmìje nìsu zle .... su žìvòtinje.	ali
b. Ùčitelj .... nè zna kolìko ìma đàka.	ako
c. Mala Màra pjevā .... ptica .... ptica nè	čak
pjevā .... mala Màra.	kao
d. .... Màra vodì psa Žućka u škòlu, ... pas	jer
i đàci ìgrajū loptē zajedno za vrijème	onda
òdmora.	već
e. Ùčitelj kàžē da je najbolje u pètak .... sve	
su Màrine žìvòtinje kod kuće.	

а. Змйје нйсу зле .... су жѝвòтиње.	али
б. Ỳчитељ .... нè зна колѝко ѝма ђàка.	ако
в. Мала Мàра певā .... птица .... птица нè	чак
певā .... мала Мàра.	као
г. .... Мàра водѝ пса Жуђка у шкòлу, ...	јер
пас и ђàци ѝграjȳ лоптē заједно за врème	онда
òдмора.	већ
д. Ỳчитељ кàжē да је најбоље у пètак	
све су Мàрине жѝвòтиње код куђē.	

C7

List the time-related expressions found in the dialogues in 5A2, 5A3, 5A4 and 5C1 and then explain the grammar of each one.

Example: The phrase *u četiri sàta* in 5A2 is an accusative expression of time.

Answer to the question on p. 75: The story is written in Serbian ijekavian.

VOCABULARY

oko + *Gen*	around
zèmlja	country

For help in answering these questions consult the maps below and the map at the beginning of the book.

1. [B,C] Jèsu li Sȑbija i Cȓna Gòra sada jèdna zèmlja ili dvije?
   [S] Да ли су Србија и Црна Гора сада једна земља или две?

2. [B,C] Kòji su neki od srpskih i crnògorskih gradòva?
   [S] Који су неки од српских и црногорских градова?

3. [B,C] Kàko se zòvu rijèke koje tèku kroz Cȓnu Goru?
   [S] Како се зову реке које теку кроз Црну Гору?

4. [B,C] Kàko se zòvu rijèke koje tèku kroz Sȑbiju?
   [S] Како се зову реке које теку кроз Србију?

5. [B,C] Kòje su zèmlje oko Cȓne Gòre?
   [S] Које су земље око Црне Горе?

6. [B,C] Kòje su zèmlje oko Sȑbije?
   [S] Које су земље око Србије?

📖 Priča: Albahari

Read Part II of the story "Osam malih priča o mojoj ženi" by David Albahari (p. 341).

Šesta lekcija • Lesson Six

VOCABULARY

država	state	stol, stola [C]	table
dvadeset	twenty	sunce	the sun
kat [C]	floor, story	sunčev sistem [B,S]	the solar system
kružiti, kružim	to circle, to orbit (I)	sunčev sustav [C]	the solar system
mesec	the moon	sustav [C]	system
mjesec	the moon	svemir [B,C,S]	universe
na + Loc	in, on, at	šesti, šesto, šesta	sixth
nalaziti se, nalazim se	to be located (I)	tačan, tačno, tačna [B,S]	precise
nebo	sky	točan, točno, točna [C]	precise
planet, planeta [C]	planet	torba	bag, sack
planeta [B,S]	planet	u + Loc	in, at
pod, poda	floor	usred + Gen	in the middle of
prostorija	premises, room, area	vasiona [B,S]	universe
sistem, sistema [B,C,S]	system	vrata (pl form)	door
soba	room	zemlja	earth, soil
sprat [B,S]	floor, story	zgrada	building
stajati, stojim	to stand (I)	zvezda	star
sto	hundred	zvijezda	star
sto, stola [B,S]	table		

U ZGRADI

Bosnian	Croatian	Serbian
1. Gdje se nalaze *sto i stolice?*	1. Gdje se nalaze *stol i stolice?*	1. Где се налазе *сто и столице?*
2. *Sto* stoji na *podu*, a *stolice* su oko *stola*.	2. *Stol* stoji na *podu*, a *stolice* su oko *stola*.	2. Сто стоји на поду, а *столице* су око *стола*.
1. A gdje se nalazi *sto* u *sobi?*	1. A gdje se nalazi *stol* u *sobi?*	1. А где се налази *сто* у *соби?*
2. *Sto* je pored *zida* ali daleko od *table*, usred *sobe*.	2. *Stol* je pored *zida* ali daleko od *ploče*, usred *sobe*.	2. *Сто* је поред *зида* али далеко од *табле*, усред *собе*.
1. Koliko je centimetara od *stola* do *table?*	1. Koliko je centimetara od *stola* do *ploče?*	1. Колико је центиметара од *стола* до *табле?*
2. Tačno sto dvadeset centimetara.	2. Točno sto dvadeset centimetara.	2. Тачно сто двадесет центиметара.
1. A gdje je *ta soba?*	1. A gdje je *ta soba?*	1. А где је *та соба?*
2. Na *prvom spratu*.	2. Na *prvom katu*.	2. На *првом спрату*.
1. Gdje je *taj sprat?*	1. Gdje je *taj kat?*	1. Где је *тај спрат?*
2. U *ovoj zgradi*.	2. U *ovoj zgradi*.	2. У *овој згради*.

✒☞ **First do this exercise using three sequences**: **1)** stolica, prozor, vrata, prostorija, grad, država; **2)** olovka, rečnik [E] rječnik [J], čaša, torba, **and 3)** planet [C] planeta [B,S] zemlja, nebo, sunce, sunčev sistem [B,S] sustav [C], zvezda [E] zvijezda [J], svemir [B,C,S] vasiona [B,S]. **For 3) you will need the phrase** kružiti oko "revolve around." **Then go** on to locate objects and people in the room, the place you live, and the universe, stating what they are next to, near to, far from, on, and in.

Building

Dubrovnik State Archive

 GRAMMAR

* Locative case *

The endings of the locative singular [Lsg] are *-u* for masculine and neuter nouns, and *-i* for feminine nouns. Adjective endings are *-om* for masculine and neuter, and *-oj* for feminine. The ending *-om* appears as *-em* after "soft" consonants, but the ending *-oj* does not change form. [66a] The forms *moj, tvoj, svoj* can keep or lose the syllable *-je-* in these endings: for instance, the Lsg of *moj* is either *mom* or *mojem*. [66b]

	masculine	neuter	feminine -a	feminine -cons
Nsg	*naš velik grad*	*naše dobro selo*	*naša dobra zemlja*	*naša fina ljubav*
Lsg	*našem velikom gradu*	*našem dobrom selu*	*našoj dobroj zemlji*	*našoj finoj ljubavi*

* Usage of the locative case *

The locative case is used exclusively after prepositions, including *pri, o, po* and others. [68] It is also used after *na* and *u*. The identity of the case after these prepositions is critical to their meaning: if the accusative follows, the meaning is motion: "onto" or "into" [55a], but if the locative follows, the meaning is location: "on," "in" or "at." [67] Individual words keep their identity as "*u*-words" or "*na*-words" in either instance. Normally *u*-words are those which take "in" in English and *na*-words are those which take "on" or "at" in English, but some phrases simply need to be learned as idioms. [67b] The chart below gives examples, particularly of the way words with broadly similar meanings can differ as to the choice of *u* or *na*.

u-words		*na*-words	
škola	school	*sveučilište* [C] *univerzitet* [B,S]	university
smena [E] *smjena* [J]	shift, rotation		
grad	city	*fakultet*	university dept.
bioskop [S] *kino* [B,C]	cinema	*predavanje*	lecture
država	country	*koncert*	concert
kancelarija [B,C,S]	office	*ostrvo* [B,S] *otok* [B,C]	island
ured [B,C]		*odmor*	vacation
kazalište [C] *pozorište* [B,S]	theater	*ručak*	lunch
kafana [B,S] *kavana* [C]	coffeehouse	*kolodvor* [C] *stanica* [B,S]	station
momenat [B,S]	moment	*slika*	picture
trenutak [B,C,S]			
		sever [E] *sjever* [J]	north
		prozor	window
svemir [B,C,S] *vasiona* [B,S]	universe	*nebo*	sky

In a few instances a word can be used with either *u* or *na*, but with different meanings, as in *u selu* "in [a particular] village" vs. *na selu* "in the countryside"; *u sudu* "in the courthouse" vs. *na sudu* "in court," etc.

* Irregular plurals *

The word *vrata* is neuter plural, but is used with singular meaning. Thus *vrata su otvorena* means "the door is open," regardless of the fact that all the relevant words (subject, verb, adjective) are plural. [75]

VOCABULARY

apsolvent	5th yr. student	polagati, polažem	to take [exams] (I)
beogradski	Belgrade *(adj.)*	položiti, položim	to pass [exams] (P)
februar [B,S]	February	predavanje	lecture
godina	year	radi se o + *Loc*	it's a matter of
godinu dana	[for] a year	sarajevski, sarajevsko, sarajevska	Sarajevo *(adj.)*
ispit	exam	semestar, semestra	semester
januar [B,S]	January	siječanj, siječnja [C]	January
juli, jula [B,S]	July	slušati, slušam	to attend, to listen (I)
kasan, kasno, kasna	late	srpanj, srpnja [C]	July
koledž	college	studirati, studiram	to study (I)
letnji, letnje, letnja	summer *(adj.)*	sveučilište [C]	university
listopad [C]	October	školska godina	school year
ljetni, ljetno, ljetna	summer *(adj.)*	tek	only, just
mesec; *Gpl* meseci	month	trajati, trajem	to last, to endure (I)
mjesec; *Gpl* mjeseci	month	univerzitet, univerziteta [B,S]	university
o + *Loc*	about	usmen, usmeno, usmena	oral
o čemu se radi?	what's it about?	veljača [C]	February
oktobar, oktobra [B,S]	October	zagrebački, zagrebačko, zagrebačka	Zagreb *(adj.)*
pismeni, pismeno, pismena	written	završavati se, završavam se	to end (I)
po + *Loc*	according to	zimski, zimsko, zimska	winter *(adj.)*, wintry
počinjati, počinjem	to begin (I)	značiti, značim	to mean (I)
		život, života	life

UNIVERZITET [B,S]   SVEUČILIŠTE [C]

Bosnian

1. O čemu se radi u tvojoj knjizi?
2. Čitala sam o studentskom životu na Sarajevskom univerzitetu.
1. I kakav je njihov život po toj knjizi?
2. U knjizi piše da studenti imaju puno usmenih, a malo pismenih ispita.
1. A od kada do kada traje školska godina?
2. Zimski semestar počinje tek u mjesecu oktobru i završava se u januaru.
1. A ljetni?
2. Ljetni semestar počinje u februaru i završava se u julu.
1. Zaista kasno počinju i kasno završavaju!
2. Jeste, ali u julu nema više predavanja, već su samo ispiti.
1. A koliko godina obično studiraju studenti u Sarajevu?
2. Predavanja se slušaju četiri godine, a onda su studenti apsolventi godinu dana.
1. Šta znači "apsolvent"?
2. Apsolventi ne slušaju predavanja, već samo polažu ispite dok ih sve ne polože.

Croatian

1. O čemu se radi u tvojoj knjizi?
2. Čitala sam o studentskom životu na Zagrebačkom sveučilištu.
1. I kakav je njihov život po toj knjizi?
2. U knjizi piše da studenti imaju puno usmenih, a malo pismenih ispita.
1. A od kada do kada traje školska godina?
2. Zimski semestar počinje tek u mjesecu listopadu i završava se u siječnju.
1. A ljetni?
2. Ljetni semestar počinje u veljači i završava se u srpnju.
1. Zaista kasno počinju i kasno završavaju!
2. Jest, ali u srpnju nema više predavanja, već su samo ispiti.
1. A koliko godina obično studiraju studenti u Zagrebu?
2. Predavanja se slušaju četiri godine, a onda su studenti apsolventi godinu dana.
1. Što znači "apsolvent"?
2. Apsolventi ne slušaju predavanja, već samo polažu ispite dok ih sve ne polože.

<u>Serbian</u>

1. O čemu se rȁdī u tvòjoj knjizi?
2. Čìtala sam o stùdentskōm žìvotu na Beògradskōm univerzitètu.
1. I kàkav je njihov žìvot po tòj knjizi?
2. U knjizi pȋšē da stùdenti ìmajū pùno ȕsmenīh, a malo pìsmenīh ìspīta.
1. A od kàda do kàda trajē škȍlska godina?
2. Zȉmskī semestar pòčinje tek u mèsēcu oktòbru i zàvršava se u jànuāru.
1. A lȅtnjī?
2. Lȅtnjī sèmestar pòčinje u febrùaru i zàvršava se u jùlu.
1. Zȁista kàsno pòčinju i kàsno zàvršavaju!
2. Jèste, ali u jùlu nèma vȉše predávanja, već su samo ìspiti.
1. A kòlìko gòdina òbičnō stùdìraju studenti u Beògradu?
2. Predávanja se slùšajū čètiri gȍdine, a ònda su stùdenti apsòlventi gȍdinu dána.
1. Šta znȁčī "apsolvent"?
2. Apsòlventi nè slùšajū predávanja, već samo pòlažu ìspite dok ih sve ne pòlože.

✎ **First** rehearse this conversation and perform it. Then redo the exchange so that it describes studying at an American university or college (*koledž*).

Self-study learners: Note the names of the months, the use of prepositions, and especially the words that require the preposition *na* vs. those that require the preposition *u*.

THE MONTHS **[67d]**

B,S: *janùar, februàr, mart, àpril, maj, jùni, jùli, àvgust, septèmbar, oktòbar novèmbar, dècembar.*
C: *sijèčanj, vèljača, òžujak, trávanj, svìbanj, lȉpanj, sȑpanj, kòlovōz, rùjan, lȉstopād, stùdenī, prȍsinac.*

Alternate form [B,C]: Ordinal numbers, (*prvī mjèsēc, drȕgī mèsēc...*), often given as Roman numerals, and often used without the noun *mèsēc* [E] *mjèsēc* [J]. **[124b]**

University in Belgrade
Faculty of Philosopy

University in Zagreb

⚙ GRAMMAR

* Past tense, introduction *

The past tense is composed of an auxiliary verb and a participle. The auxiliary is identical to the present tense of *biti*. The participle is called the L-participle because its characteristic marker is the consonant *-l-*. For verbs whose infinitives end in *-iti* or *-ati*, drop the *-ti* and add the L-participle endings directly. **[69]** The endings of this participle are like those of adjectives ending in *-o* (such as *dèbeo, dèbelo, dèbela*). **[16c]** The L-participle agrees with the subject in number and gender. In 1st and 2d person the ending depends on the gender of the person speaking (1st) or spoken to (2nd). **[69]** Here are the L-participles of *biti* and *čìtati*:

	masculine	neuter	feminine	masculine	neuter	feminine
singular	bio	bȉlo	bȉla	čìtao	čìtalo	čìtala
plural	bȉli	bȉla	bȉle	čìtali	čìtala	čìtale

* Verbal usage, continued *

Verbs used in the present tense are usually imperfective, but perfective verbs can be used after conjunctions. Some conjunctions, like *dok*, have different meanings depending on the aspect of the following verb. Thus, the sentence *mi jedemo jabuke dok ti ne jedeš ništa* (imperfective verb) means "we're eating apples WHILE you're not eating anything"; whereas the sentence *studenti polažu ispite dok ih ne polože* (perfective verb) means "students take exams UNTIL they pass them." [70b] The particle *se* can be added to an active verb to make it intransitive and passive. For example, the sentence *studenti slušaju predavanja* is an active sentence with the meaning "students listen to lectures," while the sentence *predavanja se slušaju* is a passive sentence with the meaning "lectures are listened to." [74]

* Forms of the locative case, continued *

The locative form of *tko / ko* is *kòme*, and that of *što / šta* is *čèmu*. [66c] Feminine nouns in *-a* whose stem ends in *-k*, *-g* or *-h* usually shift it to *-c, -z,* or *-s*, respectively, before the Lsg ending *-i*. Some nouns do not make the shift. It is not usually possible to predict which nouns these are; one must learn this fact along with the meaning of the noun. [66a]

				stem in –*k*	stem in -*g*	stem in -*h*
Nom	*ko* [B,S] *tko* [C]	*šta* [B,S] *što* [C]		(Nsg / Lsg)	(Nsg / Lsg)	(Nsg / Lsg)
Acc	*koga*	[= Nom]		*ruka / ruci*	*knjiga / knjizi*	*svrha / svrsi*
Gen	*koga*	*čega*		*Amerika / Americi*	*snaga / snazi*	
Loc	*kome*	*čemu*	[but]	*Bosanka / Bosanki*	*papiga / papigi*	*epoha / epohi*

* Time expressions *

The preposition *u* plus the name of a month locates an event in that month. The name of the month can be used alone, or it can be followed by the noun *mesec* [E] *mjesec* [J] "month." [67d] Duration of time is expressed in the accusative without a preposition; for instance, *mesec* [E] *mjesec* [J] *dana* means "for a month." If the unit is a single one, a noun in the genitive specifying the unit of time usually follows; for instance *godinu dana* "for a year" or *sat vremena* "for an hour." [71] To speak of an event that began in the past but still goes on, use the present tense and the adverb *već* (whose basic meaning is "already"). Thus the BCS present tense in the sentence *žive tu već godinu dana* corresponds to English present perfect continuous in the sentence "they have been living here for a year." [106a]

* Ordinal numbers *

Cardinal numbers ("one, two, three," etc.) count something, while ordinal numbers ("first, second, third," etc.) specify the place of something in a series. Ordinal numbers in BCS are adjectives. Most are formed by adding the long-form adjective endings directly to the cardinal number. The words for "first" and "second" are different, however, and there are certain minor changes in others. Below are the ordinals for 1 through 12, in the masculine nominative singular form. [109, 123b]

1st	*prvi*	4th	*četvrti*	7th	*sedmi*	10th	*deseti*
2nd	*drugi*	5th	*peti*	8th	*osmi*	11th	*jedanaesti*
3rd	*treći*	6th	*šesti*	9th	*deveti*	12th	*dvanaesti*

VOCABULARY

baš mi je drago!	I am truly delighted!	sjèditi, sjèdīm	to be sitting (I)
bolje	better	slabo	poorly, weakly
jùče [B,S]	yesterday	slati, šaljēm	to send (I)
jùčer [C]	yesterday	slika	photo, picture
pozdrav	greeting	star, staro, stara	old
pozdravljati, pozdravljām	to greet (I)	staviti, stavīm	to put (P)
sad, sada	now	strog, strogo, stroga	strict
sam, samo, sama	on one's own, by oneself	upravo	just, right now
sat vremena	[for] an hour	već	already
sèdeti, sèdīm	to be sitting (I)		

KAKO TI JE?

Bosnian
1. Šta ti je bȉlo jùče?
2. *Nešto mi nìje bȉlo dobro.*
1. Kàko ti je sad?
2. Bolje mi je.
1. Šta radīš? Kòme pīšeš?
2. Sjèdīm sama òvdje već sat vremena i pīšem *svòjoj sestri*. A ti, šta radīš?
1. I ja sjèdīm sam i pīšem nekome pȉsmo.
2. Kome ti pīšeš?
1. Pīšem svom *starōm prijatelju*.
2. Baš mi je drago! A o čemu mu pīšeš?
1. Šaljēm mu pozdrave i pīšem mu o sebi i o *Bosni*.
2. Pozdravljām ga i ja! Zanìmljivo! Upravo sam stavila slike *Crne Gòre* u pȉsmo *sestri*.

Croatian
1. Što ti je bȉlo jùčer?
2. *Nešto mi nìje bȉlo dobro.*
1. Kàko ti je sad?
2. Bolje mi je.
1. Što radīš? Kòme pīšeš?
2. Sjèdīm sama òvdje već sat vremena i pīšem *svòjoj sestri*. A ti, što radīš?
1. I ja sjèdīm sam i pīšem nekome pȉsmo.
2. Kome ti pīšeš?
1. Pīšem svòjem *starōm prijatelju*.
2. Baš mi je drago! A o čemu mu pīšeš?
1. Šaljēm mu pozdrave i pīšem mu o sebi i o *Hrvatskoj*.
2. Pozdravljām ga i ja! Zanìmljivo! Upravo sam stavila slike *Crne Gòre* u pȉsmo *sestri*.

Serbian
1. Шта ти је бȉло јȳче?
2. *Нешто ми нȳје било добро.*
1. Кàко ти је сад?
2. Бòље ми је.
1. Шта радȳш? Кòме пȳшеш?
2. Сèдȳм сама òвде вȇћ сȃт времена и пȳшем *свòјој сèстри*. А тȳ, шта радȳш?
1. И јȃ сèдȳм сам и пȳшем некоме пȳсмо.
2. Коме ти пȳшеш?
1. Пȳшем свом *старȏм прȳјатељу*.
2. Баш ми је дрȃго! А о чему му пȳшеш?
1. Шȃљем му поздраве и пȳшем му о себи и о *Србȳји*.
2. Поздрȃвљам га и ја! Занȳмљиво! Управо сам ставила слике *Црнē Гȍрē* у пȳсмо *сèстри*.

🖝 **Replace**: *sestra* **with** brat, majka, otac, **replace** *stari prijatelj* **with** dragi profesor, stroga profesorica [B,C] profesorka [S], **and replace** *Crna Gora* **with the names of other places, such as** Bosna i Hercegovina, Hrvatska, Kosovo, Republika Srpska, Srbija, Vojvodina, Južna Amèrika.

🖝 **Replace**: *Nešto mi nìje bȉlo dobro* **with** Bȉlo mi je slabo **or** Bȉlo mi je loše **or** Bȉlo mi je grozno.

Pictures of Montenegro:

Boka Kotorska

The Montenegrin coast near Boka Kotorska

 **GRAMMAR**

* Dative case *

The forms of the dative singular [Dsg] are exactly the same as those of the locative singular, including the fact of consonant shifts in stems ending in -*k*, -*g* or -*h*. **[66a]** The dative case has many different uses. One is indirect object, as in *pišem pismo sestri* "I am writing a letter to my sister." **[73a]** Another is to speak of states or feelings. English identifies the person experiencing these as the subject, but BCS identifies this person in the dative case, as in *bolje mi je* "I'm better," or *dosadno mu je* "he's bored." **[73g]** The state is always expressed as an adverb, and the verb is always 3rd singular. In the past tense the verb is always neuter, as in *bilo im je dosadno* "they were bored." **[104e]**

* Dative and locative personal pronouns *

There are full (long form) pronouns for both dative and locative case meanings. **[66d]** These full forms include a "reflexive" form, which means "oneself." Only the dative case has clitic (short form) pronouns. **[66e]** "Reflexive" clitic forms will be learned later. **[98]**

FULL FORMS	SINGULAR			PLURAL		
	Nom	Gen	Dat-Loc	Nom	Gen	Dat-Loc
1st sg	*ja*	*mene*	*meni*	*mi*	*nas*	*nama*
2nd sg	*ti*	*tebe*	*tebi*	*vi*	*vas*	*vama*
reflexive		*sebe*	*sebi*			
3rd sg masc / neut	*on / ono*	*njega*	*njemu*	*oni / ona*	*njih*	*njima*
3rd sg fem	*ona*	*nje*	*njoj*	*one*	*njih*	*njima*

CLITIC FORMS	SINGULAR			PLURAL		
	[Nom]	Gen	Dat	[Nom]	Gen	Dat
1st sg		*me*	*mi*		*nas*	*nam*
2nd sg		*te*	*ti*		*vas*	*vam*
3rd sg masc. / neut.		*ga*	*mu*		*ih*	*im*
3rd sg fem		*je*	*joj*		*ih*	*im*

* Word order *

Clitics must occur in a strict order, namely: LI - [aux] - [dat] - [acc/gen] - SE - JE. The capitalized words refer to actual clitics (JE is 3rd singular), and those in brackets refer to grammatical categories ([aux] means all clitic forms of *biti* except *je*). **[64, 76]** Examples showing this rule are *dajem mu ga* "I give it to him" (in which [dat] precedes [gen]), *šta ti je bilo?* "what was the matter with you?" (in which [dat] precedes JE), and *ne tiče ga se* "it doesn't concern him" (in which [gen] precedes SE).

* The form *sam*, *samo*, *sama* *

Used as a pronoun, the word *sam* means "by oneself, alone." Used as an adjective, it emphasizes the identity of something or someone, as in *na samome danu* "on the very day." Note that the pronoun is distinguished from the clitic form *sam* "[I] am" or the adverb *samo* "only" by its long root vowel. **[72c]**

ᕫA4 ⊙51,52

VOCABULARY

čini mi se	it seems to me	mnogi, mnogo, mnoga	many
činiti se, čini se	to seem (I)	riba	fish
govoriti, govorim	to speak (I)	slan, slano, slana	salty
hrana	food	stavljati, stavljam	to put (I)
Japan, Japana	Japan	susjed [B,C]	neighbor *(m)*
jelo	dish [of food]	susjeda [B,C]	neighbor *(f)*
jelovnik	menu	svaki	every
kiseo, kiselo, kisela	sour	svaki dan	every day
komšija [B,S]	neighbor *(m)*	sviđati se, sviđam se + *Dat*	to appeal to (I)
komšinica [B,S]	neighbor *(f)*	sviđa mi se [to]	I like [that]
kuhati, kuham [B,C]	to cook (I)	uvek	always
kuvati, kuvam [S]	to cook (I)	uvijek	always
ljut, ljuto, ljuta	hot, spicy	vrsta	type
meso	meat		

ŠTA TI SE SVIĐA? [B,S]   ŠTO TI SE SVIĐA? [C]

Bosnian
1. Sviđaju li ti se više *slatka* ili *slana* jela? *Moja mama* odlično kuha sve vrste hrane.
2. Meni se više sviđaju *slatka* jela.
1. Voliš li *meso?*
2. Sviđaju mi se mnoga jela, ali ne volim *meso.*
1. *Mama* mi je iz *Argentine.* Ona uvijek govori da se *meso* mora svaki dan stavljati na jelovnik!
2. Izvinite, ali čini mi se da se *meso* ne mora jesti.

Croatian
1. Sviđaju li ti se više *slatka* ili *slana* jela? *Moja mama* odlično kuha sve vrste hrane.
2. Meni se više sviđaju *slatka* jela.
1. Voliš li *meso?*
2. Sviđaju mi se mnoga jela, ali ne volim *meso.*
1. *Mama* mi je iz *Argentine.* Ona uvijek govori da se *meso* mora svaki dan stavljati na jelovnik!
2. Oprostite, ali čini mi se da se *meso* ne mora jesti.

Serbian
1. Da li ti se više sviđaju *slatka* ili *slana* jela? *Moja mama* odlično kuva sve vrste hrane.
2. Meni se više sviđaju *slatka* jela.
1. Da li voliš *meso?*
2. Sviđaju mi se mnoga jela, ali ne volim *meso.*
1. *Mama* mi je iz *Argentine.* Ona uvek govori da se *meso* mora svaki dan stavljati na jelovnik!
2. Izvinite, ali čini mi se da se *meso* ne mora jesti.

ᕫ **Replace** *mama* **with** susjed [B,C] komšija [B,S] **or** susjeda [B,C] komšinica [B,S], **and replace** *slatki, slani* **with** kiseli, ljuti. **Replace** *meso* **with** riba, **and** *Argentina* **with** Japan.

ᕫ **Do** the exercise again, this time using plural pronouns instead of *ti* and *ja*.

Roasts, A la carte, Grill, Prepared Food

Always fresh meat

⚙ GRAMMAR

* The words "like" and "love" *

The verb *voleti* [E] *voljeti* [J] carries the basic meaning "love." It also means both "love and "like" when used before an infinitive, and is used when the state of "liking" is an enduring one. The idea "like" in the sense "take a liking to" is expressed by the verbs *sviđati se* and *dopadati se*. The grammar of these verbs differs sharply from English "like" in that the person or thing which is liked appears as the subject of the sentence, and the person who does the liking appears in the dative case. For example, "I like her" in BCS is *ona mi se sviđa* (literally, "she is pleasing to me"). **[73d]**

* Other uses of the dative *

Some verbs take what looks like a direct object in the dative case. For instance, the object of *odgovarati* "answer" (and of certain other verbs) must be in the dative case. **[73b]** Short form dative pronouns also can be used to indicate possession. Thus, "my brother" can be said either as *brat mi* or *moj brat*. The first is somewhat more informal, and is used when the idea of possession has already been mentioned. **[73e]**

The state of Montenegro proclaimed its independence in 2006. The Montenegrin constitution adopted in late 2007 proclaimed the official language to be Montenegrin, and in early 2008 the government set up a council to codify this language. Despite these official acts, however, it is too early to speak in systematic terms of a Montenegrin language. The establishment of a standard language requires both a lengthy process of codification decisions and a period during which the codification choices are validated by the community which they represent. Furthermore, both these processes rest upon a linguistic awareness with historical roots going back at least several generations. In the case of Montenegrin, the movement to create a separate language can be dated only as far back as 1993. Although one can speak of a distinct Montenegrin cultural identity, the issue of whether the language of Montenegro should be Serbian or Montenegrin, and the actual form the latter should take if and when it is accepted fully by the Montenegrin community, continues to be a matter of discussion. Also of relevance is the fact that each of the three existing standards (Bosnian, Croatian, and Serbian) makes reference to a cultural history associated with a distinctly separate religion. Montenegro, by contrast, does not represent a fourth separate religion but rather shares this part of its cultural history with Serbia.

For all these reasons no attempt is made here to present [M] alongside [B], [C] and [S] as a fourth linguistic standard. Montenegrin culture is represented at several points in the book (see pp. 85, 96, 239, 292-296) and the linguistic traits of Montenegrin are discussed in more detail on p. 296.

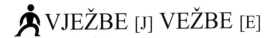 VJEŽBE [J] VEŽBE [E]

B1

Fill in each blank with the locative form of the word found in the immediately following sentence, Pay attention to the choice of prepositions!

Example: [B] Gdje je knjiga? Knjiga je (na) .... Knjiga je na stolu. Gdje je sto?, etc.
[C] Gdje je knjiga? Knjiga je (na) .... Knjiga je na stolu. Gdje je stol?, etc.
[S] Gde je knjiga? Knjiga je (na) .... Knjiga je na stolu. Gde je sto?, etc.

Bosnian
1. Gdje je sto?
   Sto je u ....
2. Gdje je soba?
   Soba je u ....
3. Gdje je zgrada?
   Zgrada je na ....
4. Gdje je fakultet?
   Fakultet je u ....
5. A gdje je grad?
   Grad je u ....

Croatian
1. Gdje je stol?
   Stol je u ....
2. Gdje je soba?
   Soba je u ....
3. Gdje je zgrada?
   Zgrada je na ....
4. Gdje je fakultet?
   Fakultet je u ....
5. A gdje je grad?
   Grad je u ....

Serbian
1. Где је сто?
   Сто је у ....
2. Где је соба?
   Соба је у ....
3. Где је зграда?
   Зграда је на ....
4. Где је факултет?
   Факултет је у ....
5. А где је град?
   Град је у ....

For #5 enter the name of the state you live in. Replace this sequence with: 1) reč [E] riječ [J], (na) papir, (u) knjiga, (u) torba, (u) auto; 2) vrata, (u) zid, (na) kat [B,C] sprat [B,S], (u) zgrada.

Keep a list for yourself of the nouns you encounter which are used with *na*.

B2

Fill in the blanks with the correct past tense forms of the verbs in parentheses.

Bosnian and Serbian
1. Šta .... juče .... (raditi)?
2. Juče .... (pisati) pismo.
1. O čemu .... (pisati)?
2. .... o *tebi i sebi.*

Croatian
1. Što .... jučer .... (raditi)?
2. Jučer .... (pisati) pismo.
1. O čemu .... (pisati)?
2. .... o *tebi i sebi.*

Replace *pisati pismo* **with** čitati knjigu, gledati film. **Replace** *tebi i sebi* **with** mesec [E] mjesec [J], nebo, sunce **and other topics of your choice.**

B3

Give the forms requested of these verbs (1st singular present, and the 3rd person past tense forms for masculine singular, neuter singular, feminine singular, and masculine plural).

	1st sg. pres.	masc.sg.past	neut.sg.past	fem.sg.past	masc.pl.past
biti					
čekati					
čitati					
dolaziti					
gledati					
kupiti					
kupovati					
kružiti					
misliti					
moliti					
odgovarati					
pisati					
raditi					
slati					
spavati					
staviti					
stavljati					
znati					

B4

Bosnian and Croatian
1. Evo *čaše*. Na *stolu* je.
2. Stavljam *je* na *rječnik*.
1. Sada je na *rječniku*.

Serbian
1. Ево *чаше*. На *столу* је.
2. Стављам *је* на *речник*.
1. Сада је на *речнику*.

☞ **Replace this sequence with:**

1) reč [E] riječ [J], (na) papir, (u) knjiga, (u) torba, (u) auto;

2) vrata, (u) zid, (na) kat [B,C] sprat [B,S], (u) zgrada.

B5

Bosnian and Serbian
1. Kȁko je *Elvisu* dȁnas?
2. Dȁnas *mu* je tȅško.
1. Zašto?
2. Zȁto̱ što dȁnas ȉma̱ usmeni̱ ȉspit.
1. Da li sve zna̱?
2. Čȉni̱ *mu* se da ništa nȅ zna̱!

Croatian
1. Kȁko je *Elvisu* dȁnas?
2. Dȁnas *mu* je tȅško.
1. Zašto?
2. Zȁto̱ što dȁnas ȉma̱ usmeni̱ ȉspit.
1. Zna̱ li sve?
2. Čȉni̱ *mu* se da ništa nȅ zna̱!

☛ **Replace**: *Elvis* **first with** Ȁmila, **then with the pair** Elvis i Ȁmila.

B6

1. Kȍja̱ ti se jela svi̱đaju̱?
2. Kȍja̱ ti se jela ne svi̱đaju̱?
3. Čȉja̱ ti se hra̱na svi̱đa?
4. Kȍje̱ ti se životinje svi̱đaju̱?
5. Kakve ti se ȍlo̱vke svi̱đaju̱?

1. Кȍја̱ ти се јела свȕђају̱?
2. Кȍја̱ ти се јела не свȕђају̱?
3. Чȕја̱ ти се хра̱на свȕђа?
4. Кȍје̱ ти се животиње свȕђају̱?
5. Какве ти се ȍло̱вке свȕђају̱?

☛ **Ask each** other these questions and refer to the dialogue in A4, or to the glossary, for vocabulary.

Self-study learners: Replace *ti* in the above questions with *mu, joj, im, nam, vam.* Then compose answers to these questions, paying particular attention to the grammatical requirements of the verb *svi̱đati se.*

B7

Bosnian, Croatian and Serbian
1. *Mama* mi je *Hrvȁtica.* Ȍdakle̱ je tvȍja *mama?*
2. Mȍja *mama* je iz *Argenti̱ne̱.* A *tata* mi je Ȅngle̱z.

☛ **Replace** *Hrvȁtica* **with** Bȍsa̱nka, Crnȍgorka, Srpkinja; Ȅnglez **with** Amerikȁnac; *Argenti̱na* **with** Bugarska̱, Grčka̱, Mađarska̱. **Switch** *tata* **and** *mama.* **Also use** Bȍsa̱nac, Crnogȍrac, Hrvȁt, Srbin.

6th of August Street

✍ DOMAĆA ZADAĆA [B,C] DOMAĆI ZADATAK [S]

C1

Replace the word in parentheses with svo̱j, nje̱gov, nje̱n [B,S] nje̱zin [C], njihov, **choosing both the appropriate form and providing it with the right endings.**

<u>Bosnian</u>

Elvis i A̱mila či̱taju knjige u ško̱li.

Elvis či̱ta .... (Elvisovu) knjigu, a A̱mila či̱ta .... (A̱milinu) knjigu.

O̱na že̱li či̱tati .... (Elvisovu) knjigu, a ne .... (A̱milinu).

Elvis ne že̱li či̱tati .... (A̱milinu) knjigu, već .... (Elvisovu).

Tu̱ su i njihovi prijatelji Zla̱ta i Sead.

O̱ni ne̱maju .... (ni Zla̱tine ni Seadove) knjige, a ne že̱le či̱tati .... (ni Elvisove ni A̱miline) knjige.

Oba prijatelja gledaju zidove, pro̱zore, sto̱ i ta̱blu u ra̱zredu, i čekaju Elvisa i A̱milu.

<u>Croatian</u>

Da̱nijel i Ma̱rta či̱taju knjige u ško̱li.

Da̱nijel či̱ta .... (Da̱nijelovu) knjigu, a Ma̱rta či̱ta .... (Ma̱rtinu) knjigu.

O̱na že̱li či̱tati .... (Da̱nijelovu) knjigu, a ne .... (Ma̱rtinu).

Da̱nijel ne že̱li či̱tati .... (Ma̱rtinu) knjigu, već .... (Da̱nijelovu).

Tu̱ su njihovi prijatelji Ti̱jana i Hṟvoje.

O̱ni ne̱maju .... (ni Ti̱janine ni Hṟvojeve) knjige, a ne že̱le či̱tati .... (ni Da̱nijelove ni Ma̱rtine) knjige.

Oba prijatelja gledaju zidove, pro̱zore, sto̱l i ploču u ra̱zredu, i čekaju Da̱nijela i Ma̱rtu.

<u>Serbian</u>

Da̱nilo i Sve̱tlana či̱taju knjige u ško̱li.

Da̱nilo či̱ta .... (Da̱nilovu) knjigu, a Sve̱tlana či̱ta .... (Sve̱tlaninu) knjigu.

O̱na že̱li či̱tati .... (Da̱nilovu) knjigu, a ne .... (Sve̱tlaninu).

Da̱nilo ne že̱li da či̱ta .... (Sve̱tlaninu) knjigu, već .... (Da̱nilovu).

Tu̱ su i njihovi drugovi Bra̱nka i Aleksa̱ndar.

O̱ni ne̱maju .... (ni Bra̱nkine ni Ale̱ksa̱ndrove) knjige, a ne že̱le da či̱taju .... (ni Da̱nilove ni Sve̱tlanine) knjige.

Oba druga gledaju zidove, pro̱zore, sto̱ i ta̱blu u ra̱zredu, i čekaju Da̱nila i Sve̱tlanu.

C2

Ask each other these questions:

Bosnian	Croatian	Serbian
1. Kakve ispite imaju studenti na Sarajevskom univerzitetu?	1. Kakve ispite imaju studenti na Zagrebačkom sveučilištu?	1. Какве испите имају студенти на Београдском универзитету?
2. Koliko godina obično studiraju studenti u Sarajevu?	2. Koliko godina obično studiraju studenti u Zagrebu?	2. Колико година обично студирају студенти у Београду?
3. Kada počinje zimski semestar?	3. Kada počinje zimski semestar?	3. Када почиње зимски семестар?
4. Kada se završava ljetni semestar?	4. Kada se završava ljetni semestar?	4. Када се завршава летњи семестар?
5. Šta rade studenti kada su apsolventi?	5. Što rade studenti kada su apsolventi?	5. Шта раде студенти када су апсолвенти?
6. Koliko mjeseci traje školska godina?	6. Koliko mjeseci traje školska godina?	6. Колико месеци траје школска година?

C3

Hrana

Connect the word to the food it represents:

hljeb	meso	riba	jabuka	narandža	sir	pecivo	kruška	čaj	mlijeko	slatkiš
kruh				naranča					mleko	
hleb				pomorandža						

C4

Insert the verb given in parentheses below the line in its appropriate present-tense form.

1. [B,C] Oni .... zajedno na fakultetu svakog četvrtka.
   [S] Они .... заједно на факултету сваког четвртка.
   (raditi / радити)

2. [B,C] Već mjesec dana .... filmove svaki dan.
   [S] Већ месец дана .... филмове сваки дан.
   ([mi] gledati / [ми] гледати)

3. [B] Vi nam .... iduće sedmice.
   [C] Vi nam .... idućeg tjedna.
   [S] Ви нам .... идуће недеље.
       (dolaziti / долазити)

4. [B,C] Prijateljice .... nekoga po gradu.
   [S] Другарице .... некога по граду.
       (tražiti / тражити)

5. [B,C] Roditelji .... misliti na nas.
   [S] Родитељи .... да мисле на нас.
       (voljeti / волети)

6. [B] Mi .... jabuke, a oni .... narandže, dok vi ne .... ništa.
   [C] Mi .... jabuke, a oni .... naranče, dok vi ne .... ništa.
   [S] Ми .... јабуке, а они .... поморанце, док ви не .... ништа.
       (jesti / јести)   (jesti / јести)   (jesti / јести)

7. [B,C] Student .... rječnik svojem prijatelju.
   [S] Студент .... речник своме пријатељу.
       (kupovati / куповати)

8. [B,C] Na usmenom ispitu profesori .... , a mi ....
   [S] На усменом испиту професори .... , а ми ....
       (pitati / питати)   (odgovarati / одговарати)

9. [B,C] a. Ja ne .... !   b. Ti .... !   Ti ne .... , a oni .... ? To nije dobro.
   [S] a. Ja не .... !   b. Ти .... !   Ти не .... , а они .... ? То није добро.
       (moći / моћи)   (morati / морати)   (moći / моћи)   (moći / моћи)

10. [B,C] Rijeke Sava, Dunav, Drina i Drava .... uz granice, ali rijeka Bosna ne .... uz granicu.
    [S] Реке Сава, Дунав, Дрина и Драва .... уз границе, али река Босна не .... уз границу.
        (teći / тећи)   (teći / тећи)

C5

Translate sentence (a) of each set into English, and then translate the following sentence or sentences into B, C, or S, using the first as a model:

1. a. [B,C] Nema mačaka u ovoj kući.
      [S] Нема мачака у овој кући.
   b. There is no water in this cup.
   c. There are no animals in this city.

2. a. [B,C] Sestra joj je iz Kalifornije.
      [S] Сестра joj je из Калифорније.
   b. Our brother is from Hungary.
   c. His father is from Montenegro.

3. a. [B,C] Òni stavljaju pìsmo u tòrbu. Pìsmo je u tòrbi.
   [S] Они стављају пѝсмо у тòрбу. Пѝсмо је у тòрби.
   b. We are putting money into the bag. The money is in the bag.
   c. He is putting pencils into the bag. The pencils are in the bag.

4. a. [B] Tàbla je na zìdu, pored stòla, dalèko od vráta.
   [C] Plòča je na zìdu, pored stòla, dalèko od vráta.
   [S] Тàбла је на зѝду, поред стòла, далèко од врáта.
   b. The window is on the wall, by the blackboard, far from the table.
   c. The many-colored snake is at home, the blue bird is in the schoolroom, but the little yellow
      dog is next to the black cat.

5. a. [B,C] Mìrjani je tèško.
   [S] Мѝрјани је тèшко.
   b. Zlatan feels cold.
   c. Danilo feels well.

6. a. [B,C] Profesori slùšaju stùdente i stùdenti slùšaju profesore.
   [S] Профèсори слùшају стùденте и стùденти слùшају профèсоре.
   b. Pupils listen to elementary-school teachers, and elementary-school teachers
      listen to pupils.
   c. Aunts listen to sisters, sisters listen to aunts.

7. a. [B,C] Mì ih pìtamo, a òni nam odgovàraju.
   [S] Мѝ их пѝтамо, а òни нам одговàрају.
   b. They ask us, we answer them.
   c. He asks her, she answers him.

8. a. [B] Prostòrija je u zgràdi, zgrada je na fakultètu, fakùltet je na planèti Zèmlji,
      planèta Zèmlja krùži oko Súnca, a Súnce je usred svemíra.
   [C] Prostòrija je u zgràdi, zgrada je na fakultètu, fakùltet je na planètu Zèmlji,
      planet Zèmlja krùži oko Súnca, a Súnce je usred svemíra.
   [S] Простòрија је у згрàди, зграда је на факултèту, факùлтет је на планèти Зèмљи,
      планèта Зèмља крùжи око Súнца, а Súнце је усред свемѝра.
   b. The table is in the room, the room is at the university, the university is in the city,
      the city is in the state.

9. a. [B,C] Ìdēm iz jèdnē zgràdē u drùgū.
   [S] Ѝдēм из јèднē згрàдē у дрùгу.
   b. I am from New York. Are you from New Orleans?
   c. This is a fish from the Adriatic Sea.

10.a. [B,C] Kolìko si sáti putòvala od Parìza do Lòndōna?
   [S] Колѝко си сáти путòвала од Парѝза до Лòндōна?
   b. How do they go from the Moon to the Sun?
   c. This is a letter from your friend from France.

11.a. [B,C] Dànas mòrām ìći s òvog poluòtoka na ònaj.
   [S] Дàнас мòрāм да идем са òвог полуòстрва на онò.
   b. He takes the pencil from the table.
   c. This is a French-English dictionary [literally: a dictionary from French into English].

C6

Replace vòljeti **in the following sentences by** svìđati se, **making any other necessary changes.**
Example: Volīm mèdvjede. **becomes**   Mèdvjedi mi se svìđajū.

1. [B,C] Volīš li predávanja na fakultètu?
   [S] Da li volīš predávanja na fakultètu?
2. Volīm velika vráta.
3. Volīm tvog psa i tvoj pas me voli.
4. Òni volē slàtka jela, ali vi ih nè volīte.
5. Zar crna mačka volī šàrenu zmìju?
6. Màrin učitelj nè voli Màrine živòtinje u škòli.

C7

Fill in the blanks below with the correct dative - locative form of the word in parentheses, and mark in each instance whether the meaning is dative or locative. Then write out the sentence in full.

1. Pišem pismo .... (svòja majka).

2. Vráta se nàlazē na .... (vìsoki zid) u .... (škòlska soba).

3. (Ònaj grozni profesor) .... se ne svìđaju naša pìtanja.

4. Kùpujēm knjigu .... (svoj òtac).

5. Òn žìvī u .... (Južna Amèrika), a òna žìvī u .... (Fràncuska).

6. Čìtam knjigu o .... (plàva rèka). [E]

   Čìtam knjigu o .... (plàva rijèka). [J]

7. .... (Òna žèna) nìje dànas dobro.

8. Mèso se svìđa i .... (pas) i .... (mačka), ali ne i .... (màjmun).

9. Profesor mnogo gòvorī o .... (matemàtika).

10. Ako je i .... (òn) i .... (ti) slabo, idèmo kući odmah.

🌐 Geografska pitanja [B,C,S] Zemljopisna pitanja [C]

VOCABULARY

istok	east	poluotok [B,C]	peninsula
nekoliko	several	slovenački, slovenačko, slovenačka [B,S]	Slovenian
obala	coast, shore	slovenski, slovensko, slovenska [C]	Slovenian
područje	region, area	više	a lot [of]
poluostrvo [B,S]	peninsula	zapad	west

Bosnian and Croatian

Hrvatska se ne sastoji od više djelova kao Srbija (Srbija i Vojvodina), ili Bosna i Hercegovina (Federacija i Republika Srpska), već ima nekoliko područja.

Serbian

Хрватска се не састоји од више делова као Србија (Србија и Војводина), или Босна и Херцеговина (Федерација и Република Српска), већ има неколико подручја.

1. [B,C] Koja se područja nalaze na zapadu Hrvatske uz Jadransko more?

   [S] Која се подручја налазе на западу Хрватске уз Јадранско море?

2. [B,C] Koji je poluotok blizu Italije?

   [S] Које је полуострво близу Италије?

3. [B,C] Koje se područje nalazi na istoku Hrvatske, uz Dunav i srpsku granicu?

   [S] Које се подручје налази на истоку Хрватске, уз Дунав и српску границу?

4. [B,C] Kako se zove dio hrvatske obale od Rijeke do Zadra?

   [S] Како се зове део хрватске обале од Ријеке до Задра?

5. [B,C] Koje je područje između Zagreba i slovenske granice?

   [S] Које је подручје између Загреба и словеначке границе?

Note that *Mađarska* is spelled *Madjarska* on the map above. It is common practice to use the sequence **dj** when the letter **đ** is not available in one's word processing software. In general, however, the use of **đ** is preferable, since **đ** and **dj** are in fact distinct sounds. In addition, whereas certain words can be spelled both ways (such as *Mađarska* or *Madjarska*), many B, C, and S ijekavian words (such as *djeca*, *djevojka* or *gdje*) can only be spelled with **dj**. In the developing Montenegrin standard, however, it is now the norm to spell these ijekavian words with the letter **đ**.

📖 Priča: Albahari

Read Part III of the story "Osam malih priča o mojoj ženi" by David Albahari (p. 342).

Sedma lekcija • Lesson Seven

briga	worry	nikada	never
budi bez brige	don't worry	omlet	omelet
često	often	pahuljice *(pl form)*	cereal flakes
doručak, doručka	breakfast	paprika	pepper (vegetable)
doručkovati, doručkujem	to eat breakfast (I/P)	paradajz [B,C,S]	tomato
džem	jam	ponekad	sometimes
išta, ičega	anything	puter [B,S]	butter
jaje, jajeta	egg	rajčica [C]	tomato
jaje na oko	egg sunnyside up	s, sa + *Instr*	with
kajgana	scrambled eggs	sebe	self
kiselo mleko	yogurt-like beverage	sedmi, sedmo, sedma	seventh
kiselo mlijeko	yogurt-like beverage	spremati, spremam	to prepare (I)
kobasica	sausage	spremiti, spremim	to prepare (P)
limun	lemon	svež, sveže, sveža	fresh
maslac [B,C,S]	butter	svjež, svježe, svježa	fresh
med	honey	šećer	sugar
naravno	naturally	tost	toast
ni	neither	ukusan, ukusno, ukusna	tasty

DORUČAK

Bosnian

1. Šta jedeš za doručak? Želiš li jesti sa mnom? Mogu nešto da spremim za tebe i za sebe.
2. Obično jedem pahuljice.
1. Sa čim ih spremaš?
2. S mlijekom i šećerom. A ti?
1. Često doručkujem crni hljeb sa svježim sirom i zelenom paprikom, a ponekad i kobasicom, ali nikada ne jedem pahuljice.
2. A šta piješ?
1. Uvijek pijem kafu s toplim mlijekom. A ti?
2. Ja pijem čaj bez ičega.
1. Zar ga ne piješ ni sa šećerom ni sa mlijekom ni sa limunom!? Kako možeš piti takav čaj?
2. Naravno da mogu. Budi bez brige!

Croatian

1. Što jedeš za doručak? Želiš li jesti sa mnom? Mogu nešto spremiti za tebe i za sebe.
2. Obično jedem pahuljice.
1. S čim ih spremaš?
2. S mlijekom i šećerom. A ti?
1. Često doručkujem crni kruh sa svježim sirom i zelenom paprikom, a ponekad i kobasicom, ali nikada ne jedem pahuljice.
2. A što piješ?
1. Uvijek pijem kavu s toplim mlijekom. A ti?
2. Ja pijem čaj bez ičega.
1. Zar ga ne piješ ni sa šećerom ni s mlijekom ni s limunom!? Kako možeš piti takav čaj?
2. Naravno da mogu. Budi bez brige!

Serbian

1. Šta jedeš za doručak? Da li želiš da jedeš sa mnom? Mogu nešto da spremim za tebe i za sebe.
2. Obično jedem pahuljice.
1. Sa čim ih spremaš?
2. Sa mlekom i šećerom. A ti?
1. Često doručkujem crni hleb sa svežim sirom i zelenom paprikom, a ponekad i kobasicom, ali nikada ne jedem pahuljice.
2. A šta piješ?
1. Uvek pijem kafu sa toplim mlekom. A ti?
2. Ja pijem čaj bez ičega.
1. Zar ga ne piješ ni sa šećerom ni sa mlekom ni sa limunom!? Kako možeš da piješ takav čaj?
2. Naravno da mogu. Budi bez brige!

✍ **Other breakfast foods:** jaje na oko, jedno jaje, kiselo mleko [E] mlijeko [J], maslac [B,C,S] puter [B,S], med, paradajz [B,C,S] rajčica [C], tost, voće; **and the phrases** slatki džem, ukusni omlet, velika kajgana. **Describe your own breakfast habits: what you usually eat and what you never eat.**

Self-study learners: Pay attention to the way that *s* and *sa* are used and to the endings of the nouns and adjectives that follow them. Note the declension of the word *što* or *šta*, especially the instrumental form *čime*, and the declension of the related word *išta*, especially the genitive form *ičega*.

Bread

Burek

Rolls

Flaky pastry

Various
cakes

 GRAMMAR

* Instrumental case *

The ending of the instrumental singular [Isg] is -*om* for feminine nouns in -*a*. For masculine and neuter nouns it is -*om* (which appears as -*em* after a soft consonant). The adjective ending is -*im* for masculine-neuter and -*om* for feminine. No shift occurs after soft consonants in the feminine forms. [79a] The Isg ending of feminine nouns in a consonant is either -*i* or -*u*, the latter accompanied by certain changes in the preceding consonant. Most such nouns occur with both endings, but some only with the ending -*i*. Only the -*u* endings are illustrated below; the -*i* endings are exactly like the Gsg and DLsg of these nouns. [79b]

	masculine	neuter	feminine -a	feminine -cons.
Nsg	*važan grad / muž*	*lepo selo / more*	*naša zemlja*	*vaša reč / kost*
Isg	*važnim gradom / mužem*	*lepim selom / morem*	*našom zemljom*	*vašom rečju / košću*

* The instrumental case of pronouns *

In interrogative pronouns (right), and in 1st and 3rd singular personal pronouns (below), there are two forms of the instrumental: a shorter and a longer one. There are only full form personal pronouns. In the plural, Dat, Loc and Instr all have the same ending. Prepositions ending in a consonant must add -*a* before *mnom*. All prepositions take the accent before *mnom*: *sa mnom, preda mnom*. [79c-d] The words *ništa* "nothing," *nešto* "something," *išta* "anything [at all]" and *svašta* "all sorts of" are declined like *šta* [B,S] *što* [C]. [62, 92]

	WHO	WHAT
Nom	*tko / ko*	*što / šta*
Acc	*koga*	*što / šta*
Gen	*koga*	*čega*
Dat-Loc	*kome*	*čemu*
Instr	*kim, kime*	*čim, čime*

FULL FORMS		Singular				Plural		
	Nom	Gen	Dat-Loc	Instr		Nom	Gen	Dat-Loc-Instr
1.sg	*ja*	*mene*	*meni*	*mnom, mnome*		*mi*	*nas*	*nama*
2.sg	*ti*	*tebe*	*tebi*	*tobom*		*vi*	*vas*	*vama*
reflexive		*sebe*	*sebi*	*sobom*				
3.sg masc/neut	*on / ono*	*njega*	*njemu*	*njim, njime*		*oni / ona*	*njih*	*njima*
3.sg fem.	*ona*	*nje*	*njoj*	*njom, njome*		*one*	*njih*	*njima*

The instrumental case is used with several prepositions, the most frequently occurring of which is *s* "with." If the following word begins with *s, z, š,* or *ž,* this preposition must take the form *sa.* In B it sometimes appears as *sa* in other instances as well, and in S it usually takes the form *sa* regardless of the shape of the word which follows. [80a]

Bus and tram tickets

VOCABULARY

autobus	bus	prokockati	to gamble away (P)
avion, aviona [B,C,S]	airplane	prometni [C]	traffic
bicikl	bicycle	put, puta	journey; way
bojati se, bojim se + *Gen*	to fear (I)	radi + *Gen*	for the sake of
budućnost, budućnosti *(f)*	future	saobraćajni [B,S]	traffic
godinama	for years	skup, skupo, skupa	expensive
hodati, hodam	to walk (I)	suprug	spouse *(m)*
imati pravo	to be right (I)	supruga	spouse *(f)*
kilometar, kilometra	kilometer	tramvaj	tram
kola *(pl form)*	car	u neku ruku	in a sense, in a way
kolima	by car	ugodan, ugodno, ugodna	convenient
mlad, mlado, mlađa	young	vlak [C]	train
motocikl	motorcycle	voz [B,S]	train
muž	husband	vozač, vozača	driver
nemoj	don't	voziti, vozim	to drive (I)
nesreća	accident, calamity	voziti se, vozim se	to ride [in a vehicle] (I)
opasan, opasno, opasna	dangerous	vožnja	ride, drive *(noun)*
pa	so, and	zdravlje	health
pravo	right *(noun)*	zrakoplov [C]	airplane
pred + *Instr.*	in front of	žuriti se, žurim se	to hurry (I)

ČIME IDEŠ NA POSAO?

Bosnian
1. Čime ideš ponedjeljkom na *posao?*
2. Obično idem *tramvajem.*
1. A utorkom?
2. Utorkom *supruga* i ja uvijek idemo zajedno i žurimo se, pa se vozimo *autom.*
1. *Kolima?* Dakle ti si vozač! Zar to nije skupo?
2. Skupo jeste, ali je ugodno! Godinama već vozim.
1. A biciklom ili motociklom? To je dobro za zdravlje.
2. Biciklom mogu, ali mi se čini opasno voziti se motociklom. Bojim se saobraćajne nesreće.
1. U neku ruku imaš pravo. Mlad si! Pred tobom je budućnost. Nemoj to prokockati!
2. Radi zdravlja volim hodati dva kilometra od kuće do posla kad je lijepo vrijeme.

Croatian
1. Čime ideš ponedjeljkom na *posao?*
2. Obično idem *tramvajem.*
1. A utorkom?
2. Utorkom *supruga* i ja uvijek idemo zajedno i žurimo se, pa se vozimo *autom.*
1. *Kolima?* Dakle ti si vozač! Zar to nije skupo?
2. Skupo jest, ali je ugodno! Godinama već vozim.
1. A biciklom ili motociklom? To je dobro za zdravlje.
2. Biciklom mogu, ali mi se čini opasno voziti se motociklom. Bojim se prometne nesreće.
1. U neku ruku imaš pravo. Mlad si! Pred tobom je budućnost. Nemoj to prokockati!
2. Radi zdravlja volim hodati dva kilometra od kuće do posla kad je lijepo vrijeme.

Serbian

1. Чи́ме и̏деш по̀не̏де̏љко̄м на *по̀сао*?

2. О̀бично и̏де̄м *трамва̏је̄м*.

1. А у̏то̄рко̄м?

2. У̏то̄рко̄м *супру̀га* и ја̑ у̏ве̄к и̏де̄мо за̏је̏дно, и жу̀рӣмо се, па се во̀зӣмо *а̏уто̄м*.

1. *Ко̀лӣма*? Да̏кле̄, ти̑ си во̀зач! За̑р то̑ ни̏је ску̀по?

2. Ску̀по је̏сте̄, али је пр̏ија̏тно! Го̀динама ве̄ћ во̏зӣм.

1. А би̏циклом или мо̀тоциклом? То̑ је до̀бро за здра̏вље.

2. Би̏циклом мо̀гу, али ми се чи̏нӣ о̀пасно во̀зити се мо̀тоциклом. Бо̀јӣм се саобра̏ћа̄јне̄ несре̏ће̄.

1. У не̏кӯ ру̏ку и̏ма̄ш пра̏во. Мла̑д си! Пред тобо̑м је жи̏вот. Не̏мо̄ј то̑ про̀коцкати.

2. Ра̏ди здра̏вља во̀лӣм да хо̏да̄м два̑ кило̀метра од ку̏ће̄ до по̀сла кад је ле̏по вре̏ме.

☞ **Work up a skit loosely based on this exercise, about going on a trip. Replace** *supruga* **with** suprug **or** muž, *posao* **with** put, **and** *tramvaj* **and** *auto* **with** autobus, avion [B,C,S] zrakoplov [C], vlak [C] voz [B,S], peške [S] pješice [B,C].

GRAMMAR

* Use of the instrumental case *

The instrumental is used in a number of adverbial expressions. It can express the means of transport: for instance, *ja idem tramvajem, ona ide biciklom, a on ide kolima* "I go by tram, she goes by bicycle, and he goes by car." [81a] It is also used to express the time of a regular, repeated action; for instance, *ona radi kasno utorkom* "she works late on Tuesdays." Used in the plural with a noun of time, it expresses a period of long duration which still continues; in this meaning it is used with a present tense verb and the adverb *već*; for instance, *već godinama razmišljam o tome* "I've been thinking about that for years." [81b]

* Prepositions with the instrumental *

Most other prepositions which take the instrumental case refer to physical (or metaphorical) location. Among these are *pred* "before," *nad* "above" and *za* "behind"; the latter is often seen in the idiom *za stolom* "at the table." [80b]

* Verbs of transport *

Three verbs share the general meaning "take [someone or something] [somewhere]." If the object is an animate being capable of moving under its own steam, one of two verbs is used, the choice of which depends on the means of transport. If the movement is by foot, one uses *voditi* and if it is by vehicle, one uses *voziti*. The third verb, *nositi*, is used if the object to be taken is inanimate or an animate being which must be carried, such as an infant. The verb *voziti* "drive" is used in several different ways. As a transitive verb it takes an Acc object, which can signify either a passenger, as in *voziti ženu na posao* "drive [one's] wife to work," or a type of vehicle, as in *voziti auto* "drive a car." As an intransitive verb, accompanied by *se*, it can mean either simply "ride" (as opposed to "drive"), or "ride/go by vehicle," with the vehicle specified in the Instr, as in *voziti se autom* "drive a car" or *voziti se biciklom* "ride a bike." [84a]

* Negative imperative *

A negative command ("Don't....") is expressed by the form *nemoj* (plural *nemojte*) followed by either the infinitive or *da* + present tense, as in *nemoj to prokockati / nemoj to da prokockaš*, both of which mean "Don't gamble it away." [78e] As in other instances of infinitive meaning, C nearly always uses the infinitive form, S usually uses *da* + present tense, and B uses both.

* Negated *moći* vs. *morati* *

In the affirmative, *moći* means "can, be able to," and *morati* means "must, be obliged to." But with negation, the meanings shift. The English idea "must not" is expressed by negated *moći*, whereas negated *morati* means only "not be obliged to." For example: *ne možeš tako!* "You mustn't [do it] that way!" vs. *ne moraš tako* "You don't have to [do it] that way." Negated *moći* also continues to mean "not be able to," as in *ne mogu tako* "I can't [do it] that way." [142]

VOCABULARY

akcioni film	action movie	odneti, odnesem	to take away (P)
crtani film	animated film	odnijeti, odnesem	to take away (P)
dokumentarac, dokumentarca	documentary [film]	ovamo	[toward] here
duhovit, duhovito, duhovita	witty	požuriti, požurim	to hurry up (P)
hajde	let's [+ verb]; let's go	pusti me na miru!	leave me be!
k, ka + Dat	to, toward	pustiti, pustim	to release, to let go (P)
kaput, kaputa	coat	razumeti, razumem	to understand (I/P)
limunada [B,S]	romantic comedy	razumjeti, razumijem	to understand (I/P)
ljubić [B,C]	romantic comedy	reći [reknem]	to say (P)
ma nemoj!	you don't say!	sluga (m)	servant
ma, daj!	come on!	slušati	to hear, to listen to (I)
mir	peace	spavanje	sleep; sleeping
neka + 3rd person verb	let [someone] + verb	spavati, spavam	to sleep (I)
nemojmo	let's not	triler	thriller

MA NEMOJ!

Bosnian
1. Molim te, dođi ovamo i daj mi *jabuku*.
2. Izvoli *jabuku!*
1. Hvala! I sada požuri! Idi do *Redžije* i odnesi joj ovu knjigu.
2. Ma nemoj! Pusti me na miru! Nisam ti ja sluga!
1. Dobro, razumijem. Čuj, idem sam do nje sa knjigom!
2. Što se mene tiče, radi šta hoćeš.
1. Nemojmo tako. Kaži, možemo li te *Redžija* i ja voditi u kino?
2. Ne da mi se. Neka ona ide s tobom. Meni se spava. Pojedi tu *jabuku* i idite u kino.
1. Ma, daj! Kakvo spavanje! Hajde da gledamo neki *duhoviti film*. Uzmi kaput pa idemo!

Croatian
1. Molim te, dođi ovamo i daj mi *jabuku*.
2. Izvoli *jabuku!*
1. Hvala! I sada požuri! Idi k *Ines* i odnesi joj ovu knjigu.
2. Ma nemoj! Pusti me na miru! Nisam ti ja sluga!
1. Dobro, razumijem. Čuj, idem sam k njoj s knjigom!
2. Što se mene tiče, radi što hoćeš.
1. Nemojmo tako. Reci, možemo li te *Ines* i ja voditi u kino?
2. Ne da mi se. Neka ona ide s tobom. Meni se spava. Pojedi tu *jabuku* i idite u kino.
1. Ma, daj! Kakvo spavanje! Hajde da gledamo neki *duhoviti film*. Uzmi kaput pa idemo!

Serbian
1. Molim te, dođi ovamo i daj mi *jabuku*.
2. Izvoli *jabuku!*
1. Hvala! A sada požuri! Idi do *Ane* i odnesi joj ovu knjigu.
2. Ma nemoj! Pusti me na miru! Nisam ti ja sluga!
1. Dobro, razumem. Slušaj, idem sam do nje sa knjigom!
2. Što se mene tiče, radi šta hoćeš.
1. Nemojmo tako. Kaži, da li *Ana* i ja možemo da te vodimo u bioskop?
2. Ne ide mi se. Neka ona ide s tobom. Meni se spava. Pojedi tu *jabuku* i idite u bioskop.
1. Ma, daj! Kakvo spavanje! Hajde da gledamo neki *duhoviti film*. Uzmi kaput pa idemo!

ઝ☞ **Replace** *jabuka* **with** keks, jagoda, smokva. **Replace** *Ana, Ines, Redžija* **with** tata, Siniša, Hamdija, Luka, mama. **Replace** *duhoviti film* **with** akcioni film, crtani film, dokumentarac, limunada [B,S] ljubić [B,C], triler.

 **GRAMMAR**

* The imperative mood, continued *

To form the imperative stem, drop the final vowel of the 3rd plural present. If what remains is -*j*, leave it alone; otherwise add -*i*. **[78a]** This form is the singular imperative, used with persons one speaks to as *ti*. To form the plural imperative (used with persons one speaks to as *vi*), add the syllable -*te*. **[78b]** To form the "inclusive imperative," often translated as "let's... ," add the syllable -*mo*. This latter meaning is more frequently expressed by the word *hajde* followed by the infinitive (or *da* + present). **[78c]** The sequence *neka* + 3rd person verb is translated "let...", for example *neka uđe* "let him in / have him come in." **[78d]** The verb *reći* "say" is used rarely in the present tense but frequently in the imperative: *reci, recite, recimo*.

infinitive	3rd pl present	sg imperative	pl imperative	inclusive
dati	*daju*	*daj*	*dajte*	*dajmo*
kupovati	*kupuju*	*kupuj*	*kupujte*	*kupujmo*
doći	*dođu*	*dođi*	*dođite*	*dođimo*
odneti [E] *odnijeti* [J]	*odnesu*	*odnesi*	*odnesite*	*odnesimo*
uzeti	*uzmu*	*uzmi*	*uzmite*	*uzmimo*

* Verbs of transport, continued *

The basic transport verbs *nositi*, *voditi*, and *voziti* mean, "carry," "lead by foot," and "take by vehicle," respectively. Their perfective partners preserve these basic meanings, but are formed from different stems; furthermore, they only occur with prefixes. For example: *odneti* [E] *odnijeti* [J] (1st sg. *odnesem*) "carry [away]," *odvesti* (1st sg. *odvedem*) "lead [away]," and *odvesti* (1st sg. *odvezem*) "drive [away]." **[84a]**

* "Inclinational" se-verbs *

To express the idea that a person feels like performing (or not performing) a particular action, use the 3rd singular form of the verb plus *se*, and identify the person in the dative case; for instance *meni se spava* "I feel sleepy," or *nama se ne ide* "we don't feel like going." If the action is not specified but is understood from the context, the phrase *ne da se* (+ dative) is often used in Bosnian and Croatian, as in *ne da mi se* "I'm not in the mood." In Serbian, however, this phrase means "I don't feel like giving [it]." **[82b]**

* Prepositions meaning "to [a person]" *

Movement toward a person (or toward a person's place of residence) is expressed in Croatian by the preposition *k* (+ dative); if the following word begins with *k* or *g*, this preposition takes the form *ka*. For instance, *idi k Ani* "go to Ana;" *idimo ka Goranu* "let's go to Goran's [house]." Bosnian and Serbian use prepositions with the genitive for this meaning: *do* for the idea of "to a person" and *kod* for the idea of "to a person's house." Thus *idi do Ane*, but *idimo kod Gorana*. **[84b]**

* Aspect, continued *

Most verbs have separate forms for perfective and imperfective. A few use the same form in both perfective and imperfective meanings, however. Examples are *čuti* "hear," *videti* [E] *vidjeti* [J] "see," *ručati* "eat lunch," *razumeti* [E] *razumjeti* [J] "understand." **[83a]**

Amusing slang usage. There is no affirmative expression corresponding to the negative form *nemoj*. But B, C, and S colloquial usage has at times included the option of responding to *Ma nemoj!* with the ungrammatical yet popular *Ma moj!* or *Ma da moj!* This is surprisingly similar to the English colloquial habit of responding to "No way!" with "Way!"

VOCABULARY

biblioteka [B,S]	library	muzika [B,C,S]	music
ceo, celo, cela	whole	početak, početka	beginning
ceo dan	all day	poseban, posebno, posebna	special
cijel (or cio), cijelo, cijela	whole	rano	early
cijeli dan	all day	sat; satovi [C]	class
čas; časovi [B,S]	class	sredina	middle
glazba [C]	music	stan	apartment
jezička laboratorija [B,S]	language lab	studentski dom,	student dormitory
jezični laboratorij [C]	language lab	studentskog doma	
knjižnica [C]	library	svejedno	all the same
kompjuter [B,S]	computer	svejedno mi je	I don't care
kompjutor [C]	computer	ujutro [B,C]	in the morning
kraj	end	ujutru [B,S]	in the morning

ČIME PIŠEŠ?

Bosnian
1. Čime pišeš?
2. Obično pišem olovkom.
1. A gdje učiš?
2. Kad nemam časove ponekad učim u sobi, ali često idem u jezičku laboratoriju.
1. Svaki dan ima svoj početak, sredinu i kraj. Kada najbolje učiš?
2. Posebno volim učiti rano ujutro. Ne mogu učiti noću. A ti, kad najbolje učiš?
1. Svejedno mi je, ujutro, popodne ili uveče. A kada slušaš muziku?
2. Muziku slušam cijeli dan.

Croatian
1. Čime pišeš?
2. Obično pišem olovkom.
1. A gdje učiš?
2. Kad nemam satove ponekad učim u sobi, ali često idem u jezični laboratorij.
1. Svaki dan ima svoj početak, sredinu i kraj. Kada najbolje učiš?
2. Posebno volim učiti rano ujutro. Ne mogu učiti noću. A ti, kad najbolje učiš?
1. Svejedno mi je, ujutro, popodne ili navečer. A kada slušaš glazbu?
2. Glazbu slušam cijeli dan.

Serbian
1. Чиме пишеш?
2. Обично пишем оловком.
1. А где учиш?
2. Кад немам часове понекад учим у соби, али често идем у језичку лабораторију.
1. Сваки дан има свој почетак, средину и крај. Када најбоље учиш?
2. Посебно волим да учим рано ујутру. Не могу да учим ноћу. А ти, кад најбоље учиш?
1. Свеједно ми је, ујутру, поподне или увече. А када слушаш музику?
2. Музику слушам цео дан.

☞ **Replace** olovka with fino pero, hemijska [B,S] kemijska [C] olovka, kompjuter [B,S] kompjutor [C], obična olovka; **replace** soba with studentski dom, stan; **replace** jezička laboratorija [B,S] jezični laboratorij [C] with kafana [B,S] kavana [C], knjižnica [C] biblioteka [B,S].

☞ **Redo** the exercise so that it reflects your own study habits.

☞ **Retell** the exercise in the past tense.

> The word for "pencil," olovka, comes from the word for "lead," olovo. After olovka came to mean "general writing implement," there emerged the phrase hemijska [B,S] kemijska [C] olovka meaning "ball-point pen," and this led to the formation of the phrase obična olovka, with the specific meaning "pencil."

GRAMMAR

* Instrumental of means *

The instrumental is used alone without a preposition in certain meanings expressed by English "with." It is this usage, by which one identifies the tool or the means used to accomplish an action, which gives the instrumental case its name. For instance, *pišem plavom olovkom* "I write with a blue pencil." **[81a]** Be careful to avoid the tendency to use the preposition *s / sa* in this meaning.

* Variation in suffixes and gender of nouns *

The same adjective root often uses different suffixes in different areas, as in the example *jezički* [B,S] vs. *jezični* [C]. When nouns are borrowed from another language, they sometimes are placed in different gender classes. For instance, the nouns meaning "laboratory" and "planet" are feminine in B and S, but masculine in C: *laboratorija* [B, S] *planeta* [B, S] vs. *laboratorij* [C] *planet* [C]. **[172a]**

The words for "where." There are three question words which mean "where". These are *gde* [E] *gdje* [J], *kamo*, and *kuda*. It used to be the case that their meanings were clearly distinguished throughout the region: *gde* [E] *gdje* [J] referred to location, *kamo* referred to the goal of one's movement ("where to"), and *kuda* referred to the path taken ("which way"). Although these meanings are still seen in the adverbs *ovamo* "over here, to here," and *ovuda* "this way, by this path," the distinction is gradually being lost in the words meaning "where." Officially, C still distinguishes *kamo* "where to" from *kuda* "which path," but Croats freely use *kuda* in the meaning "where to" as well. In B and S, both *kuda* and *gde* [E] *gdje* [J] are used in the meaning "where to," and the idea "which path" is expressed in B,C, and S by the phrase *kojim putem*. The whole process is similar to English, which is losing the distinction between "whither" and "where."

Trams on Ban Jelačić Square in Zagreb.

🏃 VJEŽBE [J] VEŽBE [E]

B1

Questions to ask each other:

Bosnian	Croatian	Serbian
1. Sa čim piješ kȁfu?	1. S čim piješ kȁvu?	1. Sa čim piješ kȁfu?
2. Sa čim piješ čaj?	2. S čim piješ čaj?	2. Sa čim piješ čaj?
3. Sa čim spremaš jȁja?	3. S čim spremaš jȁja?	3. Sa čim spremaš jȁja?
4. Sa čim spremaš omlet?	4. S čim spremaš omlet?	4. Sa čim spremaš omlet?

☞ **In your answers,** use the vocabulary from the dialogue in A1.

B2

Bosnian	Croatian	Serbian
1. Zar nemaš s kim ići *u grad*?	1. Zar nemaš s kim ići *u grad*?	1. Зар немаш с ким да идеш *у град*?
2. Nemam.	2. Nemam.	2. Немам.
1. Onda hajde sȁ mnom!	1. Onda hajde sȁ mnom!	1. Онда хајде сȁ мном!

☞ **Replace** *u grad* **with** na sveučilište [C] univerzitet [B,S], u bioskop [S] kino [B,C], u kazalište [C] pozorište [B, S].

B3

Bosnian	Croatian	Serbian
1. Čime voliš putòvati?	1. Čime voliš putòvati?	1. Čime voliš da putuješ?
2. Volim da putujem *vozom*.	2. Volim putòvati *vlȁkom*.	2. Volim da putujem *vozom*.
1. Znaš li *ga* sama voziti?	1. Znaš li *ga* sama voziti?	1. Da li znaš sama da *ga* voziš?
2. Ne, ne. Ja se vozim a neko drugi mora da bude vozač.	2. Ne, ne. Ja se vozim a netko drugi mora biti vozač.	2. Ne, ne. Ja se vozim a neko drugi mora da bude vozač.

☞ **Replace** *vlȁk* [C] *voz* [B,S] **with** kola or ȁuto, avìon [B,C,S] zrakoplov [C].

B4

Bosnian	Croatian	Serbian
1. Predȁ *mnom* je *budućnost*!	1. Predȁ *mnom* je *budućnost*!	1. Предȁ *мном* је *будућност*!
2. A šta misliš da *radiš* sa *svojom budućnošću*?	2. A što misliš *raditi* sa *svojom budućnošću*?	2. А шта мислиш да *радиш* са *својом будућношћу*?
1. Danima već mislim o *putu*.	1. Danima već mislim o *putu*.	1. Данима већ мислим о *путу*.
2. Pa onda *putuj*! Nikad se nȅ zna šta nosi sutra!	2. Pa onda *putuj*! Nikad se nȅ zna što nosi sutra!	2. Па онда *путуј*! Никад се нȅ знȁ шта носи сутра!

☞ **Rewrite the conversation six different ways, so that the speaker is not** *ja* **but rather** ti, vi, mi, on, ona, **or** oni, **changing the verbs accordingly in each rewrite. Replace** *svoja budućnost* **with** ova crna noć, ovaj lepi [E] lijepi [J] život, ova velika ljubav; **replace** *put* **and** *putovati* **with** ljubav **and** voleti [E] voljeti [J]; sveučilište [C] univerzitet [B,S], **and** učiti.

B5

Bosnian	Croatian	Serbian
1. Dȍbro jȕtro! Mȍramo se žúriti *u škȍlu* jer dȁnas ȉmamo *velȉk ȉspit*.	1. Dȍbro jȕtro! Mȍramo se žúriti *u škȍlu* jer dȁnas ȉmamo *velȉk ȉspit*.	1. Dȍbro jȕtro! Mȍramo da se žúrimo *u škȍlu* jer dȁnas ȉmamo *velȉk ȉspit*.
2. Dȍbro jȕtro. Nȅ možete tȁko br̥zo. Pr̥vo mȍrate dȍručkovati radi zdrȁvlja. Nȅ mȍrate ništa piti, ali mȍrate jesti. A tek ondȁ možete ići *u škȍlu*.	2. Dȍbro jȕtro. Nȅ možete tȁko br̥zo. Pr̥vo mȍrate dȍručkovati radi zdrȁvlja. Nȅ mȍrate ništa piti, ali mȍrate jesti. A tek ondȁ možete ići *u škȍlu*.	2. Dȍbro jȕtro. Nȅ možete tȁko br̥zo. Pr̥vo mȍrate dȍručkovati radi zdrȁvlja. Nȅ mȍrate ništa piti, ali mȍrate da jedȅte. A tek ondȁ možete da idȅte *u škȍlu*.
1. *Nȅ dȍlazi u ȍbzir.* Nȅ možemo dȍručkovati zbog *ȉspita*. Mȍramo odmȁh ȉći. Dovȋđenja.	1. *Nȅ dȍlazi u ȍbzir.* Nȅ možemo dȍručkovati zbog *ȉspita*. Mȍramo odmȁh ȉći. Dovȋđenja.	1. *Nȅ dȍlazi u ȍbzir.* Nȅ možemo da dȍručkujemo zbog *ȉspita*. Mȍramo odmȁh da idȅmo. Dovȋđenja.
2. Dȍbro, dȍbro. Nȅ mȍrate dȍručkovati ako ne žȅlite. Dovȋđenja.	2. Dȍbro, dȍbro. Nȅ mȍrate dȍručkovati ako ne žȅlite. Dovȋđenja.	2. Dȍbro, dȍbro. Nȅ mȍrate dȍručkovati ako ne žȅlite. Dovȋđenja.

☞ **Replace** *u škȍlu* **with** na pȍsao **and** *velȉk ȉspit* **with** tȅžak prȍblem. **You may replace** *Nȅ dȍlazi u ȍbzir* **with** Pustite nas na mȉru! Ma nȅmoj! Ma, daj! Nȉsam vam ja slȕga! **but be aware that these expressions are not courteous. Read the explanation on p. 101 about the negation of** mȍći **and** mȍrati.

B6

1. Mȍlim te, ȕzmi *obȉčnu ȍlovku*!	1. Мȍлим те, ȳзми *обȉчнȳ ȍловку*!
2. Ȅvo, ȉmam *je*.	2. Ȅво, ȉмам *je*.
1. Sȁda *pȉši* njȏme!	1. Сȁда *пȉши* њȏме!
2. *Pȉšem.*	2. *Пȉшем.*

☞ **Replace** *obȉčnȁ ȍlovka* **with** br̥zi vlȁk [C] vȍz [B,S], mȁli tramvȁj, **and** *pȉsati* **with** ići, vȍziti, putȍvati.

B7

Bosnian	Croatian	Serbian
1. Kȁda ȉmaš jȅzičkȅ vjȅžbe na fakultȅtu?	1. Kȁda ȉmaš jȅzičnȅ vjȅžbe na fakultȅtu?	1. Kȁda ȉmaš jȅzičkȅ vȅžbe na fakultȅtu?
2. Ȍbično ih ȉmam ponȅdjeljkom, srijȅdom i pȅtkom ujutro.	2. Ȍbično ih ȉmam ponȅdjeljkom, srijȅdom i pȅtkom ujutro.	2. Ȍbično ih ȉmam ponȅdeljkom, srȅdom i pȅtkom ujutro.
1. A kȁda slušaš predávanja?	1. A kȁda slušaš predávanja?	1. A kȁda slušaš predávanja?
2. Njȋh ȉmam ȍbično po pȍdne, ȕtorkom i četvr̥tkom.	2. Njȋh ȉmam ȍbično po pȍdne, ȕtorkom i četvr̥tkom.	2. Njȋh ȉmam ȍbično po pȍdne, ȕtorkom i četvr̥tkom.
1. A kȍje drugȅ čȁsove ȉmaš?	1. A kȍje drugȅ sȁtove ȉmaš?	1. A kȍje drugȅ čȁsove ȉmaš?
2. Slušȁm ih nekoliko još.	2. Slušȁm ih nekoliko još.	2. Slušȁm ih nekoliko još.
1. A kȁda ondȁ ȕčiš?	1. A kȁda ondȁ ȕčiš?	1. A kȁda ondȁ ȕčiš?
2. Kasno navečȅ, i sȕbotom i nȅdjeljom.	2. Kasno navečȅr, i sȕbotom i nȅdjeljom.	2. Kasno uvečȅ, i sȕbotom i nȅdeljom.

☞ **Adapt** this to describe your own week and the way in which you organize your days.

✍ DOMAĆA ZADAĆA [B,C] DOMAĆI ZADATAK [S]

C1

First practice the dialogue in A1 outside of class so that you can perform it in class as a skit. Then write a paragraph about what you eat for breakfast on Mondays, Saturdays and Sundays.

C2

Insert the appropriate preposition:

1. Dobar život je .... tobom.
        (in front of)

2. Oni sutra putuju .... Njujorka .... Bostona.
        (from)   (to)

3. Majka mi je .... San Franciska.
        (from)

4. Hajde .... mnom .... grad!
     (with)   (to)

5. Uzmi olovku .... stola.
        (from)

6. Daj mi knjigu .... torbe.
        (from)

7. Piši pismo .... papiru.
        (on)

8. [B] Stavi onaj komad papira .... teku a ne .... teku!
   [C] Stavi onaj komad papira .... bilježnicu a ne .... bilježnicu!
   [S] Stavi onaj komad papira .... svesku a ne .... svesku!
                            (on)   (in)

9. Kaži mu .... svojoj ljubavi iz mladih dana!
        (about)

10. [B,C] Razumiješ sve .... rječnika!
    [S] Razumeš sve .... rečnika!
        (without)

11. Daj joj doručak .... osam sati!
        (before)

12. [B,S] Sunce je .... Sunčevog sistema.
    [C] Sunce je .... Sunčeva sustava.
        (in the middle of)

C3

Make ten short sentences in which you combine the nouns and adjectives in column A with an imperative formed from one of the verbs in column B. Make at least two negative sentences.

Example: **A.**   **B.**
                          šaren, zmija   pogledati
          becomes   Pogledaj šarenu zmiju!

A	**B**
1. sladak, jelo	pisati
2. debeo, pismo	dati
3. šaren, tramvaj	voziti se
4. dosadan, čovek [E] čovjek [J]	ići
5. dobar, život	spremiti
6. odličan, film	biti
7. tužan, muzika [B,S] glazba [C]	slušati
8. lep [E] lijep [J], grad	pogledati
9. duhovit, knjiga	prokockati
10. plav, vlak [C] voz [B,S]	uzeti

C4

1. Provide some examples from Lesson 6 showing how the locative case is used.
2. Describe the uses of the dative case. Give three examples of datives from Lessons 6 and 7, one with a preposition.
3. Find examples in the A exercises of this lesson of the use of the instrumental, both with and without a preposition.
4. List four prepositions which take the genitive case.
5. What ways of expressing time have been introduced in Lessons 6 and 7?
6. What changes sometimes happen to the consonants **k**, **g** and **h**? Give three examples each of this process, first for masculine nouns in the nominative plural and then for feminine nouns in the dative-locative singular. Why do you think this change happens?

C5

Translate into B, C, or S:

1. The judge listens to the lawyer.
2. Go to the bank!
3. Her dad understands her.
4. They read their book, and I read their book.
5. Let's not drink our tea with milk or with sugar or with lemon.
6. Look at me, listen to me, talk with me!
7. We saw neither bears nor dogs.
8. Many animals live in this world, but there are no animals here in this room now.

C6

Translate the first sentence of each set into English, and the two following sentences into B, C, or S, using the first as a model:

1. a. [B,C] Zar ne razumiješ francuski?
   [S] Зар не разумеш француски?
   b. Don't you understand English?
   c. Don't you have your own life?

2. a. [B,C] Godinama čitam Prousta i Krležu.
   [S] Годинама читам Пруста и Крлежу.
   b. For days I have been riding on the tram.
   c. For months he has been driving his own car.

3. a. [B] Utorkom obično učim u biblioteci.
   [C] Utorkom obično učim u knjižnici.
   [S] Уторком обично учим у библиотеци.
   b. Usually on Saturdays I eat meat.
   c. On Wednesdays I always have a lecture in the afternoon.

4. a. [B] Pišem na njenom kompjuteru, a ne na svom.
   [C] Pišem na njezinu kompjutoru, a ne na svojem.
   [S] Пишем на њеном компјутеру, а не на свом.
   b. She wrote letters to her sister all day.
   c. We are listening to our music, not yours.

5. a. Neka ide ako želi!
   b. Let them read their books at home. Let's go to the movies!
   c. Let her write her homework and then let her go to sleep.

   Try translating the short sentence: *Budi svoj*!

Miroslav Krleža (mentioned in #2) is Croatia's most prolific 20th century writer. A dramatist, novelist, poet, essay writer, satirist, and lexicographer, he is best known abroad for the two novels which have been translated into English, *Na rubu pameti* (*On the Edge of Reason*) and *Povratak Filipa Latinovicza* (*The Return of Philip Latinovicz*).

C7

Redo these sentences as negatives and translate them into English:

1. [B,C] Volim jesti jaja i pahuljice i kobasice za doručak.

   [S] Volim da jedem jaja i pahuljice i kobasice za doručak.

2. [B,C] Uvijek pijem čaj s limunom i šećerom.

   [S] Uvek pijem čaj sa limunom i šećerom.

3. Godinama se bojim zmija.

4. [B,C] Hòćeš li? Mòžemo!

   [S] Dà li hòćeš? Mòžemo!

5. [B,C] Pred njȋm je lijèpa budùćnost!

   [S] Pred njȋm je lèpa budùćnost!

6. [B] Pètkom ìmajū cijèlī dȃn predávanja i čàsove.

   [C] Pètkom ìmajū cijèlī dȃn predávanja i sàtove.

   [S] Pètkom ìmajū ceo dȃn predávanja i čàsove.

7. Dòbro ti je tȍ za zdrȁvlje.

8. Mòžeš sve što žèlīš u žìvòtu.

☺☹ Aforizmi Dušana Radovića

See the note below about the series of aphorisms, to be presented over the next several lessons. These aphorisms provide incentives for lively conversations. Think about each one as you read it, and bring a question to class to ask a fellow classmate. Use phrases such *as O čèmu se rȁdī? Čìnī mi se... Ne čìnī mi se* and the like.

VOCABULARY

афòризам, афòризма	aphorism	òтjецати поред [B,C]	to flow around (I)
дáље	further	прòтицати, прòтичēм [B,S]	to flow through (I)
нáроднӣ, нáродно, нáродна	national	прòтjецати, прòтjечēм [B,C]	to flow through (I)
òтицати, òтичēм [B,S]	to drain away (I)	рȅд	line [of people]
òтицати поред [B,S]	to flow around (I)	све вишȅ	more and more
òтjецати, òтjечēм [B,C]	to drain away (I)		

Пред Нáроднōм библиотèкōм je рȅд, али за трамвȃj. Рȅд je и пред Нáроднӣм музèjēм, али за аутòбус.

Сȁва све вишȅ прòтичē к р о з Бèоград, а Дунав и дáље òтичē п о р е д Бèограда.

To help students practice Cyrillic and to acquaint them with Serbian life and humor, Lessons 7-14 include aphorisms by Belgrade humorist and talk show host Dušan Radović, taken from his 1970s morning radio show called *Beògrade, dòbro jutro (Good morning, Belgrade)*. His brand of quirky (and often dark) humor became famous throughout the former Yugoslavia. An understanding of several of these aphorisms will be aided by knowledge of culture, history or geography, as can be illustrated by the second of the two aphorisms above. Within the borders of the former Yugoslavia, the Sava was a purely domestic river, traversing Slovenia and Croatia on its way to Belgrade, where it flows into the Danube. By contrast, the Danube is an international river, linking Vienna, Budapest and Belgrade as it flows toward the Black Sea. With this in mind, one can see that Radović is suggesting that the Danube circumvents Belgrade because it is far too worldly a waterway to flow through the middle of the city the way the Sava does.

Note the spacing of the words *kroz* and *pored* in the Radović aphorisms. Such typographical s p a c i n g is often used for emphasis in BCS in place of *italics*.

Vintage postcard of Belgrade: view of the *ušće* from Kalemegdan Park

A view toward the *ušće* from Kalemegdan Park, 2005

> The confluence *(ušće)* of the Danube and Sava rivers is located in the center of Belgrade. The ancient fortress of Kalemegdan towers on the hillside above this spot. It is now the city's most well-known park. The statue "Victory," by Ivan Meštrović, stands high above the *ušće*.

📖 Priča: Albahari

Read Part IV of the story "Osam malih priča o mojoj ženi" by David Albahari (p. 342).

Osma lekcija • Lesson Eight

ćèrka, *DLsg* ćèrki; *Gpl* ćèrki [S]	daughter	pod + *Instr*	under
kćèrka, *DLsg* kćèrki; *Gpl* kćèrki [B,C]	daughter	sin	son
kći, *Asg* kćer, *Gsg* kćeri [B,C,S] *(f)*	daughter	siv*	gray
lav	lion	strašan, strašna	terrible
miš	mouse	strpljenje	patience
mladìć, mladìća	boy	strpljiv	patient
mùdar, mùdra*	wise	veseo, vesela	cheerful
nad + *Instr*	above	vrèdan, vrèdna	diligent, valuable
osmi	eighth	vrijèdan, vrijèdna	diligent, valuable
pametan, pametna	intelligent		

STRPLJENJE

Bosnian and Croatian

Djèvojke strpljivo sjède za stolom.
Pod *djevojkama* su *stolice*.
Dòrùčak je u *djèvojkama*.
Profesorica gledà *djèvojke*.
Djèvojke ùčè od *profesorice*.
A *profesorica* ùči od *djèvojaka*.
Dobar dàn, *profesorice!*

Serbian

Дèвојке стрпљиво сèдe за столом.
Под *дèвојкама* су *столице*.
Дòручак је у *дèвојкама*.
Профèсорка гледà *дèвојке*.
Дèвојке ùчè од *профèсорке*.
А *профèсорка* ùчи од *дèвојака*.
Добар дàн, *профèсорко!*

☞ **Replace the pair** *dèvojke* [E] *djèvojke* [J] **and** *profesorica* [B,C] *profèsorka* [S] **with the following pairs: a)** pametnè ćèrke [S] kćèrke [B,C] kćeri [B,C,S] **and** mùdra majka; **b)** strašni lavovi **and** sivi miš; **c)** vesèli sinovi **and** ozbiljni òtac; **d)** vrèdni [E] vrijèdni [J] mladìći **and** dosadni profesor.

☞ **Replace** *pod* with nad **and replace** *stolice* with làmpe.

☞ **Once you've used each of these examples, reverse the singulars and plurals of each pair. For example, instead of** *strašni lavovi* **and** *sivi miš*, **use:** strašni lav **and** sivi miševi.

> * Starting with Lesson 8, only the masculine form is given for adjectives whose feminine and neuter forms are made simply by adding -*a* and -*o* (or -*e*) respectively. If a change in the stem occurs, either in spelling or in accent, then both the masculine and feminine forms are given. Thus only the masculine *siv* is given, since the feminine *siva* and neuter *sivo* are entirely predictable. But for the adjective *mùdar*, the feminine form is *mùdra* is also given, since it is not completely predictable. Using the feminine form, however, one is able to predict with certainty that the neuter form is *mùdro*.

Forbidden
access
to non-employees

 **GRAMMAR**

* Plural case forms *

Although the dative, locative and instrumental cases are considered to have distinct meanings in the plural, just as they do in the singular, the form is the same for all three in any one noun. Feminine nouns in -*a* take the ending -*ama* and all other nouns take the ending -*ima*. Masculine nouns whose stems end in -*k*, -*g*, -*h* make the same consonant shift in DLIpl as in Npl. The ending for all adjectives in these three cases is -*im*. [86] At this point, the student should review all singular and plural case forms for nouns, adjectives, and pronouns. Sample declensions can be found on pp. 323-329. [89a-c]

	masculine	neuter	feminine –a	feminine -cons.
Npl	*dobri đaci / gradovi*	*mala sela*	*dobre žene*	*fine stvari*
Apl	*dobre đake / gradove*	*mala sela*	*dobre žene*	*fine stvari*
DLIpl	*dobrim đacima / gradovima*	*malim selima*	*dobrim ženama*	*finim stvarima*

* Vocative case, continued *

The vocative case is the form of the noun used to address a person (and, much more rarely, an object). Not all nouns have a separate vocative case, and the ones which do often have variant endings. Masculine nouns in -*k*, -*g*, -*h* usually shift the consonant to -*č*, -*ž*, -*š* before the ending -*e*, and masculine nouns ending in a "soft" consonant often take the ending -*u*. A number of two-syllable feminine nouns take the ending -*o*. Feminine nouns ending in -*ica*, however, usually (but not always) take the ending -*e*. Feminine nouns in a consonant rarely form the vocative, since they refer almost exclusively to objects or concepts. When they are used in poetic contexts, however, especially in metaphorical reference to a person, they take the ending -*i*. For instance: *moja ljubavi* "[oh] my love!." The vocative of neuter nouns, and all plural nouns, is identical to the nominative. [88]

	masculine				feminine –a		fem -cons.
Nominative sg	*momak*	*Bog*	*duh*	*prijatelj*	*djevojka*	*učiteljica*	*ljubav*
Vocative	*momče*	*Bože*	*duše*	*prijatelju*	*djevojko*	*učiteljice*	*ljubavi*

Sarajevo lies in a valley surrounded by mountains, and was thus well suited to the Winter Olympic Games held there in 1984. Residential neighborhoods, many of them rebuilt since the war, climb up the surrounding hillsides.

VOCABULARY

braća *(sg form)*	brothers	gospoda *(sg form)*	gentlemen
dèca *(sg form)*	children	mìran, mìrna	calm
dète, deteta	child	nemìran, nemìrna	restless
dijète, djèteta	child	nestrpljènje	impatience
djèca *(sg form)*	children		

NESTRPLJENJE

<u>Bosnian and Croatian</u>

Mìrna djèca strpljivo sjède za stòlom.
Pod mìrnom djecòm su stolice.
Dòručak je u mìrnoj djèci.
Nemìrno dijète gleda mìrnu djècu.
Nemìrno dijète uči od mìrne djèce.
A mìrna djèca uče od nemìrnog djèteta.
Dobar dan, djèco!

<u>Serbian</u>

Mìrna dèca strpljivo sède za stòlom.
Pod mìrnom decòm su stolice.
Dòručak je u mìrnoj dèci.
Nemìrno dète gleda mìrnu dècu.
Nemìrno dète uči od mìrne dèce.
A mìrna dèca uče od nemìrnog dèteta.
Dobar dan, dèco!

☞ **First replace** nemìrno dète [E] dijète [J] **and** mìrna dèca [E] djèca [J] **with a)** dobri brat **and** zla braća; **b)** mladi gospodin **and** stara gospoda.

☞ **Then replace** mìrna djèca **with** mìrno dijète, **and** nemìrno dijète **with** nemìrna djèca.

⚙ GRAMMAR

* Neuter nouns with added syllable -et- *

Some neuter nouns add the syllable -et before G, DL and I singular case endings. Among them are names of certain males, objects and the young of the species. **[89b, 89d]**

NAsg	dète [E]	dijète [J]	jáje	dùgme	tèle	Brane
Gsg	dèteta	djèteta	jàjeta	dùgmeta	tèleta	Braneta
DLsg	dètetu	djètetu	jàjetu	dùgmetu	tèletu	Branetu
Isg	dètetom	djètetom	jàjetom	dùgmetom	tèletom	Branetom
	"child"		"egg"	"button"	"calf"	[name]

* Irregular plurals of dète / dijète, brat, gospòdin *

The plurals of these nouns are SINGULAR in form. They follow the declension of feminine nouns in -a, and adjectives modifying them take feminine singular endings. But these nouns have PLURAL meaning, and always take plural verbs. For instance: naša dèca igraju zajedno "our children are playing together." **[90]**

Nom	dèca [E]	djèca [J]	braća	gospòda
Acc	dècu	djècu	braću	gospòdu
Gen	dèce	djèce	braće	gospòde
Dat-Loc	dèci	djèci	braći	gospòdi
Instr	dècom	djècom	braćom	gospòdom
Voc	dèco	djèco	braćo	gospòdo
	children		brothers	gentlemen

VOCABULARY

bàlkanski	Balkan	osim + *Gen*	except
čuti se, čujem se	to talk to each other (I/P)	osim toga	besides
dalmàtinski	Dalmatian	pòvremeno	now and then
inostranstvo [B,S]	foreign lands	preko + *Gen*	across, over, via
inozemstvo [C]	foreign lands	razmišljati, razmišljam	to consider (I)
internet	internet	rođak	relative
ìstarski	Istrian	slavònski	Slavonian
jàviti se, jàvim se + *Dat*	to get in touch with (P)	sreća	happiness, fortune
javljati se, javljam se + *Dat*	to get in touch with (I)	telèfon, telefòna	telephone
kosovski	Kosovo *(adj.)*	vojvòđanski	Vojvodina *(adj.)*

JAVI SE!

Bosnian

1. Kàkva sreća! Pìsmo od *roditèlja!*
2. Čuješ li se često sa svojim *roditeljima?*
1. Javljam im se òbičnim pìsmom, a pòvremeno i telefònom.
2. Òbičnim pìsmom? Zašto? Zar nìsi razmišljao da im kupiš kompjuter?
1. Ne, zatò što im volim pìsati pìsma, a osim toga oni ne žèle ìmati kompjuter.
2. A kàko se javljaš *studentima u inostranstvu?*
1. Uvijek im se javljam preko *interneta.*

Croatian

1. Kàkva sreća! Pìsmo od *roditèlja!*
2. Čuješ li se često sa svojim *roditeljima?*
1. Javljam im se òbičnim pìsmom, a pòvremeno i telefònom.
2. Òbičnim pìsmom? Zašto? Zar nìsi razmišljao da im kupiš kompjutor?
1. Ne, zatò što im volim pìsati pìsma, a osim toga oni ne žèle ìmati kompjutor.
2. A kàko se javljaš *studentima u inozemstvu?*
1. Uvijek im se javljam preko *interneta.*

Serbian

1. Каква срећа! Писмо од *родитеља!*
2. Да ли се чујеш често са својим *родитељима?*
1. Јављам им се обичним писмом, а повремено и телефоном.
2. Обичним писмом? Зашто? Зар ниси размишљао да им купиш компјутер?
1. Не, зато што волим да им пишем писма, а осим тога они не желе да имају компјутер.
2. А како се јављаш *студентима у иностранству?*
1. Увек им се јављам преко *интернета.*

☛ **Replace**: *ròditelji* with braća, dèca [E] djèca [J], ćèrke [S] kćeri [B,C,S] kćèrke [B,C], rođaci, sèstre, sinovi.

☛ **Replace** *stùdenti u inostranstvu* [B,S] *u inozemstvu* [C] **with**: bàlkanski, bòsanski, crnògorski, dalmàtinski, hrvàtski, ìstarski, kosovski, slavònski, srpski, **or** vojvòđanski stùdenti.

☛ **Use** this exercise as a model to describe how you communicate with your family and friends.

(No parking) ...except on the sidewalk

 **GRAMMAR**

* *Se*-verbs, continued *

The particle *se* has a number of different meanings. One is to add to a verb the general meaning of English "each other." This appears in various ways in the English translation. Thus, *čuti se* means "be in touch" (usually by phone), and *videti se* [E] *vidjeti se* [J] means "meet, get together." **[87a]** For some basic verbs, the particle *se* is simply part of their meaning. If such verbs take an object, this object will be in a case other than the accusative. For example, the verb *javljati se* (perfective *javiti se*) "get in touch with" takes a dative object. The means of communication need not be specified; if it is, the instrumental case is used. For instance: *javljam joj se telefonom* "I call her on the phone / communicate with her by phone." **[87b]**

A4 ⊙67,68

VOCABULARY

ispod + *Gen*	beneath, under	sag [C]	rug
ispred + *Gen*	in front of	sat	clock
iza + *Gen*	behind	sobni	room *(adj.)*
iznad + *Gen*	up above	strana	side
katedra	lectern, podium	strop [C]	ceiling
lampa; *Gpl* lampi	lamp	stropni [C]	ceiling *(adj.)*
nasuprot + *Dat*	opposite	svetlo	light
plafon [B,S]	ceiling	svjetlo	light
plafonski [B,S]	ceiling	tepih [B,S]	rug
profesorski	professorial		

SOBA

Bosnian
1. Gdje se nalazi *naša tabla?*
2. *Naša tabla* je u sobi na zidu ispred studenata i blizu profesora, kod profesorske katedre.
1. Na sredini zida je, a taj zid je između dva druga zida iza vrata.
2. Do prozora je s jedne strane, a pored vrata s druge strane, iznad poda, ispod plafona i ispod lampi, i nasuprot vama i pred nama.
1. Pred kim?
2. Pred nama.

Croatian
1. Gdje se nalazi *naša ploča?*
2. *Naša ploča* je u sobi na zidu ispred studenata i blizu profesora, kod profesorske katedre.
1. Na sredini zida je, a taj zid je između dva druga zida iza vrata.
2. Do prozora je s jedne strane, a pored vrata s druge strane, iznad poda, ispod stropa i ispod lampi, i nasuprot vama i pred nama.
1. Pred kim?
2. Pred nama.

Serbian
1. Gde se nalazi *naša tabla?*
2. *Naša tabla* je u sobi na zidu ispred studenata i blizu profesora, kod profesorske katedre.
1. Na sredini zida je, a taj zid je između dva druga zida iza vrata.
2. Do prozora je s jedne strane, a pored vrata s druge strane, iznad poda, ispod plafona i ispod lampi, i nasuprot vama i pred nama.
1. Pred kim?
2. Pred nama.

☞ **The responses** given above represent only a few of several possible ways to answer the questions posed. Try shifting them around, so as to create a different response for each question.

☞ **Replace** *naša ploča* [C] *tabla* [B,S] **with**: naš profesor, ovaj sto [B,S] stol [C], plafonska svjetla [B] plafonska svetla [S] stropna svjetla [C], sat, sobna vrata, tvoja stolica, veliki sag [C] tepih [B,S], vredni [E] vrijedni [J] studenti.

☞ **Using the map** at the beginning of the textbook as a guide, describe the position of cities, rivers and other topographical features with reference to one another, using these prepositions.

* Review of prepositions *

Each preposition takes a particular case. Since most prepositions take the genitive case, it makes good sense to memorize which prepositions take other cases, and then to use the genitive as the default case. **[93]** Many prepositions refer to physical location, but a number are used in other meanings as well. For instance, the phrase *s jedne strane* can mean either "on one side [of something]" (physical location) or "on the one hand" (abstract concept). **[157c]** Some prepositions which take the instrumental, such as *pred* "before," *pod* "under," *nad* "above," *među* "between, among," and *za* "behind," also have compound forms which take the genitive. These are *ispred, ispod, iznad, između* and *iza*. **[157b]**

A view across Zagreb from Novi Zagreb in the south to Mt. Medvednica in the north. The Sava River runs from east to west along the southern perimeter of the city (just along the row of poplars seen in the middle of the photograph). The oldest part of the city lies along finger ridges extending from the mountain slopes toward the Sava River plain.

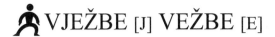# VJEŽBE [J] VEŽBE [E]

B1

Bosnian	Croatian	Serbian
Bosanski jezik je izuzetno zanimljiv.	*Hrvatski jezik* je izuzetno zanimljiv.	*Српски језик* је изузетно занимљив.
Svakim danom sve više volim *bosanski jezik.*	Svakim danom sve više volim *hrvatski jezik.*	Сваким даном све више волим *српски језик.*
Razmišljam o *bosanskom jeziku.*	Razmišljam o *hrvatskom jeziku.*	Размишљам о *српском језику.*
Bez *bosanskog jezika* nema sreće.	Bez *hrvatskog jezika* nema sreće.	Без *српског језика* нема среће.
Pjevam pjesme *bosanskom jeziku.*	Pjevam pjesme *hrvatskom jeziku.*	Певам песме *српском језику.*
Sa *bosanskim jezikom* divno je živjeti.	S *hrvatskim jezikom* divno je živjeti.	Са *српским језиком* дивно је живети.
O, *bosanski jeziče!*	O, *hrvatski jeziče!*	О, *српски језиче!*

☞ **Replace** *bosanski jezik, hrvatski jezik* or *srpski jezik* with: duga noć, hladno pivo, moj/svoj udžbenik za bosanski **or** udžbenik za hrvatski **or** udžbenik za srpski, naš dragi kolega, slatko jelo, strašni lav, velika ljubav.

B2

Bosnian and Croatian	Serbian
Balkanski jezici su izuzetno zanimljivi.	*Balkanski jezici* su izuzetno zanimljivi.
Svakim danom sve više volim *balkanske jezike.*	Svakim danom sve više volim *balkanske jezike.*
Razmišljam o *balkanskim jezicima.*	Razmišljam o *balkanskim jezicima.*
Bez *balkanskih jezika* nema sreće.	Bez *balkanskih jezika* nema sreće.
Pjevam pjesme *balkanskim jezicima.*	Pevam pesme *balkanskim jezicima.*
S *balkanskim jezicima* divno je živjeti.	S *balkanskim jezicima* divno je živeti.
O, *balkanski jezici!*	O, *balkanski jezici!*

☞ **Replace** *balkanski jezici* with domaće zadaće [B,C] domaći zadaci [S], mali (**or** veliki) gradovi, mali psi, nove cipele, teška pitanja, šarene mačke. **Continue** this exercise by inserting adjectives and nouns of your own choice.

B3

Ask each other these questions. In your answers, use the prepositions, nouns and pronouns which were suggested in the dialogue in A4.

1. [B] S kim se vozite svakog jutra? Zašto?
   [C] S kim se vozite svakoga jutra? Zašto?
   [S] Sa kim se vozite svakog jutra? Zašto?

2. Koliko je duga vaša vožnja svaki dan?

3. [B,C] Kome se sviđa voziti se biciklom, a kome voziti se kolima? Zašto?
   [S] Kome se sviđa da se vozi biciklom, a kome da se vozi kolima? Zašto?

4. Čime se javljate svojim prijateljima? Telefonom, pismom ili preko interneta? Zašto?

5. Zar ne pišete pisma svojim prijateljima? Zašto?

6. [B,C] Pored čega sjedite sada? Zašto?
   [S] Pored čega sedite sada? Zašto?

7. [B,S] Šta slušate svakog dana? Zašto?
   [C] Što slušate svakoga dana? Zašto?

B4

Ask each other to locate objects in the classroom, using questions such as the following as prompts.

Self-study learners: Note the position of various objects in your room or house, and then ask yourself questions about their location. Rearrange things to make the distribution more interesting and to require you to use as many prepositions as possible.

1. [B,C] Ispod čega je stolica?
   [S] Испод чега је столица?

2. [B,C] Pored koga je prozor?
   [S] Поред кога је прозор?

3. [B] Na čemu je tepih?
   [C] Na čemu je sag?
   [S] На чему је тепих?

4. [B,C] Pored čega je knjiga?
   [S] Поред чега је књига?

5. [B,C] S kim ona sjedi?
   [S] Са ким она седи?

6. [B] Iznad čega su plafonska svjetla?
   [C] Iznad čega su stropna svjetla?
   [S] Изнад чега су плафонска светла?

7. [B] Ispred čega je tabla?
   [C] Ispred čega je ploča?
   [S] Испред чега је табла?

8. [B,C] Nasuprot čemu su vrata?
   [S] Насупрот чему су врата?

B5

Bosnian and Croatian	Serbian
1. Sat je na zidu.	1. Сат је на зиду.
2. Rječnik se nalazi na stolu.	2. Речник се налази на столу.
3. Sam sam.	3. Сам сам.
4. Imam pismo od moje tetke!	4. Имам писмо од моје тетке!
5. Brat mi je visok čovjek.	5. Брат ми је висок човек.

☞ **Make** past-tense versions. Provide both a masculine and a feminine version for #3 and #4.

☞ **Rewrite** these sentences as negatives.

☞ **Now redo** all sentences you have just created, this time putting all the nouns in the plural.

B6

Practice with the various ways to express possession (which include the possessive adjective, the genitive case and the dative case).
State the idea of possession twice, first using the name alone (a), and then using the entire phrase (b).

> **Example**: Čija je ova olovka? (moja prijateljica Mirjana)
> a. Ovo je Mirjanina olovka.
> b. Ovo je olovka moje prijateljice Mirjane.

1. Čiji je taj crveni auto? (tvoja sestra Dušanka)
2. Čije je to pitanje? (naš profesor Haris)
3. Čija je ova noć? (njena [B,S] njezina [C] prijateljica [B,C,S] drugarica [S] Nada)
4. Čiji je taj strašni pas? (njihov advokat [B,S] odvjetnik [B,C] Dušan)
5. Čije je to veliko znanje? (njegova devojka [E] djevojka [J] Željka)
6. Čija je ova šarena mačka? (vaš kolega Željko)

B7

1. Kako se kaže *sudac* na bosanskom i srpskom?	1. Како се каже *судац* на босанском и српском?
2. Kako se kaže *advokat* na hrvatskom?	2. Како се каже *адвокат* на хрватском?
3. Kako se kaže *Španjolska* na srpskom?	3. Како се каже *Шпањолска* на српском?
4. Kako se piše *Washington* na srpskom?	4. Како се пише *Washington* на српском?
5. Kako se kaže *Evropa* na hrvatskom?	5. Како се каже *Европа* на хрватском?
6. Kako se kažu *Greece* i *Hungary* na bosanskom, hrvatskom i srpskom?	6. Како се кажу *Greece* и *Hungary* на босанском, хрватском и српском?
7. Kako se kaže *kazalište* na srpskom?	7. Како се каже *казалиште* на српском?
8. Kako se kaže *bioskop* na hrvatskom i bosanskom?	8. Како се каже *биоскоп* на хрватском и босанском?
9. Kako se kaže *kasa* na hrvatskom?	9. Како се каже *каса* на хрватском?
10. Kako se kaže *kat* na srpskom i bosanskom?	10. Како се каже *кат* на српском и босанском?
11. Kako se kaže *sveučilište* na bosanskom i srpskom?	11. Како се каже *свеучилиште* на босанском и српском?

☞ **Play** this as a game. One team asks a question, hoping to stump the other team with a word they might not remember.

✍ DOMAĆA ZADAĆA [B,C] DOMAĆI ZADATAK [S]

C1

Fill in the blanks with the appropriate time expression, and translate the sentences into English:

1. [B,C] .... uvijek idem na predavanja popodne.
   [S] .... увек идем на предавања поподне.
   [fill in the weekday of your choice]

2. [B,C] .... u .... idem s prijateljima na more.
   [S] .... у .... идем с друговима на море.
   (Every year)   [fill in the month of your choice]

3. [B,C] .... nisam razmišljala o svojoj ljubavi.
   [S] .... нисам размишљала о својој љубави.
   (For months)

4. [B,C] .... idem na koncert u ....
   [S] .... идем на концерт у ....
   (This week)   [fill in a weekday of your choice]

5. [B,C] Često idem u kino ....
   [S] Често идем у биоскоп ....
                    (on Fridays)

6. [B,C] .... je čekao da mu se javiš telefonom.
   [S] .... је чекао да му се јавиш телефоном.
   (For days)

7. [B,C] .... joj se javio, ali nije bila kod kuće pa se nisu čuli.
   [S] .... joj се javio, али није била код куће па се нису чули.
   (Yesterday)

C2

Fill in the blanks with the appropriate forms of the words in parentheses. For verbs, use only present tense. Then write out the whole story.

Bosnian

Haris i Nada su momak i djevojka. Oni su .... (studenti). U .... (jul), kada .... (završavati se) ljetni semestar, Haris .... (ići) sam .... (voz) iz .... (Tuzla) u .... (Sarajevo), a Nada .... (ići) iz .... (Tuzla) .... (kola) na .... (Hvar) sa .... (mama i tata). Dok su Haris i Nada na .... (put), Harisu je dobro, ali Nadi nije. Haris .... (javljati se) .... (Nada) iz .... (Sarajevo) preko .... (internet). Nada .... (javljati se) .... (Haris) .... (telefon). Haris razumije .... (Nada). Nada želi biti sa .... (Haris). Hvar je lijep, ali poslije dva .... (dan) .... (Nada) nije lijepo na .... (Hvar) bez .... (Haris). Ni .... (Haris) nije u .... (Sarajevo) lijepo bez .... (Nada). Haris .... (kazati) .... (Nada) da .... (doći) u .... (Sarajevo) .... (trajekt i autobus). Náda .... (dòlaziti) sa .... (Hvȁr) u .... (Sȁrajevo) i Hàris .... (ìći) (Náda) (dòčekati) na .... (stànica). Onda̱ Hàris .... (ìći) po .... (grȁd) sa .... (Náda) i .... òni (razgovàrati) o .... (Hàrisov pu̱t) i o .... (Nȁdin pu̱t). Náda .... (biti) deset .... (da̱n) kod .... (Àmila), ... (svòja tetka), a Hàris .... (biti) kod .... (Elvis), ... (svo̱j àmidža). Pos-lije .... (to̱) Hàris i Náda .... (ìći) u .... (Tuzla) .... (vo̱z).

Croatian

Žȅljko i Jasna su mòmak i djèvojka. Òni su .... (stùdenti). U .... (srpanj), kàda .... (završȁvati se) ljetni̱ sèmestar Žȅljko .... (ìći) sa̱m .... (vlȁk) iz .... (Varàždi̱n) u .... (Zȁgreb), a Jasna .... (ìći) iz .... (Varàždi̱n) .... (kola) na .... (Hvȁr) s .... (mama i tata). Dok su Žȅljko i Jasna na .... (pu̱t), Žȅljku je dobro, ali Jasni nȉje. Žȅljko .... (jàvljati se) .... (Jasna) iz .... (Zȁgreb) preko .... (ìnternet). Jasna .... (jàvljati se) .... (Žȅljko) .... (telèfo̱n). Žȅljko razùmije .... (Jasna). Jasna žèli̱ biti sa .... (Žȅljko). Hvȁr je lijȇp, ali poslije dva̱ .... (da̱n) .... (Jasna) nȉje lijȇpo na .... (Hvȁr) bez .... (Žȅljko). Ni .... (Žȅljko) nȉje u .... (Zȁgreb) lijȇpo bez .... (Jasna). Žȅljko .... (kȁzati) .... (Jasna) da .... (do̱ći) u .... (Zȁgreb) .... (tràjekt i autòbus). Jasna .... (dòlaziti) sa .... (Hvȁr) u .... (Zȁgreb) i Žȅljko .... (ìći) (Jasna) (dòčekati) na .... (kolodvȍr). Onda Žȅljko .... (ìći) po .... (grȁd) s .... (Jasna) i .... òni (razgovàrati) o .... (Žȅljkov pu̱t) i o .... (Jasnin pu̱t). Jasna .... (biti) deset .... (da̱n) kod .... (Náda), ... (svòja tetka), a Žȅljko .... (biti) kod .... (Domagoj), ... (svo̱j stric). Poslije .... (to̱) Žȅljko i Jasna .... (ìći) u .... (Varàždi̱n) .... (vlȁk).

Serbian

Dùšan i Dùšanka su mòmak i dèvojka. Òni su .... (stùdenti). U .... (juli), kàda .... (završȁvati se) .... (letnji̱ sèmestar) Dùšan .... (ìći) sa̱m .... (vo̱z) iz .... (Nȉš) u .... (Beògrad), a Dùšanka .... (ìći) iz .... (Nȉš) .... (kola) u .... (Cṟna Gòra) sa .... (mama i tata). Dok su Dùšan i Dùšanka na .... (pu̱t), Dùšanu je dobro, ali Dùšanki nȉje. Dùšan .... (jàvljati se) .... (Dùšanka) iz .... (Beògrad) preko .... (ìnternet). Dùšanka .... (jàvljati se) .... (Dùšan) .... (telèfo̱n). Dùšan razùme̱ .... (Dùšanka). Dùšanka žèli̱ da bude̱ sa .... (Dùšan). Cṟna Gòra je lèpa, ali posle dva̱ .... (da̱n) .... (Dùšanka) nȉje lèpo u .... (Cṟna Gòra) bez .... (Dùšan). Ni .... (Dùšan) nȉje lèpo u (Beògrad) bez .... (Dùšanka). Dùšan .... (kȁzati) .... (Dùšanka) da .... (do̱ći) u .... (Beògrad) .... (autòbus). Dùšanka (dòlaziti) iz .... (Cṟna Gòra) u .... (Beògrad) i Dùšan .... (ìći) (Dùšanka) (dòčekati) na .... (stànica). Onda Dùšan .... (ìći) po .... (grȁd) sa .... (Dùšanka) i .... òni (razgovàrati) o .... (Dùšanov pu̱t) i o .... (Dùšankin pu̱t). Dùšanka .... (biti) deset .... (da̱n) kod ....

(Ana), ... (svȍja tȅtka), a Dȕšan .... (biti) kod .... (Sȑđan), ... (svȏj strȋc). Posle ....
(tȍ) Dȕšan i Dȕšanka .... (ȉći) u .... (Nȋš) .... (vȍz).

C3

Replace each italicized noun or name in the sentence with a pronoun (full form or clitic, as required), changing the word order where necessary. Then write out the whole sentence.

1. [B,C] Mjȅsēc krȕžī oko *zèmlje,* a zèmlja krȕžī oko *sȗnca.*
   [S] Mȅsēc krȕžī oko *zèmlje,* a zèmlja krȕžī oko *sȗnca.*

2. Žȅljka šȁljē *Gòranu* krȁtko pȋsmo, a Gòran šȁljē *Žȅljki* dȕgo pȋsmo.

3. Jȅlo od *kobàsicē* i *jája* òdličnō je za dòručak.

4. [B,S] Jȁvili smo se *ròditeljima,* ali se nȋsmo čȕli sa njima.
   [C] Jȁvili smo se *ròditeljima,* ali se nȋsmo čȕli s njima.

5. [B,C] Slȕšajū *svòje profèsore* cijȅlī dȃn.
   [S] Slȕšajū *svòje profèsore* cȅo dȃn.

6. [B] Pȋjēmo *mlijéko* svȁkī dȃn, ali nȉkada nè pijēmo *kàfu.*
   [C] Pȋjēmo *mlijéko* svȁkī dȃn, ali nȉkada nè pijēmo *kàvu.*
   [S] Pȋjēmo *mlȅko* svȁkī dȃn, ali nȉkada nè pijēmo *kàfu.*

7. Od *pròzora* do *vráta* nȉje dalèko, vȅć je dalèko od *pròzora* do nȁs!

8. U *novìnama* ȉmā *zanìmljivīh stvárī.*

C4

Fill in each blank with the appropriate form of the word in parentheses. Where you see an exclamation point with the verb, use the imperative.

1. .... (slȕšati!) me! Jája se ne .... (mòrati) jesti svȁkī dȃn!
2. Zar Ines .... (ne poznávati) mòju sèstru?
3. .... (pȉsati!) svòjim sèstrama dànas, a brȁći sutra!
4. Kàda .... (pòčinjati) tvȏj nòvī pòsao?
5. [B] Štȁ hòćeš da .... (mȋ, jesti) za rȕčak dànas?
   [C] Štȍ hòćeš da .... (mȋ, jesti) za rȕčak dànas?
6. [B] U kolìko sȁti navèče u četvŕtak .... (òni, gledati) film?
   [C] U kolìko sȁti navèčer u četvŕtak .... (òni, gledati) film?

1. .... (слушати!) ме! Јаја не .... (мȍрати) да се једу сваки дан!
2. Зар Инес .... (не познавати) мȍју сестру?
3. .... (писати!) свȍјим сестрама данас, а браћи сутра!
4. Када .... (почињати) твȍј нови посао?
5. Шта хоћеш да .... (ми, јести) за ручак данас?
6. У колико сȁти увече у четврстак .... (они, гледати) филм?

☞ **Use** past tense for #6.

C5

Translate the first sentence into English. Then translate the ones that follow it into B, C, or S, using the first as a model.

1. a. [B,C] Daj djèci vòća, glädna su!
   [S] Daj dèci vòća, glädna su!
   b. Write a letter to the children.
   c. Listen! Your house is very beautiful with that red door and those windows!

2. a. Njihova dvȃ brata žívē kod ròditelja, ali òstala braća nìsu vȉšē kod kućē.
   b. Put a picture into the letter for your brothers.
   c. Get in touch with your brothers about their homework.

3. a. [B,S] Ìmam i svòg psa i tvòg psa. Šta da rȃdīm sa tvòjim psom?
   [C] Ìmam i svòjeg psa i tvòjeg psa. Što da rȃdīm s tvòjim psom?
   b. Please bring me both your cat and my mouse.
   c. Nada is reading both his book and her book.

4. a. Pred njima je dobar žìvot, ali predà mnȏm su problèmi.
   b. She works outside all day in front of the building.
   c. Below the floor is another room on another floor (story).

C6

Identify the number (singular or plural) of each of the following nouns. If it is singular, give the plural form, and if it is plural, give the singular form.

vlȁk	brat
žìvoti	zidovi
pìsma	đȁci
dèvojke [E], djèvojke [J]	pas
dète [E], dijète [J]	ljùbavi
mòmci	sȋn
lav	rȅč [E], rijȇč [J]
supruga	znȃnje
vȍz	rečníci [E], rječníci [J]
ljȗdi	knjiga
pìtanja	òtac
nȍć	suprug
kljȗč	

C7

For each aspect pair given below, state which of the two is perfective and which is imperfective.

1. kupòvati	kúpiti	3. ùzeti	ùzimati	5. dòći	dòlaziti
2. polòžiti	polágati	4. jesti	pòjesti	6. sprèmati	sprèmiti

VOCABULARY

бака [B,C,S]	grandma	нена [B]	grandma
баба [S]	grandma	разлог	reason
благо вама!	lucky you!	тући, тучем	to spank, to beat (I)
глупљи, глупље, глупља	stupider	унук	grandson, grandchild
деда	grandpa		

Благо бабама и дедама који имају унуке. Тешко нама који имамо децу.

Ако већ тучете децу, туците их без разлога, јер су сви други разлози глупљи.

✍ **Bring** a question on each aphorism to class. Use questions with:

a) (ne) sviđati se

b) (ne) činiti se

c) O čemu se radi

d) Zar .... ?

📖 Priča: Albahari

Read Part V of the story "Osam malih priča o mojoj ženi" by David Albahari (p. 343).

Deveta lekcija • Lesson Nine

VOCABULARY

àustrijskī	Austrian	pòrodica [B,S]	family
bòravak, bòravka	sojourn, stay	pròleće	spring
dèvetī	ninth	pròljeće	spring
ìspitnī	exam *(adj.)*	rok	period, deadline
jèzik	language	sànjati, sànjam	to dream (I)
kìneskī	Chinese	slàvenskī [B,C]	Slavic
lèto	summer	slòvenskī [B,S]	Slavic
ljèto	summer	stànovati, stànujēm	to reside (I)
mèsēc dána	[for] a month	stùdijskī	study *(adj.)*
mjèsēc dána	[for] a month	Šàngaj	Shanghai
Mòskva	Moscow	zìma	winter
òbitelj [C] *(f)*	family		

ŠTA ĆEŠ RADITI? [B,S]   ŠTO ĆEŠ RADITI? [C]

Bosnian
1. Šta ćeš ráditi preko *ljeta?*
2. Poslije ìspitnog roka ìći ću u *Pàriz* na mjesèc dána.
1. Dívno! Šta ćeš tamo ráditi?
2. Bit će tȍ stùdijskī bòravak. Sànjam o tome već godìnama!
1. A šta ćeš ùčiti dok si u *Parìzu?*
2. Ùčit ću govòriti *francùskī jèzik* ì dan ì noć. I jest ću, nàravno, *francùska jela!*
1. A gdje ćeš stànovati?
2. Stanòvat ću kod jèdne *francùske pòrodice.*

Croatian
1. Što ćeš ráditi preko *ljeta?*
2. Poslije ìspitnog roka ìći ću u *Pàriz* na mjesèc dána.
1. Dívno! Što ćeš tamo ráditi?
2. Bit će tȍ stùdijskī bòravak. Sànjam o tome već godìnama!
1. A što ćeš ùčiti dok si u *Parìzu?*
2. Ùčit ću govòriti *francùskī jèzik* i dan ì noć. I jest ću, nàravno, *francùska jela!*
1. A gdje ćeš stànovati?
2. Stanòvat ću kod jèdne *francùske òbitelji.*

Serbian
1. Šta ćeš da rádiš preko *leta?*
2. Posle ìspitnog roka ću da idèm u *Pàriz* na mesèc dána.
1. Dívno! Šta ćeš tamo da rádiš?
2. Bíće tȍ stùdijskī bòravak. Sànjam o tome već godìnama!
1. A šta ćeš da ùčiš dok si u *Parìzu?*
2. Ùčiću da govòrim *francùskī jèzik* i dan ì noć. I ješću, nàravno, *francùska jela!*
1. A gde ćeš da stànuješ?
2. Stanòvaću kod jèdne *francùske pòrodice.*

𝒥☞ **Replace** *leto* [E] *ljeto* [J] **with** jesèn, pròleće [E] pròljeće [J], zìma.

𝒥☞ **Replace** *Pàriz* **with** 1. Bèč, 2. Šàngaj, 3. Mòskva; **replace** *francùski jèzik* **with** 1. nèmačkī [E] njèmačkī [J] jèzik, 2. kìneskī jèzik, 3. slàvenske [B,C] slòvenske [B,S] jèzike **and** *francùska òbitelj* [C] *pòrodica* [B,S] **and** *francùska jela* **with** 1. àustrijska òbitelj [C] pòrodica [B,S] **and** àustrijska jela; 2. kìneska òbitelj [C] pòrodica [B,S] **and** kìneska jela; 3. rùska òbitelj [C] pòrodica [B,S] **and** rùska jela.

 GRAMMAR

* The future tense *

The future is a compound tense, formed by adding an auxiliary to the infinitive (or its replacement, the sequence *da* + present). The auxiliary, which functions like "will" in English, has both full and clitic forms. The clitic forms are used predominantly; for the full forms (and negative future), see the next section. The full forms, although identical to the conjugated forms of *hteti* [E] *htjeti* [J], do not in this instance mean "want." Instead they carry only the meaning of future tense [95a]

Future tense auxiliaries

FULL		CLITIC	
hoću	hoćemo	ću	ćemo
hoćeš	hoćete	ćeš	ćete
hoće	hoće	će	će

* Word order in the future and variant spellings *

As a clitic, the future auxiliary must come in second position. But the infinitive portion of the future may be anywhere in the sentence. If the infinitive begins the sentence the auxiliary must come immediately after it. In this case, infinitives ending in *-ti* are shortened and the unit "infinitive + clitic" is pronounced together. C keeps the *-t* of the infinitive and writes the two forms separately (*učit ću*), but S drops the *-t* and writes the two as one word (*učiću*). Infinitives ending in *-sti* shift the *-st-* to *-šć-* when they are joined with the future clitic; this pronunciation is heard everywhere, but appears in spelling only in S (*ješću* [S] but *jest ću* [C]). In all such instances, B can use both spellings. Note that infinitives ending in *-ći* are written separately everywhere (*ići ću*). [95a]

* The preposition *na* in future time expressions *

English uses "for" to express the length of time covered by an action. In BCS, the preposition choice depends on the meaning. If the focus is on an intended endpoint, use *na* + Acc, as in *ići ću u Pariz na godinu dana* "I'm going to Paris for a year." [100] But if it concerns simply of a unit of time, use the Acc without a preposition, as in *ona će biti godinu dana u Parizu* "she'll be in Paris for a year." [71]

Caution!
Plaster falling

češljati	to brush, comb (I)	ȍstati, ȍstanem	to remain (P)
čist	clean	počèšljati	to brush, comb (P)
dòma [C]	[toward] home	pògledati se	to look at oneself (P)
istī	same	pòlaziti	to set out, to go (I)
izglèdati, ìzglēdām	to appear (I)	prati, perēm	to wash (I)
jao	oh no!	prljav	dirty
kao	as	probúditi, probúdīm	to awaken (P)
krènuti, krènēm	to go, to set out (P)	pròvesti se, pròvedēm se	to spend [time] (P)
krétati, krèćēm	to get moving (I)	[ìmati] pùne rúke pòsla	to be very busy
kȕći [B,C,S]	[toward] home	rúka; Gpl. rúkū	hand, arm
lìce	face	ùmiti se, ùmijēm se	to wash one's face (P)
nȅprijatan, nȅprijatna [B,S]	uncomfortable	umívati se, ùmīvām se	to wash one's face (I)
nèugodan, nèugodna [B,C]	uncomfortable	ùredan, ùredna	tidy
nèuredan, nèuredna	messy	vrátiti se, vrátīm se	to return (P)
oglèdalo [B,C,S]	mirror	zȑcalo [C]	mirror
òprati, òperēm	to wash (P)	zȗb; zȗbi	tooth

POGLEDAJ SE!

Bosnian
1. Pogledaj se u oglèdalo!
2. Žèliš li rȅći da sam nèuredna? Jao, nèugodno mi je!
1. Istā si kao uvijek! Lìce ti je prljavo. Počèšljaj se, ùmij se, operi rùke, pa ćeš onda izglèdati bolje!
2. Glèdaj dok se češljam, ùmīvam se i perēm rùke. Sàda sam ùredna i lìce mi je čisto! Hòćeš li sa mnȍm krènuti u grȁd?
1. Nèću. Žèlim ostati kod kùće jer imam pùne rùke pòsla. Hòćeš li prati zùbe?
2. Nèću sad. Jȅst ću dok sam vani, pa ću ih prati prije spávanja. Zdravo! Žùri mi se! Krèćem! Vrȁtit ću se kùći poslije 11 sȁti!
1. Lijèpo se pròvedi. Ako mi se ne spáva, čekat ću te. Nemoj me probúditi ako spávam.

Croatian
1. Pogledaj se u zȑcalo!
2. Žèliš li rȅći da sam nèuredna? Jao, nèugodno mi je!
1. Istā si kao uvijek! Lìce ti je prljavo. Počèšljaj se, ùmij se, operi si rùke, pa ćeš onda izglèdati bolje!
2. Glèdaj dok se češljam, ùmīvam se i perēm si rùke. Sàda sam ùredna i lìce mi je čisto! Hòćeš li sa mnȍm krènuti u grȁd?
1. Nȅ ću. Žèlim ostati kod kùće jer imam pùne rùke pòsla. Hòćeš li prati zùbe?
2. Nȅ ću sad. Jȅst ću dok sam vani, pa ću ih prati prije spávanja. Bok! Žùri mi se! Krèćem! Vrȁtit ću se dòma poslije 11 sȁti!
1. Lijèpo se pròvedi. Ako mi se ne spáva, čekat ću te. Nemoj me probúditi ako spávam.

Serbian
1. Погледај се у оглèдало!
2. Да ли жèлиш да кàжеш да сам нèуредна? Јао, нèпријатно ми је!
1. Истā си као увек! Лùце ти је прљаво. Почèшљај се, умùј се, опери рùке, па ћеш онда да изглèдаш боље!
2. Глèдај док се чешљам, умùвам се и перем рùке. Сàда сам ùредна и лùце ми је чисто! Хòћеш ли сà мном да крèнеш у грȁд?
1. Нèћу. Жèлим да остàнем код кùће јер ùмам пùне рùке посла. Да ли ћеш да перèш зùбе?
2. Нèћу сад. Јешћу док сам напољу, па ћу их прати пре спàвања. Ћао! Крèћем! Жùри ми се! Врàтићу се кùћи после 11 сȁти.
1. Лèпо се пròведи! Ако ми се не спȁва, чекàћу те. Нèмој да ме пробùдиш ако спȁвам.

🙰 **Redo** in a plural version, as if 1. and 2. are each several people rather than single individuals.

 **GRAMMAR**

* Questions and negation in the future tense *

Questions expecting a "yes-no" answer use the full form of the auxiliary and the particle *li* (in either the form *hoćeš li...* or *da li hoćeš...*). **[95b]** If a question begins with a word such as *kada* or *šta* [B,S] *što* [C], the clitic auxiliary is used. The negative future uses only a full-form negative auxiliary; there is no short form. The forms *neću*, etc. - now spelled *ne ću* (etc.) in Croatian - are thus identical in form to negated *hteti* or *htjeti*, but mean only negative future **[95a]**

Negative future	
neću [B,S] / *ne ću* [C]	*nećemo* [B,S] / *ne ćemo* [C]
nećeš [B,S] / *ne ćeš* [C]	*nećete* [B,S] / *ne ćete* [C]
neće [B,S] / *ne će* [C]	*neće* [B,S] / *ne će* [C]

* Word order in the future tense *

The particle *li* is the only clitic which precedes the future tense auxiliary: all other clitics must follow it. The full form auxiliary takes first position in a question, followed by *li*, and then by other clitics: *Hoćeš li im se javiti?* **[102]**

li precedes fut. aux.	other clitics follow fut.aux.
Da li ćeš im se javiti?	*Mi ćemo im se javiti.*
Da li će joj ga dati?	*Oni će mu ih pokazati.*

* Double meanings of *hteti* [E] *htjeti* [J] *

The clitic forms of this verb have only future tense meaning. But the full forms signify both future tense and "want." Context of usage usually is enough to tell which is meant; if necessary one can use *želeti* [E] *željeti* [J] to specify the meaning "want." The negative forms *neću* [B,S] *ne ću* [C] etc. mean both "won't" (negative future) and "not want"; one must again know from context which meaning is intended. **[95c]**

* Reflexive verbs *

The particle *se* functions as direct object when the verb indicates action performed upon one's own person, for example in verbs such as *češljati se, umiti se, brijati se*. It is only verbs like these that are truly "reflexive." Croatian can also use the reflexive dative particle *si* in a "possessive" sense (as in *perem si zube* "I clean my teeth"), but only (of course) if there is a direct object to be "possessed." **[97]**

* The particle *se* with verbs *

Because the particle *se* was originally used only as the clitic form of the reflexive pronoun object *sebe*, it has become customary to use the term "reflexive verb" for a verb which is accompanied by *se*. In fact only a very few verbs (such as *obući se* "get [oneself] dressed") are true reflexive verbs. Now, however, the particle *se* is used with many additional meanings. For instance, it can make a verb impersonal, **[140]** "inclinational," **[82a]** intransitive, **[98]** "non-causative," **[98]** passive, **[139]** or reciprocal. **[87a]** The chart below illustrates how *se* can add each of these meanings to a verb which lacks that particular meaning when it occurs without *se*. There are also several verbs which never occur without *se*, such as *bojati se* "be afraid," *baviti se* "be occupied with" *dogoditi se* "happen," *nalaziti se* "be located," and others. **[87b]**

	with *se*		without *se*	
Impersonal	*Tamo se dobro jede.*	One eats well there.	*Ne jedem meso.*	I don't eat meat.
Inclinational	*Ne ide mi se.*	I don't feel like going.	*Idemo sad.*	We're going now.
Intransitive	*Djeca se igraju.*	The children play.	*Igra šah.*	He's playing chess.
Non-causative	*Budim se rano.*	I wake up early.	*Majka me budi.*	Mother awakens me.
Passive	*Kako se to kaže?*	How is that said?	*Kaži nešto!*	Say something!
Reciprocal	*Oni se vole.*	They are in love.	*Volim ga.*	I love him.
Reflexive	*Obucite se!*	Get dressed!	*Obukla je lutku.*	She dressed her doll.

* Aspect, continued *

The aspect of a verb is often a matter of focus. Aspect choice in the future depends upon whether the speaker focuses on the general fact of future action or the completion of a specific action. Reference to the fact of action alone is expressed by imperfective verbs, for instance: *šta* [B,S] *što* [C] *ćeš raditi tamo?* "what will you do there?" or *učiću* [B,S] *učit ću* [C] *francuski* "I'll study French." By contrast, focus on the completion of an action is expressed by perfective verbs, as in *kad ćeš mi se javiti?* "when will you call me?" or *hoćeš li se kasno vratiti?* "will you be back late?" In a few instances the difference in aspectual meaning (of action in progress vs. completed action) comes across in the English translation. For instance, the imperfective verb *učiti* means "study" in English, while its perfective partner *naučiti* means "learn."

 A3

A3   ☉73,74

VOCABULARY

baš	precisely	netko [C]	someone
ide [mi] se	[I] feel like going	niko [B,S]	no one
deliti, delim	to divide up (I)	nitko [C]	no one
dijeliti, dijelim	to divide up (I)	podeliti, podelim	to split (*e.g.* costs) (P)
gubiti	to waste, to lose (I)	podijeliti, podijelim	to split (*e.g.* costs) (P)
hoćeš-nećeš	like it or not	podstanar	tenant, subletter
ići u podstanare	to become a tenant	režije [C] (*pl form*)	utility bills
iznajmiti, iznajmim [B,S]	to rent (P)	savršen	perfect
kirija [B,S]	rent	stanarina [B,C,S]	rent
možda	perhaps	stanovanje	living, residing
na jesen [B]	in the autumn	trošak, troška; troškovi	expense(s)
na jesen [S,C]	in the autumn	unajmiti, unajmim [C]	to rent (P)
neko [B,S]	someone		

STANOVANJE

Bosnian
1. Gdje ćeš stanovati na jesen?
2. Ostat ću u studentskom domu. A ti?
1. Neću se vratiti u dom. Ove godine idem u podstanare. Baš sada tražim stan. Hoćeš li dijeliti sobu s nekim u studentskom domu?
2. Ne želim ni sa kim stanovati, ali hoćeš-nećeš moraš! A ti?
1. Vidjet ću. Možda ću iznajmiti stan sa nekim studentima i podijeliti s njima troškove i kiriju.
2. Ne da mi se ići u stanare. Savršeno mi odgovara tu blizu. Neću morati gubiti vrijeme i hodati daleko na predavanja.

Croatian
1. Gdje ćeš stanovati na jesen?
2. Ostat ću u studentskom domu. A ti?
1. Ne ću se vratiti u dom. Ove godine idem u podstanare. Baš sada tražim stan. Hoćeš li dijeliti sobu s nekim u studentskom domu?
2. Ne želim ni s kim stanovati, ali hoćeš-ne-ćeš-moraš! A ti?
1. Vidjet ću. Možda ću unajmiti stan s nekim studentima i podijeliti s njima režije i stanarinu.
2. Ne da mi se ići u stanare. Savršeno mi odgovara tu blizu. Ne ću morati gubiti vrijeme i hodati daleko do predavanja.

Serbian
1. Gde ćeš stanovati na jesen?
2. Ostaću u studentskom domu. A ti?
1. Neću da se vratim u dom. Ove godine idem u podstanare. Baš sada tražim stan. Da li ćeš deliti sobu s nekim u studentskom domu?
2. Ne želim ni sa kim da stanujem, ali hoćeš-nećeš moraš! A ti?
1. Videću. Možda ću da iznajmim stan sa nekim studentima i podeliti s njima troškove i kiriju.
2. Ne ide mi se u podstanare. Savršeno mi odgovara tu blizu. Neću morati da gubim vreme i da hodam daleko na predavanja.

☞ **Retell** this as a conversation about your own housing plans.

Self-study learners: When you write a version about your own housing plans, be sure to use forms of the future tense. Note the instrumental forms *kim* and *nekim* and *ni s kim*.

131
Deveta lekcija   Lesson Nine

⚙ GRAMMAR

* Negated prepositional phrases *

The negative pronouns *ništa* "nothing" and *niko* [B,S] *nitko* [C] "no one" consist of two parts. When they occur as objects of prepositions, the preposition comes between the two parts. [93b]

Affirmative		Negative	
o nečemu	about something	ni o čemu	about nothing
od nekoga	from someone	ni od koga	from no one
s nekim	with someone	ni s kim	with no one

* "Something, anything," etc. *

Pronouns such as *nešto* "something," *neko* [B,S] *netko* [C] "someone," *negde* [E] *negdje* [J] "somewhere," are formed by adding the prefix *ne-* to the interrogative pronouns *šta* or *što*, *ko* or *tko*, and *gde* or *gdje*, in a manner parallel to the formation of the negative pronouns *ništa* "nothing," *niko* or *nitko* "no one," and *nigde* or *nigdje* "nowhere." A similar series is created by adding the prefixes *i-* and *sva-*, which yields such as *išta* "anything at all," *svašta*, "all sorts of things," and the like. [62]

* "What" clauses *

When the idea translated by English "what" or "that" corresponds to an entire clause, BCS frequently uses the phrase *to što*. This is translated variously - sometimes as English "what" and sometimes as the entire English phrase "the fact that..." Thus, the sentence *meni ne odgovara to što radiš* corresponds to English "what you're doing does not suit me," whereas the sentence *savršeno mi odgovara to što ne moram ići tamo* corresponds to "the fact that I don't have to go there suits me just fine." [99]

Zagreb train station [Glavni kolodvor]

Belgrade train station [Železnička stanica]

baba [B,S]	grandmother	mìnut [B,S]	minute
bàka [B,C,S]	grandmother	minùta [C]	minute
bez obzíra na	regardless (of)	po njȉh	for them, to get them
ded	grandfather	pòći, pòđem	to set out, to go (P)
djed	grandfather	pola trȉ	2:30
jasan, jasna	clear, obvious	stȉći, stȉgnem	to arrive (P)
kolèga *(m)*	colleague	tata	Dad *(m)*
mama	Mom		

NA STANICI [B,S]   NA KOLODVORU [C]

Bosnian

1. Kàda će *tvòji ròditelji* dòći da vȉde tvȏj nȍvi stân?
2. Stȉći će sutra vȍzom na željezničkū stànicu u pola trȉ.
1. Hòćeš li *ih* dòčekati?
2. Hòću, jasno. Polàzim na stànicu u dva sàta. Hòćeš li i tȋ pòći sa mnȏm po *njȉh?*
1. Ne mògu, jer sam na predávanju, ali se mòme bratu idȅ. On *tvòje ròditelje* vòli, i žèli *ih* dòčekati sà tobȏm.
2. Zar ȍn nȅma puno pòsla ȍve sèdmice?
1. Ȉma, ali će ìći sà tobȏm bèz obzíra na tȍ.

Croatian

1. Kàda će *tvòji ròditelji* dòći vȉdjeti tvȏj nȍvi stân?
2. Stȉći će sutra vlȁkom na kolodvȍr u pola trȉ.
1. Hòćeš li *ih* dòčekati?
2. Hòću, jasno. Polàzim na kolodvȍr u dva sàta. Hòćeš li i tȋ pòći sa mnȏm po *njȉh?*
1. Ne mògu, jer sam na predávanju, ali se mòjem bratu idȅ. On *tvòje ròditelje* vòli, i žèli *ih* dòčekati s tobȏm.
2. Zar ȍn nȅma puno pòsla ovog tjȅdna?
1. Ȉma, ali će ìći s tobȏm bez obzíra na tȍ.

Serbian

1. Када ће *твоји родитељи* да дођу да виде твој нови стан?
2. Стићи ће сутра возом на железничку станицу у пола три.
1. Да ли ћеш да их дочекаш?
2. Хоћу, јасно. Полазим на станицу у два сата. Хоћеш ли и ти да пођеш са мном по њих?
1. Не могу, јер сам на предавању, али се мом брату иде. Он *твоје родитеље* воли, и жели да их дочека са тобом.
2. Зар он нема пуно посла ове недеље?
1. Има, али ће да иде са тобом без обзира на то.

🙷 **Replacements for** *roditelji*: tvȏj kolèga, mòje dète [E] dijète [J] **or** mòja dèca [E] djèca [J], njègov ded [E] djed [J], njèna bàka [B] njȅzina bàka [C] njȅna baba [S], vȁš brat **or** vȁša bràća, njihov tata.

Every region has its own colloquial words for **father** and, in a few instances, for **mother** as well. In some parts of Bosnia children call their father *bȁbo*, in Dalmatia, *ćáća* or *pápo*, in the Zagorje area around Zagreb *jápa*, and in Belgrade, *ćȁle*. In Bosnia children sometimes call their mother *nána*, while in Belgrade *kȅva* is used as slang for mother. Teenagers throughout the region address their parents as *stára* ("old woman") and *stári* ("old man"), and together as *stárci* ("oldsters").

The exclamation *jao*, meaning "ouch / oh no / alas" is one of many BCS exclamations. Another is *joj*, best translated as "oops." The word *ovaj* is often used when a speaker of B, C, or S is groping for a word or thought. Beyond these, there are numerous interjections used to punctuate speech. Bosnian uses *bȍna* and *bȍlan* (usually considered to be forms of the word *bolan*, "painful") as a form of address, similar to the way "man" is used in colloquial American English. In Serbian, speakers often add *bre* for emphasis, much as "you know" or "like" are used by speakers of English. Some Croatian and Bosnian speakers pepper their speech with the interrogative *je li?* or its contractions, *jel'?, jel'da?* or *jel'te?*.

🏃 VJEŽBE [J] VEŽBE [E]

> **Note**: As in other uses of the infinitive, the infinitive portion of the future tense may be expressed by the infinitive itself (*ja ću ìći*) or by the sequence *da* + present (*ja ću da idem*). Here too, C almost always uses the infinitive, while S uses both options. Accordingly the C as presented in this book uses only the infinitive; and although the S as presented herein uses both, those students working on Serbian are strongly urged to use every opportunity to practice using the "*da* + present" option, as it takes time to learn.

B1

Bosnian	Croatian	Serbian
1. Hoćete li ìći *u kìno* večeras?	1. Hoćete li ìći *u kìno* večeras?	1. Да ли ħете да идете *у биоскоп* вечерас?
2. Da, ìći ćemo od *5 sàti* na predstavu.	2. Da, ìći ćemo od *5 sàti* na predstavu.	2. Да, ићи ħемо од *5 сàти* на представу.
1. A kad ćete pòći òd kuće da stignete *u kìno* u *pēt?*	1. A kad ćete pòći od kuće da stignete *u kìno* u *pēt?*	1. А кад ħете да пòђете од куħе да стигнете *у биоскоп* у *пēт?*
2. Pòći ćemo u *4 sàta i 10 minùta.*	2. Pòći ćemo u *4 sàta i 10 minùta.*	2. Пòħи ħемо у *4 сàта и 10 минýта.*

☞ **Replace** *u bioskop* [S] *u kìno* [B,C] **with** na predàvanje, **replace** *večeras* **with** dànas **or** jutròs, **and change the times accordingly**.

B2

☞ **Change** the above exchange so that it represents a conversation a) between you and a person you know as *ti*, b) between two single individuals, c) between two groups. Do this by replacing the 1st and 2nd person plural forms above by a) 1st and 2nd singular, b) 3rd singular, and c) 3rd plural

☞ **Redo** B1 as a conversation about your own evening plans.

B3

Bosnian	Croatian	Serbian
1. Kàži, šta ti odgòvara više, *kìno* ili *pozorìšte* večeras?	1. Rèci, što ti odgòvara više, *kìno* ili *kazalìšte* večeras?	1. Kàži, šta ti odgòvara više, *bioskop* ili *pozorìšte* večeras?
2. Više mi odgòvara *pozorìšte*, a tebi?	2. Više mi odgòvara *kazalìšte*, a tebi?	2. Više mi odgòvara *pozorìšte*, a tebi?
1. Ja više volim *kìno*. A Hamdija? Šta on žèli da radi?	1. Ja više volim *kìno*. A Damir? Što on žèli radìti?	1. Ja više volim *bioskop*. A Milorad? Šta on žèli da radi?
2. Uvìjek je isti. Svejèdno mu je. Odgòvara mu to što odgòvara i nama.	2. Uvijek je isti. Svejèdno mu je. Odgòvara mu to što odgòvara i nama.	2. Uvek je isti. Svejèdno mu je. Odgòvara mu to što odgòvara i nama.

☞ **Replace** *bioskop* [S] *kìno* [B,C], *kazalìšte* [C] *pozorìšte* [B,S] **with** film **or** glàzba [C] mùzika [B,C,S].
☞ **Use** a woman's name instead of the man's. Switch the exercise to the plural.

B4

Bosnia	Croatian	Serbian
1. Šta obično radiš kad dođeš kući popodne?	1. Što obično radiš kad dođeš doma popodne?	1. Шта обично радиш кад дођеш кући поподне?
2. *Perem ruke.*	2. *Perem si ruke.*	2. *Перем руке.*
1. A kada *ruke opereš* danas šta ćeš onda?	1. A kada *ruke opereš* danas što ćeš onda?	1. А када *руке опереш* данас, шта ћеш онда?
2. Onda ću ručati sa prijateljicom.	2. Onda ću ručati s prijateljicom.	2. Онда ћу да ручам са другарицом.
1. A poslije ručka?	1. A poslije ručka?	1. А после ручка?
2. Onda ću oprati zube.	2. Onda ću oprati zube.	2. Онда ћу да оперем зубе.

☞ **Replace**: *prati* and *oprati ruke* with *umivati* and *umiti lice*; *češljati se* and *počešljati se*.

☞ **Retell** the exercise using other activities.

B5

Bosnian	Croatian	Serbian
1. Kada ćeš mi *se javiti?*	1. Kada ćeš mi *se javiti?*	1. Kada ćeš da mi *se javiš?*
2. *Javit* ću ti *se* sutra u pola četiri.	2. *Javit* ću ti *se* sutra u pola četiri.	2. *Javiću* ti *se* sutra u pola četiri.
1. A kako *ćeš* mi se *javiti* sutra?	1. A kako *ćeš* mi se *javiti* sutra?	1. A kako *ćeš* mi se *javiti* sutra?
2. *Javit* ću ti *se telefonom.*	2. *Javit* ću ti *se telefonom.*	2. *Javiću* ti *se telefonom.*

☞ **Replace** *javiti se* with *vratiti se* and *telefon* with *kola*.

☞ **Rewrite** the exercise in the plural.

B6

Bosnian	Croatian	Serbian
1. O *čemu* ćeš *pisati sestri?*	1. O *čemu* ćeš *pisati sestri?*	1. О чему ћеш да *пишеш* сестри?
2. Ni o *čemu*. Ne *piše* mi *se* sada. Sutra ću *joj* o *nečemu pisati.*	2. Ni o *čemu*. Ne *piše* mi *se* sada. Sutra ću *joj* o *nečemu pisati.*	2. Ни о *чему*. Не *пише* ми *се* сада. Сутра ћу *да joj пишем* о *нечему*.
1. A zašto ti se sada ne *piše?*	1. A zašto ti se sada ne *piše?*	1. А зашто ти се сада не *пише?*
2. Zato što mi se spava.	2. Zato što mi se spava.	2. Зато што ми се спава.

☞ **Switch the** *šta* [B,S] *što* [C] **to** *ko* [B,S] *tko* [C]. **Replace** *pisati* with *govoriti*, **and** *sestra* with *brat*.

B7

Working with a partner from class (if you are not able to work together in person, collaborate over the phone or by e-mail), write your own version of one of the four A dialogues in Lesson 9. Rehearse it together so that the two of you can perform your version for the other students in class. Include props where appropriate.

Self-study learners: Find the verbs in this lesson accompanied by the particle *se*, and determine in each instance the particular type of meaning added by this particle. Go back over previous lessons and search for such verbs there too.

✍ DOMAĆA ZADAĆA [B,C] DOMAĆI ZADATAK [S]

C1

Rewrite in the future tense:

Bosnian	Croatian	Serbian
1. Idemo u kino.	1. Idemo u kino.	1. Идемо у биоскоп.
2. Čitaju knjige.	2. Čitaju knjige.	2. Читају књиге.
3. Pišeš li pismo?	3. Pišeš li pismo?	3. Да ли пишеш писмо?
4. Hana i Hamdija putuju vozom u New York u utorak.	4. Sanja i Darko putuju vlakom u New York u utorak.	4. Марко и Саша путују возом у Њујорк у уторак.
5. Ines stanuje kod svoje tetke.	5. Iva stanuje kod svoje tetke.	5. Марија станује код своје тетке.
6. I ja moram da kupim psa!	6. I ja moram kupiti psa!	6. И ја морам да купим пса!

C2

Translate into B, C, or S:

1. For months I have been preparing for this test.
2. Don't you want to buy a dog?
3. At 5:30 on Tuesday afternoon I will go to the theater.
4. I like large cities more than small cities.
5. This semester I will be a tenant, and I will rent an apartment.
6. We are students at the university and we listen to professors in lectures.
7. I have no apples or plums but I have a lot of oranges and walnuts.
8. I'm feeling poorly. And you?

C3

Connect each word in the two left columns with the correct English translation in the right column, and mark each word as B, C, and/or S. If you find a word that you have not yet encountered in one of the lessons, look it up in the glossary at the back of the book.

1. tko	15. nigdje	who
2. što	16. neko	someone
3. iko	17. igdje	no one
4. kada	18. nigde	anyone
5. gdje	19. nešto	what
6. išta	20. igde	something
7. šta	21. ikada	nothing
8. nekada	22. niko	anything
9. ko	23. negdje	where
10. ništa	24. nitko	somewhere
11. gde	25. negde	nowhere
12. netko		anywhere
13. itko		when
14. nikada		sometime
		never
		ever

Translate the first sentence (or sequence of sentences) in each group into English. Then translate the two that follow it into B, C, or S, using the first as a model.

1. a. [B,C] Svȉđaju joj se Beatlesi.
   [S] Svȉđaju joj se Bitlsi.
   b. They like a good breakfast.
   c. I like the Balkan languages.

2. a. Nè spava̱ im se.
   b. We feel like working.
   c. She feels like studying.

3. a. [B] Hòćete li sȁ mnom pȍći ȕ grad? Mȍže! Idȇmo.
   [C] Hòćete li sȁ mnom pȍći u grad? Mȍže! Idȇmo.
   [S] Da li hòćete da pȍđete sȁ mnom u grad? Mȍže! Idȇmo.
   b. Will you wash your hands? OK! I am washing them.
   c. Will you wash your face? OK! I am washing it.

4. a. [B,C] Hòćete li nešto dȍručkovati? Ne, hvȁla, pojest ću nešto u gra̱du.
   [S] Da li hòćete nešto da dȍručkuje̱te? Ne, hvȁla, poješću nešto u gra̱du
   b. She will eat dinner at seven-thirty in the evening.
   c. They will drink tea and eat cookies at 4 p.m.

5. a. [B,C] Jȁvit ću joj se sutra u čètiri.
   [S] Jȁviću joj se sutra u čètiri.
   b. They will contact them in the morning.
   c. She will contact us after school.

6. a. [B,S] Ȕzmi tȍrbom sa stȍla! Ȉdi sa tȍrbom od jȅdne strȃ̱ne zgradȇ do drugȇ i trȁži svȍje stvȁri, pa onda̱ dȍđi do mene i ȕzmi mȍju ȍlovku iz tȍrbe!
   [C] Ȕzmi tȍrbu sa stȍla! Ȉdi s tȍrbom od jȅdne strȃ̱ne zgradȇ do drugȇ i trȁži svȍje stvȁri, pa onda̱ dȍđi k meni i ȕzmi mȍju ȍlovku iz tȍrbe!

   b. 1. Please take the pencil from the book.
      2. But where is the pencil: in the book or on the book?
      1. There it is on the book, there by the window.
      2. Here, I will take it from the book.

   c.1. Let them drive from Boston to Cleveland.
      2. Yes, but why to Cleveland? Why not from Boston to Montreal?
      1. Because her mother is from Boston and his father is from Cleveland.
      2. Now I understand. And where are you from?
      1. I am from Minneapolis, but my parents are from Vienna.

7. a. [B] Hȍćeš li novine čȉtati odma̱h u kolima, ili kod kućȇ za deset minu̱ta?
   [C] Hȍćeš li novine čȉtati odma̱h u kolima, ili kod kućȇ za deset minu̱ta?
   [S] Da li hȍćeš čȉtati novine odma̱h u kolima, ili kod kućȇ za deset minu̱ta?

b. 1. Where is my bag?
    2. It is on the door. Why are you looking for your bag?
    1. Because my newspaper is in it, and I want to read it.

c. Why is he going from door to door? He is searching for a neighbor.

C5

Complete these sentences using the words in parentheses.

1. Nè pij̱u čaj .... (sa, ništa).
2. Sutra ujutro ću se vidjeti .... (sa, neko).
3. Ne̱mamo ništa u kući za doru̱čak. Ka̱ko ćeš spre̱miti doru̱čak .... (od, ništa)?
4. Òna ne žeḻi .... (sa, niko) da iḏe u ki̱no.
5. Vidi̱m da im̱aš pi̱smo .... (od, neko)!
6. Òni znaj̱u nešto .... (o, nešto).
7. Mi̱ vam nè mo̱ramo govòriti .... (o, ništa).

1. Nè pij̱u čaj .... (s, ništa).
2. Sutra ujutro ću se vidjeti .... (s, netko).
3. Ne̱mamo ništa u kući za doru̱čak. Ka̱ko ćeš spre̱miti doru̱čak .... (od, ništa)?
4. Òna ne žeḻi .... (s, nitko) da iḏe u ki̱no.
5. Vidi̱m da im̱aš pi̱smo .... (od, netko)!
6. Òni znaj̱u nešto .... (o, nešto).
7. Mi̱ vam nè mo̱ramo govòriti .... (o, ništa).

1. Нѐ пиј̱у чај .... (са, ништа).
2. Сутра ујутро ћу се видети .... (са, неко).
3. Нѐмамо ништа у кући за доручак. Како ћеш да спрѐмиш доручак .... (од, ништа)?
4. Она не жѐл̱и .... (са, нико) да иде у биоскоп.
5. Видим да им̱аш пи̱смо .... (од, неко)!
6. Они знај̱у нешто .... (о, нешто).
7. Ми̱ не мо̱рамо да вам говòримо .... (о, ништа).

C6

Create two sentences in the future tense using a pronoun from column A, a verb from column B, and a phrase from column C. The first should begin with the pronoun, while the second should begin with the verb and not include any pronouns.

Example: mi, im̱ati, vremena.   a. Mi̱ ćemo im̱ati vremena.
                                    b. [B,C] Ìmat ćemo vremena.
                                       [S] Ìmaćemo vremena.

A	B	C
1. òna	ìći	u gra̱d
2. mi̱	pi̱sati	pi̱smo
3. ti̱	se̱deti [S] sjèditi [B,C]	pored vra̱ta
4. òni	razm̱išljati	o tebi
5. vi̱	ùčiti	ba̱lkanske j̱ezike
6. o̱n	jesti	kru̱ške i jabuke
7. ja̱	putòvati	u Lòndon
8. òni	mo̱ći	govòriti fraṉcuski
9. mi̱	stanòvati	u studentsḵom do̱mu

C7

If these are the answers, what are the questions?

1. [S] Чини ми се да није лијепо становати у студентском дому.
   [B,C] Čini mi se da nije lijepo stanovati u studentskom domu.

2. [S] Не свиђају ми се предавања рано ујутру.
   [B,C] Ne sviđaju mi se predavanja rano ujutro.

3. [S] Сутра ћемо да идемо у Бијело Поље.
   [B,C] Sutra ćemo ići u Bijelo Polje.

4. [S] Сада је 5 сати и 35 минута и вријеме је за чај.
   [B,C] Sada je 5 sati i 35 minuta i vrijeme je za čaj.

5. [S] Моји родитељи ће да стигну сутра у Сарајево у три поподне на жељезничку станицу.
   [B] Moji roditelji će stići sutra u Sarajevo u tri popodne na željezničku stanicu.
   [C] Moji roditelji će stići sutra u Sarajevo u tri popodne na kolodvor.

Bijelo Polje, Montenegro (1930s)

The above exercise demonstrates the use of Serbian ijekavian, and functions as a reminder of the fact that ijekavian is frequently written in Cyrillic. In speech as in writing, ijekavian is the norm for Serbs in Bosnia and in southwestern Serbia, and for all speakers living in Montenegro.

C8

Make a family tree using B, C, or S labels, with the names of the following relatives from your own family:

maternal and paternal grandparents
paternal and maternal uncles and their wives
aunts (maternal or paternal) and their husbands
your parents, brothers and sisters

VOCABULARY

Баново брдо	a hilly Belgrade neighborhood	поштен	fair
богзна	like, really [God knows]	продавати, продајем	to sell (I)
Карабурма	a hilly Belgrade neighborhood	раме; рамена	shoulder
не изгледа богзна како	doesn't look like much	ранији	earlier
невољан, невољна	listless	слегати, слежем	to shrug [shoulders] (I)
одиграти се	to play (P)	слијегати, слијежем	to shrug [shoulders] (I)
Партизан	Partisan soccer team	упитан, упитна	quizzical
погачица	bread roll	утакмица	[sports] game
поновно [C]	again	Црвена звезда	Red Star soccer team
поново [B,C,S]	again		

Ако ћемо поштено, Београд овог јутра не изгледа богзна како. Гледамо га упитно, а он невољно слеже раменима Карабурме и Бановог брда: данас му не иде, Београд данас нема свој дан.

Вечерас ће се поново одиграти једна од ранијих утакмица између Црвене звезде и Партизана. Продаваће се оне исте погачице и кафа.

☞ **List** the time expressions used in these aphorisms.

☞ **Bring** a question on each aphorism to class.

Crvena zvezda and *Partizan* are arch-rival Belgrade soccer teams. The rivals in Croatian soccer are *Dinamo* (Zagreb) and *Hajduk* (Split), while the traditional rivals in Bosnia and Herzegovina are *Željezničar* and *Sarajevo* (both of them Sarajevo teams).

Dušan Radović's radio show was broadcast from the top floor of a Belgrade skyscraper, from a studio which commanded a sweeping view of the city. He often spoke of the city's appearance, its mood, and the weather, from this vantage point.

📖 Priča: Albahari

Read Part VI of the story "Osam malih priča o mojoj ženi" by David Albahari (p. 344).

Deseta lekcija • Lesson Ten

centar, centra	center	podne, podneva	noon
ćevapčići	grilled minced meat	popodne	in the afternoon
deseti	tenth	pre podne	[in the] late morning
društvo	company, friends	prije podne	[in the] late morning
izaći, izađem; izašao [B,C,S]	to go out (P)	put, puta	time, instance
izići, iziđem; izišao [B,C]	to go out (P)	restoran, restorana	restaurant
izvrstan, izvrsna	excellent	uopće [B,C]	in general, at all
jedanput	once	uopšte [B,S]	in general, at all
naći se, nađem se; našao se	to meet [with] (P)	večerati	to dine, to eat supper (I/P)
naručiti, naručim	to order (P)		

KOD CHARLIEA [B,C]   KOD ČARLIJA [S]

Bosnian
1. Šta si radila u petak?
2. Prije podne sam bila na fakultetu.
1. A poslije toga?
2. Popodne sam išla u grad i našla se sa društvom.
1. A da li si sa njima izašla uveče?
2. Jesam. Večerali smo u restoranu.
1. Kako se zvao restoran, gdje se nalazi i šta ste naručili?
2. Zove se "Kod Charliea," nalazi se u centru grada, a jeli smo ćevapčiće i pili pivo.
1. Da li ti je to prvi put u tom restoranu?
2. Ne, bila sam tamo već jedanput ranije.
1. Da li je bilo problema sa hranom u restoranu?
2. Ne, nije uopće bilo problema. Sve je bilo izvrsno. Onda sam došla kući autobusom.

Croatian
1. Što si radila u petak?
2. Prije podne sam bila na fakultetu.
1. A poslije toga?
2. Popodne sam išla u grad i našla se s društvom.
1. A jesi li s njima izašla navečer?
2. Jesam. Večerali smo u restoranu.
1. Kako se zvao restoran, gdje se nalazi i što ste naručili?
2. Zove se "Kod Charliea," nalazi se u centru grada, a jeli smo ćevapčiće i pili pivo.
1. Je li ti to prvi put u tom restoranu?
2. Ne, bila sam tamo već jedanput ranije.
1. Je li bilo problema s hranom u restoranu?
2. Ne, nije uopće bilo problema. Sve je bilo izvrsno. Onda sam došla kući autobusom.

Serbian
1. Шта си радила у петак?
2. Пре подне сам била на факултету.
1. А после тога?
2. Поподне сам ишла у град и нашла се са друштвом.
1. А да ли си са њима изашла увече?
2. Јесам. Вечерали смо у ресторану.
1. Како се звао ресторан, где се налази и шта сте наручили?
2. Зове се "Код Чарлија," налази се у центру града, а јели смо ћевапчиће и пили пиво.
1. Да ли ти је то први пут у том ресторану?
2. Не, била сам тамо већ једанпут раније.
1. Да ли је било проблема са храном у ресторану?
2. Не, није уопште било проблема. Све је било изврсно. Онда сам дошла кући аутобусом.

🙰 **Redo** the exercise with male subjects for both speakers.

🙰 **Redo** the exercise with a feminine plural or masculine plural subject for speaker #2.

Traditionally, if one person invites another out for coffee, a drink, a meal, or to a movie or other form of entertainment, the person making the invitation generally expects to foot the bill. This is most often the case when the word *zvati* or *voditi* is used in the invitation, as in *zovem te na kafu* or *vodim te na kavu*. The invitation is less clearly defined if it embraces a group of people and uses phrases such as *idemo na kavu!* or *hajdemo svi u bioskop večeras!* In such cases, each person usually pays his or her own way.

Ćevapčići Grill, Sarajevo

 GRAMMAR

* Verb types *

The easiest way to build verbal vocabulary is by recognizing a verb's conjugation type. There are 16 basic types, which are defined by the relationship between infinitive and present tense. **[103a]** Type 1 includes *a*-conjugation verbs, and Types 2-4 include *i*-conjugation verbs. All the rest are *e*-conjugation verbs. Some verbs of types 13 and 15b can have alternate present tense forms in *-nem*. A very few verbs have irregular present tense forms. One must take care to learn both infinitive and present tense: for instance, *dovesti* (1sg. pres. *dovedem*) is type 13, but *dovesti* (1sg. pres. *dovezem*) is type 14. For a reference list of all verbs presented in this book, categorized according to verb types, see Appendix 9 (pp. 359-366).

Type	infinitive	1sg pres	Type	infinitive	1sg pres.
1	*igrati*	*igram*	9	*poznavati*	*poznajem*
2	*staviti*	*stavim*	10	*brati*	*berem*
3	*videti* [E] *vidjeti* [J]	*vidim*	11	*uzeti*	*uzmem*
4	*držati*	*držim*	12	*smeti* [E] *smjeti* [J]	*smem* [E] *smijem* [J]
5	*pisati*	*pišem*	13	*jesti*	*jedem*
6	*piti*	*pijem*	14	*tresti*	*tresem*
7	*krenuti*	*krenem*	15a	*teći*	*tečem*
8a	*kupovati*	*kupujem*	15b	*pomoći*	*pomognem*
8b	*kazivati*	*kazujem*	16	*doći*	*dođem*

* Past tense *

The past tense consists of an auxiliary (the present tense of *biti*) and the L-participle. To form the L-participle of types 1 and 2 verbs, drop the *-ti* of the infinitive and add the L-participle endings, [69] and follow the same procedure to form the L-participle of types 3-12. The ijekavian form of the masculine singular participle of types 3 and 12 ends in *-io*. To form the L-participle of types 13-16, drop the final vowel of the 3rd plural PRESENT and add the L-participle endings, inserting *a* before the masculine singular ending *-o*. Type 16 verbs (including *ići*) replace the stem final consonant with *š*. Type 13 verbs drop the stem final consonant and do not insert *a* in the masculine singular. The verb *hteti* [E] *htjeti* [J] follows type 12, and *moći* follows type 15a. The verb *doneti* [E] *donijeti* [J] follows type 12 in the past tense but type 14 in the present tense. The L-participle of *umreti* [E] *umrijeti* [J] is *umro*, *umrla*, etc. (with *r* functioning as a vowel). Verbs which add *n* in the present tense (such as *pasti*, *padnem* "fall" *and pomoći*, *pomognem* "help") drop this consonant in the past tense. [104a] The chart below lists only masculine and feminine singular, since all the other forms can be predicted from the feminine singular.

Type/infin.	3 (*videti* [E])	(*vidjeti* [J])	12 (*hteti* [E])	(*hteti* [J])	14/12 (*doneti* [E])	(*donijeti* [J])
masculine sg	*video*	*vidio*	*hteo*	*htio*	*donio*	*donio*
feminine sg	*videla*	*vidjela*	*htela*	*htjela*	*donela*	*donijela*

	7 (*krenuti*)	13 (*pasti*)	14 (*dovesti*)	15a (*teći*)	15b (*pomoći*)	16 (*doći*)
masculine sg	*krenuo*	*pao*	*dovezao*	*tekao*	*pomogao*	*došao*
feminine sg	*krenula*	*pala*	*dovezla*	*tekla*	*pomogla*	*došla*

* Usage of the past tense *

The past tense auxiliary is equivalent to the present tense of *biti*. The clitic form is used in most instances, while the full form is used to ask questions, to show emphasis or in single-word answers, and the negated form of *biti* expresses negation. [104b] If two past tense forms have the same subject and occur near each other in the same clause, the auxiliary need not be repeated. For example, one can say either *išla sam i našla se s društvom* (with only one instance of the auxiliary *sam*) or *išla sam i našla sam se s društvom* (with two instances of it). The auxiliary can also be dropped in certain narrative styles, such as fairy tales. [104c] When the 3rd singular auxiliary *je* occurs next to *se*, what is known as "se-merger" occurs: the *je* is dropped. Thus one says *vratio sam se* "I came back," but *vratio se* "he came back." [111a] When particular emphasis is desired, C may keep the *je*, and say *vratio se je*. [111b] When the feminine singular accusative clitic *je* occurs adjacent to the 3rd singular auxiliary *je*, it is replaced by *ju*. Thus one says *ti se je upoznao* "you made her acquaintance," but *on ju je upoznao* "he made her acquaintance." [104c, 111a]

* Past and future tense of "existential" *ima* and *nema* *

The past tense of *ima* is *bilo je*, and the past tense of *nema* is *nije bilo*. [104e] The future tense of these existential verbs is likewise formed with the verb *biti*: the future of *ima* is *biće* / *bit će*, and the future of *nema* is *neće biti*. [95d]

Entrance

Exit

VOCABULARY

izgùbiti, ìzgubīm	to lose (P)	pòglāvlje	chapter
izgùbiti glȁvu	to panic (P)	poznȁti	to be familiar with (P)
kontrolnī [zadàtak]	test	pročìtati	to read (P)
napìsati, napȋšēm	to write (P)	prošlī	previous, last
napòkon	finally	trèćī	third
naùčiti, nàučīm	to learn (P)	ùspeti, ùspēm	to succeed (P)
òdlaziti	to leave (I)	ùspjeti, ùspijēm	to succeed (P)
òpet	again	verovàtan, verovàtna [S]	probable
òtīći, òdēm; òtišao	to leave (P)	vjerojàtan, vjerojàtna [C]	probable
pȁdati	to fall; to fail [exam] (I)	vjerovàtan, vjerovàtna [B]	probable
pȁsti, pȁdnēm; pao	to fall; to fail [exam] (P)		

PISATI I NAPISATI

Bosnian
1. Pìšēš li *dòmaću zàdaću?*
2. Ne, vèć sam *ih* napìsao.
1. Vjerovȁtno čìtāš *trèćē pòglāvlje* u udžbèniku.
2. Ne, vèć sam *ga* pročìtao.
1. Da li ondà polàžēš *ìspit iz bòsanskōga* u ponèdjeljak?
2. Da! Jer prošlòg pùta nìsam polòžio, vèć sam izgùbio glȁvu i pao.
1. Òdlazīš li òpet dànas na fakùltet?
2. Ne. Òtišao sam u pètak. Dànas ùčīm cijèlog dàna kod kùće.
1. Bravo, jer ćeš tàko sve naùčiti i nèćeš vìšē padȁti!
2. Bit će mi drȁgo napòkon ùspjeti!

Croatian
1. Pìšēš li *dòmaću zàdaću?*
2. Ne, vèć sam *je* napìsao.
1. Vjerojȁtno čìtāš *trèćē pòglāvlje* u udžbèniku.
2. Ne, vèć sam *ga* pročìtao.
1. Polàžēš li ondà *ìspit iz hrvȁtskōga* u ponèdjeljak?
2. Da! Jer prošlòga pùta nìsam polòžio, vèć sam izgùbio glȁvu i pao.
1. Òdlazīš li òpet dànas na fakùltet?
2. Ne. Òtišao sam u pètak. Dànas ùčīm cijèlog dàna kod kùće.
1. Bravo, jer ćeš tàko sve naùčiti i nèćeš vìšē padȁti!
2. Bit će mi drȁgo napòkon ùspjeti!

Serbian
1. Da li pìšēš *dòmaće zadàtke?*
2. Ne, vèć sam *ih* napìsao.
1. Verovȁtno čìtāš *trèćē pòglāvlje* u udžbèniku.
2. Ne, vèć sam *ga* pročìtao.
1. Da li ondà polàžēš *ìspit iz srpskòg* u ponèdeljak?
2. Da! Jer prošlòg pùta nìsam polòžio, vèć sam izgùbio glȁvu i pao.
1. Da li òdlazīš òpet dànas na fakùltet?
2. Ne. Òtišao sam u pètak. Dànas ùčīm cèlog dàna kod kùće.
1. Bravo, jer tàko ćeš sve naùčiti i nèćeš vìšē padȁti!
2. Bìće mi drȁgo napòkon da ùspēm!

❦☞ **Replace** *dòmaća zàdaća* [B,C] *dòmaćī zadàtak* [S] **with** prȉča; *trèćē pòglāvlje* **with** pȋsmenā vȅžba [E] vjȅžba [J]; *ìspit iz bòsanskōga* **or** *ìspit iz hrvȁtskōga* **or** *ìspit iz srpskòg* **with** kontrolnī iz gramàtike.

❦☞ **Redo** the exercise with female subjects.

 **GRAMMAR**

* Word order in the past tense *

Any time there is more than one clitic present, all of them must occur in a specific order. The order can be visualized in terms of six possible slots (see box below). [64] The question particle *li* always comes in slot 1, and verbal auxiliaries (both future and past tense) in slot 2. Object pronouns come in slot 3 (dative) and slot 4 (genitive-accusative), respectively. The particle *se* comes in slot 5. The hardest to remember is that the 3rd singular auxiliary must come in slot 6 (instead of in slot 2 with all the other auxiliaries): this is called the "*je*-final" rule. [104c, 111a] Thus, one says *ti si mu ga dala* "you [f.] gave it to him" [order 2-3-4] but *ona mu ga je dala* "she gave it to him" [order 3-4-6]. Here is a chart summarizing the order of clitics:

1	2	3	4	5	6
li	all auxiliaries other than *je*	dative object pronouns	genitive-accusative object pronouns	*se*	3rd singular auxiliary *je*

* Verbal aspect, continued *

The imperfective aspect describes either an action in progress, a repeated action, or the general fact of an action. It can be translated by the English progressive tenses only in the first of these meanings. Imperfective verbs are most frequent in the present tense. In the past and future tenses they express both one of the above meanings, and the fact of past or future action without specific focus on completion. Perfective verbs by definition contain the idea of closure, and usually describe single completed actions; this is their most frequent use in the past and future tenses. Aspect is often a function of the verb's meaning, as some verbs are inherently more disposed to the idea of perfective (such as "arrive") while others more inherently disposed to the idea of imperfective (such as "do" or "live"). [106b] It can also happen that the perfective and imperfective partners correspond to different verbal meanings in English. The chart below illustrates the use of imperfective verbs in present and past tenses.

Imperfective aspect	Present tense	Past tense
ongoing	*Pišeš li pismo nekome?* "Are you writing a letter to someone?"	*Dugo si pisao.* "You were writing for a long time."
repeated	*On često piše majci.* "He writes to his mother often."	*Ranije je pisao svaki dan.* "He used to write every day."
fact	*Taj pisac dobro piše.* "That author writes well."	*Mnogo sam pisao danas.* "I wrote a lot today."

At this point the student should review verb vocabulary and learn aspect partners for the most common verbs. Normally the same English verb translates both partners of a pair, but in some instances the two correspond to different English verbs. In some pairs the perfective is marked by a prefix [96b, 146c] and in others the difference between the two is marked by a suffix. Suffixation is the more complex process since it almost always involves a change in conjugation type and usually one or more other processes as well. [96a, 147a] For instance, the imperfective verb *davati* differs from its perfective partner *dati* in terms of verb type (type 1 vs. type 9 - whose marker is in fact the suffix *-va*). The imperfective *polagati* differs from the perfective *položiti* in four different ways –in verb type (type 5 vs. type 2), in the stem final consonant (-*ž* vs. -*g*), in the stem vowel itself (*o* vs. *a*), and in the length of this vowel. Motion verbs keep the same prefix in both aspects, but the root is different: *otići* vs. *odlaziti* "leave," *doći* vs. *dolaziti* "come," and the like. [54]

The charts on the next page give examples of prefixation and suffixation. After studying them, the student should begin to review the different types of aspect relationships by leafing through this book's glossary.

145

Deseta lekcija   Lesson Ten

PREFIXATION				SUFFIXATION		
imperfective	*jesti*	eat		imperfective	*padati*	fall [often], be falling
perfective	*pojesti*	eat [up]		perfective	*pasti*	fall [once]
imperfective	*učiti*	study		imperfective	*polagati*	put, take an exam
perfective	*naučiti*	learn		perfective	*položiti*	put down, pass an exam

TYPES OF SUFFIXATION

perfective	type	imperfective	type	other changes	
dati	1	*davati*	9	suffix -*va*	give
poznati	1	*poznavati*	9	suffix -*va*	know
ostati	5/10	*ostajati*	5	suffix -*aj*	stay
uključiti	2	*uključivati*	8b	suffix –*iva*	include
svideti se [E] *svidjeti se* [J]	3	*sviđati se*	1	consonant shift	be pleasing to
osjetiti se	2	*osjećati se*	1	consonant shift	feel
pustiti	2	*puštati*	1	consonant shift	let, allow
odgovoriti	2	*odgovarati*	1	stem vowel shift	answer

* Subjectless sentences *

Subjectless sentences are those without a grammatical subject. Some types, such as impersonal sentences, lack a grammatical subject altogether, [140] while others have a "logical subject" in some case other than the nominative. The unifying feature is that all such sentences have 3rd singular verbs in the present tense and neuter singular L-participles in the past tense. [141] Subjectless sentences with the dative are of several sorts, including those with inclinational *se*-verbs, *sviđati se* and *činiti se*. [141b] Subjectless sentences with the genitive usually concern measurement of some sort. [141c] Subjectless sentences with the accusative express the identity of a person experiencing an emotion such as shame, worry, fear or the like. [105]

	present	past	
impersonal	*Ne može se reći.*	*Nije se moglo reći.*	It can't / couldn't be said.
(dative)	*Dobro mi je.*	*Dobro mi je bilo.*	I am / was fine.
(genitive)	*Mnogo ih ima.*	*Mnogo ih je bilo.*	There are / were a lot of them.
(accusative)	*Strah me je.*	*Strah me je bilo.*	I am / was afraid.

In the center of Zagreb; everything for your eyes

The vocabulary and reading for this section are on the next two pages. Turn the page now and read the poem. After that, come back to this page and do the exercises based on the poem.

1. [B,C] Naučite ovu pjesmu napamet.

   [S] Naučite ovu pesmu napamet.

2. [B,C] Napišite novu verziju pjesme: umjesto *lava* stavite *lavicu*, i umjesto muškog imena *Brana* stavite žensko ime *Branka*.

   [S] Napišite novu verziju pesme: umesto *lava* stavite *lavicu*, i umesto muškog imena *Brana* stavite žensko ime *Branka*.

3. [B,C] Objasnite je li ova pjesma na bosanskom, hrvatskom ili srpskom? Po čemu znate?

   [S] Objasnite da li je ova pesma na bosanskom, hrvatskom ili srpskom? Po čemu znate?

4. [B,C] Opišite oba lika u pjesmi: lava i Branu. Kako izgledaju, koliko su mladi ili stari, koje su im osnovne crte, i kako se osjećaju?

   [S] Opišite oba lika u pesmi: lava i Branu. Kako izgledaju, koliko su mladi ili stari, koje su im osnovne crte, i kako se osećaju?

5. [B,C] Razmislite o lavu i o Brani. Je li Branu strah lava, ili lava strah Brane?

   [S] Razmislite o lavu i o Brani. Da li je Branu strah od lava, ili lava strah od Brane?

6. [B,C] Zašto Brana zapravo briše lava s papira? Sumnja li u svoje sposobnosti crtanja? A vi? Kako vi ocjenjujete Branine sposobnosti crtanja?

   [S] Zašto Brana zapravo briše lava sa papira? Da li sumnja u svoje sposobnosti crtanja? A Vi? Kako Vi ocenjujete Branine sposobnosti crtanja?

7. [B] Ko je zbilja glavni lik ove pjesme, Brana ili lav? Zbog čega ste to zaključili?

   [C] Tko je zbilja glavni lik ove pjesme, Brana ili lav? Zbog čega ste to zaključili?

   [S] Ko je zbilja glavni lik ove pesme, Brana ili lav? Zbog čega ste to zaključili?

8. [B] Šta je laž, a šta je istina u pjesmi?

   [C] Što je laž, a što je istina u pjesmi?

   [S] Šta je laž, a šta je istina u pesmi?

The idea of fear can be expressed either by the verbs *plašiti se* "be frightened of" and *bojati se* "to fear," or by a subjectless sentence with accusative logical subject, of the form *strah me je* (meaning "I am afraid"). The construction with *strah me je* is normally used more with concrete objects, as is *plašiti se*, whereas *bojati se* is used with abstract contexts. With all three, that which one fears is expressed in the genitive case. In the *strah me je* construction the preposition *od* is added in S and may optionally be added in B and C. Thus one says *bojim se visine* "I am afraid of heights," *plašim se miševa* "I am frightened of mice," and either *strah me je zmija* or *strah me je od zmija* "I am afraid of snakes."

VOCABULARY

bio jednom	once there was...	opisati, opišem	to describe (P)
brisati, brišem	to erase (I)	osećati se	to feel (emotion) (I)
crta	feature, trait	osjećati se	to feel (emotion) (I)
crtanje	drawing	osnovni	basic
dok ne	until	oštar, oštra	sharp
guma	eraser	pesma	poem, song
istina	truth	pjesma	poem, song
izbrisati, izbrišem	to erase (P)	pogled	look, gaze
laž *(f)*	falsehood, lie	razmisliti	to ponder, to think (P)
lik	character	sposobnost, sposobnosti *(f)*	capability
ljut	angry	strah	fear
milost, milosti *(f)*	mercy	strah [ga] je	[he] is afraid
muški	masculine, male	sumnjati, sumnjam	to doubt (I)
napamet	by heart	uho; uši, *Gpl* ušiju [B,C,S]	ear
narogušen	bristling	umesto + *Gen*	instead of
naučiti napamet	to memorize (P)	umjesto + *Gen*	instead of
noga; *Gpl* nogu	leg, foot	uvo; uši, *Gpl* ušiju [S]	ear
objasniti, objasnim	to explain (P)	verzija	version
oblak	cloud	zaključiti, zaključim	to conclude (P)
oceniti, ocenim	to judge (P)	zapravo	actually
ocenjivati, ocenjujem	to evaluate (I)	zbilja	really, truly
ocijeniti, ocijenim	to judge (P)	zbog + *Gen*	because of, due to
ocjenjivati, ocjenjujem	to evaluate (I)	ženski	feminine, female
oko; oči, *Gpl* očiju	eye		

"Bio jednom..." (the phrase is always used without the past tense auxiliary), the equivalent of "Once upon a time...," is one of the most common ways to start a BCS story with a male protagonist. The form of the first word of this set opening depends upon the identity of the protagonist. If the protagonist is female, the tale will begin with *"Bila jednom... ,"* while a tale with a neuter protagonist starts with *"Bilo jednom..."*. Less frequently, one finds tales with a group as protagonists. Such tales would begin *"Bili jednom..."*.

Bio jèdnom jèdan lav

Dušan Radović

Bio jèdnom jèdan lav.
Kàkav lav?
Strȁšan lav! Narогušen i ljȕt sav.
Strȁšno, strȁšno!

Ne pȉtajte šta je jeo. Tȁj je jȅo šta je hteo.
Tramvȁj ceo, i oblȁka jèdan deo.

Strȁšno! Strȁšno!

Ìšao je na trȋ noge.
Gledao je na trȋ oka.
Slušao je na trȋ uva.
Strȁšno! Strȁšno!

Zȕbi oštrȋ, poglȅd zao,
Ȍn za milȍst nȉje znao.
Strȁšno! Strȁšno!

Dok ga Brȁna jèdnog dȁna
Nȉje gùmоm ìzbrisao.
Strȁšno! Strȁšno!

bolestan, bolesna	sick	pisanje	writing
boleti, boli	to hurt (I)	po mom mišljenju	in my opinion
boljeti, boli	to hurt (I)	pomagati, pomažem + *Dat*	to help (I)
čuvaj se!	be careful	pomoći; pomognem; pomogao + *Dat*	to help (P)
čuvati, čuvam	to keep, to protect (I)	razbuditi se, razbudim se	to wake up fully (P)
dosta	enough	prst; *Npl* prsti, *Gpl* prstiju	finger, toe
glava	head	rame; ramena	shoulder
koleno	knee	skupa [C]	together
koljeno	knee	slagati se, slažem se	to agree (I)
kosa	hair	stomak, stomaka [S]	belly, gut
lakat; laktovi	elbow	stopalo	foot, sole of foot
leđa *(pl form)*	back	šaka	hand, fist
mišljenje	opinion, thinking	trbuh [B,C]	belly, gut
način	way, manner	umoran, umorna	tired
naročito	especially	verovati, verujem + *Dat*	to believe (I)
na taj način	[in] that way	vjerovati, vjerujem + *Dat*	to believe (I)
nos, nosa	nose	vrat	neck
nožni palac	big toe	zaboraviti	to forget (P)
obrva	eyebrow	zdrav	healthy
odvesti, odvezem	to transport [away] (P)	želudac, želuca	stomach
palac, palca	thumb, big toe		

BOLE ME I NOGE I RUKE!

Bosnian
1. Pomozi mi, molim te! Bole me i *noge* i ruke i *leđa*, a naročito *prsti!*
2. Jesi li bolestan?
1. Ne, čini mi se da sam zdrav, samo umoran. Ne mogu nositi ove *knjige*.
2. Čuvaj se! Pomoći ću ti! Ali ako ja tebi pomažem, ti isto meni moraš pomoći.
1. U pisanju zadataka? Hajde da učimo zajedno. Po mom mišljenju, ja i ti ćemo na taj način najlakše sve objasniti.
2. Slažem se. Glava me već boli od učenja. Prvo ćemo odnijeti *knjige*, onda ću te odvesti kod sebe kući kolima, pa ćemo tamo skupa učiti.
1. Pomogla nam je prošlog puta i *kafa!* Moram se razbuditi. Spava mi se.
2. Vjeruj mi, nisam na to zaboravila! Ako te ne boli i trbuh, imam dosta *kafe* i za tebe i za sebe.

Croatian
1. Pomozi mi, molim te! Bole me i *noge* i ruke i *leđa*, a naročito *prsti!*
2. Jesi li bolestan?
1. Ne, čini mi se da sam zdrav, samo umoran. Ne mogu nositi ove *knjige*.
2. Čuvaj se! Pomoći ću ti! Ali ako ja tebi pomažem, ti isto meni moraš pomoći.
1. U pisanju zadaća? Hajde da učimo zajedno. Po mom mišljenju, ja i ti ćemo na taj način najlakše sve objasniti.
2. Slažem se. Glava me već boli od učenja. Prvo ćemo odnijeti *knjige*, onda ću te odvesti k sebi doma kolima, pa ćemo tamo skupa učiti.
1. Pomogla nam je prošlog puta i *kava!* Moram se razbuditi. Spava mi se.
2. Vjeruj mi, nisam na to zaboravila! Ako te ne boli i trbuh, imam dosta *kave* i za tebe i za sebe.

Tricky translation: *Želudac* is the precise word for "stomach," while the words *stomak* [S] and *trbuh* [B,C] refer more generally to the overall abdominal area, and are often translated as "belly" or "gut," but also "stomach." *Ruka* means both "hand" and "arm," and *noga* means both "foot" and "leg." The more precise terms for "hand" and "foot" are *šaka* and *stopalo*, respectively. **[110a]**

Serbian

1. Помози ми, молим те! Боле ме и *ноге* и руке, *леђа*, а нарочито *прсти!*

2. Да ли си болестан?

1. Не, чини ми се да сам здрав, само уморан. Не могу да носим ове *књиге.*

2. Чувај се! Помоћи ћу ти! Али ако ја теби помажем, ти исто мени мораш да помогнеш.

1. У писању задатака? Хајде да учимо заједно. По мом мишљењу, ја и ти ћемо на тај начин најлакше све да објаснимо.

2. Слажем се. Глава ме већ боли од учења. Прво ћемо да однесемо *књиге*, онда ћу да те одвезем код себе кући колима, па ћемо тамо заједно да учимо.

1. Помогла нам је прошлог пута и *кафа!* Морам да се разбудим. Спава ми се.

2. Веруј ми, нисам на то заборавила! Ако те не боли и стомак, имам доста *кафе* и за тебе и за себе.

☞ **Replace** *prsti* **with** palci.

☞ **Replace** *noga* **with** koleno [E] koljeno [J], **and** *leđa* **with** ramena.

☞ **Replace** *knjige* **with** rečnici [E] rječnici [J], stolice, stolovi.

☞ **Replace** *kafa* [B,S] *kava* [C] **with** vino, pivo.

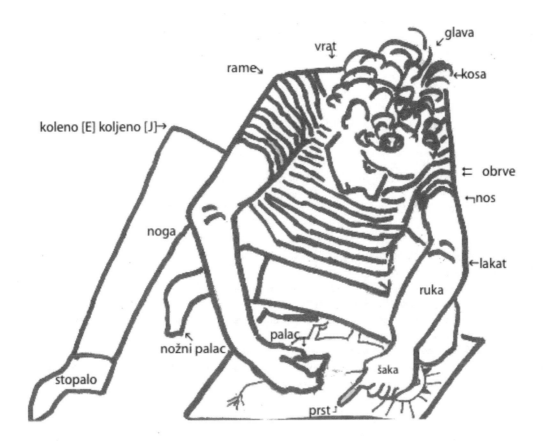

 **GRAMMAR**

* Verbal nouns *

Nouns can be formed from verbal roots by adding the suffix *-nje* preceded by a long vowel. If the verb's infinitive ends in *-ati*, that vowel is *a*. Otherwise it is *e*, which can (but does not always) cause a change in the stem-final consonant. **[112c]** These nouns usually refer to the ongoing process of an action but they can also refer to the fact of an action. **[108, 116]** For more on this type of consonant shift, see p. 163.

Suffix: *-anje*			Suffix: *-enje*		
infinitive	verbal noun		infinitive	verbal noun	
čitati	čitanje	reading	učiti	učenje	learning
pisati	pisanje	writing	misliti	mišljenje	thinking, opinion
crtati	crtanje	drawing	objasniti	objašnjenje	explanation

* The human body *

A number of nouns referring to parts of the body have irregular forms. The words meaning "eye" and "ear" are neuter in the singular. Their plural forms, however, are feminine, with the endings of feminine nouns in a consonant, and with Gpl. in *-iju*. The singular of "ear" is *uho* [B,C] or *uvo* [S] (although *uho* is also used). Several other paired body parts have Gpl. forms in *-u*. **[110a]**

Nsg	Asg	Gsg	DLsg	Isg	NApl	Gpl	DLIpl	
oko	oko	oka	oku	okom	oči	očiju	očima	eye
uho	uho	uha	uhu	uhom	uši	ušiju	ušima	ear
uvo	uvo	uva	uvu	uvom	uši	ušiju	ušima	ear
ruka	ruku	ruke	ruci	rukom	ruke	ruku	rukama	hand, arm
noga	nogu	noge	nozi	nogom	noge	nogu	nogama	leg, foot

When a body part "hurts," the body part itself is the subject of the sentence, and the person who feels the pain in his or her body is expressed in the accusative case. The verb is *boleti / boljeti*. Thus, for instance, *noge me bole* "my feet hurt," or *glava je boli* "her head hurts." **[110b]**

* Verbs of transport *

As seen in Lesson 7, BCS has three different verbs meaning "take [something or someone] [somewhere]," all rhyming with each other to an extent, and all with largely predictable meanings. Thus, if one is taking an object, or a living being that must be carried (such as a baby), the verbal root *nos-* is used. The other two concern a living being capable of moving under its own power. If one is "taking" this being somewhere on foot, the verbal root *vod-* is used, but if the movement is by vehicle, the verbal root *voz-* is used. The imperfective verbs all end in *-iti*. In their perfective partners, which exist only in prefixed form, the roots are *-nes-*, *-ved-*, and *-vez-*, respectively. The most neutral perfective is with the prefix *od-*. Other prefixes such as *do-*, *u-*, *pre-*, *iz-*, are added to both members of the pair, creating in each instance a frequently used new aspect pair with often abstract meanings. Below, this process is illustrated using the prefix *pre-*. **[107]**

	IMPERFECTIVE		PERFECTIVE	
	infinitive	1sg pres.	infinitive	1sg pres.
carry	nositi	nosim	odneti [E] odnijeti [J]	odnesem
take (on foot), lead	voditi	vodim	odvesti	odvedem
take (by vehicle)	voziti	vozim	odvesti	odvezem
transmit, pass on	prenositi	prenosim	preneti [E] prenijeti [J]	prenesem
translate	prevoditi	prevodim	prevesti	prevedem
transport	prevoziti	prevozim	prevesti	prevezem

🚶 VJEŽBE [B,C] VEŽBE [S]

B1

Bosnian	Croatian	Serbian
1. Šta si radio u subotu i nedjelju?	1. Što si radio u subotu i nedjelju?	1. Шта си радио у суботу и недељу?
2. Preko vikenda sam išao na *koncert* i *učio*.	2. Preko vikenda sam išao na *koncert* i *učio*.	2. Преко викенда сам ишао на *концерт* и *учио*.
1. I jesi li *naučio* sve?	1. I jesi li *naučio* sve?	1. И да ли си *научио* све?
2. Jesam ovog puta! Pao sam na ispitu prošlog petka, ali neću sad pasti.	2. Jesam ovoga puta! Pao sam na ispitu prošlog petka, ali ne ću sad pasti.	2. Јесам овог пута! Пао сам на испиту прошлог петка, али нећу сад да паднем.

🖝 **Replace** *koncert* **with** (u) bioskop [S] (u) kino [B,C], (u) kazalište [C] (u) pozorište [B,S] **and** *učiti* (I) *naučiti* (P) **with** čitati (I) pročitati (P); pisati (I) napisati (P).

🖝 **Redo** the exercise so that #2 is a female speaker.

B2

Ask each other these questions in the past tense. After that, then make each one into a question about the future.

Bosnian	Croatian	Serbian
1. Šta si radio preko vikenda?	1. Što si radio preko vikenda?	1. Šta si radio preko vikenda?
2. Šta si radila u ponedjeljak popodne?	2. Što si radila u ponedjeljak popodne?	2. Šta si radila u ponedeljak popodne?
3. Kako su ti profesori pomogli prije ispita?	3. Kako su ti profesori pomogli prije ispita?	3. Kako su ti profesori pomogli pre ispita?
4. Šta si pročitala preko ljeta?	4. Što si pročitala preko ljeta?	4. Šta si pročitala preko leta?
5. Da li si napisao cijelu domaću zadaću za danas?	5. Jesi li napisao cijelu domaću zadaću za danas?	5. Da li si napisao celi domaći zadatak za danas?
6. Šta si gledao u kinu prošlog petka?	6. Što si gledao u kinu prošlog petka?	6. Šta si gledao u bioskopu prošlog petka?

B3

Bosnian, Croatian	Serbian
1. Jao, *glava* me boli!	1. Jao, *глава* ме боли!
2. Bole li te i *trbuh* i *glava*?	2. Да ли те боле и *стомак* и глава?
1. Ne, samo me glava boli, ali boli strašno!	1. Не, само ме глава боли, али боли страшно!

🖝 **Replace** *glava* and *trbuh* or *stomak* with

a) oči **and** uši **and** nos

b) šake **and** prsti **and** palci

c) stopala **and** prsti **and** nožni palci

d) leđa **and** vrat **and** ramena

🖝 **Remember** to make any appropriate adjustments to the verbs.

B4

Bosnian	Croatian	Serbian
1. Nema *običnih olovaka* nigdje u ovoj sobi!	1. Nema *običnih olovaka* nigdje u ovoj sobi!	1. Nema *običnih olovaka* nigde u ovoj sobi!
2. Juče ujutro ih je bilo, ali jutros kad sam se probudio više ih nije bilo.	2. Jučer ujutro ih je bilo, ali jutros kad sam se probudio više ih nije bilo.	2. Juče ujutro ih je bilo, ali jutros kad sam se probudio više ih nije bilo.
1. A da li je bilo *hemijskih olovaka* u onoj *torbi* jutros?	1. A je li bilo *kemijskih olovaka* u onoj *torbi* jutros?	1. A da li je bilo *hemijskih olovaka* u onoj *torbi* jutros?
2. Da, bilo ih je u ovoj *torbi,* ali sad ih nema.	2. Da, bilo ih je u ovoj *torbi,* ali sad ih nema.	2. Da, bilo ih je u ovoj *torbi,* ali sad ih nema.
1. Izgleda da smo ih zbilja izgubili.	1. Izgleda da smo ih zbilja izgubili.	1. Izgleda da smo ih zbilja izgubili.

☞ **Replace** *olovke* **with** kratka pisma, nemački [E] njemački [J] udžbenici, slatke kruške.

☞ **Replace** *torba* **with** prostorija, sto [B,S] stol [C], soba, zgrada.

☞ **Use** this exchange as a model for narrating an instance when you lost something.

Self-study learners: Pay attention to the way *nema, bilo* and *nije bilo* are used.

B5

Bosnian and Croatian	Serbian
1. *Profesori* nam *pomažu,* ali mi *njima* ne *pomažemo!*	1. *Професори* нам *помажу,* али ми њима не *помажемо!*
2. Zašto *im* ne *pomažete?*	2. Зашто им не *помажете?*
1. Zato što još ne znamo dosta o ovom pitanju!	1. Зато што још не знамо доста о овом питању!
2. Učite pa ćete naučiti!	2. Учите па ћете да научите!

☞ **Redo** this conversation in the past tense. Keep the verb *pomoći* but use the singular forms *profesor, profesorica* [B,C] *profesorka* [S]

B6

a. **Make a present tense version of exercise** B5, **replacing** *pomagati* **with** govoriti **(in the case of** profesori**) and** odgovarati **(in the case of** mi**). Then make a past-tense version of it, replacing** *pomoći* **with** govoriti **(in the case of** profesori**) and** odgovoriti **(in the case of** mi**).**

b. **Make both present and past tense versions of the same exercise, this time replacing** *pomagati* **and** *pomoći* **with** verovati [E] vjerovati [J].

B7

Work in pairs to come up with fifteen examples of time expressions, five each using the accusative, the genitive, and the instrumental.

Self-study learners: Go back over the last several lessons and make a list of the different sorts of time expressions you have seen. What sorts of generalizations can you make about the ways different cases are used to express the idea of time?

✍ DOMAĆA ZADAĆA [B,C] DOMAĆI ZADATAK [S]

C1

Translate:

1. We will have friends in France and Greece. We had friends in England and Germany.
2. They will go by car through New York. They went by train through North America.
3. I will eat meat. He ate four apples and six oranges.
4. I will go to Argentina for a month.
5. With whom will you live in the fall? Last year I lived with a friend.
6. Will you explain this to me? I don't understand.

C2

For each blank in the following sentences, choose the correct aspectual form from the pair of verbs in parentheses at the end of the sentence, and supply it with the endings required by the sentence.

1. [B,C] .... mi ..... odmah! Svaki dan ja ti .... , a ti mi ..... nìsi .... već mjesec dana.

   [S] .... mi ..... odmah! Svaki dan ja ti .... , a ti mi ..... nìsi .... već mesec dana.
      (javljati se, javiti se)

2. Koliko puta moram .... ovaj ispit da ga .... ? (polagati, položiti)

3. [B,C] Kad me zoveš, uvijek .... ali prošlog petka nisam mogla ....   (dolaziti, doći)

   [S] Kad me zoveš, uvek .... ali prošlog petka nisam mogla ....   (dolaziti, doći)

4. [B,C] .... u grad! Sada mi .... na fakultet, a poslije ćemo i mi .... u grad. (polaziti, poći)

   [S] .... u grad! Sada mi .... na fakultet, a posle ćemo i mi .... u grad.   (polaziti, poći)

5. On satima već .... Kada će taj roman .... ?   (čitati, pročitati)

6. [B,C] Ti uvijek meni rukom .... divna pisma, ali sam ja danas tebi .... pismo preko

   interneta!   (pisati, napisati)

   [S] Ti uvek meni rukom .... divna pisma, ali sam ja danas tebi .... pismo preko interneta!
      (pisati, napisati)

7. [B] Juče ste joj .... hljeb, jaja i mlijeko. Danas joj mi .... šećer, kafu i čaj.

   [C] Jučer ste joj .... kruh, jaja i mlijeko. Danas joj mi .... šećer, kavu i čaj.

   [S] Juče ste joj .... hleb, jaja i mleko. Danas joj mi .... šećer, kafu i čaj.
      (kupovati, kupiti)

8. .... mu! Oni su mu već ....   (odgovarati, odgovoriti)

9. [B] Obično ujutro .... mnogo soka od narandže, ali juče sam .... dvije čaše mlijeka.

   [C] Obično ujutro .... mnogo soka od naranče, ali jučer sam .... dvije čaše mlijeka.

   [B] Obično ujutro .... mnogo soka od pomorandže, ali juče sam .... dve čaše mleka.
      (piti, popiti)

10. Kad .... krušku, dođi ovamo!   (jesti, pojesti)

11. .... stan! Strašno je neuredan.   (spremati, spremiti)

12. [B,C] Pet sati je. Vrijeme mi je da ....   (odlaziti, otići)

    [S] Pet sati je. Vreme mi je da ....   (odlaziti, otići)

13. [B,C] Jesi li .... lice?   (prati, oprati)

    [S] Da li si .... lice?   (prati, oprati)

14. .... novac za benzin.   (uzimati, uzeti)

15. On je nekoliko puta .... na ovom ispitu.   (padati, pasti)

16. [B] Ako .... kompjuter ovdje na sto, bit će mi bolje raditi.   (stavljati, staviti)

    [C] Ako .... kompjutor ovdje na stol, bit će mi bolje raditi.   (stavljati, staviti)

    [S] Ako .... kompjuter ovde na sto, biće mi bolje raditi.   (stavljati, staviti)

17. [B] Nikad nećeš znati kako .... to što radim.   (ocjenjivati, ocijeniti)

    [C] Nikad ne ćeš znati kako .... to što radim.   (ocjenjivati, ocijeniti)

    [S] Nikad nećeš znati kako .... to što radim.   (ocenjivati, oceniti)

C3

Translate the first sentence in each group into English. Then translate the two that follow it into B, C or S using the first sentence as a model.

1. a. Pojeo je tramvaj ceo.
   b. We ate five pears.
   c. Once there was a lioness and she ate a part of a cloud.

2. a. Dovezli smo vam teške stvari kolima, a lake stvari smo vam nosili u rukama.
   b. We carried the child to the restaurant.
   c. We brought you this beautiful chair by train.

3. a. Nije bilo više vremena.
   b. There were no pears in the house.
   c. There were no things in the car.

4. a. Prošle subote smo joj pomogli.
   b. Today I am helping you.
   c. They helped the people.

5. a. Svejedno im je.
   b. It doesn't matter to us.
   c. It does matter to me.

6. a. Zašto ne ješ? Zbog toga što nisam gladna.
   b. Why aren't you sleeping? Because it is three o'clock in the afternoon.
   c. Why aren't you writing your homework assignment? Because it isn't interesting.

C4

Match word to picture. Note that one picture may illustrate more than one word!

stopala nòga prst obrve lȉce oči glȁva uho [B,C] palac nȍs kòsa rȕka šaka kòleno [E]
uvo [S]   kòljeno [J]

C5

Insert a noun related to a part of the body after each number. Write the number out in words.
glȁva, oko, nòga, palac, prsti, rȕka, stòmak [S] tȑbuh [B,C], uho [B,C] uvo [S], vrat, želùdac.

For example: sedam glȁva

1

2

3

4

5

6

7

8

9

10

C6

1. Which of the masculine body-part nouns have plurals ending in *-ovi* or *-evi*?
2. Which of the body-part nouns have genitive plurals ending in *-u*?
3. Which of these words has a phonetic change in the dative/locative singular?
4. Which of these words has a phonetic change in the nominative plural?
5. Of the body part names you have learned so far, which one is used only in the plural form?
6. List all the neuter nouns among the body-part vocabulary, singular and plural.

☺☹ Aforizmi Dušana Radovića

VOCABULARY

довољан, довољна	enough	последњи	final, last
жалостан, жалосна	sorrowful	пошљедњи	final, last
место	place	пресретан, пресретна [B,C]	overjoyed
мјесто	place	пресрећан, пресрећна [S]	overjoyed
наћи, нађем; нашао	to find (P)	родити се	to be born (P)
паркирање	parking	стићи, стигнем	get around to

Неко је јутрос срећан, пресрећан, јер је нашао место за паркирање. Неко други је тужан и жалостан, јер му се родило женско дете.

Последњи је дан друге школске недеље. Ђаци још нису стигли да не уче, нису имали довољно времена.

🌟☞ **Bring** a question on each aphorism to class, incorporating one or more of these phrases:

a. Zar ....?

b. Zbog čega .... ?

c. Objasnite ....

d. [B,S] Šta ste zaključili? [C] Što ste zaključili?

e. O čemu se radi?

f. [B,C] Čini li vam se .... ? [S] Da li vam se čini .... ?

📖 Priča: Albahari

Read Part VII of the story "Osam malih priča o mojoj ženi" by David Albahari (p. 344).

Jedanaesta lekcija • Lesson Eleven

VOCABULARY

gotovo	that's that!	rešen	resolved
haljina	dress	rešiti	to resolve (P)
hlače [B,C] *(pl form)*	pants, trousers	riješen	resolved
jedanaesti	eleventh	riješiti	to resolve (P)
košulja	shirt	smatrati, smatram	to consider (I)
pantalone [S] *(pl form)*	pants, trousers	šešir, šešira	hat
pokušati	to try (P)	važan, važna	important
rasprava	discussion	završen	finished
rečen, rečena	said	završiti, završim	to finish (P)

VAŽNO, VAŽNIJE, NAJVAŽNIJE

<u>Bosnian</u>
1. Tvoje *pitanje* je bilo *važno* ali moje je bilo *važnije!*
2. Tačno, ali je moje *pitanje* svakako bilo *zanimljivije!*
3. Dosta je rečeno. Moje *pitanje* je i *važnije* i *zanimljivije* od vaših, i gotovo!
1. [*turning to fourth student*] Ti nam pokušaj reći: ko je od nas imao *najzanimljivije pitanje?*
4. Riješena je stvar! Rasprava je završena! Zaključio sam da svako smatra svoje *pitanje najzanimljivijim!*

<u>Croatian</u>
1. Tvoje je *pitanje* bilo *važno* ali moje je bilo *važnije!*
2. Točno, ali je moje *pitanje* svakako bilo *zanimljivije!*
3. Dosta je rečeno. Moje je *pitanje* i *važnije* i *zanimljivije* od vaših, i gotovo!
1. [*turning to fourth student*] Ti nam pokušaj reći: tko je od nas imao *najzanimljivije pitanje?*
4. Riješena je stvar! Rasprava je završena! Zaključio sam da svatko smatra svoje *pitanje najzanimljivijim!*

<u>Serbian</u>
1. Твоје *питање* је било *важно* али је моје било *важније!*
2. Тачно, али је моје *питање* свакако било *занимљивије!*
3. Доста је речено. Моје *питање* је и *важније* и *занимљивије* од ваших, и готово!
1. [*turning to fourth student*] Ти покушај да нам кажеш: ко је од нас имао *најзанимљивије питање?*
4. Решена је ствар! Расправа је завршена! Закључио сам да свако сматра своје *питање најзанимљивијим!*

⤷ **Instead of** *pitanje*, *važni*, *zanimljivi*, **use a)** haljina - šarena, elegantna; **b)** hlače [C] pantalone [B,S] - debele, tople; **c)** kaput - veliki, lepi [E] lijepi [J]; **d)** košulja - duga, tanka; **e)** šešir - visoki, dobri.

Note that there are four different speakers in this exercise, not just the usual two.

He's finished!

 **GRAMMAR**

* Passive participles *

Passive participles are adjective-like words made from verbs; they refer to completed actions. To form the passive participle, add the correct participle marker either to the infinitive stem (found by dropping *-ti*) or to the present stem (found by dropping the final vowel of 3rd pl.pres.). Then add regular adjectival endings.

* Verb types and the formation of passive participles *

There are three different participle markers: *-n*, *-t*, and *-en*. A knowledge of verb types (see the verb chart on p. 142) is very helpful in remembering which verb takes which marker. The marker *-n* is found in most verbs whose infinitive ends in *-ati* (types 1, 4, 5, 8, and 10), and the participle is made by adding the marker *-n* to the infinitive stem. The marker *-t* is found exclusively in verbs of types 7 and 11, and is frequently used in verbs of type 6; it is added to the infinitive stem. The most complex of the three is the marker *-en*, which is found in verbs with infinitives in *-iti* and a number of others as well. To form these participles, add the marker directly to the present stem of verbs of types 13, 14, and 16. Before adding it to the present stem of verbs of types 2, 3, and 15, however, change the stem-final consonant to its softened variant (found in the chart on p. 163). Although the passive participle forms must be learned individually for certain verbs, the system summarized in the chart below works for the vast majority of verbs. The abbreviations PM and C' in the chart below mean "participle marker" and "consonant softening," respectively.

PM	Type	infinitive	3rd pl. present	passive participle	
-n-	1	*pregledati*	*pregledaju*	*pregledan*	checked, examined
	4	*održati*	*održe*	*održan*	held
	5	*napisati*	*napišu*	*napisan*	written
	8	*organizovati*	*organizuju*	*organizovan*	organized
	10	*sabrati*	*saberu*	*sabran*	gathered
-t-	7	*opsednuti*	*opsednu*	*opsednut*	besieged
	11	*zauzeti*	*zauzmu*	*zauzet*	busy, taken
-en-	13	*pojesti*	*pojedu*	*pojeden*	eaten, consumed
	14	*odvesti*	*odvezu*	*odvezen*	driven, taken
		donijeti	*donesu*	*donesen*	brought
	16	*pronaći*	*pronađu*	*pronađen*	discovered
C' *-en-*	2	*postaviti*	*postave*	*postavljen*	placed
	3	*videti / vidjeti*	*vide*	*viđen*	seen
	15	*izvući*	*izvuku*	*izvučen*	drawn out
-t- / -en-	6	*popiti*	*popiju*	*popit / popijen*	drunk [up]
		naliti	*naliju*	*nalit / naliven*	poured [over]
-t- / -n-	(1)	*poslati*	*pošalju*	*poslat / poslan*	sent

* Comparison of adjectives *

Adjectives come in three degrees of comparison: positive, comparative, and superlative (as in English "good, better, best"). To form the BCS comparative degree, add a suffix to the adjective stem, and to form the superlative degree, place the particle *naj-* in front of the comparative form. Comparatives and superlatives are treated as regular adjectives, except that they occur only in the long form (masc. *-i*, etc.). Adverbs are formed from the Nsg neuter comparative or superlative form. [113] Four adjectives express comparison by a different word altogether, [113c] and a number of adjectives follow a model to be seen in the grammar to A2. All others use the suffix *-ij*. The accent is always short rising on the syllable preceding this suffix. [113a] Examples in the left-hand column below are given in the dictionary form, Nsg. masc. short form.

	Positive	[stem]	Comparative	Superlative	
suffix -ij-	važan	važn-	važniji	najvažniji	important (more, most)
	star	star-	stariji	najstariji	old, older, oldest
	zanimljiv	zanimljiv-	zanimljìviji	najzanimljìviji	interesting (more, most)
different word	dobar		bolji	najbolji	good, better, best
	loš		gori	najgori	bad, worse, worst
	velik		veći	najveći	big, bigger, biggest
	mali, malen		manji	najmanji	small, smaller, smallest
[see A-2]	visok	vis-	viši	najviši	tall, taller, tallest

A cafe on Tkalčićeva St. near Zagreb's main square.

Cafe, Novi Sad

A cafe inside Diocletian's palace, Split

VOCABULARY

atmosfèra	ambience	prìjatan, prìjatna	pleasant
bȍlji	better	prȉlog	side dish
čèkanje	waiting	prȍstor	space
dòbiti, dòbijēm	to get (P)	rázličīt	different, distinct
dòduše	furthermore	rȍštilj	grill
dogòvorēn	agreed	sàlata	salad
dogòvoriti se, dogòvorīm se	to agree (P)	sàsvīm	completely
jèdan drugòme	to one another	slàstica [C]	dessert
júha [C]	soup	slȉčan, slȉčna	similar
kùhar [B,C]	cook	specijàlitēt, specijalitéta	speciality
kùvar [S]	cook	sùpa [B,S]	soup
mànjē	less	trèbati	to need (I)
mànjī	smaller	ùdoban, ùdobna	comfortable
nègo	than	uporéditi [B,S], upòredīm	to compare (P)
poréđēnje [B,S]	comparison	ùsporedba [C]	comparison
pòslastica [B,S]	dessert	usporéditi [B,C], uspòredīm	to compare (P)
pòtrēban, pòtrēbna	necessary	vegetarijànskī	vegetarian
prèdjelo	appetizer		

DVA RESTORANA

<u>Bosnian</u>

1. Hàjde da uspòredīmo *òva dvà restoràna.* Jèsu li *jèdan drugòme* slȉčni ili *rázličiti?*

2. Dȍbro. Za pòčetak rèci mi, *kòjī* ti se vȉše svȋđa, a *kòjī* ti se mànjē svȋđa?

1. Po mȏm mišljênju nȋsu ùopšte *slȉčni jèdan drugȏm.* *Ȍvaj restòran* mi se mànjē svȋđa.

2. Zášto? U *ȍvom* su bȍlja jèla nego u *ònōme.*

1. Slȁžēm se. Ali se tȁmo čȅka krȁće. U *ȍvom restoránu* je tȅže dòbiti stȍ nego u *ònōm.* Tȁmo se ȍsjećām bȍljē.

2. *Ònaj restòran* jèste vȅćī od *òvōga.*

1. Gdjȅ je udòbnija atmosfèra?

2. Atmosfèra je mànjē ùdobna u *ònōm.*

1. Dogȍvoreno: *ȍvaj restòran* ȉmā bȍlja jèla. Dòduše, čȅka se dȕže i tȅže je dòbiti stȍ, i *mànjī* je, ali ȉmā udòbniju atmosfèru. *Ònaj restòran* ȉmā gòra jèla, čȅka se krȁće, lȁkšē je dòbiti stȍ, i *vȅćī* je.

2. Dàklē, na krȁju, *ȍvom restoránu* trèbajū vȅćī prȍstor i vȉše stolòva, a *ònom restoránu* trèbajū bȍlja jèla i prìjatnija atmosfèra! Mȍrām zaključȉti da su *òva dvà restoràna* sàsvīm *rázličita.*

<u>Croatian</u>

1. Hàjde da uspòredīmo *òva dvà restoràna.* Jèsu li *jèdan drugòme* slȉčni ili *rázličiti?*

2. Dȍbro. Za pòčetak rèci mi, *kòjī* ti se vȉše svȋđa, a *kòjī* ti se mànjē svȋđa?

1. Po mȏm mišljênju nȋsu ùopće *slȉčni jèdan drugòme.* *Ȍvaj restòran* mi se mànjē svȋđa.

2. Zášto? U *ȍvom* su bȍlja jèla nego u *ònōme.*

1. Slȁžēm se. Ali se tȁmo čȅka krȁće. U *ȍvom restoránu* je tȅže dòbiti stȏl nego u *ònōm.* Tȁmo se ȍsjećām bȍljē.

2. *Ònaj restòran* jèst vȅćī od *òvōga.*

1. Gdjȅ je udòbnija atmosfèra?

2. Atmosfèra je mànjē ùdobna u *ònōm.*

1. Dogȍvoreno: *ȍvaj restòran* ȉmā bȍlja jèla. Dòduše, čȅka se dȕže i tȅže je dòbiti stȏl, i *mànjī* je, ali ȉmā udòbniju atmosfèru. *Ònaj restòran* ȉmā gòra jèla, čȅka se krȁće, lȁkšē je dòbiti stȏl, i *vȅćī* je.

2. Dàklē, na krȁju *ȍvom restoránu* trèbajū vȅćī prȍstor i vȉše stolòva, a *ònom restoránu* trèbajū bȍlja jèla i prìjatnija atmosfèra! Mȍrām zaključȉti da su *òva dvà restoràna* sàsvīm *rázličita.*

✍☞ **Self-study learners:** Note the use of *nego* and *od*, *ȍvaj* and *ònaj*, *ali* and *a* in drawing comparisons.

Serbian

1. Hajde da uporedimo *ova dva restorana*. Da li su *slični jedan drugom* ili *različiti?*
2. Dobro. Za početak reci mi, *koji* ti se više sviđa, a *koji* ti se manje sviđa?
1. Po mom mišljenju nisu uopšte *slični jedan drugome*. *Ovaj restoran* mi se manje sviđa.
2. Zašto? U *ovom* su bolja jela nego u *onom*.
1. Slažem se. Ali se tamo čeka kraće. U *ovom restoranu* je teže dobiti sto nego u *onom*. Tamo se osećam bolje.
2. *Onaj restoran* jeste *veći* od *ovoga*.
1. Gde je udobnija atmosfera?
2. Atmosfera je manje udobna u *onom*.
1. Dogovoreno: *ovaj restoran* ima bolja jela. Doduše, čeka se duže i teže je dobiti sto, i *manji* je, ali ima udobniju atmosferu. *Onaj restoran* ima gora jela, čeka se kraće, lakše je dobiti sto, i *veći* je.
2. Dakle, na kraju, *ovom restoranu* su potrebni veći prostor i više stolova, a *onom restoranu* trebaju bolja jela i prijatnija atmosfera. Moram da zaključim da su *ova dva restorana* sasvim *različita*.

☞ **Draw** your own comparisons between **a)** ovo, ono predavanje; **b)** ova, ona škola; **c)** bosanski [B] hrvatski [C] srpski [S] jezik, francuski jezik; **d)** život na selu, život u gradu.

⚙ GRAMMAR

* Comparison of adjectives expressed by consonant softening *

Many adjectives add the meaning "comparative" by "softening" (= changing the shape of) the stem-final consonant. To do this, simply replace the consonant in the dictionary form of the word (the "base" consonant) by its "softened" variant, as shown in the chart below. Such changes occur in the formation of comparative and superlative adjectives, passive participles, verbal nouns, the instrumental singular of feminine nouns in a consonant, and certain other words. The soft version of *-st-* is *-šć-*, more rarely *-št-*. [112c]

base	k	g	h	c	s	z	t	d	p	b	v	m	n	l	sl	sn	zn	zd	st	st
soft	č	ž	š	č	š	ž	ć	đ	plj	blj	vlj	mlj	nj	lj	šlj	šnj	žnj	žđ	šć	št

Adjectives which express comparison in this way replace the stem-final consonant by its softened variant. If the adjective stem ends in *-ak* or *-ok*, this syllable is usually dropped first. [113b] As in other adjectives, the superlative is formed by adding *naj-* to the comparative form. Three adjectives add the suffix *-š*. [113a] Although a number of adjectives have several meanings, only one is given for each in the chart below.

	Positive	[stem]	Comparative	Superlative	
suffix -š-	*lep* [E] *lijep* [J]		*lepši, ljepši*	*najlepši, najljepši*	nice, nicer, nicest
	mek		*mekši*	*najmekši*	soft, softer, softest
	lak		*lakši*	*najlakši*	easy, easier, easiest
softening	*brz*		*brži*	*najbrži*	fast, faster, fastest
	čest		*češći*	*najčešći*	often (more, most)
	dug		*duži*	*najduži*	long, longer, longest
	glup		*gluplji*	*najgluplji*	stupid, stupider, stupidest
	jak		*jači*	*najjači*	strong, stronger, strongest
	mlad		*mlađi*	*najmlađi*	young, younger, youngest
	tih		*tiši*	*najtiši*	quiet, quieter, quietest
	kratak	*krat-*	*kraći*	*najkraći*	short, shorter, shortest
	težak	*tež-*	*teži*	*najteži*	hard, harder, hardest
	nizak	*niz-*	*niži*	*najniži*	low, lower, lowest
	debeo	*debl-*	*deblji*	*najdeblji*	fat, fatter, fattest
	tanak	*tan-*	*tanji*	*najtanji*	thin, thinner, thinnest

* Comparison of adverbs *

Comparative and superlative adverbs are equivalent to the corresponding neuter singular adjective forms. In two instances, the neuter singular adjective and the adverb have the same form but different meanings.

ADJECTIVE (neuter singular)			ADVERB		
vìsoko	*vȉše*	*nàjviše*	*mnȍgo*	*vȉše*	*nàjviše*
tall	taller	tallest	many	more	most
màlo	*mànje*	*nàjmanje*	*màlo*	*mànje*	*nàjmanje*
small	smaller	smallest	few, little	less	least

* Comparison "than" *

Comparison "than" is expressed by *od* + Gen, as in *òvaj grȁd je vèćī od ònoga* "this city is bigger than that one." One can also use *nego* (and must use *nego* if a verb follows). What follows *nego* must be a grammatical match to what precedes, as in *bȍlje je u òvōm mestu nego u ònōm* "it's better in this place than in that one." *Mànje* can be combined with an adjective or adverb in a manner parallel to English "less," as in *mànje je ùgodno* "it's less comfortable." [114] The BCS word meaning "more," however (*vȉše*) cannot normally be combined with adjectives or adverbs; one must use the comparative forms presented above.

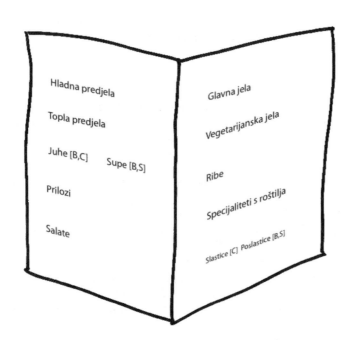

Hladna predjela

Topla predjela

Juhe [B,C]   Supe [B,S]

Prilozi

Salate

Glavna jela

Vegetarijanska jela

Ribe

Specijaliteti s roštilja

Slastice [C] Poslastice [B,S]

* "One another" *

The idea "one another" is expressed by the phrase *jèdan drȕgi*. The first component of this phrase is usually in the nominative, while the second is in whatever case the sentence requires. Thus, in the phrase *slȉčan jèdan drȕgōme* "similar to one another," the second component must be in the dative case. This phrase is also often used in the meaning "each other." For more discussion, see pp. 237 and 259. [160]

* The verb *trebati* *

The verb *trebati* means "need." The one who needs something is in the dative, and what s/he needs is the subject of the sentence, as in *trèbajū mi òlōvke* "I need pencils." In Croatian and Bosnian one can also use *trebati* like English "need," as in *jā trèbām nove òlōvke*. [119]

* Names of professionals *

Words ending in *-ik*, *-ač*, *-ar* (and other less frequently used suffixes) identify a person who does a particular job. They refer either to the profession in general terms or to a specific male praticing that profession. In some cases there is a separate word for a female practitioner of the profession; in others the general word is used. B, C, and S sometimes have different words for the same profession. The following gives examples according to Serbian and Croatian preferences. The Bosnian preference is noted as [B]; if no notation is given, it means Bosnian uses both words. An asterisk (*) means the form is ekavian (consult the other side of the table or the glossary for the corresponding ijekavian word). [121b]

STRUKE • PROFESSIONS

Profession	C (male/general)	(female)	S (male/general)	(female)
architect	arhitekt [B]		arhitekta	
actor	glumac	glumica	glumac	glumica
artist	umjetnik	umjetnica	umetnik *	umetnica *
baker	pekar	pekarica	pekar	pekarica
barber	brijač [B]		berberin	
biologist	biolog		biolog	
boss	šef	šefica	šef	šefica
butcher	mesar [B]		kasapin, mesar	
carpenter	stolar		tesar	
chemist	kemičar	kemičarka	hemičar [B]	hemičarka [B]
clerk	činovnik	činovnica	činovnik	činovnica
	pisar		pisar	
composer	skladatelj	skladateljica	kompozitor [B]	kompozitorka [B]
cook	kuhar [B]	kuharica [B]	kuvar	kuvarica
dancer	plesač	plesačica	igrač	igračica
dentist	zubar	zubarica	zubar	zubarka
director	direktor,	direktorica,	direktor	direktorica
	ravnatelj	ravnateljica		
doctor	liječnik,	liječnica,	lekar,* [B]	lekarka,*
	doktor	doktorica	doktor	doktorica, doktorka
driver	vozač		vozač	
electrician	električar	električarka	električar	električarka
farmer	poljoprivrednik		poljoprivrednik	
housekeeper		domaćica		domaćica
lawyer	odvjetnik		advokat	
manager	upravnik,	upravnica,	upravnik [B]	upravnica
	upravitelj	upraviteljica		
mechanic	strojar, mehaničar		mehaničar [B]	
minister [gov't.]	ministar	ministrica	ministar	
musician	glazbenik	glazbenica	muzičar [B]	muzičarka [B]
nurse	bolničar	bolničarka,	bolničar	bolničarka,
		medicinska		medicinska sestra
		sestra		
painter	slikar	slikarica	slikar	slikarka [B]
pharmacist	apotekar,	apotekarica	apotekar,	apotekarka [B]
	farmaceut		farmaceut	
poet	pjesnik	pjesnikinja	pesnik *	pesnikinja *
president	predsjednik	predsjednica	predsednik *	predsednica *
priest (Catholic)	svećenik		sveštenik	
priest (Orthodox)	pop		pop	
scholar	znanstvenik,	znanstvenica	naučnik [B]	
	učenjak [B]			
sculptor	kipar	kiparica	vajar	vajarka
soldier	vojnik		vojnik	
teacher	nastavnik,	nastavnica,	nastavnik,	nastavnica,
	učitelj	učiteljica	učitelj	učiteljica
thief	lopov		lopov	
veterinarian	veterinar		veterinar	
waiter	konobar	konobarica	konobar,	konobarica,
			kelner [B]	kelnerica [B]
worker	radnik	radnica	radnik	radnica
writer	pisac	spisateljica	pisac	spisateljica

VOCABULARY

barem	at least	plan grada	map of town
baviti se + *Instr*	to do, to occupy oneself with (I)	razni	various
glumica	actress	sećati se + *Gen*	to remember (I)
hronika [B,S]	chronicle	sjećati se + *Gen*	to remember (I)
inženjer, inženjera	engineer	stati, stanem	to stop (P)
kako kada	depends on when	struka	profession
kronika [C]	chronicle	taksi	taxi
matematičar	mathematician	taksiranje	taxi driving
moguće	possible	taksist [C]	taxi driver
na primer	for example	taksista [B,S]	taxi driver
na primjer	for example	travnički	Travnik *(adj.)*
nameravati, nameravam	to intend (I)	ubuduće	in the future
namjeravati, namjeravam	to intend (I)	vozačka dozvola	driver's license
nauka [B,S]	science	zadovoljan, zadovoljna	satisfied
ni... ni...	neither... nor...	zarađivati, zarađujem	to earn (I)
novinar	journalist	znanost, znanosti [C] *(f)*	science

STRUKA I POSAO

Bosnian

1. Šta radiš?
2. Čitam roman *Travnička hronika* pisca Ive Andrića.
1. A, sjećam se tog romana! I ja sam ga čitala prije mnogo godina. Ali nisam na to mislila, već sam te namjeravala pitati čime se baviš!
2. A to! Po struci sam *inženjer*, ali vozim taksi.
1. Je li moguće?! Jesi li time zadovoljan? Da li se taksiranjem barem dobro zarađuje?
2. Kako kada! Najbolje noću.
1. A čime se bave tvoji prijatelji?
2. Svi su taksisti, ali imaju razne struke.
1. Na primjer?
2. Jedna je *ljekarka*, jedan je *matematičar,* jedan je *tesar,* ali svi imaju vozačku dozvolu i plan grada. Čime se ti baviš?
1. Upravo sam završila fakultet političkih nauka, ali nije bilo posla kao *novinar* ranije, nema ga ni sada, i neće ga biti ni ubuduće.
2. Stani! Idi položiti vozački ispit. Trebat će ti vozačka dozvola. Uvijek možeš biti *taksista!*

Croatian

1. Što radiš?
2. Čitam roman *Travnička hronika* pisca Ive Andrića.
1. A, sjećam se tog romana! I ja sam ga čitala prije mnogo godina. Ali nisam na to mislila, već sam te namjeravala pitati čime se baviš!
2. A to! Po struci sam *inženjer*, ali vozim taksi.
1. Je li moguće?! Jesi li time zadovoljan? A zarađuje li se barem dobro taksiranjem?
2. Kako kada! Najbolje noću.
1. A čime se bave tvoji prijatelji?
2. Svi su taksisti, ali imaju razne struke.
1. Na primjer?
2. Jedna je *liječnica*, jedan je *matematičar,* jedan je *stolar,* ali svi imaju vozačku dozvolu i plan grada. Čime se ti baviš?
1. Upravo sam završila fakultet političkih znanosti, ali nije bilo posla kao *novinar* ranije, nema ga ni sada, i neće ga biti ni ubuduće.
2. Stani! Idi položiti vozački ispit. Trebat će ti vozačka dozvola! Uvijek možeš biti *taksist!*

Serbian

1. Шта радиш?

2. Читам роман *Травничка хроника* писца Иве Андрића.

1. А, сећам се тог романа. И ја сам га читала пре много година. Али нисам на то мислила, већ сам намеравала да те питам чиме се бавиш!

2. А то! По струци сам *инжењер*, али возим такси.

1. Да ли је могуће?! Да ли си тиме задовољан? Да ли се са таксирањем барем добро зарађује?

2. Како када! Најбоље ноћу.

1. А чиме се баве твоји пријатељи?

2. Сви су *таксисти*, али су разних струка.

1. На пример?

2. Једна је *лекарка*, један је *математичар,* један је *тесар*, али сви имају возачку дозволу и план града. Чиме се ти бавиш?

1. Управо сам завршила факултет политичких наука за *новинаре*, али није било посла раније, нема га сада, и неће га бити ни убудуће.

2. Стани! Иди да положиш возачки испит. Требаће ти возачка дозвола. Увек можеш бити *таксиста!*

✍️ **Write** your own conversation between two people discussing employment. Use as resources the vocations italicized in 11A and on p. 165, and the list of disciplines on p. 208. Be sure to include in your conversation the question *Čime se baviš?*

Ivo Andrić was awarded the Nobel Prize for Literature in 1961. He is best known for short stories, the novella *Prokleta avlija* (*The Damned Yard*), and three novels: *Na Drini ćuprija* (*The Bridge on the Drina*), *Gospođica* (*The Woman from Sarajevo*), and *Travnička hronika* (translated into English as *Bosnian Chronicle, Bosnian Story,* and, most recently, *Days of the Consuls*). He wrote all three novels under house arrest during World War II, and published them all in 1945, after the war ended. Andrić considered himself a Yugoslav writer, and wrote chiefly about Bosnia.

⚙️ GRAMMAR

* The instrumental case, continued *

The instrumental case is used for the second object after verbs like *smatrati, činiti* and others, as in *mi ga smatramo pametnim* "we consider him [to be] intelligent," or *to će ga činiti vojnikom* "that will make him [into] a soldier." The verb *baviti se* followed by the instrumental case means "be occupied with," and is the usual way of identifying an occupation or a frequently undertaken activity. Thus, *čime se bavite?* means "what do you do?" and *ona se bavi crtanjem* means "she [regularly] draws." **[81d]**

Saddlemaker and Beltmaker

Lawyer

Knowledge

☉91,92

VOCABULARY

dovoljan, dovoljna	sufficient	radno mjesto	place of employment
ležati, ležim	to lie, to be lying (I)	razumevanje	understanding
nego šta! [B,S]	you'd better believe it!	razumijevanje	understanding
nego što! [C]	you'd better believe it!	red	line, queue
neizvesnost, neizvesnosti (f)	uncertainty	savetovati se	to get advice (I)
neizvjesnost, neizvjesnosti (f)	uncertainty	savjetovati se	to get advice (I)
nikad se ne zna	you never know	sesti, sednem	to sit down (P)
odnos	attitude, relationship	sjesti, sjednem	to sit down (P)
osoblje	staff, personnel	služba za zapošljavanje	employment office
pada [mi] na pamet	it occurs [to me]	smetati, smetam + Dat	to bother (I)
poduzeće [B,C]	business, company	stati, stanem	to stand up (P)
preduzeće [B,S]	business, company	učenje	study, learning
prema + Dat	toward	znanje	knowledge
radno mesto	place of employment	zvanje	vocation

TREBA MI POSAO!

Bosnian

1. Sjednite tu! Pomozite mi! Treba mi bolji posao. Ne zarađujem dovoljno!
2. Razumijem. Sigurno te je strah od neizvjesnosti!
1. Nije me strah ničega i ne treba mi vaše razumijevanje. Treba mi posao!
2. Ali pitanje je hoćeš li dobro radno mjesto u nekom preduzeću naći ako sjediš ovdje.
1. Ne sjedim nego ležim. Ovako mogu lakše gledati televiziju.
2. Još gore! Stani na noge! Smeta mi tvoj odnos prema poslu! Dosta je čekanja! Trebaju ti učenje i znanje!

Croatian

1. Sjednite tu! Pomozite mi! Treba mi bolji posao. Ne zarađujem dovoljno!
2. Razumijem. Sigurno te je strah od neizvjesnosti!
1. Nije me strah ni od čega i ne treba mi vaše razumijevanje. Treba mi posao!
2. Ali pitanje je hoćeš li dobro radno mjesto u nekom poduzeću naći ako sjediš ovdje.
1. Ne sjedim nego ležim. Ovako mogu lakše gledati televiziju.
2. Još gore! Stani na noge! Smeta mi tvoj odnos prema poslu! Dosta je čekanja!

Serbian

1. Sedite tu! Pomozite mi! Treba mi bolji posao. Ne zarađujem dovoljno!
2. Razumem. Sigurno te je strah od neizvesnosti!
1. Nije me strah ni od čega i ne treba mi vaše razumevanje. Treba mi posao!
2. Ali pitanje je da li ćeš naći dobro radno mesto u nekom preduzeću ako sediš ovde.
1. Ne sedim nego ležim. Ovako mogu lakše da gledam televiziju.
2. Još gore! Stani na noge! Smeta mi tvoj odnos prema poslu! Dosta je čekanja! Trebaju ti učenje i znanje!

1. Treba da stojim u redu u službi za zapošljavanje?
2. Nego šta! Treba da se savjetuješ s osobljem u službi. Valja pokušati!
1. Ne pada mi na pamet. Stvari će već krenuti same od sebe. Meni previše ne smeta ovakav život.
2. Samo ti lezi i gledaj televiziju! Nikad se ne zna!

Trebaju ti učenje i znanje!
1. Trebam stajati u redu u službi za zapošljavanje?
2. Nego što! Trebaš se savjetovati s osobljem u službi. Valja pokušati!
1. Ne pada mi na pamet. Stvari će već krenuti same od sebe. Meni ne smeta previše ovakav život.
2. Samo ti lezi i gledaj televiziju! Nikad se ne zna!

1. Treba da stojim u redu u službi za zapošljavanje?
2. Nego šta! Treba da se savetuješ s osobljem u službi. Valja pokušati!
1. Ne pada mi na pamet. Stvari će već krenuti same od sebe. Meni ne smeta previše ovakav život.
2. Samo ti lezi i gledaj televiziju! Nikad se ne zna!

🖝 **Play** this interchange as a skit, rehearsing it outside of class so that you can peform it in class without referring to the text.

🖝 **Self-study learners:** Note the use of *treba* and *valja*, the imperatives, the comparatives, the phrases *nego šta / što* and *ne pada mi na pamet*, and the use of *smetati*.

Croatian

Pharmaceutical Society

Pharmaceutical Herald
Editorial Board and Administration

Pharmacy

⚙ GRAMMAR

* The verb *trebati*, continued *

The BCS verb *trebati* means "need." When it is followed by a verb, the meaning is that someone needs to do something. There are two ways to express this meaning. According to the more frequently used one, the form *treba* is unchanging and the action is expressed by *da* + present tense, as in *ti treba da učiš večeras* "you need to study tonight." In Croatian and Bosnian, this meaning of "need" can also be expressed as in English: the person who needs to do something is the subject of the conjugated verb *trebati*, and either form of the infinitive can follow. Thus, one can say either *ti trebaš učiti večeras* or *ti trebaš da učiš večeras*. When the idea is a subjectless one, there is no variation. One can use only 3rd sg. *treba* followed by infinitive or equivalent, as in *treba čekati* "it's necessary to wait."

* Verbs of body position *

There are two different sets of verbs meaning "sit," "stand," and "lie." One expresses stasis (the fact of being IN a position), and the other describes motion (INTO the position). The motion verbs all have present tense forms in *-nem* (etc.) and the stasis verbs all have present tense form in *-im* (etc.). The stasis verb "sit" belongs to type 3 in ekavian (*sedeti, sedim*) but to type 2 in ijekavian (*sjediti, sjedim*). **[120]**

	SIT		STAND	LIE
stasis	*sedeti (sedim)*	*sjediti (sjedim)*	*stajati (stojim)*	*ležati (ležim)*
motion	*sesti (sednem)*	*sjesti (sjednem)*	*stati (stanem)*	*leći (legnem)*

Open Monday to Friday.

Hours of operation: weekdays, 8 a.m. to 3 p.m.

⩗ VJEŽBE [J] VEŽBE [E]

B1

Bosnian	Croatian	Serbian
1. Kȁko si?	1. Kȁko si?	1. Ка̏ко си?
2. *Sretna* sam.	2. *Sretna* sam.	2. *Сре̏ħна* сам.
1. Eh, svakȁko sam ja *srȅtniji* od tebe.	1. Eh, svakȁko sam ja *srȅtniji* od tebe.	1. Ех, свака̏ко сам ја *сре̏ħнију* од тебе.
2. Ne, ne, ja̠ sam *srȅtnija*. A ti̠ si ma̠nje *sretan*!	2. Ne, ne, ja̠ sam *srȅtnija*. A ti̠ si ma̠nje *sretan*!	2. Не, не, ја̠ сам *сре̏ħнија*. А ти си ма̏ње *сре̏ħан*.

☞ **Replace** *sretni* [B,C] *srećni* [S] **with**: dobri̠, duhȍviti, le̠pi [E] lije̠pi [J], loši̠, pametni̠, slatki̠, strȁšni, visoki̠.

☞ **Redo** this exercise first in the past tense, and then in the future tense.

B2

Use the menu items on p. 163 as a basis for a discussion comparing two or more restaurants.

B3

Bosnian	Croatian	Serbian
1. Čȉme ćeš se baviti kad zȃvršiš fakul̠tȅt?	1. Čȉme ćeš se baviti kad zȃvršiš fakul̠tȅt?	1. Čȉme ćeš da se baviš kad zȃvršiš fakul̠tȅt?
2. Žȅlim da bude̠m *doktor*. A ti?	2. Žȅlim biti *liječnik*. A ti̠?	2. Žȅlim da bude̠m *lekar*. A ti̠?
1. Ja̠ žȅlim da bude̠m *slikar*.	1. Ja̠ žȅlim biti *slikar*.	1. Ja̠ žȅlim da bude̠m *slikar*.
2. Od *slika* se ne žȉvi!	2. Od *slika* se ne žȉvi!	2. Od *slika* se ne žȉvi!
1. Eh, mȍžda ću zarȃđivati kao *konobar* ili *taksista*.	1. Eh, mȍžda ću zarȃđivati kao *konobar* ili *taksist*.	1. Eh, mȍžda ću da zarȃđujem kao *kelner* ili *taksista*.

☞ **Replace** *doktor* [B] *liječnik* [C] *lekar* [S], *konobar* [B,C,S] *kelner* [B,S], *taksist* [C] *taksista* [B,S] **with nouns denoting other vocations and types of artistic creativity.**

☞ **Possible replacements:**

a) kompozitor [B,S] skladatelj [C] **and** glȃzba [C] muzika [B,S].

b) arhitekt [C] arhitekta [B,S], **and** zgrada.

c) pȉsac **or** spisatȅljica **and** rȍman.

d) pesnik [E] pjesnik [J] **and** pȍezija.

B4

Bosnian and Serbian	Croatian
Nȅma *znȃnja* bez učȅnja.	Nȅma *znȃnja* bez učȅnja.
Nȉje nikada rȁnije bȉlo *znȃnja* bez učȅnja.	Nȉje nikada rȁnije bȉlo *znȃnja* bez učȅnja.
A nȅće ni biti *znȃnja* bez učȅnja ubȕduće.	A ne̠ će ni biti *znȃnja* bez učȅnja ubȕduće.

☞ **Replace** *znȃnje* **and** *učȅnje* **with** a) dȍručak **and** novine; **b)** dȍbro društvo **and** dobro jelo; **c)** ȍdgovor **and** pȉtanje.

B5

Bosnian	Croatian	Serbian
1. Šta ti treba za sreću?	1. Što ti treba za sreću?	1. Шта ти треба за срећу?
2. Ne treba mi mnogo.	2. Ne treba mi puno.	2. Не треба ми много.
1. Kao šta, na primjer?	1. Kao što, na primjer?	1. Као шта, на пример?
2. Na primjer, trebaju mi *dobro jelo* i *topla soba.*	2. Na primjer, trebaju mi *dobro jelo* i *topla soba.*	2. На пример, требају ми *добро јело* и *топла соба.*
1. Meni trebaju: *prijatelji, dobro društvo, fine stvari,* a ponajviše mi treba *novac!*	1. Meni trebaju: *prijatelji, dobro društvo, fine stvari,* a najviše mi treba *novac!*	1. Мени требају: *пријатељи, добро друштво, фине ствари,* а понајвише ми треба *новац!*
2. Meni *novac* nije važan. Samo mi stvara probleme!	2. Meni *novac* nije važan. Samo mi stvara probleme!	2. Мени *новац* није важан. Само ми ствара проблеме!
1. A čega te je strah?	1. A čega te je strah?	1. А од чега те је страх?
2. Strah me je *neizvjesnosti!*	2. Strah me je *neizvjesnosti!*	2. Страх ме је од *неизвесности!*

☞ **Replace the italicized words that refer to** *sreća* **with** jesen, leto [E] ljeto [J], ljubav, poezija, proleće [E] proljeće [J], put, zima. **Replace** *neizvesnost* [E] *neizvjesnost* [J] **with**: dosadna predavanja, loš posao, neozbiljne kolege.

B6

Bosnian and Croatian	Serbian
1. *Sjedni tu!*	1. Седи ту!
2. Hvala, hoću!	2. Хвала, хоћу!
1. I dok *sjediš, pročitaj ovo pismo!*	1. И док седиш, *прочитај ово писмо!*
2. Zašto?	2. Зашто?
1. Važno je!	1. Важно је!

☞ **Replace** *sesti* [E] *sjesti* [J] **and** *sedeti* [E] *sjediti* [J] **with** leći **and** ležati, stati **and** stajati. **Replace** *pročitaj ovo pismo* **with another command.**

B7

Ask each other these questions:

1. [B,S] Šta ti najviše smeta u životu, i zašto?
   [C] Što ti najviše smeta u životu, i zašto?

2. [B,S] Šta ti najviše odgovara u životu i zašto?
   [C] Što ti najviše odgovara u životu, i zašto?

3. [B,C] Sjećaš li se svojih prijatelja iz škole? Kako su se zvali? Gdje su sada?
   [S] Da li se sećaš svojih prijatelja iz škole? Kako su se zvali? Gde su sada?

4. Koju struku smatraš najboljom, a koju najgorom? Zašto?

5. [B,C] Kȁko se ȍsjećaš dok ùčīš gramȁtiku -- veselīm ili tȕžnīm?
   [S] Kȁko se ȍsećaš dok ùčīš gramȁtiku -- veselīm ili tȕžnīm?

6. [B,C] Čȅga te je nȁjvišē strȁh?
   [B,C,S] Od čȅga te je nȁjvišē strȁh?

Self-study learners: Practice the use of comparatives and superlatives. Locate (or imagine) a series of similar objects, moods, and situations; and describe them with respect to one another. Compose several sentences using the *smȁtrati* with two objects (as in English "I consider him a genius").

ZAUZETO / Occupied, 1999
Public installation, National Gallery of Bosnia and Herzegovina, Sarajevo, 1999

✍ DOMAĆA ZADAĆA [B,C] DOMAĆI ZADATAK [S]

C1

Rewrite the *Pas i mačka* story (5A1) in the past tense, and rewrite exercise 5B6 in the future tense.

C2

First go down the two left hand columns and mark each word as either a noun (N) or a verb (V). Then go down the two right hand columns and mark each word as an adjective (Adj) or an adverb (Adv). For words which might be either adjective or adverb, give both markings. Then join the words into pairs - either as "verb + adverb" or "adjective + noun," making three pairs of each type. Finally, form the comparative and the superlative of the adjectives and adverbs and write out the resulting phrases. Note: adjectives are given here as in dictionaries (masculine singular short form).

Example:

N or V	Adjective or Adverb	same with comparative	same with superlative
pas (**N**)	zelen (**Adj**)	zeleniji pas	najzeleniji pas
govoriti (**V**)	važno (**Adv**)	ona govori važnije	ona govori najvažnije

Noun or Verb?		**Adjective or Adverb?**	
pitanje	reč	loše	mnogo
ljubav	auto	dug	velik
sveučilište	sjediti	debeo	zanimljivo
rječnik	noć	kiseo	šaren
činiti	univerzitet	glup	srećno
amidža	čekanje	brzo	kratak
biti	jesti	dobro	težak
pismo	stvar	visok	tužan
osećati se	stric	ružno	lak
tata	doći	malo	sretno

C3

Translate these sentences into B, C, or S. Then rewrite each first in the future, then in the past tense.

1. I am a student.
2. We are eating breakfast.
3. He is writing a letter.
4. They are listening to professors.
5. People can see a movie here.
6. Rivers flow through Belgrade, Zagreb and Sarajevo.
7. What is the dog called?

C4

Translate into B, C, or S:
1. I am talking now with my friend in town.
2. She is talking with her friend in town now.
3. She is talking with his friend in town now.
4. She will see her friend in town tonight.
5. She will see his friend in town tonight.

6. They will see their friends in town tonight.
7. Her friend saw her yesterday.
8. Her friend saw him yesterday.
9. Their friends saw them yesterday.

C5

ODJEĆA [J] ODEĆA [E]

Connect word to image:

kȁpūt   košulja   cȉpela   šȅšȉr   hlače   pantalȍne   hȁljina

C6

Translate the first sentence into English, and the next two into B, C, or S, using the first as a model:

1. a. Odmah mi trebaju pȁre!
   b. I need my car now!
   c. She needs a friend.

2. a. Nȉje bȉlo problȅma s učenjem jȅzika.
   b. There won't be any problems with studying the language.
   c. There wasn't time to eat breakfast.

3. a. [B,S] Šta im je?
      [C] Što im je?
   b. What is up with us?
   c. What is up with you?

4. a. [B,C] Sjedni tu s nama! Hvȁla, hoću. Dugo već stojȋm.
      [S] Sedi tu s nama! Hvȁla, hoću. Dugo već stojȋm.
   b. Lie down! Thanks, but I have been lying down a long time.
   c. Get up! Thanks, I have been sitting a long time.

5. a. [B,C] Ne sjećȁm ga se.
      [S] Ne sećȁm ga se.
   b. Do you remember me?
   c. They remembered the good old days.

6. a. [B,C] Strah ju je aviȍna.
      [B,C,S] Strah ju je od aviȍna.
   b. They are afraid of snakes.
   c. We are afraid of homework.

7. a. Po mȍm mišljenju, Ȁndrićev romȁn *Travnȋčka hronika* je boljȋ od romȁna *Na Drini ćuprija*.
   b. In our opinion, small dogs are more pleasant than large dogs.
   c. In his opinion, larger cities are more interesting than smaller cities.

8. a. Čini mi se da je lav strašniji nego što je Brana.
   b. It seems to us that Brana is more frightening than the lion is.
   c. That idea is more beautiful than this one is.

9. a. [B] Vjerovatno će ti se manje spavati ako popiješ kafu.
      [C] Vjerojatno će ti se manje spavati ako popiješ kavu.
      [S] Verovatno će ti se manje spavati ako popiješ kafu.
   b. I am less hungry than you are.
   c. We were less happy before than we are now.

10. a. Bolje išta nego ništa.
    b. Better late than never.
    c. Better safe than sorry.

C7

Fill in vocations from the STRUKA list in A3

1. [B,C] Sandra uči da bude .... Ako ne može naći posao, radit će kao ....
   [S] Sandra uči da bude .... Ako ne može da nađe posao, radiće kao ....
2. Najbolji posao je .... , ali ni .... nije loše.
3. [B,C] Najgore radno mjesto je ...., a najteže radno mjesto je ....
   [S] Najgore radno mesto je ...., a najteže radno mesto je ....
4. Najzanimljivije zvanje je ....
5. Najlakše zvanje je ....
6. Bolje je biti .... nego ....
7. Gore je biti .... nego ....

☺☹ Aforizmi Dušana Radovića

VOCABULARY

догодити се, догоди се	to happen (P)	обећати	to promise (P)
изнервирати се, изнервирам се	to get irritated (P)	плашити се + *Gen*	to be frightened of (I)
незнање	ignorance	постављати питање	to pose a question (I)
нервирати се, нервирам се	to be irritated (I)		

Ако се плашите одговора – не постављајте питања. Није свако знање лепше од незнања.

Обећајте себи да се данас нећете нервирати без обзира на то шта вам се догоди. Па тек ако вам се баш ништа не догоди, можете се због тога вечерас мало изнервирати.

🐦 **Bring** a question on each aphorism to class, incorporating one or more of these phrases:
a) Zbog čega .... ?

b) [B,C] Smatrate li .... ? [S] Da li smatrate .... ?

c) Po vašem mišljenju ....

📖 Priča: Albahari

Read Part VIII of the story "Osam malih priča o mojoj ženi" by David Albahari (p. 345).

Dvanaesta lekcija • Lesson Twelve

 A1

VOCABULARY

budući da	since	namještaj	furniture
cimer	roommate *(m)*	natkasna [B,S]	nightstand, bedside table
cimerica [B,C]	roommate *(f)*	noćni ormarić [B,C]	nightstand, bedside table
cimerka [B,S]	roommate *(f)*	odnosno	or rather, that is
čaršaf [B]	bed sheet	otprilike	approximately
čaršav [S]	bed sheet	paviljon, paviljona	wing of building
ćebe, ćebeta [S]	blanket	pisaći	writing *(adj.)*
deka [B,C]	blanket	plahta [C]	bed sheet
dnevni	daily	pokrivač [C]	blanket
držati, držim	to hold (I)	po prilici	approximately
dvanaesti	twelfth	po sobi	per room
godišnji	annual	posteljina	bedding
hiljada	thousand	prosečan, prosečna	average *(adj.)*
hiljadu	one thousand	prosječan, prosječna	average *(adj.)*
ispadati	to transpire (I)	tisuća	thousand
jastuk	pillow	tisuću	one thousand
koji	which, who, that	trećina	a / one third
krevet	bed	urediti, uredim	to arrange, to set up (P)
množiti	to multiply (I)	zajednički	shared, common
nameštaj	furniture		

STUDENTSKI DOM

<u>Bosnian</u>

Studenti koji stanuju u studentskom domu moraju urediti svoje sobe prije početka semestra. Svaki student ima cimera i svaka studentica ima cimerku. Dakle, od namještaja svaka soba treba da ima 2 kreveta, 2 noćna ormarića, 2 pisaća stola, 2 lampe, i 2 mala tepiha. Svaki student donosi sa sobom svoju posteljinu: jastuk, čaršafe, deku. Soba se dijeli na 3 dijela: jedna trećina sobe je za pisaće stolove i lampe, druga trećina je za krevete, noćne ormariće, i male tepihe, a treći dio je zajednički prostor. Kako svaki paviljon studentskog doma ima 150 soba, tako paviljon mora imati 300 kreveta, 300 noćnih ormarića, 300 pisaćih stolova, 300 lampi i 300 malih tepiha. Budući da svaki student ima 15-ak udžbenika, to znači da studenti drže otprilike 30 udžbenika po sobi, ili oko 4.500 udžbenika po paviljonu. Studenti treba da uče prosječno 4 sata dnevno u svojim sobama. Množeći to sa 180 dana u školskoj godini, ispada da 1 student treba da uči 720 sati, odnosno 2 studenta treba da uče 1.440 sati, a 5 studenata treba da uči 3.600 sati godišnje. Treba reći i da svaki studentski dom ima 9 paviljona.

Croatian

Studenti koji stanuju u studentskom domu moraju urediti svoje sobe prije početka semestra. Svaki student ima cimera i svaka studentica ima cimericu. Dakle, od namještaja svaka soba treba imati 2 kreveta, 2 noćna ormarića, 2 pisaća stola, 2 lampe, i 2 mala saga. Svaki student donosi sa sobom svoju posteljinu: jastuk, plahte, pokrivač. Soba se dijeli na 3 dijela: jedna trećina sobe je za pisaće stolove i lampe, druga trećina je za krevete, noćne ormariće, male sagove, a treći dio je zajednički prostor. Kako svaki paviljon studentskog doma ima 150 soba, tako paviljon mora imati 300 kreveta, 300 noćnih ormarića, 300 pisaćih stolova, 300 lampi i 300 malih sagova. Budući da svaki student ima 15-ak udžbenika, to znači da studenti drže po prilici 30 udžbenika po sobi, ili oko 4.500 udžbenika po paviljonu. Studenti trebaju učiti prosječno 4 sata dnevno u svojim sobama. Množeći to s 180 dana u školskoj godini, ispada da 1 student treba učiti 720 sati, odnosno 2 studenta trebaju učiti 1.440 sati, a 5 studenata treba učiti 3.600 sati godišnje. Treba reći i da svaki studentski dom ima 9 paviljona.

Serbian

Studenti koji stanuju u studentskom domu moraju da urede svoje sobe pre početka semestra. Svaki student ima cimera i svaka studentkinja ima cimerku. Dakle, od nameštaja svaka soba treba da ima 2 kreveta, 2 natkasne, 2 pisaća stola, 2 lampe, i 2 mala tepiha. Svaki student donosi sa sobom svoju posteljinu: jastuk, čaršave, ćebe. Soba se deli na 3 dela: jedna trećina sobe je za pisaće stolove i lampe, druga trećina je za krevete, natkasne i male tepihe, a treći deo je zajednički prostor. Kako svaki paviljon studentskog doma ima 150 soba, tako paviljon mora da ima 300 kreveta, 300 natkasni, 300 pisaćih stolova, 300 lampi i 300 malih tepiha. Budući da svaki student ima 15-ak udžbenika, to znači da studenti drže otprilike 30 udžbenika po sobi, ili oko 4.500 udžbenika po paviljonu. Studenti treba da uče prosečno 4 sata dnevno u svojim sobama. Množeći to sa 180 dana u školskoj godini, ispada da 1 student treba da uči 720 sati, odnosno 2 studenta treba da uče 1.440 sati, a 5 studenata treba da uči 3.600 sati godišnje. Treba i da se kaže da svaki studentski dom ima 9 paviljona.

✍☞ **Write out** the numbers in the above passage as words. Identify the case and number of each noun following a number, and explain why each takes the case and number it does. Read the passage through several times and then answer the related questions in exercise B1, on p. 191.

 **GRAMMAR**

* Cardinal numbers, review *

Cardinal numbers are used for counting (1, 2, 3, etc.). The number 1 is an adjective, agreeing with the noun that follows it (*jedan, jedno, jedna*). The number 2 has one form if a masculine or neuter noun follows (*dva*) and another if a feminine noun follows (*dve* [E] *dvije* [J]). No other numbers are affected by the gender of the following noun. Multiples of 100 either add the cardinal numbers directly, in a single word, or count the word *stotina*; alternate forms of 200 and 300 are used in Bosnian and Serbian. Multiples of 1000 count the word *tisuća* [C] or *hiljada* [B,S]. When any of the words *stotina, hiljada, tisuća* is used to name the number it is in Nsg, but when it is used in counting it is in Asg (in the chart below these words are given in the form used to count). Compounds are made by adding numbers directly, as in English. **[123a]**

100	*sto ; stotinu*	300	*tristo* [B,C,S]	600	*šeststo*	1,000	*tisuću* [C]
200	*dvjesto / dvesto* [B,C,S]		*trista* [B,S]	700	*sedamsto*		*hiljadu* [B,S]
	dvjesta / dvesta [B,S]	400	*četiristo*	800	*osamsto*	1,000,000	*milijun* [C]
[or]	*dve / dvije stotine*	500	*petsto*	900	*devetsto*		*milion* [B,S]

23	*dvadeset tri*	137	*sto trideset sedam*
103	*sto tri ; stotinu tri*	1,500	*tisuću petsto* [C] *hiljadu petsto* [B,S]
3,650	*tri tisuće šeststo pedeset* [C]	5,817	*pet tisuća osamsto sedamnaest* [C]
	tri hiljade šeststo pedeset [B,S]		*pet hiljada osamsto sedamnaest* [B,S]

* Agreement with cardinal numbers *

The number 1 is followed by the singular form of the noun counted. The numbers 2-4 are followed by the "counting form," which for nouns is like the Gsg (except that the feminine ending *-e* is not long). Modifiers of masculine and neuter nouns all take the ending *-a* (no length), and modifiers of feminine nouns all take the ending *-e* (no length). The numbers 5-20 are followed by the Gpl. The form of a noun following a compound number is determined by the final digit. Thus, 21, 51, 1001, 7251, etc. are all followed by the SINGULAR form of the noun, and numbers such as 22, 43, 252, 7984, etc. are all followed by the counting form. All other numbers are followed by the Gpl. **[124a]**

Singular

1	*jedan pametan student*	21	*dvadeset jedan pametan student*
1	*jedna dobra knjiga*	351	*trista pedeset jedna dobra knjiga*
1	*jedno malo selo*	3951	*tri tisuće devetsto pedeset jedno malo selo* [C]
			tri hiljade devetsto pedeset jedno malo selo [B,S]

Counting form

| 2 | *dva pametna studenta* | 34 | *trideset četiri pametna studenta* |
| 2 | *dvije* [J] *dve* [E] *dobre knjige* | 542 | *petsto četrdeset dvije* [J] *dve* [E] *dobre knjige* |

Genitive plural

| 5 | *pet pametnih studenata* | 12 | *dvanaest pametnih studenata* |
| 9 | *devet dobrih knjiga* | 475 | *četiristo sedamdeset i pet dobrih knjiga* |

* Fractions and approximative numbers *

Except for the words "quarter" and "half," the denominator portion of a fraction is formed by adding the suffix *-ina* to the stem of the ordinal number. The numerator then counts this number. Approximative numbers ("ten or so") are formed by adding the suffix *-ak* to the cardinal number. The word for "half" is *polovica* [C] *polovina* [B,S] and the word for "quarter" is either *četvrt* or *četvrtina*. **[123d]**

Fractions

3rd (m.sg.)	*treći*	>	1/3	*jedna trećina*	2/3	*dve* [E] *dvije* [J] *trećine*		
8th (m.sg.)	*osmi*	>	1/8	*jedna osmina*	3/8	*tri osmine*	5/8	*pet osmina*

Approximatives

10	*deset*	>	10 or so	*desetak*
15	*petnaest*	>	about 15	*petnaestak*
100	*sto*	>	100 or so	*stotinjak*

* The relative conjunction *koji* as subject *

As a question word, the pronominal adjective *koji* means "which" or "what." As a relative conjunction, it corresponds to the English conjunctions "who, whom, which, that" as used in sentences such as "the students WHO live there have to arrange their rooms themselves" or "do you know the woman THAT is coming into the room." English can sometimes omit these conjunctions but BCS must always include them. In each instance, the form of the relative conjunction *koji* must agree in gender and number with the word it refers to. In the BCS version of the first English sentence, it refers to the noun "students" and must thus be *koji* (masc pl): *studenti KOJI stanuju tamo moraju sami urediti svoje sobe*. But in the BCS version of the second English sentence it refers to the noun "woman" and must thus be *koja* (fem sg): *poznaješ li ženu KOJA ulazi u sobu?"* The case of *koji* depends on its role within its own clause. In each of these two sentences it is the subject within its own clause and is therefore in the nominative case. **[128]**

* Present verbal adverb *

The present verbal adverb is created by adding the unchanging suffix *-ći* to the 3rd plural present form of a verb of the imperfective aspect. This adverb identifies an action occurring simultaneously with that of the main verb (no matter what its tense); both verbs must refer to the subject of the sentence. Thus the sentence *vozeći se autobusom čita novine* means "she reads the paper while riding the bus," while the sentence *ranije je čitala novine vozeći se autobusom* means "she used to read the paper while riding the bus." The present verbal adverb can also denote mild causative relationships, as in *množeći to sa 180, dobijamo 720* "multiplying that by 180, we get 720." The adverb formed from *biti* takes its stem from *budem*, for example *budući vojnik, zna o ratu* "being a soldier, he knows about war." The related conjunction *budući da* means "since, insofar as." **[129, 138a]** True verbal adverbs are unchanging in form. However, a number of them have taken on double duty as adjectives, often undergoing a subtle change in meaning. When they are used as adjectives, they take all adjectival endings. Some examples are *idući* "next," *sljedeći* "next, following," *vodeći* "leading, top," *mogući* "possible," *odgovarajući* "relevant, corresponding." **[138c]**

Shopping in Zagreb, Ilica

Shopping in Sarajevo, Baščaršija

Shopping in Belgrade, Knez Mihailova St.

VOCABULARY

bombon, bombona [B,C]	[piece of] candy	porculanski [B,C]	porcelain
bombona [B,S]	[piece of] candy	posuđe [B,C]	dishes
br.	№	potom	then, later
cveće *coll.*	flowers	pozdraviti se	to greet one another (P)
cvijeće *coll.*	flowers	pratiti	to follow, to accompany (I)
drago kamenje *coll.*	precious stones	pričati, pričam	to talk, to chat (I)
dućan, dućana [B,C,S]	store	pružiti	to offer (P)
ići svojim putem	to go one's own way	pružiti ruku	to extend one's hand
izlog	store window, display	pušač, pušača	smoker
jedni drugima	to one another	pušiti	to smoke (I)
kafić, kafića	small café	radnja [B,C,S]	store
kamenje *coll.*	stones, rocks	razgovarati, razgovaram	to converse (I)
kila [C]	kilogram	razgovor	conversation
kilo [B,S]	kilogram	s nogu	standing
košarkaški	basketball *(adj.)*	sudovi [B,S]	dishes
kupovina	shopping	svi	all, everyone
lokal, lokala	local bar, restaurant	šank	bar, counter
meč	sports match	šetnja	stroll, walk
međutim	however	trgovina [B,C,S]	store
naći, nađem	to find (P)	ući, uđem	to enter (P)
nakon + *Gen.*	after	ulica	street
naporan, naporna	strenuous	uparkirati, uparkiram	to park (P)
navratiti, navratim	to drop by (P)	utakmica	sports match
obližnji	nearby	uživati, uživam	to enjoy
otvoriti, otvorim	to open (P)	zatim	thereafter, then
pokloniti	to give [a gift] (P)	zatvoriti, zatvorim	to close (P)
porcelanski [S]	porcelain		

KUPOVINA

<u>Bosnian</u>

Izašavši iz svojih kuća u *pola pet*, *tri žene* su išle ulicom, pričale i uživale u šetnji. *Četiri* plava i žuta *automobila* su se uparkirala blizu njih. Vrata su se otvorila i izašla su *četvorica visokih muškaraca* u *četiri i četrdeset pet*. Svi su pružili jedni drugima ruke, pozdravili se i veselo razgovarali. Zatim je *njih sedmoro* ušlo u veliku trgovinu u Hrastovoj ulici *br. 21*. Dvanaest mačaka i *jedanaest* pasa gledalo ih je iz izloga. Ušavši u trgovinu, *žene* su kupile *muškarcima* po *jednog* psa i *jednu* mačku, dok su *muškarci ženama* kupili *cvijeće* i kilo bombona te im odmah poklonili. A potom su se te *tri žene*, svaka sa svojim *cvijećem*, našle sa još *šest*, i nakon naporne kupovine, *njih devet* je otišlo u obližnji kafić na kafu i razgovor. Međutim, *njih četvorica* su navratila do najbližeg lokala, pušači među njima su pušili za šankom, svaki je nešto popio s nogu, i pratili su košarkaški meč na televiziji. Nakon meča se zatvorio lokal i svaki od njih je otišao svojim putem.

<u>Croatian</u>

Izašavši iz svojih kuća u *pola pet, tri žene* su išle ulicom, pričale i uživale u šetnji. *Četiri* plava i žuta *automobila* su se uparkirala blizu njih. Vrata su se otvorila i izašla su *četvorica visokih muškaraca* u *tri četvrt pet.* Svi su pružili jedni drugima ruke, pozdravili se i veselo razgovarali. Zatim je *njih sedmero* ušlo u veliki dućan u Hrastovoj ulici *br. 21. Dvanaest* mačaka i *jedanaest pasa* gledalo ih je iz izloga. Ušavši u dućan, *žene* su kupile *muškarcima* po *jednog* psa i *jednu* mačku, dok su *muškarci ženama* kupili *cvijeće* i kilu bombona te im odmah poklonili. A potom su se te *tri žene*, svaka sa svojim *cvijećem*, našle s još *šest*, i, nakon naporne kupovine, *njih devet* je otišlo u obližnji kafić na kavu i razgovor. Međutim, *njih četvorica* su navratila do najbližeg lokala, pušači među njima su pušili za šankom, svaki je nešto popio s nogu, i pratili su košarkašku utakmicu na televiziji. Nakon utakmice se zatvorio lokal i svaki od njih je otišao svojim putem.

<u>Serbian</u>

Изашавши из својих кућа у *пола пет, три жене* су ишле улицом, причале и уживале у шетњи. *Четири* плава и жута *аутомобила* су се упаркирала близу њих. Врата су се отворила и изашла су *четворица* високих *мушкараца* у *четири и четрдесет пет.* Сви су пружили једни другима руке, поздравили се и весело разговарали. Затим је *њих седморо* ушло у велику радњу у Храстовој улици *бр. 21. Дванаест* мачака и *једанаест* паса гледало их је из излога. Ушавши у радњу, *жене* су купиле *мушкарцима* по *једног* пса и *једну* мачку, док су *мушкарци женама* купили *цвеће* и кило бомбона, те им одмах поклонили. А потом су се те *три жене*, свака са својим *цвећем*, нашле са још *шест*, и, после напорне куповине, *њих девет* је отишло у оближњи кафић на кафу и разговор. Међутим, *њих четворица* су навратила до најближег локала, пушачи међу њима су пушили за шанком, сваки је нешто попио с ногу, и пратили су кошаркашку утакмицу на телевизији. Након утакмице се затворио локал и сваки од њих је отишао својим путем.

☞ **Retell this story, replacing** *žena* **with** lekarka [S] liječnica [C] ljekarka [B,S] **or other female vocations, and replacing** *muškarac* **with** lekar [S] liječnik [C], ljekar [B,S] **or other male vocations (see p. 165 for suggestions). Replace** cveće [E] cvijeće [J] **with** drago kamenje, porcelanski sudovi [S] porculansko posuđe [B,C].

The word *televizor* refers to the television set as a piece of equipment, and the word *televizija* refers to that which is watched on the television set.

Open 24 hours

Please close the door!

The words for 'store' or 'shop' used below are only three of a family of synonyms. For instance, while Bosnian speakers use *trgovina*, they also say *samoposluga*, *prodavnica* and *dućan*; and while Serbian speakers often say *radnja*, they also use the words *samousluga*, *prodavnica*, *and dućan*. Croatian speakers use *samoposluga*, *trgovina*, *radnja*, *dućan* or *prodavaonica*.

Store

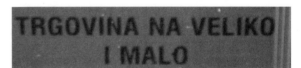

Wholesale and retail trade

Store

Store

⚙ GRAMMAR

* Agreement with cardinal numbers *

Nouns following 1 (or compound numbers ending in 1) are singular. If such a phrase is the subject of the sentence, the verb is also singular. Nouns following 2-4 (or compound numbers ending in 2-4) take the counting form. If such a phrase is the subject of the sentence, the verb is plural, but the L-participle of the past tense takes the counting form. Nouns following other numbers take Gpl. If such a phrase is the subject of the sentence, the verb is singular, and the L-participle of the past tense is neuter singular. Numbers do not change form after a preposition. For examples, see the following chart.

1	1 dobar student uči	1 student je učio	241 student uči	241 student je učio
2-4	2 dobra studenta uče	2 studenta su učila	243 studenta uči	243 studenta su učila
5+	5 dobrih studenata uči	5 studenata je učilo	257 studenata uči	257 studenata je učilo

* Group numbers *

There are two additional sets of numbers referring to groups. One describes groups of male humans only, while the other describes groups of mixed gender (or more rarely, groups of objects). Groups of female humans are referred to by the cardinal numbers alone. All group numbers are formed from the same stem. The ending *-ica* is used for the number referring to males. The endings *-oro* [B,S] and *-ero* [C] form the number referring to mixed groups. **[123c]**

	(mixed group)		(males only)
2	*dvoje*		*dvòjica*
both	*oboje*		*obòjica*
3	*troje*		*tròjica*
4	*četvero* [C]	*četvoro* [B,S]	*četvòrica*
5	*petero* [C]	*petoro* [B,S]	*petòrica*
6	*šestero* [C]	*šestoro* [B,S]	*šestòrica*
7	*sedmero* [C]	*sedmoro* [B,S]	*sedmòrica*

The counted noun or pronoun is in the Gpl. Thus: *na̱s dvoje* "the two of us [one male, one female]," *va̱s trojica* "the three of you [males]," *troje dèce̱* [E] *djèce̱* [J] "three children," *četvòrica učènika̱* "four [male] pupils." When a mixed-gender phrase is the subject, a present tense verb is plural, but a past tense verb is neuter singular. Thus: *njih petero* [C] *petoro* [B,S] *dobro ra̱de̱* (present) but *njih petero* [C] *petoro* [B,S] *je dobro ra̱dilo* (past) "the five of them work[ed] well." Group nouns in *-ica* are declined like feminine singular nouns; for example, *rekao je petòrici da òstane̱* "he told the five [males] to stay." If such a noun is the subject, the verb is plural, but the L-participle of the past tense is feminine singular; for example *njih trojica dobro ra̱de̱* (present) but *njih trojica su dobro ra̱dila* "the three of them work[ed] well." A group of females is counted by the feminine count form plus a plural verb, thus *tri žène dobro ra̱de̱* (present) and *tri žène su dobro ra̱dile* (past) "the three women work[ed] well." **[124d]**

* Past verbal adverb *

The past verbal adverb is formed by dropping the *-o* from the masculine singular L-participle of a perfective verb and adding the unchanging suffix *-vši*. This adverb identifies an action which was completed prior to the action of the main verb; both it and the main verb must refer to the subject of the sentence. For example, *rèka̱vši to, izášao je iz sobe* means "having said that, he left the room." **[129, 138b]** Past verbal adverbs are used only in written style; only one (*bívši* "former") has become a full-fledged adjective. **[138c]**

* Collective nouns *

Collective nouns are singular nouns which refer to objects seen as an indivisible group. Most such nouns are neuter singular, e.g. *cvȅće* [E] *cvijȅće* [J] "flowers," *drvȅće* "trees," *lišće* "leaves," *kàme̱nje* "stones," *grànje* "branches," and the like. Regular plurals exist (such as *cvetovi* [E] *cvjetovi* [J], *drvèta*, and the like) but these plural forms are used relatively rarely, since when such objects are visualized as individual units they usually occur after numbers. **[115]** Another type of collective, which refers to small or young creatures seen as a group (often with endearing overtones), is feminine singular. Thus *ùnuča̱d* "small grandchildren" (sg. *ùnuče*). The collective form *momča̱d* (derived from *momče* "lad") is now most frequently used in the meaning "[sports] team."

Croatian bill from the transitional years in the early 1990s, when the currency still bore the name *dìna̱r* (and not yet *kùna*), and when inflation was still very high. Note the accusative case, *tìsu̱ću hrvàtski̱h dìna̱ra*, in the denomination. The accusative is used whenever the numbers 100 and 1000 (*stotinu*, *hìljadu* [B,S] or *tìsu̱ću* [C]) function to count something, and therefore is always used on currency and coins.

VOCABULARY

čestitati, čestitam	to congratulate (I)	rođendan	birthday
godište	year of birth	setiti se + *Gen*	to remember (P)
napuniti	to complete (a year) (P)	sjetiti se + *Gen*	to remember (P)
na žalost	unfortunately	slaviti	to celebrate (I)
ništa za to	it doesn't matter, it's nothing	smeti, smem	to dare; may; be allowed (I)
obaveza [B,S]	obligation	smjeti, smijem	to dare; may; be allowed (I)
običaj	custom	srećan put [B,S]	bon voyage
obiteljski [C]	familial	sretan put [B,C]	bon voyage
obveza [C]	obligation	što *(conjunction)*	that
odlučiti, odlučim	to decide (P)	unapred	in advance
porodični [B,S]	familial	unaprijed	in advance
poštovati, poštujem	to respect, to honor (I)	valja	ought; should (I)
propustiti, propustim	to miss [an opportunity] (P)	valjati	to be worth
proslava	celebration	žao [mi] je	[I'm] sorry
Rim	Rome		

KOLIKO IMAŠ GODINA?

Bosnian

1. Koliko imaš godina?
2. Ja sam '84. godište. Napunit ću *21 g. na ljeto*.
1. Kada ti je rođendan?
2. Rođendan mi je osamnaestog avgusta.
1. Putujem baš *osamnaestog osmog* u Rim. Hoćeš li sa mnom?
2. Na žalost ne mogu. Odlučila sam ostati tu. Imam obavezu prema svojima. Ne smijem propustiti proslavu rođendana kod svojih.
1. Ali sigurno slaviš rođendan kod svojih već godinama?
2. Porodične običaje valja poštovati!
1. Kad budeš slavila rođendan, sjetit ćeš se mene i bit će ti žao što nisi sa mnom pošla u Rim!
2. Ništa za to. Sretan ti put!
1. A tebi unaprijed čestitam rođendan.
2. Hvala!

Croatian

1. Koliko imaš godina?
2. Ja sam '84. godište. Napunit ću *21 g. na ljeto*.
1. Kada ti je rođendan?
2. Rođendan mi je osamnaestog kolovoza.
1. Putujem baš *osamnaestog osmog* u Rim. Hoćeš li sa mnom?
2. Na žalost ne mogu. Odlučila sam ostati tu. Imam obvezu prema svojima. Ne smijem propustiti proslavu rođendana kod svojih.
1. Ali sigurno slaviš rođendan kod svojih već godinama?
2. Obiteljske običaje valja poštovati!
1. Kad budeš slavila rođendan, sjetit ćeš se mene i bit će ti žao što nisi sa mnom pošla u Rim!
2. Ništa za to. Sretan ti put!
1. A tebi unaprijed čestitam rođendan.
2. Hvala!

Serbian

1. Koliko imaš godina?
2. Ja sam '84. godište. Napuniću *21 g. na leto*.
1. Kada ti je rođendan?
2. Rođendan mi je osamnaestog avgusta.
1. Putujem baš *osamnaestog avgusta* u Rim. Da li hoćeš sa mnom?
2. Na žalost ne mogu. Odlučila sam da ostanem tu. Imam obavezu prema svojima. Ne smem da propustim proslavu rođendana kod svojih.
1. Ali sigurno slaviš rođendan kod svojih već godinama?
2. Porodične običaje valja poštovati!
1. Kad budeš slavila rođendan, setićeš se mene i biće ti žao što nisi sa mnom pošla u Rim!
2. Ništa za to. Srećan ti put!
1. A tebi unapred čestitam rođendan.
2. Hvala!

☞ **Replace** 21. g. **with your own age; replace** osamnaesti avgust [B,S] kolovoz [C] **with the date of your birthday, and give your own** 'godište'. **If appropriate, replace** *na leto* [E] *na ljeto* [J] **with one of the following:** na jesen, na proleće [E] na proljeće [J], na zimu.

Self-study learners: Pay special attention to the way dates, age and birthdays are expressed.

⚙ GRAMMAR

* Ordinal numbers in naming dates *

Ordinal numbers identify a place in a series (1st, 2nd, 3rd, etc.). They are most frequently used in stating dates. The day of the month is named with a Gsg. ordinal number followed by the month name in the genitive. "March 8th," therefore, is *osmog marta* [B,S] *osmog ožujka* [C] *osmog trećeg* [B,C]. If the date is given using a numeral, a period is written after it, as in 8. *marta* [B,S] 8. *ožujka* [C] 8. *trećeg* [B,C] **[124b]**

* Discussing one's age *

There are several ways to state one's age. To say "he is 21," for instance, one can use either the dative (*njemu je dvadeset jedna godina*) or *imati* + direct object (*on ima dvadeset jednu godinu*). One can also use the noun *godište* modified by the ordinal number of one's year of birth, as in *Ja sam 87.* [= *osamdeset sedmo*] *godište* "I was born in '87." The verb *napuniti* is used to mark a birthday, as in *sutra će napuniti 31 godinu* "he'll turn 31 tomorrow." **[124e]** A period following a number indicates that the word is an ordinal rather than a cardinal; thus *87 godina* means "87 years" but *87. godina* means "the 87th year." **[124b]**

* The "exact future" *

In addition to what is sometimes called the first future, that formed with *hteti* or *htjeti*, there is a second future tense. It is composed of the auxiliary *budem* plus the L-participle. In principle, it can be made from all verbs; in practice it is usually formed only from imperfective verbs, and is used only after conjunctions with potential future meaning such as *kad* "when," *ako* "if," *čim* "as soon as," and others. The meaning is exactly the same as when the present tense form of a perfective verb is

	singular	plural
1st masc.	*budem radio*	*budemo radili*
1st fem.	*budem radila*	*budemo radile*
2nd masc.	*budeš radio*	*budete radili*
2nd fem.	*budeš radila*	*budete radile*
3rd masc.	*bude radio*	*budu radili*
3rd neut.	*bude radilo*	*budu radila*
3rd fem.	*bude radila*	*budu radile*

used after one of these conjunctions. The exact future allows imperfective verbs to express more "closure" than they would otherwise. For example, the exact future in the sentence *kad budeš slavila rođendan, bit će ti žao što nisi pošla sa mnom u Rim* "when you celebrate your birthday you'll be sorry you didn't come to Rome with me," puts more specific focus on the concrete occurrence of the envisioned event than would the present tense (*kad slaviš*...). **[130, 144a]** For more on conditional "if" sentences, see Lesson 13.

* The conjunction *što* *

The conjunction usually encountered in the meaning "that" is *da*. After verbs expressing emotion, however, the conjunction *što* is often used. For instance, *znam da je došao* "I know that he came," but *žao mi je što nije mogao doći* "I'm sorry [that] he couldn't come." **[143g]**

* Words meaning "ought, might, may" *

Verbs expressing degrees of possibility or obligation are followed by another verb denoting the action that should, can, or must be undertaken. These verbs can have a number of different meanings. The verb *trebati*, for instance, means either "need" or "should" depending on the context, **[119, 127]** and the verb *smeti* [E] *smjeti* [J] can mean both "dare" (as in *ne smem to propustiti* "I don't dare miss it") and "may" (as in *smijem li zamoliti malo hladne vode?* "may / might I ask for a little cold water?"). **[142]** The verb *valjati* is an exception: it has this sort of meaning only in subjectless sentences. When it is used with a subject, it means "be good" (as applied to food, behavior or the like), as in *ove jabuke više ne valjaju, treba ih baciti* "these apples are no longer any good, one must toss them out." But when it is used in a subjectless sentence, it has the same meaning as *treba*. Thus, for instance, *ne valja zakasniti* means "one had better not be late," and *njihove običaje valja poštovati* means "one should respect their customs." **[127]**

VOCABULARY

atentat, atentata	assassination	Prvi svetski rat	World War I
dogoditi se, dogodi se	to happen, to occur (P)	Prvi svjetski rat	World War I
Drugi svetski rat	World War II	rat	war
Drugi svjetski rat	World War II	savez	union
izvršiti atentat (na)	to assassinate (P)	sjedinjen	united
nadvojvoda	archduke	sjediniti, sjedinim	to unite (P)
napasti, napadnem	to attack (P)	snaga	power, force
nezavisnost, nezavisnosti *(f)*	independence	svetski	world *(adj.)*
Osovina	axis	svjetski	world *(adj.)*
proglasiti, proglasim	to proclaim (P)		

ŠTA SE DOGODILO? [B,S]   ŠTO SE DOGODILO? [C]

1. a. Šta se dogodilo *4. jula hiljadu sedamsto sedamdeset šeste godine?*
b. Sjedinjene Američke Države *su proglasile svoju nezavisnost.*
2. a. Šta se dogodilo *7. decembra 1941. g. ?*
b. *Snage Osovine su napale* Pearl Harbor.
3. a. Šta se dogodilo *22. XI 1963. g.?*
b. Lee Harvey Oswald je *izvršio atentat na* predsjednika Johna Kennedya.

1. a. Što se dogodilo *4. srpnja tisuću sedamsto sedamdeset šeste godine?*
b. Sjedinjene Američke Države *su proglasile svoju nezavisnost.*
2. a. Što se dogodilo *7. prosinca 1941. g. ?*
b. *Snage Osovine su napale* Pearl Harbor.
3. a. Što se dogodilo *22. XI 1963. g.?*
b. Lee Harvey Oswald *je izvršio atentat na* predsjednika Johna Kennedya.

1. a. Шта се догодило *4. јула хиљаду седамсто седамдесет шесте године?*
b. Сједињене Америчке Државе *су прогласиле своју независност.*
2. a. Шта се догодило *7. децембра 1941. г.?*
b. *Снаге Осовине су напале* Перл Харбор.
3. a. Шта се догодило *22. XI 1963. г.?*
b. Ли Харви Освалд *је извршио атентат на* председника Џона Кенедија.

🐎 **Replace the date in 1a) with November 29, 1943, and use the clues that follow to describe what happened on that day**: Josip Broz Tito, nezavisnost Jugoslavije. **Replace the date in 2a) with April 6, 1941, and use these clues to complete the exercise:** Beograd, Drugi svetski [E] svjetski [J] rat. **Finally, replace the date in 3a) with June 28, 1914, and use these clues to answer the question**: Gavrilo Princip, Nadvojvoda Ferdinand, njegova žena Sofija, Prvi svetski [E] svjetski [J] rat.

⚙ GRAMMAR

* Ordinal numbers, continued *

Compound ordinal numbers are as in English, in that only the final segment is ordinal. Thus, English "eight hundred forty SEVENTH" is parallel to BCS *osamsto četrdeset SEDMI*. Compound ordinals are most frequently used when naming a year, and only the final ordinal number takes a case form. This case form is almost always genitive singular feminine (modifying the Gsg noun *godine*, which can but need not be included). "March 8, 1981" is thus *osmog marta hiljadu devetsto osamdeset prve* [*godine*] [B,S] *osmog ožujka tisuću devetsto osamdeset prve* [*godine*] [C]. Frequently the abbreviation *g.* is used in place of *godine*. If the number is given as a numeral, a period indicates that it is an ordinal: *8. mart 1981. g.* **[124b]**

* Aorist and imperfect *

There are two other past tense forms in BCS, both of which are now relatively archaic and are found primarily in literary texts, especially older ones. Both are single-word tense forms. The aorist is used to relate individual actions completed in a sequence, and the imperfect is used to describe background states, or continuous actions going on in the background. In form, one must take care to differentiate the 3pl aorist from the 3sg imperfect. Within each tense, the 2nd and 3rd singular always use the same form. For certain verbs the 3rd singular present and 3rd singular aorist look alike. [122, 150] In spoken Serbian and Bosnian, one hears the aorist of certain verbs, such as *biti* and *reći*, with some frequency. Nearly all BCS speakers will use the colloquial phrase *odoh ja* (literally, "I went away") in the sense "I'm out of here."

	AORIST						IMPERFECT	
inf.	*svratiti*	*nazvati*	*reći*	*ući*	*dati*	*biti*	*stajati*	*biti*
1 sg	*svratih*	*nazvah*	*rekoh*	*uđoh*	*dadoh*	*bih*	*stajah*	*bijah*
2-3sg	*svrati*	*nazva*	*reče*	*uđe*	*dade*	*bi*	*stajaše*	*bijaše*
1 pl	*svratismo*	*nazvasmo*	*rekosmo*	*uđosmo*	*dadosmo*	*bismo*	*stajasmo*	*bijasmo*
2 pl	*svratiste*	*nazvaste*	*rekoste*	*uđoste*	*dadoste*	*biste*	*stajaste*	*bijaste*
3 pl	*svratiše*	*nazvaše*	*rekoše*	*uđoše*	*dadoše*	*biše*	*stajahu*	*bijahu*

Tricky translation: The word "independence" is translated differently depending on the meaning. Throughout the region, *samostalnost* is used to mean "personal independence" (e.g. living on one's own), while *nezavisnost* is used to mean political independence; C also uses *samostalnost* in this latter meaning as well.

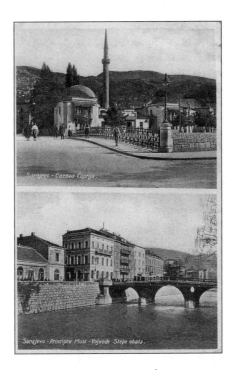

Vintage postcard of *Careva ćuprija* (Emperor's Bridge) in Sarajevo. Below, the bridge known for years as *Principov most* (Princip Bridge) now called *Latinska ćuprija* (Latin Bridge), site of the assassination of Archduke Franz Ferdinand by Gavrilo Princip on June 28, 1914.

VJEŽBE [J] VEŽBE [E]

B1

Refer back to the text in A1, and answer the following questions based on that text. Then answer these or similar questions with respect to your own living situation (house, dormitory, or apartment).

1. [B,C] Zašto studenti moraju urediti svoje sobe?
    [S] Zašto studenti moraju da urede svoje sobe?

2. S kim stanuje svaki student?

3. [B,C] Zašto svaka studentska soba mora imati namještaj?
    [S] Zašto svaka studentska soba mora da ima nameštaj?

4. Koliko ima paviljona u studentskom domu?

5. Koliko ima soba u svakom paviljonu?

6. [B] Koliko ima tepiha u jednom paviljonu, a koliko u cijelom domu?
    [C] Koliko ima sagova u jednom paviljonu, a koliko u cijelome domu?
    [S] Koliko ima tepiha u jednom paviljonu, a koliko u celom domu?

7. Zašto ima udžbenika u sobama?

8. [B] Koliko sati sedmično uče studenti? Dakle, koliko sati mjesečno?
    [C] Koliko sati tjedno uče studenti? Dakle, koliko sati mjesečno?
    [S] Koliko sati nedeljno uče studenti? Dakle, koliko sati mesečno?

9. [B,C] Koliko sati treba 10 studenata učiti godišnje?
    [S] Koliko sati treba 10 studenata da uči godišnje?

B2

Review the passage in A2, locate the phrases or sentences that have numbers as their subject (such as *Tri žene su išle...*), and mark the gender and number (singular or plural) of the L-participle in each of these sentences (for instance, in this example it is feminine plural). Finally, retell the story, replacing all the numbers (including the times of day and the street number), by other numbers.

B3

Answer the following questions with respect to the content of A2.

1. [B,C] Koliko je bilo sati kada su žene izašle iz svojih kuća?
    [S] Колико је било сати када су жене изашле из својих кућа?

2. [B,C] Koliko minuta kasnije su muškarci izašli iz automobila?
    [S] Колико минута касније су мушкарци изашли из аутомобила?

3.   [B] Koliko ih je ušlo u veliku trgovinu?
         [C] Koliko ih je ušlo u veliki dućan?
         [S] Колико их је ушло у велику радњу?

4.   [B] Koji je broj one velike trgovine?
         [C] Koji je broj onog velikog dućana?
         [S] Који је број оне велике радње?

5.   [B,C] Koji je broj vaše kuće ili stana?
         [S] Који је број ваше куће или стана?

6.   [B,C] Koji je vaš broj telefona?
         [S] Који је ваш број телефона?

7.   [B] Šta su žene kupile u trgovini i za koga?
         [C] Što su žene kupile u dućanu i za koga?
         [S] Шта су жене купиле у радњи и за кога?

8.   [B] Šta su muškarci kupili u trgovini i za koga?
         [C] Što su muškarci kupili u dućanu i za koga?
         [S] Шта су мушкарци купили у радњи и за кога?

9.   [B,C] Koliko je bilo životinja u izlogu?
         [S] Колико је било животиња у излогу?

10.   [B,C] S kim su se našle te tri žene?
         [S] Са ким су се нашле те три жене?

11.   [B] A šta su onda sve te žene radile?
         [C] A što su onda sve te žene radile?
         [S] А шта су онда све те жене радиле?

12.   [B] A šta su onda svi ti muškarci radili?
         [C] A što su onda svi ti muškarci radili?
         [S] А шта су онда сви ти мушкарци радили?

B4

Bosnian	Croatian	Serbian
1. Koliko ima *studenata koji uče bosanski* na fakultetu?	1. Koliko ima *studenata koji uče hrvatski* na fakultetu?	1. Колико има *студената који уче српски* на факултету?
2. Ima ih desetak.	2. Ima ih desetak.	2. Има их десетак.
1. A koliko ima *studenata koji uče francuski*?	1. A koliko ima *studenata koji uče francuski*?	1. А колико има *студената који уче француски*?
2. Ima ih nekoliko stotina.	2. Ima ih nekoliko stotina.	1. Има их неколико стотина.
1. A koliko ih ima *koji uče španjolski*?	1. A koliko ih ima *koji uče španjolski*?	2. А колико их има *који уче шпански*?
2. Ima ih nekoliko hiljada!	2. Ima ih nekoliko tisuća!	1. Има их неколико хиљада!

☞ **Replace the italicized words with** 1) studenti koji stanuju u svom stanu, **and** 2) studenti koji stanuju kod svojih, 3) studenti koji stanuju u domu **and adjust the numbers accordingly.**

B5

Bosnian

1. Ìmam 2 *hȉljade* eu̯ra u banci!
2. Odlično! Ja ìmam samo *hȉljadu*, ali i *hȉljadu* eu̯ra je ipak nešto.
1. Kȁko da ne! Kad budem ìmao 5 *hȉljada*, kȕpit ću sebi starȋ *àuto!*
2. Ja žèlim kȕpiti novȋ *àuto*, pa mi trebaju *hȉljade* i *hȉljade!*

Croatian

1. Ìmam 2 *tȉsuće* eu̯ra u banci!
2. Odlično! Ja ìmam samo *tȉsuću*, ali i *tȉsuću* eu̯ra je ipak nešto.
1. Kȁko da ne! Kad budem ìmao 5 *tȉsuća*, kȕpit ću si starȋ *àuto!*
2. Ja žèlim kȕpiti novȋ *àuto*, pa mi trebaju *tȉsuće* i *tȉsuće!*

Serbian

1. Ìmam 2 *hȉljade* evra u banci!
2. Odlično! Ja ìmam samo *hȉljadu*, ali i *hȉljadu* evra je ipak nešto.
1. Kȁko da ne! Kad budem ìmao 5 *hȉljada*, kȕpiću sebi starȋ *àuto!*
2. Ja žèlim da kȕpim novȋ *àuto*, pa mi trebaju *hȉljade* i *hȉljade!*

☞ **Replace** *hȉljada* [B,S] *tȉsuća* [C] **with** stotina; **replace** *àuto* **with** kompjùter [B,S] kompjùtor [C].

The word "Europe" is *Evrȍpa* in Serbian and *Eu̯rȍpa* in Croatian; Bosnian uses both spellings. Similarly, the word for the basic unit of European currency is spelled *euro* in Croatian and *evro* in Serbian, again with both spellings used in Bosnian. The word is a masculine noun: *jèdan euro* [B,C] *jèdan evro* [B,S].

B6

Bosnian and Croatian

1. Kȍje si gȍdište?
2. Ja sam *'71.* gȍdište. Ìmam *trȉdesȇt tri* .... A tȋ?
1. Ja sam *'63.* gȍdište, takȍ da ìmam *čètrdesȇt dvȉje* ....
2. Znȁči da sam *dvànaȇst* .... stàriji od tebe!

Serbian

1. Кȍје си гȍдиште?
2. Ја сам *'71.* гȍдиште. Ѝмам *трȉдесȇт три* .... А ти?
1. Ја сам *'63.* гȍдиште, такȍ да ѝмам *чѐтрдȅсȇт двȅ* ....
2. Знȁчи да сам *двàнаȇст* .... стàрији од тебе.

☞ **Fill in** the blank with the proper form of the noun *godina*. Then replace the ages and years above with your own.

B7

Bosnian and Croatian

1. Kad *ti* je rođendȃn?
2. Rođendȃn *mi* je ....
1. Onda *ti* ùnaprȋjed čèstitam rođendȃn!
2. Hvȁla. A kad je *tȅbi*?
1. *Mèni* je ....
2. Onda i ja *tȅbi* čèstitam!

Serbian

1. Kad *ti* je rođendȃn?
2. Rođendȃn *mi* je ....
1. Onda *ti* ùnaprȅd čèstitam rođendȃn!
2. Hvȁla. A kad je *tȅbi*?
1. *Mèni* je ....
2. Onda i ja *tȅbi* čèstitam!

☞ **Once** you have practised this using your own birthdays, change it to refer to other classmates and their birthdays.

✍ DOMAĆA ZADAĆA [B,C] DOMAĆI ZADATAK [S]

C1

Compose eight short sentences in the past tense. The subject of each sentence should be one of the numbers in the first column plus a phrase composed of one of the adjectives in the second column plus the adjacent noun in the third column. Write out all the numbers in words. Note that adjectives appear in the list in the customary dictionary-entry form (masculine singular short form); you will need to put the proper endings on each of the adjectives.

Example:

Clue: 5   gladan   podstanar   **Possible answer:** Pet gladnih podstanara je jelo u restoranu.

2	suh [B,C] suv [S]	orah
11	nemački [E] njemački [J]	gradovi
33	težak	godina
51	debeo	mačka
84	studentski	pisaći stolovi
100	gladan	životinja
104	naporan	dan
500	grčki	student
1000	brz	vlak [C] voz [B,S]
1001	divan	noć
2000	pametan	električar

C2

Answer these questions, writing the numbers out in words:

1. Koliko ima studenata u vašoj grupi?

2. [B,S] Koliko ima studentkinja u vašoj grupi?

   [C] Koliko ima studentica u vašoj grupi?

3. [B,S] Koliko ima studenata na vašem univerzitetu?

   [C] Koliko ima studenata na vašem sveučilištu?

4. [B,S] Koliko ima profesora na vašem univerzitetu?

[C] Koliko ima profesora na vašem sveučilištu?

5. Koliko ima ljudi u vašem gradu?

6. Koliko ste imali pasa kad ste bili mali?

7. Koliko ima stvari u ovoj sobi?

8. Koliko ste visoki (u centimetrima)?

9. Koliko ste teški (u kilama)?

C3

Fill in the blank with the requested phrases, and then write the sentence out in full.

1. U .... držala je novac, a u .... je držala olovku i papir.
   (first bag)   (second bag)

2. [B] Kao .... ću pisati zadaću, kao .... ću čitati, a kao .... ću spremati vježbe.
   [C] Kao .... ću pisati zadaću, kao .... ću čitati, a kao .... ću spremati vježbe.
   [S] Kao .... ću pisati zadatak, kao .... ću čitati, a kao .... ću spremati vježbe.
      (first)   (second)   (third)

3. Oni su stajali na .... , a ja sam stajao ispod njih na .... , a ona je bila na ....
   (fifth floor)   (fourth floor)   (third floor)

C4

Write out five dates and state why they are important to you. Use the "question and answer" format seen in A4 as a guide.

C5

Write a short paragraph describing a room and its furnishings that you remember. Use the verbs *sećati* se [E] *sjećati se* [J] and *setiti se* [E] *sjetiti se* [J]).

C6

Translate into B, C, or S:

1. Four smart dentists worked in this building.

2. We don't need breakfast.

3. Five happy taxi drivers were reading novels by Ivo Andrić.

4. We need an apartment in New York.

5. Twenty-two tall bakers sat in their cars.

6. She needs the study of the Hungarian language.

7. A hundred and forty-four apples were red, and five were yellow.

8. I need your understanding.

9. Sixty-one ugly bosses will write letters.

10. He needs happiness.

11. Twelve elegant actors were in the theater.

12. Ninety-two sad dancers were standing in the rain.

13. You need me, and I need you.

14. A thousand euros will not be enough.

15. Six rivers flowed through the country.

C5

Namještaj [J] Nameštaj [E]

Connect word to object

sto   sat   lampa   pisaći stol   jastuk   stol   pisaći sto   stolica

☺☹ Aforizmi Dušana Radovića

VOCABULARY

испричати, испричам	to relate, to tell (P)
решавати, решавам	to address [a problem], to grapple with (I)
рјешавати, рјешавам	to address [a problem], to grapple with (I)

Не можемо живети без других људи. Једни нам стварају, а други решавају проблеме.

Страшно је то кад имате нешто важно да испричате, а немате коме.
А још је страшније кад имате коме, а немате шта.

✍ **Bring** a question on each aphorism to class, incorporating one or more of these phrases:

a. Objasnite ....

b. Zar ....

c. [B,C] Slažete li se s Dušanom Radovićem o .... ?

   [S] Da li se slažete sa Dušanom Radovićem o .... ?

📖 Priča: Bazdulj

Read Part I of the story "Ljubav na španjolski način" by Muharem Bazdulj (p. 347).

Trinaesta lekcija • Lesson Thirteen

∾A1   ⊙7,8

dobro došli	welcome	prazan, prazna	empty
drugo	else	preporučiti, preporučim	to recommend (P)
gost	guest	prijati + *Dat*	to appeal [to] (I)
hodnik	hallway	rado	gladly
kolač, kolača	cake	sipati [B,S]	to serve a beverage (I)
ljubazan, ljubazna	kind	to već da	that's much better
ponuditi	to offer (P)	točiti [C]	to serve a beverage (I)
poslužiti, poslužim	to serve (P)	trinaesti	thirteenth
pozvati, pozovem	to invite (P)	zamoliti, zamolim	to request, to ask for (P)
pozvati u goste	to invite for a visit (P)		

DOBRO DOŠLI!

<u>Bosnian</u>

1. Gospodine, dobro došli! Biste li bili tako ljubazni da pođete sa mnom iz hodnika u sobu?
2. Bilo bi mi drago! Hvala što ste me pozvali u goste!
1. Izvolite, sjedite! Sa čim bih vas mogla ponuditi?
2. Gospođo, strašno sam žedan. Smijem li zamoliti malo hladne vode?
1. Naravno! Sa ledom ili bez?
2. Sa puno, puno leda!
1. Izvolite, gospodine! A da li nešto drugo želite popiti ili pojesti? Možda vina i kolača?
2. Hvala, gospođo. Sviđa mi se ono crno vino. Da li biste bili tako ljubazni da mi sipate?
1. Izvolite gospodine! Bolja je puna nego prazna čaša! Preporučila bih i ovaj kolač. Da li smijem da vas poslužim?
2. Hvala, gospođo, rado bih malo kolača. Ali, molim vas, manje! Još manje! To već da. A vi?
1. Ne bi mi prijalo slatko, hvala. Najviše mi odgovara ovo vino.

<u>Croatian</u>

1. Gospodine, dobro došli! Biste li bili tako ljubazni da pođete sa mnom iz hodnika u sobu?
2. Bilo bi mi drago! Hvala što ste me pozvali u goste!
1. Izvolite, sjedite! S čim bih vas mogla ponuditi?
2. Gospođo, strašno sam žedan. Smijem li zamoliti malo hladne vode?
1. Naravno! S ledom ili bez?
2. S puno, puno leda!
1. Izvolite, gospodine! A želite li nešto drugo popiti ili pojesti? Možda vina i kolača?
2. Hvala, gospođo. Sviđa mi se ono crno vino. Biste li bili tako ljubazni da mi točite?
1. Izvolite gospodine! Bolja je puna nego prazna čaša! Preporučila bih i ovaj kolač. Smijem li da vas poslužim?
2. Hvala, gospođo, rado bih malo kolača. Ali, molim vas, manje! Još manje! To već da. A vi?
1. Ne bi mi prijalo slatko, hvala. Najviše mi odgovara ovo vino.

<u>Serbian</u>

1. Gospodine, dobro došli! Da li biste bili tako ljubazni da pođete sa mnom iz hodnika u sobu?
2. Bilo bi mi drago! Hvala što ste me pozvali u goste!
1. Izvolite, sedite! Sa čime bih vas mogla ponuditi?
2. Gospođo, strašno sam žedan, da li smem da zamolim za čašu hladne vode?
1. Naravno! Sa ledom ili bez?
2. Sa puno, puno leda!
1. Izvolite, gospodine! A da li nešto drugo želite popiti ili pojesti? Možda vina i kolača?
2. Hvala, gospođo. Sviđa mi se ono crno vino. Da li biste bili tako ljubazni da mi sipate?
1. Izvolite gospodine! Bolja je puna nego prazna čaša! Preporučila bih i ovaj kolač. Da li smem da vas poslužim?
2. Hvala, gospođo, rado bih malo kolača. Ali, molim vas, manje! Još manje! To već da. A vi?
1. Ne bi mi prijalo slatko, hvala. Najviše mi odgovara ovo vino.

197
Trinaesta lekcija   Lesson Thirteen

👉 **Bring** food and other relevant props to class and perform this skit from memory, staying as close to the original as the props you provide allow.

Self-study learners: While working on this exercise note the forms of the conditional, *bih, bi, bi, bismo, biste, bi,* and the phrases of politeness. Also notice the use of *odgovàrati* and *prìjati.*

GRAMMAR

* The conditional mood *

The conditional mood is used with many of the same meanings as the English conditional. It is composed of the L-participle and a form similar to the aorist of *biti.* The clitic and full forms of this auxiliary look alike on the printed page; in speech, the full forms are accented but the clitic forms are not. Clitics are used in in most instances, and full forms are used for asking questions and in single-word answers. The forms given in the chart must be used in writing and in careful speech. In informal speech, only the auxiliary *bi* is used. **[131]**

	singular	plural
1st masc.	*bih rȁdio*	*bismo rȁdili*
1st fem.	*bih rȁdila*	*bismo rȁdile*
2nd masc.	*bi rȁdio*	*biste rȁdili*
2nd fem.	*bi rȁdila*	*biste rȁdile*
3rd masc.	*bi rȁdio*	*bi rȁdili*
3rd neut.	*bi rȁdilo*	*bi rȁdila*
3rd fem.	*bi rȁdila*	*bi rȁdile*

One use of the conditional is in so-called politeness formulas. Just as it is more polite in English to use the conditional (as in "I WOULD LIKE some cake") rather than the indicative (as in "I WANT some cake"), BCS uses the conditional *žèlela* [E] *žèljela* [J] *bih kolȁča* instead of the indicative *žèlim kolȁča.* **[133b]**

* The word "welcome" *

The English phrase "welcome" is translated literally into BCS, given that one breaks the English one down into its two components, "well" and "come." The second word of the BCS phrase is spoken differently depending on the relationship. If the person arriving is someone you would normally address as *ti,* then you should greet this person with the phrase *dobro dòšao* (for a man) or *dobro dòšla* (for a woman). Otherwise, the phrase *dobro dòšli* should be used (to a group, or to someone normally addressed as *vi*). When written as a single word, the phrase functions as an adjective, as in *òna je dobrodòšla* "she is [a] welcome [guest]."

Introductions are made as follows: In rapid sequence, the person initiating the introduction looks directly at the other person and then says *"Dobar dȁn!"* while extending the right hand and speaking his or her name (first name in an informal setting and full name in a formal setting). Friends greet by kissing on alternate cheeks. This is done twice by speakers of Bosnian and Croatian, and three times by speakers of Serbian.

Sarajevo: Buildings from the Austro-Hungarian period, after 1878.

Zagreb: a view of St. Mark's Church and the
Parliament (Sabor) of Croatia.

Belgrade: the Parliament (Narodna Skupština) of Serbia

Trinaesta lekcija   Lesson Thirteen

čim	as soon as	skloniti, sklonim	to put away (P)
čim prije [B,C]	as soon as possible	sledeći	next
doneti, donesem	to bring (P)	sljedeći	next
donijeti, donesem	to bring (P)	spustiti, spustim	to put down (P)
makar	at least	sveza [C]	connection
mušterija	customer	što pre [S]	as soon as possible
početi, počnem	to begin (P)	što prije [B,C,S]	as soon as possible
popraviti	to repair (P)	u redu	O.K., fine
pre	earlier	u svezi [C]	in relation to
prije	earlier	u vezi [B,S]	in relation to
sebičan, sebična	selfish	veza [B,C,S]	connection

EVO KOMPJUTERA! [B,S]   EVO KOMPJUTORA! [C]

Bosnian

1. [*carrying a heavy box*] Evo, donio sam vaš kompjuter. Popravljen je. Gdje da ga spustim?
2. Molim vas stavite ga tamo na pisaći sto.
1. Ako hoćete da ga stavim na sto, morali biste skloniti sve vaše stvari sa stola!
2. Odmah, ali mogu li vas ponuditi s kafom prije toga?
1. Ne, hvala. Već sam popio danas. Žuri mi se. [*groaning under the weight of the box*] Ako biste sklonili stvari mogao bih početi raditi.
2. Naravno! Ali kad ste već tu, možete li mi objasniti neke stvari u vezi s kompjuterom?
1. [*groaning*] Molim vas, rekli ste da ćete skloniti te stvari! Nemojte biti neozbiljni! Moram čim prije otići kod sljedeće mušterije.
2. U redu, [*clearing the desk*] sklonio sam ih. Žao mi je što ne možete ostati makar par minuta duže!

Croatian

1. [*carrying a heavy box*] Evo, donio sam vaš kompjutor. Popravljen je. Gdje da ga spustim?
2. Molim vas stavite ga tamo na pisaći stol.
1. Ako hoćete da ga stavim na stol, morali biste skloniti sve vaše stvari sa stola!
2. Odmah, ali mogu li vas ponuditi s kavom prije toga?
1. Ne, hvala. Već sam popio danas. Žuri mi se. [*groaning under the weight of the box*] Ako biste sklonili stvari mogao bih početi raditi.
2. Naravno! Ali kad ste već tu, možete li mi objasniti neke stvari u svezi s kompjutorom?
1. [*groaning*] Molim vas, rekli ste da ćete skloniti te stvari! Nemojte biti neozbiljni! Moram čim prije otići do sljedeće mušterije.
2. U redu, [*clearing the desk*] sklonio sam ih. Žao mi je što ne možete ostati makar par minuta duže!

Serbian

1. [*carrying a heavy box*] Ево, донео сам ваш компјутер. Поправљен је. Где да га спустим?
2. Молим вас ставите га тамо на писаћи сто.
1. Ако хоћете да га ставим на сто, морали бисте да склоните све ваше ствари са стола!
2. Одмах, али да ли могу да вас понудим са кафом пре тога?
1. Не, хвала. Већ сам попио данас. Жури ми се. [*groaning under the weight of the box*] Ако бисте склонили те ствари могао бих почети да радим.
2. Наравно! Али кад сте већ ту, да ли можете да ми објасните неке ствари у вези са компјутером?
1. [*groaning*] Молим вас, казали сте да ћете да склоните те ствари! Немојте бити неозбиљни! Морам што пре да одем код следеће муштерије.
2. У реду, [*clearing the desk*] склонио сам их. Жао ми је што не можете да останете макар пар минута дуже!

☞ **Play** this conversation, on your feet, using a box for the computer. Go through it again with #1 as a female repair person. Then change the number of people involved, first so that there are two repair people, and then so that there are two people receiving them.

☞ **Rework** the conversation so that it is informal, using *ti* instead of *vi*.

⚙ GRAMMAR

* Use of the conditional in "toned-down" statements or requests *

The conditional mood is often used, as in English, to soften the force of a statement or request. Both the sentences *morate skloniti stvari* and *morali biste skloniti stvari* state that someone must move his/her things, but the first is much more abrupt. The difference is the same as that between English "you have to move your things" and "you would need to move your things." **[133a]**

* Indirect discourse *

When speech is quoted directly, the verb remains in the same tense as in the quoted speech, as in, for instance "you said, 'I WILL move those things'." When speech is quoted indirectly and placed in a subordinate clause after a past tense verb, English must change the tense of the quoted speech. Thus, the indirect version of this English sentence is "you said you WOULD move those things." In the BCS versions of these sentences, however, the quoted speech remains in the same tense, whether it is a direct quote or an indirect one. The direct is *rekli ste 'ja ĆU skloniti te stvari',* and the indirect is *rekli ste da ĆETE skloniti te stvari.* **[135]** English speakers must pay particular attention to this difference between BCS and English.

* *Da* introducing proposed actions *

The conjunction *da* usually follows a verb, and introduces a clause containing a second verb. The second clause may be one of fact, as in *znam da je on Amerikanac* (the relationship of fact is indicated by the conjunction "that" in the English translation "I know that he's an American"). But *da* can also introduce a subordinate clause of purpose, as in *želim da učimo zajedno* (here the relationship of purpose indicated by the preposition "to" in the English translation "I want us to study together"). If *da* stands alone before the main verb of a sentence, the idea of purpose is presented as a potential action. This frequently takes the form of a question, as in *kako da dođem do trga?* "how [can] I get to the square?" and *da to spustim na pod?* "[should] I put this on the floor?" It can also take the form of a suggestion, as in *da popijemo nešto!* "let's have something to drink!" **[143e]**

Stopping permitted up to 3 minutes

VOCABULARY

brinuti, brinem	to worry	pojam, pojma	concept
čarobnjak, čarobnjaka	wizard, magician	pojaviti se, pojavim se	to appear (P)
ipak	nevertheless	polako	take it easy, slow down
kralj, kralja	king	poslovan, poslovna	business (adj.)
materijal, materijala	documents, papers	primerak, primerka	copy
nekih pedesetak	some fifty-odd	primjerak, primjerka	copy
nemam pojma	I have no idea	pripremiti, pripremim	to prepare (P)
noćas	tonight, last night	reputacija	reputation
obraditi, obradim	to work through (P)	sastanak, sastanka	meeting
ostali	remaining	stranica	page
ovako	like this, as it is	šteta	a shame, too bad
partner, partnera	partner		

POLAKO ...

Bosnian

1. Ako pročitam tvoje materijale noćas, dat ću ti ih sutra ujutro rano na poslu.
2. Koliko još imaš stranica?
1. Pa, nekih pedesetak.
2. Bolje bi ipak bilo kad bi to pročitao - najkasnije do osamnaest i trideset. Treba mi moj primjerak materijala da bih ih obradio s kolegom večeras u devetnaest i trideset.
1. Svejedno mi je. Neka ih kolega obradi sam.
2. Sjeti se moje reputacije! Šta će reći ostali poslovni partneri kad im dođem nepripremljen sutra na sastanak?
1. Polako. Nemam pojma šta će reći. Neka kažu šta hoće. Da sam čarobnjak mogao bih da ih pročitam do večeras. Šteta što nisam.
2. A ja, da sam kralj, ne bih brinuo! Ovako, ne smijem ni da se pojavim sutra.

Croatian

1. Ako pročitam tvoje materijale noćas, dat ću ti ih sutra ujutro rano na poslu.
2. Koliko još imaš stranica?
1. Pa, nekih pedesetak.
2. Bolje bi ipak bilo kad bi to pročitao - najkasnije do osamnaest i trideset. Treba mi moj primjerak materijala da bih ih obradio s kolegom večeras u devetnaest i trideset.
1. Svejedno mi je. Neka ih kolega obradi sam.
2. Sjeti se moje reputacije! Što će reći ostali poslovni partneri kad im dođem nepripremljen sutra na sastanak?
1. Polako. Nemam pojma što će reći. Neka kažu što hoće. Da sam čarobnjak mogao bih ih pročitati do večeras. Šteta što nisam.
2. A ja, da sam kralj, ne bih brinuo! Ovako, ne smijem se ni pojaviti sutra.

Serbian

1. Ako pročitam tvoje materijale noćas, daću ti ih sutra ujutro rano na poslu.
2. Koliko još imaš stranica?
1. Pa, nekih pedesetak.
2. Bolje bi ipak bilo kad bi to pročitao - najkasnije do osamnaest i trideset. Treba mi moj primerak materijala da bih ih obradio s kolegom večeras u devetnaest i trideset najkasnije.
1. Svejedno mi je. Neka ih kolega obradi sam.
2. Seti se moje reputacije! Šta će reći ostali poslovni partneri kad im dođem nepripremljen sutra na sastanak?
1. Polako. Nemam pojma šta će da kažu. Neka kažu šta hoće. Da sam čarobnjak mogao bih da ih pročitam do večeras. Šteta što nisam.
2. A ja, da sam kralj, ne bih brinuo! Ovako, ne smem ni da se pojavim sutra.

☞ **Make** your own version, based loosely on this exchange, of a conversation between two people, one of whom owes the other a book the other needs to study for an exam, or some money, or a coveted item of clothing.

Self-study learners: Note the use of the perfective form *pročitati,* the verbal forms *treba, neka, setiti se* [E] *sjetiti se* [J], *smeti* [E] *smjeti* [J] and the phrases *nemam pojma* and *šteta što....*

GRAMMAR

* Conditional sentences *

The conditional mood takes its name from sentences which articulate a condition, together with its presumed result, in the form "If A .... then B." There are three different kinds of such sentences, and the differences between them are marked not only by the verb form but also by the conjunction used to express the idea "if." When the speaker fully expects the condition to be fulfilled, s/he uses the conjunction *ako* plus an indicative form of the verb (present or past tense); for instance, *ako pročitam sve do večeras, mogu vam dati knjigu* "if I read everything through before this evening, I can give you the book." **[132a]** If the fulfillment of the condition is possible but uncertain, the speaker usually uses the conjunction *kad*, and the conditional mood in both clauses of the sentence; for instance, *bolje bi bilo kad biste to pročitali do večeras* "it would be better if you were to read it through by this evening." **[132b]** If the condition is purely hypothetical or otherwise unfulfillable, the speaker uses the conjunction *da* followed by the present tense, with the verb of the second clause in the conditional mood; for instance, *da sam čarobnjak, mogao bih to sve pročitati do večeras* "if I were a magician, I'd be able to read it all by this evening." **[132c]**

* Conditional of purpose *

The conditional mood after the conjunction *da* emphasizes the purpose or goal of an action. An example is *treba mi to da bih ga obradila večeras* "I need it so that I can work on it this evening." **[134b]** This is the single use of the BCS conditional that has no parallel in English. Students may think of this meaning as an English quasi-conditional of the sort "...that I might work on it" or the like, in order to learn it more easily.

VOCABULARY

ako nemate ništa protiv	if you've no objections	odvesti, odvezem	to take by vehicle (P)
autobuski [B,S]	bus *(adj.)*	poništiti	to stamp, to void (P)
autobusni [C]	bus *(adj.)*	pravo [S]	straight ahead
desni	right [= not left] *(adj.)*	proći, prođem	to pass (P)
gradski	city *(adj.)*	protiv + *Gen*	against
itekako	definitely	ravan, ravna [B,C]	straight
karta	ticket	ravno [B,C]	straight ahead
kiosk	newspaper stand	sići, siđem	to get off (P)
kolegica [B,C]	female colleague	skrenuti, skrenem	to turn (P)
koleginica [B,S]	female colleague	trebalo bi	ought
kraj + *Gen*	next to, by	trg	[city] square
levi	left *(adj.)*	ulica	block; street
lijevi	left *(adj.)*	uputstva	instructions
odavde	from here	zahvalan, zahvalna	grateful

UPUTSTVA

Bosnian

1. Molim vas, kako da dođem odavde do glavnog trga?
2. Nije teško. Objasnit ću vam. Prvo na kiosku treba kupiti autobusku kartu koju ćete dati vozaču autobusa. On će tu kartu poništiti. Proći ćete nekih desetak ulica do treće stanice. Na trećoj stanici treba sići.
1. A kad siđem jesam li onda na trgu na kojem treba da budem?
2. Odmah ćete vidjeti trg ravno ispred sebe. Ne bi trebalo skrenuti ni lijevo ni desno. A zašto idete na trg, ako smijem da pitam?
1. Smijete! Tražim Gradsku kafanu. Rekla mi je kolegica da je zgrada koju ću vidjeti kraj Gradske kafane vrlo lijepa.
2. Kako da ne. To je zgrada u kojoj ja stanujem! Mogu vas tamo odvesti svojim kolima ako nemate ništa protiv.
1. Bila bih vam itekako zahvalna!

Croatian

1. Molim vas, kako da dođem odavde do glavnog trga?
2. Nije teško. Objasnit ću vam. Prvo na kiosku treba kupiti autobusnu kartu koju ćete dati vozaču autobusa. On će tu kartu poništiti. Proći ćete nekih desetak ulica do treće stanice. Na trećoj stanici treba sići.
1. A kad siđem jesam li onda na trgu na kojem trebam biti?
2. Odmah ćete vidjeti trg ravno ispred sebe. Ne bi trebalo skrenuti ni lijevo ni desno. A zašto idete na trg, ako smijem pitati?
1. Smijete! Tražim Gradsku kavanu. Rekla mi je kolegica da je zgrada koju ću vidjeti kraj Gradske kavane vrlo lijepa.
2. Kako da ne. To je zgrada u kojoj ja stanujem! Mogu vas tamo odvesti svojim kolima ako nemate ništa protiv.
1. Bila bih vam itekako zahvalna!

Tickets for public transportation or inter-city travel can usually be purchased in the bus, tram, or train from the driver or a conductor. But they will be less expensive if purchased at a newspaper kiosk (for city buses or trams) or at the terminal (for intercity bus or train travel). See p. 99 for examples of bus tickets.

<u>Serbian</u>

1. Мо̏л̣им вас, ка̏ко да до̂ђем о̏давде до гла̏вно̑г трга?

2. Ни̏је те̏шко. Обја̏снићу вам. Прво̄ на киоску тре̏ба̄ да кӯпите а̏утобускӯ ка̏рту ко̏јӯ ћете да да̄те воза̄чу ау̏то̏буса. Он ће тӯ ка̏рту пони̏штити. Про̂ћи ћете неки̏х десе̏так ули̏ца до тре̏ће̄ ста̏нице̄. На тре̏ћо̄ј ста̏ници тре̏ба̄ да си̏ђете.

1. А кад си̏ђем да ли сам о̏нда̄ на тргу на ко̏је̄м тре̏ба̄ да бу̏де̄м?

2. О̏дма̄х ћете ви̏дети трг пра̏во и̏спред себе. Не̏ би тре̏бало скре̄нути ни ле̏во ни де̏сно. А за̏што и̏де̄те на трг ако сме̑м да пи̏та̄м?

1. Сме̏те! Тра̏жӣм Гра̏дскӯ ка̏фа̄ну. Ка̏зала ми је коле̏гиница да је згра̏да ко̏јӯ ћу да ви̏дӣм крај Гра̏дске̄ ка̏фа̄не̄ вр̏ло ле̏па.

2. Ка̏ко да не. То̏ је згра̏да у ко̏јо̄ј ја̄ ста̏нӯје̄м! Мо̏гу да вас о̏две̄зе̄м та̏мо сво̏јӣм ко̏лима ако не̏ма̄те ни̏шта про̏тив.

1. Би̏ла бих вам итека̏ко заxва̏лна!

📖 **Use** this sketch as the basis for giving each other instructions for how to find something in a city.

Self-study learners: Go over this exchange carefully and note the vocabulary used to give instructions for taking a bus ride and finding a location.

City parking. Bus station. Ticket sales. Welcome.

Tickets sold by the driver.

Zagreb, City Cafe.

 **GRAMMAR**

* The relative conjunction *koji*, continued *

The gender and number of the relative conjunction *koji* are determined by the word it refers to, which is called its antecedent. In the sentence *studenti koji stanuju tamo moraju urediti svoje sobe* (seen on p. 180), it is the masculine plural noun *studenti* which requires masculine plural endings on *koji*. Similarly, in the sentence *poznaješ li ženu koja ulazi u sobu* it is the feminine singular noun *žena* which requires feminine singular endings on *koja*. But the antecedent determines only number and gender; it is the grammar of the clause in which *koji* occurs that determines what case it is in. In both of these sentences, the relative conjunction *koji* is the subject within its own clause (a fact which is seen also in the English "the students WHO live here...." and "...the woman WHO is coming into the room"); thus the case is nominative. [128a] But a relative conjunction must take whatever case the clause requires. For instance, it is accusative in the sentence *zgrada KOJU ćete videti* [E] *vidjeti* [J] *na glavnom trgu je moja* "the building WHICH you will see on the main square is mine," and locative in the sentence *to je zgrada u KOJOJ ja stanujem* "that's the building I live in [in WHICH I live]." The gender and number of each of these relative conjunctions is feminine singular, of course, since in both instances the antecedent is the feminine singular noun *zgrada*.

In forming such sentences, English speakers must not only remember to follow all the rules of case, number and gender, but they must also remember the more basic rule, which is to insert a relative conjunction whenever the grammar requires it. The fact that most English speakers would omit "that" or "which" (and would phrase the above sentences as "the building you'll see on the square is mine" or "that's the building I live in") requires extra effort in learning to form BCS relative clauses. [136a]

* Compound conjunctions *

Many English prepositions are used in an adverbial sense. This accounts for the fact that they can function grammatically both as prepositions and as conjunctions. For example, when the English word "before" is used in an adverbial phrase of time (as in "before lunch"), it is a preposition. But when it is followed by a clause containing a verb (as in "before he arrived"), it is a conjunction. BCS must use different words in these two instances. If what follows is a noun or a pronoun, BCS uses a preposition. But if what follows is a clause, BCS must use a conjunction.

Most conjunctions are simple words, like *da*, *što*, *ako*, *kad*, and the like. But when the idea expressed by a preposition also serves as a conjunction, then BCS creates a compound conjunction by adding a specific phrase after the preposition. The most frequent such phrases are *nego što* (which does not change) or *to što* (in which *to* must take the case endings required by the sentence). For example, the phrases "before lunch" and "after lunch" are expressed with prepositions: *pre* [E] *prije* [J] *ručka* and *posle* [E] *poslije* [J] *ručka*. But when the idea "before" is expressed as a conjunction, one must add *nego što*, as in *završila sam sve pre* [E] *prije* [J] *nego što je on stigao* "I finished everything before he arrived." Similarly, the idea "after" as a conjunction requires *to što*, and the prepositional portion of the conjunction requires *to* to be in the genitive. Thus one says *zvala je nakon toga što je otišao* "she called after he left." Many other prepositions are related to conjunctions in this manner: for example, *došli smo zbog vas* "we came because of you" vs. *došli smo zbog toga što moramo s vama razgovarati* "we came because we have to speak with you." [143b]

🏃 VJEŽBE [J] VEŽBE [E]

B1

Bosnian and Croatian	Serbian
1. Dobar dan! Ja sam Sonja Pašić.	1. Добар дан! Ја сам Соња Пашић.
2. Drago mi je. Margaret Smith.	2. Драго ми је. Маргарет Смит.

☞ **Practice** introducing yourself to someone, shaking hands as you say your name.

Bosnian and Croatian	Serbian
1. Hoćete li pušiti?	1. Да ли хоћете пушити?
2. Žao mi je, ali ne pušim, hvala.	2. Жао ми је, али не пушим, хвала.

☞ **Self-study learners**: note that the phrases *drago mi je* and *žao mi je* are particularly important.

Bosnian and Croatian	Serbian
1. Hoćete li još kolača?	1. Да ли хоћете још колача?
2. Hvala, ali ne mogu više.	2. Хвала, али не могу више.

☞ **Practice** offering each other things and refusing politely.

Bosnian	Croatian	Serbian
1. Šta biste željeli popiti?	1. Što biste željeli popiti?	1. Шта бисте желели да попијете?
2. Svejedno mi je, *kafu* ili *čaj*.	2. Svejedno mi je, *kavu* ili *čaj*.	2. Свеједно ми је, кафу или чај.

☞ **Replace the** *kafa* [B,S] *kava* [C] **and** *čaj* **with other beverages:** mineralna voda, pivo, sok, vino.

> When a person is offered food or drink in the BCS region, s/he often refuses the first offer so as not to seem overly eager. Your host may assume you are doing the same if you decline an offer for food or drink. Should you find that the offer is made repeatedly despite your refusal, this is because your host would feel impolite doing otherwise. The response *hvala, ne mogu* is a courteous one. However, it is considered impolite to say simply *neću* [B,S] or *ne ću* [C],

B2

Bosnian	Croatian	Serbian
1. Da li bi htjela nešto da *pojedeš* za večeru?	1. Bi li htjela nešto *pojesti* za večeru?	1. Да ли би хтела нешто да *поједеш* за вечеру?
2. Hvala, bih! Strašno sam *gladna*!	2. Hvala, bih! Strašno sam *gladna*!	2. Хвала, бих! Страшно сам *гладна*!
1. Čime te mogu poslužiti? Imam *finog mesa*.	1. Čime te mogu poslužiti? Imam *finog mesa*.	1. Чиме могу да те послужим? Имам *финог меса*.
2. Na žalost, *meso* mi se ne *jede* zbog toga što sam *jela* dosta *mesa* danas za ručak. Može li nešto drugo?	2. Na žalost, *meso* mi se ne *jede* zbog toga što sam *jela* dosta *mesa* danas za ručak. Može li nešto drugo?	2. На жалост, *месо* ми се не *једе* због тога што сам *јела* доста *меса* данас за ручак. Да ли може нешто друго?
1. Kako da ne! Može, bez problema.	1. Kako da ne! Može, bez problema.	1. Како да не! Може, без проблема.

☞ **Replace** *fino meso* **with** belo [E] bijelo [J] vino, crni hljeb [B,S] crni kruh [C] crni hleb [S], ćevapčići, hladno pivo, jaje, maslac, slatki kolač. **When speaking of beverages, use** žedan, popiti **and** piti.

Bosnian
1. Kada biste htjeli, mogli biste svi biti odlični profesori *slavistike*!
2. A šta ako bismo htjeli biti profesori nečeg drugog?
1. Ni to ne bi bilo loše. Čega biste htjeli biti profesori?
2. Ako bi sve bilo po meni, htio bih da budem profesor *jezika* i *književnosti*, zbog toga što to najviše volim.
3. A ja bih bio profesor *hemije*, zato što to najviše žele moji roditelji.

Croatian
1. Kada biste htjeli, mogli biste svi biti odlični profesori *slavistike*!
2. A što ako bismo htjeli biti profesori nečeg drugoga?
1. Ni to ne bi bilo loše. Čega biste htjeli biti profesori?
2. Ako bi sve bilo po meni, htio bih biti profesor *jezika* i *književnosti*, zbog toga što to najviše volim.
3. A ja bih bio profesor *kemije*, zato što to najviše žele moji roditelji.

Serbian
1. Kada biste hteli, mogli biste svi biti odlični profesori *slavistike*!
2. A šta ako bismo hteli biti profesori nečeg drugog?
1. Ni to ne bi bilo loše. Čega biste hteli biti profesori?
2. Ako bi sve bilo po meni, hteo bih da budem profesor *jezika* i *književnosti*, zbog toga što to najviše volim.
3. A ja bih bio profesor *hemije*, zato što to najviše žele moji roditelji.

☛ **Replace** the italicized disciplines with ones from the following list.

VOCABULARY

anglistika	English language and literature	kemija [C]	chemistry
arhitektura	architecture	kineziologija [C]	physical education
biologija	biology	književnost, -osti (f)	literature
bogoslovija	theology	likovna umetnost, -osti (f)	fine arts
dramske umetnosti (f)	theater arts	likovna umjetnost, -osti (f)	fine arts
dramske umjetnosti (f)	theater arts	lingvistika [B,C,S]	linguistics
društvene nauke [B,S]	social sciences	mašinstvo [B,S]	mechanical engineering
društvene znanosti [C]	social sciences	matematika	mathematics
ekonomija	economics	medicina	medicine
elektrotehnika	electrical engineering	muzika [B,C,S]	music
filologija [B,S]	philology	pedagogija	teaching
filozofija	philosophy	političke nauke [B,S]	political science
fizička kultura [B,C,S]	physical education	političke znanosti [C]	political science
fizika	physics	poljoprivreda	agriculture
geografija	geography	povijest [C] (f)	history
germanistika	Germanic languages and literatures	pravo	law
		prirodne nauke [B,S]	natural science
glazba [C]	music	prirodne znanosti [C]	natural science
hemija [B,S]	chemistry	psihologija	psychology
historija [B]	history	romanistika	Romance languages and literatures
informatika	computer science		
istorija [S]	history	slavistika	Slavic languages and literatures
jezikoslovlje [C]	linguistics	stomatologija	dentistry
južnoslavistika	South Slavic languages and literatures	strojarstvo [C]	mechanical engineering
		šumarstvo	forestry

↑ GALLERY ↑

PROFESSIONAL LITERATURE

social sciences, economics,

law, medicine, natural sciences

SUBSCRIPTION TO AND ORDERING OF

FOREIGN PUBLICATIONS.

B4

Bosnian	Croatian	Serbian
1. Izvoli sjesti! Da popijemo malo kafe.	1. Izvoli sjesti! Da popijemo malo kave.	1. Изволи, седи! Да попијемо мало кафе.
2. Baš mi prija kafa sada.	2. Baš mi prija kava sada.	2. Баш ми прија кафа сада.
1. Da li bi je željela piti sa šećerom ili bez?	1. Bi li je željela piti sa šećerom ili bez?	1. Да ли би желела да је пијеш са шећером или без?
2. Molila bih sa šećerom ali bez mlijeka, hvala.	2. Molila bih sa šećerom ali bez mlijeka, hvala.	2. Молила бих са шећером али без млека, хвала.

☞ **Rework** the conversation so that it is about having beer or wine and cake or *ćevapčići*.

B5

1. Kako bi bilo kad bi *zarađivala* više *novca*?
2. To ne bi bilo loše.
1. A kako bi bilo kad bi *zarađivala* manje *novca*?
2. To ne bi bilo dobro.

☞ **Replace** *zarađivati više novca* **with** čitati više knjiga, kupiti više stvari, položiti više ispita, slušati više predavanja.

B6

Ask each other these and similar questions:

<u>Bosnian</u>
1. Šta bi najviše volio jesti?
2. Kuda bi najviše voljela putovati?
3. Koliko bi najviše želio zarađivati?
4. Kada bi mogao ići u Bosnu i Hercegovinu?
5. Šta bi bilo bolje: uvijek biti student ili završiti fakultet?

<u>Croatian</u>
1. Što bi najviše volio jesti?
2. Kamo bi najviše voljela putovati?
3. Koliko bi najviše želio zarađivati?
4. Kada bi mogao ići u Hrvatsku?
5. Što bi bilo bolje: uvijek biti student ili završiti fakultet?

<u>Serbian</u>
1. Шта би највише волео да једеш?
2. Куда би највише волела да путујеш?
3. Колико би највише желео зарађивати?
4. Када би могао да идеш у Србију?
5. Шта би било боље: увек бити студент или завршити факултет?

B7

<u>Bosnian</u>
1. Šta ti je?
2. *Glava* me boli.
1. Treba ti *čaša hladne vode*!
2. Svejedno mi je. Kada bih *popila čašu hladne vode*, *glava* bi me boljela još više!

<u>Croatian</u>
1. Što ti je?
2. *Glava* me boli.
1. Treba ti *čaša hladne vode*!
2. Svejedno mi je. Kada bih *popila čašu hladne vode*, *glava* bi me boljela još više!

<u>Serbian</u>
1. Шta ti je?
2. *Glava* me boli.
1. Treba ti *čaša hladne vode*!
2. Svejedno mi je. Kada bih *popila čašu hladne vode*, *glava* bi me bolela još više!

☛ **Replace** *glava* **with** ruka, noga, stomak [B,S] trbuh [C], lakat, leđa.

☛ **Replace** *popiti čašu hladne vode* **with** staviti led, popiti aspirin, umiti se hladnom vodom.

✍ DOMAĆA ZADAĆA [B,C] DOMAĆI ZADATAK [S]

C1

Work up a skit in which characters are getting to know one another. Use the polite phrases from A1.

C2

Write a paragraph (100 words) on one of the following themes:

Šta bih radila da imam vremena i novca?

Šta bi radio da ima vremena i novca?

Šta bismo radili da imamo vremena i novca?

C3

Fill in the blanks with the appropriate form of the conditional:

1. [B,C] Kada .... cijelu domaću zadaću svaki dan .... odličan student.
   [S] Kada .... celi domaći zadatak svaki dan .... odličan student.
      (ti, napisati)   (biti)

2. [C]   Ne .... loše da dođeš k nama sutra po podne na ručak.
   [B,S] Ne .... loše da dođeš kod nas sutra po podne na ručak.
         (biti)

3. [B,C] O takvim stvarima .... govoriti.
   [S]   O takvim stvarima .... da se govori.
                  (ne treba)

4. [B,C] Da .... predsjednica ili predsjednik Amerike, ... puno posla.
   [S]   Da .... predsednica ili predsednik Amerike, ... puno posla.
         (ti, biti)   (imati)

5. [B,S] Da li .... tako ljubazni da pođete sa mnom?
   [C] Biste li .... tako ljubazni da pođete sa mnom?
            (vi, biti)

6. .... život da vozim motocikl.
   (ja, prokockati)

C4

Take each of the phrases below and make it into a hypothetical conditional.

Example: ja / pìlòt
[B,C] Da sam pìlòt, putòvala bih cìjèlè gòdinè avìonom!
[S] Da sam pìlòt, putòvala bih cèlè gòdinè avìonom!

1. mì / francùzi
2. òni / dobrì
3. vì / šezdèsèt gòdina
4. jà / trì gòdine
5. òna / čàrobnjàk

1. ми / францу̀зи
2. о̀ни / добрѝ
3. вѝ / шездѐсѐт го̀дина
4. jà / трѝ го̀дине
5. о̀на / чаро̀бњак

C5

Translate the first sentence into English and the next two into B, C, or S, following the example of the first.

1. a. [B,C] Biste li bìli tàkò ljùbazni sjèsti óvdje do njè?
      [S] Да ли бисте бѝли тако̀ љу̀базни да сѐдите о̀вде до ње?
   b. Would you be so kind as to open that door? Thank you! Now, would you open this door?
   c. Would you be so kind as to help us and give us your hand?

2. a. [B,C] Kad bih mògla polòžiti ìspìt, òdmah bih òtišla ga polàgati!
      [S] Кад бих мо̀гла поло̀жити испѝт, о̀дмах бих о̀тишла да га по̀лажем!
   b. If we could prepare Japanese food, we would eat well.
   c. If you could study 20 hours each day, you would be an excellent student!

3. a. [B] Da si žìvio prìje stotinu gòdìna, vjerovàtno vìšè nè bi bio žìv!
      [C] Da si žìvio prìje stotinu gòdìna, vjerojàtno vìšè nè bi bio žìv!
      [S] Да си жѝвео пре сто̀ го̀дина, веро̀ватно вишѐ нѐ би био жѝв!
   b. If I were a magician, I would never worry about anything.
   c. If we were children, we would play ball all day.

4. a. [B,C] Bòlè me i nòge i rùke. Smìjem li te zamòliti za pòmoć?
      [S] Бо̀лѐ ме и но̀ге и ру̀ке. Да ли смѐм да те за̀молим за по̀моћ?
   b. My stomach hurts. If I were to drink warm milk it would hurt less.
   c. My head hurts, but it will hurt less if I lie down.

5. a. [B,C] Čìme se baviš? Bavìm se pràvom.
      [S] Чѝме се бавѝш? Бавѝм се пра̀вом.
   b. What do they do? They work in medicine.
   c. What does she do? She works in geography.

C6

Answer the following questions (based on A1, A2, A3 and A4).

A1

1. [B,C] Zbog čega je gospodin zamolio malo hladne vode?
   [S] Због чега је господин замолио за мало хладне воде?

2. [B,C] Zašto je gospođa pitala gospodina želi li nešto drugo popiti ili pojesti?
   [S] Зашто је госпођа питала господина да ли жели нешто друго попити или појести?

3. [B,C] Pored toga što gospodin pije crno vino, hoće li i nešto pojesti?
   [S] Поред тога што господин пије црно вино, да ли хоће и нешто појести?

4. [B,C] Zašto se gospođi čini da je bolja puna nego prazna čaša?
   [S] Зашто се госпођи чини да је боља пуна него празна чаша?

5. [B,C] Zar će gospođa piti samo vino? Zašto?
   [S] Зар ће госпођа пити само вино? Зашто?

A2

1. [B] Šta bi trebalo učiniti tako da čovjek može spustiti kompjuter?
   [C] Što bi trebalo učiniti tako da čovjek može spustiti kompjutor?
   [S] Шта би требало да се учини тако да човек може да спусти компјутер?

2. [B,C] Zašto treba skloniti sve stvari sa stola?
   [S] Зашто треба да се склоне све ствари са стола?

3. [B,C] Zbog čega je čovjek ljut?
   [S] Због чега је човек љут?

A3

1. [B,C] Zašto trebaju broju 2 materijali?
   [S] Зашто требају броју 2 материјали?

2. [B,C] Zar broj 1 nije kralj?
   [S] Зар број 1 није краљ?

3. [B] Šta će reći poslovni partneri kad broj 1 dođe nepripremljen na sastanak?
   [C] Što će reći poslovni partneri kad broj 1 dođe nepripremljen na sastanak?
   [S] Шта ће да кажу пословни партнери кад број 1 дође неприпремљен на састанак?

A4

1. [B,C] Zbog čega broj 1 traži glavni trg?
   [S] Због чега број 1 тражи главни трг?

2. [B] Pored čega na glavnom trgu stoji Gradska kafana?
   [C] Pored čega na glavnome trgu stoji Gradska kavana?
   [S] Поред чега на главном тргу стоји Градска кафана?

3. [B,C] O čemu su broj 1 i broj 2 razgovarali?
   [S] О чему су број 1 и број 2 разговарали?

Trinaesta lekcija   Lesson Thirteen

☺☹ Aforizmi Dušana Radovića

VOCABULARY

анони̏мно̄ст, анони̏мности (f)	anonymity	нескро̀ман, нескро̏мна	immodest
вре̏дно̄ст, вре̏дности (f)	value	обjекти̏ван, обjекти̏вна	objective
вриjѐдно̄ст, вриjѐдности (f)	value	по̀сти̏ћи, по̀сти̏гне̄м	to accomplish (P)
глу̏по̄ст, глу̏пости (f)	stupidity	спа̀сити, спа̏сӣм [C]	to save (P)
инсисти̏ра̄ње	insistence	спа̀сти, спа̀се̄м [B,S]	to save (P)

Ко jе и̏мао сре̏ће̄ да се jу̏тро̄с про̀бу̏дӣ у Бѐогра̏ду, мо̏же смѐтрати да jе за да̏нас до̀во̏љно постигао у жи̏во̏ту. Сва̏ко̄ да̏ље инсисти̏ра̄ње на jо̏ш не̏чему, би̏ло би нѐскро̏мно.

Да су мно̏гӣ љу̏ди без врѐдности би̏ли паметни и обjекти̏вни, никад нѐ би по̏стигли о̏но̄ што су постигли. Мно̏ге̄ jе само глу̏по̄ст спа̏сла од анони̏мности.

✍ **Bring** a question on each aphorism to class, incorporating one or more of these phrases:

a. Zbog čèga .... ?

b. Objàsnite .... ?

c. [B,C] Čìni̠ li vam se da .... ? [S] Da li vam se čìni̠ da ....?

d. Zar .... ?

📖 Priča: Bazdulj

Read Part II of the story "Ljùbav na španjolski nàčin" by Muharem Bazdulj (p. 348).

Četrnaesta lekcija • Lesson Fourteen

VOCABULARY

čas	moment	poređati, poređam [B,S]	to line up (P)
četrnaesti	fourteenth	poslednji	final, last
čvrst	firm	posljednji	final, last
dići [dignuti], dignem	to raise (P)	preliti, prelijem	to pour over (P)
dizati, dižem	to raise (I)	primaknuti, primaknem	to bring closer (P)
dno, dna	bottom	priprema	preparation
doliti, dolijem	to add liquid (P)	recept	recipe
drška [B,S]	handle	samleti, sameljem	to grind (P)
držak, drška [C]	handle	samljeti, sameljem	to grind (P)
džezva	[Turkish] coffee pot	sastojak, sastojka	ingredient
fildžan [B]	[Turkish] coffee cup	sekunda	second (unit of time)
hitan, hitna	urgent	sitan, sitna	tiny, fine
istog časa	that very moment	skuhati [B,C]	to bring to a boil (P)
istog trena	that very moment	skuvati [S]	to bring to a boil (P)
izmešati, izmešam	to stir up, to mix (P)	sleći se [slegnuti se], slegnem se	to settle (P)
izmiješati, izmiješam	to stir up, to mix (P)	srknuti, srknem	to sip (P)
kahva [B]	coffee	šalica [B,C]	cup
kašika [B,S]	spoon	šolja [B,S]	cup
kašičica [S]	small spoon	šporet [B,S]	stove
kašikica [B]	small spoon	štednjak [B,C]	stove
mleti, meljem	to grind (I)	tada	then, at that time
mljeti, meljem	to grind (I)	talog	dregs, sediment
odliti, odlijem	to pour off (P)	tren	moment
oprema	equipment	uhvatiti	to take hold of (P)
ostaviti	to leave [behind] (P)	vatra	stove burner; fire
pažljiv	careful	vreo, vrela	hot
pena	foam	vrh	top
pjena	foam	zagrabiti	to scoop up (P)
ponovno [C]	again	zaslladiti, zasladim	to sweeten (P)
ponovo [B,S]	again	želja	wish
popeti se, popnem se	to climb (P)	žlica [C]	spoon
poredati, poredam [B,C]	to line up (P)	žličica [C]	small spoon

Recommendation: For Lessons 14 and 15, where the exercise is too long to fit on the same page with the vocabulary box, make a photocopy of the vocabulary page to use while you work on the exercise.

RECEPT ZA KAHVU [B] KAVU [C] KAFU [S]

BOSNIAN

Sastojci: voda, šećer (po želji), sitno mljevena kahva
               (tražite da se kahva samelje što je sitnije moguće)
Oprema: jedna džezva, četiri fildžana, jedna kašika
Vrijeme pripreme: 5-6 minuta

Staviti punu džezvu vode na šporet. Primaknuti jedan prazan fildžan. Čim se voda skuha, treba odliti malo skuhane vode u taj fildžan i skloniti džezvu sa vatre. Ako želite kahvu* sa šećerom, sad treba zasladiti vrelu vodu sa dvije kašikice šećera, vratiti džezvu na vatru na svega par sekundi, i zatim ponovo skloniti džezvu sa vatre. Dok je džezva na strani, treba zagrabiti pet punih kašika mljevene kahve i dodati ih u vrelu vodu. Kašikom dobro izmiješati kahvu i vodu. Onda treba čvrsto uhvatiti dršku džezve i vratiti džezvu na vatru. Zatim se pažljivo prati kako se kahva diže u džezvi. Kad se digne do samog vrha, hitno treba da se skloni sa vatre, istog časa. Onda se čeka dva-tri minuta sve dok se kahva ne slegne u džezvi. Onda se još jedanput vrati džezva na vatru, i opet se skloni čim se kahva digne do vrha. Onda se posljednji, treći put džezva vrati na vatru dok se posljednji put kahva ne popne do vrha džezve. Tad treba skloniti džezvu na stranu sa kuhanom kahvom, uzeti fildžan s odlitom vodom i preliti tu vodu preko skuhane kahve, dok je još u džezvi. Zatim se poredaju četiri fildžana jedna do druge. Staviti po jednu kašikicu pjene u svaki fildžan. Kad se podijeli sva pjena, onda se dolije kahva do vrha svakog fildžana. Talog se ostavi da se slegne. Treba srknuti malo da vidite da li je kahva dovoljno slatka. Na kraju, kada se kahva popije, onda se čita budućnost iz taloga koji ostaje na dnu fildžana.

---

* **Note** the spelling of the Bosnian word "coffee" in this passage. It is spelled here *kahva*, though elsewhere in this book *kafa* is the Bosnian spelling used. This is just one of a number of alternate choices of spelling, pronunciation and vocabulary that have become part of broader usage since 1990. Because most speakers of Bosnian say *kafa* most of the time, that spelling is given precedence in this book. The spelling *kahva* is used in this exercise to direct attention to the fact of variant possibilities, and to the fluidity of the linguistic situation in Bosnia and Herzegovina, Croatia, Montenegro, and Serbia.

Sàstojci: vòda, šéćer (po žèlji), sitno mljèvena kàva
(tràžite da se kàva samelje što je sitnije moguće)
Oprema: jèdna džezva, čètiri šalice, jèdna žlica
Vrijème pripreme: 5-6 minuta

Staviti punu džezvu vòde na štednjak. Primàknuti jèdnu praznu šalicu. Čim se vòda skuha, treba òdliti malo skuhane vòde u tu šalicu i sklòniti džezvu s vatre. Ako žèlite kàvu sa šèćerom, sad treba zaslàditi vrelu vodu s dvije žlìčice šèćera, vràtiti džezvu na vatru na svega par sekùndi, i zàtim ponòvno sklòniti džezvu s vatre. Dok je džezva na strani, treba zàgrabiti pet punih žlìca mljèvene kàve i dòdati ih u vrelu vodu. Žlìcom dobro izmijèšati kàvu i vodu. Onda treba čvrsto ùhvatiti držak džezve i vràtiti džezvu na vatru. Zàtim se pàžljivo prati kàko se kàva diže u džezvi. Kad se digne do samog vrha, hitno treba da se skloni s vatre, istog trena. Onda se čeka dvije-tri minùte sve dok se kàva ne slegne u džezvi. Onda se još jedànput vrati džezva na vatru, i òpet se skloni čim se kàva digne do vrha. Onda se pòsljednji, treći put džezva vrati na vatru dok se pòsljednji put kàva ne popne do vrha džezve. Tad treba sklòniti džezvu na stranu sa kuhanom kàvom, ùzeti šalicu s òdlitom vòdom i prèliti tu vodu preko skuhane kàve, dok je još u džezvi. Zàtim se porèdaju čètiri šalice jèdna do druge. Staviti po jèdnu žlìčicu pjene u svaku šalicu. Kad se podijèli sva pjena, onda se dolije kàva do vrha svake šalice. Tàlog se òstavi da se slegne. Treba srknuti malo da vidite je li kàva dòvoljno slatka. Na kraju, kàda se kàva pòpije, onda se čita budùćnost iz tàloga koji òstaje na dnu šalice.

Састојци: вода, шећер (по жељи), ситно млевена кафа
(тражите да се кафа самеље што је ситније могуће)
Опрема: једна џезва, четири шоље, једна кашика
Време припреме: 5-6 минута

Ставити пуну џезву воде на шпорет. Примакнути једну празну шољу. Чим се вода скува, треба одлити мало скуване воде у ту шољу и склонити џезву са ватре. Ако желите кафу са шећером, сад треба засладити врелу воду са две кашичице шећера, вратити џезву на ватру на свега пар секунди, и затим поново склонити џезву са ватре. Док је џезва на страни, треба заграбити пет пуних кашика млевене кафе и додати их у врелу воду. Кашиком добро измешати кафу и воду. Онда треба чврсто ухватити дршку џезве и вратити џезву на ватру. Затим се пажљиво прати како се кафа диже у џезви. Кад се дигне до самог врха, хитно треба да се склони са ватре, истог часа. Онда се чека два-три минута све док се кафа не слегне у џезви. Онда се још једанпут врати џезва на ватру, и опет се склони чим се кафа дигне до врха. Онда се последњи, трећи пут џезва врати на ватру док се последњи пут кафа не попне до врха џезве. Тад треба склонити џезву на страну са куваном кафом, узети шољу с одливеном водом и прелити ту воду преко скуване кафе, док је још у џезви. Затим се поређају четири шоље једна до друге. Ставити по једну кашичицу пене у сваку шољу. Кад се подели сва пена, онда се долије кафа до врха сваке шоље. Талог се остави да се слегне. Треба сркнути мало да видите да ли је кафа довољно слатка. На крају, када се кафа попије, онда се чита будућност из талога који остаје на дну шоље.

☞ **Groups** of two or three students should make coffee while giving each other the instructions. If you are unable to find the proper coffee pot, use a small, ordinary pot. In order to get coffee beans that are ground as finely as possible (like confectioner's sugar), have them ground at the setting for Turkish coffee.

Self-study learners: Follow the instructions given in the textbook and make coffee. As you read the instructions, note how infinitives, impersonal verbs with *se*, and the verb *treba* are used in the giving of instructions. Also note the use of conjunctions such as *čim* and *dok*, as well as adverbs and adverbial phrases such as *zatim*, *onda*, *tad*, and *na kraju*, in describing the process.

⚙ GRAMMAR

* Infinitives in the function of imperative *

Infinitives are often encountered in contexts such as recipes and instruction manuals, where they convey the basic meaning of a command. The use of the infinitive makes the command a more impersonal one than if an imperative were used. Many such infinitives, in fact, represent shortened forms of subjectless sentences with *treba* such as *treba staviti* "one should put" and *treba zasladiti* "one needs to sweeten."

* Active vs. passive sentences *

Active sentences are those in which the subject performs an action. Frequently they are also transitive: this means they contain a direct object, which describes the direct result of the action. In all active sentences the focus is on the actor and the action. Examples are *Ana je pronašla mačku* "Anna found a cat" (transitive), *majka sipa kafu* "mother is pouring coffee" (transitive), *učitelj je rekao da će biti ispit* "the teacher said there'll be an exam" (intransitive). Grammatically, each has a subject (Ana, mother, teacher) who performs an action (found, pours, said). In passive sentences, by contrast, the focus is either on the fact of the action or on its result; the actor is not usually mentioned. Passive versions of the above sentences are *pronađena je mačka* "a cat was found," *kafa se sipa* "coffee is being poured," and *rečeno je da će biti ispit* "it was said there'll be an exam." By comparing the first two active and passive sentences, one sees that the object of a transitive verb (cat, coffee) has become the subject of a passive verb. When an active sentence is intransitive, it has no object, and its passive version is subjectless (English often uses "it" in such cases).

* Formation of passive and impersonal sentences *

There are two types of passive sentences. One contains a form of the verb *biti* accompanied by a passive participle, and the other contains a verb plus the particle *se*. In both, the subject identifies something which is the logical object of an action (a cat that was found, or coffee that is being poured). If the focus of the verb is to describe the action, then a *se*-verb is usually chosen. Like any verb, it must agree with its subject, for example *kafa se sipa* "coffee is poured" [singular] vs. *jabuke se jedu* "apples are eaten" [plural]. If the focus is on the result of the action, then a sequence of *biti* + passive participle is usually chosen. Both segments must agree with the subject: the form of *biti* as a verb, and the passive participle as an adjective. For example, in *pronađena je mačka*, the subject (*mačka*) is 3rd singular feminine, the verb (*je*) is 3rd singular, and the participle (*pronađena*) is feminine singular. Such sentences frequently put the participle first, especially if the emphasis is on the result of an action. Most verbal ideas express the passive using one type of sentence (*biti* + passive participle) or the other (*se*-verb). Only a very few can use both. One of these is *roditi se*: both *ona se rodila 1973 g.* and *ona je rođena 1973 g.* mean "she was born in 1973." **[139]**

In impersonal sentences, the focus is also either on the fact of an action or its result. But there is a major grammatical difference – they are subjectless. Like in passives, the verb is either a *se*-verb or a sequence of *biti* + passive participle, but unlike in passives, the verb is only 3rd singular and any participial forms must be neuter singular. The exact meaning of an impersonal sentence is somewhat harder to render into English, because English requires a subject. Usually such sentences are translated with "it," or the impersonal "one" or "you"; sometimes plurals such as "people" or the impersonal "they" are used. For example: *od slika se ne živi* "one can't live from pictures [alone]," *nikad se ne zna* "you never know," *dugo se čekalo* "they waited a long time," *okupljalo se u centru grada* "people gathered in the center of town," *dogovoreno je* "it's agreed." Note that in all these examples the verb is 3rd singular. If it is a *se*-verb, then the L-participle of the past tense is neuter singular (*okupljalo*) and any passive participle is neuter singular (*dogovoreno*).

The relationship between a passive sentence and its corresponding active version is relatively clear: the object of an active sentence becomes the subject of a passive sentence, whether the verb is accompanied by *se* or a passive participle. But it is often harder to see the relationship between an impersonal sentence and an active sentence communicating similar information. This is because in such sentences one is concerned only with the action - such as in *stišalo se* "everything quieted down" - or the state, such as in *nije bilo sigurno* "it wasn't certain." **[140]**

Founded in 1827

No smoking

No parking

VOCABULARY

bespomoćan, bespomoćna	helpless	padavine [B,S] *(pl form)*	precipitation
cesta [B,C]	road	pola	half
čas... čas	one moment ... the next	prespavati, prespavam	to sleep over (P)
gostionica	tavern	pretvarati, pretvaram	to turn into (I)
granuti, grane	to burst forth (P)	prolepšati se	to get nicer (P)
hotel	hotel	proljepšati se	to get nicer (P)
isplatiti se, isplati se	to be worthwhile (P)	put [B,C,S]	road, trip
izvješće [C]	report	putovanje	journey, trip
izveštaj [S]	report	rastajati se, rastajem se	to part ways (I)
izvještaj [B,S]	report	razići se, raziđem se	to disperse (P)
jak	strong	razvedriti se, razvedrim se	to clear up (P)
kiša	rain	reda radi	as one ought
kraj, kraja	region	saznati	to find out (P)
mesto	place, town	situacija	situation
mjesto	place, town	skloniti se, sklonim se	to take shelter
mrak	dark	službeni put	business trip
nadati se, nadam se	to hope (I)	sneg	snow
naići [na], naiđem [na]	to happen upon (P)	snijeg	snow
nalet	gust [*e.g.* of wind]	sutradan	the next day
nastaviti	to continue (P)	svratiti, svratim	to stop by (P)
natrag	back *(adv.)*	uslov [B,S]	condition
nevreme	foul weather, storm	uvjet [B,C]	condition
nevrijeme	foul weather, storm	vesti *(pl form)*	news
nijednom	never, not once	vetar, vetra	wind
očajan, očajna	miserable, despairing	vijesti *(pl form)*	news
oluja	storm	vjetar, vjetra	wind
onde	there, in that place	vraćati se, vraćam se	to return (I)
ondje	there, in that place	vremenska prognoza	weather report
padaline [C] *(pl form)*	precipitation	znatan, znatna	considerable

OLUJA

BOSNIAN   *Vraćajući se* kući kolima oko pet i petnaest naveče nakon službenog puta u drugom gradu, dvije koleginice su naišle na oluju s jakim padavinama, čas snijeg, čas kiša, a da stvar bude gora, padao je mrak. *Skrenuvši* sa puta i *(svratiti)* do najbližeg mjesta do pola šest, sklonile su se u jednu gostionicu. *(Gledati)* kroz prozor gostionice kako se snijeg pretvara u nalete kiše i vjetra, očajno su razmišljale da li se isplati putovati dalje. *(Jesti)* ondje večeru, i *(piti)* vina, razgovarale su o svojoj situaciji. *(Znati)* da se ne može voziti po takvoj oluji, odlučile su prespavati u obližnjem hotelu. *(Osjećati se)* bespomoćne, slušale su vijesti, vremensku prognozu i izvještaj o stanju na cestama. *(Javiti se)* svojima oko pola devet, otišle su spavati, *(nadati se)* da će se sutradan vrijeme proljepšati, tako da mogu nastaviti putovanje. I zaista, *(probuditi se)* vrlo rano u pet do pet, saznale su na vijestima da su uvjeti na cesti znatno bolji. *(Voziti)*, vidjele su da su se oblaci razišli, sunce granulo i dan se razvedrio. *(Žuriti se)* natrag, nisu stale nijednom na putu, sve do svog grada gdje su stigle u dvadeset do jedanaest. Javile su se reda radi na poslu i onda *(rastajati se)* svaka se vratila svojoj kući.

CROATIAN   *Vraćajući se* kući kolima oko pet i petnaest navečer nakon službenog puta u drugom gradu, dvije kolegice su naišle na oluju s jakim padalinama, čas snijeg, čas kiša, a da stvar bude gora, padao je mrak. *Skrenuvši* s puta i *(svratiti)* do najbližeg mjesta do pola šest, sklonile su se u jednu gostionicu. *(Gledati)* kroz prozor gostionice kako se snijeg pretvara u nalete kiše i vjetra, očajno su razmišljale isplati li se putovati dalje. *(Jesti)* ondje večeru, i *(piti)* vina, razgovarale su o svojoj situaciji. *(Znati)* da se ne može voziti po takvoj oluji, odlučile su prespavati u obližnjem hotelu. *(Osjećati se)* bespomoćne slušale su vijesti, vremensku prognozu i izvješće o stanju na cestama. *(Javiti se)* svojima oko pola devet, otišle su rano spavati, *(nadati se)* da će se sutradan vrijeme proljepšati, tako da mogu nastaviti putovanje. I zaista, *(probuditi se)* vrlo rano u pet do pet, saznale su na vijestima da su uvjeti na cesti znatno bolji. *(Voziti)*, vidjele su kako su se oblaci razišli, sunce granulo i dan se razvedrio. *(Žuriti se)* natrag, nisu stale nijednom na putu, sve do svoga grada gdje su stigle u dvadeset do jedanaest. Javile su se reda radi na poslu i onda *(rastajati se)* svaka se vratila svojoj kući.

SERBIAN   *Vraćajući se* kući kolima oko pet i petnaest naveče posle službenog puta u drugom gradu, dve koleginice su naišle na oluju s jakim padavinama, čas sneg, čas kiša, a da stvar bude gora, padao je mrak. *Skrenuvši* sa puta i *(svratiti)* do najbližeg mesta do pola šest, sklonile su se u jednu gostionicu. *(Gledati)* kroz prozor gostionice kako se sneg pretvara u nalete kiše i vetra, očajno su razmišljale da li se isplati da putuju dalje. *(Jesti)* onde večeru, i *(piti)* vina, razgovarale su o svojoj situaciji. *(Znati)* da se ne može voziti po takvoj oluji, odlučile su da prespavaju u obližnjem hotelu. *(Osećati se)* bespomoćne, slušale su vesti, vremensku prognozu i izveštaj o stanju na putevima. *(Javiti se)* svojima oko pola devet, otišle su da spavaju, *(nadati se)* da će se sutradan vreme prolepšati, tako da mogu da nastave putovanje. I zaista, *(probuditi se)* vrlo rano u pet do pet, saznale su na vestima da su uslovi na putevima znatno bolji. *(Voziti)*, videle su da su se oblaci razišli, sunce granulo i dan se razvedrio. *(Žuriti se)* natrag, nisu stale nijednom na putu, sve do svog grada gde su stigle u dvadeset do jedanaest. Javile su se reda radi na poslu i onda *(rastajati se)* svaka se vratila svojoj kući.

Verbs: svratiti, gledati, jesti, piti, znati, osećati se [E] osjećati se [J],
            javiti se, nadati se, probuditi se, voziti, žuriti se, rastajati se.

☞ **Replace** each italicized infinitive by the appropriate verbal adverb. The first two verbs in the text [*vraćajući se* and *skrenuvši*] have been done for you as examples. Form the adverbs first, from the list above, and then insert them into the text. Note the aspect of each verb, and remember that past verbal adverbs are formed only from perfective verbs form, and present verbal adverbs only from imperfective verbs. Thus, the only verbal adverb which can be formed from the imperfective verb *vraćati se* is the present verbal adverb *vraćajući se*, and the only verbal adverb which can be formed from the perfective verb *skrenuti* is the past verbal adverb *skrenuvši*.

Note: the frequency of these forms in the above story is far greater than in normal writing. The story has been composed expressly in this way in order to give you practice with verbal adverbs.

GRAMMAR

* Passive participles, past and present verbal adverbs *

The present verbal adverb is formed by adding the ending *-ći* to the 3rd plural present form, and the past verbal adverb is formed by adding *-vši* to the masculine L-participle minus the final *-o* (review the grammar sections on pp. 180 and 185. respectively). Passive participles (to be drilled in the next section) are formed by adding one of the participle markers *-t*, *-n* or *-en* to the appropriate verb stem (review p. 160).

* Telling time, continued *

"Half past" the hour can be expressed as the hour plus 30 minutes (*jedan i trideset* "1:30"). Much more frequently, however, it is expressed in terms of the following hour, by the unchanging form *pola* plus the name of the hour (*pola dva* "1:30"). The preposition *u* occurs before this expression as before other expressions of time (*u pola tri* "at 2:30", *u tri i petnaest* "at 3:15"). **[61c]**

A3

VOCABULARY

besvestan, besvesna	unconscious	preživeti, preživim	to survive (P)
besvjestan, besvjesna	unconscious	preživjeti, preživim	to survive (P)
bolnica	hospital	prijaviti, prijavim	to report (P)
bolnički	hospital *(adj.)*	prolaznik	passerby
hitna kola	ambulance	pronaći, pronađem	to find (P)
hitna pomoć *(f)*	911	roditi se, rodim se	to be born (P)
izjava	statement	sinoć	last night
javnost, javnosti *(f)*	the general public	slučaj; slučajevi	case
obavestiti, obavestim	to inform (P)	slučajan, slučajna	random, chance
obavijestiti, obavijestim	to inform (P)	srećom	luckily
par	pair, couple	stanje	condition
pločnik [C]	sidewalk	širok, široka	broad, wide
poginuti, poginem	to perish (P)	trotoar, trotoara [B,S]	sidewalk
policija	police	uprava	administration
policijski	police *(adj.)*	utvrditi, utvrdim	to establish (P)
pomoć *(f)*	aid, help		

CRNA HRONIKA [B,S]   CRNA KRONIKA [C]

Bosnian

Sinoć oko osam sati slučajni prolaznici *su pronašli* ženu i muškarca kako leže u besvjesnom stanju na širokom trotoaru pored ceste. Prolaznici *su pozvali* hitnu pomoć i *prijavili su* slučaj policiji. Vozač hitnih kola *odvezao je* par u bolnicu. Kasnije, u izjavi za javnost, činovnici bolničke i policijske uprave *su utvrdili* da su to brat i sestra. Žena *se rodila* 1973. g. a muškarac *se rodio* 1975. g. *Rekli su* da srećom par nije poginuo, već su preživjeli tešku saobraćajnu nesreću. Policijska uprava *je obavijestila* njihovu porodicu.

CROATIAN

Sinoć oko osam sati slučajni prolaznici *su pronašli* ženu i muškarca kako leže u besvjesnom stanju na širokom pločniku pored ceste. Prolaznici *su pozvali* hitnu pomoć i *prijavili su* slučaj policiji. Vozač hitnih kola *odvezao je* par u bolnicu. Kasnije, u izjavi za javnost, činovnici bolničke i policijske uprave *su utvrdili* da su to brat i sestra. Žena *se rodila* 1973. g. a muškarac *se rodio* 1975. g. *Rekli su* da srećom par nije poginuo, već su preživjeli tešku prometnu nesreću. Policijska uprava *je obavijestila* njihovu obitelj.

SERBIAN

Синоћ око осам сати случајни пролазници *су пронашли* жену и мушкарца како леже у бесвесном стању на широком тротоару поред пута. Пролазници су *позвали* хитну помоћ и *пријавили су* случај полицији. Возач хитних кола *одвезао је* пар у болницу. Касније, у изјави за јавност, чиновници болничке и полицијске управе су *утврдили* да су то брат и сестра. Жена *се родила* 1973. г., а мушкарац *се родио* 1975. г. *Рекли су* да срећом пар није погинуо већ су преживели тешку саобраћајну несрећу. Полицијска управа *је обавестила* њихову породицу.

> On the last page of the daily news in Bosnia and Herzegovina, Croatia, Montenegro, and Serbia, one often finds a section with brief news items about accidents, crimes, natural disasters, or other catastrophic events of local, national or international significance - usually with the title *Crna hronika* [B,S] *Crna kronika* [C].

← Industrial zone ↑ Bus Terminal
Hospital

☞ **1. Make** the passive participle of each of the verbs listed below. 2. Having reviewed the grammar on passive sentences (p. 219), look at how each (italicized) verb is used actively in the text above and think how to turn it into a passive phrase including a passive participle. 3. Make the above text passive: replace each active verb with a passive participle phrase.

Verbs: obavestiti se [E] obavijestiti se [J], odvesti, pozvati, pronaći, prijaviti, reći, roditi se, utvrditi.

Example (for the verb obavestiti se [E] obavijestiti se [J])
1. obavešten [E] obaviješten [J]
2. obaveštena je [E] obaviještena je [J]
3. [B] Policijska uprava *je obavijestila* njihovu porodicu **becomes**: Njihova porodica je obaviještena.
   [C] Policijska uprava *je obavijestila* njihovu obitelj **becomes**: Njihova obitelj je obaviještena.
   [S] Policijska uprava *je obavestila* njihovu porodicu **becomes**: Njihova porodica je obaveštena.

No dumping of dirt or trash

No walking and releasing of dogs

A4

VOCABULARY

dolazak, dolaska	arrival	primetiti, primetim	to notice (P)
gust	dense	primijetiti, primijetim	to notice (P)
izdaleka	from afar	radovati se, radujem se + *Dat*	to be glad (I)
izlet	excursion	shvatiti	to grasp, to understand (P)
jesenski [C]	autumnal	stišati se	to quiet down (P)
jesenji [B,S]	autumnal	stizati, stižem	to arrive (I)
konačan, konačna	final	učenik	pupil, student
magla	fog	uskoro	soon thereafter
nestati, nestanem	to disappear (P)	zabrinut	worried
očekivati, očekujem	to expect (I)	zabrinutost, zabrinutosti *(f)*	concern, anxiety
odjednom	suddenly	zakasniti, zakasnim	to be late (P)
okupljati, okupljam	to gather (I)	zakašnjenje	delay
posve	completely	zvuk	sound
povratak, povratka	return		

MAGLA

BOSNIAN

Jesenja magla je bila gusta te noći, pa niko ništa *nije vidio*. Od magle *su se* svi zvukovi *stišali* pa niko ništa *nije čuo*. Zabrinuti ljudi *su se okupljali* na željezničkoj stanici ali *nisu govorili*. Čekali *su* povratak učenika i nastavnika sa školskog izleta. *Očekivali su* djecu u devet sati uveče, ali zbog magle *nisu bili* sigurni hoće li voz zakasniti ili ne. Nakon sat vremena zakašnjenja, ljudi *su* odjednom *primijetili* voz kako stiže izdaleka. Zabrinutost roditelja je nestala čim *su shvatili* da će se djeca uskoro pojaviti. Djeca *su* konačno *stigla* na stanicu u deset i pedeset pet. Svi *su se* radovali dolasku voza. Na kraju, kad su djeca sišla sa voza, svi *su* posve *zaboravili* strah i *pošli* kući na spavanje.

CROATIAN

Jesenska magla je bila gusta te noći, pa nitko ništa *nije vidio*. Od magle *su se* svi zvukovi *stišali* pa nitko ništa *nije čuo*. Zabrinuti ljudi *su se okupljali* na kolodvoru ali *nisu govorili*. *Čekali su* povratak učenika i nastavnika sa školskog izleta. *Očekivali su* djecu u devet sati navečer, ali zbog magle *nisu bili* sigurni hoće li vlak zakasniti ili ne. Nakon sat vremena zakašnjenja, ljudi *su* odjednom *primijetili* vlak kako stiže izdaleka. Zabrinutost roditelja je nestala čim *su shvatili* da će se djeca uskoro pojaviti. Djeca *su* konačno *stigla* na kolodvor u deset i pedeset pet. Svi *su se radovali* dolasku vlaka. Na kraju, kad su djeca sišla s vlaka, svi *su* posve *zaboravili* strah i *pošli* kući na spavanje.

SERBIAN

Jesenja magla je bila gusta te noći, pa niko ništa *nije video*. Od magle *su se* svi zvukovi *stišali* pa niko ništa *nije čuo*. Zabrinuti ljudi *su se okupljali* na železničkoj stanici ali *nisu govorili*. *Čekali su* povratak učenika i nastavnika sa školskog izleta. *Očekivali su* decu u devet sati uveče, ali zbog magle *nisu bili* sigurni da li će voz da zakasni ili ne. Nakon sat vremena zakašnjenja, ljudi *su* odjednom *primetili* voz kako stiže izdaleka. Zabrinutost roditelja je nestala čim *su shvatili* da će se deca uskoro pojaviti. Deca *su* konačno *stigla* na stanicu u deset i pedeset pet. Svi *su se radovali* dolasku voza. Na kraju, kad su deca sišla sa voza, svi *su* posve *zaboravili* strah i *pošli* kući na spavanje.

☞ **Make** the italicized verbs in the passage above passive (and, if appropriate, impersonal; review p. 219 on the difference between passives and impersonals). Note that nearly all verbs in this passage will require constructions with *se*. The only exceptions are impersonal sentences whose main verb is *biti*, and the verb *zaboraviti*.

The railway of Bosnia and Herzegovina

The railway of the Republic of Srpska

VJEŽBE [J] VEŽBE [E]

B1

Bosnian and Croatian	Serbian
1. Kàko se dòlazi do tvòje kùće?	1. Kàko se dòlazi do tvòje kùće?
2. Ide̲ se glavno̲m ulico̲m je̲dan kilometar.	2. Ide̲ se glavno̲m ulico̲m je̲dan kilometar.
1. A onda̲?	1. A onda̲?
2. Onda̲ treba̲ skrȅnuti lije̲vo kod glávno̲g trga.	2. Onda̲ treba̲ skrȅnuti le̲vo kod glávno̲g trga.
1. A kad skre̲nem lije̲vo, šta onda̲?	1. A kad skre̲nem le̲vo, šta onda̲?
2. Onda̲ treba̲ ȉći rávno do slje̲de̲će ulice̲ desno, i tu̲ u̲ći.	2. Onda̲ treba̲ ȉći pravo do sle̲de̲će ulice̲ desno, i tu̲ u̲ći.
1. Kòji je bro̲j tvòje kùće?	1. Kòji je bro̲j tvòje kùće?
2. Bro̲j 72.	2. Bro̲j 72.

✍ **Give** directions for how to get somewhere, using this exchange as a model.

B2

Working with each other in class, turn each sentence into an impersonal sentence with *se*. Then translate the resulting sentence into English (note that sentences such as these can often be translated in several ways). Read through the examples carefully before doing the exercise.

Example 1 (present tense)
> Lju̲di gòvore̲ da me varȁš.   **becomes**
>> Gòvori̲ se da me varȁš.
>>> [NB, this is the title of a popular song sung by Zvonko Bogdan.]

> **Possible translations:**   They say that you are cheating on me.
>   It is being said that you are cheating on me.
>   Rumor has it that you are cheating on me.

Example 2 (past tense with transitive verb)
> [B] Rado smo čìtali nje̲n ròma̲n.
> [C] Rado smo čìtali nje̲zin ròma̲n.
> [S] Радо смо читали њен роман.

>   **becomes**
>> [B] Nje̲n ròma̲n se rado čìtao.
>> [C] Nje̲zin ròma̲n se rado čìtao.
>> [S] Њен роман се радо читао.

> **Possible translations:**   People enjoyed reading her novel.
>   Her novel was being eagerly read.

Example 3 (past tense example with intransitive verb)
> U osam sȁti mnogi lju̲di su ȉšli kolima u̲ gra̲d.   **becomes**
>> [B,C] U osam sȁti ȉšlo se kolima u̲ gra̲d.
>> [S] У осам сȁти ишло се колима у град.

> **Possible translation:**   There was a lot of automobile traffic going into town at eight o'clock.

1. [B] Òni gòvorē o njègovom pòslu.

   [C] Òni gòvorē o njègovu pòslu.

   [S] Òни гòворē о њèговом пòслу.

2. [B,C] Svi dànas prìčajū o tom nòvōm fìlmu.

   [S] Сви дàнас прìчајū о том нòвōм фùлму.

3. [B,C] Ìdēmo òvōm ùlicōm do tvòjē kùćē.

   [S] Ùдēмо òвōм ùлицōм до твòјē кùћē.

4. [B,C] Òna kàžē da je vàni hlàdno.

   [S] Òна кàжē да је хлàдно нàпољу.

5. [B,C] Rādimo kàko trebà.

   [S] Рādимо кàко требà.

6. [B,C] Òne znàjū sve o njìhovīm problèmima.

   [S] Òне знàjū све о њùховūм проблèмима.

7. [B] Šèfovi razmìšljajū o tòme šta ćē sùtra nòvine da pìšū.

   [C] Šèfovi razmìšljajū o tòme što ćē sùtra nòvine pìsati.

   [S] Шèфови размùшљају о тòме шта ћē сùтра нòвине да пùшū.

8. [B,C] Ljùdi su razgovàrali o nàma.

   [S] Љùди су разговàрали о нàма.

9. [B] Vòzovi su ìšli bŕzo.

   [C] Vlàkovi su ìšli bŕzo.

   [S] Вòзови су ùшли бŕзо.

10. [B,C] Svi su slùšali nàjnòvijū pjèsmu.

    [S] Сви су слùшали нàjнòвијū пèсму.

Tricky translation: In the early 1990s, one of the Croatian political parties, the *Hrvatska Demokratska Zajednica* (Croatian Democratic Union), made wide use of the slogan *Zna se, HDZ*. It would be possible to translate this slogan into English as "It is known – the HDZ," or even "One knows – the HDZ" (that is, as an impersonal passive). But a more natural English translation would be "Everybody knows: the HDZ."

B3

Working with each other in class, rewrite each sentence below so that it contains a passive participle. Then translate the resulting sentence into English.

1. Urèdili smo sobu bez tvòjē pòmoći.
2. Kùpio je trì knjìge.
3. Ùzeli su njègovu tòrbu.
4. Vìdela [E] Vìdjela [J] sam ga.
5. Pòpili smo pêt pìva.
6. Gospòdin Kòvač je nàpisao pìsmo Gospòđi Brkić.

B4

Working with each other in class, turn each sentence below into a passive sentence with *se* and then translate the resulting sentence into English.

1. Vidjeli smo visoku zgradu tamo.
2. Gledali smo film.
3. Popili su čašu vode.
4. Sklonila je stvari sa stola.
5. Kolega je sinoć obradio materijale.

1. Видели смо високу зграду тамо.
2. Гледали смо филм.
3. Попили су чашу воде.
4. Склонила је ствари са стола.
5. Колега је синоћ обрадио материјале.

B5

Redo the following (slightly adapted) version of 7A1, replacing verbs by impersonals and *se*- passives.

Bosnian
1. Šta jedeš za doručak? Želiš li jesti? Mogu nešto da spremim za tebe.
2. Obično jedem pahuljice.
1. Sa čim ih spremaš?
2. Sa mlijekom i šećerom.
1. Često doručkujem crni hljeb sa svježim sirom i zelenom paprikom.
2. A šta piješ?
1. Uvijek pijem kafu sa toplim mlijekom.
2. Ja pijem čaj bez ičega.
1. Kako možeš piti takav čaj?
2. Naravno da mogu.

Croatian
1. Što jedeš za doručak? Želiš li jesti? Mogu nešto spremiti za tebe.
2. Obično jedem pahuljice.
1. S čim ih spremaš?
2. S mlijekom i šećerom.
1. Često doručkujem crni kruh sa svježim sirom i zelenom paprikom.
2. A što piješ?
1. Uvijek pijem kavu s toplim mlijekom.
2. Ja pijem čaj bez ičega.
1. Kako možeš piti takav čaj?
2. Naravno da mogu.

Serbian
1. Šta jedeš za doručak? Da li želiš da jedeš? Mogu nešto da spremim za tebe.
2. Obično jedem pahuljice.
1. Sa čim ih spremaš?
2. Sa mlekom i šećerom.
1. Često doručkujem crni hleb sa svežim sirom i zelenom paprikom.
2. A šta piješ?
1. Uvek pijem kafu sa toplim mlekom.
2. Ja pijem čaj bez ičega.
1. Kako možeš da piješ takav čaj?
2. Naravno da mogu.

B6

Pair up with another student, and retell together, in the form of indirect narration, one or more of the following exercises: 1A3, 1A4, 2A1, 2A2, 2A3, 2A4.

Example: 1A1 in the form of indirect narration
1. Broj jedan pozdravlja broj dva.
2. Broj dva pita broj jedan ko [B,S] tko [C] je.
1. Broj jedan odgovara da je student i da se zove ....
2. Broj dva kaže da se zove ....

 Note: At this point it will be helpful to review the rules of clitic ordering on p. 86. The basic rule of thumb is that all clitics in a subordinate clause must immediately follow *da*. For example:
> Broj jedan kaže da JE student
> Broj dva kaže da SE zove ....

✍ DOMAĆA ZADAĆA [B,C] DOMAĆI ZADATAK [S]

C1

The following review exercise is best done as at least three separate assignments. Teachers and self-study learners should choose the order which best corresponds to their needs for review.

Give the following information for each verb below
  a) its meaning (translate it into English)
  b) its aspect (state whether it is perfective or imperfective)
  c) its verb type (using the categories given on p. 142 and in Appendix 9)
        [Note that the infinitive *odvesti* is listed twice: these are two separate verbs!]
Then for each verb give the following forms
  d) present verbal adverb (for imperfectives) or past verbal adverb (for perfectives)
  e) passive participle (do this only for verbs marked with *)

čekati	naći*	opisati *	popiti *	razumjeti	staviti *
dati	nalaziti se	oprati *	popraviti *	reći *	stavljati
davati *	napasti *	osećati	poslužiti *	rešavati	studirati *
doći	napisati *	osjećati	postavljati *	rešiti *	stvarati *
držati	napuniti *	ostati	postaviti *	rješavati	sumnjati
govoriti	naručiti *	otići	poštovati *	riješiti *	sviđati se
gubiti	naučiti *	padati	pozdraviti *	sanjati *	točiti *
hteti	navratiti	pasti	poznavati	sećati se	trajati
htjeti	nervirati se	pisati *	pozvati *	setiti se	učiti *
ići	nestati	piti *	preporučiti *	sipati *	umivati se
ispadati	obavestiti *	plašiti *	pričati	sjećati se	urediti *
ispričati *	obavijestiti*	početi *	probuditi *	sjetiti se	uzeti *
izaći	obećati *	počinjati	pročitati *	skloniti *	uzimati *
izbrisati *	objasniti*	poći	prodavati	slagati se	uživati
izgledati	obraditi *	podeliti *	proglasiti *	slegati	večerati
izići	oceniti *	podijeliti *	prokockati *	slijegati	voziti *
iznajmiti *	ocenjivati	pogledati *	propustiti *	slati	vraćati se
javiti *	ocijeniti *	pogledati	provesti *	slušati	vratiti *
javljati se	ocjenjivati	pojaviti se	pružiti *	smatrati *	zaboraviti *
kazati *	očekivati *	pojesti*	pustiti	smetati *	zaključiti *
kružiti *	odgovarati	pokloniti *	pušiti	smeti	zamoliti *
kuhati *	odigrati *	pokušati *	putovati	smjeti	zarađivati
kupiti *	odlaziti	polagati	raditi *	spremati	završavati
kupovati	odlučiti *	polaziti	razbuditi se	spremiti *	završiti *
kuvati *	odneti *	položiti *	razgovarati	spustiti *	značiti
ležati	odnijeti *	pomagati	razmisliti *	stajati	živeti
misliti *	odvesti *	pomoći	razmišljati	stanovati	živjeti
moliti *	odvesti *	ponuditi *	razumeti		

ZABRANJENO JE NAGNUTI SE KROZ PROZOR

Forbidden to lean out the window

C2

Which of the sentences below contain which of the following forms?
a) passive participles b) present verbal adverbs c) past verbal adverbs d) impersonal or passive *se*.
Mark the sentences appropriately. Then translate each sentence into English.

1. [B,C] Kako je ranije rečeno, doručak bez novina nije pravi doručak.

   [S] Како је раније речено, доручак без новина није прави доручак.

2. [B,C] Kako se kaže bioskop na hrvatskom?

   [S] Како се каже биоскоп на хрватском?

3. [B] Kupivši nove olovke i teke, pošla je na prvi dan škole.

   [C] Kupivši nove olovke i bilježnice, pošla je na prvi dan škole.

   [S] Купивши нове оловке и свеске, пошла је на први дан школе.

4. [B,C] Postavljajući pitanja, đaci saznaju odgovore.

   [S] Постављајући питања, ђаци сазнају одговоре.

5. [B,C] Stvarajući probleme, ljudi ih rješavaju.

   [S] Стварајући проблеме, људи их решавају.

6. [B,C] Ako će se španjolski jezik učiti kako treba, studenti trebaju svaki dan pisati domaće zadaće.

   [S] Ако ће се шпански језик учити како треба, студенти треба сваки дан да раде домаће задатке.

7. [B] Mlijeko je popito, hljeb je pojeden, ali još ima jabuka.

   [C] Mlijeko je popito, kruh je pojeden, ali još ima jabuka.

   [S] Млеко је попијено, хлеб је поједен, али још има јабука.

8. [B,C] Gospođa je željela biti ljubazna, ponudivši gospodina s kolačem.

   [S] Госпођа је желела да буде љубазна, понудивши господина са колачем.

C3

Translate these sentences into B, C, or S. Write two versions each for sentences 8 and 10, one which suggests that the idea is purely hypothetical (you will never be a mechanic, or it is impossible to eat your dinner in ten minutes), and the other which suggests that these things could actually happen.

1. Having written the letter, I put it into an envelope.
2. Having contacted her customers, the manager answered their questions.
3. The lawyer, thinking about something, forgot to finish reading his newspaper.
4. All worries were forgotten when the exam was finished.
5. The flowers were purchased, the coffee drunk, and the friends were driven home.
6. A hand was offered.
7. To make tea, first you boil the water, then you pour it over the tea, then you wait three to five minutes. Add sugar and milk at the end as you wish.
8. If I were a mechanic, I would be kind to my customers.
9. Would you be so kind as to pour me a glass of juice?
10. If we were to finish eating our dinner quickly, we would arrive at the theater at 7:30.

On the internet, find the website of one or more of the newspapers listed below, and search under *Crna hronika* [B,S] *Crna kronika* [C]. Choose an article of roughly 100-200 words and print it out. Then make a list of the passive participles, impersonal *se*-constructions, and verbal past and present adverbs you find. For each of these, state the infinitive of the verb it is formed from and its aspect. Finally, translate the article into English.

Bosanske dnevne novine
> *Dnevni Avaz   Oslobođenje*

Crnogorske dnevne novine
> *Dan   Glas Crnogorca   Pobjeda*

Hrvatske dnevne novine
> *Vjesnik   Večernji list   Jutarnji list   Novi list*
> *Glas Istre   Glas Slavonije   Slobodna Dalmacija*

Srpske dnevne novine
> *Borba, Politika   Dnevne novosti   Danas*

Newspaper kiosk, Rijeka

VOCABULARY

је ли чему?	is it worth anything?	пљу̏штати	to rain cats and dogs (I)
је̏дино	only	посма̏трати, посма̏трам [B,S]	to observe (I)
ка̏пати	to drip (I)	преста̏јати, престо̏јим	to go on standing (P)
ли̏ти, ли̏је̄м	to pour (I)	пре̏стати, пре̏стане̄м	to stop (P)
Ма̏рс	Mars	прома̏трати, прома̏трам [C]	to observe (I)
Па̏лата Бео̏град	the Belgrade "Palace" building	ро̏сити	to drizzle (I)

Киша је и ка̏пала, и ро̏сила, и па̏дала, и ли̏ла, и пљу̏штала... Само још ни̏је пре̏стала. Сто̏јимо на на̏јвишем про̏зору Па̏лате̄ Бео̏град, посма̏трамо наш град под ја̏ко̄м ки̏шо̄м и мисли̏мо: и̏ма̄ ли живо̏та на Ма̏рсу и је ли чему?

Бе̏рбери и зубни̏ лека̏ри преста̏јаће и о̏ва̄ј да̏н на но̏гама. О̏ни се̏де̄ је̏дино кад о̏дӯ је̏дни код други̏х.

🖎 **Retell** the aphorism in your own words. Start with the words: Dušan Radović ka̋že̎ da je kiša ....

Palata Beograd is the name of the building from where Dušan Radović broadcast his morning radio show "Beograde, Dobro jutro!", the venue where these aphorisms were first heard. The studio was on the 16th floor of the building, which gave him a sweeping view of the city.

📖 Priča: Bazdulj

Read Part III of the story "Ljubav na španjolski način" by Muharem Bazdulj (p. 349).

Petnaesta lekcija • Lesson Fifteen

A1   ⊙ Use the DVD in the slipcase at the back of the book.

RJEČNIK [J] REČNIK [E]

brzina	speed	poleteti, poletim	to fly off (P)
častiti	to treat (I/P)	poletjeti, poletim	to fly off (P)
čuven, čuvena	famous	ponajviše	most of all
daljina	distance	posetilac, posetioca	visitor
dubina	depth	posjetilac, posjetioca	visitor
duet, dueta	duet	poželeti, poželim	to wish for (P)
dvostruk	double, twofold	poželjeti, poželim	to wish for (P)
egzibicija	show	pretvarati se, pretvaram se	to pretend (I)
ekavica	ekavian	prevariti	to deceive, to trick (P)
gledalac, gledaoca [B,C,S]	spectator	pritom	in so doing
gledatelj [C]	spectator	prolećni [B,S]	spring (adj.)
igra [B,S]	dance	proljetni [C]	spring (adj.)
igrati [B,S]	to dance	pronaći, pronađem [B,S]	to invent
ijekavica	ijekavian	propeler, propelera	propeller
iskoristiti	to use, to exploit (P)	proraditi, proradim	to start functioning (P)
istovremen	simultaneous	radostan, radosna	joyous
izjadati se	to complain (P)	rastužiti se, rastužim se	to become sad (P)
izumjeti, izumijem [B,C]	to invent (P)	razveseliti	to cheer [someone] (P)
izvoditi, izvodim	to perform (I)	režiser, režisera	[film] director
jednodušan, jednodušna	unanimous	rođaka	female relative
kapa	cap	snažan, snažna	powerful
leteti, letim	to fly (I)	spreman, spremna	prepared
letjeti, letim	to fly (I)	spremanje	cleaning
letenje	flight	srce	heart
ljubak, ljupka	cute	svršiti, svršim	to end, to finish (P)
ljubimac, ljubimca	favorite, pet	šaljiv	jocular, joking
misaon	thought-related	tačka [B,S]	[performance] number
moriti	to torment (I)	talas [B,S]	wave
naime	namely	točka [C]	[performance] number
napustiti, napustim	to abandon	tuga	sorrow
neobičan, neobična	unusual	tugovati, tugujem	to grieve (I)
no	but	u [name] + Gen	belonging to
obnoviti, obnovim	to renew (P)	uzalud	in vain
odleteti, odletim	to fly away (P)	v.	see [abbr. for vidi]
odletjeti, odletim	to fly away (P)	val, valovi [B,C]	wave
ostrvo [S]	island	vazduh [B,S]	air
otok [B,C]	island	veselje	merriment
petnaesti	fifteenth	vinuti se, vinem se	to soar (P)
pingvin, pingvina	penguin	za + Instr	for, after
pingvinski	penguin (adj.)	za uzvrat	in return
ples [B,C]	dance	zadiviti, zadivim	to thrill (P)
plesati, plešem [B,C]	to dance (I)	zadivljen	admiring
počistiti	to clean up (P)	zoološki vrt	zoo
podignuti [podići], podignem	to lift, raise (P)	zov	call
pohvaliti se, pohvalim se	to boast (P)	zrak [B,C]	air
polarno more	polar sea		

Crtani film: PINGVIN CHARLIE
priča: Hanna Kraatz
režiser: B. Kolar

U Baltazar-gradu nalazio se lijepi zoološki vrt. A u njemu – Pingvin Charlie – ljubimac svih posjetilaca. Charlie je bio uvijek spreman da razveseli gledaoce svojim šaljivim plesom. Pritom je točno znao što je kome najdraže. Pa je upravo to i izvodio. Charlie se radovao svakome, no najradije je plesao za profesora Baltazara, a on bi ga za uzvrat častio limunadom s puno, puno leda.

Međutim Charliea je u dubini srca morio teški problem. On naime nije mogao letjeti. Gledajući svoje rođake ptice kako lete, Charlie je svaki put poželio da se vine u zrak, ali je to uvijek žalosno svršilo! Saznavši za njegovu tugu, ostale su se ptice pretvarale kao da i same ne znaju letjeti. No sve je bilo uzalud. Charlie je i dalje tugovao.

Jednoga dana izjadao se profesoru Baltazaru. Baltazar je shvatio da mu mora pomoći. Profesor Baltazar izumio je neobičnu "leti-kapu." Čim ju je Charlie stavio na glavu, proradio je propeler i podigao ga je u zrak! Kapa je naime radila na misaone valove, a želja za letenjem u Charliea bila je tako snažna, da je propeler radio punom brzinom. Cijelog dana Charlie je izvodio egzibicije pred zadivljenim rođakama, a kad je pala noć pošao je umoran na spavanje.

Iz dana u dan letio je sve bolje. Navratio je i do profesora Baltazara da mu se pohvali.

Charlie je osjetio zov daljina. Letio je sve dalje i dalje, čak i preko mora. No uvijek se vraćao na vrijeme za spavanje. A onda je došao dan velikog proljetnog spremanja u zoološkom vrtu, kad on ostaje zatvoren da bi se sve moglo počistiti, urediti i obnoviti. Charlie je to iskoristio da odleti još dalje, gdje još nikada nije bio. Odletio je i više se nije vratio!

Svi su se rastužili, a ponajviše profesor Baltazar. Zato je poletio da ga pronađe.

Našao ga je daleko usred polarnog mora na jednom malom otoku Pingvinske zemlje. A s njim je bila i Šarlota, ljupka pingvinka! Charlie je našao ljubav svoga života i nije ju htio napustiti. A kako Šarlota nije mogla letjeti... E tu se Charlie prevario! Radosno su svi poletjeli natrag u Baltazar-grad! U gradu, u vrtu, veselju nije bilo kraja! A Charlie i Šarlota su sada plesali svoju čuvenu točku – u duetu, što je bilo i dvostruko ljepše, po jednodušnom mišljenju cijelog Baltazar-grada.

☞ **Classroom students and self-study learners alike:** First watch *Pingvin Charlie* twice without reading the written version of the story given above. Then read the story through carefully. Now, watch the cartoon two more times, the first time without consulting the written version, the second time while consulting it. Watch the cartoon a final time without the text.

 **GRAMMAR**

* Aspect choice and verbal meaning *

Any one verb carries not only its dictionary meaning, but also the meaning added by the choice of verbal aspect. When a speaker uses an imperfective verb, s/he chooses to indicate one of three basic ideas: that the action is currently ongoing, that it is frequently repeated, or that it is a general fact. Examples of imperfective verbs are *on je i dalje tugovao* "he continued to grieve" (ongoing), *on je plesao za profesora* "he danced for the professor" (repeated), and *tamo se nalazio lijepi vrt* "a lovely garden was located there" (general fact). **[145a]** When a speaker uses a perfective verb, the most frequent intended meaning is of a single, self-contained (usually completed) action. Examples of perfective verbs are *shvatio je da mu mora pomoći* "he realized that he had to help him," *izumio je neobičnu leti-kapu* "he invented an unusual flying cap," and *proradio je propeler* "the propeller began to work." A perfective verb can also denote a repeated action if there is sufficient emphasis on the fact that the action was completed each time. For example, the perfective verbs in *svaki put je poželio da se vine u zrak, ali je to uvijek žalosno svršilo* each refer to repeated instances of a single completed action: "each time he wanted (= had a desire) to rise up into the air but it always (= every time) ended unhappily." **[145b]**

* Aspect and narrative *

Aspect choice also carries a meaning beyond the level of an individual sentence. Whenever past events are narrated as a connected series of, the choice of aspect functions to organize the narrative. Verbs which advance the action are almost always perfective, while those which set the scene and describe the background against which the action occurs are almost always imperfective. Most narratives begin with a section which sets the place, introduces characters, and describes their normal actions – all with verbs in the imperfective aspect. Once the background has been established, the central action of the story begins, frequently introduced by a phrase such as *jednoga dana...* followed by a verb in the perfective aspect ("one day [something happened]."). Backgrounded narration can also be related in the present tense. This usage, called the "historic present," is much more frequent in BCS than in English, and is considered excellent literary style. **[145c]**

* *Sve* plus the comparative *

When the form *sve* is followed by a comparative adjective or adverb, it refers to a gradual and steady increase of the attribute in question. Thus the phrase *sve bolje* means "better and better," and the phrase *sve više* means "more and more." **[114a]**

 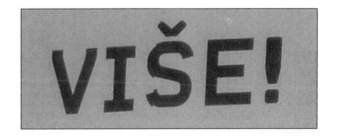

RJEČNIK [J] REČNIK [E]

ama baš ništa	absolutely nothing	prepričati, prepričam	to retell, to narrate (P)
buduće vreme	future tense	preraditi, preradim	to rework, to redo (P)
buduće vrijeme	future tense	pretežak, preteška	too difficult
istraživati, istražujem	to explore, to research (I)	rečenica	sentence
izraz	expression	sopstven [B,S]	own
jedan po jedan	one by one	stati, stanem	to start (P)
nijedan, nijedna	not a single one	tišina	silence
oblik	form	unositi, unosim	to enter, to inscribe (I)
ponaosob	individually	uraditi, uradim [B,S]	to do [and complete] (P)
poruka	message	uzbuđenje	excitement
postaviti	to pose, to place (P)	vlastit [B,C]	own

KONTROLNI TEST

Bosnian

Na času za vrijeme kontrolnog:

1. Tišina! Pišite! Nemojte stati i nemojte pričati .... sa .... (jedni drugi). Svako od vas neka sam uradi vlastiti kontrolni.
2. Ali profesore, imamo pitanja. Sve u svemu nismo ama baš ništa razumjeli.
1. Ako imate pitanja, pitajte mene, a ne .... (jedan drugi).
2. Ne razumijemo nijedno pitanje. .... (Sva pitanja) su nam (pretežak).
1. Molim vas, pogledajte bolje. Od .... (sva pitanja), prva četiri uopšte nisu teška.
2. Tačno, ali sa .... (sva ostala) imamo ozbiljne probleme.
1. U redu. Razgovarat ću s vama ponaosob, ali nemojte razgovarati .... sa .... (jedni drugi).
2. Namjeravamo slati poruke od .... do .... (jedni drugi). Može li tako?
1. Ne može, već svi vi morate jedan po jedan doći do mene sa .... (sva svoja pitanja). Ne zaboravite! Imate svega još pet minuta do kraja kontrolnog.
2. Studentski život, u .... (sva svoja ljepota), uvijek je pun uzbuđenja!

Croatian

Na satu za vrijeme kontrolnoga:

1. Tišina! Pišite! Nemojte stati i nemojte pričati .... s .... (jedni drugi). Svatko od vas neka sam piše vlastiti kontrolni.
2. Ali profesore, imamo pitanja. Sve u svemu nismo ama baš ništa razumjeli.
1. Ako imate pitanja, pitajte mene, a ne .... (jedan drugi).
2. Ne razumijemo nijedno pitanje. .... (Sva pitanja) su nam (pretežak).
1. Molim vas, pogledajte bolje. Od .... (sva pitanja), prva četiri uopće nisu teška.
2. Točno, ali sa .... (sva ostala) imamo ozbiljne probleme.
1. U redu. Razgovarat ću s vama ponaosob, ali nemojte razgovarati .... s .... (jedni drugi).
2. Namjeravamo slati poruke od .... do .... (jedni drugi). Može li tako?
1. Ne može, već svi vi morate jedan po jedan doći k meni sa .... (sva svoja pitanja). Ne zaboravite! Imate svega još pet minuta do kraja kontrolnoga.
2. Studentski život, u .... (sva svoja ljepota), uvijek je pun uzbuđenja!

Serbian

На часу за време контролног:

1. Тишина! Пишите! Немојте да станете и немојте да причате .... са .... (једни други). Свако од вас нека сам уради сопствени контролни.

2. Али професоре, имамо питања. Све у свему нисмо ама баш ништа разумели.

1. Ако имате питања, питајте мене, а не .... (један други).

2. Не разумемо ниједно питање. .... (Сва питања) су нам (претежак).

1. Молим вас, погледајте боље. Од .... (сва питања), прва четири уопште нису тешка.

2. Тачно, али са .... (сва остала) имамо озбиљне проблеме.

1. У реду. Разговараћу са вама понаособ, али немојте разговарати .... са .... (једни други).

2. Намеравамо да шаљемо поруке од .... до .... (једни други). Може ли тако?

1. Не може, већ сви ви морате један по један доћи до мене са .... (сва своја питања). Не заборавите! Имате свега још пет минута до краја контролног.

2. Студентски живот, у .... (сва своја лепота), увек је пун узбуђења!

☞ **Fill in** the blanks the appropriate forms of the words or phrases in parentheses.

 **GRAMMAR**

* "Each other" *

The English phrase "each other" is translated into BCS in two different ways. One is with a *se*-verb, as in *oni se vole* "they are in love (= they love each other)," or *oni se stalno svađaju* "they are constantly arguing [with one another]." **[126]** The other is with the phrase *jedan drugi* (singular) or *jedni drugi* (plural). *Jedan drugi* refers to two persons (or objects) while *jedni drugi* refers to groups of persons or objects. One must take care in translating English sentences such as "they help each other," since BCS must specify whether "they" refers only to two persons, as in *oni pomažu jedan drugome*, or to a larger group, as in *oni pomažu jedni drugima*. The second component of this phrase is in whatever case the sentence requires. For instance, the verb in *pomažu jedan drugome* requires the dative, whereas the prepositions in *ulaze jedan za drugim* "they enter in succession [= one after another]" and *sede* [E] *sjede* [J] *udaljeni jedan od drugoga* "they are sitting apart from one another," require the instrumental and the genitive, respectively. The first component of the phrase (*jedan* or *jedni*) is usually in the nominative, but not always. For instance, it is the object of a preposition in the phrase *slati poruke od jednih do drugih* "to send messages to one another." **[160]**

* Stati *

The perfective verb *stati* has several quite different meanings. It has been seen already (p. 166) in the meaning "stop," and is seen on the next page (sentence 5) in the meaning "start." In the first meaning it is frequently used alone (as in *stani!* "stop!"). In the second meaning, it is followed by an imperfective verb denoting the action which is beginning, as in *stati ispitivati* "to begin testing / examining." **[101]**

* Sav "all," sve "everything," and svi "everyone" *

The pronominal adjective *sav* means "all, the entire." The forms *sve* and *svi* (given in capital letters in the chart) do double duty: they can either modify nouns (that is, act as adjectives) or stand alone as pronouns. The Nsg neuter pronoun *sve* means "everything," and the Npl masculine pronoun *svi* means "everyone" **[36b, 91b]** as in *sve je bilo dobro* "everything was all right," and *svi su bili tužni* "everyone was sad."

	Singular			Plural		
	masc.	neut.	fem.	masc.	neut.	fem.
Nom	sav	*SVE*	sva	*SVI*	sva	sve
Acc	(N / G)	sve	svu	sve	sva	sve
Gen	svega	svega	sve	svih	svih	svih
Dat/Loc	svemu	svemu	svoj	svim	svim	svim
Instr	svim	svim	svom	svim	svim	svim

Note: in addition to the forms in the chart, there is the shorter form *svem*, and the longer form *svima* (see Appendix 4, p. 327).

237

Petnaesta lekcija   Lesson Fifteen

🚶 VJEŽBE [B,C] VEŽBE [S]

Starting with this lesson, instructions for the B exercises are given in B, C, and S.

B1

[B] Evo pȉtanja kòja trebā da pòstavite jèdni drùgima.
  Potrèbnē rijèči ćete nàći u rjèčnīku kod vjèžbē A2

[C] Evo pȉtanja kòja trebate pòstaviti jèdni drùgima.
  Potrèbnē rijèči ćete nàći u rjèčnīku kod vjèžbē A2

[S] Ево пȉтања кȍја требȃ да пȍставите јȅдни друȁгима.
  Потрèбнē рȅчи ћете нȁћи у речнȉку код вежбе A2.

1. [B,C] Gdje stànuje Pìngvin Charlie na pòčētku, u srèdini, i na kràju crtànog filma?

   [S] Где стàнује Пȉнгвин Чàрли на почȅтку, у средѝни, и на крају цртàног филма?

2. [B,C] Čìme se bavi Pìngvin Charlie, a čìme profèsor Baltazar?

   [S] Чȉме се бави Пȉнгвин Чàрли, а чȉме професор Балтазар?

3. [B,C] Zašto je Pìngvin Charlie tùžan dok žìvi sȁm u zoòloškom vrtu?

   [S] Зашто је Пȉнгвин Чàрли тȕжан док жȉви сȁм у зоòлошком врту?

4. [B,C] Kàko su mu htjèle pòmoći njègove ròđake ptice s jèdne strȁne, a profèsor Baltazar s drùge?

   [S] Кàко су хтеле да му пȍмогну његове рȍђаке птице с јȅднē страȁне, а професор Балтазар са другȅ?

5. [B] Šta se dogòdilo čim je Charlie stao ispitìvati radosti letènja?

   [C] Što se dogòdilo čim je Charlie stao ispitìvati radosti letènja?

   [S] Шта се догȍдило чим је Чàрли стао да испȉтујē радости летѐња?

6. [B,C] Kàko su se òsjećali svi u Baltazar-grȁdu kad je Charlie odlètio?

   [S] Кàко су се òсећали сви у Балтазар-граȁду кад је Чàрли одлѐтео?

7. [B] Čim je dòbio lèti-kapu od profesora Baltazara, Charlie je mogao odlètjeti bȉlo kuda. Zbog čèga je pošao baš na pòlarno mȍre?

    [C] Čim je dòbio lèti-kapu od profesora Baltazara, Charlie je mogao odlètjeti bȉlo kamo. Zbog čèga je pošao baš na pòlarno mȍre?

    [S] Чим је дòбио лèти-капу од профèсора Балтазара, Чàрли је мòгао да одлèти бȉло где. Због чèга је пòшао баш на пòларно мȍре?

8. [B,C] Kàko se òsjećao profesor Baltazar kad je Charlie òtišao?

    [S] Кàко се òсећао профèсор Балтазар кад је Чàрли òтишао?

9. [B] Kùda je zàtim òtišao profesor Baltazar, i zašto?

    [C] Kamo je zàtim òtišao profesor Baltazar, i zašto?

    [S] Где је зàтим òтишао профèсор Балтазар, и зашто?

10. [B] Tko je Šarlòta i òdakle je?

    [C] Ko je Šarlòta i òdakle je?

    [S] Ко је Шарлòта и òдакле је?

11. [B,C] Kàko je ùspio profesor Baltazar vràtiti Charliea i Šarlòtu u Baltazar-grȁd?

    [S] Кàко је ùспео профèсор Балтазар да врȁти Чàрлија и Шарлòту у Балтазар-грȁд?

12. [B] Šta je bȉlo novo u zoòloškom vrtu nakon toga?

    [C] Što je bȉlo novȍ u zoòloškom vrtu nakon toga?

    [S] Шта је бȉло ново у зоòлошком врту после тога?

B2

[B,S] **Preprìčajte** "Pingvìna Charliea" u svòjoj sòpstvenoj verziji.

[C] **Preprìčajte** "Pingvìna Čarlija" u svòjoj vlàstitoj verziji.

B3

[B,C] **Prepričajte** vježbe 3A2, 3A3, 3A4, 4A2, 4A3, 4A4 u parovima.

[S] **Препричајте** вежбе 3А2, 3А3, 3А4, 4А2, 4А3, 4А4 у паровима.

B4

Prevedite ove rečenice na engleski.

1. Ostale su se ptice pretvarale kao da i same ne znaju letjeti.

2. [B,C] Pingvin Charlie se pretvarao kao da mu je svejedno leti li ili ne.

   [S] Pingvin Čarli se pretvarao kao da mu je svejedno da li leti ili ne.

3. Govori mu kao da razumiješ o čemu se radi!

4. [B,C] Zar ima pingvina koji mogu letjeti kao da su ptice?

   [S] Zar ima pingvina koji mogu da lete kao da su ptice?

5. [B] Zbog čega su se pretvarali kao da ne znaju bosansku gramatiku?

   [C] Zbog čega su se pretvarali kao da ne znaju hrvatsku gramatiku?

   [S] Zbog čega su se pretvarali kao da ne znaju srpsku gramatiku?

6. [B] Čim ju je vidio, Charlie je znao da mu je Šarlota ljubav njegovog života.

   [C] Čim ju je vidio, Charlie je znao da mu je Šarlota ljubav njegova života.

   [S] Čim ju je video, Čarli je znao da mu je Šarlota ljubav njegovog života.

B5

Self-study learners: Watch a film in B, C, or S
    See suggestions at http://www.bcsgrammarandtextbook.org/Textbook/movies.shtml)
or find another cartoon about Profesor Baltazar
    (relevant links at http://www.bcsgrammarandtextbook.org/Textbook/baltazar.shtml)

✍ DOMAĆA ZADAĆA [B,C] DOMAĆI ZADATAK [S]

C1

There are many places in the text of PINGVIN CHARLIE where a verb, phrase or preposition requires a particular case. In the text below, first translate the words in parentheses, and then use the story as a model to put them into the case required by each sentence.

Example: Charlie se radovao .... (all the birds) **becomes**

Charlie se radovao sv<u>i</u>m pticama.

1. .... (one day) P<u>i</u>ngv<u>i</u>n Charlie se <u>i</u>zjadao .... (his best friend).

2. U zo<u>o</u>lošk<u>om</u> vrtu P<u>i</u>ngv<u>i</u>n Charlie je bio ljub<u>i</u>mac .... (of all the viewers).

3. Dok je Charlie č<u>a</u>stio profesora Baltazara .... (dance), profesor Baltazar je č<u>a</u>stio Charliea .... (orange juice).

4. Profesor Baltazar je shvatio da treb<u>a</u> p<u>o</u>moći .... (Šarlota).

5. .... (All day) Charlie je pl<u>e</u>sao pred .... (admiring people of Baltazar-town).

6. Šarl<u>o</u>ta se pohv<u>a</u>lila .... (other penguins) na <u>o</u>toku .... (in the polar sea) da id<u>e</u> u Baltazar-gr<u>a</u>d.

7. [S] Charlie i Šarl<u>o</u>ta su b<u>i</u>li .... (prepared) l<u>e</u>teti sve bolj<u>e</u>.
   [B,C] Charlie i Šarl<u>o</u>ta su b<u>i</u>li .... (prepared) l<u>e</u>tjeti sve bolj<u>e</u>.

8. Kad su se vr<u>a</u>tili u zo<u>o</u>lošk<u>i</u> vrt .... (dance) n<u>i</u>je b<u>i</u>lo kr<u>a</u>ja.

C2

Analyze the grammar of the Pingvin Charlie story (A1). For each verb, state whether it is imperfective (I) or perfective (P), and explain the meaning of the aspect in each particular instance: why is that aspect chosen rather than the other? Then identify all the verbal nouns, passive participles, and verbal adverbs (marking them as VN, PP, and VA, respectively).

C3

Translate these sentences into B, C, or S:

1. All in all, this animated film is funnier than that one.
2. In all her joy, she forgot what she said.
3. Everyone who watched the film became sad.
4. The merriment lasted until the next morning.
5. They studied all day, however they didn't learn the poem by heart.
6. He saw her.

C4

Together with another student from your class, compose a short conversation (100 words) on one of the three themes below, and then perform it in class.

Self-study learners: compose two conversations, one from the point of view of one participant (or set of participants) and another from the point of view of the other(s).

1. [B,C] Razgovor između profesora Baltazara i Charliea o tome kȁko se Charlie žȅli vȉnuti u zrȁk, a nè može.

   [S] Разговор између професора Балтазара и Чарлија о томе кȁко Чарли жȅли да се вȉне у ваздух, а нè може.

2. [B,C] Razgovor između Charliea i Šarlȍte u trenȕtku kad ȍna treba prvi put polȅtjeti, i vrȁtiti se s Charlieom u Baltazar-grȁd.

   [S] Разговор између Чарлија и Шарлȍте у тренȕтку кад ȍна треба први пут да полȅти, и да се врȁти са Чарлијем у Балтазар-грȁд.

3. [B] Razgovor između Charliea i Šarlȍte s jȅdne strȁne i ljȕdi u Baltazar-grȁdu s drugȅ strȁne poslije njihovog pȍvratka.

   [C] Razgovor između Charliea i Šarlȍte s jȅdne strȁne i ljȕdi u Baltazar-grȁdu s drugȅ strȁne poslije njihova pȍvratka.

   [S] Разговор између Чарлија и Шарлȍте са јȅдне стрȁне и љȕди у Балтазар-граду са другȅ стрȁне после њиховог пȍвратка.

📖 Priča: Bazdulj

Pročìtati čètvrti dio iz priče "Ljȕbav na španjolski nȁčin" Muhȁrema Bazdulja (str. 350).
Pročìtati čètvrti deo iz priče "Ljȕbav na španjolski nȁčin" Muhȁrema Bazdulja (str. 350).

Šesnaesta lekcija • Lesson Sixteen

ᔓA1

RJEČNIK [J] REČNIK [E]

administracija	administration	poduzeti, poduzmem [B,C]	to undertake (P)
anketa	survey	poneti, ponesem	to take (P)
baciti, bacim	to throw (P)	ponijeti, ponesem	to take (P)
čudo; čuda *or* čudesa	miracle, wonder	ponosan, ponosna	proud
divna li čuda	what a miracle	postavljati	to pose (I)
dnevna soba	living room	posuditi, posudim	to borrow (P)
dopadati se	to be appealing to (I)	potruditi se, potrudim se	to make an effort (P)
dospeti, dospijem	to arrive at (P)	preduzeti,	to undertake (P)
dospjeti, dospijem	to arrive at (P)	preduzmem [B,S]	
ekipa	crew	prihvatiti	to accept (P)
festival, festivala	festival	prilika	opportunity
i tako dalje (*abbr.* itd.)	and so forth, etcetera	projekat, projekta [S]	project
interesirati,	to interest (I)	projekt [B,C]	project
interesiram [B,C]		rezervirati, rezerviram [C]	to reserve (I/P)
interesovati,	to interest (I)	rezervisati,	to reserve (I/P)
interesujem [B,S]		rezervišem [B,S]	
jedno	approximately	skoknuti, skoknem	to hop (P)
kino-dvorana	cinema hall	smisliti	to devise (P)
komotan, komotna	comfortable	sprovesti, sprovedem	to conduct (P)
korak	step	sročiti, sročim	to compose (P)
krcat	crammed, packed	stipendija	stipend, scholarship
lenj, lenja [S]	lazy	stipendiranje	funding
lijen [B,C]	lazy	stran	foreign
mogućnost, -osti (*f*)	possibility	sudjelovati,	to participate (I)
nabaviti	to obtain (P)	sudjelujem [B,C]	
ne budi lenj [S]	not to be lazy	šesnaesti	sixteenth
ne budi lijen [B,C]	not to be lazy	teret	burden
nekakav, nekakva	some kind of	toliko	so much
ničiji	no one's	treća godina	junior year
nije bogzna šta	isn't much (God knows)	učestvovati, učestvujem [S]	to participate (I)
nije ni za baciti	[it's] not to be sneezed at	ulaznica	entrance ticket
odavno	a long time ago	upoznati	to get to know (P)
odgledati	to view all (P)	većina	majority
odobriti, odobrim	to approve (P)	video	VCR
odsek	university department	videoteka	video store
odsjek	university department	zadnji	last, furthest back
odsesti, odsjednem	to be a guest (P)	zainteresiran [B,C]	interested
odsjesti, odsjednem	to be a guest (P)	zainteresovan [B,S]	interested
plan	plan		

243

Šesnaesta lekcija   Lesson Sixteen

PISMO O DOLASKU NA FILMSKI FESTIVAL

Dragi moji tetko i teče!   5. april 2005.g.

Prvo da vas pozdravim od tate i mame i Majde. Svi smo dobro, i nadam se da ste i vi dobro. Kao što sigurno već znate, studiram film na jednom koledžu u našem gradu, i budući da sam bio ponekad i vrijedan, dospio sam čak i do treće godine!

Na mom odsjeku se pojavila mogućnost stipendiranja studenata koji ponude zanimljive projekte. A ja ti, ne budi lijen, sjednem pa smislim mali projektić za ovo ljeto, i, divna li čuda, prihvatili su! Daće mi nešto novaca, nije bogzna šta, ali nije ni za baciti, i evo me u Sarajevo k vama! Prvo da vas pitam, smijem li kod vas odsjesti jedno dva mjeseca, od 1. jula do 1. septembra? Spavaću u dnevnoj sobi i na podu ako treba. Znam da nemate puno prostora. Pomoći ću vam oko svega, a sudjelovaću i u troškovima oko hrane i drugih stvari. Ne želim vam biti na teretu. Znam da vi tamo ne živite tako komotno kao mi ovdje.

Plan mi je da skoknem do Motovuna na filmski festival krajem jula, a svakako moram biti u Sarajevu za vrijeme sarajevskog festivala sredinom avgusta. Sročio sam nekakvu anketu, odobrili su je ovdje u administraciji mog koledža, s pitanjima koja ću postavljati raznim ljudima u kafićima, na ulici, i tako dalje, o tome jesu li uopšte gledali neki bosanski film, ako jesu, onda koji, i koji im se najviše dopadao od onih koje su gledali i zbog čega.

Gledao sam već odavno one čuvene kao što su *Sjećaš li se Dolly Bell* i *Otac na službenom putu* Emira Kusturice, i *Savršeni krug* Ademira Kenovića. Ne mogu vam opisati koliko smo svi mi koji smo iz Bosne u Americi bili ponosni kad je Tanović dobio Oskara za najbolji strani film za *Ničiju zemlju*! Krcate su bile sve američke kino-dvorane. Sad je krenuo novi val bosanskih filmova, ali ih nisam imao priliku da gledam, pa se nadam dok sam u Sarajevu kod vas da ću ih moći barem posuditi iz videoteke ili od nekoga. Nadam se da imate video ili DVD kod kuće!

Već sam preduzeo korake da nabavim ulaznice za sarajevski festival jer sam čuo da se teško nabave u zadnji čas. Jeste li i vi zainteresovani? Mogu i za vas rezervisati ako vas interesuje, preko interneta. I naravno, ako mi se pruži prilika da upoznam neke režisere ili ljude iz njihovih ekipa, ništa ne bih imao protiv. Od mene se očekuje da sprovedem svoju anketu, i odgledam većinu filmova na tim festivalima. Kada se vratim, moram o tome nešto da napišem.

Eto, toliko za sad. Jako se radujem što ću vas uskoro vidjeti!

Voli vas,

Dino

Photographs of Sarajevo

RJEČNIK [J] REČNIK [E]

Amerika, Americi	America	planirati, planiram	to plan (I)
blagovaonica [C]	dining room	pomenuti [B,S]	to mention (P)
cvrkutati, cvrkućem	to chirp (I)	povezivati, povezujem	to connect (I)
čuditi se	to be amazed (I)	predsoblje	front hall
drugo	other	prost	simple
igračka	toy	rasti, rastem	to grow (I)
igrati se, igram se	to play (I)	raširiti, raširim	to spread (P)
ispričati, ispričam	to talk fully (P)	razlika	difference
kuhinja	kitchen	rođeni	close kin
kupaonica [C]	bathroom	sestrica	little sister
kupatilo [B,S]	bathroom	spavaća soba	bedroom
nekada	once [in the past]	spomenuti, spomenem [B,C]	to mention (P)
nuditi	to offer (I)	sport [B,S]	sports
obezbediti, obezbedim [S]	to secure, to provide (P)	šport [C]	sports
		studij	[course of] study
obezbijediti, obezbijedim [B,S]	to secure, to provide (P)	toliko	so many
		trpezarija [B,S]	dining room
obradovati, obradujem	to delight (P)	uglavnom	mainly
Olimpijada	Olympic Games	ugostiti, ugostim	to host (P)
omladina	young people	uključiti, uključim	to turn on (P)
osetiti	to feel (P)	W.C. [B,C,S] *(pron. ve-ce)*	toilet
osigurati [C]	to secure, to provide (P)	zagrliti	to embrace (P)
		zahod [C]	toilet
osjetiti	to feel (P)	zapamtiti	to remember (P)
ostava	pantry, closet	živ	alive

ODGOVOR IZ SARAJEVA

Dragi naš Dino,

Da samo znaš koliko si nas obradovao svojim pismom i time što planiraš da dođeš. Prosto ne možemo da vjerujemo da ćemo našeg Dinu opet nakon toliko godina vidjeti. Bio si mali kada si s roditeljima otišao u Ameriku i, kako je onda, te davne '92. izgledalo, na početku rata, mislili smo da te možda više nikada nećemo vidjeti. Ali, eto, dao Bog, pa smo svi, i vi tamo i mi ovdje, zdravi i živi. Slike su i telefoni jedno, a drugo je zagrliti svoga i ugostiti ga, kao nekada, kada ni slutiti nismo mogli da će do svega ovoga doći.

Sjedimo i čitamo tvoje pismo, pa se sve čudimo: naš Dino na studiju za režisera. Kao da te sada gledamo kako se sa sestricom Majdom igraš, ovdje u trpezariji. Raširili igračke ispod stola, pa sve nešto cvrkućete. Kada ti je mama ovdje bila prije dvije godine, pričala nam je o svemu, kako rastete i u kakve škole idete. Rekla nam je da si više za sport nego za knjigu, za razliku od tvoje sestre, ali vidimo da si se našao u tome što studiraš i to nam je drago.

Dragi naš Dino, ma kako možeš i da pitaš možeš li kod nas biti? Izgleda da je u Americi to tako. Da i najrođenijeg pitaš i nudiš mu novac. Lijepo je što na to misliš, ali si ti naš, a ne neki student podstanar. Mami pokaži šta sam ti napisala, pa ćeš vidjeti šta će ti reći. Samo ti nama dođi. I ovo je tvoj dom, a ne samo taj tamo u Americi.

Neke od filmova što si spomenuo gledali smo na televiziji. Video nikada nismo imali, a to drugo, taj DVD, ja to ne bih znala ni uključiti. Ima to ovdje, mislim, jedan komšija, pa možemo kod njega da navratimo i gledamo.

Lijepo je što svoj studij povezuješ s Bosnom. Mnogo se ovdje ovih godina filmova snimilo, uglavnom o ratu. A i o čemu bi drugom? Neka svijet i tako vidi i zapamti šta se dogodilo.

Sarajevo je opet puno omladine i života, a za vrijeme festivala osjetimo da smo u centru svijeta. Bilo je tako i za vrijeme Olimpijade. Ti se još nisi bio ni rodio. Što se karata tiče, ne brini. Imam ja jednog prijatelja koji još radi na Televiziji. Novinar je i sigurno će imati ideju kako da ti obezbijedimo karte.

Bilo bi još mnogo toga o čemu bismo ti rado pisali. Imaćemo vremena da se o svemu ispričamo. Javi nam kada tačno stižeš.

Puno vas sve volimo!

Tetka i tetak

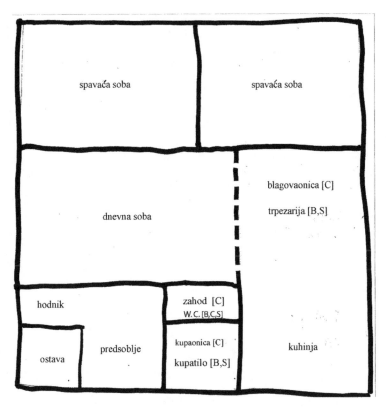

The apartment of Dino's aunt and uncle

RJEČNIK [J] REČNIK [E]

adresa	address	postdiplomski studij [B,S]	graduate study
boraviti	to stay (I)	posvetiti, posvetim	to dedicate (P)
čitaonica	reading room	poštovan	respected, esteemed
dogodine	next year	poštovanje	respect, esteem
dopustiti, dopustim	to permit (P)	predati	to submit (P)
financiranje [C]	financial support	preuraniti	to act too soon (P)
finansiranje [B,S]	financial support	pribaviti	to get hold of (P)
folklor, folklora	folklore	privatna soba	private room
formular, formulara	form	proputovati, proputujem	to travel through (P)
gostovati, gostujem	to be a guest (I)	provesti, provedem	to carry out (P)
hostel	hostel	putem	by means of
informacija	information	rad	piece of writing
instanca	institution	referada	registrar's office
iskaznica	membership card	smeštaj	accommodation
istraživanje	research	smještaj	accommodation
istraživački	research (adj.)	smotra	festival, review
izdavati, izdajem	to rent briefly (I)	smotra folklora	folklore festival
izvor	source	stručnjak	expert
izvorni	original (adj.)	stupiti, stupim	to step (P)
jedini	one and only	stupiti u vezu	to get in touch (P)
kogod	someone [or other]	sveučilišni [C]	university (adj.)
konac, konca	end	tema	theme, topic
lokacija	location	temelj	foundation
magistarski rad	master's thesis	terenski	field [work] (adj.)
molba	request, application	tijekom [C]	during
momentalno [B,S]	at the moment	tkogod [C]	someone [or other]
nacionalni	national	tokom [B,S]	during
najpre	first of all	tradicija	tradition
najprije	first of all	trenutačno [C]	at the moment
obalni	coastal	trud	effort
obratiti se, obratim se	to turn to (P)	turistička agencija	tourist agency
obzir	consideration	učiniti se, učini se	to seem (P)
obzirom na or s obzirom na	in regards to	uložen	invested
odgovoriti, odgovorim	to answer (P)	univerzitetski [B,S]	university (adj.)
odgovarajući	corresponding	uostalom	after all
okvirni	approximate	uputiti, uputim	to direct [to] (P)
pokrenuti, pokrenem	to start (P)	zahvaljivati, zahvaljujem	to thank (I)
posetiti	to visit (P)	zanima me	[it] interests me
posjetiti	to visit (P)	zanimati, zanimam	to interest (I)
poslijediplomski studij [C]	graduate study		

PISMO O ISTRAŽIVAČKOM RADU U HRVATSKOJ

Poštovani gospodine profesore,

Dopustite mi da se najprije predstavim. Studentica sam na poslijediplomskom studiju slavistike na sveučilištu u Indiani i odlučila sam da svoj magistarski rad posvetim hrvatskoj književnosti. Trenutačno slušam predavanja kod profesora Jeguljića, koji mi je i dao Vaše ime i adresu, i preporučio mi da Vam se obratim. Naime, idućeg bih ljeta rado došla na Vaš fakultet i provela istraživanje na temu "Živa tradicija usmene književnosti danas u Hrvatskoj." Ovo bi istraživanje bilo temelj mojega magistarskog rada. Na Vašem bih fakultetu bila mjesec dana, od 15. svibnja do 15. lipnja, a potom bih proputovala kroza sve krajeve Hrvatske (svakako namjeravam posjetiti obalna područja Primorja i Dalmacije, Dalmatinsku zagoru, Posavinu, istočnu Slavoniju i Istru). Tijekom ovoga terenskog rada, koji bi trajao do konca srpnja, snimala bih razne vrste žive usmene književnosti. Na kraju bih posjetila i Smotru folklora u Zagrebu.

The pavilion in the Zrinjevac Promenade, often used as a stage
during the Folklore Festival every July in Zagreb

Imala bih nekoliko molbi. Prvo, bila bih Vam veoma zahvalna kad biste mi pomogli da pronađem smještaj dok sam u Zagrebu. Ne znam ima li Vaš fakultet osiguran smještaj za strane studente koji kod Vas gostuju; ako nema, možete li mi preporučiti neku turističku agenciju koja izdaje privatne sobe? Najradije bih stanovala kod kakve obitelji ili pak u studentskom domu, ali ako to nije moguće, mogla bih spavati i u hostelu.

Budući da je tema moga istraživanja iz područja kojim se i Vi već duže vrijeme bavite, zanima me biste li mi mogli preporučiti nekoliko lokacija gdje bih mogla snimiti izvorni materijal. Možda trenutačno i neki odsjeci na Vašemu fakultetu rade na sličnim projektima? Ako da, koji su to odsjeci i kome da se na tim odsjecima obratim? Da li da im se javim telefonom, pismom ili pak putem interneta?

Možete li mi Vi ili tkogod u referadi Vašeg fakulteta pribaviti iskaznicu za Nacionalnu i sveučilišnu knjižnicu i druge veće knjižnice i čitaonice u gradu?

Budući da do moga dolaska u Hrvatsku ima još osam mjeseci, možda će Vam se učiniti da sam malo preuranila sa svim ovim pitanjima. Međutim, da bih osigurala potreban novac za svoj boravak, moram najprije odgovarajućim instancama u Americi predati molbu za financiranje cijelog projekta; u njihovu formularu moram navesti da sam već stupila u vezu s odgovarajućim stručnjacima, da znam gdje ću boraviti i da sam već sve pokrenula da bi projekt bio što uspješniji. S obzirom na to da molbu moram predati do konca godine, molila bih Vas da mi se barem s okvirnim informacijama javite što prije.

Slavonian village

Pretpostavljam da ne ćete moći odgovoriti na sva moja pitanja, ali budući da mi je profesor Jeguljić ovdje u Indiani dao samo Vašu adresu, Vi ste mi trenutačno jedini izvor informacija. Uostalom, ako i ne budete mogli odgovoriti na neka od mojih pitanja, sigurna sam da ćete me znati uputiti onim osobama ili službama koje će to moći.

Unaprijed zahvaljujem na Vašoj pomoći i uloženom trudu u vezi s mojim studijskim boravkom dogodine u Hrvatskoj.

U Bloomingtonu, 15. listopada 2005.

S poštovanjem,

Andrea Smithson

When you are writing a formal letter to a single person you may capitalize the letter "V" on all the forms of *Vi* and *Vaš*. Although many native speakers feel this to be a quaint and antiquated custom, the current language guides still recommend doing it. Do not capitalize the "V" when the *vi* refers to more than one person. One also sometimes comes across instances of capital "T" (*Ti* and *Tvoj*) in correspondence. However, this is much more old-fashioned, and far less common in today's usage.

RJEČNIK [J] REČNIK [E]

baština	legacy	naposljetku	finally, in closing
besplatan, besplatna	free of charge	neposredan,	direct
bogat	rich	neposredna [B,C,S]	
cena	price	pohađati, pohađam	to attend (I)
cijena	price	polaznik	person taking a course
doista	truly	popriličan, poprilična	considerable
dosadašnji	previous	porazgovarati,	to talk briefly (P)
etnologija	ethnology	porazgovaram	
gospođica	Miss	potvrda	confirmation
iako	although	pridoneti, pridonesem	to contribute (P)
istražiti, istražim	to investigate (P)	pridonijeti, pridonesem	to contribute (P)
izdati	to issue (P)	priključiti se, priključim se	to join (P)
iznajmljivati,	to rent [to] (I)	pristupačan, pristupačna	accessible
iznajmljujem		razdoblje	period [of time]
izniman, iznimna [C]	exceptional	slobodan, slobodna	free, unhindered
izravan, izravna [C]	direct	srdačan, srdačna	heartfelt, warm
izuzetan, izuzetna [B,C,S]	exceptional	stranac, stranca	foreigner
jednomesečni	one-month	tečaj [B,C,S]	course [e.g. language]
jednomjesečni	one-month	telefonski	telephone *(adj.)*
katedra	university dept.	učlaniti se, učlanim se	to join (P)
književni	literary	unajmljivati, unajmljujem	to rent [from] (I)
kurs [B,S]	course [e.g. language]	zanimati se, zanimam se	to be engaged in (I)
naposletku	finally, in closing		

ODGOVOR IZ ZAGREBA

Poštovana gospođice Smithson,

Hvala Vam na Vašemu pismu. Moram Vam reći da mi je doista drago da se netko u Americi zanima za usmenu hrvatsku književnost. Kao što znate, usmena književnost u Hrvatskoj ima dugu tradiciju, ali do sada svi njezini oblici nisu bili dovoljno istraženi. Siguran sam da će Vaše istraživanje pridonijeti još boljem razumijevanju te iznimno bogate i zanimljive književne baštine.

Što se Vaših pitanja tiče, mislim da Vam mogu pomoći u svemu što Vas zanima. Krenimo od smještaja. U Zagrebu postoji nekoliko studentskih domova u kojima biste mogli odsjesti, ali se bojim da u razdoblju u kojem ćete Vi biti ovdje ne će biti slobodnih soba. Naime, u to vrijeme još traju predavanja i ispiti tako da su svi domovi puni. Kao što ste rekli, druga je mogućnost da živite s nekom obitelji, ali, na žalost, ovdje nema mnogo obitelji koje se bave tim poslom. Budući da u Zagrebu namjeravate ostati mjesec dana, preporučio bih Vam da unajmite stan. Imam prijatelja čija sestra iznajmljuje svoj stan za vrlo pristupačnu cijenu. Razmislite o tome i ako se odlučite unajmiti taj stan, javite mi se pa ću Vam poslati telefonski broj prijateljeve sestre.

Na našem se fakultetu trenutačno radi na nekoliko projekata iz područja koje Vas zanima i mislim da biste im se bez problema mogli priključiti. Jedan projekt vodi Katedra za stariju hrvatsku književnost, a drugi Odsjek za etnologiju. Najbolje će Vam biti da se obratite izravno njima, a i ja ću porazgovarati sa svojim kolegama na tim odsjecima. Oba su ta projekta počela prije nekoliko godina i prikupljeno je već poprilično materijala.

Svi naši i gostujući studenti mogu se besplatno učlaniti u Nacionalnu i sveučilišnu knjižnicu i ostale veće knjižnice u gradu. Potrebno je samo da imate dvije slike i potvrdu da sudjelujete u projektu na našem fakultetu. Tu će Vam potvrdu izdati u našoj referadi.

Dalmatian village

Iako ćete za svoga boravka dosta vremena posvetiti svome istraživačkom radu, preporučio bih Vam da usput pohađate i tečaj hrvatskoga jezika. Na našem se fakultetu održavaju jednomjesečni tečajevi hrvatskoga za strance i dosadašnji su polaznici bili veoma zadovoljni.

Nadam se da sam uspio odgovoriti na sve što Vas je zanimalo. Ako imate bilo kakvih drugih pitanja, slobodno mi se opet javite.

Naposljetku, pozdravite mojega kolegu i dobrog prijatelja Jeguljića. Mi se znamo još od studentskih dana i neko smo se vrijeme dosta družili. Recite mu da mi se javi kad opet bude u Zagrebu.

Vidimo se dogodine u Hrvatskoj!

U Zagrebu, 28. listopada 2005.
Srdačan pozdrav,

Marko Knjižić

Split, Diocletian's Palace

Zagreb, Zrinjevac Promenade

RJEČNIK [J] REČNIK [E]

angažirati se, angažiram se [C]	to get involved (I/P)	porijeklo	origin
angažovati se, angažujem se [B,S]	to get involved (I/P)	pozorišni [B,S]	theater *(adj.)*
		predavati, predajem	to teach (I)
Beograđanin	resident of Belgrade	provesti, provedem	to spend *[e.g. time]* (P)
doseliti se, doselim se	to move to (P)	savet	advice
eventualan, eventualna	possible	savjet	advice
interesantan, interesantna	interesting	sedmični [B,S]	weekly
kazališni [C]	theater *(adj.)*	sjajan, sjajna	marvelous
koštati	to cost (I)	smisao, smisla	sense, meaning
kupati se, kupam se	to swim, to bathe (I)	stepen [B,S]	degree
nada	hope	stupanj [C]	degree
nedeljni [S]	weekly	suviše	too much
obilaziti	to tour (I)	temperatura	temperature
obnavljati, obnavljam	to renew (I)	tjedni [C]	weekly
obraćati se	to address (I)	trajanje	duration
odvažiti se, odvažim se	to muster courage (P)	umeren	moderate *(adj.)*
okolina	surroundings	umjeren	moderate *(adj.)*
opteretiti	to burden (P)	uobičajen	customary
plaža	beach	usavršiti, usavršim	to perfect (P)
poreklo	origin	vrućina	heat

ПИСМО О КУРСЕВИМА ЗА УЧЕЊЕ ЈЕЗИКА У БЕОГРАДУ

Поштовани господине Поповићу,   9. фебруар 2005.

Пишем Вам из Америке. Професор Анђић, који предаје код нас на универзитету, дао ми је Ваше име и адресу пре пар месеци и препоручио да Вам се јавим ако будем имала икаква питања у вези с мојим евентуалним доласком у Београд после краја летњег семестра. Сада сам се сетила његовог савета и одважила да Вам пишем.

Ево како је дошло до овог путовања: пореклом сам из Србије. Моји баба и деда су се доселили из Крагујевца у Питсбург почетком прошлог века, што је додуше доста давно, али се у нашој кући још увек говори српски. Код професора Анђића, овде на факултету, почела сам да обнављам граматику и, како ми је то доста добро пошло за руком, одлучила сам да се ангажујем око доласка у Београд сад на лето, па Вам се овим путем обраћам с неколико питања.

Шта бисте ми препоручили што се тиче течајева за странце који желе да усаврше језик? Ако их има, колико би могао да кошта течај у трајању од 4-5 недеља? Спремна сам да похађам чак и три пута недељно ако се тако нешто нађе.

Волела бих да проведем викенде тако што бих обилазила интересантна места и крајеве у Србији и околини. Да ли можете нешто у том смислу да ми препоручите? Волела бих да знам какав је Београд за време лета. Шта се тих месеци дешава у граду? Волим да идем у позориште и чула сам да Београд има сјајан позоришни живот, али ме занима да ли има представа и преко лета?

Knez Mihailova Street, Belgrade

Какво је уобичајено време у то доба године? Има ли великих врућина или су температуре умерене? Шта раде Београђани кад је 35 степени или још топлије? Да ли има неких плажа где се купају?

Семестар ми се овде у Америци завршава средином маја. Могла бих да будем у Београду већ од, рецимо, 20. маја, и да останем око два и по до три месеца. Морам да се вратим кући најкасније до 15. августа да бих се припремала за следећу школску годину. Смештај ми не представља никакав проблем, јер сам преко даљих рођака нашла где ћу да станујем.

У нади да Вас нисам сувише оптеретила питањима, унапред Вам захваљујем на труду и срдачно Вас поздрављам.

Ана Ђурић

RJEČNIK [J] REČNIK [E]

atraktivan, atraktivna	attractive	početni	initial
bara	marshland	podatak; podaci	datum, data
bašta [B,S]	garden	pojedinačan, pojedinačna	individual
biti u mogućnosti da	to be able to	poseta [S]	visit
dodatan, dodatna	additional	posjet [B,C]	visit
događaj	event	predak; preci	ancestor
dojam, dojma [C]	impression	prestonica [S]	capital city
dozvoliti, dozvolim	to allow (P)	prijestolnica [B,C]	capital city
drage volje	gladly	približiti se, približim se	to approach (P)
glazbeni [C]	musical	primorski	coastal
grupa	group	priredba	performance
intenzivan, intenzivna	intensive	rad	work
javljanje	contact, writing	rashladiti se, rashladim se	to cool off (P)
jezero	lake	redovan, redovna	regular
kanjon	river gorge	samostan	Catholic monastery
konverzacijski [B,C]	conversational	sezona	season
konverzacioni [B,S]	conversationa	spomenik	monument
koristan, korisna	useful	srednjevekovni [S]	medieval
kupalište	place to swim	srednjevjekovni [B]	medieval
kurs	course, *e.g.* language	srednjovjekovni [C]	medieval
lista	list	širom	throughout, across
mada	although	takav, takva	that sort of
manastir	Orthodox monastery	tip	type, kind
muzički [B,C,S]	musical	toplota	warmth, heat
na otvorenom	on an outdoor stage	tvrđava	fortress
nagovestiti, nagovestim	to alert, to hint (P)	uprkos + *Dat*	despite
nagovijestiti, nagovijestim	to alert, to hint (P)	utisak, utiska [B,S]	impression
nipošto	by no means	uveravati, uveravam	to assure (I)
obilaženje	tour	uvjeravati, uvjeravam	to assure (I)
održavati, održavam	to hold (I)	viđenje	seeing
opredeliti, opredelim	to choose (P)	volja	will
opredijeliti, opredijelim	to choose (P)	vrt [C]	garden
organizirati, organiziram [C]	to organize (I/P)	zaći, zađem	to go behind, to set [of the sun] (P)
organizovati, organizujem [B,S]	to organize (I/P)		
osnov [B,S]	basis	zamirati	to die down (I)
osnova [C]	basis	zanimanje	interest
otputovati, otputujem	to leave on a trip (P)	zavisan, zavisna [B,S]	dependent [on]
ovisan, ovisna [C]	dependent [on]	znamenitost, -osti *(f)*	place of interest
planina	mountain	žurba	hurry

ODGOVOR IZ BEOGRADA

20. februar 2005.
Beograd

Draga gospođice Đurić,

Sa zanimanjem sam pročitao Vaše pismo. Profesor Anđić mi je već nagovestio mogućnost Vašeg javljanja. Vrlo rado ću Vam pomoći, koliko mogu, u pripremi Vaše posete Beogradu, i uveravam Vas da mi to nije nikakav teret.

Počnimo od pitanja u vezi s letnjim tečajevima srpskog jezika za strance. Nekoliko škola stranih jezika nudi takve kurseve, na nivoima od početnog do konverzacionog. Letnji tečajevi su uglavnom intenzivnog tipa, uključujući i do pet dana nedeljno po tri sata. Ako smem da primetim, moj utisak na osnovu Vašeg pisma je da biste Vi trebalo da se opredelite za neki od viših nivoa. Osim toga, neke od škola nude mogućnost rada s profesorima u manjim grupama, ili pojedinačno, što mislim da bi Vam moglo biti naročito korisno. Moram da Vam se izvinim što, u žurbi da Vam što pre odgovorim, nisam još uvek prikupio tačne podatke o cenama, ali nadam se da ću i te informacije biti u mogućnosti da Vam uskoro ponudim.

S obzirom da nameravate da ostanete između dva i po i tri meseca, mislim da ćete imati dovoljno vremena za obilaženje znamenitosti u Beogradu i oko njega. Mada sam grad ima dosta muzeja i spomenika vrednih viđenja, nipošto ne bi trebalo da propustite da posetite još neke gradove, na primer, Novi Sad i Smederevo, kao i grad Vaših predaka, Kragujevac, zatim, zavisno od interesovanja, neke od prirodnih lepota (Obedsku baru, kanjon Tare, planine Zlatibor ili Kopaonik), kao i neke od srednjovekovnih manastira (na primer, Studenicu ili Sopoćane, oba na listi svetske baštine UNESCO). Ako Vam planovi i obaveze dozvole, mislim da bi bilo dobro da, makar i na nekoliko dana, otputujete do Crne Gore, gde su veoma zanimljivi stara prestonica Cetinje, te primorski grad Kotor i planina Durmitor, koji su oba takođe na pomenutoj listi UNESCO. Osim toga, poseta Crnoj Gori bi Vam pružila priliku da se malo rashladite na moru.

Što me dovodi do Vašeg pitanja u vezi s vremenskim prilikama. Leta u Beogradu su, naime, najčešće veoma topla, i temperature u julu i avgustu mogu da se približe i četrdesetom stepenu. Većina Beograđana se tada uputi na Adu Ciganliju, gde se na jezeru nalazi veliko javno kupalište. Kada sunce zađe, bašte mnogih restorana i kafana širom grada Vam mogu pomoći da pobegnete od vrućine.

Church of the Blessed Virgin, Studenica Monastery, Serbia.
Built in the late 12th century at the behest of Stevan Nemanja
(Župan of Serbia, 1168-1196)

Uprkos toploti, kulturni život u gradu ne zamire. Mada se redovna pozorišna sezona završava početkom leta, u julu i avgustu se održavaju festivali na kojima imate i pozorišnih i muzičkih priredbi. To su veoma često događaji napolju, na otvorenom, na zanimljivim lokacijama kao što je stara tvrđava Kalemegdan, što ih čini posebno atraktivnim.

Nadam se da će Vam ove informacije biti dovoljne za početak, a ja ću drage volje odgovoriti na sva Vaša dodatna pitanja. Neke će stvari biti lakše organizovati kad dođete ovamo.

Srdačno Vas pozdravljam,

Stojan Popović

The algebraic formula for converting Fahrenheit to Celsius is: Tc = (5/9) multiplied by (Tf-32)
[Tc = temperature in degrees Celsius, Tf = temperature in degrees Fahrenheit].
A handy shortcut: keep several equivalent temperatures in mind as guidelines
0° C = 32°F   10° C = 50° F   21° C = 70° F   33° = 90°F   40°C = 104°F   100°C = 212°F

The Petrovaradin Fortress

The Danube flowing through Novi Sad

🏃 VJEŽBE [J] VEŽBE [E]

B1

[B,C] **Pripr̀èmajte** uloge, i vȍdite sljèdèće razgovòre.

[S] **Pripr̀èmajte** uloge, i vȍdite slèdèće razgovòre.

1. [B] Neka svaki od stùdenāta ȕzmē ulogu jèdnog od pošìljača pìsāmā, pa neka razgovàraju o tome kàko će pìsati svòje pìsmo, šta trebā rèći, i zbog čèga.

   [C] Neka svaki od stùdenāta ȕzmē ulogu jèdnog od pošìljalača pìsāmā, pa neka razgovàraju o tome kàko će pìsati svòje pìsmo, što trebā rèći, i zbog čèga.

   [S] Neka svaki od stùdenāta ȕzmē ulogu jèdnog od pošìljača pìsāmā, pa neka razgovàraju o tome kàko će da pìšū svòje pìsmo, šta trebā da se kȁžē i zbog čèga.

2. [B,C] Neka stùdenti (Dino, Andrea i Ana) pìtaju jèdno drugo o planovima i projektima.

   [S] Neka stùdenti (Dino, Andrea i Ana) pìtaju jèdno drugo o planovima i projektima.

3. [B,C] Neka stric i strina, Mȁrko i Stòjana, razgovàraju o tome kàko će stùdentima pòmoći.

   [S] Neka stric i strina, Mȁrko i Stòjana, razgovàraju o tome kàko će stùdentima da pòmognū.

4. Neka stùdenti razgovàraju o tome kàko im je bȉlo kàda su se vràtili kući.

Grammar note. As seen on p. 237, the general idea "each other" is expressed by a phrase containing a form of *jèdan* and a form of *drugi*. If both (or all) persons concerned are male, or if no specific reference to gender is made, then both forms are masculine; and if both or all persons concerned are female, then both forms are feminine. But if the group is of mixed gender, then neuter forms are used, as in *Mȁrko i Ana pìtaju jèdno drugo* "Marko and Ana ask each other," or *òni idù jèdno za drugim* "they follow one another."

B2

[B,C] **Pripr̀ìčati** vjèžbe 9A1, 9A2, 9A3, 9A4, 10A1, 10A2, 10A3 u parovima.

[S] **Препр̀ичати** вежбе 9A1, 9A2, 9A3, 9A4, 10A1, 10A2, 10A3 у паровима.

✍ DOMAĆA ZADAĆA [B,C] DOMAĆI ZADATAK [S]

C1

Go through the letters and make a list of the greetings, dates, and other stock letterwriting phrases.

C2

Write a letter to Stojan Popović, Marko Knjižić, or Dino's uncle and aunt, thanking them for their advice and the time they took to make your summer project a success.

C3

Translate this letter into B, C, or S:

Dear Ms. Kovačević,   Atlanta, March 2, 2006

My colleagues and I are medical students in the United States and we would like to come to visit your country. We are very interested in seeing two or three large general hospitals and several smaller ones, and, if possible, we'd be very glad to talk to some medical students. We thought we might come over in June and July. Would it be possible for us to spend two or three weeks visiting the major cities in the area? I know that you, too, are a medical student because several of your friends are students here with us at school. They gave me your name and address and recommended you as someone who might be willing to help us find accommodations and arrange for our stay.

The travel won't be a problem because we are happy to travel by bus or train. We have enough money to stay in small hotels or hostels. As far as knowledge of your language is concerned, as you can see from this letter, I have been studying [B, C or S] for two semesters and have learned enough to write a letter like this one, and I can converse a little, though I am still afraid of serious conversation. Do medical students there speak English? I hope so!

In return, we would like to help you come to visit the United States next year, and we would be glad to make similar plans for your visit in gratitude for your help to us.

Thanks in advance for your time, and I hope that we are not burdening you too much with our questions!

Sincerely,
Mark "Haso" Stern, Jane "Jana" Donnelly and Tom "Toma" Fuller

C4

1. Go through the six letters in this lesson (two each in 16A1, 16A2 and 16A3) and find one or all of the following:
(a) sentences using the conditional mood (b) complex sentences using the *da* conjunction (c) complex sentences using the *što* conjunction (d) examples of sentences using *koji* (e) examples of verbs which require the use of genitive, dative or instrumental (such as *da vam se javim*).
2. Go through "Ljubav na španjolski način" for forms of *sav, sve, sva*.

📖 Priča: Bazdulj

[B,C] **Pročitati** peti dio iz priče "Ljubav na španjolski način" Muharema Bazdulja (str. 352).
[S] **Pročitati** peti deo iz priče "Ljubav na španjolski način" Muharema Bazdulja (str. 352).

Sedamnaesta lekcija • Lesson Seventeen

⊙16

RJEČNIK [J] REČNIK [E]

dečak, dečaka	boy	sedamnaesti	seventeenth
dječak, dječaka	boy	umreti, umrem; umro, umrla	to die (P)
domovina	homeland	umrijeti, umrem; umro, umrla	to die (P)
lažljiv	fake, lying	zalupiti	to slam (P)
lepotica	beauty	zver (f)	beast
ljepotica	beauty	zvijer (f)	beast
ostavljati	to leave (I)		

LJEPOTICA I ZVIJER
Ferida Duraković (1957-)

Lažljiva ljepotica
Zalupila je vratima
Konačno
Kao Domovina
I nestala
U Istoriju.

Lažljiva, dakle, ljepotica
I Domovina
Imaju nešto zajedničko:
Obje za sobom ostavljaju
Dječake
Koji će umrijeti
Zbog njih.

rat 1991

RJEČNIK [J] REČNIK [E]

fraza	phrase	stih	line of verse
glagol	verb	strofa	stanza
imenica	noun	upotrebljavati, upotrebljavam	to use (I)
označiti, označim	to mark, to identify (P)	veznik	conjunction
predlog	preposition	zamenica	pronoun
prijedlog	preposition	zamjenica	pronoun
pridev	adjective	zaokružiti, zaokružim	to encircle (P)
pridjev	adjective	znak	sign, mark
prilog	adverb		

GRAMATIKA

1. [B,C] Označite gramatičke oblike u pjesmi, upotrebljavajući sljedeće znakove:
   (G) glagoli; (I) imenice; (P) pridjevi; (PR) prilozi; (PD) prijedlozi; (Z) zamjenice;
   (V) veznici; (B) brojevi.
   [S] Означите граматичке облике у песми, употребљавајући следеће знакове:
   (Г) глаголи; (И) именице; (П) придеви; (ПР) прилози; (ПД) предлози; (З) заменице;
   (В) везници; (Б) бројеви.

2. [B,C] Zaokružite subjekt svake rečenice ili fraze (ima ih šest).
   [S] Заокружите субјекат сваке реченице или фразе (има их шест).

3. [B,C] Označite koliko ima strofa.
   [S] Означите колико има строфа.

4. [B,C] Označite koliko ima stihova.
   [S] Означите колико има стихова.

PITANJA

Bosnian
1. Zbog čega je lažljiva ljepotica zalupila vratima?
2. Poslije čega je Domovina nestala u historiju?
3. Po čemu je lažljiva ljepotica slična Domovini?
4. Postoji li neka veza između dječaka koji će umrijeti zbog ljepotice i dječaka koji će umrijeti za Domovinu?

Croatian
1. Zbog čega je lažljiva ljepotica zalupila vratima?
2. Poslije čega je Domovina nestala u povijest?
3. Po čemu je lažljiva ljepotica slična Domovini?
4. Postoji li neka sveza između dječaka koji će umrijeti zbog ljepotice i dječaka koji će umrijeti za Domovinu?

Serbian
1. Због чега је лажљива лепотица залупила вратима?
2. После чега је Домовина нестала у историју?
3. По чему је лажљива лепотица слична Домовини?
4. Да ли постоји нека веза између дечака који ће умрети због лепотице и дечака који ће умрети за Домовину?

The walls of the National Library (formerly the Town Hall) in Sarajevo, all that is left standing of the library after it was shelled and burned during the war.

Promenade by the National Library ruins along the Miljacka, Sarajevo.

The words for **history** in B, C, and S are *hìstorija* [B], *povìjest* [C], and *ìstorija* [S]. Bosnian usage vacillates between *ìstorija* and *hìstorija*, although Bosnian grammarians (and most recent usage) tend to prefer the latter. This fact, of apparent change in progress, explains the seeming discrepancy between the usage by the modern Bosnian poet F. Duraković of the form *ìstorija*, and the usage in this textbook's lessons of the form *hìstorija*. The title of the poem by A. G. Matoš, to be found in Lesson 18, illustrates change over a longer time period. Namely, the spelling of the second word in the title of the poem *Jèsenje veče* is no longer encountered in modern Croatian, which now uses only the spelling *večer*.

RJEČNIK [J] REČNIK [E]

biljka	plant	stoljeće [B,C]	century
boravište	dwelling place	svet	world
duša	soul	svijet	world
izjednačivati se, izjednačujem se	to become equal (I)	svršavati, svršavam	to end (I)
kamen	stone	'tica (poetic)	= ptica
k'o (poetic)	= kao	uskrsnuće	resurrection
milijun, milijuna [B,C]	million	uzdignuće	ascension
milion, miliona [B,S]	million	uzlet	ascent
narod [B,C,S]	people, nation	večan, večna	eternal
nebo	heaven; sky	večnost, večnosti (f)	eternity
ostati nam je	we must remain	vek [S]	century
poumreti, poumrem	to die off [one by one] (P)	vera	faith
poumrijeti, poumrem	to die off [one by one] (P)	vijek [B,S]	century
puk [C]	people, folk	vječan, vječna	eternal
rodbina	relatives, kin	vječnost, vječnosti (f)	eternity
s, sa + Acc	over to	vjera	faith
s onu stranu	over to the other side	zauvek	forever
seoba	migration	zauvijek	forever
smrt (f)	death		

ZEMLJA
A. B. Šimić (1898-1925)

Toliko stoljeća su narodi u nebo vjerovali
i ovaj svijet im bješe kratko boravište
iza kojeg ih vječni život čeka.

Toliko stoljeća su narodi u nebo odlazili
Seoba milijuna s onu stranu zvijezda
K'o 'tice, duše su se dizale sa zemlje u vječnost.

Životinje i biljke samo
ostajahu s kamenjem na zemlji
zauvijek.

Al' vjere poumriješe
sve jedna za drugom
i saznadosmo: nema neba
ni uzdignuća, ni uzleta ni uskrsnuća
i svaki uzlet opet svršava na zemlji.

Na zemlji nam je ostati zauvijek.
Životinje i biljke naša su rodbina
i kamen samo naš najdalji brat.

U smrti svi se izjednačujemo.

Mostar and the famous bridge over the Neretva River, built in 1565 by the Ottoman architect known as Mimar Hajrudin. The bridge was destroyed in the recent war [1993] and rebuilt by UNESCO in 2004.

Jajce, Central Bosnia, early 20th century

RJEČNIK [J] REČNIK [E]

današnji	today's	gramatički	grammatical
davni	distant (in time)	prošlost, prošlosti (f)	the past
dešavati se, dešava se [B,S]	to happen (I)	zaključak, zaključka	conclusion
događati se, događa se [B,C]	to happen (I)		

GRAMATIKA

1. [B,C] Označite gramatičke oblike u pjesmi, upotrebljavajući sljedeće znakove: (G) glagoli; (I) imenice; (Z) zamjenice [svih vrsta]; (P) pridjevi; (PR) prilozi; (PD) prijedlozi; (V) veznici; (B) brojevi.
   [S] Označite gramatičke oblike u pesmi, upotrebljavajući sledeće znakove: (G) glagoli; (I) imenice; (Z) zamenice [svih vrsta]; (P) pridevi; (PR) prilozi; (PD) predlozi; (V) veznici; (B) brojevi.

2. [B,S] Zaokružite subjekat svake rečenice ili fraze (ima ih četrnaest).
   [C] Zaokružite subjekt svake rečenice ili fraze (ima ih četrnaest).

3. Označite koliko ima strofa.

4. Označite koliko ima stihova.

PITANJA

Bosnian

1. Šta su radili ljudi kada su umrli u davnoj prošlosti, po pjesmi "Zemlja"?
2. Ko ili šta je ostajalo na zemlji, i zašto?
3. Budući da se nešto promijenilo, ljudi su saznali nešto novo. Šta se promijenilo i šta su saznali?
4. Šta se, po Šimiću, dešava u današnjem vremenu kada se umre? Slažete li se vi lično sa zaključkom ove pjesme?
5. Koje godine se rodio A. B. Šimić, a koje godine je umro? Dakle, koliko je imao godina kad je umro?

Croatian

1. Što su radili ljudi kada su umrli u davnoj prošlosti, po pjesmi "Zemlja"?
2. Tko ili što je ostajalo na zemlji, i zašto?
3. Budući da se nešto promijenilo, ljudi su saznali nešto novo. Što se promijenilo i što su saznali?
4. Što se, po Šimiću, događa u današnjem vremenu kada se umre? Slažete li se vi osobno sa zaključkom ove pjesme?
5. Koje godine se rodio A. B. Šimić, a koje godine je umro? Dakle, koliko je imao godina kad je umro?

Serbian

1. Šta su radili ljudi kada su umrli u davnoj prošlosti, po pjesmi "Zemlja"?
2. Ko ili šta je ostajalo na zemlji, i zašto?
3. Budući da se nešto promenilo, ljudi su saznali nešto novo. Šta se promenilo i šta su saznali?
4. Šta se, po Šimiću, dešava u današnjem vremenu kada se umre? Da li se vi lično slažete sa zaključkom ove pesme?
5. Koje godine se rodio A. B. Šimić, a koje godine je umro? Dakle, koliko je imao godina kad je umro?

RJEČNIK [J] REČNIK [E]

bog, boga	god	raspeti, raspnem	to crucify (P)
bono	painfully [*i.e.* bolno]	rumen, rumena	ruddy, glowing red
ćutati, ćutim [B,S]	to be silent (I)	san, sna	dream, sleep
drhtati, dršćem	to tremble (I)	sur, sura	grey
hrid *(f)*	cliff	školj	small island, atoll
iskati, ištem	to seek (I)	trnuti, trnem	to extinguish, to go out (I)
jecati, jecam	to sob (I)	ubog	miserable, poor
klečati, klečim	to kneel (I)	uzdah	sigh
kostur	skeleton	vrh + *Gen*	at the top of
krš	karst, barren landscape	zadnji	last
moliti, molim	to pray (I)	zrak [B,S]	ray
prohladan, prohladna	chilly	zraka [C]	ray
pučina	open sea	zvono	bell

VEČE NA ŠKOLJU
Aleksa Šantić (1868-1924)

Pučina plava
Spava,
   Prohladni pada mrak.
Vrh hridi crne
Trne
   Zadnji rumeni zrak.

I jeca zvono
Bono,
   Po kršu dršće zvuk;
S uzdahom tuge
Duge
   Ubogi moli puk.

Kleče kosturi
Suri
   Pred likom boga svog –
Ištu... No tamo
Samo
   Ćuti raspeti bog ...

I san sve bliže
Stiže.
   Prohladni pada mrak.
Vrh hridi crne
Trne
   Zadnji rumeni zrak.

RJEČNIK [J] REČNIK [E]

doba	time period *(neut.)*	razotkriti, razotkrijem	to find out, to discover (P)
dočaravati, dočaravam	to conjure up (I)	smestiti	to situate (P)
naslov	title	smjestiti	to situate (P)
odlika	feature	uticati, utičem [B,S]	to influence (I)
radnja	plot, storyline, action	utjecati, utječem [B,C]	to influence (I)

GRAMATIKA

1. [B,C] Označite gramatičke oblike u svakoj strofi pjesme, upotrebljavajući sljedeće znakove:
   (G) glagoli; (I) imenice; (Z) zamjenice [svih vrsta]; (P) pridjevi; (PD) prilozi; (PG) prijedlozi;
   (V) veznici.

   [S] Означите граматичке облике у свакој строфи песме, употребљавајући следеће знакове:
   (Г) глаголи; (И) именице; (З) заменице [свих врста]; (П) придеви; (ПД) прилози; (ПГ) предлози;
   (В) везници.

2. [B,C] Zaokružite subjekt svake rečenice ili fraze (ima ih dvanaest).
   [S] Заокружите субјекат сваке реченице или фразе (има их дванаест).

3. [B,C] Koja od ove tri pjesme ima najviše strofa i najviše stihova? Koja ih ima najmanje?
   [S] Која од ове три песме има највише строфа и највише стихова? Која их има најмање?

PITANJA

1. [B,C] Gdje je smještena radnja ove pjesme?
   [S] Где је смештена радња ове песме?

2. [B] Budući da pjesma opisuje veče, šta saznajemo iz samog naslova o tome kako to doba dana utiče na atmosferu koju dočarava pjesma?
   [C] Budući da pjesma opisuje večer, što saznajemo iz samoga naslova o tome kako to doba dana utječe na atmosferu koju dočarava pjesma?
   [S] Будући да песма описује вече, шта сазнајемо из самог наслова о томе како то доба дана утиче на атмосферу коју дочарава песма?

3. [B] Šta znamo o ljudima u pjesmi?
   [C] Što znamo o ljudima u pjesmi?
   [S] Шта знамо о људима у песми?

4. [B,C] Koje godine se rodio Aleksa Šantić, a koje godine je umro?
   [S] Које године се родио Алекса Шантић, а које године је умро?

5. [B] Postavite svoja sopstvena dva pitanja o pjesmi.
   [C] Postavite svoja vlastita dva pitanja o pjesmi.
   [S] Поставите своја сопствена два питања о песми.

Islands off the Dalmatian coast

The above three poems were chosen both for the grammatical challenges they pose to students, and to provide examples of verse from three of the cultural traditions of Bosnia. But a shared theme of the Šimić and Šantić poems also raises an interesting issue. In the years following World War I, many artists and writers felt there should be separation between the powers of church and state in the newly formed country of Yugoslavia. Both Šimić and Šantić were followers of the anticlericalist movement, which espoused spirituality over organized religion. Spirituality and the nature of God are frequent themes in Šimić's brief opus. In his poem, Aleksa Šantić also articulates a strong commitment to social issues. He wrote both romantic and patriotic poetry in addition to the poem quoted here, which describes life in impoverished island communities off the Dalmatian coast, and which was dedicated to Dalmatian poet Ivo Ćipiko.

℘A4

RJEČNIK [J] REČNIK [E]

brojan, brojna	numerous	posmrtan, posmrtna	posthumous
gornji	above, upper	postojanje	existence
Jugoslavija	Yugoslavia	preobraženje	transfiguration, transformation
koristiti	to use (I)	stvoriti, stvorim	to create (P)
nastanak, nastanka	origin, emergence	tama	darkness
nestanak, nestanka	disappearance	tekst	text
objaviti, objavim	to publish (P)	u gostima	visiting, being a guest
objavljivati, objavljujem	to publish (I)	za razliku od	unlike
period	period, time	zbirka	collection

NASTANAK I NESTANAK

Ova tri pjesnika su iz Bosne i Hercegovine. Ferida Duraković je iz Sarajeva, a druga dvojica su iz Hercegovine: Aleksa Šantić je iz Mostara, a A. B. Šimić je iz malog mjesta blizu Mostara koje se zove Drinovci. Pjesma Feride Duraković je objavljena u knjizi *Srce tame,* koja se pojavila 1998. u Sarajevu. Šimićevu pjesmu je posmrtno objavio njegov brat Stanislav budući da je Šimić umro vrlo mlad. Za vrijeme svog života je objavio svega jednu zbirku pjesama, *Preobraženja.* Za razliku od Šimića, Šantić je dugo živio i objavio brojne pjesme, pripovijetke i dramske tekstove, a Duraković pjesme još uvijek objavljuje. Sve troje piše za vrijeme postojanja Jugoslavije: Šantić i Šimić na samom nastanku, a Duraković u nestanku.

☞ **Prevedite** gornji tekst na engleski.

Radimlje near Stolac: a well-known *stećak*, surrounded by several others

Throughout the countryside of Bosnia and Herzegovina are scattered tombstones with striking images chiseled upon them. The word referring to such a stone is *stećak* (plural *stȩćci*). For many years it was thought that these stones were created by followers of the medieval Bosnian Church (or of one of its presumed offshoots, the Bogomil movement), and the stones had been associated with the general idea of heresy that had surrounded both these ill-understood organizations. In recent years, the *stećak* has come to be seen as part of a much more broadly based tradition, embracing Bosnians of all faiths from medieval times onward, who have consequently come to interpret them as part of their shared cultural heritage on all levels. In 1878, when the Austro-Hungarian Empire took over the administration of Bosnia and Herzegovina, it sought to promote a post-Ottoman, pan-Bosnian identity, and the *stećak* was one of the symbols used to establish this identity. The Bosnian poet Mak Dizdar, who is seen by many Bosnians as their national voice, bases much of his poetic opus on the *stećak* inscriptions.
For more on Dizdar and other literary figures connected with Bosnia, consult the "additional reading" lists at   http://www.bcsgrammarandtextbook.org/

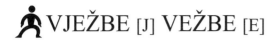 VJEŽBE [J] VEŽBE [E]

B1

[B,C] **Podijelite** ove tri pjesme među studentima, i neka svaki student nauči jednu od njih napamet.

[S] **Podelite** ove tri pesme među studentima, i neka svaki student nauči jednu od njih napamet.

B2

[B,C] **Prepričajte** vježbe 5A1, 5A2, 5A3, 6A1, 6A2, 6A3, 6A4 u parovima.

[S] **Препричајте** вежбе 5A1, 5A2, 5A3, 6A1, 6A2, 6A3, 6A4 у паровима.

B3

[B,C] **Vježbajte** u parovima. Stvorite jednu rečenicu od svake dvije, koristeći se veznikom *koji*.

[S] **Vežbajte** u parovima. Stvorite jednu rečenicu od svake dve, koristeći se veznikom *koji*.

1. [B] To je učiteljica moje kćerke. Vidio sam je juče u školi.

   [C] To je učiteljica moje kćeri. Vidio sam je jučer u školi.

   [S] То је учитељица моје ћерке. Видео сам је јуче у школи.

2. [B] Da li je to tvoj daidža? Jesi li kod njega sedmicu dana bila u gostima?

   [C] Je li to tvoj ujak? Jesi li kod njega tjedan dana bila u gostima?

   [S] Да ли је то твој ујак? Да ли си код њега недељу дана била у гостима?

3. [B,C] Vidim rijeku pred sobom. Idem prema rijeci.

   [S] Видим реку пред собом. Идем према реци.

4. [B] Taj čovjek je iz Chicaga. On je dobar prijatelj mog komšije.

   [C] Taj čovjek je iz Chicaga. On je dobar prijatelj mojeg susjeda.

   [S] Тај човек је из Чикага. Он је добар друг мог комшије.

5. [B] Zàlupila je vràtima làžljiva ljepòtica. Làžljiva ljepòtica je nèstala u històriju.

    [C] Zàlupila je vràtima làžljiva ljepòtica. Làžljiva ljepòtica je nèstala u povijȇst.

    [S] За̀лупила је вра̀тима ла̏жљива лепо̀тица. Ла̏жљива лепо̀тица је нѐстала у и̏сто̏рију.

6. [B,C] Na̋rodi su u nebo vjerovali. Na̋rodima je òvaj svijȇt bio kratko bòravište.

    [S] На̋роди су у небо веровали. На̋родима је о̀ва̑ј све̑т био кратко бо̀равиште.

7. [B,C] Žìvòtinje i biljke òstajahu na zèmlji zàuvijek. Žìvòtinje i biljke naša su rodbina.

    [S] Живо̀тиње и би̏љке о̀стаја̄ху на зѐмљи за̀уве̄к. Живо̀тиње и би̏љке наша су родбина.

8. [B,C] Ubogi pȗk moli s uzdàhom dugȇ túgē. Ubogom pȗku san sve bližē stižē.

    [S] Убоги пȗк моли с уздàхом дугȇ ту̀гȇ. Убого̄м пȗку сан све ближȇ стижȇ.

✍ DOMAĆA ZADAĆA [B,C] DOMAĆI ZADATAK [S]

C1

RJEČNIK [J] REČNIK [E]

aorist	aorist [*verb tense*]	prošlo vrijeme	past tense
bezdan, bezdna	abyss	pust, pusta	barren
božji	divine	sadašnje vreme	present tense
duh	spirit	sadašnje vrijeme	present tense
imperfekt	imperfect [*verb tense*]	Stari zavet	Old Testament
nazvati, nazovem	to call (P)	Stari zavjet	Old Testament
negacija	negation	Sveto pismo	Holy Scripture
obličje	shape	svetlost, svetlosti (f)	light
primer	example	svjetlost, svjetlosti (f)	light
primjer	example	videlo	heavenly body
prošlo vreme	past tense	vidjelo	heavenly body

Prevedite svaku prvu rečenicu na engleski, a ostale rečenice na B, C, ili S.

1. a. [B,S] Petoro ljudi je išlo na košarkašku utakmicu.
   [C] Petero ljudi je išlo na košarkašku utakmicu.
   b. The two children returned to their home.
   c. The five of them* sang a song together.
       [*a group of young men and women]

2. a. Samo su se pozdravili s nama reda radi.
   b. She wrote him a letter for the sake of love.
   c. Please, don't do that for my sake!

3. a. Očekujući težak ispit, učili su i dan i noć.
   b. Having bought flowers, she went to a bar and drank a glass of water.
   c. Having returned the books, they wrote their report.

4. a. Sedmorica su radila zajedno godinama.
   b. The two (men) were happy.
   c. We watched *The Dirty Dozen* yesterday.

5. a. [B,C] Ljudi su obaviješteni na vrijeme.
       [S] Ljudi su obavešteni na vreme.
   b. The dinner was eaten, the water was drunk.
   c. All in all, it was concluded that the event was very successful.

6. a. Čitalo se u novinama da je situacija sada znatno bolja.
   b. It was expected that they would arrive at midnight.
   c. It seemed that the rain would never stop.

7. a. [B,C] Rekli su da će snijeg i kiša padati cijeli dan.
       [S] Rekli su da će sneg i kiša padati ceo dan.
   b. We said that they liked roses more than tulips.
   c. He said that she contacted us over the internet.

8. a. [B] Može li bȉlo ko pȉsati pjesme?
   [C] Može li bȉlo tko pȉsati pjesme?
   [S] Da li može bȉlo ko da pȋše pesme?
   b. They will go anywhere and do anything.
   c. He did not want to talk to anyone.

C2

1. U počȅtku stvorȋ Bog nebo i zemlju. 2. A zȅmlja bješe bez oblȉčja i pȕsta, a bješe tȁma nad bezdanom: i duh bõžji dizȁše se nad vodȍm. 3. I reče Bog: neka budȅ svjetlȍst. I bȉ svjetlȍst. 4. I vidjȅ Bog svjetlȍst da je dobra; i rastavȋ Bog svjetlȍst od tȁme; 5. I svjetlȍst nazvȁ Bog dȁn, a tȁmu nazvȁ nȍć. I bȉ večȅ i bȉ jutro, dȁn prvȋ.

✍ Označite svaki glagol u gȍrnjem tekstu sa 'A' za aorist, ili 'I' za imperfekt.

Below: The first page of the *Svȅto pȋsmo*, *Stari zȁvjet*, translated by Đuro Daničić. Vienna, 1909.

PRVA KNJIGA MOJSIJEVA

KOJA SE ZOVE POSTANJE.

GLAVA 1.

U početku stvori Bog nebo i zemlju. 2. A zemlja bješe bez obličja i pusta, i bješe tama nad bezdanom: i duh Božji dizaše se nad vodom.

3. I reče Bog: neka bude svjetlost. I bi svjetlost.

4. I vidje Bog svjetlost da je dobra; i rastavi Bog svjetlost od tame;

5. I svjetlost nazva Bog dan, a tamu nazva noć. I bi veče i bi jutro, dan prvi.

6. Po tom reče Bog: neka bude svod posred vode, da rastavlja vodu od vode.

7. I stvori Bog svod, i rastavi vodu pod svodom od vode nad svodom; i bi tako.

8. A svod nazva Bog nebo. I bi veče i bi jutro, dan drugi.

9. Po tom reče Bog: neka se sabere voda što je pod nebom na jedno mjesto, i neka se pokaže suho. I bi tako.

10. I suho nazva Bog zemlja, a zborišta vodena nazva mora; i vidje Bog da je dobro.

11. Opet reče Bog: neka pusti zemlja iz sebe travu, bilje, što nosi sjeme, i drvo rodno, koje radja rod po svojim vrstama, u kojem će biti sjeme njegovo na zemlji. I bi tako.

12. I pusti zemlja iz sebe travu, bilje, što nosi sjeme po svojim vrstama, i drvo, koje radja rod, u kojem je sjeme njegovo po njegovijem vrstama. I vidje Bog da je dobro.

13. I bi veče i bi jutro, dan treći.

14. Po tom reče Bog: neka budu vidjela na svodu nebeskom, da dijele dan i noć, da budu znaci vremenima i danima i godinama;

15. I neka svijetle na svodu nebeskom, da obasjavaju zemlju. I bi tako.

16. I stvori Bog dva vidjela velika: vidjelo veće da upravlja danom, i vidjelo manje da upravlja noću, i zvijezde.

17. I postavi ih Bog na svodu nebeskom da obasjavaju zemlju,

18. I da upravljaju danom i noću, i da dijele svjetlost od tame. I vidje Bog da je dobro.

19. I bi veče i bi jutro, dan četvrti.

20. Po tom reče Bog: neka vrve po vodi žive duše, i ptice neka lete iznad zemlje pod svod nebeski.

21. I stvori Bog kitove velike i sve žive duše što se miču, što provrvješe po vodi po vrstama svojim, i sve ptice krilate po vrstama njihovijem. I vidje Bog da je dobro;

22. I blagoslovi ih Bog govoreći: radjajte se i množite se, i napunite vodu po morima, i ptice neka se množe na zemlji.

23. I bi veče i bi jutro, dan peti.

24. Po tom reče Bog: neka zemlja pusti iz sebe duše žive po vrstama njihovijem, stoku i sitne životinje i zvijeri zemaljske po vrstama njihovijem. I bi tako.

25. I stvori Bog zvijeri zemaljske po vrstama njihovijem, i stoku po vrstama njezinijem, i sve sitne životinje na zemlji po vrstama njihovijem. I vidje Bog da je dobro.

26. Po tom reče Bog: da načinimo čovjeka po svojemu obličju, kao što smo mi, koji će biti gospodar od riba morskih i od ptica nebeskih i od stoke i od cijele zemlje i od svijeh životinja što se miču po zemlji.

27. I stvori Bog čovjeka po obličju svojemu, po obličju Božijemu stvori ga; muško i žensko stvori ih.

C3

Odgòvorite na pòstavljena pìtanja.

Prìmer [E] **prìmjer** [J] **pìtanja:**

    Kolìko vas je na čàsu bòsanskog?   [vas = stùdenata]
    Kolìko vas je na sàtu hr̀vatskoga?   [vas= stùdenata]
    Kolìko vas je na čàsu srpskòg?   [vas = stùdenata]

Prìmer [E] **prìmjer** [J] **òdgovora:**   Ìma nas petero.

1. [B,C] Kolìko nas je na svìjetu?   [nas = ljùdi]
   [S] Kolìko nas je na svètu?   [nas = ljùdi]

2. Kolìko ih je u sòbi?   [ih = stòlica]

3. [B] Kolìko vas je na cijèlom univerzitètu?   [vas = slàvista]
   [C] Kolìko vas je na cijèlom sveučìlištu?   [vas = slàvista]
   [S] Kolìko vas je na cèlom univerzitètu?   [vas = slàvista]

4. Kolìko ih je u pr̀vom ràzredu òsnovne škòle?   [ih = đàka]

5. Kolìko ih je u Amèrici?   [ih = ljùdi]

6. Kolìko ih je u òvoj lèkciji?   [ih = pèsama; pjèsama]

7. [B,C] Kolìko ih je u svìm òvim pjesmama?   [ih = stìhova]
   [S] Kolìko ih je u svìm òvim pesmama?   [ih = stìhova]

C4

[B,C] **Prerádite** òve rečènice tàko da budu a) u prošlòm vrèmenu, i b) i u prošlòm vrèmenu
       i u negàciji.
[S] **Прерáдите** òве речèнице тàко да буду а) у прошлòм времену, и б) и у прошлòм времену
       и у негàцији.

1. [B] Trèba òdmah ìći u tr̀govinu kòja je do mòje zgràde.
   [C] Trèba òdmah ìći u dùćan kòji je do mòje zgràde.
   [S] Трèба òдмах да се ѝде у рàдњу кòја је до мòје зграде.

2. [B,C] Kàko se pìše vàše ìme?
   [S] Кàко се пѝше ваше име?

3. [B] Baš nam se jèdu òni kolàči kòji su jùče pèčeni.
   [C] Baš nam se jèdu òni kolàči kòji su jùčer pèčeni.
   [S] Баш нам се јèду òни колàчи кòји су јùче пèчени.

4. [B] Mòže se òtvoreno govòriti o tòme šta se dògađa u nàšem drùštvu.
   [C] Mòže se òtvoreno govòriti o tòme što se dògađa u nàšem drùštvu.
   [S] Мòже òтворено да се говòри о тòме шта се дòгађа у нàшем друштву.

5. [B] Budući da smo svi ovdje prijatelji, osjećam se kao da sam kod kuće.
   [C] Budući da smo svi ovdje prijatelji, osjećam se kao da sam doma.
   [S] Будући да смо сви овде пријатељи, осећам се као да сам код куће.

C5

[B,C] **Napišite** tekst (oko 200 riječi) o filmu koji vam se nije sviđao. Prvo treba prepričati o čemu se radilo u filmu, a tek onda treba objasniti zašto vam se nije sviđao.

[S] **Napišite** tekst (oko 200 reči) o filmu koji vam se nije sviđao. Prvo treba da se prepriča o čemu se radilo u filmu, a tek onda treba da se objasni zašto vam se nije sviđao.

The Bosnian state of today covers roughly the same area as the medieval kingdom of Bosnia, which was founded around 1180 and fell to the Turks in 1463. Shortly before this, *Herceg* ("Duke") Stjepan had established his dukedom as an independent unit; this entity came to be known as Herzegovina. Although Bosnia was transformed into a province within the Ottoman Turkish empire, it retained both its borders and its name relatively unchanged, and functioned for the Ottomans as the center of "Turkey in Europe." Both the current name (Bosnia and Herzegovina) and the current borders were assigned in 1878 by the Congress of Berlin. Despite the transition from an Ottoman province to a protectorate administered by Austro-Hungary, Bosnia and Herzegovina continued to be a clearly defined place with a composite name and a composite identity, both of which it has retained throughout the 20th century and into the 21st.

📖 Priča: Bazdulj

Pročitati šesti deo iz priče "Ljubav na španjolski način" Muharema Bazdulja (str. 353).
Pročitati šesti dio iz priče "Ljubav na španjolski način" Muharema Bazdulja (str. 353).

Osamnaesta lekcija • Lesson Eighteen

☉19

RJEČNIK [J] REČNIK [E]

bivati, bivam	to be (I)	olovan, olovna	leaden
crneti se, crnim se	to be black, to look black (I)	osamnaesti	eighteenth
crnjeti se, crnim se	to be black, to look black (I)	plivati	to swim (I)
gluh [B,C]	deaf	rana	wound
gluv [B,S]	deaf	samac, samca	loner
gluhijem (archaic)	= gluhim	sena	shadow
go, gola [B,S]	bare, naked	sjena	shadow
gol [C]	bare, naked	skrivati, skrivam	to conceal (I)
gord	proud	slep	blind
gorski	hilly, mountainous	slijep	blind
grana	branch	slutiti, slutim	to sense dimly (I)
jablan	poplar	snivati, snivam	to dream (I)
kućica	little house	strana	slope, side
lisje	leaves (i.e. lišće)	suh [B,C]	dry
ljudski	human	suv [B,S]	dry
mokar, mokra	wet	suhijem (archaic)	= suhim
monoton	monotonous	suton	dusk
motriti	to gaze (I)	šaptati, šapćem	to whisper (I)
mračan, mračna	dark, gloomy	taman, tamna	dark
mreti, mrem	to die (i.e. umreti)	toranj, tornja	tower
mrijeti, mrem	to die (i.e. umrijeti)	utonuti, utonem	to sink (P)
mrk	gloomy	vrana	crow
nemir	restlessness	vrba	willow
njiva	plowed field		

JESENJE VEČE

Antun Gustav Matoš

Olovne i teške snove snivaju
Oblaci nad tamnim gorskim stranama;
Monotone sjene rijekom plivaju,
Žutom rijekom među golim granama.

Iza mokrih njiva magle skrivaju
Kućice i toranj; sunce u ranama
Mre i motri kako mrke bivaju
Vrbe, crneći se crnim vranama.

Sve je mračno, hladno; u prvom sutonu
Tek se slute ceste, dok ne utonu
U daljine slijepe ljudskih nemira.

Samo gordi jablan lisjem suhijem
Šapće o životu mrakom gluhijem,
Kao da je samac usred svemira.

RJEČNIK [J] REČNIK [E]

nacrtati	to draw (P)	prizor	scene
odrediti, odredim	to determine (P)	stalo [mu je] do +Gen	it matters to [him]
podcrtati [C]	to underline (P)	umirati	to be dying (I)
podvući, podvučem [B,S]	to underline (P)	zamisliti, zamislim	to imagine (P)
pojava	appearance		

GRAMATIKA

1. [B,C] Zaokružite sve glagole u pjesmi.
   [S] Zaokružite sve glagole u pesmi.

2. [B,S] Odredite šta je subjekat svake rečenice ili fraze.
   [C] Odredite što je subjekt svake rečenice ili fraze.

3. [B,S] Podvucite svaku pojavu instrumentala.
   [C] Podcrtajte svaku pojavu instrumentala.

4. Koja rečenica počinje s frazom u akuzativu?

PITANJA

1. [B,C] Nad čim se nalaze oblaci?
   [S] Над чим се налазе облаци?

2. [B,C] Odakle su monotone sjene koje rijekom plivaju, odnosno od čega su sjene?
   [S] Одакле су монотоне сене које реком пливају, односно од чега су сене?

3. [B] Šta skrivaju magle koje su iza mokrih njiva?
   [C] Što skrivaju magle koje su iza mokrih njiva?
   [S] Шта скривају магле које су иза мокрих њива?

4. [B,C] Možete li zaključiti zašto Matoš ovdje upotrebljava riječ "rana"? Da biste zamislili prizor koji dočarava pjesma, treba se sjetiti sunca koje još nije sasvim zašlo iza oblaka,
   [S] Да ли можете да закључите зашто Матош овде употребљава реч "рана"? Да бисте замислили призор који дочарава песма, треба да се сетите сунца које још није сасвим зашло иза облака.

5. [B,C] Čime se crne vrbe pored kojih teče rijeka?
   [S] Чиме се црне врбе поред којих тече река?

6. [B,C] Gdje se nalaze ljudi u prve dvije strofe?
   [S] Где се налазе људи у прве две строфе?

7. [B] Gdje idu ceste koje se tek slute?
   [C] Kamo idu ceste koje se tek slute?
   [S] Где иду путеви који се тек слуте?

8. [B,C] Kakav je Matošev jablan?
   [S] Какав је Матошев јаблан?

Poplar

9. [B,C] Zašto je g̲ordi̲ jabl̲a̲n stao šaptati gl̲u̲h̲i̲m mr̲a̲kom?
   [S] Зашто је г̲о̲р̲д̲и̲ јабл̲а̲н стао да шапће глу̲вим мр̲а̲ком?

10. [B] Do čèga je Matošu stalo u òv̲o̲j pjesmi? Drug̲i̲m riječima, šta mu je najvàžnije̲?
    [C] Do čèga je Matošu stalo u òv̲o̲j pjesmi? Drug̲i̲m riječima, što mu je najvàžnije̲?
    [S] До чèга је Матошу стало у ов̲о̲ј песми? Друг̲и̲м рèчима, шта му је највàжније̲?

Nàcrtajte obl̲ake, g̲orske̲ stràne, ž̲ùt̲u rijèku, gol̲e gràne koj̲e̲ se crn̲e̲ vranama, mokr̲e̲ njive, kućice, t̲oranj, màglu, ceste, i jabl̲a̲n.

A sculpture by the artist Ivan Kožarić of A. G. Matoš on a park bench.
The sculpture is located in Zagreb's Gornj̲i̲ gr̲a̲d (Upper Town).

RJEČNIK [J] REČNIK [E]

čelo	brow; forehead	strastan, strasna	passionate
misao, misli *(f)*	thought	veđa	eyelid
ozariti, ȍzarīm	to illuminate, to glow (P)	vjeđa	eyelid
plakati, plačēm	to cry (I)	zublja	torch
potiti	to perspire (I)	žariti, žarīm	to burn (I)
samoća	solitude		

NOTTURNO
Tin Ujević

Noćas se moje čelo žari,
noćas se moje vjeđe pote;
i moje misli san ozari,
umrijet ću noćas od ljepote.

Duša je strasna u dubini,
ona je zublja u dnu noći;
plačimo, plačimo u tišini,
umrimo, umrimo u samoći.

St. Jacob's Cathedral in Šibenik. Both the building and the wreath of portrait
on it are the work of Juraj Dalmatinac (15th c.)

Dubrovnik

RJEČNIK [J] REČNIK [E]

kriv	wrong	protagonist [B,C]	protagonist
ljubavni	love (*adj.*)	protagonista [B,S]	protagonist
ponašati se, ponašam se	to behave (I)	razlikovati, razlikujem	to distinguish (I)
priroda	nature		

PITANJA

1. [B] Kako se osjeća protagonista ove pjesme?
   [C] Kako se osjeća protagonist ove pjesme?
   [S] Kako se oseća protagonista ove pesme?

2. [B,C] Zašto mu je stalo čelo žariti baš noćas?
   [S] Zašto mu je stalo čelo da žari baš noćas?

3. [B,C] Je li mu drago ili krivo što se tako osjeća?
   [S] Da li mu je drago ili krivo što se tako oseća?

4. [B,C] Kome on zapravo pjeva ovu pjesmu?
   [S] Kome on zapravo peva ovu pesmu?

5. [B,C] Do čega je pjesniku najviše stalo?
   [S] Do čega je pesniku najviše stalo?

6. [B,C] Je li ovo ljubavna pjesma?
   [S] Da li je ovo ljubavna pesma?

7. [B,C] Kako se razlikuju duša u ovoj pjesmi i narod u Šimićevoj pjesmi?
   [S] Kako se razlikuju duša u ovoj pesmi i narod u Šimićevoj pesmi?

8. Kako Ujević piše o smrti a, za razliku od njega, kako o smrti pišu Šimić i Duraković?

9. Kako Ujević piše o životu a, za razliku od njega, kako o životu pišu Duraković, Šimić i Šantić?

10. [B,C] Usporedite doba dana u Matoševoj, Ujevićevoj i Šantićevoj pjesmama.
    [S] Uporedite doba dana u Matoševoj, Ujevićevoj i Šantićevoj pesmama.

RJEČNIK [J] REČNIK [E]

Austro-Ugarska	Austria-Hungary	poći za rukom + *Dat*	to be able to do
bespoštedan, bespoštedna	unrelenting	podučavati, podučavam	to tutor (I)
begunac, begunca	fugitive	postati, postanem	to become (P)
bjegunac, bjegunca	fugitive	posvetiti se, posvetim se	to dedicate oneself (P)
blizak, bliska	close, intimate	poznat	known, famous
boemski	bohemian	prerasti, prerastem	to outgrow (P)
članak, članka	article (news)	preseliti se, preselim se	to move (P)
dan danas	(to) this very day	prevoditi, prevodim	to translate (I)
esej, eseja	essay	prevođenje	translation [activity]
fašistički	fascist	prevod	translation [text]
gde god	wherever	prijevod	translation [text]
gdje god	wherever	primati, primam	to receive (I)
grlo	throat	progoniti, progonim	to persecute (P)
isprva	at first	proslaviti	to celebrate (P)
izbivanje	time spent away	rak	cancer
kako... tako	both... and	rodom	by birth
kazniti	to punish (P)	samrt *(f)*	deathbed
komunist [C]	communist	seliti se, selim se	to move (I)
komunista [B,S]	communist	shodno tome	therefore
kritika	criticism	sonet, soneta	sonnet
kultura	culture	spajati, spajam	to connect (I)
ličnost, ličnosti *(f)*	personality	sukobiti se	to clash (P)
moderan, moderna	modern	suparnik	rival
monarhija	monarchy	suparništvo	rivalry
nadimak, nadimka	nickname	saradnja [B,S]	cooperation
nadživeti, nadživim	to outlive (P)	suradnja [C]	cooperation
nadživjeti, nadživim	to outlive (P)	svirati, sviram	to play
napuštati, napuštam	to abandon (I)		[an instrument] (I)
nedostajati,	to be missed by (I/P)	ubrzo	soon thereafter
nedostajem + *Dat* *		uoči + *Gen*	on the eve of
Nezavisna Država	Independent State	uspevati, uspevam	to succeed (I)
Hrvatska [*abbr.* NDH]	of Croatia	uspijevati, uspijevam	to succeed (I)
novinski	news-related	violončelo	cello
objavljivanje	publication [activity]	vlada	government
oboleti, obolim	to fall ill (P)	vlast *(f)*	power
oboljeti, obolim	to fall ill (P)	vodeći	leading
odseliti se, odselim se	to move away (P)	voditi, vodim	to register (I)
okupator, okupatora	occupying forces	vojni	military *(adj.)*
okupiti se	to gather around (P)	vojska	army
plaća [B,C]	salary	zabrana	ban
plata [B,S]	salary	zameriti se	to offend (P)
pobeći, pobegnem	to flee (P)	zamjeriti se	to offend (P)
pobjeći, pobjegnem	to flee (P)		

* Tricky translation: The verb *nedostajati* takes a dative logical subject. In other words, what English speakers would interpret as the object of "to miss" is the BCS subject, while the person who misses something (the subject in English) appears in the dative case. Thus the sentence *nedostajao mu je Zagreb* means "he missed Zagreb."

MATOŠ I UJEVIĆ

Antun Gustav Matoš se rodio 1873. u Tovarniku, malom mjestu blizu Šida u Srijemu. S 19 godina pobjegao je u Srbiju da ne bi služio u vojsci Austro-Ugarske. Proveo je sljedeće tri godine u Beogradu, svirajući violončelo, podučavajući đake i studente i radeći kao novinar i pisac. Međutim, kako se svojim bespoštednim kritikama zamjerio drugim piscima, napušta Beograd i seli u Pariz 1899. u kojem živi punih pet godina. Gdje god da je boravio, pisao je eseje, pjesme i pripovijetke i objavljivao ih u raznim časopisima, kako u Hrvatskoj, tako i u Bosni. Nedostajao mu je Zagreb ali budući da ga je austrougarska vojna vlast još uvijek vodila kao bjegunca, nije mu odmah pošlo za rukom da se vrati, pa je nakon Pariza proveo još četiri godine u Beogradu. Vraća se napokon u Zagreb 1908. i tamo živi sve do svoje smrti, 1914. A. G. Matoš se proslavio svojim esejima i pjesmama, a naročito svojim sonetima. U Zagrebu je ubrzo nakon povratka postao vodeća ličnost kulture. Smatra se prvim modernim hrvatskim pjesnikom. U godinama prije njegove smrti okupili su se oko njega zagrebački pjesnici i pisci, među kojima je bio i Tin Ujević.

Augustin Ujević (1891-1955), poznat pod nadimkom Tin, rodom je iz Dalmatinske Zagore. Matoša je upoznao u Zagrebu, dok je bio student. Isprva su bili bliski prijatelji, ali su se oštro sukobili i razišli kao suparnici. Ujević nije nikada sasvim prerastao svoje suparništvo s Matošem makar ga je nadživio za više od četrdeset godina. I Ujević je čuven po tome što se često selio. Otišao je u Pariz 1913. i tamo je ostao do kraja Prvog svjetskog rata, radeći i kao prevoditelj i kao pisac. Živeći boemskim životom jedva je uspijevao spajati kraj s krajem, pa se 1919. vratio u Zagreb. Zatim se odselio u Beograd gdje je s kraćim izbivanjima boravio do 1930. kada se preselio u Sarajevo. Vratio se u Zagreb tek uoči Drugoga svjetskog rata. U vrijeme NDH stao je raditi kao prevoditelj novinskih članaka i shodno tome primao plaću od fašističke vlade, pa su ga poslije rata zbog suradnje s okupatorom komunisti kaznili s petogodišnjom zabranom objavljivanja vlastitih pjesama i tekstova. Za to vrijeme se, dakle, posvetio književnu prevođenju, najviše s francuskoga i engleskoga. I dan danas ljudi čitaju njegove prijevode Whitmana, Poea, Conrada, Prousta i Sartrea. Oboljevši od raka grla, i dalje je prevodio Prousta čak i dok je ležao u bolnici na samrti. Za života objavio je pet zbirki pjesama, a učenici i studenti u Hrvatskoj još uvijek uče njegove stihove napamet.

🖎 **Prevedite** gornji tekst na engleski.

> **Grammar note.** The particle *god*, added to a question word, means roughly the same as English "-ever." Thus *kad god* "whenever," *gde god* [E] *gdje god* [J] "wherever," *koliko god* "however much," and so on. **[134a, 143k]** The word *bilo* can be added before any of these words in much the same meaning, thus *bilo šta* [B,S] *bilo što* [C] "whatever" *bilo koga pitaš* "whomever you ask," and the like. **[143k]**

🏃 VJEŽBE [B,C] VEŽBE [S]

B1

[B,C] **Naučite** ove dvije pjesme napamet.
[S] **Naučite** ove dve pesme napamet.

B2

[B,C] **Prepričajte** vježbe 7A1, 7A2, 7A3, 7A4, 8A3, 8A4 u parovima.
[S] **Препричајте** вежбе 7A1, 7A2, 7A3, 7A4, 8A3, 8A4 у паровима.

B3

[B,C] **Prevedite,** koristeći se veznikom *koji*. Gdje god ima dvije rečenice (br. 6-10), prvo
prevedite te dvije rečenice, pa onda napravite od njih jednu rečenicu koristeći se veznikom *koji*.
[S] **Prevedite,** koristeći se veznikom *koji*. Gde god ima dve rečenice (br. 6-10), prvo prevedite te
dve rečenice, pa onda napravite od njih jednu rečenicu koristeći se veznikom *koji*.

1. Is that the woman to whom you spoke yesterday?
2. The possibilities were explained to artists, to whom nothing is difficult.
3. They answered one another in letters which were longer and longer.
4. She left the room in which she was standing.
5. The husband saw his wife whom he loved.
6. Baltazar is a professor. He invented a 'leti-kapa.'
7. The man had a dog. The dog he had was smart.
8. Ujević is a poet. He is the poet we are reading.
9. They are my friends. Yesterday I helped my friends.
10. Baltazar-grad is a city. In that city every question is resolved.
    (make two versions of this sentence, one with a passive participle, and the other with a *se*-verb)

B4

Odgovorite na ova pitanja koristeći se veznikom *da bi*.

1. [B] Šta treba Pingvinu Charlieu da bi letio?
   [C] Što treba Pingvinu Charlieu da bi letio?
   [S] Šta treba Pingvinu Čarliju da bi leteo?

2. [B] Šta treba lažljivoj ljepotici da bi nestala u historiju?
   [C] Što treba lažljivoj ljepotici da bi nestala u povijest?
   [S] Šta treba lažljivoj lepotici da bi nestala u istoriju?

3. [B,S] Šta treba narodima da bi otišli u nebo?
   [C] Što treba narodima da bi otišli u nebo?

4. [B,S] Šta treba gordom jablanu da bi šaptao o životu?
   [C] Što treba gordom jablanu da bi šaptao o životu?

5. [B] Šta treba pjesniku da bi umirao u noći?
   [C] Što treba pjesniku da bi umirao u noći?
   [S] Šta treba pesniku da bi umirao u noći?

6. [B] Šta morate naučiti da biste bili spremni za ispit krajem semestra?
   [C] Što morate naučiti da biste bili spremni za ispit krajem semestra?
   [S] Šta morate da naučite da biste bili spremni za ispit krajem semestra?

7. [B] Šta morate raditi preko ljeta da ne biste zaboravili bosanski?
   [C] Što morate raditi preko ljeta da ne biste zaboravili hrvatski?
   [S] Šta morate da radite preko leta da ne biste zaboravili srpski?

Dubrovnik city walls

The verse epic *Judita,* published in 1501 by the Split poet Marko Marulić, was the first work of literature to
appear in print in Croatian. For the next century and a half, there was a great amount of literary activity in
Croatian along the Adriatic coast and on the islands. Although much of language of this Renaissance poetry
is viewed today as somewhat archaic, that of the comedies by Marin Držić, written in the 1550s, is suffi-
ciently close to today's Croatian that the plays are still read and performed. The coastal area was important
culturally until the early 19th century, when it passed from Venetian to Austro-Hungarian control after the
Napoleonic conquest. By 1830, the focus of cultural life in the Croatian lands had shifted to Zagreb.
For more information about on Croatian culture and Croatian literature in English, consult the "additional
reading" lists at   http://www.bcsgrammarandtextbook.org/

✍ DOMAĆA ZADAĆA [B,C] DOMAĆI ZADATAK [S]

C1

[B,C] **Napišite** tekst (oko 200 riječi) o jelu koje ne volite. Objasnite zašto ga ne volite.

[S] **Napišite** tekst (oko 200 reči) o jelu koje ne volite. Objasnite zašto ga ne volite.

C2

Prevedite svaku prvu rečenicu na engleski, a ostale rečenice na B, C, ili S.

1. a. Trči kao da letiš!
   b. They should study as if this is the exam of their life.
   c. "Live as if you will die tomorrow but learn as if you will live forever."
      -- Mahatma Gandhi [B,C] Gandi [S]

2. a. Njih dvojica su godinama bili suparnici.
   b. The three of them* are excellent poets.   (* group containing both men and women)
   c. The ten of them** were friends.

      (**write three different translations: i) "them" = a group of men,
      ii) "them" = a group of women, iii) "them" = a group of both men and women)

3. a. [B,C] Prije nego što su se vratili u Zagreb, i Matoš i Ujević su živjeli u nekoliko gradova.
      [S] Pre nego što su se vratili u Zagreb, i Matoš i Ujević su živeli u nekoliko gradova.
   b. After she slammed the door, the lying beauty vanished into history.
   c. Before the chilly darkness fell, a bell sobbed.

4. a. [B,C] Budući da su magle skrivale kućice i toranj, cesta se nije mogla jasno vidjeti.
      [S] Budući da su magle skrivale kućice i toranj, put se nije mogao jasno videti.
   b. Since she was from a small place, she didn't like living in a big city.
   c. The poet's brow is burning, since he will die of beauty tonight.

5. a. [B] Kad god putujemo vozom, uvijek čitamo novine.
      [C] Kad god putujemo vlakom, uvijek čitamo novine.
      [S] Kad god putujemo vozom, uvek čitamo novine.
   b. Wherever you live, you are with us.
   c. Whomever you write to, send my regards.

6. a. Nije mu stalo ni do čega.
   b. She cared for him.
   c. We cared for them.

7. a. [B,C] Koliko god je učio, nije nikada uspio naučiti francuski.
      [S] Koliko god je učio, nije nikada uspeo da nauči francuski.
   b. Whatever you want, you can have.
   c. Call me whenever you need me.

📖 Priča: Bazdulj

[B,C] **Pročitati** sedmi deo iz priče "Ljubav na španjolski način" Muharema Bazdulja (str. 354).

[S] **Pročitati** sedmi dio iz priče "Ljubav na španjolski način" Muharema Bazdulja (str. 354).

Devetnaesta lekcija • Lesson Nineteen

RJEČNIK [J] REČNIK [E]

devètnaestī	nineteenth	prijèći, prijéđem	to go across (P)
nèstajati, nèstajēm	to disappear (I)	prenòćiti, prènoćīm	to spend the night (P)
nèžan, nèžna	tender	slàvūj, slavúja	nightingale
njèžan, njèžna	tender	smȇh, smȇha	lfraughter
prag	threshold	smijȇh, smijȇha	laughter
prèći, prèđem	to go across (P)		

OČIJU TVOJIH DA NIJE
Vasko Popa

Òčijū tvòjīh da nìje
Nè bi bȉlo neba
U slepȏm našem stȁnu

Smȇha tvòga da nȇmā
Zidovi nè bi nikad
Iz òčijū nèstajali

Slavùjā tvòjīh da nìje
Vrbe nè bi nikad
Nèžnē preko praga prèšle

Rùku tvòjīh da nìje
Sȕnce nè bi nikad
U snu našem prenòćilo.

RJEČNIK [J] REČNIK [E]

àpstraktan, àpstraktna	abstract (*adj.*)	određen	certain, definite
celìna	whole	pesnički	poetic
cjelìna	whole	pjesnički	poetic
celòvit	complete	"nepočin-polje"	"unrest-field"
cjelòvit	complete	počinuti, počinem	to rest (P)
cìklus	cycle	poetski	poetic
dlan	palm of hand	polje	field
figùra	figure	poput + *Gen*	similar to
funkcionìrati, funkcionìram [B,C]	to function (I)	postojeći	existing
funkcionìsati, funkcionìšem [B,S]	to function (I)	prvobitan, prvobìtna	initial
ìskaz	statement	razina [C]	level
izràziti, ìzrazim	to express (P)	sadržati, sadržim	to contain (P)
karàkter	character	složen	complex
kora	bark	stilski	stylistic
koren	root	šator	tent
korijen	root	upečatljiv	striking
nazìvati, nàzivam	to call (I)	zamisao, zamisli (*f*)	concept
nìvo, nivòa [B,C,S]	level		

ВАСКО ПОПА

Васко Попа је један од најоригиналнијих и најпознатијих српских песника. Све песме Васка Попе су кратки, целовити песнички искази, али истовремено свака његова песма је и део веће песничке целине коју сам песник назива циклус. На апстрактнијем нивоу, и сам циклус функционише као дужа, сложена песма. Песма *Очију твојих да није* је део циклуса *Далеко у нама*, који је првобитно објављен у књизи *Кора* (1953). Све песме у овом циклусу су љубавног карактера. Једна од најпознатијих песама у овом циклусу садржи стих: *Да ли ћу моћи / на овом непочин-пољу / Да ти подигнем шатор од својих дланова*. Попут многих својих упечатљивих стилских фигура, Попа је сам створио израз *непочин-поље* од постојећих словенских корена да би изразио одређену поетску замисао. Исти израз се потом јавља као наслов Попине следеће збирке песама (1956). Касније његове књиге, објављене између 1968. и 1982., биле су занимљиве не само за њихове упечатљиве слике, већ и за сложене односе између песама у циклусу и циклуса у књизи.

Belgrade apartment buildings at night in the snow

Belgrade: St. Mark's Church

RJEČNIK [J] REČNIK [E]

izgovoriti, izgovorim	to pronounce (P)	poniziti, ponizim	to humiliate (P)
izricati, izričem	to pronounce, to declare (I)	presuda	verdict, sentence
lagati, lažem	to tell a lie (I)	radije	more readily
lažan, lažna	false	slabost, slabosti (f)	weakness
milosrdan, milosrdna	merciful	unesrećiti	to make unhappy (P)
milosrđe	mercy	uvrediti, uvredim	to insult (P)
nazreti, nazrem	to catch sight of (P)	uvrijediti, uvrijedim	to insult (P)
obrazina	mask	zderati, zderem	to tear off (P)
pomilovanje	clemency, pardon		

ZA LAŽI IZGOVORENE IZ MILOSRĐA
Desanka Maksimović

Tražim pomilovanje
za one koji nemaju snage
zlome kazati da je zao
niti rđavome da je rđav,
za onoga kome je žao
čoveka istinom unesrećiti,
za ljude koji lažu iz milosrđa.
Za čoveka koji će ponižen biti
radije nego koga da ponizi,
za onoga koji i kad nazre
obrazinu kome na licu
nema srca da je zdere,
za ljude koji ne mogu da uvrede
ni čoveka druge misli i vere,
za one koji nikad ne bi mogli
drugome presude da izriču,
kojima se sve sudije čine stroge,
za svaku milosrdnu lažnu priču
i slične njima slabosti mnoge.

RJEČNIK [J] REČNIK [E]

autorica [B,C]	[female] author	nekolicina	a few
autorka [S]	[female] author	podnaslov	subheading
car	emperor	pojedinac, pojedinca	individual
diskusija	discussion	posedovati, posedujem	to possess (I)
društven	social	posjedovati, posjedujem	to possess (I)
glas	voice	potraga	search
grupirati, grupiram [B,C]	to group (I/P)	potreba	need
grupisati, grupišem [B,S]	to group (I/P)	pravda	justice
identificirati [C]	to identify (I/P)	predstavljati	to represent (I)
identifikovati,	to identify (I/P)	ravnoteža	balance
identifikujem [B,S]		remek-delo	masterpiece
inače	otherwise	remek-djelo	masterpiece
izreći, izreknem	to articulate (P)	sloboda	freedom
kršiti, kršim	to violate [law or rule] (I)	tumač, tumača	interpreter
lirski	lyrical	zakon	law
moćan, moćna	powerful	zakonik	code of laws
neimenovan	unnamed	zakonodavac, zakonodavca	lawmaker

ДЕСАНКА МАКСИМОВИЋ

Књига песама *Тражим помиловање* (1964) сматра се ремек-делом српске песникиње Десанке Максимовић. Састоји се од 59 песама које су груписане око теме изречене у поднаслову књиге *Лирске дискусије са Душановим Закоником*. У песмама налазе се два поетска гласа: један је глас Цара Душана, најмоћније личности српске историје, који је познат између осталог и по томе што је објавио законик 1349. године. Као законодавац, глас Цара Душана представља државу и потребу за друштвеним редом у људском животу. Други је глас неименованог песника који тражи милосрђе од Цара за оне који су кршили (или би могли да крше) закон. Глас представља појединца и потребу за личном слободом у људском животу. Многим тумачима се чини да је Душанов глас мушки, а да песник поседује женски глас, јер се зна да је ауторка жена. У само неколицини песама, међутим, песников глас јасно може да се идентификује као женски. Књига је иначе о потрази за равнотежом између државе и појединца, између правде и милосрђа.

Emperor Dušan   The Code of Laws
of Emperor Dušan

The medieval Serbian state, under the rule of the Nemanja dynasty, reached its peak with the reign of Stefan Dušan the Mighty (1331-1355), who was crowned "Emperor of the Serbs and Greeks" in 1346. At its height, Dušan's empire stretched from the Sava and the Danube in the north to the Gulf of Corinth in the south. Serbia under the Nemanja dynasty is known for its achievements in literature, architecture and painting. Perhaps its most notable achievement, however, is the Law Code *(zakonik)* established by Dušan in 1349 and 1354. After Dušan's sudden death in 1355 the empire gradually disintegrated, and the growing might of the Ottoman Turks led to their eventual conquest of Serbia. The memory of the medieval state and its achievements kept Serbian identity alive through the long centuries of Ottoman rule.

For more about Serbian history, culture, and Serbian literature in English translation, consult the "additional reading" lists at   http://www.bcsgrammarandtextbook.org/

A3

RJEČNIK [J] REČNIK [E]

bedem	rampart	nevolja	trouble
besediti *(archaic)*	to talk (I)	obigrati	to ride around, to fly around (P)
besjediti *(archaic)*	to talk (I)	ostareo, ostarela	elderly
beli dan	broad daylight	ostario, ostarjela	elderly
bijeli dan	broad daylight	postelja	bed
dohvatiti	to grab hold of (P)	povrnuti, povrnem	to return (P)
dozivati, dozivam	to call out to (I)	putalj *(archaic)*	steed
glas	word, news	skočiti, skočim	to jump (P)
golem	enormous	strela	arrow
hajduk, hajduka	brigand	strijela	arrow
izneti, iznesem	to carry out (P)	svičice *(archaic)*	undergarment
iznijeti, iznesem	to carry out (P)	tamnica	dungeon
izvideti, izvidim	to scout (P)	ubiti, ubijem	to kill (P)
izvidjeti, izvidim	to scout (P)	učiniti, učinim	to make, to do (P)
izvijati, izvijam	to soar (I)	upaziti	to notice (P)
knjiga	epistle, letter	uraniti	to get up early (P)
kukati	to moan, to keen	vakat, vakta	age, time
kukavica	cuckoo	vilen	wild, fiery
kula	tower	začuti se, začujem se	to suddenly be heard (P)
lagan	light	zakukati	to burst into wails; to coo like a cuckoo bird (P)
lastavica	swallow		
mek	soft	zeman, zemana *(archaic)*	time
nakititi	to decorate (P)	zlato	gold

SIBINJANIN JANKO U TAMNICU U TATARINU GRADU
Stanko Pižurica

[...]
Zakukala kukavica crna
U Sibinju gradu bijelome   **Sibinj**: a Croatian town in Slavonia near the
A na kulu Banović Sekule   border with Bosnia
Kad joj vakta ni zemana nema   **Sekul Banović**: the protagonist
O Mitrovu jesenjemu danu.   **Mitrov dan**: St. Dimitrius Day, November 8th
Pređe zore i bijela dana   **pređe** [= pred]

Nà to čuo Banović Sekule

Đe spàvaše u postelju meku   **đe** [= gdje]

pa kad čuo kukavicu crnu

Skoči Sekul nà noge lagane

Samo gòlo u gòlu košulju

E na njemu bijele svičice

Pa dò'vati od zlata strijèlu   **dò'vati** [= dòhvati]

Iznese je pred bijelu kùlu

Òbigraje prèbijelu kùlu   **òbigraje** [= òbigra]

A gledaše na bèdemu kùli

Đe će crnu viđet' kukavicu.   **viđet'** [= vidjeti]

Kad pògleda na pròzor od kùle

E ùgleda òstarilu màjku   **òstarila** [=òstarjela]

E đe kuka, ka' i kukavica   **ka'** [= kao]

A ìzvija ka' i lastavica.

A kad viđe Banović Sekule   **viđe** [= vidje]

Strijèlu je zlatnu òstavijo   **òstavijo** [= òstavio]

Pa dòziva òstarjelu màjku

Stàra màjko da te Bog ùbije

Što si jutros ùranila màjko

Na bijelu od kamena kùlu

O jèsenju Mitrovome dànu   **o** + *Loc*: on, at

Kàka ti je gòlema nèvolja   **kàka** [= kàkva]

Ko je tebe žàlos' učìnijo   **žàlos'** [= žàlost]   **učìnijo:** [= učìnio]

Za žìvòta Banović Sekule

Kad to zàču òstarila Jànja

Stàra Jànja Sekulina màjka

Ta ovàko sinu bèsidila   **bèsidila** [= bèsjedila]

No moj sine Banović Sekule

Ako kukam i nèvolja mi je

Moj Sekule moj jèdini sine

Ti nijèsi sine ùpazijo –   **nijèsi** [= nìsi]

Ìmala sam brata jèdinoga   **ùpazijo** [=ùpazio]

Brata mòga od Sibìnja Jànka

Evo ìma dvànaes' gòdina   **dvànaes'** [= dvànaest]

Kad je Janko pòš'o u 'ajdùke.   **pòš'o** [= pòšao]   **'ajdùk** [= hàjduk]

Na njègova vilena putàlja

Nema Janka ni od Janka glàsa.

Pa moj sine Banović Sekule

Čètrdes' sam nàkitila knjiga   **čètrdes'** [čètrdeset]

Na čètrdes' bijelìjeh gràda   **bijelìjeh** [bijelìh]

Tr<u>a</u>̀žila sam po knjigama J<u>a</u>nka
Svak<u>a</u> mi se natr<u>a</u>g pȍv<u>r</u>n<u>u</u>la
E, k<u>a</u>̀žuj<u>u</u> n<u>e</u>m<u>a</u> tamo J<u>a</u>nka.   **k<u>a</u>̀žuj<u>u</u>** [k<u>a</u>̀zuj<u>u</u>]

[...]

A page from the transcription of the epic poem sung by Stanko Pižurica

Šćepan Prkaćin singing epic verse and
accompanying himself on the gusle.

RJEČNIK [J] REČNIK [E]

aluminijski	aluminum	otvarati, otvaram	to open (I)
blago	treasure	pevač, pevača	singer
digitalni	digital	pevati	to compose verse (I)
disk	disk	pjevač, pjevača	singer
epski	epic *(adj.)*	pjevati	to compose verse (I)
forma	form	podstaći, podstaknem	to encourage (P)
glazbalo [C]	musical instrument	posledica	consequence
gusle *(pl. form)*	gusle (one-stringed instrument)	posljedica	consequence
		postepen	gradual
hrišćanski [B,S]	Christian *(adj.)*	predstaviti	to present (P)
instrument [B,C,S]	musical instrument	prenositi, prenosim	to transmit (I)
interesovanje [B,S]	interest	presudan, presudna	decisive, fateful
izučavati, izučavam	to make a study of (I)	prikupiti	to bring together (P)
jedinstven	unique	sakupljati, sakupljam [B,S]	to collect, to amass (I)
jednožičan, jednožična	one-stringed	sastaviti	to assemble (P)
junački	heroic	saznavati, saznajem	to learn, to glean (I)
južnoslavenski [C]	South Slavic *(adj.)*	skupljati, skupljam [B,C]	to collect, to amass (I)
južnoslovenski [B,S]	South Slavic *(adj.)*	Slaven, Slavena [B,C]	Slav
koleno	generation	Sloven, Slovena [B,S]	Slav
koljeno	generation	snimiti, snimim	to record (P)
kršćanski [C]	Christian *(adj.)*	spevati	to compose verse (P)
kulturan, kulturna	cultural	spjevati	to compose verse (P)
metrički	metrical	tradicionalan, tradicionalna	traditional
muslimanski	Muslim *(adj.)*	ukoliko	inasmuch as
narodni	of the people, national	umetnički	artistic
očuvati, očuvam	to preserve (P)	umjetnički	artistic
osećaj	feeling	unutra	inside
osjećaj	feeling	vladavina	rule
osmanski	Ottoman	značaj	significance

EPSKA POEZIJA

Junačka epska poezija je važan dio južnoslovenske kulturne baštine. U toku dugog perioda osmanske vladavine, južni Sloveni su koristili epsku poeziju da bi očuvali svoju istoriju i osjećaj za sopstvenu kulturu. Epske pesme, koje su spjevane u posebnoj metričkoj formi korišćenoj samo za epsku poeziju i pjevane uz "gusle," tradicionalni jednožični instrument, prenesene su sa koljena na koljeno. 1814. godine Vuk Stefanović Karadžić je učinio nešto od presudnog značaja kada je počeo sakupljati i objavljivati srpske narodne pjesme. Predstavivši ovaj tradicionalni umjetnički oblik svjetskoj javnosti, Vuk je i podstakao interesovanje za prikupljanje kulturnog "blaga" i to interesovanje traje do dana današnjeg. Najveću i najjedinstveniju zbirku epskih pjesama, međutim, sastavila su dva američka naučnika, Milman Peri* i Albert Lord, snimivši pjesme kako od hrišćanskih tako i od muslimanskih pjevača u Crnoj Gori, Srbiji i Bosni na aluminijske diskove tridesetih godina dvadesetog vijeka. Ova zbirka se čuva na Univerzitetu Harvard i postepeno se objavljuje u digitalnom obliku preko interneta.

Ukoliko neko želi više da sazna o radu Perija i Lorda, i o epskoj tradiciji koju su izučavali, taj može da pogleda knjigu *The Singer of Tales*, Harvard University Press, May, 2000.

*The English spelling is Milman Parry. The website of the archive which bears his name (the Milman Parry Collection of Oral Literature) is: http://chs119.harvard.edu/mpc/

Photographs of Montenegro

Note about the language of Montenegro: The most characteristic mark of Montenegrin is its systematically ijekavian character, which includes not only ijekavian forms but also negated forms of *biti* (*nijesam*, *nijesi*, etc.) and certain adjectival endings such as *starijem* (instead of *starim*), which are considered archaic elsewhere in BCS but are the norm in Montenegrin. The sound sequences pronounced elsewhere in ijekavian regions as *tj* and *dj* are pronounced by Montenegrins as *ć* and *đ*, for instance *ćerati*, *đevojka*, *đe* (instead of *tjerati*, *djevojka*, [g]dje). There are also a number of words (and pronunciations) that are felt to be characteristically Montenegrin, such as *sjutra* "tomorrow" and *zboriti* "speak." In overall terms, Montenegrin vocabulary has much more in common with Serbian than with Bosnian or Croatian. Students wishing to focus on Montenegrin should learn forms marked [J] and [S] in this book and consult http://www.bcsgrammarandtextbook.org/ for more information.

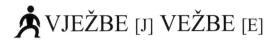 VJEŽBE [J] VEŽBE [E]

B1

[B,C] **Podijelite** ove tri pjesme među studentima, i neka svaki student nauči jednu od njih napamet. Treba svega 20-ak stihova naučiti od pjesme Stanka Pižurice.

[S] **Поделите** ове три песме међу студентима, и нека сваки студент научи једну од њих напамет. Треба свега 20-ак стихова да се научи од песме Станка Пижурице.

B2

[B,C] **Prepričajte** vježbe 9A1, 9A2, 9A3, 9A4, 10A1, 10A2, 10A3 u parovima.

[S] **Prepričajte** vežbe 9A1, 9A2, 9A3, 9A4, 10A1, 10A2, 10A3 u parovima.

B3

PITANJA

1. OČIJU TVOJIH DA NIJE

a. [B,C] Pjesma se otvara s riječima *Očiju tvojih da nije / Ne bi bilo neba.* Iz ovih riječi saznajemo, dakle, da neba ima u stanu kao posljedica toga što postoje oči jedne osobe. Čega, osim očiju i neba, još ima u ovoj pjesmi?

   [S] Песма се отвара са речима *Очију твојих да није / Не би било неба.* Из ових речи сазнајемо, дакле, да неба има у стану као последица тога што постоје очи једне особе. Чега, осим очију и неба, још има у овој песми?

b. [B] Šta nam pjesma govori o stanu?
   [C] Što nam pjesma govori o stanu?
   [S] Шта нам песма говори о стану?

c. [B,C] Kakav je odnos u pjesmi između svijeta vani i života unutra?
   [S] Какав је однос у песми између света напољу и живота унутра?

2. ZA LAŽI IZGOVORENE IZ MILOSRĐA:

a. [B,C] Koliko ima vrsti ljudi u pjesmi za koje pjesnik traži milosrđe?
   [S] Koliko ima vrsti ljudi u pesmi za koje pesnik traži milosrđe?

b. [B,C] Biste li vi imali snage zlome reći da je zao? Jeste li ikada to i učinili?
   [S] Da li biste vi imali snage zlome kazati da je zao? Da li ste to ikada i ucinili?

c. [B] Biste li radije bili poniženi nego da nekog ponizite?
   [C] Biste li radije bili poniženi nego nekog poniziti?
   [S] Da li biste radije bili poniženi nego da nekog ponizite?

d. [B] Biste li vi mogli da budete sudija i da izričete presude?
   [C] Biste li vi mogli biti sudac i izricati presude?
   [S] Da li biste vi mogli da budete sudija i da izričete presude?

e. [B] Ko vam je bliži po prirodi, car Dušan sa svojim zakonikom, ili pjesnik sa svojom potrebom
    za milosrđem?
   [C] Tko vam je bliži po prirodi, car Dušan sa svojim zakonikom, ili pjesnik sa svojom potrebom
    za milosrđem?
   [S] Ko vam je bliži po prirodi, car Dušan sa svojim zakonikom, ili pesnik sa svojom potrebom
    za milosrđem?

3. SIBINJANIN JANKO U TAMNICU U TATARINU GRADU

a. [B,C] Kako se zove mjesto gdje živi Sekul Banović?
   [S] Како се зове место где живи Секул Бановић?

b. [B] Šta je probudilo Sekula Banovića? Šta je mislio da čuje, a šta je stvarno čuo?
   [C] Što je probudilo Sekula Banovića? Što je mislio da čuje, a što je stvarno čuo?
   [S] Шта је пробудило Секула Бановића? Шта је мислио да чује, а шта је стварно чуо?

c. [B,C] Kako njemu majka objašnjava zbog čega je zakukala na bijeloj kuli?
   [S] Како њему мајка објашњава због чега је закукала на белој кули?

d. [B] Šta se dogodilo majčinom bratu Janku?
   [C] Što se dogodilo majčinom bratu Janku?
   [S] Шта се догодило мајчином брату Јанку?

e. [B] Šta je majka učinila da bi Janka pronašla?
   [C] Što je majka učinila da bi Janka pronašla?
   [S] Шта је мајка учинила да би Јанка пронашла?

Murat Zunić (singer from the Bihać region) performing an epic poem

✍ DOMAĆA ZADAĆA [B,C] DOMAĆI ZADATAK [S]

C1

Prevèdite na B, C, ili S:

1. In order to study BCS, you must do your homework every day.

2. She is the woman I saw at the store.

3. In order to go to Croatia, Serbia, or Bosnia and Herzegovina you should travel by plane.

4. Think as if you were ten years younger!

5. Anyone would have written the homework better than we did.

6. Wherever you go, be happy!

7. The hand you are writing with is your stronger hand.

8. In order to be able to read Serbian Cyrillic easily, you must practice frequently.

9. Whenever I think of you, I say your name.

10. They are going to see a movie in which everybody is sad in the end.

11. With whom are you traveling this summer? With the sister who arrived here from Zagreb, or with the brother whose house you are living in?

12. What kind of milk do you drink your coffee with?

13. Whenever he danced, he delighted the viewers.

14. Please use your own furniture, and I will use mine.

C2

Prevèdite na B, C, or S:

Vasko Popa was born in 1922 in a small Serbian village near the Serbian-Romanian border. In 1940 he moved to Belgrade to study Romance languages and literatures. Then World War II began. Because of the war he studied in Bucharest and Vienna. He returned to the University of Belgrade after the war, and graduated in 1949 in French studies. His first book, *Kora,* in which the poem *Òčiju tvòjih da nìje* appeared, was published in 1953. He spent years working on each of his eight collections of poetry. All of his books have been beautifully translated into English.

Desanka Maksimović was born in 1898 in central Serbia in the village of Brankovina, where she lived as a child, the eldest of eight. In 1918, at the end of World War I, when she was twenty, her family moved to Belgrade, the city in which she lived until the end of her life. She studied comparative literature at Belgrade University and started writing poetry while she was a student.

Her first book of verse was published in Belgrade in 1924. After that, she was an active poet for more than seventy years. Her book *Tražim pomilovanje* was her most popular. She published her last collection of poetry (its title is *Pamtiću sve*) in 1988 when she was ninety years old, and died five years later, in 1993.

Stanko Pižurica. It is known that Stanko Pižurica was from the village of Rovca near Ivangrad in Montenegro, and that he was 65 years old when his singing was recorded by Milman Parry in the town of Kolašin on June 25, 1935. Therefore one concludes that he was born in 1870. It is known that he was not able to read or write.

C3

[B] **Napišite** kratak tekst (200 riječi) o tome gdje biste putovali po Bosni i Hercegovini, Hrvatskoj i / ili Srbiji, i što biste radili dok ste tamo. Ako nećete moći putovati po tim krajevima u bližoj budućnosti, pišite o tome šta biste radili da možete.

[C] **Napišite** kratak tekst (200 riječi) o tome gdje biste putovali po Bosni i Hercegovini, Hrvatskoj i / ili Srbiji, i što biste radili dok ste tamo. Ako ne ćete moći putovati po tim krajevima u bližoj budućnosti, pišite o tome što biste radili da možete.

[S] **Napišite** kratak tekst (200 reči) o tome gde biste putovali po Bosni i Hercegovini, Hrvatskoj i / ili Srbiji, i šta biste radili dok ste tamo. Ako nećete moći da putujete po tim krajevima u bližoj budućnosti, pišite o tome šta biste radili da možete.

📖 Priča: Bazdulj

[B,C] **Pročitajte** osmi dio iz priče "Ljubav na španjolski način" Muharema Bazdulja (str. 356).
[S] **Pročitajte** osmi deo iz priče "Ljubav na španjolski način" Muharema Bazdulja (str. 356).

Dvadeseta lekcija • Lesson Twenty

U zagrljaju rijeke

Miro Gavran

 |

⊙39

RJEČNIK [J] REČNIK [E]

buka	noise	poslepodne, poslepodneva	afternoon
dopirati, dopirem	to reach, to get through to (I)	poslijepodne, poslijepodneva	afternoon
		pretraga [B,C]	medical test
dostojanstvo	dignity	prevaliti, prevalim	to cover, to pass (P)
dvadeseti	twentieth	prodreti, prodrem	to penetrate (P)
ispitivanje [B,S]	medical test	prodrijeti, prodrem	to penetrate (P)
kućna nega	home care	proziran, prozirna	transparent
kućna njega	home care	svojevrstan, svojevrsna	of a kind
nejestiv	inedible	trosed	three-seat sofa
neuverljiv	unconvincing	trosjed	three-seat sofa
neuvjerljiv	unconvincing	umirivati, umirujem	to soothe, to calm (I)
odavati, odajem	to betray (I)	vreva	bustle
oporavak, oporavka	convalescence	zavesa	curtain
otpustiti, otpustim	to release (P)	zavjesa	curtain
pacijent	[hospital] patient	zagrljaj	embrace

Danas su u našu sobu smjestili još jednog pacijenta. Zove se Šimun. Čini mi se da je prevalio sedamdesetu godinu. Njegovo lice odaje mir, svojevrsno dostojanstvo. Dugu i bogatu životnu priču.

Premda sam iz liječnikovih riječi zaključio da je ozbiljno bolestan, on kao da se ne boji ničega. Poslat će ga na sve moguće pretrage, i to hitno, još ovo poslijepodne. Žure se, veoma se žure.

Sada nas je u sobi šestoro. Ako bude sreće, za tjedan dana će me otpustiti na kućnu njegu. Liječnik je zadovoljan mojim oporavkom.

Hrana je grozna. Nejestiva. Smeta mi buka koja dopire kroz prozor. Bolnice bi trebali graditi daleko od gradske vreve. Smeta mi sunce koje prodre kroz neuvjerljive prozirne zavjese. Tako bih volio biti doma – u svojoj sobi, na trosjedu. Slušati umirujuću glazbu, čitati novine, igrati se s kćerkom, razgovarati sa suprugom.

RJEČNIK [J] REČNIK [E]

bolesnički	patient-related	optuživati, optužujem	to accuse (I)
čuđenje	surprise	oteti se, otmem se	to escape (P)
dim	smoke	oženiti, oženim	to marry (P)
dodirnuti, dodirnem	to touch (P)	pecanje	fishing
fabrika [B,S]	factory	pravilo	rule
gubitak, gubitka	loss	prekinuti, prekinem	to interrupt (P)
izmenjivatii, izmenjujem	to alternate (I)	priviknuti se, priviknem se	to get used to (P)
izmjenjivati, izmjenjujem	to alternate (I)	prodati	to sell (P)
izvući se, izvučem se	to wiggle out (P)	promeniti, promenim	to change (P)
jednoličan, jednolična	monotonous	promijeniti, promijenim	to change (P)
krivac, krivca	culprit	protekli	last [period of time]
lebdeti, lebdim	to hover (I)	ritam, ritma	rhythm
lebdjeti, lebdim	to hover (I)	slagati, slažem	to arrange (I)
mašinski [B,S]	mechanical	smiraj	tranquility
miris	smell, fragrance	strojarski [C]	mechanical
mozaik	mosaic	škrt	meager
nastaviti	to continue (P)	tvornica [B,C]	factory
nećak	nephew	uz	up, along
nepunih 15 godina	not quite 15	vinograd	vineyard
odživeti, odživim	to live out (P)	vršnjakinja	woman of same age
odživjeti, odživim	to live out (P)	zreo, zrela	mature
opravdati	to justify (P)	životan, životna	vital

Stojimo u dnu bolesničkog hodnika. Šimun i ja. Pušimo, razgovaramo. Dugi dimovi se izmjenjuju s kratkim rečenicama. Od škrtih informacija slažem mozaik njegova života.

Do prije dvadeset godina živio je u Iloku, gradiću na Dunavu. Imao je velik vinograd... Oženio je svoju vršnjakinju – od devetnaeste godine živjeli su mirno i sretno.

Nisu imali djecu – prihvatili su to kao Božju volju, ne tražeći krivca, ne optužujući ni nebo ni sebe.

Svake nedjelje išao je na pecanje, na Dunav, uživajući u trenucima provedenim uz rijeku. Osjećao je da se samo ondje tišina može dodirnuti rukom, a duša naći smiraj nakon napornog radnog tjedna.

Jednoga dana njegov brat i supruga poginuli su u prometnoj nesreći. Iza njih ostala su dva sina – Josip je imao dvanaest godina, a Marko nepunih petnaest.

Nije želio da nećaci nakon gubitka roditelja izgube i grad u kojem su rođeni – prodao je svoju kuću i vinograd i preselio se u Zagreb.

Promijenio je način života. Otvorio je trgovinu i odlučio osigurati svojim nećacima dobar život i najbolje školovanje.

- Divni su to dečki. Sada su već zreli ljudi. Oženjeni, jedan ima sina, drugi kćerku. Upoznat ćete ih, kad mi dođu u posjet.

- Nisu još bili?! – otelo mi se pitanje i čuđenje što ga u ova tri dana nisu posjetili nećaci.

-Vjerojatno imaju mnogo obaveza. Josip predaje na Strojarskom fakultetu, a Marko je ravnatelj tvornice – pokušao ih je Šimun opravdati.

Potom je nastavio sa svojom životnom pričom. U proteklih dvadeset godina pokušavao se priviknuti na ritam velikog grada – nedostajao mu je njegov vinograd i pecanje na Dunavu.

Prošle jeseni umrla mu je supruga. Nakon toga više se ničemu nije znao radovati. Osjećao se da je odživio život do kraja.

Uspjelo mu je i jednom i drugom nećaku kupiti udobne stanove, pomoći im da se dobro pripreme za život koji je bio pred njima.

Medicinska sestra je prekinula naš razgovor:

- Gospodo pušači, još samo vas dvojicu čekamo. Vrijeme je za večeru.

Zar baš moramo večerati – pokušao sam se izvući, jer je jednoličan miris hrane lebdio hodnikom.

- Morate. Pravila su pravila.

 III

RJEČNIK [J] REČNIK [E]

blizina	nearness	po cimetu	of cinammon
cimet	cinnamon	poljubac, poljupca	kiss
dosegnuti, dosegnem	to reach (P)	posetiteljica	female visitor
dovesti, dovedem	to bring (P)	posjetiteljica	female visitor
goditi	to please (I)	prepoznavati, prepoznajem	to recognize (I)
izlazak, izlaska	exit	raspitivati se, raspitujem se	to inquire (I)
nadvladati, nadvladam	to overcome (P)	skorašnji	forthcoming
nalaz	finding, report	smejati se, smejem se [S]	to laugh (I)
napraviti	to make (P)	smijati se, smijem se [B,C]	to laugh (I)
naprotiv	on the contrary	spoznati	to realize (P)
nasloniti	to lean, to rest (P)	svakidašnjica	everyday life
nužan, nužna	necessary	štrudla	strudel
očaj	despair	veoma	very
operacija	operation	veseliti se	to be glad (I)
osmeh	smile	zahvaliti se, zahvalim se	to thank (P)
osmijeh	smile	zamirisati, zamiriše	to start smelling (P)
osmogodišnji	eight-year	zavist (f)	envy
pažnja	attention		

Nedugo iza doručka došla mi je u posjet supruga. Dovela je i našu kćerku. Obradovao sam se njihovoj blizini, njihovim glasovima i osmijesima. Tek u bolnici spoznao sam koliko njih dvije znače, koliko ih volim.

Supruga mi je donijela štrudlu od jabuka, koju je jutros za mene napravila. Cijela soba je zamirisala po cimetu. Godila mi je njezina pažnja. Zahvalio sam joj se dugim nježnim poljupcem.

Moja osmogodišnja kćerka popela se na moj krevet i naslonila glavu na jastuk, kao da smo doma.

Razgovaramo, smijemo se. Vesele se što za pet dana izlazim iz bolnice. Prenose mi pozdrave prijatelja koji su se proteklih dana raspitivali o mome zdravlju.

Odjednom mi je postalo neugodno što sa ženom pričam o izlasku iz bolnice, o povratku u svakidašnjicu, dok na susjednom krevetu leži Šimun za čije današnje nalaze liječnici su rekli da su veoma loši i da je nužna hitna operacija.

- Šimune, da vas upoznam. Ovo je moja supruga, a ovo je naša kćerka.

Šimun im uz osmijeh pruži ruku. Na licu mu ne prepoznajem zavist zbog mog skorašnjeg izlaska iz bolnice, niti zbog mojih posjetiteljica. Naprotiv, kao da je sretan zbog moje sreće.

Hoću li ja dosegnuti takav mir kad budem u njegovim godinama? Hoću li ja imati snage nadvladati strah i očaj kad se jednog dana primakne moj kraj?

RJEČNIK [J] REČNIK [E]

bol	pain (f)	predložiti, predložim	to propose (P)
drzak, drska	rude, insolent	pregled	medical examination
gotovo	almost	prekosutra	day after tomorrow
istinski	truly	prepisati, prepišem	to sign over (P)
izgledi	prospects	prići, priđem	to come over to (P)
iznenaditi, iznenadim	to surprise (P)	predlog	proposal
ležaj	bed	prijedlog	proposal
nagovarati, nagovaram	to urge (I)	priličan, prilična	considerable
naslednik	heir	progovoriti, progovorim	to speak out (P)
nasljednik	heir	razotkriti se, razotkrijem se	to disclose oneself (P)
netaktičan, netaktična	tactless	riskantan, riskantna	risky
obići, obiđem	to circumvent; to visit (P)	rub	edge
oporuka	will	susresti, susretnem	to meet (P)
othraniti, othranim	to rear, to nurture (P)	svedok, svedoka	witness
pomirljiv	conciliatory	svjedok, svjedoka	witness
pošten	honest, honorable	zainteresiranost, -osti [B,C]	interest, concern (f)
poćutati, poćutam [B,S]	to fall silent briefly (P)	zainteresovanost, -osti [B,S]	interest, concern (f)
		zakonski	legal
pošutjeti, pošutim [C]	to fall silent briefly (P)	zapanjiti, zapanjim	to astonish (P)
potrošiti, potrošim	to spend, to waste (P)	započeti, započnem	to start in (P)

Poslije podne se pojavio Marko.

Brzim korakom prišao je Šimunovu krevetu, pružio mu ruku, sjeo na rub ležaja i započeo razgovor, kao da pred sobom ima poslovnog partnera, a ne strica koji ga je othranio.

Osjećao sam da u njegovim pitanjima o Šimunovu zdravlju nema istinske zainteresiranosti za to kako se osjeća njegov stric.

Držao sam novine pred sobom, ne mogavši ih čitati, jer sam slučajno bio svjedok njihova razgovora.

Marko je na trenutak pošutio, a potom netaktično progovorio:

- Doktor kaže da prekosutra moraš na operaciju.

- Na žalost, moram.

- Kaže da će biti prilično riskantno. Da si zakasnio gotovo dva mjeseca.

- Znam.

- Da si otišao na pregled prije mjesec dana kad se javila prva bol, kad sam te nagovarao na to, sada bi imao bolje izglede.

- Bolje ne misliti o tome što bi bilo da je bilo – pomirljivo odgovori Šimun.

- Vidiš, htio sam ti nešto predložiti.

- Reci.

- Možda bi bilo dobro da prije operacije napišeš oporuku.

- Oporuku?! Zašto? Ako umrem, ti i Josip sve dijelite na dva dijela. Vi ste mi jedini nasljednici. Zakonski je sve jasno.

- Nije te ni obišao. On ima sigurniji posao od moga. Na njega si potrošio više nego na mene. Njemu si platio i postdiplomski studij u inozemstvu. Mislim da bi bilo pošteno da svoj stan prepišeš na mene.

- Misliš da bi to bilo pošteno!? – zapanjeno je ponovio Šimun, iznenađen drskim prijedlogom.

- Da. Ako se odlučiš, sutra ću ti doći u posjet s odvjetnikom. Donijet ćemo prijedlog oporuke. Razmisli do sutra. Ne moraš odmah reći svoje mišljenje.

Moj pogled se susreo sa Šimunovim. Bilo mu je neugodno što se pred mojim očima njegov nećak Marko razotkrio u pravom svjetlu.

 V

⊙43

RJEČNIK [J] REČNIK [E]

celokupan, celokupna	entire	prije negoli	before
cigareta	cigarette	prineti, prinesem	to bring up to (P)
cjelokupan, cjelokupna	entire	prinijeti, prinesem	to bring up to (P)
drven	wooden	prošetati, prošetam	to take a walk (P)
dulje	longer	pušenje	smoking
fotografija	photograph	raniti	to wound (P)
hiniti, hinim [C]	to feign (I)	razočarati se, razočaram se	to be disappointed (P)
izdržati, izdržim	to endure (P)	ribič, ribiča	fisherman
izdanje [B,C,S]	edition	rečni	river (adj.)
izvući, izvučem	to extract (P)	riječni	river (adj.)
kimnuti, kimnem	to nod (P)	sabrati, saberem	to collect (P)
lešinar	vulture	shvaćati	to grasp (I)
lukav	sly	skupiti se	to curl up (P)
malen	small	stil	style
naklada [C]	edition	sapatnik [B,S]	fellow sufferer
nasledstvo	inheritance	supatnik [C]	fellow sufferer
nasljedstvo	inheritance	suptilan, suptilna	subtle
obasjavati, obasjavam	to cast light on (I)	svetiljka	lamp
operirati, operiram [B,C]	to operate (I/P)	svjetiljka	lamp
operisati, operišem [B,S]	to operate (I/P)	štampati [B,S]	to print (I)
označivač, označivača	marker	tiskati [C]	to print (I)
pogledati	to glance at (P)	ugasiti, ugasim	to extinguish (P)
popušiti	to have a smoke (P)	umetnuti, umetnem	to insert, to put into (P)
potpisati, potpišem	to sign (P)	usnuti, usnem	to fall asleep (P)
praviti se [B,C,S]	to feign, to pretend (I)	uzvodno	upstream
premda	although	zaćutati, zaćutam [B,S]	to fall suddenly silent (P)
pribor za pecanje	fishing gear	zašutjeti, zašutim [C]	to fall suddenly silent (P)

Sutradan, nakon doručka, pojavio se Josip. Imao je iste ideje kao i njegov brat. Razlikovali su se samo po stilu.

Josip je bio suptilniji, lukaviji, manje izravan. Mnogo dulje od Marka hinio je zabrinutost za Šimunovo zdravlje, prije negoli je postavio pitanje nasljedstva, prije negoli je predložio da još tog poslijepodneva dovede svoga odvjetnika i da stric potpiše već pripremljenu oporuku.

Bilo mi je tužno gledati Šimunovo razočarano lice. Skupio se na krevetu poput ranjene životinje nad kojom kruže nestrpljivi lešinari.

Nisam više izdržao.

Izišao sam na hodnik prošetati i popušiti cigaretu, premda mi nije bilo ni do šetnje, ni do pušenja.

Noć je.

305
Dvadeseta lekcija   Lesson Twenty

Svi moji supatnici spavaju. Svi osim Šimuna. Samo njegova noćna svjetiljka škrto obasjava knjigu koju drži u ruci.

Primijetio je moj pogled.

- Ako Vam smeta, ugasit ću svjetlo – predložio je.

- Ne, ne. I tako mi se ne spava – odgovorio sam.

Sutra u podne će ga operirati. Noć uoći operacije teško je usnuti. Tako je bilo i prije moje operacije.

- Što čitate?

- Pjesme. *Pjesme o vodi*, tako se zove knjiga. Jedan moj prijatelj, ribič, prije petnaestak godina sabrao je u ovoj knjizi sve pjesme o vodi do kojih je mogao doći. Knjigu je tiskao u svojoj nakladi, u samo stotinjak primjeraka. Nije je prodavao. Cjelokupnu nakladu podijelio je svojim prijateljima. Ne rastajem se od nje već godinama. Trećina pjesama posvećena je Dunavu, mojoj rijeci.

Zašutio je na trenutak.

- Ondje sam bio najsretniji. Živjeti uz rijeku, to je tako posebno. Uz rijeku je sve lakše. Ne znam shvaćate li me?

Kimnuo sam glavom.

Šimun je iz knjige izvukao fotografiju koja je bila umetnuta kao označivač stranica.

- Pogledajte!

Uzeo sam fotografiju i prinio je očima. Na njoj se vidjela malena drvena kuća na riječnoj obali.

- Tu smo se okupljali. Svake nedjelje. U toj kućici smo držali pribor za pecanje. Dva-tri kilometra uzvodno od Iloka.

🙰 VI   ⊙44

RJEČNIK [J] REČNIK [E]

dijeta	diet	onamo	there, in that direction
izlaziti, izlazim	to go out, to leave (I)	oporaviti se	to recover (P)
izuzeti, izuzmem	to exclude (P)	opraštati, opraštam	to bid farewell (I)
kriv	guilty	optimizam, optimizma	optimism
ličiti, ličim (na) [B,S]	to resemble (I)	otkriti, otkrijem	to discover (P)
ma šta [B,S]	no matter what	pokazati, pokažem	to demonstrate (P)
ma što [C]	no matter what	sakriti, sakrijem	to conceal (P)
materijalan, materijalna	material *(adj.)*	sličiti (na) [B,C]	to resemble (I)
mučan, mučna	agonizing	suditi, sudim	to judge (I)
nagao, nagla	sudden	suđen	destined
nagovoriti, nagovorim	to urge (P)	šaptom	in a whisper
nasmejati se, nasmejem se	to laugh a lot (P)	tih	quiet
nasmijati se, nasmijem se	to laugh a lot (P)	valjda	probably
odgojiti, odgojim	to raise (P)	zapitati, zapitam	to inquire (P)
odjeća	clothing	žudnja	longing
odmahnuti, odmahnem	to wave away (P)		

Govorio je tiho, šaptom, da ne probudi ostale. Govorio je kao da se opraštamo, o vremenima prošlim, o godinama u kojima je njegov život bio čvrsto u njegovim rukama.

- Danas sam sretniji od vas.

- Zašto? – zapitao sam.

- Na dijeti sam cijeli dan. Zbog operacije. Nisam morao jesti bolesničku hranu.

Nasmijali smo se obojica.

- Sutra ujutro dolaze moji nećaci, dolaze me posljednji put nagovoriti da potpišem oporuku kojom jedan drugoga žele izuzeti od nasljedstva. To mi je mučnije od same operacije. Čuli ste ih, zar ne?

Kimnuo sam glavom.

- Takva su valjda sad vremena. Ja sam vjerojatno kriv što im je žudnja za materijalnim iznad ljudskog. Nisam ih dobro odgojio.

- Niste vi zato krivi. Neke se stvari događaju, ma što mi činili da se ne dogode. Tako je valjda suđeno.

Bacio je još jedan pogled na fotografiju.

- Ne žalim ni za čim osim za Dunavom. Žao mi je što ga više neću vidjeti, tako mi je žao...

- Ne govorite na taj način. Nakon operacije, kad se oporavite, možemo zajedno otići onamo, na pecanje.

Odmahnuo je rukom.

- Moji nalazi su loši. Čak ni moj liječnik nije pokazao očekivani optimizam. A i sam osjećam da je moja priča završena.

Nisam znao što odgovoriti. U boji njegova glasa nisam mogao otkriti ni strah ni tugu.

Naglo je skrenuo razgovor na mene.

- Imate lijepu obitelj. Kćerka vam više sliči na suprugu.

- To se i meni čini.

- Vidi se da vas istinski vole. A i vi njih.

- Teško bi to bilo sakriti.

- I ne treba. Kad izlazite?

- Trebao bih u srijedu. Ali zamolit ću liječnika da me pusti dan prije. U utorak mi je rođendan.

- Koji?

- Četrdeseti.

 VII   ⊙45

RJEČNIK [J] REČNIK [E]

beg	escape	odjeća	clothing
bijeg	escape	odvratiti, odvratim	to retort (P)
čuvar, čuvara	guard, watchman	optužiti, optužim	to accuse (P)
dežuran, dežurna	on duty	ormarić	small cupboard
galama	ruckus	pratnja	escort
ispitivati, ispitujem	to question (I)	prebacivati, prebacujem	to pass on, to transfer (I)
izvikati se, izvičem se	to yell at length (P)	predstojnik [odela]	head [of a ward]
krivnja	guilt	predstojnik [odjela]	head [of a ward]
mnoštvo	multitude	trag	trace
nasilan, nasilna	violent	uspaničiti se	to panic (P)
obijanje	break-in	vikati, vičem	to shout (I)
odeća	clothing	zatvor	prison

Probudila me galama. Dežurna sestra je bila uspaničena. Liječnik je vikao na nju, a ona je prebacivala krivnju na noćnog čuvara. Došao je i predstojnik odjela. Svi su postavljali mnoštvo pitanja, ne nalazeći odgovor.

Šimun je nestao.

Uzalud su ga tražili po bolnici, po gradu.

Ormarić s njegovom odjećom bio je u hodniku, otvoren i prazan. Nije bilo tragova nasilnog obijanja.

Oko devet sati pojavio se Šimunov nećak Marko u pratnji svoga odvjetnika.

Kad je saznao da mu nema strica, izvikao se na predstojnika odjela. Optužio ga je što bolje ne čuvaju pacijente uoči operacije.

- Zar ne shvaćate da može umrijeti prije nego što mi potpiše oporuku!

- Gospodine, ovo nije zatvor nego bolnica. Uostalom, ne zanima me nikakva oporuka nego moj pacijent – odvratio mu je predstojnik.

Uskoro je došla policija. Ispitivali su nas znamo li kamo je Šimun mogao otići. Zanimalo ih je o čemu je dan uoči bijega pričao s nama.

Ništa im nisam otkrio. Nijednu jedinu rečenicu.

❧ VIII ⊙46

RJEČNIK [J] REČNIK [E]

dah	breath	protrnuti, protrnem	to go numb (P)
darovati, darujem	to give a gift (I)	puštanje	release
datum	date	ribarska kućica	fishermen's hut
delovati, delujem	to act (I)	ribički štap	fishing rod
djelovati, djelujem	to act (I)	sagnuti se, sagnem se	to lean over (P)
iščitati	to read to the end (P)	skroman, skromna	modest, humble
izmisliti	to fabricate (P)	skrovit	secretive, mysterious
jučerašnji	yesterday's *(adj.)*	štap, štapa	rod, staff, cane
mahnuti, mahnem	to wave (P)	šuma	forest
naježiti se, naježim se	to get goose bumps (P)	trošan, trošna	run down, worn
navesti, navedem	to state (P)	ugledati	to catch sight of (P)
nedvosmislen	unambiguous	ukazivati, ukazujem	to point out (I)
neizmjeran, neizmjerna	immeasurable	upisati, upišem	to write in (P)
nizvodno	downstream	uvući, uvučem	to pull in (P)
objašnjenje	explanation	vlažan, vlažna	moist, damp
okrenuti, okrenem	to turn [over] (P)	zabrinuti, zabrinem	to worry (P)
potpis	signature	zaključati	to lock (P)
postaja [C]	station	završetak, završetka	end
posveta	dedication	zbogom	farewell

Deset dana potom, vozeći se autobusom u Slavoniju, čitao sam novine. U Crnoj kronici sam ugledao Šimunovu fotografiju, uz tekst kojim se mole svi koji su ga vidjeli da to prijave najbližoj policijskoj postaji. Ispod toga su naveli izjave njegovih zabrinutih nećaka.

Hodajući uzvodno od Iloka uz Dunav uspjelo mi je pronaći ribarsku kućicu s fotografije. Kućica je bila znatno trošnija nego što je izgledala na fotografiji.

Nisam znao samome sebi objasniti zašto sam sada ovdje. Ali, ta rijeka i taj čovjek uvukli su me u svoju priču, i morao sam doći.

Nisam mogao objasniti svojoj ženi zašto samo tri dana nakon puštanja na kućnu njegu polazim na put, nisam joj mogao reći istinu, jer istina često djeluje tako neuvjerljivo. Zato sam izmislio da polazim na službeni put.

Vrata nisu bila zaključana.

U skromnoj prostoriji bilo je nekoliko ribičkih štapova, stol i tri stolice.

Na stolu je bila knjiga.

Šimunova knjiga.

Okrenuo sam prvu stranicu. Protrnuo sam kad sam pročitao posvetu. Pisalo je:

"Dragi Petre, mladi moj prijatelju, znao sam da ćete me potražiti, i zato Vam darujem knjigu koju sam neizmjerno volio. Umjesto objašnjenja, umjesto moga zbogom, pjesma s 37. stranice reći će Vam sve."

Vaš Šimun

Okrenuo sam 37. stranicu, i u jednom dahu iščitao kratku pjesmu:

U ZAGRLJAJU RIJEKE

Ne tražite me prijatelji,
Na dalekim cestama,
U skrovitim šumama,
U hladnim gradovima.
Ja sam tu – posve blizu.
Uzvodno i nizvodno
Od vašeg srca.
Rijeka koju sam volio,
Sada me grli,
Dok izvor mi se
Ukazuje na ušću.

Naježio sam se od stihova i poruke koja mi je tako nedvosmisleno bila upućena.

Ponovno sam okrenuo stranicu s posvetom. Ispod Šimunova potpisa bio je upisan jučerašnji datum.

Nedaleko od kućice, u vlažnoj zemlji, pronašao sam tragove cipela koji su vodili prema rijeci.

Došao sam do same obale, sagnuo se i dodirnuo prstima hladnu vodu, a potom mahnuo prema ušću ne znajući pozdravljam li ja to Dunav ili Šimuna. Ili oboje.

ZAVRŠETAK

🏃 VJEŽBE [J] VEŽBE [E]

BI

1. [B] Šta se zna o Šimunu a šta o Petru? Zašto su zajedno?
   [C] Što se zna o Šimunu a što o Petru? Zašto su zajedno?
   [S] Шта се зна о Шимуну а шта о Петру? Зашто су заједно?

2. [B] Ko je bolesniji od njih dvojice?
   [C] Tko je bolesniji od njih dvojice?
   [S] Ко је болеснији од њих двојице?

3. [B,C] Kakva je hrana u bolnici?
   [S] Каква је храна у болници?

4. [B] Šta Petru smeta? Zašto? Gdje bi radije bio i šta bi radio da je tamo?
   [C] Što Petru smeta? Zašto? Gdje bi radije bio i što bi radio da je tamo?
   [S] Шта Петру смета? Зашто? Где би радије био и шта би радио да је тамо?

BII

1. O čemu razgovaraju Šimun i Petar?

2. Prepričajte Šimunov život.

3. [B,S] Šta misli Petar o Šimunu?
   [C] Što misli Petar o Šimunu?

BIII

1. [B] Šta se dogodilo kad su došle Petrova supruga i kći? O čemu su razgovarali?
   [C] Što se dogodilo kad su došle Petrova supruga i kći? O čemu su razgovarali?
   [S] Шта се догодило кад су дошле Петрова супруга и кћи? О чему су разговарали?

2. [B,C] Zašto je Petru odjednom neugodno?
   [S] Зашто је Петру одједном неугодно?

3. [B] Sviđa li se Šimunu Petrova porodica?
   [C] Sviđa li se Šimunu Petrova obitelj?
   [S] Да ли се Шимуну свиђа Петрова породица?

BIV

1. [B,C] Kako se ponaša Šimunov nećak Marko kada obilazi Šimuna, i o čemu želi razgovarati? Zašto?
   [S] Kako se ponaša Šimunov nećak Marko kada obilazi Šimuna, i o čemu želi da razgovara? Zašto?

2.   [B] Šta je trebao ranije Šimun učiniti, po Markovom mišljenju?
     [C] Što je trebao ranije Šimun učiniti, po Markovu mišljenju?
     [S] Šta je trebao ranije Šimun da učini, po Markovom mišljenju?

BV

1.   [B,C] Kako se ponaša Šimunov nećak Josip kad posjećuje Šimuna? Kako su Josip i Marko slični, a kako različiti?
     [S] Како се понаша Шимунов нећак Јосип кад посећује Шимуна? Како су Јосип и Марко слични, а како различити?

2.   [B,C] Zašto se kasnije Šimunu ne spava?
     [S] Зашто се касније Шимуну не спава?

3.   [B,C] Čim se Šimun bavi kada mu se ne spava?
     [S] Чим се Шимун бави када му се не спава?

4.   [B,C] Na kojoj rijeci je Šimun volio ići na pecanje s prijateljima? Gdje se nalazi ta rijeka?
     [S] На којој реци је Шимун волео да иде на пецање с пријатељима? Где се налази та река?

BVI

1.   [B,S] Šta misli Šimun o svojim nećacima? Zašto?
     [C] Što misli Šimun o svojim nećacima? Zašto?

2.   [B,C] Zašto se Šimun veseli kad ne može jesti?
     [S] Zašto se Šimun veseli kad ne može da jede?

3.   Za čim Šimun žali?

BVII

1.   Zbog čega je ljekar vikao na dežurnu sestru?
     Zbog čega je liječnik vikao na dežurnu sestru?
     Због чега је лекар викао на дежурну сестру?

2.   Kako su razgovarali predstojnik odjela i Šimunov nećak Marko? Zašto?
     Како су разговарали предстојник одела и Шимунов нећак Марко? Зашто?

BVIII

1.   [B,S] Kuda Petar putuje? Zašto?
     [C] Kamo Petar putuje? Zašto?

2.   [B,C] Koju knjigu pronalazi Petar, i gdje?
     [S] Koju knjigu pronalazi Petar, i gde?

3.   Kako se priča završava?

✍ DOMAĆA ZADAĆA [B,C] DOMAĆI ZADATAK [S]

C1

1. Retell one of the eight segments of the story.

2. Translate one of the segments of the story.

C2

1. Analyze the verbal usage (aspect, tense) in sections III and IV.

2. Find the participles, verbal adverbs and verbal nouns in section II.

3. Find the subjectless sentences in section V.

4. Find the conditional forms in section IV and translate each sentence where there is conditional usage.

5. Find every instance of a number that is used in the story, and describe the verbs and cases governed by these numbers.

6. Analyze the prepositional usage in section III or VIII. Write out the phrases with prepositions, noting which case each preposition takes.

❧ Abbreviations used in the appendices

1, 2, 3	first, second, third (person)
A, Acc	accusative case
A-G	accusative and genitive
AJ	[in verb charts: adjective-like forms (L-participle and passive participle)]
Apl	accusative plural
Asg	accusative singular
AV	[in verb charts: adverbial forms (present and past verbal adverb)]
[B]	Bosnian usage
[B,C]	Bosnian and Croatian usage
[B,C,S]	Bosnian, Croatian and Serbian usage (where there also exists another word or phrase which is used in only one or two of the others)
[B,S]	Bosnian and Serbian usage
[C]	Croatian usage
CF	counting form
D, Dat	dative case
DL	dative and locative
DLsg	dative-locative singular
DLIpl	dative-locative-instrumental plural
[E]	ekavian word or words
f, fem.	feminine
G, Gen	genitive case
GDLVsg	genitive, dative, locative and vocative singular
Gpl	genitive plural
Gsg	genitive singular
(I)	imperfective aspect
(I/P)	both imperfective and perfective aspect
I, Instr	instrumental case
incl.	inclusive imperative
Isg	instrumental singular
[J]	ijekavian word or words
[J] [B/S]	ijekavian words specific to Bosnian and Serbian ijekavian usage
L, Loc	locative case
L-I	locative and instrumental
L-part	L-participle (used in compound tense formations)
m, masc.	masculine
n, neut.	neuter
N	nominative
N	[in verb charts: non-conjugating forms (infinitive and verbal noun)]
NApl	nominative - accusative plural
Npl	nominative plural
Nsg	nominative singular
(P)	perfective aspect
pass. part.	passive particle
pl	plural
[S]	Serbian usage
sg	singular
v.	see (abbreviation of *vidi*)
V	[in verb charts: conjugated forms (present, aorist, imperfect and imperative)]
Vsg	vocative singular

The Latin alphabet

Latin		Cyrillic		English equivalent	Latin		Cyrillic		English equivalent
A	a	А	а	father	L	l	Л	л	left
B	b	Б	б	bet	Lj	lj	Љ	љ	million
C	c	Ц	ц	its	M	m	М	м	met
Č	č	Ч	ч	church	N	n	Н	н	net
Ć	ć	Ћ	ћ	chick [gotcha!]	Nj	nj	Њ	њ	canyon
D	d	Д	д	dent	O	o	О	о	or
Dž	dž	Џ	џ	junk	P	p	П	п	speck
Đ	đ	Ђ	ђ	ginger [didja see it?]	R	r	Р	р	[trilled r]
E	e	Е	е	met	S	s	С	с	sent, center
F	f	Ф	ф	fed	Š	š	Ш	ш	sugar
G	g	Г	г	get	T	t	Т	т	step
H	h	Х	х	Bach	U	u	У	у	flute
I	i	И	и	machine	V	v	В	в	vet
J	j	Ј	ј	yes, boy	Z	z	З	з	zen
K	k	К	к	sketch	Ž	ž	Ж	ж	treasure

The Cyrillic alphabet

Cyrillic		Latin		English equivalent	Cyrillic		Latin		English equivalent
А	а	A	a	father	Н	н	N	n	net
Б	б	B	b	bet	Њ	њ	Nj	nj	canyon
В	в	V	v	vet	О	о	O	o	or
Г	г	G	g	get	П	п	P	p	speck
Д	д	D	d	dent	Р	р	R	r	[trilled r]
Ђ	ђ	Đ	đ	ginger [didja see it?]	С	с	S	s	spent, center
Е	е	E	e	met	Т	т	T	t	step
Ж	ж	Ž	ž	treasure	Ћ	ћ	Ć	ć	chick [gotcha!]
З	з	Z	z	zen	У	у	U	u	flute
И	и	I	i	machine	Ф	ф	F	f	fed
Ј	ј	J	j	yes, boy	Х	х	H	h	Bach
К	к	K	k	sketch	Ц	ц	C	c	its
Л	л	L	l	left	Ч	ч	Č	č	church
Љ	љ	Lj	lj	million	Џ	џ	Dž	dž	junk
М	м	M	m	met	Ш	ш	Š	š	sugar

✑ Appendix 2   A selection of women's and men's names

Some women's names

Aìda [B,C]

Àmila [B]

Ana [C,S]

Anka [C]

Ànkica [C,S]

Azra [B,C]

Biljana [S]

Bòjana [C,S]

Brànka [C,S]

Dijàna [B,C,S]

Dràgana [S,C]

Dùbravka [C,S]

Dušànka [S]

Dželìla [B]

Edìta [B,C,S]

Emìna [B]

Gòrdana [C,S]

Grozdana [S]

Hana [B]

Ines [C,S]

Ìva [C,S]

Ìvana [C,S]

Jadrànka [C,S]

Jasna [B,C,S]

Jovana [S]

Ljìljana [C,S]

Ljubica [C,S]

Màra [C,S]

Marìja [C, S]

Màrta [C,S]

Merìma [B]

Mèrsiha [B]

Mìra [B,C,S]

Mìrjana [B,C,S]

Nàda [B,C,S]

Ràda [S]

Ràdmila [S]

Rajka [S]

Redžija [B]

Sanja [B,C]

Saša [B,C,S]

Selma [B]

Snèžana [S]

Snjèžana [B,C,S]

Stàka [S]

Svètlana [B,S]

Svjètlana [B,C,S]

Tìjana [C,S]

Zehra [B]

Zlàta [B,C,S]

Zòra [C,S]

Zvjèzdana [C]

Žèljka [C]

Some men's names

Aleksàndar [C,S]

Àlija [B]

Ànte [C]

Àntun [C]

Brànimir [C]

Brànislav [S]

Brànko [S,C]

Dàmir [B,C]

Dàmjan [C,S]

Dànijel [C]

Danilo [S]

Dàrko [C]

Dobrilo [S]

Dùšan [S]

Đorđe [S]

Elvis [B]

Èmir [B]

Gòran [B,C,S]

Grgur [C]

Hajrùdin [B]

Hàmdija [B]

Hàris [B]

Hàsan [B]

Hrvoje [C]

Ìnoslav [C]

Ìvan [C,S]

Ìvica [C]

Ìvo [C]

Ìzet [B]

Jàsmin [B]

Jòvan [S]

Jovica [S]

Juraj [C]

Lùka [S,C]

Ljudèvit [C]

Màrko [C,S]

Mèhmed [B]

Milorad [S]

Mìrko [S]

Miroslav [C,S]

Mirza [B]

Nenàd [C,S]

Nermin [B]

Nìkola [C,S]

Pètar [C,S]

Predrag [S]

Ràjko [S]

Saša [B,C,S]

Senad [B]

Sìniša [C,S]

Slobòdan [C,S]

Srđan [S]

Tòmislav [C,S]

Vlàda [S]

Vlàdimir [C,S]

Vlàdo [B,C]

Zlàtan [B,C,S]

Zòran [C,S]

Žàrko [C,S]

Žèljko [C,S]

Živoràd [S]

A [A]   Африка *Африка*   април *април*   дан *дан*

А а   Африка   *април*   *дан*

Б [B]   Босна *Босна*   босански *босански*   добар *добар*

Б б   Босна   *босански*   *добар*

В [V]   Војводина *Војводина*   висок *висок*   твој *твој*

В в   Војводина   *висок*   *твој*

Г [G]   Грета *Грета*   географија *географија* август *август*

Г г   Грета   *географија*   *август*

Д [D]   Дубровник *Дубровник*   децембар *децембар*   среда *среда*

Д д   Дубровник   *децембар*   *среда*

Ђ [Đ]   Ђорђе *Ђорђе*   ђак *ђак*   мађарски *мађарски*

Ђ ђ   Ђорђе   *ђак*   *мађарски*

Е [E]   Европа *Европа*   енглески *енглески*   један *један*

Е е   Европа   *енглески*   *један*

Ж [Ž]   Жаклина *Жаклина*   жена *жена*   може *може*

Ж ж   Жаклина   *жена*   *може*

З [Z]   Загреб *Загреб*   за *за*   кроз *кроз*

З з   Загреб   *за*   *кроз*

И [I]   Италија *Италија*   имати *имати*   молим *молим*

И и   Италија   *имати*   *молим*

319
Appendices

Ј [J] Југославија *Југославија*	јануар *јануар*	моје *моје*
Ј ј Југославија	*јануар*	*моје*
К [K] Косово *Косово*	ко *ко*	српски *српски*
К к Косово	*ко*	*српски*
Л [L] Лондон *Лондон*	леп *леп*	али *али*
Л л Лондон	*леп*	*али*
Љ [Lj] Љубљана *Љубљана*	љубав *љубав*	недеља *недеља*
Љ љ Љубљана	*љубав*	*недеља*
М [M] Македонија *Македонија*	март *март*	нема *нема*
М м Македонија	*март*	*нема*
Н [N] Нови Сад *Нови Сад*	новембар *новембар*	речник *речник*
Н н Нови Сад	*новембар*	*речник*
Њ [Nj] Њујорк *Њујорк*	његов *његов*	питање *питање*
Њ њ Њујорк	*његов*	*питање*
О [O] Орегон *Орегон*	октобар *октобар*	лош *лош*
О о Орегон	*октобар*	*лош*
П [P] Подгорица *Подгорица*	петак *петак*	ципела *ципела*
П п Подгорица	*петак*	*ципела*
Р [R] Румунија *Румунија*	руски *руски*	црн *црн*
Р р Румунија	*руски*	*црн*

C [C] Србија *Србија*	септембар *септембар*	писмо *писмо*
С с Србија	септембар	писмо

Т [T] Тексас *Тексас*	тата *тата*	четвртак *четвртак*
Т т Тексас	тата	четвртак

Ћ [Ć] Ћуприја *Ћуприја*	ћирилица *ћирилица*	кућа *кућа*
Ћ ћ Ћуприја	ћирилица	кућа

У [U] Уганда *Уганда*	уторак *уторак*	јун *јун*
У у Уганда	уторак	јун

Ф [F] Француска *Француска*	фебруар *фебруар*	кафа *кафа*
Ф ф Француска	фебруар	кафа

Х [H] Хрватска *Хрватска*	хлеб *хлеб*	њихова *њихова*
Х х Хрватска	хлеб	њихова

Ц [C] Црна гора *Црна гора*	црвен *црвен*	француски *француски*
Ц ц Црна Гора	црвен	француски

Ч [Č] Чикаго *Чикаго*	човек *човек*	мачка *мачка*
Ч ч Чикаго	човек	мачка

Џ [Dž] Џули *Џули*	џез *џез*	уџбеник *уџбеник*
Џ џ Џули	џез	уџбеник

Ш [Š] Шарлота *Шарлота*	шта *шта*	ваше *ваше*
Ш ш Шарлота	шта	ваше

MASCULINE animate nouns

Nsg	konj	muž	junak	pratilac	Srbin	Turčin
Asg	konja	muža	junaka	pratioca	Srbina	Turčina
Gsg	konja	muža	junaka	pratioca	Srbina	Turčina
DLsg	konju	mužu	junaku	pratiocu	Srbinu	Turčinu
Isg	konjem	mužem	junakom	pratiocem	Srbinom	Turčinom
Vsg	konju	mužu	junače	pratioče	Srbine	Turčine
CF	konja	muža	junaka	pratioca	Srbina	Turčina
Npl	konji	muževi	junaci	pratioci	Srbi	Turci
Apl	konje	muževe	junake	pratioce	Srbe	Turke
Gpl	konja	muževa	junaka	pratilaca	Srba	Turaka
DLIpl	konjima	muževima	junacima	pratiocima	Srbima	Turcima

MASCULINE inanimate nouns

Nsg	dan	grad	posao	zadatak	put
Asg	dan	grad	posao	zadatak	put
Gsg	dana	grada	posla	zadatka	puta
DLsg	danu	gradu	poslu	zadatku	putu
Isg	danom	gradom	poslom	zadatkom	putem *
Vsg	dane	grade	posle	zadatke	pute
CF	dana	grada	posla	zadatka	puta
Npl	dani	gradovi	poslovi	zadaci	putevi*
Apl	dane	gradove	poslove	zadatke	puteve*
Gpl	dana	gradova	poslova	zadataka	puteva*
DLIpl	danima	gradovima	poslovima	zadacima	putevima*

* putem, putevi *etc.* [B,C,S]   putom, putovi, *etc.* [C]

NEUTER nouns

Nsg	selo	polje	pismo	gnijezdo *	ime	jaje
Asg	selo	polje	pismo	gnijezdo	ime	jaje
Gsg	sela	polja	pisma	gnijezda	imena	jajeta
DLsg	selu	polju	pismu	gnijezdu	imenu	jajetu
Isg	selom	poljem	pismom	gnijezdom	imenom	jajetom
Vsg	selo	polje	pismo	gnijezdo	ime	jaje
CF	sela	polja	pisma	gnijezda	imena	jaja
Npl	sela	polja	pisma	gnijezda	imena	jaja
Apl	sela	polja	pisma	gnijezda	imena	jaja
Gpl	sela	polja	pisama	gnijezda	imena	jaja
DLIpl	selima	poljima	pismima	gnijezdima	imenima	jajima

* gnijezdo *etc.* [J]   gnezdo *etc.* [E]

FEMININE nouns in -a

Nsg	ruka	knjiga	djevojka *	tetka	borba	učiteljica
Asg	ruku	knjigu	djevojku	tetku	borbu	učiteljicu
Gsg	ruke	knjige	djevojke	tetke	borbe	učiteljice
DLsg	ruci	knjizi	djevojci	tetki	borbi	učiteljici
Isg	rukom	knjigom	djevojkom	tetkom	borbom	učiteljicom
Vsg	ruko	knjigo	djevojko	tetka	borbo	učiteljice
NApl	ruke	knjige	djevojke	tetke	borbe	učiteljice
Gpl	ruku	knjiga	djevojaka	tetaka / tetki	borba / borbi	učiteljica
DLIpl	rukama	knjigama	djevojkama	tetkama	borbama	učiteljicama

* djevojka *etc.* [J]   devojka *etc.* [E]

FEMININE nouns in a consonant

Nsg	stvar	noć	radost	ljubav	misao	kći *
Asg	stvar	noć	radost	ljubav	misao	kćer
GDLVsg	stvari	noći	radosti	ljubavi	misli	kćeri
Isg	stvari / stvarju	noći / noću	radošću / radosti	ljubavi / ljubavlju	misli / mišlju	kćeri / kćerju
NApl	stvari	noći	radosti	ljubavi	misli	kćeri
Gpl	stvari	noći	radosti	ljubavi	misli	kćeri
DLIpl	stvarima	noćima	radostima	ljubavima	mislima	kćerima

* kćerka [B,C,S]   kći [B,C]   ćerka [S]

MALE names

N	Pètar	Nìkola	Hŕvoje	Đòrđe	Brane	Rȁnko	Ìvo
A	Pètra	Nìkolu	Hŕvoja	Đòrđa	Braneta	Rȁnka	Ìvu
G	Pètra	Nìkolē	Hŕvoja	Đòrđa	Braneta	Rȁnka	Ìvē
DL	Pètru	Nìkoli	Hŕvoju	Đòrđu	Branetu	Rȁnku	Ìvi
I	Pètrom	Nìkolōm	Hŕvojem	Đòrđem	Branetom	Rȁnkom	Ìvōm
V	Petre	Nìkola	Hŕvoje	Đòrđe	Brane	Rȁnko	Ivo

FEMALE names

N	Nàda	Vèsna	Drȁgica	Ìnes
A	Nàdu	Vèsnu	Drȁgicu	Ìnes
G	Nàdē	Vèsnē	Drȁgicē	Ìnes
DL	Nàdi	Vèsni	Drȁgici	Ìnes
I	Nàdōm	Vèsnōm	Drȁgicōm	Ìnes
V	Nàdo	Vèsna	Drȁgice	Ìnes

NAME AND SURNAME

N	Nìkola Ìlić	Ìvo Lalić	Rȁnko Bugàrski	Ana Pàvić	Ìnes Kȕna
A	Nìkolu Ìlića	Ìvu Lalića	Rȁnka Bugàrskog	Anu Pàvić	Ìnes Kȕnu
G	Nìkolē Ìlića	Ìvē Lalića	Rȁnka Bugàrskog	Anē Pàvić	Ìnes Kȕnē
DL	Nìkoli Ìliću	Ìvi Laliću	Rȁnku Bugàrskom	Ani Pàvić	Ìnes Kȕni
I	Nìkolom Ìlićem	Ìvom Lalićem	Rȁnkom Bugàrskim	Anōm Pàvić	Ìnes Kȕnom
V	G. Ìliću	G. Laliću	G. Bugàrski	Gđo Pàvić	Gđo Kȕna

Adjective declension: paradigms

DESCRIPTIVE ADJECTIVES

	Masculine		Neuter		Feminine	
	short	long	short	long	short	long
Nsg	dȍbar	dȍbri	dȍbro	dȍbrō	dòbra	dòbrā
	loš	lȍši	lȍše	lȍšē	lòša	lòšā
Asg	dȍbar *	dȍbri *	dȍbro	dȍbrō	dòbru	dòbrū
	loš *	lȍši *	lȍše	lȍšē	lòšu	lòšū
Npl	dȍbri	dȍbri	dȍbra	dȍbrā	dȍbre	dȍbrē
	lȍši	lȍši	lòša	lòšā	lòše	lòšē
Apl	dȍbre	dȍbre	dȍbra	dȍbrā	dȍbre	dȍbrē
	lòše	lòšē	lòša	lòšā	lòše	lòšē

* inanimate only

	Masculine-Neuter			Feminine	
---	short	long	longer	short	long
Gsg	dòbra *	dobr<u>o</u>g *	dobr<u>o</u>ga *		dòbr<u>e</u>
	lòša *	loš<u>e</u>g *	loš<u>e</u>ga *		lòš<u>e</u>
DLsg	dòbru	dobr<u>o</u>m	dobr<u>o</u>me, dobr<u>o</u>mu		dòbr<u>o</u>j
	lòšu	loš<u>e</u>m	loš<u>e</u>mu		lòš<u>o</u>j
Isg		dobr<u>i</u>m			dobr<u>o</u>m
		loš<u>i</u>m			lòš<u>o</u>m
CF	dobra			dobre	
	loša			loše	

* and animate accusative

	Masculine-Neuter-Feminine	
---	long	longer
Gpl	dobr<u>i</u>h	
	loš<u>i</u>h	
DLIpl	dobr<u>i</u>m	dobr<u>i</u>ma
	loš<u>i</u>m	loš<u>i</u>ma

PRONOMINAL ADJECTIVES

	Masculine		Neuter		Feminine	
Nsg	kòji	nek<u>i</u>	kòj<u>e</u>	nek<u>o</u>	kòja	nek<u>a</u>
Asg	kòji *	nek<u>i</u> *	kòj<u>e</u>	nek<u>o</u>	kòju	nek<u>u</u>
Npl	kòji	nek<u>i</u>	kòja	nek<u>a</u>	kòj<u>e</u>	nek<u>e</u>
Apl	kòj<u>e</u>	nek<u>e</u>	kòja	nek<u>a</u>	kòj<u>e</u>	nek<u>e</u>

* inanimate only

	Masculine – Neuter				Feminine	
---	long		longer			
Gsg	kòj<u>e</u>g *	nek<u>o</u>g *	kòj<u>e</u>ga *	nek<u>o</u>ga *	kòj<u>e</u>	nek<u>e</u>
	k<u>o</u>g *		k<u>o</u>ga *			
DLsg	kòj<u>e</u>m,	nek<u>o</u>m	kòj<u>e</u>mu,	nek<u>o</u>mu	kòj<u>o</u>j	nek<u>o</u>j
	k<u>o</u>m		k<u>o</u>mu			
Isg	kòj<u>i</u>m,	nek<u>i</u>m			kòj<u>o</u>m	nek<u>o</u>m
	k<u>i</u>m					

* and animate accusative

	Masculine - Neuter – Feminine			
---	long		longer	
Gpl	kòj<u>i</u>h	nek<u>i</u>h		
DLIpl	kòj<u>i</u>m	nek<u>i</u>m	kòj<u>i</u>ma	nek<u>i</u>ma

DEMONSTRATIVE PRONOMINAL ADJECTIVES

	Masculine		Neuter		Feminine	
Nsg	ovaj	taj	ovo	to	ova	ta
Asg	ovaj *	taj *	ovo	to	ovu	tu
Npl	ovi	ti	ova	ta	ove	te
Apl	ove	te	ova	ta	ove	te

* inanimate only

	Masculine – Neuter				Feminine	
	long		longer			
Gsg	ovog *	tog *	ovoga *	toga *	ove	te
DLsg	ovom	tom	ovome, ovomu**	tome, tomu**	ovoj	toj
Isg	ovim	tim		time	ovom	tom
CF	ova	ta			ove	te

* and animate accusative   ** [C] only

	Masculine – Neuter – Feminine			
	long		longer	
Gpl	ovih	tih		
DLIpl	ovim	tim	ovima	tima

	Masculine		Neuter		Feminine	
Nsg	kakav	sav	kakvo	sve	kakva	sva
Asg	kakav *	sav *	kakvo	sve	kakvu	svu
Npl	kakvi	svi	kakva	sva	kakve	sve
Apl	kakve	sve	kakva	sva	kakve	sve

* inanimate only

	Masculine – Neuter				Feminine	
	long		longer			
Gsg	kakvog *		kakvoga *	svega *	kakve	sve
DLsg	kakvom	svem	kakvomu	svemu	kakvoj	svoj
Isg	kakvim	svim		svima	kakvom	svom

* and animate accusative

	Masculine - Neuter – Feminine			
	long		longer	
Gpl	kakvih	svih	sviju	
DLIpl	kakvim	svim	svima	

POSSESSIVE PRONOMINAL ADJECTIVES

	Masculine		Neuter		Feminine	
Nsg	moj	naš	moje	naše	moja	naša
Asg	moj *	naš *	moje	naše	moju	našu
Npl	moji	naši	moja	naša	moje	naše
Apl	moje	naše	moja	naša	moje	naše

* inanimate only

	Masculine – Neuter				Feminine	
	long		longer			
Gsg	mojeg *	našeg *	mojega *	našega *	moje	naše
	mog *		moga *			
DLsg	mojem,	našem	mojemu,	našemu	mojoj	našoj
	mom		mome, momu			
Isg	mojim	našim			mojom	našom

* and animate accusative

	Masculine - Neuter – Feminine			
	long		longer	
Gpl	mojih	naših		
DLIpl	mojim	našim	mojima	našima

	Masculine		Neuter		Feminine	
Nsg	njegov	mamin	njegovo	mamino	njegova	mamina
Asg	njegov *	mamin *	njegovo	mamino	njegovu	maminu
Npl	njegovi	mamini	njegova	mamina	njegove	mamine
Apl	njegove	mamine	njegova	mamina	njegove	mamine

* inanimate only

	Masculine – Neuter				Feminine	
	short		long			
Gsg	njegova*	mamina *	njegovog *	maminog *	njegove	mamine
DLsg	njegovu	maminu	njegovom	maminom	njegovoj	maminoj
Isg			njegovim	maminim	njegovom	maminom

* and animate accusative

	Masculine - Neuter – Feminine			
	long		longer	
Gpl	njegovih	maminih		
DLIpl	njegovim	maminim	njegovima	maminima

Declension of pronouns

PERSONAL PRONOUNS, singular

	1st full	1st clitic	2nd full	2nd clitic	reflexive full	reflexive clitic	3rd masc. / neut. full	3rd masc. / neut. clitic	3rd feminine full	3rd feminine clitic
N	ja		ti				on / ono		ona	
A	mene	me	tebe	te	sebe	se	njega	ga	nju	je, ju
G	mene	me	tebe	te	sebe	se	njega	ga	nje	je
D	meni	mi	tebi	ti	sebi	[si]	njemu	mu	njoj	joj
L	meni		tebi		sebi		njemu		njoj	
I	mnom, mnome		tobom		sobom		njim, njime		njom, njome	

PERSONAL PRONOUNS, plural

	1st full	1st clitic	2nd full	2nd clitic	3rd masc. / neut. / feminine full	3rd masc. / neut. / feminine clitic
N	mi		vi		oni / ona / one	
A-G	nas	nas	vas	vas	njih	ih
D	nama	nam	vama	vam	njima	im
L-I	nama		vama		njima	

INTERROGATIVE PRONOUNS and words derived from them

	long	longer	long	longer	long	longer	long	longer
N	ko / tko		neko / netko		šta / što		ništa	
A	kog	koga	nekog	nekoga	šta / što		ništa	
G	kog	koga	nekog	nekoga		čega	ničeg	ničega
D		kome, komu		nekome, nekomu				
L	kom	kome	nekom	nekome		čemu	ni o čem	ni o čemu
I	kim	kime	nekim	nekime	čim	čime	ničim	ničime

BEZ	+ Gen	*without*
BLIZU	+ Gen	*near, close to*
DO	+ Gen	*to, next to, up to*
ISPOD	+ Gen	*under*
ISPRED	+ Gen	*in front of*
IZ	+ Gen	*from, out of*
IZA	+ Gen	*behind*
IZMEĐU	+ Gen	*between, among*
IZNAD	+ Gen	*above*
K, KA	+ Dat	*to, towards*
KOD	+ Gen	*at, by, with; to*
KROZ	+ Acc	*through*
NA	+ Acc	*to, onto*
NA	+ Loc	*on, at*
NAD	+ Instr	*over, above*
NAKON	+ Gen	*after*
NASUPROT	+ Dat	*opposite, across from*
O	+ Loc	*about, concerning*
OD	+ Gen	*from, of*
OKO	+ Gen	*around*
PO	+ Acc	*per, each*
PO	+ Loc	*according to, around, in*
POD	+ Instr	*under*
PORED	+ Gen	*beside, next to*
POSLE POSLIJE	+ Gen	*after*
PRE PRIJE	+ Gen	*before*
PRED	+ Instr	*before, in front of*
PREKO	+ Gen	*across*
PREMA	+ Dat	*toward, according to*
PRI	+ Loc	*near, by, with, at*
S, SA	+ Gen	*from, down from, off of*
S, SA	+ Instr	*with*
U	+ Acc	*to, into, on*
U	+ Loc	*in, at*
UZ	+ Acc	*alongside, up, along*
ZA	+ Acc	*for*
ZA	+ Instr	*behind*
ZBOG	+ Gen	*because of, due to*

PREPOSITIONS BY CASE

Accusative	kroz, na, u, uz, za
Genitive	bez, blizu, do, iz, kod, nakon, od, oko, pored, posle [E] poslije [J], pre [E] prije [J], preko, s (*or* sa), zbog
	ispod, ispred, iza, između, iznad
Dative	k (*or* ka), nasuprot, prema
Locative	na, o, po, pri, u
Instrumental	nad, pod, pred, s (*or* sa), za

The following charts summarize the forms of a verb. Each verb has two forms that act as a noun (N), in that they name an activity (the infinitive and the verbal noun). Each verb also has two sets of forms that function as adjectives (AJ), the passive participle and the L-participle, and two forms that function as adverbs (AV), the past and present verbal adverbs. The remaining forms are verbal (V), the three tenses and the imperative mood.

In theory, any one verb will have a separate form corresponding to each of the boxed slots in the inventory diagram below. Although this does not always happen in practice, most verbs do indeed occur in nearly all the possible forms. "Holes" in the pattern are usually a function of aspect or transitivity, since these two features of a verb's meaning affect its ability to express the nuances inherent in the particular forms. In each case, an attempt was made to choose head verb which would give the fullest range of forms. Where the verb in question lacks one or more of the forms, the slot is filled by a form from another verb of the same type. Appendix 9 (pp. 358-366) presents all the verbs introduced in lesson vocabularies and grammar sections, organized according to conjugational type, and gives information about accentuation.

Verb inventory

N		infinitive						verbal noun
V	present	1sg	2sg	3sg	1pl	2pl	3pl	
	aorist	1sg	2sg	3sg	1pl	2pl	3pl	
	imperfect	1sg	sg	3sg	1pl	2pl	3pl	
	imperative		sg		incl.	pl		
AJ	L-participle	m.sg	n.sg	f.sg	m.pl	n.pl	f.pl	
	passive participle	m.sg	n.sg	f.sg	m.pl	n.pl	f.pl	
AV	verbal adverb	present vbl.adv.			past vbl. adv.			

Type 1 (gledati)

N		gledati					gledanje
V	present	gledam	gledaš	gleda	gledamo	gledate	gledaju
	aorist	gledah	gleda	gleda	gledasmo	gledaste	gledaše
	imperfect	gledah	gledaše	gledaše	gledasmo	gledaste	gledahu
	imperative		gledaj!		gledajmo!	gledajte!	
AJ	L-participle	gledao	gledalo	gledala	gledali	gledala	gledale
	pass. part.	gledan	gledano	gledana	gledani	gledana	gledane
AV		gledajući			[pogledavši]		

Type 2 (nositi)

N		nositi					nošenje
V	present	nosim	nosiš	nosi	nosimo	nosite	nose
	aorist	nosih	nosi	nosi	nosismo	nosiste	nosiše
	imperfect	nošah	nošaše	nošaše	nošasmo	nošaste	nošahu
	imperative		nosi!		nosimo!	nosite!	
AJ	L-participle	nosio	nosilo	nosila	nosili	nosila	nosile
	pass. part.	nošen	nošeno	nošena	nošeni	nošena	nošene
AV		noseći			nosivši		

Type 3 (videti) [E]

N		videti					viđenje
V	present	vidim	vidiš	vidi	vidimo	vidite	vide
	aorist	videh	vide	vide	videsmo	videste	videše
	imperfect	viđah	viđaše	viđaše	viđasmo	viđaste	viđahu
	imperative		vidi!		vidimo!	vidite!	
AJ	L- participle	video	videlo	videla	videli	videla	videle
	pass. part.	viđen	viđeno	viđena	viđeni	viđena	viđene
AV		videći			videvši		

Type 3 (vidjeti) [J]

N		vidjeti					viđenje
V	present	vidim	vidiš	vidi	vidimo	vidite	vide
	aorist	vidjeh	vidje	vidje	vidjesmo	vidjeste	vidješe
	imperfect	viđah	viđaše	viđaše	viđasmo	viđaste	viđahu
	imperative		vidi!		vidimo!	vidite!	
AJ	L- participle	vidio	vidjelo	vidjela	vidjeli	vidjela	vidjele
	pass. part.	viđen	viđeno	viđena	viđeni	viđena	viđene
AV		videći			vidjevši		

Type 4 (držati)

N		držati					držanje
V	present	držim	držiš	drži	držimo	držite	drže
	aorist	držah	drža	drža	držasmo	držaste	držaše
	imperfect	držah	držaše	držaše	držasmo	držaste	držahu
	imperative		drži!		držimo!	držite!	
AJ	L- participle	držao	držalo	držala	držali	držala	držale
	pass. part.	držan	držano	držana	držani	držana	držane
AV		držeći			državši		

Type 5 (pisati)

N		pisati					pisanje
V	present	pišem	pišeš	piše	pišemo	pišete	pišu
	aorist	pisah	pisa	pisa	pisasmo	pisaste	pisaše
	imperfect	pisah	pisaše	pisaše	pisasmo	pisaste	pisahu
	imperative		piši!		pišimo!	pišite!	
AJ	L- participle	pisao	pisalo	pisala	pisali	pisala	pisale
	pass. part.	pisan	pisano	pisana	pisani	pisana	pisane
AV		pišući			pisavši		

Type 6 (piti)

N		piti					pijenje
V	present	pijem	piješ	pije	pijemo	pijete	piju
	aorist	pih	pi	pi	pismo	piste	piše
	imperfect	pijah	pijaše	pijaše	pijasmo	pijaste	pijahu
	imperative		pij!		pijmo!	pijte!	
AJ	L- participle	pio	pilo	pila	pili	pila	pile
	pass. part.	[popit]	[popito]	[popita]	[popiti]	[popita]	[popite]
		[popijen]	[popijeno]	[popijena]	[popijeni]	[popijena]	[popijene]
AV		pijući			[popivši]		

Type 7 (krenuti)

N		krenuti					[svanuće]
V	present	krenem	kreneš	krene	krenemo	krenete	krenu
	aorist	krenuh	krenu	krenu	krenusmo	krenuste	krenuše
	imperfect	[tonjah]	[tonjaše]	[tonjaše]	[tonjasmo]	[tonjaste]	[tonjahu]
	imperative		kreni!		krenimo!	krenite!	
AJ	L- participle	krenuo	krenulo	krenula	krenuli	krenula	krenule
	pass. part.	[dignut]	[dignuto]	[dignuta]	[dignuti]	[dignuta]	[dignute]
AV		[dižući]			krenuvši		

Types 8a-8b (kupovati, kazivati)

Type 8a

N		kupovati					kupovanje
V	present	kupujem	kupuješ	kupuje	kupujemo	kupujete	kupuju
	aorist	kupovah	kupova	kupova	kupovasmo	kupovaste	kupovaše
	imperfect	kupovah	kupovaše	kupovaše	kupovasmo	kupovaste	kupovahu
	imperative		kupuj!		kupujmo!	kupujte!	
AJ	L- participle	kupovao	kupovalo	kupovala	kupovali	kupovala	kupovale
	pass. part.	kupovan	kupovano	kupovana	kupovani	kupovana	kupovane
AV		kupujući			kupovavši		

Type 8b

N		kazivati					kazivanje
V	present	kazujem	kazuješ	kazuje	kazujemo	kazujete	kazuju
	aorist	kazivah	kaziva	kaziva	kazivasmo	kazivaste	kazivaše
	imperfect	kazivah	kazivaše	kazivaše	kazivasmo	kazivaste	kazivahu
	imperative		kazuj!		kazujmo!	kazujte!	
AJ	L- participle	kazivao	kazivalo	kazivala	kazivali	kazivala	kazivale
	pass. part.	kazivan	kazivano	kazivana	kazivani	kazivana	kazivane
AV		kazujući			kazivavši		

Type 9 (davati)

N		dàvati					dávanje
V	present	dajem	daješ	daje	dajemo	dajete	daju
	aorist	davah	dava	dava	davasmo	davaste	davaše
	imperfect	davah	davaše	davaše	davasmo	davaste	davahu
	imperative		daj!		dajmo!	dajte!	
AJ	L- participle	davao	davalo	davala	davali	davala	davale
	pass. part.	davan	davano	davana	davani	davana	davane
AV		dajući			davavši		

Type 10 (brati)

N		brati					branje
V	present	berem	bereš	bere	beremo	berete	beru
	aorist	brah	bra	bra	brasmo	braste	braše
	imperfect	brah	braše	braše	brasmo	braste	brahu
	imperative		beri!		berimo!	berite!	
AJ	L- participle	brao	bralo	brala	brali	brala	brale
	pass. part.	bran	brano	brana	brani	brana	brane
AV		berući			bravši		

Type 11 (uzeti)

N		uzeti					[poduzéće]*
V	present	uzmem	uzmeš	uzme	uzmemo	uzmete	uzmu
	aorist	uzeh	uze	uze	uzesmo	uzeste	uzeše
	imperfect	[kunijah]	[kunijaše]	[kunijaše]	[kunijasmo]	[kunijaste]	[kunijahu]
	imperative		uzmi!		uzmimo!	uzmite!	
AJ	L-participle	uzeo	uzelo	uzela	uzeli	uzela	uzele
	pass. part.	uzet	uzeto	uzeta	uzeti	uzeta	uzete
AV		[kunući]			uzevši		

* poduzeće [B,C]   preduzeće [B,S]

Type 12 (umeti) [E]

N		umeti					uméće
V	present	umem	umeš	ume	umemo	umete	umeju
	aorist	umeh	ume	ume	umesmo	umeste	umeše
	imperfect	umejah	umejaše	umejaše	umejasmo	umejaste	umejahu
	imperative		umej		umejmo	umejte	
AJ	L- participle	umeo	umeelo	umela	umeli	umela	umele
	pass. part.						
AV		umejući			umevši		

Type 12 (umjeti) [J]

N		umjeti					umijeće
V	present	umijem	umiješ	umije	umijemo	umijete	umiju
	aorist	umjeh	umje	umje	umjesmo	umjeste	umješe
	imperfect	umijah	umijaše	umijaše	umijasmo	umijaste	umijahu
	imperative		umij		umijmo	umijte	
AJ	L- participle	umio	umjelo	umjela	umjeli	umjela	umjele
	pass. part.						
AV		umijući			umjevši		

Type 13 (jesti)

N		jesti					jedenje
V	present	jedem	jedeš	jede	jedemo	jedete	jedu
	aorist	jedoh	jede	jede	jedosmo	jedoste	jedoše
	imperfect	jeđah	jeđaše	jeđaše	jeđasmo	jeđaste	jeđahu
	imperative		jedi!		jedimo!	jedite!	
AJ	L- participle	jeo	jelo	jela	jeli	jela	jele
	pass. part.	jeden	jedeno	jedena	jedeni	jedena	jedene
AV		jedući			jedavši		

Type 14 (tresti)

N		tresti					tresenje
V	present	tresem	treseš	trese	tresemo	tresete	tresu
	aorist	tresoh	trese	trese	tresosmo	tresoste	tresoše
	imperfect	tresah	tresaše	tresaše	tresasmo	tresaste	tresahu
	imperative		tresi!		tresimo!	tresite!	
AJ	L- participle	tresao	treslo	tresla	tresli	tresla	tresle
	pass. part.	tresen	treseno	tresena	treseni	tresena	tresene
AV		tresući			tresavši		

Types 15a-b (teći, stići)

Type 15a

N		teći					tečenje
V	present	tečem	tečeš	teče	tečemo	tečete	teku
	aorist	tekoh	teče	teče	tekosmo	tekoste	tekoše
	imperfect	tecijah	tecijaše	tecijaše	tecijasmo	tecijaste	tecijahu
	imperative		teci!		tecimo!	tecite!	
AJ	L- participle	tekao	teklo	tekla	tekli	tekla	tekle
	pass. part.	tečen	tečeno	tečena	tečeni	tečena	tečene
AV		tekući			[tekavši]		

Type 15b

N		stići					stizanje
V	present	stignem	stigneš	stigne	stignemo	stignete	stignu
	aorist	stigoh	stiže	stiže	stigosmo	stigoste	stigoše
	imperfect	stizah	stizaše	stizaše	stizasmo	stizaste	stizahu
	imperative		stigni!		stignimo!	stignite!	
AJ	L- participle	stigao	stiglo	stigla	stigli	stigla	stigle
	pass. part.	[strižen]	[striženo]	[strižena]	[striženi]	[strižena]	[strižene]
AV			stižući			stigavši	

Type 16 (doći)

N		doći					
V	present	dođem	dođeš	dođe	dođemo	dođete	dođu
	aorist	dođoh	dođe	dođe	dođosmo	dođoste	dođoše
	imperfect	[iđah]	[iđaše]	[iđaše]	[iđasmo]	[iđaste]	[iđahu]
	imperative		dođi!		dođimo!	dođite!	
AJ	L- participle	došao	došlo	došla	došli	došla	došle
	pass. part.	[nađen]	[nađeno]	[nađena]	[nađeni]	[nađena]	[nađene]
AV			[idući]			došavši	

The verb hteti [E]

N		hteti					htenje
V	present	ću	ćeš	će	ćemo	ćete	će
		hoću	hoćeš	hoće	hoćemo	hoćete	hoće
		neću	nećeš	neće	nećemo	nećete	neće
	aorist	hteh	hte	hte	htesmo	hteste	hteše
		htedoh	htede	htede	htedosmo	htedoste	htedoše
	imperfect	hoćah	hoćaše	hoćaše	hoćasmo	hoćaste	hoćahu
		hotijah	hotijaše	hotijaše	hotijasmo	hotijaste	hotijahu
AJ	L- participle	hteo	htelo	htela	hteli	htela	htele
AV			hoteći			htevši	

The verb htjeti [J]

N		htjeti					htjenje
V	present	ću	ćeš	će	ćemo	ćete	će
	(full)	hoću	hoćeš	hoće	hoćemo	hoćete	hoće
	(negated)	neću	nećeš	neće	nećemo	nećete	neće
	aorist	htjeh	htje	htje	htjesmo	htjeste	htješe
	(or)	htjedoh	htjede	htjede	htjedosmo	htjedoste	htjedoše
	imperfect	hoćah	hoćaše	hoćaše	hoćasmo	hoćaste	hoćahu
	(or)	hotijah	hotijaše	hotijaše	hotijasmo	hotijaste	hotijahu
AJ	L- participle	htio	htjelo	htjela	htjeli	htjela	htjele
AV			hoteći			htevši	

The verb biti

N		biti					
V	present	sam	si	je	smo	ste	su
	(full)	jèsam	jèsi	jeste *	jèsmo	jèste	jèsu
	(negated)	nìsam	nìsi	nìje	nìsmo	nìste	nìsu
		bud̲e̲m	bud̲e̲š	bud̲e̲	bud̲e̲mo	bud̲e̲te	bud̲u̲
	aorist	bih	bi	bi	bismo	biste	biše
	imperfect [E]	bej̲a̲h	bej̲a̲še	bej̲a̲še	bej̲a̲smo	bej̲a̲ste	bej̲a̲hu
	imperfect [J]	bij̲a̲h	bij̲a̲še	bij̲a̲še	bij̲a̲smo	bij̲a̲ste	bij̲a̲hu
	imperative		budi!		budimo!	budite!	
AJ	L- participle	bio	bȉlo	bȉla	bȉli	bȉla	bȉle
AV		budući			bivši		

* jeste [B,S]   jest [C]

📖 I ⊙23

VOCABULARY

brati, berem	to pick (I)	nikada	never
cveće	flowers	nogomet [C]	soccer
cvijeće	flowers	pijaca [B,S]	marketplace
fudbal [B,S]	soccer	sanjati, sanjam	to dream (I)
ići, idem	to go (I)	skupljati, skupljam, skupljaju	to collect (I)
igrati, igram, igraju	to play (I)	spavati, spavam, spavaju	to sleep (I)
ljubavni	romance	tržnica [B,C]	marketplace

Moja žena bere cveće.

Ja skupljam marke.

Moja žena čita ljubavne romane.

Ja igram fudbal.

Moja žena gleda televiziju.

Ja idem na pijacu.

Moja žena dugo spava.

Ja nikada ne sanjam.

📖 II ⊙24

VOCABULARY

Da li tebi nešto treba? [S]	Do you need something?	samoposluga [B,C]	self-service grocery store
doručak, doručka	breakfast	samousluga [B,S]	self-service grocery store
meni se jede	I feel like eating	šunka	ham
kajgana	scrambled eggs	Treba li ti nešto? [B,C]	Do you need something?
kamilica	chamomile	zaboraviti, zaboravim	to forget (P)

Moja žena ide u samouslugu.

- Moram da kupim hleb i mleko - kaže ona. - Da li tebi nešto treba?

- Kupi šunku - kažem. - Volim šunku za doručak.

- Meni se jede kajgana - kaže moja žena.

- Da li imamo čaj od kamilice? pitam.

- Mislim da nemamo.

- Ne zaboravi da ga kupiš.

341

- A novine - pita moja žena - da li da kupim novine?

- Doručak bez novina - kažem - nije pravi doručak.

📖 III ⊙25

VOCABULARY

brinuti, brinem	to worry (I)	odlijetati, odlijećem	to fly away (I)
buktinja	torch	ostajati, ostajem	to remain (I)
ćutati, čutim [B,S]	to be silent (I)	park	park
dodavati, dodajem	to add (I)	pogledaj!	look! (P)
izgledati, izgledam	to seem (I)	satima	for hours
izgleda	it seems	sličiti, sličim (na) [B,C]	to resemble (I)
jedino	only	smešiti se, smešim se	smile (I)
kao da	as if	smiješiti se, smiješim se	smile (I)
klupa	bench	što	that
krošnja	tree top	šutjeti, šutim [B,C]	to be silent
ličiti, ličim (na) [B,S]	to resemble (I)	vrabac, vrapca	sparrow
lišće coll.	foliage, leaves	zlato	gold
nastavljati, nastavljam	to continue (I)	žaliti, žalim	to feel sorry (I)
odletati, odlećem	to fly away (I)	žalim što	I'm sorry that

Moja žena i ja sedimo na klupi. Klupa je u parku.

- Volim jesen - kaže moja žena.

- Jesen je uvek lepa - kažem.

- Pogledaj lišće - nastavlja moja žena. - Izgleda kao da je od zlata.

- Neke krošnje - kažem, - liče na buktinje.

- Mogu satima da ih gledam, dodaje moja žena.

Ja malo ćutim, a onda kažem - Jedino žalim što odleću ptice.

- Ne brini - smeši se moja žena - ostaju nam vrapci.

📖 IV ⊙26

VOCABULARY

buket, buketa	bouquet	prodavačica	saleswoman
ću	I will	radnja	store, shop
koštati	to cost (I)	ruža	rose
lala [B,S]	tulip	tulipan [B,C]	tulip
nisam ih video	I didn't see them	umotati	to wrap up (P)
nisam ih vidio	I didn't see them	venčanje	wedding
pogledati	to look at (P)	vjenčanje	wedding
pokazivati, pokazujem	to show (I)		

Kupujem buket ruža za moju ženu.

- Te ruže su divne - kaže prodavačica. - I nisu skupe.

"Osam malih priča o mojoj ženi" – *David Albahari*

Umotajte ih, molim vas, u lep papir - kažem.

- Svakako - kaže prodavačica. - Da li ih nosite nekome na venčanje?"

- Ruže su za moju ženu.

- O - kaže prodavačica. - Ona sigurno voli ruže.

- Sviđaju joj se i lale - kažem - ali nisam ih video u radnji.

- Tamo su - pokazuje prodavačica - pored kase. Da li želite da ih pogledate?

- Ipak ću uzeti ruže - kažem. - Koliko košta sedam crvenih ruža?

📖 V   ⊙27

VOCABULARY

baš	truly, really	posle	afterwards
budilnik [B,S]	alarm clock	poslije	afterwards
budilica [B,C]	alarm clock	prsten; prstenovi	ring
čelo	forehead	teretana	gym for lifting weights
gospodar, gospodara	lord, master	trčati, trčim	to run (I)
jedva čekam	I can hardly wait	uskoro	soon
karta	ticket	ustajati, ustajem	to get up, to rise (I)
kasnije	later	zaboravan	forgetful
krenuti, krenem	to get going (P)	zvoniti, zvonim	to ring (I)
lupiti se	to strike oneself (P)		

Moj budilnik zvoni u šest sati.

- Zašto ustaješ tako rano? pita moja žena.

- Idem u teretanu da vežbam - kažem.

- Zar ne možeš kasnije da ideš?

- Posle žurim na posao.

- A uveče?

- Uveče idemo u bioskop - kažem. - Već imamo karte.

Moja žena se lupi po čelu. - Baš sam zaboravna! Šta gledamo?

- Treći deo 'Gospodara prstenova'.

- Jedva čekam da ga vidim - kaže moja žena. Onda pogleda na sat. - Moraš uskoro da kreneš.

- Mogu da trčim do teretane - odgovaram. - I to je vežba.

"Osam malih priča o mojoj ženi" – David Albahari

VOCABULARY

brisati, brišem	to wipe, to erase (I)	prestajati, prestajem	to stop (I)
da imam	if I had	put [tri puta]	time [three times]
da li bi me više voleo?	would you love me more?	rep	tail
drvo, drveta	tree	slagati, slažem	to arrange (I)
dvorište	yard	slikati	take a picture (I)
foto-aparat, foto-aparata	camera	sudovi [B,S]	dishes
krpa	dishtowel	tanjir, tanjira [B,S]	plate
ostavljati	to leave, to set aside (I)	tanjur, tanjura [C]	plate
podizati, podižem	to raise (I)	veverica	squirrel
polica	shelf	vjeverica	squirrel
posuđe *coll.* [C]	dishes	zatim	thereafter

Moja žena pere sudove i peva.

Ja brišem čaše i tanjire. Zatim ih slažem na policu.

U dvorištu, na drvetu, sedi veverica.

Ostavljam krpu, uzimam foto-aparat i slikam je tri puta.

Moja žena prestaje da peva. - Mene nikada ne slikaš tri puta - kaže ona.

- Ti nisi veverica - kažem.

- Naravno da nisam - kaže moja žena. Onda me pogleda. - Da li bi me više voleo da imam rep?

- Volim te i bez repa - kažem, podižem foto-aparat i slikam je četiri puta.

VOCABULARY

alo	hello [on the phone]	prohujao, prohujala	swept away
držati, držim	to hold (I)	slušalica	telephone receiver
izveštaj [S]	report	spuštati, spuštam	to hang up (I)
izvještaj [B]	report	stranica	page
izvješće [C]	report	šetnja	stroll
maramica	handkerchief	telefonirati, telefoniram	to telephone (I/P)
ni toliko	not even this much	vihor	gale-strength wind
pozdraviti	to greet (P)		

Svakog dana, tačno u podne, telefoniram mojoj ženi.

- Alo - kaže moja žena.

- Zdravo - kažem. - Kako si? Šta radiš?

- Dobro sam - kaže moja žena. Čitam knjigu.

- Šta čitaš?

- Roman 'Prohujalo s vihorom'.

"Osam malih priča o mojoj ženi" – David Albahari

- To je tužna knjiga - kažem.

- Dok čitam - kaže moja žena - držim maramicu u ruci.

- Koliko još imaš do kraja?

- Pedeset stranica - odgovara ona, - možda ni toliko.

- A kada ih pročitaš – pitam - šta onda misliš da radiš?

- Idem u šetnju sa Ljubicom.

- Pozdravi Ljubicu - kažem.

- A ti - pita moja žena - kada dolaziš kući?

- Kada napišem izveštaj - kažem i spuštam slušalicu.

📖 VIII   ⊙30

VOCABULARY

birati, biram, biraju	to select (I)	igla	needle
bluza	blouse	konac, konca	thread
daska za peglanje	ironing board	kuhinja	kitchen
duga	rainbow	obući, obučem	to put on clothing (P)
dugme, dugmeta [B,S]	button	prišivati, prišivam	to sew on (I)
gumb [C]	button	uvlačiti, uvlačim	to draw in (I)

Moja žena sedi u kuhinji i uvlači konac u iglu. Onda bira dugme za svoju bluzu. Bluza je bela. I konac je beo. Samo je dugme crveno. Moja žena prišiva crveno dugme na belu bluzu. Malo posle, ona stavlja bluzu na dasku za peglanje. Vidim da je svako dugme druge boje. Kada obuče bluzu, moja žena izgleda kao beli oblak iza šarene duge.

"Osam malih priča o mojoj ženi" – David Albahari

Appendix 8: LJUBAV NA ŠPANJOLSKI NAČIN *Muharem Bazdulj*

VOCABULARY

čin	act	polako	slowly
će	"went"	povod	reason, occasion
dres	sports uniform	poznat	known
frizerka	hairdresser	pred + *Acc*	in front of
fudbalski klub [B,S]	soccer team	prići priđem	to come over to (P)
gimnazija	secondary school	prozvati, prozovem	to call, to dub (P)
gimnazijalac, gimnazijalca	high school student	replika	reply
hvala na pitanju	thanks for asking	stići, stignem; stigao, stigla	to arrive (P)
klimati glavom	to nod (I)		
latinoamerički	Latin American *(adj.)*	strani jezik	foreign language
mesto	place	španski [B,S]	Spanish
metar, metra	meter	španjolski [B,C]	Spanish
mjesto	place	tečaj	course [of study]
nizvodno	downstream	ubiti, ubijem	to kill (P)
nogometni klub [B,C]	soccer team	učenik	pupil, student
objaviti, objavim	to announce (P)	upitati, upitam	to inquire (P)
odevati, odevam	to don, to clothe (I)	upoznati se	to get acquainted (P)
odijevati, odijevam	to don, to clothe (I)	valjda	probably
osmehnuti, osmehnem	to flash a smile (P)	završni	final
osmjehnuti, osmjehnem	to flash a smile (P)	želela bi	[she] would like to
plavuša	blonde	željela bi	[she] would like to
pohađati, pohađam	to attend [a class] (I)		

Goran stoji pred Centrom za učenje stranih jezika u sarajevskoj ulici Obala Kulina Bana. To je duga ulica uz rijeku. Stotinjak metara nizvodno je mjesto na kojem je Gavrilo Princip ubio nadvojvodu Franza Ferdinanda. Taj čin, kasnije prozvan Sarajevskim atentatom, bio je povod za prvi svjetski rat.

Goran gleda na sat. Deset minuta do pet popodne. U pet sati počinje prvi čas tečaja španjolskog jezika. Goran je student književnosti. Želi naučiti španjolski jer jako voli latinoameričke pisce, naročito Borgesa.

Pred zgradu Centra stigla je i Marina. Pozdravlja Gorana klimanjem glave. Poznat joj je s fakulteta. Ona je studentica završne godine engleskog jezika, a željela bi naučiti i španjolski.

- Ovdje si zbog tečaja? - upita Goran.
- Jesam – odgovori Marina.
- Nećemo valjda biti samo nas dvoje - opet će Goran.
- Ima vremena, doći će još neko - rekla je Marina.

Uskoro im priđoše dvojica mladića, a odmah zatim i dvije djevojke. Upoznali su se. Damir, koji je stigao odjeven u dres nogometnog kluba "Real Madrid", bio je još gimnazijalac, a Vlado je radio kao konobar. Lijepa plavuša Azra bila je frizerka, dok je Sonja radila kao profesorica biologije, i to baš u gimnaziji koju je Damir pohađao.

- Dobar dan, profesorice. Kako ste? - reče Damir.
- Dobro sam, Damire, hvala na pitanju. Ovdje ti nisam profesorica, ovdje smo oboje učenici - reče Sonja.

Svi se osmjehnuše na ovu Sonjinu repliku.

- Pet je sati - objavi Vlado.
- Bolje je da uđemo - reče Azra.
Šestero mladih ljudi polako uđoše u zgradu.

VOCABULARY

dodati	to add (P)	računati	to calculate (I)
germanski	Germanic	sapunica	soap opera
grupa	group	sastav	composition
italijanski [B,S]	Italian (adj.)	serija	series
meksički	Mexican (adj.)	studij	study, studies
nagrada	award	Švedska	Sweden
nagradna igra	competition	švedski	Swedish
navijati, navijam	to root, to cheer (I)	talijanski [B,C]	Italian (adj.)
nekako	somehow	televizijski	television (adj.)
nezgodan, nezgodna	awkward	trudna	pregnant
opustiti, opustim	to relax [someone] (P)	udati se	to get married (P)
poslati, pošaljem	to send (P)	Ujedinjene Nacije [B,S]	United Nations
priznati	to admit, to confess (P)	Ujedinjeni Narodi [B,C]	United Nations
prva nagrada	first prize	upoznavati se, upoznajem se	to get to know (I)

Učitelj je bio zadovoljan što ih je samo šestero. Rekao je da se strani jezik bolje i lakše uči u manjim grupama.

- Najbolje je da se na prvom času dobro upoznamo. Nećemo danas ništa učiti, samo ćemo razgovarati - dodade učitelj.

Svi su učitelju kazali svoja imena, a zatim ih je on pitao zašto žele naučiti baš španjolski jezik. Odgovarali su jedno po jedno.

- Ja volim latinoameričku književnost, Marqueza, Cortasara, Llosu, a posebno Borgesa - rekao je Goran.

- Ja volim jezike. U gimnaziji sam učila njemački, sad završavam studij engleskog, živjela sam u Švedskoj pa znam i švedski. Sve su to germanski jezici. Željela bih naučiti i španjolski, a nekad kasnije možda i francuski te talijanski - rekla je Marina.

- Meni je malo nezgodno da priznam, ali ja želim naučiti španjolski zbog meksičkih televizijskih serija. Znam da se danas svi smiju sapunicama, a mene opet ništa tako ne opusti kad se vratim s posla - rekla je Azra.

- Ja navijam za "Real." Hoću da naučim španjolski da napišem pismo Raulu Gonzalesu i zamolim ga da mi pošalje svoj dres - rekao je Damir.

- Moja sestra se udala za španjolskog vojnika koji je bio u Sarajevu u sastavu snaga Ujedinjenih naroda. Njih dvoje sad žive u Valenciji. Sestra mi je trudna pa će ih uskoro biti troje. Nemam više braće ni sestara, samo nju, pa mi se čini da ćemo biti nekako bliže ako ja naučim španjolski - rekla je Sonja.

- Ja idem u Španjolsku na tri mjeseca. Dobio sam prvu nagradu u nagradnoj igri Coca-Cole i tri sedmice ću putovati po cijeloj Španjolskoj pa računam da bi bilo dobro da makar malo znam jezik - rekao je Vlado.

Vrijeme je brzo prošlo. Tek su se počeli upoznavati, a čas je već završio.

aerodrom [B,C,S]	airport	osnova [B,C,S]	foundation, basis
akcenat, akcenta [B,S]	accent	pogreška	mistake
akcent [B,C]	accent	poliglot [B,C]	polyglot
čitanje	reading	poliglota [B,S]	polyglot
dar, dara	gift	potrošiti, potrošim	to spend (P)
disciplina	discipline	pravilo	rule
dopuštati, dopuštam	to permit (I)	predvideti, predvidim	to foresee (P)
esej, eseja	essay	predvidjeti, predvidim	to foresee (P)
gramatički	grammatical	prekratak, prekratka	too short
greška	mistake, error	previse	too much, very much
ići nekome izvrsno	to go very well	priručnik	handbook
	for someone	promeniti, promenim	to change (P)
ionako	anyhow	promijeniti, promijenim	to change (P)
isticati, ističem	to emphasize (I)	proširivati, proširujem	expand (I)
izgovor	pronunciation	radovati, radujem	to gladden (I)
iznenađivati, iznenađujem	to surprise (I)	raspitati se, raspitam se	to ask around (P)
komentar, komentara	commentary	red vožnje	[transport] schedule
kompletan, kompletna	complete	redovan [B,C,S]	regular
koriti	to scold (I)	redovit [B,C]	regular
nabaviti	to acquire (P)	svakodnevan, svakodnevna	everyday *(adj.)*
najpre	first of all	šaliti se	to joke (I)
najprije	first of all	tvrditi, tvrdim	to claim (I)
napredak, napretka	progress	uman, umna	wise
naterati	to force (P)	uporaba [C]	use
natjerati	to force (P)	upotreba [B,C,S]	use
navesti, navedem	to induce (P)	uzalud	in vain
odnekud	from somewhere	vokabular, vokabulara	vocabulary
osnov [B,S]	foundation, basis	zračna luka [C]	airport

Bilo je predviđeno da tečaj traje osam nedjelja. Svi su najprije mislili da je to prekratko vrijeme da bi se naučile makar i osnove španjolskog jezika, no brzi ih je napredak natjerao da promijene mišljenje. Kompletna grupa je odlično učila, ali su ipak svi u nečemu bili najbolji. Marini je izvrsno išla gramatika. Učitelj je redovito isticao njezin veliki dar za gramatiku.

Marina, vidi se da ste poliglota, ali me prijatno iznenađuje to što ne dopuštate da vas neka gramatička pravila iz engleskog ili njemačkog u španjolskom navedu na pogreške - rekao je jedanput.

Goran je bio najbolji u pisanju kratkih eseja na španjolskom.

- Vidi se, Gorane, da ste već počeli čitati knjige na španjolskom jeziku i to me raduje. Mnogi tvrde da se jezik ne može naučiti bez razgovora, no šta je čitanje nego razgovor, i to razgovor sa najumnijim ljudima iz neke zemlje - kazao mu je učitelj.

Sonja je najbrže proširivala vokabular.

- Vi mora da rječnik kod kuće čitate - šalio se učitelj.

Damir je bio najvredniji u pisanju domaćih zadataka.

- To je ta školska disciplina - bio je učiteljev komentar.

Vlado je odnekud nabavio priručnik o španjolskom jeziku u svakodnevnoj upotrebi te je bez greške znao u restoranu naručiti ručak, u kafani tražiti pivo, na željezničkoj stanici ili na aerodromu se raspitati o redu vožnje. Ostalo ga nije previše ni zanimalo. Učitelj ga, međutim, nije korio.

- Vi, Vlado, najbolje znate koliko dobro želite znati jezik. Žao mi je samo što ste uzalud davali novce za tečaj. Sve ste ovo ionako mogli naučiti sami, a novce koje ste dali za tečaj mogli ste u Španjolskoj potrošiti na pivo i skupe večere - znao je reći učitelj.

Azra je imala savršen izgovor. Nakon nekoliko nedjelja učitelj joj je kazao da ima akcenat bolji i od njega samog, da bi gotovo mogla proći kao rođena Meksikanka.

- Vi ste moja mala *sinjorita* - često bi joj rekao učitelj.

RJEČNIK [J] REČNIK [E]

blag, blaga	mild, gentle	prelep	so lovely, exquisite
bližiti, bližim	to come near (I)	prelijep	so lovely, exquisite
dopadati se, dopadam se	to be likeable to (I)	prijateljstvo	friendship
dopasti se, dopadnem se	to be likeable to (P)	priznavati, priznajem	to confess, to admit (I)
doživljavati, doživljavam	to experience (I)	rastanak, rastanka	parting
družiti se, družim se	to socialize (I)	smeh	laughter
fudbaler, fudbalera [B,S]	soccer player	smijeh	laughter
glasan, glasna	loud	specifičan, specifična	specific
gle čuda	what d'ya know!	sresti, sretnem	to meet (P)
glumiti, glumim	to act [a role] (I)	sretati, srećem	to meet (I)
gužva	crowd	stvoriti, stvorim	to create (I)
igralište	playing field	svestan, svesna	aware, conscious
ikad	ever	svjestan, svjesna	aware, conscious
jedini	only	svojevrstan, svojevrsna	of a sort, special
kontakt	contact	šeretski	jocular, jokingly
matura	high sch. graduation	šetati, šetam	to stroll (I)
među + *Instr*	among	tip	type
međusoban, međusobna	mutual	tijek [C]	course, flow
mislim	I mean	tok, toka [B,S]	course, flow
nedostajati, nedostajem	to be lacking to (I)	u jedan glas	[spoken] as one
nevešt	unwitting, clumsy	u tijeku [C]	during
nevješt	unwitting, clumsy	u toku [B,S]	during
okaniti se, okanim se	to avoid, to shun (P)	umoriti se, umorim se	to get tired (I)
osvežiti se	to refresh oneself (P)	uoči + *Gen*	on the eve, before
osvježiti se	to refresh oneself (P)	uostalom	after all
ošišati se, ošišam se	to get a haircut (P)	uzviknuti, uzviknem	to shout out (P)
polaznica	attendee *(f)*	vezati, vežem	to bind (I)
polaznik	attendee *(m)*	zamišljen	absorbed in thought
povezan, povezana	connected	zapričati se, zapričam se	to start talking (P)
povezati, povežem	to connect (P)	zarumeniti se, zarumenim se	to blush (P)
prasnuti, prasnem	to burst out (P)	zezati	to tease (I)
praviti se	to pretend, to act (I)	ženska frizerka	women's hairdresser
predrasuda	prejudice		

Osma nedjelja učenja je u toku. Tečaj se bliži kraju. Svi se osjećaju slično gimnazijalcima pred maturu: kraj tečaja doživljavaju kao svojevrstan rastanak. Među svim polaznicima i polaznicama stvorilo se specifično prijateljstvo. Poslije časova se druže, odlaze jedni s drugima na kafu, šetaju zajedno. Ipak, njihovi međusobni odnosi su posve povezani s tečajem. Svako od njih ima svoje obaveze, prijateljstva, porodice, a tečaj je jedina stvar koja ih veže.

Dan uoči posljednjeg časa Goran je sreo Damira na košarkaškom igralištu. Pozdravili su se, odigrali nekoliko mečeva *jedan na jedan*, umorili se. Odlučiše se osvježiti u obližnjem kafiću. Tamo je, gle čuda, radio Vlado. Bilo je popodne, nije bilo gužve, zapravo su Goran i Damir bili jedini gosti. Sjeli su za šank i zapričali se s Vladom.

- Ovdje, dakle, radiš. Moraću češće navratiti. Nakon što tečaj završi da ostanemo u kontaktu - reče Goran Vladi.

- I meni je stvarno žao što tečaj završava. Od svih vas sad ću jedino sretati profesoricu Sonju, a nju najmanje volim vidjeti. Mislim, super je ona na španjolskom, ali je stroga na biologiji - reče Damir.

- Znam ja zbog koga će Goranu nedostajati tečaj - reče Vlado šeretski.

Goran se pravio nevješt.

- Ne razumijem - rekao je.

- Ne glumi, Gorane, bolje ti je ošišaj se - reče Vlado.

Damir prasnu u glasan smijeh.

- Vidiš da te zeza za Azru. Hajde, Gorane, svi znamo da ti se sviđa - rekao je Damir.

- Problem je samo što je ona ženska frizerka – nastavi se šaliti Vlado.

Goran se blago zarumeni i klimnu glavom.

- Sviđa mi se, priznajem, ali sam svjestan da nisam njezin tip - rekao je.

- Daj, Gorane, pa zar nikad nisi vidio kako te gleda? - uzviknuše u jedan glas Damir i Vlado.

- Ko je ikad vidio da se prelijepoj frizerki dopadne jedan običan student književnosti? Ona sanja o nekom fudbaleru ili glumcu - reče Goran.

- Gorane, okani se takvih misli i predrasuda. Uostalom, ne možeš znati dopadaš li joj se ako je ne pitaš - reče Vlado.

Goran je zamišljeno šutio.

RJEČNIK [J] REČNIK [E]

bilo šta [B,S]	anything at all	pokušavati, pokušavam	to attempt (I)
bilo što [C]	anything at all	politika	politics
cura	girl	poricati, poričem	to deny (I)
ćaskati	to chat (I)	premestiti	to shift position (P)
dečko	boy, guy	premjestiti	to shift position (P)
dosaditi, dosadim	to bore [someone] (P)	privlačiti, privlačim	to attract (P)
fotelj [B,S]	armchair	reditelj [B,S]	film, theater director
fotelja [B,C]	armchair	režiser, režisera [B,C]	film, theater director
frizerski	hairdressing *(adj.)*	rugati se, rugam se	to mock (I)
frizura	hairdo	sačekati	to wait a bit (P)
furati se, furam se	to go after (I)	salon, salona	salon (hairdresser)
glupača	stupid female	silan, silna	powerful
hauba	hood of hair-dryer	skoro	nearly, almost
isfenirati, isfeniram	to blow dry hair (P)	smeškati se	to grin (I)
izgled	appearance	smješkati se	to grin (I)
iznenađenje	surprise	strepiti, strepim	to live in fear (I)
lud, luda	crazy	sudariti se	to collide (P)
najaviti, najavim	to announce (P)	susretati, susrećem	to meet (I)
nek'	= neka	što	why (= zašto)
nešto	somewhat	tajanstveno	mysteriously
očit	obvious	ulaziti	to enter (I)
odavno	long ago	vikati, vičem	to shout (I)

U isto vrijeme dok su Goran, Vlado i Damir razgovarali u kafiću Azra, Sonja i Marina ćaskale su u frizerskom salonu. Sonja i Marina su se nešto ranije gotovo sudarile na vratima: Sonja je izlazila, a Marina ulazila.

- Kakvo iznenađenje! - rekla je Sonja.

- Super ti je frizura - rekla je Marina .

- Azra me je isfenirala, mora da i ti ideš kod nje, spomenula mi je da si i ti najavila da ćeš navratiti - rekla je Sonja.

- Da, čula sam i ranije da ona dobro radi, a po tvojoj frizuri vidim da je to zbilja tačno - rekla je Marina.

- Čuj, Azra mi kaže da joj za sat završava smjena. Ući ću s tobom i sačekati da i tebe isfenira pa možemo sve tri otići negdje na kafu - rekla je Sonja.

Uskoro je Marina bila pod haubom, Azra je stajala kraj nje, dok je Sonja sjedila na fotelji nedaleko od njih dvije.

- Kad završi tečaj ovdje ćemo se susretati nas tri - reče Sonja.

- Šteta što dečki neće biti tu - reče Azra.

- Sumnjam da će ti nedostajati Damir i Vlado - reče Marina smješkajući se.

Azra nije ni pokušavala bilo šta poricati.

- Zar je tako očito da mi se dopada? - pitala je.

- Hajde, Azra, pa nismo djeca. Jasno da je očito. Svako bi to primijetio osim glupog muškarca - reče Sonja.

- Problem je samo što ništa od toga neće biti - reče Azra.

- Što ne bi bilo? Pa ženo draga, jesi li se ti ikad pogledala u ogledalo?! Zašto prelijepe žene nikada nisu svjesne utiska koji ostavljaju? On je lud za tobom - skoro da je vikala Sonja.

- Nije stvar u izgledu. On misli da sam ja glupača. Njemu je glava puna tih nekih pisaca, pjesnika i režisera. Uvijek strepim da će mi se rugati zato što volim meksičke sapunice - reče Azra.

- Znaš šta, draga moja: pun je Filozofski fakultet cura što se furaju na iste stvari na koje se i on fura. Ako su ga takve ikad i privlačile odavno su mu dosadile. Ni ne gleda ih više. Vjeruj mi da znam - i ja na isti fakultet idem. Zaboravio bi on zbog tebe sve te silne knjige i premjestio bi se pred televizor - reče Marina.

- Ma neka njemu knjiga, dosadili su i meni muškarci što samo o politici i sportu pričaju, ali nek' mene ne pokušava promijeniti ako ste kojim slučajem u pravu kad kažete da mu se sviđam - reče Azra.

- Vidjećeš ti vrlo brzo da je to tako - reče Marina tajanstveno.

📖 VI ⊙36

RJEČNIK [J] REČNIK [E]

blesav	silly, idiotic	smejati se, smejem se [S]	to laugh (I)
diplomirati, diplomiram	to graduate (I/P)	smeten, smetena	confused
diskretan, diskretna	discreet	smijati se, smijem se [B,C]	to laugh (I)
eto	look!	spetljati se	to bumble (P)
hrabrost, hrabrosti (f)	courage	stvor, stvora	creature
iščekivanje	anticipation	šansa, Gpl. šansi	chance
iznenaditi, iznenadim	to surprise (P)	ubediti, ubedim	to convince (P)
jedva	barely	ubijediti, ubijedim	to convince (P)
nasmejati se, nasmejem se [S]	to laugh a lot (P)	urediti se, uredim se	to get dressed up (P)
		uručiti, uručim	to hand [to] (P)
nasmijati se, nasmijem se [B,C]	to laugh a lot (P)	uspešan, uspešna	successful
		uspješan, uspješna	successful
po običaju	as usual	zakazati, zakažem	to set up (P)
pojedinost, pojedinosti (f)	detail	zapanjiti, zapanjim	to astonish
popričati	to chat for a while (P)	zato	for that reason
potvrda	certificate	zaverenički	conspiratorial
potvrdan, potvrdna	affirmative	zavjerenički	conspiratorial
skupiti se	to gather [as group] (P)	završetak, završetka	end

Na dan kad je zakazan posljednji čas tečaja Goran i Marina sreli su se na fakultetu. Bilo je jutro, tečaj se po običaju trebao održati u pet popodne.

- Super je da smo se sreli, makar ćemo se vidjeti i u pet - rekao je Goran.

- I meni je drago što se vidimo. Trebam s tobom porazgovarati prije popodneva - rekla je Marina.

- I ja s tobom hoću da popričam - rekao je Goran.

- O čemu? - upita Marina.

- Znaš, ne znam kako to da kažem, budi diskretna, molim te, ali, eto, znaš, meni se sviđa Azra - rekao je Goran smeteno.

Marina se nasmijala.

- Nemam šansi kod nje. Znao sam. Mora da se zato smiješ - rekao je Goran.

- Ma ne, blesavi stvore, i ti se njoj sviđaš, ali je ona ubijeđena da nema šansi kod tebe - rekla je Marina još uvijek se smijući.

- Ozbiljna si? - pitao je Goran.

- Naravno da jesam - rekla je Marina.

Goran je čekao pet popodne u slatkom iščekivanju, a čim je završila razgovor s njim telefonom Marina je pozvala Azru.

- Budi spremna danas čuti izjavu ljubavi - rekla je Marina u slušalicu.
- Molim? - Azra je bila zapanjena.
- Sad sam pričala s Goranom. Sav se spetljao, ali mi je priznao da mu se sviđaš. Mislim da je skupio hrabrosti da to danas i tebi kaže - rekla je Marina.
- Jedva čekam pet - rekla je Azra.

U pet sati šestoro se mladih ljudi posljednji put skupilo na tečaju španjolskog jezika. Na kraju ovog časa učitelj im je trebao uručiti i potvrde o uspješno završenom tečaju. Jedna je pojedinost, međutim, iznenadila učitelja.

- Azra, ti si danas ljepša nego ikad, a i Goran se, vidim, uredio. Vas dvoje kao da ste diplomirali danas, a ne završili običan tečaj stranog jezika - rekao je učitelj.

Azra i Goran su se zarumenili, a njihovo četvero kolega su se zavjerenički osmjehnuli.

Po završetku posljednjeg časa Damir, Vlado, Sonja i Marina su se brzo razišli tako da su Azra i Goran ostali sami pred zgradom. Goran joj je na španjolskom kazao da je prelijepa i upitao je želi li biti njegova djevojka, a Azra je, također na španjolskom, odgovorila potvrdno.

📖 VII   ☉37

RJEČNIK [J] REČNIK [E]

čujan, čujna	audible	predložiti, predložim	to propose (P)
dogovor	agreement	prolaziti	to pass by (I)
fakat	indeed, truly	raja	crowd, people
filmski	pertaining to film	slučajnost,	coincidence
izaći na piće [B,C,S]	to go out for drinks (P)	slučajnosti (f)	
izići na piće [B,C]	to go out for drinks (P)	spominjati,	to mention (I)
ko tetreb zaljubiti	to fall madly in love (P)	spominjem	
ko tetrijeb zaljubiti	to fall madly in love (P)	tetreb	grouse (bird)
koja slučajnost!	what a coincidence!	tetrijeb	grouse (bird)
netremice	without blinking	viđati, viđam	to see frequently (I)
otkud	from where	venčati se	to get married (I/P)
ovuda	along this way	vjenčati se	to get married (I/P)
piće	drink; drinks	vozdra	hi [zdravo: syllables switched]
pogađati, pogađam	to guess (I)	zaljubiti se, zaljubim se	to fall in love (P)
pokvariti, pokvarim	to ruin, to spoil (P)	zbuniti, zbunim	to confuse (P)

Nedjelju dana nakon završetka tečaja Sonja je navratila u kafić u kojem je radio Vlado.

- Spominjao si da ovdje radiš, a kako sam prolazila ovuda svratih da te pozdravim - rekla je Sonja.
- Baš lijepo - rekao je Vlado.
- Viđaš li ikoga od raje s tečaja? - pitala je Sonja.
- Baš mi je jučer Goran bio - rekao je Vlado.
- Ja sam neki dan bila sa Azrom. Izgleda da im pravo dobro ide - rekla je Sonja.
- Itekako. Goran se ko tetrijeb zaljubio - rekao je Vlado.
- I Azra je luda za njim. Stvarno, prava filmska ljubav - rekla je Sonja.
- Ma k'o iz sapunice - rekao je Vlado.
- Čuj, Vlado, žurim. Ušla sam samo da te pozdravim. Odoh sad - rekla je Sonja.
- Hajde, vidimo se, dođi opet - rekao je Vlado.

Za nekoliko dana u kafić je ušla Marina.

- Hej, Vlado, kako si? - rekla je.

"Ljubav na španjolski način" – Muharem Bazdulj

- Super, baš mi je drago što si došla, ti mi jedina još nisi bila. Neki dan je svratila Sonja, Azra je juče s Goranom sjedila, a Damir mi je stara mušterija - rekao je Vlado.

- Ma baš sam došla da se s Azrom vidim. Dogovorile smo se da iziđemo na piće pa je ona predložila da se ovdje sretnemo.

Vrata kafića se otvoriše i uđe Marina.

- Ćao, ljudi, koja slučajnost - rekla je Marina.

Fakat jest. Ja čekam Azru, a ti ulaziš - rekla je Sonja.

- Pa ja se ovdje trebam sresti sa Azrom - rekla je zbunjeno Marina.

Vrata se otvoriše i pojavi se Damir.

- Vozdra, Vlado! Ćao, Marina! Dobar dan, profesorice! - rekao je.

- Da pogađam, imaš dogovor sa Azrom? - upita Vlado.

- Otkud ti to, Vlado? Trebam se s Goranom vidit, jutros me zvao - rekao je Damir.

Vrata su se ponovo otvorila, ali jedva čujno. Goran i Azra su zagrljeni ušli.

- Prijatelji, sve ćemo vam objasniti - rekao je Goran.

- Željeli smo vas skupiti sve zajedno, a ne pokvariti iznenađenje - rekla je Azra.

Marina, Sonja, Vlado i Damir su netremice gledali u njih.

- Vjenčaćemo se za desetak dana! Svi ste pozvani - rekoše Azra i Goran u jedan glas.

Vozdra/Zdravo. Colloquial usage in Bosnian and Croatian has often included a sort of slang, whose basic principle involves switching the syllables of words, in a manner similar to the switching of consonants in pig-Latin. Some other examples of popular Sarajevo words are: *žemka* for *kažem*, *đido* for *dođi*, and *žibje* for *bježi*. Though this was the most widespread in Zagreb in the 1960s, certain words have remained in usage ever since, such as *lima* for *mali*, *cobra* for *braco*, *Šomi* for *Mišo*, and *Njofra* for *Franjo*. The latter word has had a longer "shelf life" because the Croatian translation of the classic line in the Bugs Bunny cartoons, "What's up Doc?" was *Kaj te muči, Njofra?* (the word *kaj* meaning "what" in the kajkavian dialect of the greater Zagreb area). Belgrade also has an elaborate system of slang but this does not include switching the syllables of words.

"Ljubav na španjolski način" – Muharem Bazdulj

RJEČNIK [J] REČNIK [E]

aplauz	applause	otkada	ever since
bajka	fairy tale	paziti (na)	to watch out (for) (I)
bitan, bitna	essential	pljeskati, plješćem	to applaud (I)
čašičica	very small glass	poklanjati	to give [a gift] (I)
dvor, dvora	court	poljubiti, poljubim	to kiss (P)
formalan, formalna	formal	pošten	fair, honest, honorable
iskapiti, iskapim	to drink down (P)	princeza	princess
iskren	sincere	proderati se, proderem se	to shout out (P)
komunikacija	communication	proparati, proparam	to interrupt, to rip (P)
kraljević	prince	rađanje	birth
kucanje	tapping	savladati, savladam	to gain control over (I)
kum, kuma	best man	spojiti, spojim	to bond together (P)
kuma	maid/matron of honor	steći, steknem	to acquire, to get (P)
ljutiti se, ljutim se	to be angry (I)	stil	style
maloletan, maloletna	under age	svadba	wedding
maloljetan, maloljetna	under age	svedočiti, svedočim	to witness (P)
matičar	justice of peace	svjedočiti, svjedočim	to witness (P)
medeni mesec	honeymoon	tih	quiet
medeni mjesec	honeymoon	ustati, ustanem	to stand up (P)
mlada	bride	utihnuti, utihnem	to fall silent (P)
mladoženja	groom	zagrljaj	embrace
nadovezati, nadovežem	to add on (I)	zdravica	toast
narodna priča	folktale	živela! *or* živeo! *or* živeli!	long live!
oponašati, oponašam	to imitate (I)	živjela! *or* živio! *or* živjeli!	long live!

Svadba je bila mala i tiha. Došli su Goranovi i Azrini roditelji, kolege s tečaja i učitelj.

- Ovo je najljepša stvar koja mi se desila otkada vodim tečaj španjolskog jezika - rekao je.

Goranov kum je bio Vlado, a Azrina kuma Marina.

- Ti si, Damire, maloljetan, nemoj se ljutiti što nisi kum - rekao je Goran.

- Ti si, Sonja, profesorica u Damirovoj školi pa je bolje da na svadbi sjedite zajedno, da paziš na njega - rekla je Azra.

- Svi ste vi zapravo naši zajednički kumovi i kume. Volio bih da je moguće da to i formalno budete - rekao je Goran.

- Ja bih voljela da nam učitelj bude matičar - rekla je Azra.

- Ma pustite, ljudi, kao da je bitno ko su kum i kuma. Važno je da se vi volite - rekla je Sonja.

- Živjela profesorica! - proderao se Damir.

- Ovo je stvarno kao u bajci - rekla je Sonja.

- Da, bijahu jednom na španjolskom dvoru kraljević Goran i princeza Azra i gledahu jedno u drugo osam nedjelja, a kad priznaše što im srca osjećaju padoše u zagrljaj. - rekao je Damir oponašajući stil narodnih priča.

- I živjeli su dugo i sretno - nadoveza se Sonja.

Začu se zvuk kucanja čašičice o čašu. Svi utihnuše.

- Kumova zdravica - rekao je Damir.

Vlado je ustao, podigao čašu i počeo govoriti.

- Kad sam prije skoro tri mjeseca došao na prvi čas tečaja španjolskog jezika mislio sam da dolazim da bih naučio osnove komunikacije na španjolskom i tako se što bolje proveo na nagradnom putovanju. Nisam, iskreno govoreći, skoro ništa od jezika pošteno savladao, ali sam stekao petoro dragih prijatelja i svjedočio rađanju jedne velike ljubavi. Moje je nagradno putovanje za dvije osobe, a ja nemam s kim ići. Poklanjam ga Goranu i Azri. I jedno i drugo bolje govore španjolski od mene, španjolski ih je jezik spojio tako da mislim da bolji medeni mjesec od onog u Španjolskoj ne mogu ni zamisliti - rekao je.

Završetak zdravice proparao je aplauz.

- Šta plješćete, vas dvoje? Mladoženja poljubi mladu! - rekao je Vlado.

- Dobro, kume - reče Goran.

Goran i Azra se poljubiše.

- Našli su zajednički jezik - reče učitelj i iskapi čašu.

The notion of *kum* and *kuma* is an ancient one. The words are often translated as "godfather" and "godmother." However, they refer not only to the person present at the baptism of a baby (called the *kumče*), but also to the witnesses at a wedding. The *kum* and/or *kuma* are generally not blood relations, but through taking part in family ceremonies they become nearly as close as kin. The *kum* is expected to give the grandest wedding present (for decades this was the newlyweds' refrigerator) and often makes the wedding's most important toast, which is called the *kumova zdravica*.

357
"Ljubav na španjolski način" – Muharem Bazdulj

Lesson 10 (p. 142) introduces a set of verb conjugation types, whose purpose is to help those learning BCS remember conjugational forms more easily, and learn to predict with some degree of certainty the forms of verbs they will encounter in the future. These verb type numbers are used in subsequent grammar sections to explain the past tense (p. 143), aspect relationships (p. 146), and passive participles (p. 160), and are used in more detail in the companion volume, *BCS, A Grammar with Sociolinguistic Commentary*.

Following are all the verbs introduced in this book, sorted by conjugational types. Each type is represented by a model verb, for which both infinitive and 1st singular present are given. It is the relationship between these two forms which defines the type and allows one to predict for every verb in that group its present tense (and, once the rules in the above grammar sections are internalized, all other forms as well). The 1st singular present is given in those instances when its form is not unambiguously predictable from the model.

If the infinitive in the list is italicized, the accent will fall on a different syllable in the present tense. It will shift towards the beginning of the word in verbs of types 1-2, 6-9, 11 and 16; and it will shift towards the end of the word in types 10 and 13-15. Words without an accent mark also take part in these shifts: one only has to conceptualize one of these marks standing invisibly to the left of a word without an accent mark. For example:

	visible accent mark in both	visible accent mark only in one	
shift leftwards:	*govòriti, gòvorīm* (2)	*krènuti, krènēm* (7)	*dàvati, dàjēm* (9)
shift rightwards:	*dòvesti, dovèdēm* (13)	*prȁti, pèrēm* (10)	*trȅsti, trèsēm* (14)

Type 1: igrati, igram [accent shift in present does not take place in 3rd plural]

angažìrati se 16A3a
bìrati 💻A.VIII
bìvati 18A1a
crtati 10A4☙
čekati 5A2
čìtati 2A1, 6A2☙, 10A4☙
čȕvati 10A4
ćaskati 💻B.V
dati 5A2, 7A3☙, 10A2☙, 12A4☙
dešávati se 17A2b
diplomìrati 💻B.VI
dočarávati 17A3b
dòčekati 5A3
dòdati 💻B.II
dogàđati se 17A2b
dopàdati se 16A1a, 💻B.IV
dopùštati 💻B.III
dozìvati 19A3a
doživljávati 💻B.IV

funkcionìrati 19A1b
fùrati se 💻B.V
glèdati 2A2
grupìrati 19A2b
hòdati 7A2
identificìrati 19A2b
ìgrati 5C1, 15A1, 10A1☙, 💻A.I
ìgrati se 16A1b
imati 2A1, 2A1☙, 5A2
interesìrati 16A1a
isfenìrati 💻B.V
ispàdati 12A1
ispríčati 12☺, 16A1b
iščìtati 20.VIII
izglèdati 9A2, 💻A.III
izjàdati se 15A1
izmèšati 14A1

iznervìrati se 11☺
izučávati 19A3b
izvìjati 19A3a
jàvljati se 8A3
jècati 17A3a
kapati 14☺
klìmati 💻B.I
kòštati 💻A.IV
kuhati 6A4
kùpati se 16A3a
kuvati 6A4
mòrati 2A1
nàcrtati 18A1b
nàdati se 14A2
nadvládati 20.III
nagovárati 20.IV
namerávati [E]
  namjerávati [J] 11A3
napúštati 18A3
nàstavljati 💻A.III

nàterati [E]
nàtjerati [J] 💻B.III
navìjati 💻B.II
nazìvati 19A1b
nèmati 2A1, 4A1
nervìrati se 11☺
obasjávati 20.V
obèćati 11☺
òbigrati 19A3a
obnàvljati 16A3a
obràćati se 16A3a
òčuvati 19A3b
odévati [E]
  odijévati [J] 💻B.I
òdgledati 16A1a
odgovárati 5A1, 10A2☙
òdigrati se 9☺
odржávati 16A3b
okùpljati 14A4
operìrati 20.V
oponàšati 💻B.VIII
opráštati 20.VI

opravdati 20.II
organizirati 16A3b
osećati [E]
 osjećati [J] 10A3,
 10A2✿
osećati se [E]
 osjećati se [J]
 10A3
osigurati 16A1b
ostavljati 17A1a,
 📖A.VI
ošišati se 📖B.IV
otvarati 19A3b
padati 10A2,
 10A2✿
pevati [E]
 pjevati [J]
 5C1, 19A3b
pitati 3A1
planirati 16A1b
plivati 18A1a
počešljati 9A2
podcrtati 18A1b
poducavati 18A3
pogađati 📖B.VII
pogledati 20.V
 📖A.IV
pogledati 2A4
pogledati se 9A2
pohađati 16A2b,
 📖B.I
poklanjati 📖B.VIII
pokušavati 📖B.V
ponašati se 18A2b
porazgovarati
 16A2b
poredati 14A1
poređati 14A1
posmatrati 14☺
popričati 📖B.VI

postavljati 11☺,
 16A1a
pozdravljati 6A3
poznati 10A2,
 10A2✿
predati 16A2a
predstavljati
 19A2b
pregledati 11A1✿
prepričati 15A2
prespavati 14A2
pretvarati 14A2
pretvarati se 15A1
pričati 12A2
prijati 13A1
primati 18A3
prišivati 📖A.VIII
priznati 📖B.II
pročitati 10A2
prodati 20.II
prokockati 7A2
prolepšati se [E]
 proljepšati se [J]
 14A2
promatrati 14☺
proparati 📖B.VIII
prošetati 20.V
puštati 10A2✿
računati 📖B.II
raspitati se 📖B.III
razgovarati 12A2
razmišljati 8A3
razočarati se 20.V
rešavati [E]
 rješavati [J] 12☺
rezervirati 16A1a
rugati se 📖B.V
sačekati 📖B.V
sakupljati 19A3b
sanjati 📖A.I
savladati 📖B.VIII

saznati 14A2
sećati se [E]
 sjećati se [J]
 11A3
shvaćati 20.V
sipati 13A1
skrivati 18A1a
skuhati 14A1
skupljati 19A3b,
 📖A.I
skuvati 14A1
slikati 📖A.VI
slušati 6A2, 7A3
smatrati 11A1
smeškati se [E]
 smješkati se [J]
 📖B.V
smetati 11A4
snivati 18A1a
spajati 18A3
spavati 7A3, 📖A.I
spetljati se 📖B.VI
spevati [E]
 spjevati [J]
 19A3b
spoznati 20.III
spremati 7A1
spuštati 📖A.VII
sročiti 16A1a
studirati 6A2
sumnjati 10A3
sviđati se 6A4,
 10A2✿
svirati 18A3
svršavati 17A2a
šetati 📖B.IV
štampati 20.V
telefonirati 📖A.VII
tiskati 20.V
trebati 11A2
udati se 📖B.II

ugledati 20.VIII
umirati 18A1b
umivati se 9A2
umotati 📖A.IV
uparkirati 12A2
upitati 📖B.I
upotrebljavati
 17A1b
upoznati 16A1a
upoznati se 16A1a,
 📖B.I
uspevati [E]
 uspijevati [J]
 18A3
uveravati [E]
 uvjeravati [J]
 16A3b
uzimati 5A1
uživati 12A2
valjati 12A3
večerati 10A1
venčati se [E]
 vjenčati se [J]
 📖B.VII
vežbati [E]
 vježbati [J]
 2A1
viđati 📖B.VII
vraćati se 14A2
zaključati 20.VIII
zakukati 19A3a
zamirati 16A3b
zanimati 16A2a
zanimati se 16A2b
zapitati 20.VI
zapričati se 📖B.IV
završavati se 6A2
zezati 📖B.IV
znati 4A1

Type 2: staviti, stavim

baciti 16A1a
baviti se 11A3
besediti [E]
 besjediti [J]
 19A3a
bližiti 📖B.IV
boraviti 16A2a
častiti 15A1
čestitati 12A3
činiti se 6A4
čuditi se 16A1b

deliti [E]
 dijeliti [J]
 9A3
dogoditi se 11☺,
 12A4
dogovoriti se
 11A2
dohvatiti 19A3a
dolaziti 5A2
dopustiti 16A2a
dosaditi 📖B.V

doseliti se 16A3a
dozvoliti 16A3b
družiti se 📖B.IV
glumiti 📖B.IV
govoriti 6A4
gubiti 9A3
hiniti 20.V
iskapiti 📖B.VIII
iskoristiti 15A1
isplatiti se 14A2
istražiti 16A2b

izgovoriti 19A2a
izgubiti 10A2
izlaziti 20.VI
izmisliti 20.VIII
iznajmiti 9A3
iznenaditi 20.IV,
 📖B.VI
izraziti 19A1b
izvoditi 15A1
izvršiti 12A4
javiti se 8A3

360
Verb Types

kazniti 18A3
koristiti 17A4
koriti 📖B.III
kršiti 19A2b
kružiti 6A1
kupiti 2A3
ličiti 20.VI, 📖A.III
lupiti se 📖A.V
ljutiti se 📖B.VIII
misliti 3A1,
  10A4✿, 📖B.IV
množiti 12A1
moliti 17A3a
moriti 15A1
motriti 18A1a
nabaviti 16A1a,
  📖B.III
nagovestiti [E]
  nagovijestiti [J]
  16A3b
nagovoriti 20.VI
najaviti 📖B.V
naježiti se 20.VIII
nakititi 19A3a
nalaziti se 6A1
napraviti 20.III
napuniti 12A3
napustiti 15A1
naručiti 10A1
nasloniti 20.III
nastaviti 14A2
naučiti 10A2,
  10A2✿, 10A3
navratiti 12A2
nositi 5C1, 10A4✿
obavestiti [E]
  obavijestiti [J]
  14A3
obezbediti [E]
  obezbijediti [J]
  16A1b
obilaziti 16A3a
objasniti 10A3,
  10A4✿
objaviti 17A4,
  📖B.I
obnoviti 15A1
obraditi 13A3
obratiti se 16A2a
oceniti [E]
  ocijeniti [J]
  10A3
odgojiti 20.VI
odgovoriti 10A4✿,
  16A2a
odlaziti 10A2

odlučiti 12A3
odobriti 16A1a
odrediti 18A1b
odseliti se 18A3
odvažiti se 16A3a
odvratiti 20.VII
okaniti se 📖B.IV
okupiti se 18A3
oporaviti se 20.VI
opredeliti [E]
  opredijeliti [J]
  16A3b
opteretiti 16A3a
optužiti 20.VII
opustiti 📖B.II
osetiti [E]
  osjetiti [J]
  16A1b
osetiti se [E]
  osjetiti se [J]
  10A2✿
osigurati 16A2a
ostaviti 14A1
osvežiti se [E]
  osvježiti se [J]
  📖B.IV
othraniti 20.IV
otpustiti 20.I
otvoriti 12A2
ozariti 18A2a
označiti 17A1b
oženiti 20.II
paziti 📖B.VIII
plašiti se 11☺
platiti 2A4
počistiti 15A1
podeliti [E]
  podijeliti [J] 9A3
pohvaliti se 15A1
pojaviti se 13A3
pokloniti 12A2
pokvariti 📖B.VII
položiti 6A2,
  10A2✿
poljubiti 📖B.VIII
poništiti 13A4
poniziti 19A2a
ponuditi 13A1
popraviti 13A2
popušiti 20.V
posetiti [E]
  posjetiti [J]
  16A2a
poslužiti 13A1
postaviti 11A1✿,
  15A2

posuditi 16A1a
posvetiti 16A2a
posvetiti se 18A3
potiti 18A2a
potrošiti 20.IV,
  📖B.III
potruditi se 16A1a
pozdraviti 📖A.VII
pozdraviti se 12A2
požuriti 7A3
pratiti 12A2
praviti se 20.V,
  📖B.IV
predložiti 20.IV,
  📖B.VII
predstaviti 19A3b
premestiti [E]
  premjestiti [J]
  📖B.V
prenoćiti 19A1a
prenositi 10A4✿,
  19A3b
preporučiti 13A1
preraditi 15A2
preseliti se 18A3
preuraniti 16A2a
prevaliti 20.I
prevariti 15A1
prevoditi 10A4✿,
  18A3
prevoziti 10A4✿
pribaviti 16A2a
približiti se 16A3b
prihvatiti 16A1a
prijaviti 14A3
priključiti se 16A2b
prikupiti 19A3b
primetiti [E]
  primijetiti [J]
  14A4
pripremiti 13A3
privlačiti 📖B.V
probuditi 9A2
proglasiti 12A4
progoniti 18A3
progovoriti 20.IV
prolaziti 📖B.VII
promeniti [E]
  promijeniti [J]
  20.II, 📖B.III
propustiti 12A3
proraditi 15A1
proslaviti 18A3
pružiti 12A2
pustiti 7A3, 10A2✿
pušiti 12A2

raditi 2A1,
  12A3✿, 13A1✿
raniti 20.V
rashladiti se 16A3b
rastužiti se 15A1
raširiti 16A1b
razbuditi se 10A4
razmisliti 10A3
razvedriti se 14A2
razveseliti 15A1
rešiti [E]
  riješiti [J]
  11A1
roditi se 10☺,14A3
rositi 14☺
sastaviti 19A3b
seliti se 18A3
setiti se [E]
  sjetiti se [J]
  12A3
shvatiti 14A4
sjediniti 12A4
sjediti 6A3,
  11A4✿
skloniti 13A2
skloniti se 14A2
skočiti 19A3a
skupiti se 20.V
skupiti se 📖B.VI
slaviti 12A3
sličiti 20.VI, 📖A.III
slutiti 18A1a
smestiti [E]
  smjestiti [J]
  17A3b
smešiti se [E]
  smiješiti se [J]
  📖A.III
smisliti 16A1a
snimiti 19A3b
spojiti 📖B.VIII
spremiti 7A1
spustiti 13A2
staviti 6A3,10A1✿
stišati se 14A4
strepiti 📖B.V
stupiti 16A2a
stvoriti 17A4,
  📖B.IV
sudariti se 📖B.V
suditi 20.VI
sukobiti se 18A3
svedočiti [E]
  svjedočiti [J]
  📖B.VIII

svrátiti 12A4☼,
   14A2
svršiti 15A1
šaliti se 📖B.III
točiti 13A1
tražiti 3A1
tvrditi 📖B.III
ubéditi [E]
  ubijéditi [J]
   📖B.VI
učiniti 19A3a
učiniti se 16A2a
učiti 2A1, 2A1☼,
   10A2☼, 10A4☼
učlaniti se 16A2b
ugasiti 20.V
ugostiti 16A1b
uhvatiti 14A1
uključiti 10A2☼,
   16A1b

ulaziti 📖B.V
umoriti se 📖B.IV
unajmiti 9A3,
   16A2b
unesrećiti 19A2a
unositi 15A2
upaziti 19A3a
uporediti 11A2
uputiti 16A2a
uraditi 15A2
uraniti 19A3a
urediti 12A1
urediti se 📖B.VI
uručiti 📖B.VI
usavršiti 16A3a
uspaničiti se 20.VII
usporediti 11A2
utvrditi 14A3
uvlačiti 20.VII
uvrediti [E]

uvrijediti [J]
   19A2a
veseliti se 20.III
voditi 5C1,
   10A4☼, 18A3
voziti 7A2, 10A4☼
vratiti se 9A2
zaboraviti 10A4,
   📖A.II
zadiviti se 15A1
zagrabiti 14A1
zagrliti 16A1b
zahvaliti se 20.III
zakasniti 14A4
zaključiti 10A3
zalupiti 17A1a
zaljubiti se 📖B.VII
zameriti se [E]
  zamjeriti se [J]
   18A3

zamisliti 18A1b
zamoliti 13A1
zaokružiti
   17A1b
zapamtiti 16A1b
zapanjiti 20.IV,
   📖B.VI
zarumeniti se
   📖B.IV
zasladiti 14A1
zatvoriti 12A2
završiti 11A1
zbuniti 📖B.VII
značiti 6A2
zvoniti 📖A.V
žaliti 📖A.III
žariti 18A2a
žuriti se 7A2

Type 3: videti [E] vidjeti [J], vidim

boleti [E]
  boljeti [J]
   10A4
crneti se [E]
  crnjeti se [J]
   18A1a
izvideti [E]
  izvidjeti [J]
   2A2, 10A1☼,
   11A1☼, 19A3a
lebdeti [E]
  lebdjeti [J]
   20.II
leteti [E]
  letjeti [J]
   15A1

nadživeti [E]
  nadživjeti [J]
   18A3
oboleti [E]
  oboljeti [J]
   18A3
odleteti [E]
  odletjeti [J]
   5A1
odživeti [E]
  odživjeti [J]
   20.II
poleteti [E]
  poletjeti [J]
   15A1
pošutjeti 20.IV

poželeti [E]
  poželjeti [J]
   15A1
predvideti [E]
  predvidjeti [J]
   📖B.III
preživeti [E]
  preživjeti [J]
   14A3
sedeti 6A3,
   11A4☼
strepeti
svideti se [E]
  svidjeti se [J]
   10A2☼

šutjeti 📖A.III
videti [E]
  vidjeti [J]
   2A2, 10A1☼,
   11A1☼
voleti [E]
  voljeti [J]
   2A3, 3A3
zašutjeti 20.V
želeti [E]
  željeti [J]
   2A1
živeti [E]
  živjeti [J]
   5A3

Type 4: držati, držim

bojati se 7A2
ćutati 17A3a,
   📖A.III
držati 10A1☼,
   12A1, 📖A.VII
izdržati 20.V

ležati 11A4,
   11A4☼
održati 11A1☼
pljuštati 14☺
poćutati 20.IV
prestajati 14☺

sadržati 19A1b
sastojati se 4☝
stajati (stojim) 6A1,
   11A4☼, 12A4☼

trčati 📖A.V
zaćutati 20.V
zviždati 5C1

Type 5: pisati, pišem [stem-final consonant "softens" before present tense endings according to the chart on p. 163; the consonants -r- and -j- do not change.]

brisati 10A3,
📖A.VI
cvrkutati 16A1b
dizati 14A1
dopirati 20.I
drhtati (dršćem)
17A3a
funkcionisati
19A1b
grupisati 19A2b
iskati (ištem)
17A3a
isticati 📖B.III
izbrisati 10A3
izricati
19A2a
izvikati se 20.VII
kazati 5A1
kretati 9A2
lagati 19A2a
nadovezati
📖B.VIII
napisati 10A2,
11A1⚙

nasmejati se 20.VI,
📖B.VI
nasmijati se 20.VI,
📖B.VI
nedostajati 18A3,
📖B.IV
nestajati 19A1a
odletati [E]
odlijetati [J]
📖A.III
operisati 20.V
opisati 10A3
ostajati 10A2⚙,
📖A.III
oticati 7☺
otjecati 7☺
pisati 2A1, 2A1⚙,
10A1⚙, 10A4⚙
plakati 18A2a
plesati 15A1
pljeskati (plješćem)
📖B.VIII
počinjati 6A2
podizati 📖A.VI

pokazati 20.VI
polagati 6A2,
10A2⚙
pomagati 10A4
poricati 📖B.V
potpisati 20.V
povezati
📖B.IV
prepisati 20.IV
prestajati 📖A.VI,
14☺
proderati se
📖B.VIII
proticati 7☺
protjecati 7☺
rastajati se 14A2
rezervisati 16A1a
slagati 20.II,
📖A.VI
slagati se 10A4
slegati [E]
slijegati [J]
9☺

smejati se 20.III,
📖B.VI
smijati se 20.III,
📖B.VI
spominjati
📖B.VII
sretati 📖B.IV
stizati 14A4
susretati 📖B.V
šaptati 18A1a
ticati se 5A2
trajati 6A2
upisati 20.VIII
ustajati 📖A.V
uticati 17A3b
utjecati 17A3b
vezati 📖B.IV
vikati 20.VII,
📖B.V
zakazati 📖B.VI
zamirisati 20.III
zderati 19A2a

Type 6: piti, pijem

čuti 5C1
čuti se 8A3
dobiti 11A2
doliti 14A1
liti 14☺

naliti 11A1⚙
odliti 14A1
otkriti 20.VI
piti 4A4⚙, 5A1,
10A1⚙

popiti 5A4,
11A1⚙
preliti 14A1
razotkriti 17A3b
razotkriti se 20.IV

sakriti 20.VI
ubiti 19A3a, 📖B.I
umiti se 9A2
začuti se 19A3a

Type 7: krenuti, krenem [some verbs of this type have alternate infinitives of type 15b]

brinuti 13A3,
📖A.III
dignuti [or dići]
14A1
dodirnuti 20.II
dosegnuti 20.III
granuti 14A2
kimnuti 20.V
krenuti 9A2,
10A1⚙, 📖A.V
mahnuti 20.VIII
odmahnuti 20.VI
okrenuti 20.VIII

opsednuti
opsjednuti
11A1⚙
osmehnuti [E]
osmjehnuti [J]
📖B.I
počinuti 19A1b
podignuti [or
podići] 15A1
poginuti 14A3
pokrenuti 16A2a
pomenuti 16A1b

postignuti [or
postići] 13☺
povrnuti 19A3a
prasnuti 📖B.IV
prekinuti 20.II
primaknuti 14A1
priviknuti se 20.II
protrnuti 20.VIII
sagnuti se 20.VIII
skoknuti 16A1a
skrenuti 13A4
slegnuti [or sleći]
14A1

spomenuti 16A1b
srknuti 14A1
stignuti [or stići]
9A4, 10☺, 📖B.I
trnuti 17A3a
umetnuti 20.V
usnuti 20.V
utihnuti 📖B.VIII
utonuti 18A1a
uzviknuti 📖B.IV
vinuti se 15A1
zabrinuti 20.VIII

Mixture of type 5 (inf) and type 7 (pres): stati, stanem

nestati 14A4   postati 18A3   stati 11A4,   ustati 📖B.VIII
ostati 9A2, 10A2⚙   prestati 14☺   11A4⚙, 15A2

Type 8a: kupovati, kupujem

angažovati se   identifikovati   posedovati [E]   savetovati se [E]
16A3a   19A2b   posjedovati [J]   savjetovati se [J]
darovati   interesovati 16A1a   19A2b   11A4
20.VIII   *kupovati* 2A3,   poštovati 12A3   *stanovati* 9A1
delovati [E]   2A3⚙, 7A3⚙,   proputovati 16A2a   sudjelovati 16A1a
djelovati [J]   10A1⚙   *putovati* 4🌐   tugovati 15A1
20.VIII   obradovati 16A1b   radovati 📖B.III   učestvovati 16A1a
doručkovati 7A1   organizovati   radovati se 14A4   verovati [E]
gostovati   11A1⚙, 16A3b   razlikovati 18A2b   vjerovati [J]
16A2a   *otputovati* 16A3b   10A4

Type 8b: kazivati, kazujem

ispitivati 20.VII   *iznenađivati* 📖B.III   *optuživati* 20.II   *uključivati* 4🌐,
istraživati 15A2   *kazivati* 10A1⚙   *pokazivati* 📖A.IV   10A2⚙
izjednačivati 17A2a   *objavljivati* 17A4   *povezivati* 16A1b   *umirivati* 20.I
izmenjivati [E]   *ocenjivati* [E]   *prebacivati* 20.VII   *unajmljivati* 16A2b
izmjenjivati [J]   *ocjenjivati* [J]   *proširivati* 📖B.III   *zahvaljivati* 16A2a
20.II   10A3   *raspitivati se* 20.III   *zarađivati* 11A3
iznajmljivati 16A2b   *očekivati* 14A4   *ukazivati* 20.VIII

Type 9: poznavati, poznajem

davati 10A2⚙   *poznavati* 3A1,   *prepoznavati* 20.III   *upoznavati* 📖B.II
dodavati 📖A.III   3A1⚙, 10A1⚙,   *priznavati* 📖B.IV
izdavati 16A2a   10A2⚙   *prodavati* 9☺
odavati 20.I   *predavati* 16A3a   *saznavati* 19A3b

Type 10: brati, berem

brati 10A1⚙,   *oprati* 9A2   samleti [E] (sameljem)
📖A.I   poslati (pošaljem) 📖B.II   samljeti [J] (sameljem)
mleti [E] (meljem)   *pozvati* (pozovem) 13A1   14A1
mljeti [J] (meljem)   *prati* 9A2   slati (šaljem) 6A3
14A1   *prozvati* (prozovem) 📖B.I   *zvati se* (zovem se) 1A1,
nazvati (nazovem)   *sabrati* 11A1⚙, 20.V   1A1⚙
12A4⚙, 17C1

Type 11: uzeti, uzmem

izuzeti 20.VI
mreti [E] (mrem)
 mrijeti [J] (mrem)
  18A1a
nazreti (nazrem) 19A2a
oteti se 20.II
početi (počnem) 13A2
poduzeti 16A1a

popeti se (popnem se) 14A1
poumreti [E] (poumrem)
 poumrijeti [J] (poumrem)
  17A2a
preduzeti 16A1a
prodreti [E] (prodrem)
 prodrijeti [J] (prodrem)
  20.I

raspeti (raspnem) 17A3a
umreti [E] (umrem)
 umrijeti [J] (umrem)
  17A1a
uzeti 4A4⚙, 5A2, 7A3⚙,
  10A1⚙
započeti (započnem) 20.IV
zauzeti 11A1⚙

Type 12: smeti, smem [E] smjeti, smijem [J]

dospeti [E]
 dospjeti [J]
  16A1a
izumeti [E]
 izumjeti [J]
  15A1

razumeti [E]
 razumjeti [J]
  7A3
smeti [E]
 smjeti [J]
  10A1⚙, 12A3

uspeti [E]
 uspjeti [J]
  10A2

Type 13: jesti, jedem [some verbs of this type have the present tense of type 15b]

dopasti se (dopadnem se)
 📖B.IV
dovesti 20.III
jesti 4A4⚙, 5A1,
  10A1⚙, 10A2⚙
napasti (napadnem) 12A4
navesti 20.VIII, 📖B.III

odsesti (odsednem) 16A1a
odsjesti (odsjednem) 16A1a
odvesti 10A4⚙
pasti (padnem) 10A1⚙,
  10A2, 10A2⚙
pojesti 5A4, 10A2⚙,
  11A1⚙

prevesti 10A4⚙
provesti 16A2a, 16A3a
provesti se 9A2
sesti (sednem) 11A4,
  11A4⚙
sjesti (sjednem) 11A4,
  11A4⚙

sprovesti 16A1a
sresti (sretnem)
 📖B.IV

Type 14: tresti, tresem

dovesti (dovezem) 10A1⚙,
  10A4

odvesti (odvezem) 10A4,
  10A4⚙, 11A1⚙, 13A4
prerasti (prerastem) 18A3

prevesti (prevezem) 10A4⚙
tresti 10A1⚙

Mixture of type 12 (inf [long]), and type 14 (pres): doneti [E] donijeti [J], donesem

doneti [E]
 donijeti [J]
  10A1⚙, 11A1⚙,
  13A2
izneti [E]
 iznijeti [J]
  7A3, 7A3⚙,
  19A3a

odneti [E]
 odnijeti [J]
  7A3, 7A3⚙
poneti [E]
 ponijeti [J]
  16A1a

preneti [E]
 prenijeti [J]
  10A4⚙
prineti [E]
 prinijeti [J]
  20.V

pridoneti [E]
 pridonijeti [J]
  16A2b

Type 15a: teći, tečem, teku [some verbs of this type have present tense of type 15b]

mòći [mògu, možeš] 2A4,
 2A4⚙, 10A1⚙
ìzreći (ìzreknēm) 19A2b
ìzvući 20.V
ìzvući se 11A1⚙, 20.II
òbući 📖A.VIII

pòdstaći (pòdstaknēm)
 19A3b
pòdvući 18A1b
rèći (rèknēm [*rarely used*])
 7A3, 12A4⚙

stèći (stèknēm) 📖B.VIII
tèći 3⊕, 10A1⚙
tùći 8☺
ùvući 20.VIII

Type 15b: pomoći, pomognem [some verbs of this type have alternate infinitives of type 7]

dìći [*or* dìgnuti] 14A1
lèći 11A4⚙

pòbeći [E]
 pòbjeći [J]
  18A3

pòdići [*or* pòdignuti] 15A1
pomòći 10A1⚙, 10A4

pòstići [*or* pòstignuti] 13☺
slèći se [*or* slègnuti se] 14A1
stìći [*or* stìgnuti] 9A4, 10☺, 📖B.I

Type 16: doći, dođem

dòći 5A2, 7A3⚙, 10A1⚙
ìći 5A1, 📖A.I
ìzaći 10A1
ìzići 10A1
nàći 10☺, 12A2
nàći se 10A1
nàići 14A2

òbići 20.IV
òtići (òdēm) 10A2
pòći 9A4
prèći [E]
 prijèći [J]
  19A1a
prìći 20.IV, 📖B.I

pròći 13A4
prònaći 11A1⚙, 14A3, 15A1
ràzići se 14A2
sìći 13A4
ùći 12A2, 12A4⚙
zàći 18A1b

Irregular

biti 1A1, 1A1⚙, 1A4⚙, 6A2⚙, 12A4⚙
 budēm 5A3, 5A3⚙

hteti [E] htjeti [J] 5A2, 5A2⚙, 9A1⚙, 9A2⚙, 10A1

1A1

WHAT IS YOUR NAME?

1. Hi!
2. Hi. Who are you?
1. I am a student and my name is [I am called] ....
   And what is your name?
2. My name is ....

1A2

WHAT IS THIS?

1. What is this?
2. That is a pencil.
1. Is it yours?
2. Yes, it is mine.
1. No, no! It is not yours! It is hers!

1. What is this?
2. That is a textbook.
1. Is it yours?
2. Yes, it is mine.
1. No, no! It is not yours! It is hers!

1. What is this?
2. That is a letter.
1. Is it yours?
2. Yes, it is mine.
1. No! It is not yours! It is mine!

1A3

#1 and #2 are students who run into a couple, George and Mary, walking with another student, #3, and they strike up a conversation while on a stroll through a park. George and Mary have a dog, #2 is holding a cat.

HELLO!

1. Hello! [Good day!]
2. Hello! [*speaking to #1*] How sweet this dog is!
1. It is their dog [points to Mary and George], not mine. Is that your cat?
2. Yes, it's mine.
1. What is its name?
2. The cat is called Maca. And what is that sweet dog called?
3. It's called Freddy.
2. And what is your name?
1. My name is .... and what are yours?
2. Our names are .... and .... And you, what is your name?
George: My name is George, this is my wife Mary, and Freddy is ours.

My question is: How does one say George in Croatian and Serbian?
1. One says Juraj in Croatian.
2. And one says Đorđe in Serbian.
Mary: And in Bosnian?
3. Either Juraj or Đorđe.

1A4

DOG AND CAT

1. Are you a student?
2. Yes, I am a student. Are you a [female] student?
1. I am.
3. I am a [female] student, too. And George and Mary, who are they?
2. George is a professor, and Mary is a professor.
3. And their dog?
2. Their dog is not a professor. A dog isn't a person! But he is our friend.
3. Are the dog and the cat friends?
2. They are and they aren't.
1. Is George French?
2. No, he is an Englishman.
1. And what is Mary?
2. She is an Englishwoman.

2A1

STUDYING TOGETHER

1. Mehmed! (*or* Tomislav! *or* Nada!)
2. Yes?
1. Do you have the notebook?
2. I have it but I don't have the dictionary. Have you got it?
1. I have the dictionary but I don't have the notebook. Do you want us to study together tomorrow?
2. Tomorrow? On Thursday? Sorry, not on Thursday, but on Friday.
1. Fine! We'll see each other on Friday.

2A2

WHOM DO YOU SEE?

1. That man is really tall!
2. Excuse me? Who do you see?
1. I see that tall man.
2. Ah, him! He certainly is tall!

2A3

I AM BUYING A DOG

1. Hey, what are you up to?
2. I am buying a dog for my brother.
1. This yellow one here?
2. No, that red one there.
1. Why don't you want to buy the yellow dog?

2. Because my brother likes the color red!
1. Sure, the red one is OK, too!

2A4

THE STATIONERY STORE

1. Hello!
2. Hello! Can I help you?
1. Please, do you have the new German textbook?
2. We have it. Do you want it?
1. Thanks, definitely, and I want to buy a pencil.
2. Do you want this yellow one? It writes nicely.
1. Excellent! And can I buy an alphabetical notebook for a vocabulary list here?
2. We have one. Would you like to take a look at it? Here.
1. Thank you! That is all. May I pay?
2. Certainly. Here is the cash register.
1. Good-bye.
2. Good-bye!

3A1

HOW ARE YOU?

1. .... ?
2. Yes?
1. How are you?
2. Fine, and you?
1. Excellent.
2. Who are those people?
1. Those ones over there? They are our friends. Their names are Jasmin and Jasna [*or* Darko and Anka, *or* Mirko and Jovan].
2. No. I am not thinking of Jasmin and Jasna [*or* Darko and Anka, *or* Mirko and Jovan]. I know them. Who are those men over there?
1. Ah! I don't know them. Why do you ask?
2. I am asking because I am looking for a person.
1. What is his name?
2. His name is Emir Begović [*or* Ivan Božić *or* Milorad Jovanović]
1. I know Emir Begović [*or* Ivan Božić *or* Milorad Jovanović]. He isn't here today but I have his number.
2. Great! Thanks!
1. You're welcome.

3A2

GOOD NIGHT!

1. Good evening. What are you doing?
2. I'm looking out the window. What a marvelous night!
1. It is indeed. The right moment for a great love!
2. I am not thinking of love, but of poetry.
1. Of poetry? Why not of love?
2. Because I love words, and not people.
1. Good night then!

3A3

WHICH DO YOU PREFER?

1. Which do you prefer? Dogs or cats?
2. I prefer dogs. I am allergic to cats.
1. I like cats, but only some.
2. What kind of cats? Large or small?
1. I like large cats, and you? What sort of dogs do you like?
2. I like only small dogs.

3A4

WHOSE PENCILS ARE THESE?

1. Whose pencils are these?
2. Mine.
1. Which are yours?
2. All are mine.
1. The long and the short ones? Surely these long ones are yours, and the short ones are mine.
2. No. They are all mine.

4A1

WHERE ARE YOU FROM?

1. Where are your parents from?
2. My parents are from .... And yours?
1. My parents are from .... And are you also from .... ?
2. I am also from .... And you? Are you from .... as your parents are?
1. I am not. I am from ....
2. And that young woman there? Where are her parents from?
1. Her parents are from ....
2. And that young man? Where are his parents from?
1. His parents are from ....

4A2

WHO HAS OUR BOOKS?

1. Hasan [or Ante or Mirko], where is my book?
2. I've got it.
1. And Zlatan's [or Branko's or Slobodan's] book?
2. I've got his book, too.
1. And Mirjana's book?
2. I even have her book
1. Why do you have all our books?
2. Because I'm reading them.
1. And who has the book that belongs to our friend Hana [or Dijana or Grozdana]?
2. Whose?
1. Hana's [or Dijana's or Grozdana's]!
2. Ah, that book's not here. I don't know who's got it.
1. So, you do have three books, but you don't have one book?
2. That's right!

4A3

SOMETHING ELSE ...

1. .... ! Are you thirsty? Would you like a glass of juice?
2. No, thanks, I have orange juice, but I would like some cold water without ice.
1. Here's a full glass of cold water. What else would you like?
2. Two cookies, please.
1. I have these two nice cookies. Will that do?
2. That's fine, thanks!
1. Something else?
2. Thanks, nothing else.

4A4

I'M LOOKING FOR SOME THINGS

1. .... ! I am looking for some things.
2. What things?
1. First, the dictionary. Have you got it?
2. Which dictionary? From English into Bosnian [or Croatian or Serbian], or from Bosnian [or Croatian or Serbian] into English?
1. From Bosnian [or Croatian or Serbian] into English, that blue one.
2. Ah, here it is, near you! Something else?
1. Yes, next, my textbook is nowhere to be found. Do you know where it is?
2. I do [know]. There it is, away from you, over there by the notebook, next to the blackboard.
1. Next to what?
2. Next to the blackboard!
1. And then, where are my two nice pencils?
2. Both pencils are between the Bosnian [or Croatian or Serbian] dictionary and your textbook.

5A1

FIVE CATS AND FIVE DOGS

Short story: Five large cats and five fat dogs are going into town.
"Where are you going, cats?" ask the dogs.
"We are going from one house to another," say the cats.
"How many houses do you have?" ask the dogs.
"We have five little houses for five big cats," say the cats.
"Why are you going from house to house?" ask the dogs.
"To eat pears. We are hungry," answer the cats.
"A few pears or a lot of pears?" ask the dogs.
"We are taking two pears each," say the cats.

5A2

NO MONEY!

1. If there is time before lunch, I am going to the university.
2. There is time, but there's no money.
1. No money?! I'll go immediately to the bank, if you give me the car!
2. You can't take the car, because there is no gas.
1. No problem. I'm off on foot to the bank, and after the bank I am going to the university.

2. And after the university?
1. I'm back! I am coming to dinner at four o'clock!
2. As far as I am concerned, you can come at six. Dinner will be waiting for you if you want to eat it.

5A3

WHO IS COMING?

1. Next week on Wednesday at five o'clock I am going to the station to meet someone.
2. Who is coming?
1. My father's brother.
2. I know [...] means your mother's brother. Does one say [...] for your father's brother?
1. Yes! That's right. He is my paternal uncle.
2. What does he do and where does he live?
1. He is a judge and lives in Bihać [or Rijeka or Novi Sad].
2. A judge! Is your uncle's work interesting?
1. That's a matter of taste. He likes his work.
2. I want to be a lawyer.

5A4

GOING INTO TOWN

1. When can you come over tomorrow?
2. At four in the afternoon.
1. So when can we go to a movie theater to see a film?
2. At five o'clock.
1. Do you want us to go and get something to eat and drink afterwards?
2. Sure!
1. Mama, until what time may he and I be out?
3. Until ten o'clock.
1. Can't we be out until twelve?
3. Out of the question! Tomorrow is not a weekend. OK, you can be out until eleven o'clock.

6A1

IN THE BUILDING

1. Where are the table and chairs?
2. The table is [standing] on the floor and the chairs are around the table.
1. And where is the table in the room?
2. The table is by the wall but away from the blackboard, in the middle of the room.
1. How many centimeters is it from the table to the blackboard?
2. It is precisely one hundred twenty centimeters.
1. And where is the room?
2. On the first floor.
1. And where is the floor?
2. In this building.

6A2

THE UNIVERSITY

1. What is your book about?

2. I was reading about student life at Sarajevo [*or* Zagreb *or* Belgrade] University.
1. And what is their life like according to the book?
2. It says in the book that students have many oral and few written exams.
1. From when to when does the school year go?
2. The winter [fall] semester only begins in the month of October and ends in January.
1. And the summer [spring] semester?
2. The summer [spring] semester begins in February and ends in July.
1. They certainly start late and finish late!
2. Indeed, but in July there are no more lectures; there are only exams.
1. And how many years do students usually study in Sarajevo [*or* Zagreb *or* Belgrade] ?
2. Lectures are attended for four years, and then the students are 'apsolvents' for a year.
1. What does 'apsolvent' mean?
2. "Apsolvents' do not attend lectures, instead they only take exams until they pass them all.

6A3

HOW ARE YOU FEELING?

1. What was going on with you yesterday?
2. I wasn't feeling too well.
1. How are you now?
2. I'm better.
1. What are you doing? Who are you writing to?
2. I have been sitting here for an hour already, writing to my sister. And you, what are you doing?
1. I, too, am sitting and writing a letter to someone.
2. Who are you writing to?
1. I am writing to an old friend.
2. I'm so glad! And what are you writing to him about?
1. I am sending him greetings and writing to him about myself and about Bosnia.
2. My regards to him, too! How interesting! I have just put pictures of Montenegro into the letter to my sister.

6A4

WHAT DO YOU LIKE?

1 Which do you like more: sweet or savory dishes? My mother cooks all kinds of food wonderfully.
2. I like sweet dishes better.
1. Do you like meat?
2. I like many kinds of food, but I don't like meat.
1. My mother is from Argentina. She always says that meat must be put on the menu every day.
2. Excuse me, but it seems to me that it is not necessary to eat meat.

7A1

BREAKFAST

1. What do you eat for breakfast? Do you want to eat with me? I can prepare something for you and for myself.
2. I usually eat cereal.
1. What do you prepare it with?
2. With milk and sugar. And you?
1. I often have dark bread for breakfast with cottage cheese and green pepper, and sometimes sausage, but I never have cereal
2. What do you drink?

1. I always drink coffee with warm milk. And you?
2. I drink tea without anything.
1. Can it be that you drink it without sugar or milk or lemon? How can you drink such tea?
2. Of course I can. Don't worry!

7A2

HOW DO YOU GET TO WORK?

1. How do you get to work Mondays?
2. I usually go by tram.
1. And on Tuesdays?
2. On Tuesdays my wife and I always go together and we are in a hurry so we go by car.
1. By car?! So you are a driver! But isn't that expensive?
2. It is expensive, but it is pleasant! I have been driving for years.
1. What about by bicycle or motorcycle? That is good for the health.
2. I can go by bicycle, but it seems dangerous to me to ride a motorcycle. I am afraid of a traffic accident.
1. In a way you are right. You are young! The future is ahead of you. Don't gamble it away!
2. For the sake of health I like to walk the two kilometers from my house to work when the weather is nice.

7A3

DON'T!

1. Please, come over here and give me an apple.
2. Here's the apple!
1. Thanks! And now hurry! Go over to Redžija [or Ines or Ana] and take her this book.
2. Oh come on! Leave me alone! I am not your servant!
1. Fine, I understand. Listen, I am going to her with the book myself!
2. As far as I am concerned, do what you want.
1. Let's not [talk] this way. Tell me, can Redžija [or Ines or Ana] and I take you to the movies?
2. I'd rather not. Let her go with you. I feel like sleeping. Eat up that apple and be off to the movie theater.
1. Come on! Forget the sleeping! Let's go see some amusing movie. Take your coat and let's go.

7A4

WHAT DO YOU USE TO WRITE WITH?

1. What do you use to write with?
2. I usually write with a pencil.
1. And where do you study?
2. When I don't have classes sometimes I study in my room, but I often go to the language lab.
1. Every day has its beginning, middle and end. When do you study best?
2. I particularly like to study in the early morning. I cannot study late at night. And you, when do you study best?
1. It is all the same to me, in the morning, the afternoon or evening. And when do you listen to music?
2. I listen to music all day long.

8A1

PATIENCE

Girls are sitting patiently at the table.
Under the girls are chairs.

Inside the girls is breakfast.
The [female] professor looks at the girls.
The girls learn from the professor.
And the professor learns from the girls.
Hello, professor!

8A2

IMPATIENCE

Calm children are sitting patiently at the table.
Under the calm children are chairs.
Inside the calm children is breakfast.
A restless child watches the calm children.
The restless child learns from the calm children.
And the calm children learn from the restless child.
Hello, children!

8A3

GET IN TOUCH!

1. What happiness! A letter from [my] parents!
2. Do you often talk with your parents?
1. I communicate with them by letter, and sometimes by phone.
2. By letter? Haven't you considered buying them a computer?
1. No, because I like to stay in touch with them by letters, and besides they don't want to have a computer.
2. And how do you communicate with students abroad?
1. I always stay in touch with them over the internet.

8A4

THE ROOM

1. Where is our blackboard?
2. Our blackboard is in the room, on the wall, in front of the students and near the professor, by the professor's lectern.
1. It is in the middle of the wall, and that wall is between the two other walls behind the door.
2. Next to the window on the one side and the door on the other, above the floor, below the ceiling, and below the lamps, and across from us.
1. Across from whom?
2. Across from us.

9A1

WHAT WILL YOU BE DOING?

1. What will you be doing over the summer?
2. After the exam period I will be going to Paris for a month.
1. Wonderful! What will you do there?
2. It will be a study visit. I have been dreaming of this for years!
1. And what will you study while you are in Paris?
2. I will study how to speak French, day and night. And I will eat French cooking, of course.
1. And where will you stay?

2. I'll stay with a French family.

9A2

LOOK AT YOURSELF!

1. Look at yourself in the mirror!
2. Do you want to say that I am messy? Oh, how embarrassing!
1. You are the same as always. Your face is dirty. Brush your hair, wash your face and your hands, and then you'll look better!
2. Watch while I comb my hair, wash my face and hands. Now I am tidy and my face is clean! Will you go into town with me?
1. I won't. I want to stay home because I have my hands full of work. Will you brush your teeth?
2. I won't now. I'll eat while I'm out, so I'll brush them before I go to sleep. Bye! I'm in a rush! I'm off! I'll be home after eleven.
1. Have a nice time. If I'm not sleepy, I'll wait up for you. Don't wake me if I'm sleeping.

9A3

LIVING

1. Where will you be living in the fall?
2. I'll stay in the dormitory. And you?
1. I am not going back to the dorm. This year I'm going to find a place to rent. I'm looking for an apartment now. Are you going to be sharing a room with someone in the dorm?
2. I don't want to live with anyone, but want to or not, you have to! And you?
1. I'll see. Maybe I'll get an apartment with some students and share the expenses and rent with them.
2. I don't feel like looking for a place to rent. It suits me perfectly here, close by. I won't have to waste time and walk a long way to lectures.

9A4

AT THE TRAIN STATION

1. When will your parents come to see your new apartment?
2. They arrive by train tomorrow at 2:30.
1. Will you meet them?
2. Of course I will. I am leaving for the station at two o'clock. Will you go with me to meet them?
1. I can't, because I'm at a lecture, but my brother feels like going. He loves your parents and wants to greet them with you.
2. Doesn't he have a lot of work this week?
1. He does, but he will go with you, regardless.

10A1

AT CHARLIE'S

1. What did you do on Friday?
2. I was at the university in the morning.
1. And in the afternoon?
2. In the afternoon I went into town and met up with friends.
1. And did you go out with them in the evening?
2. Yes. We had dinner in a restaurant.
1. What is the restaurant called, where is it located and what did you order?

2. It is called "At Charlie's", it is in the center of town, and we ate ćevapčići and drank beer.
1. Is that your first time at that restaurant?
2. No, I was there once before.
1. Were there any problems with the food at the restaurant?
2. No, there were no problems whatsoever. Everything was excellent. Then I came home by bus.

10A2

TO WRITE AND FINISH WRITING

1. Are you doing homework assignments?
2. No, I already finished them.
1. You are probably reading the third chapter in the textbook.
2. No, I've already finished reading it.
1. Are you going to take the exam in Bosnian (*or* Serbian *or* Croatian) on Monday?
2. Yes! Because last time I didn't pass it, instead I got flustered and failed.
1. Are you going to the university again today?
2. No. I went on Friday. I am studying today at home all day.
1. Great! Because that way you will learn everything and you won't fail any more!
2. I will be pleased to succeed at last.

10A3

"ONCE THERE WAS A LION" Dušan Radović

Once upon a time there was a lion.
What kind of lion?
A terrible lion! Bristling and all furious.
Terrible! Terrible!

Don't ask what he ate.
An entire tram, and a piece of a cloud.
Terrible! Terrible!

He walked on three legs,
He looked with three eyes,
He listened with three ears.
Terrible! Terrible!

Sharp teeth, an evil gaze,
he didn't know what mercy was.
Terrible! Terrible!

Until Brana, one day,
erased him with an eraser.
Terrible! Terrible!

10A4

MY LEGS AND ARMS ACHE!

1. Help me, please! My legs and arms and back ache, and especially my fingers!
2. Are you sick?
1. No, I think I'm healthy, just tired. I can't carry these books.

2. Take care [of yourself]! I'll help you! But if I help you, you also must help me.
1. With doing the homework? Let's study together. In my opinion you and I will figure everything out the most easily that way.
2. I agree. My head is already aching from studying. First we'll carry the books, then I will drive you to my place and we'll study there together.
1. Last time coffee helped us, too. I must wake up. I'm sleepy.
2. Believe me, I haven't forgotten that! If your stomach doesn't hurt I have plenty of coffee for you and me.

11A1

IMPORTANT, MORE IMPORTANT, THE MOST IMPORTANT!

1. Your question was important, but mine was more important.
2. True, but my question was definitely more interesting!
3. Enough said. My question is more important and more interesting than yours, and that's final!
1. [turning to fourth student] You try to tell us: who of us has the most interesting question?
4. The matter is solved! The debate is done! I have concluded that each of you considers your question the most interesting!

11A2

TWO RESTAURANTS

1. Let's compare these two restaurants. Are they similar to one another or different?
2. Fine. To begin with, tell me which you like more and which you like less?
1. In my opinion, they are not at all similar to one another. This restaurant appeals to me less.
2. Why? The food is better in this one than in that one.
1. I agree. But there one waits less [time]. In this restaurant it is harder to get a table than in that one. I feel better there.
2. That restaurant is larger than this one.
1. Where is the atmosphere more pleasant?
2. The atmosphere is less pleasant in that one.
1. Agreed: this restaurant has better cooking. One waits longer, however, and it is harder to get a table, and it is smaller, but it has a more pleasant atmosphere. That restaurant has worse cooking, one waits for a shorter time, it is easier to get a table, and it is larger.
2. Therefore, this restaurant needs more space and more tables, and that restaurant needs better cooking and a more pleasant atmosphere! I must conclude that these two restaurants are completely different.

11A3

A PROFESSION AND A JOB

1. What are you doing?
2. Reading the novel *The Bosnian Chronicles* by the writer Ivo Andrić.
1. Ah, I remember that novel! I read it, too, many years ago. But I wasn't thinking of that, instead I meant to ask you what you do!
2. Oh that! By profession I am an engineer, but I drive a taxi.
1. Is it possible?! Are you satisfied with that? Do you at least make good money driving a taxi?
2. Depends on when! It's best at night.
1. And what do your friends do?
2. They are all taxi drivers, but they have various professions.
1. For example?
2. One is a physician, one is a mathematician, one is a carpenter, but they all have a driver's license and a map of the city. What do you do?

1. I have just graduated from the Faculty of Political Science, but there were no jobs for journalists before, there are none now, and there won't be any in the future either.
2. Stop! Go and pass your driver's test. You'll need your driver's license! You can always be a taxi driver!

11A4

I NEED A JOB!

1. Sit down here. Help me! I need a better job. I don't earn enough!
2. I understand. Surely you fear the uncertainty.
1. I am not afraid of anything and I don't need your understanding. I need a job!
2. But the question is whether you will find a good job in some company if you keep on sitting here.
1. I am not sitting, I am lying down. This way I can watch television more easily.
2. Worse yet! Stand up on your feet. Your attitude toward work bothers me. Enough waiting. You need studying and knowledge.
1. I should stand in line at the employment service?
2. What else?! You should get the advice of the staff at the Service. You ought to try.
1. That wouldn't even occur to me. Things will start to move of their own accord. This sort of life doesn't bother me too much.
2. Well, you just go ahead, and lie there and watch television. You never know.

12A1

THE DORMITORY

Students who live in the dormitory must arrange their own rooms before the beginning of the semester. Each [male] student has a [male] roommate and each [female] student has a [female] roommate. For furniture, therefore, each room should have two beds, two bedside tables, two desks, two lamps and two small rugs. Each student brings with himself (or herself) bedding: a pillow, sheets, a blanket. The room is divided into three parts: one third of the room is for the desks and lamps, the second third is for the beds, bedside tables and small rugs, and the third part is a shared area. Since each wing of the dormitory has 150 rooms, then, each wing must have 300 beds, 300 bedside tables, 300 desks, 300 lamps and 300 small rugs. Since every student has approximately 15 textbooks, this means that students have about 30 textbooks per room, or about 4,500 textbooks per [dormitory] wing. Students should study approximately 4 hours a day in their rooms. Multiplying that by 180 days in the school year, it turns out that one student needs to study 720 hours, i.e. two students need to study 1,440 hours, while five students need to study 3,600 hours annually. It should be said that every dormitory has nine wings.

12A2

SHOPPING

Having left their houses at half past four, three women went along the street, chatting and enjoying the stroll. Four blue and yellow cars parked nearby them. Out stepped four tall men at a quarter to five. They all extended hands to one another, greeted each other and conversed cheerfully. Then these seven people went into a large store at #21 Oak Street. Twelve cats and eleven dogs looked at them from the store window. Having entered the store, the women bought the men a dog and a cat each, while the men bought the women flowers and a kilo of candy and immediately gave them to them. And then those three women, each with her flowers, met up with six more, and after strenuous shopping, the nine of them went off to a nearby café for a cup of coffee and some conversation. The men, however, stopped in at the nearest tavern, the smokers among them smoked at the bar, each of them drank something while standing, and they watched the basketball game on television. After the game, the bar closed and each of them went his own way.

12A3

HOW OLD ARE YOU?

1. How old are you?
2. Nineteen eighty four is my year [of birth]. I'll be turning 21 this summer.
1. When is your birthday?
2. My birthday is August 18th.
1. I am traveling precisely on August 18th to Rome. Will you go with me?
2. Unfortunately I can't. I have decided to stay here. I have an obligation toward my family. I mustn't miss celebrating my birthday with my family.
1. But surely you have been celebrating your birthday with your family for years?
2. Family traditions should be respected!
1. When you are celebrating your birthday you will remember me and you will be sorry you didn't go with me to Rome.
2. Never mind. Have a great trip!
1. And I wish you a happy birthday in advance.
2. Thanks!

12A4

WHAT HAPPENED?

1. a. What happened on July 4, 1776?
   b. The United States of America proclaimed its independence.
2. a. What happened on December 7, 1941?
   b. The Axis forces attacked Pearl Harbor.
3. a. What happened on November 22, 1963?
   b. Lee Harvey Oswald assassinated President John Kennedy.

13A1

WELCOME!

1. Welcome, sir! Would you be so kind as to come with me from the hallway into the room?
2. I would be glad to! Thank you for inviting me.
1. Do sit down. What might I offer you?
2. Ma'am, I am terribly thirsty. Might I ask for a little cold water?
1. Of course! With ice or without?
2. With lots and lots of ice!
1. Here you are, sir! And do you wish to drink or eat something else? Perhaps some wine and cake?
2. Thank you, ma'am. I like that red wine. Would you be so kind as to pour me some?
1. Here you are, sir! A full glass is better than an empty one! I would recommend this cake as well. Might I serve you some?
2. Thank you, ma'am, I'd gladly have a little cake. But please, less! Even less! Now that will do nicely. And you?
1. Sweet things don't agree with me, thanks. The wine suits me best.

13A2

HERE'S THE COMPUTER!

1. [carrying a heavy box] Here, I've brought your computer. It is fixed. Where should I put it down?
2. Put it there on the desk, please.

1. If you want me to put it on the desk you will have to clear all those things of yours off !
2. Right away, but might I offer you some coffee before that?
1. No, thanks. I already had some today. I'm in a hurry. [groaning under the weight of the box] If you would clear away these things I could begin to work.
2. Naturally! But since you are already here, could you explain some things regarding the computer?
1. [groaning] Please, you said that you would clear away those things! Don't be silly! I must leave as soon as possible to go to the next customer.
2. OK. [clearing the desk] I have cleared them away. I am sorry you can't stay at least a few minutes longer!

13A3

TAKE IT EASY ...

1. If I read through your materials tonight, I'll give them to you tomorrow morning early at work.
2. How many pages do you have left?
1. Well, about fifty.
2. It would be better if you were to read them soon – by 6:30 p.m. at the latest. I need my copy of the materials to work on them with a colleague tonight at 7:30 p.m.
1. I don't care. Let the colleague work on them on his own.
2. Think of my reputation! What will the other business partners say when I appear before them at the meeting tomorrow unprepared?
1. Take it easy. I have no idea what they will say. Let them say what they will. If I were a magician I could read them [the materials] by tonight. A shame that I'm not.
2. And if I were a king, I wouldn't be worried! As it is I don't even dare make an appearance tomorrow.

13A4

INSTRUCTIONS

1. Please, how do I get from here to the main square?
2. It isn't hard. I'll explain. First, at the newspaper stand you should purchase a bus ticket, which you will give to the bus driver. He will void the ticket. You will [on the bus] pass ten blocks or so to the third stop. You should get off at the third stop .
1. And when I get off, will I then be on the square where I want to be?
2. You'll see the square immediately, right in front of you. You should not turn left or right. And why are you going to the square, if I may ask?
1. You may! I am looking for the City Café. A colleague told me that the building which I will see next to the City Café is very beautiful.
2. Indeed. That is the building where I live! I can take you there in my car if you have nothing against it.
1. I would be very grateful!

14A1

A RECIPE FOR COFFEE

Put a full [Turkish] coffee pot of water on the stove. Place an empty coffee cup near it. As soon as the water comes to a boil, you should pour a little of the boiled water off into the cup and remove the pot from the burner. If you want coffee with sugar, you should sweeten the hot water now with two small spoonfuls of sugar, return the coffee pot to the burner for just a few seconds, and then remove the pot from the burner again. While the pot is off to the side, you should scoop up five heaping spoonfuls of ground coffee and add them to the hot water. Stir the coffee and water well with the spoon. Then you should firmly grasp the handle of the coffee pot and put the pot back on the burner. Then watch closely as the coffee rises in the pot. When it gets to the very top, you should quickly take it off the burner, that instant. Then you wait two or three minutes until the coffee settles in the pot. Then put the pot back on the burner again, and then take it off again as soon as the coffee rises to the top. Then for the final, third, time put the pot back on the burner until the coffee, for the last time, rises up to the top of the coffee pot for the last time. Then you should set the coffee pot with the coffee to the side, take the coffee cup with the water you poured off, and pour this water over the coffee, while it is still in the pot. Then line up four coffee cups one next to the other. Place one small spoonful of foam into each cup. When all the foam has been divided, then you pour the coffee up to the top of each coffee cup. You leave the grounds to settle out. You need to sip a little to see if it is sweet enough. And in the end, when the coffee has been drunk, then one's future is read from the grounds which remain on the bottom of the cup.

14A2

A STORM

Returning home by car after a business trip in another city, two colleagues happened upon a storm with heavy precipitation, first snow, then rain, and to make matters worse, it was getting dark. Having turned off the road and having stopped at the nearest town by 5:30 p.m., they took shelter in a tavern. Watching through the window of the tavern as the snow turned to gusts of rain and wind, they thought miserably about whether it was worth traveling further. Eating dinner there and having had some wine, they talked about their situation. Knowing that they couldn't drive through such a storm, they decided to spend the night in a nearby hotel. Having felt helpless, they listened to the news, the weather report and the report on the condition on the motorways. Having gotten in touch with their families at about 8:30 p.m., they went to bed, hoping that the weather would be nicer the next day so that they would be able to continue their trip. And indeed, having woken up very early, at five of five, they heard on the news that the conditions on the motorways were significantly better. Driving, they saw the clouds disperse, the sun come out, and the day clear up. Hurrying back, they didn't stop once along the way, all the way to thier town where they arrived at twenty to eleven. they checked in at work for the sake of appearances, and then, parting ways, each returned to her own home.

14A3

ACCIDENT CHRONICLE

Last night at around eight o'clock, a woman and man were found lying unconscious by the side of the road. The emergency number was called and the case was reported to the police. The couple was driven to the hospital in an ambulance. Later, in a statement for the public, it was confirmed that they were brother and sister. The woman was born in 1973 and the man was born in 1975. It was said that luckily the two had not been killed, but had survived a bad traffic accident. Their family was informed.

14A4

FOG

The autumn fog was thick that night, so nothing was seen. All sounds were silenced by the fog so nothing was heard. There was gathering [people gathered] at the train station but nothing was said. The return of schoolchildren and teachers from a school excursion was anticipated. The children were expected at nine o' clock in the evening, but because of the fog it wasn't certain whether the train would be late or not. After an hour's delay, suddenly the train was noticed as it arrived from afar. The concern of the parents vanished as soon as it was understood that the children would soon appear. There was arriving [the children arrived] finally at the station at ten fifty five. There was joy at the arrival of the train. In the end, when the children stepped down off the train, the fear was completely forgotten and there was a going [everyone went] home to sleep.

In this case the more literal translation is meant to describe as closely as possible how the BCS *se*-verb passives work. In several instances, the more normal English translation is given in brackets.

✌ Key to audio recordings

The A exercises for Lessons 1-14, the poems in lessons 17, 18 and 19, and the three short stories are recorded in three CD sets, one each for Bosnian, Croatian and Serbian. Track numbers for the **regular version** are given in bold, for the slow version in non-bold.

First CD

1, 2	1A1	KAKO SE ZOVEŠ?
3, 4, 5, 6, 7, 8		
	1A2	ŠTA JE OVO? [B,S]
		ŠTO JE OVO? [C]
9, 10	1A3	DOBAR DAN!
11, 12	1A4	PAS I MAČKA
13, 14	2A1	UČITI ZAJEDNO
15, 16	2A2	KOGA VIDIŠ?
17, 18	2A3	KUPUJEM PSA
19, 20	2A4	PAPIRNICA
21, 22	3A1	KAKO STE?
23, 24	3A2	LAKU NOĆ!
25, 26	3A3	ŠTA VIŠE VOLIŠ? [B,S]
		ŠTO VIŠE VOLIŠ? [C]
27, 28	3A4	ČIJE SU OVE OLOVKE?
29, 30	4A1	ODAKLE STE?
31, 32	4A2	KOD KOGA SU NAŠE KNJIGE?
33, 34	4A3	I JOŠ NEŠTO ...
35, 36	4A4	TRAŽIM NEKE STVARI
37, 38	5A1	PET MAČAKA I PET PASA
39, 40	5A2	NEMA NOVCA!
41, 42	5A3	KO DOLAZI? [B,S]
		TKO DOLAZI? [C]
43, 44	5A4	IZLAZAK U GRAD
45, 46	6A1	U ZGRADI
47, 48	6A2	UNIVERZITET [B,S]
		SVEUČILIŠTE [C]
49, 50	6A3	KAKO TI JE?
51, 52	6A4	ŠTA TI SE SVIĐA? [B,S]
		ŠTO TI SE SVIĐA? [C]
53, 54	7A1	DORUČAK
55, 56	7A2	ČIME IDEŠ NA POSAO?
57, 58	7A3	MA NEMOJ!
59, 60	7A4	ČIME PIŠEŠ?
61, 62	8A1	STRPLJENJE
63, 64	8A2	NESTRPLJENJE
65, 66	8A3	JAVI SE!
67, 68	8A4	SOBA
69, 70	9A1	ŠTA ĆEŠ RADITI? [B,S]
		ŠTO ĆEŠ RADITI? [C]
71, 72	9A2	POGLEDAJ SE!
73, 74	9A3	STANOVANJE
75, 76	9A4	NA STANICI [B,S]
		NA KOLODVORU [C]
77, 78	10A1	KOD CHARLIEA [B,C]
		KOD ČARLIJA [S]
79, 80	10A2	PISATI I NAPISATI
81, 82	10A3	"BIO JEDNOM JEDAN LAV" – Dušan Radović
83, 84	10A4	BOLE ME I NOGE I RUKE!
85, 86	11A1	VAŽNO, VAŽNIJE, NAJVAŽNIJE
87, 88	11A2	DVA RESTORANA
89, 90	11A3	STRUKA I POSAO
91, 92	11A4	TREBA MI POSAO!

Second CD

1	12A1	STUDENTSKI DOM
2	12A2	KUPOVINA
3, 4	12A3	KOLIKO IMAŠ GODINA?
5, 6	12A4	ŠTA SE DOGODILO? [B,S]
		ŠTO SE DOGODILO? [C]
7, 8	13A1	DOBRODOŠLI!
9, 10	13A2	EVO KOMPJUTERA! [B,S]
		EVO KOMPJUTORA! [C]
11, 12	13A3	POLAKO ...
13, 14	13A4	UPUTSTVA
15	14A1	RECEPT ZA KAHVU [B]
		KAVU [C] KAFU [S]
16	17A1	"LJEPOTICA I ZVIJER" – Ferida Duraković
17	17A2	"ZEMLJA" – A. B. Šimić
18	17A3	"VEČE NA ŠKOLJU" – Aleksa Šantić
19	18A1	"JESENJE VEČE" – Antun Gustav Matoš
20	18A2	"NOTTURNO" – Tin Ujević
21	19A1	"OČIJU TVOJIH DA NIJE" – Vasko Popa
22	19A2	"ZA LAŽI IZGOVORENE IZ MILOSRĐA" – Desanka Maksimović
23-30		"OSAM MALIH PRIČA O MOJOJ ŽENI" – David Albahari
31-38		"LJUBAV NA ŠPANJOLSKI NAČIN" – Muharem Bazdulj
39-46	20.I-20.VIII	"U ZAGRLJAJU RIJEKE" – Miro Gavran

The above material was read by: Maša Čulumović, Ana Galjanić, Nada Ječmenica, Ivona Josipović, Marina Jovanović, Emir Kamenica, Mia Midenjak, Natalija Novta, Slobodan Radoman, Azra Pravdić, Obrad Šćepanović, and Toma Tasovac. There are minor discrepancies in text and pronunciation between the recorded and printed versions of the exercises.

General. This glossary includes all words used in the Textbook plus certain additional words which are in frequent use. For each word, one finds the relevant grammatical information (in italics), the English definition, notes on usage, and affiliation where relevant (in brackets). Abbreviations used are defined on p. 388.

For each entry introduced in an A-lesson vocabulary box (or a vocabulary box accompanying a homework exercise), the lesson and section number are given. When a lesson has two vocabulary boxes in each A section, these are identified by the letters a and b after the lesson and section number.

    Example: **kolegica** *f* [B,C] colleague *(f.)* 13A4

                         suton *m* dusk 18A1a

The symbol ✿ᵖ refers to examples provided in the grammar sections:

    Example: **Jugoslavija** *f* Yugoslavia 17A4✿ᵖ

The symbols ⊕, ☺ refer to words from the Geography and Aphorism sections at the ends of Lessons 1-15.

    Examples: **Posavina** *f* the Sava river valley 6⊕

                   parkiranje *n* parking 10☺

A boxed-in number refers to examples given in the boxes that provide cultural commentary.

    Example: **ovaj** *excl.* umm, uh... 9A3

The symbol 📖 refers to the stories by David Albahari or Muharem Bazdulj.

    Examples: **prodavačica** *f* saleswoman 📖A.IV

                 rastanak *m; Gsg* **rastanka** parting, farewell 📖B.IV

The symbol ↵, always given first in an entry, refers the reader to one of the Appendices.

    Example: **radost** *f; Gsg* **radosti** *Isg* **-ošću** *or* **-osti** joy ↵4 3A2

Many entries include several numbers and symbols. For instance:

                 pitanje *n* 1. question 1A2, 3A1✿ᵖ, 3A2✿ᵖ; 2. issue 1⊕

Some words in the glossary are without any number or symbol. These represent additional vocabulary, which has been included to give a broader range of expression than permitted by the Lessons.

    Example: **zebra** *f; Gpl* **zebara** *or* **zebri** 1. zebra [= animal]; 2. crosswalk

Definitions. Many words have several meanings. Some are more or less synonymous while others are quite distinct. Those judged as synonyms are separated by commas, while those seen as distinct meanings are numbered. Not all meanings of all words are listed; for this one must consult a full dictionary. In addition, not all meanings listed in the glossary are used in the Textbook; if a word is used in a particular meaning in the Textbook, the above symbols identify the point in the book where this occurs. Any necessary amplifications of a definition are given in brackets or parentheses. Related idioms are given as sub-entries.

    Examples: **pametan, pametna** *adj.* intelligent, smart 11A2

               nego *conj.* 1. but, rather 2A1; 2. than 11A2, 11A2✿ᵖ, 13A4✿ᵖ

               kvadrat *m; Gsg* **kvadrata** [geometric] square; **na kvadrat** squared (mathematics)

Different forms. Words which are marked as either ekavian or ijekavian usage are denoted as such by the symbols [E] and [J], respectively. The notations [B], [C] and [S] denote Bosnian, Croatian, and Serbian usage, respectively. Words used in two of the three are noted [B,C] or [B,S] as appropriate. Words with no marking are used throughout BCS. The notation [B,C,S] after a word means both that it is used throughout BCS, and that there exists a distinctly separate word with the same meaning which is used only in one (or two) of the others; to learn the identity of this other word one must consult the English-based glossary. The word "only" after a notation containing certain of the letters (e.g. [B,S only]) means that this meaning of the word is restricted while other meanings of it are not so restricted: for example the word **rđav** means "rusty" throughout BCS, but "bad" only in S.

Examples: **kancelarija** *f* [B,C,S] office 6A1

loš, loša; loši *adj.* [B,C,S] bad ↦4   2A2, ⌐2A2 ¬ 3A1✿ᵖ, 11A1✿ᵖ

posledica *f* [E] consequence 18A3

posljedica *f* [J] consequence 18A3

rđav *adj.* 1. bad [S only] 2A2, ⌐2A2 ¬ 2. rusty

ured *m* [C] office 6A1

Grammatical information.

Verbs are listed by the infinitive form. If the present tense is not fully predictable from the infinitive, the 1st singular present is also given (the 3rd singular is given for verbs which are used only in 3rd person). The 3rd plural present is given when it is not directly predictable from the 1st singular, as are past tense forms which are not directly predictable from the infinitive. Aspect is noted for each verb, by the symbols (I) and (P), and members of an aspectual pair are separated by a semi-colon. Biaspectual verbs are noted (I/P). In each instance of an aspectual pair, the most basic form is listed first followed by the one which is derived from it. When prefixation produces a verb with different meaning, it is listed separately and cross-referenced to the verb from which it is derived. Verbs used both with and without **se** are given within the same entry if the meaning difference is essentially one of active vs. passive or transitive vs. intransitive. Otherwise, the two are given as separate entries.

Examples: **crtati** (I); **nacrtati** (P) to draw, to sketch 18A1b, 10A4✿ᵖ

događati se *see under* **dogoditi se**

dogoditi se, dogodi se (P) 12A4, 9A2✿ᵖ; **događati se, događa se, događaju se** (I) [B,C,S] 20.VI *(3rd person only)* to happen

dovesti, dovedem; doveo, dovela (P) 20.III; **dovoditi, dovodim** (I) to bring, to lead to, to conduct *see* **voditi**

gubiti (I); **izgubiti, izgubim** (P) to lose 9A3; **izgubiti glavu** to panic, to lose one's composure 10A2

grupirati, grupiram, grupiraju (I/P) [B,C] to group 18A2

igrati, igram (I) 1. to play [a game] 5C1, 5A2✿ᵖ, 10A1✿ᵖ; 2. to dance [B,S only] 15A1; **igrati se, igram se, igraju se** (I) to play 16A1b *see also* **odigrati**

naučiti, naučim (P) to learn 10A2, 9A2✿ᵖ, 10A2✿ᵖ, *see also* **učiti**

pretvoriti (P); **pretvarati, pretvaram, pretvaraju** (I) to transform 14A2

pretvoriti se (P): **pretvarati se, pretvaram se, pretvaraju se** (I) to pretend 15A1

učiti (I) to study 2A1, 2A1✿ᵖ, 9A1✿ᵖ, 9A4✿ᵖ, 10A2✿ᵖ, 10A4✿ᵖ   *see also* **naučiti**

Nouns are listed by the nominative singular form, with gender marked as *m*, *f*, or *n*. Genitive singular forms are given for all feminine nouns in a consonant, and for all other nouns whose non-nominative forms are not directly predictable from the nominative singular. Instrumental singular is given for feminine nouns in a consonant, and nominative plural for masculine and neuter nouns which add an extra syllable in the plural or which have irregular plurals. Genitive plural is given whenever the ending is not completely predictable. Dative-Locative singular forms are given for feminine nouns ending in -**ka**, -**ga**, or -**ha**. The notation *(m., general)* and *(f.)* after names of professions and nationalities means that the first refers both to the category in general and to any one male representative of that category, while the second refers only to a female representative of that category.

Examples: **Bosanac** *m; Gsg* **Bosanca** Bosnian *(m., general)* 1A4, ⌐1A4 ¬

Bosanka *f; DLsg* **Bosanki** *Gpl* **Bosanki** Bosnian *(f.)* 1A4, 6A2✿ᵖ, ⌐1A4 ¬

doručak *m; Gsg* **doručka** breakfast 7A1

dojam *m; Gsg* **dojma** *Npl* **dojmovi** [B,C] impression 16A3

epoha *f; DLsg* **epohi** *or* **eposi** age, epoch 6A2, 6A2✿ᵖ

ime *n; Gsg* **imena** *Npl* **imena** *Gpl* **imena** name ↦4   1A2, 3A2✿ᵖ

misao *f; Gsg* **misli** *Isg* **mišlju** *or* **misli** thought ↦4   18A2

mladost *f; Gsg* **mladosti** *Isg* -**ošću** *or* -**osti** youth

Adjectives are noted *adj.*, and listed in the masculine singular short form. If there are any changes between this and other forms, the feminine singular short form is also listed. The masculine singular long form is listed only in case of accent change. If only the long form is listed, it means the adjective occurs only in that form. Words with the meaning of a noun but the form of an adjective are noted *(adj.form)*. Comparative forms are provided if they are not readily predictable (see 11A1✿).

Examples: **bolji** *adj.* better 11A2, 11A1✿ *see* **dobar**
 ceo, cela; celi *adj.* [E] whole 7A4; **ceo dan** all day 7A4
 cijel (also **cio**), **cijela; cijeli** *adj.* [J] whole 7A4; **cijeli dan** all day 7A4
 dosadan, dosadna *adj.* 1. boring, dull; 2. annoying 5A1, 6A3✿
 Engleska *f (adj. form)* England 4A1
 engleski *adj.* English 4A1
 visok, visoka; visoki *adj.* tall, high 2A2, 3A1✿, 11A1✿, 11A2✿
 viši *adj.* 1. taller; 2. higher 11A1✿

Pronouns are noted *pron.* Both full and clitic forms of personal pronouns are given; only the clitics are identified as such. Pronominal adjectives (possessives, demonstratives and the like) are noted *pron. adj.* and are given in masculine, neuter and feminine forms. See Appendix 4 for full declensions of most of these words.

Examples: **ga** *pron. (clitic)* 1. him; 2. it *(Acc-Gen)* 2A1 *see under* **on**
 naš, naše, naša *poss. pron.* our, ours 1A2
 neki, neko, neka *pron. adj.* some, any, a certain ↦4 3A3; **nekih pedesetak** fifty-some, fifty-odd, roughly fifty 13A3; **u neku ruku** in a sense, in a way 7A2
 njega *pron.* 1. him; 2. it *(Acc-Gen)* 2A2 *see under* **on, ono**

Numbers are noted *num* only if they do not function as another part of speech. In the latter case they are noted according to the part of speech which determines their form.

Examples: **četiri** *num.* four (4) 5A2, 12A1✿, 12A2✿
 četrdeset *num.* forty (40) 5A1, 5A1✿
 četvero *n.* [C] four [mixed gender] 📖B.VI, 12A2✿
 četvorica *f* four [men] 12A2✿
 četvoro *n.* [B,S] four [mixed gender] 📖B.VI, 12A2✿
 četvrti *adj.* fourth (4th) 4A1, 6A2✿, 12A3✿

Adverbs are noted *adv.*, *conjunctions* are noted *conj.*, *exclamations* are noted *excl.*, and words which resist classification are not noted as to part of speech.

Examples: **ali** *conj.* but 1A4
 alo *excl.* hello [telephone greeting] 📖A.VII
 često *adv.* often, frequently 7A1, 10A2✿
 da yes 1A2

Accentuation.

Accent is marked as in the body of the book: the underscore denotes a long vowel and the grave mark denotes a rising accent. Words with no accent mark on them have a falling accent on the first syllable. The assignment of accentual information to each individual word (whether vowels are long or short, and whether accented vowels are rising or falling) been made on the basis of the following reference works:

Hrvatski jezički savjetnik (ed. Lana Hudeček, Milica Mihaljević, Luka Vukojević; Zagreb, 1999)
Rečnik srpskohrvatskog književnog jezika, vols. 1-6 (produced by Matica srpska, 1967-1976)
Serbocroatian-English Dictionary (by Morton Benson with the collaboration of Biljana Šljivić-Šimšić; Belgrade and Philadelphia, 1971)
Veliki rječnik hrvatskoga jezika (by Vladimir Anić; Zagreb, 2003).

✑ How to use the English glossary

The English glossary includes grammatical information about English only; its primary purpose is to help the student find his or her way into the BCS glossary, where fuller grammatical information can be found about all BCS words. The English glossary also allows students to see under a single entry all the forms which may differ as to the markings noted [B], [C], [S], [B/S] [J], [E] or [J].

Synonyms are separated by commas. If a BCS aspectual pair is given, the notations (I) and (P) identify imperfective and perfective forms, respectively; the two members of an aspect pair are separated by a semi-colon. The several different meanings of words referring to profession and nationality names (general, specific male, specific female) are included within a single entry.

Those who need more information than these glossaries can provide should consult one or more of the following:

Serbocroatian-English Dictionary (by Morton Benson with the collaboration of Biljana Šljivić-Šimšić; Belgrade and Philadelphia, 1971)
English-Serbocroatian Dictionary (by Morton Benson; Belgrade and Philadelphia, 1971)
Veliki hrvatsko-engleski rječnik (by Željko Bujas; Zagreb, 1999)
Veliki englesko-hrvatski rječnik (by Željko Bujas; Zagreb, 1999)

For more information on dictionaries and grammar books, see www.bcsgrammarandtextbook.org.

✎ Abbreviations and symbols used in the glossaries

ABBREVIATIONS

abbr.	abbreviation
Acc	accusative case
adj.	adjective
adj. form	noun meaning; adjective form
adv.	adverb
Asg	accusative singular
[B]	Bosnian usage
[B,C]	Bosnian and Croatian usage
[B,C,S]	usage in Bosnian, Croatian and Serbian
[B,S]	Bosnian and Serbian usage
[C]	Croatian usage
coll.	collective
colloq.	colloquial
comp.	comparative
conj.	conjunction
Dat-Loc	dative-locative case
Dat	dative case
DLsg	dative-locative singular
DLIpl	dative-locative-instrumental plural
[E]	ekavian word or words
e.g.	for example
excl.	exclamation
f	feminine
(f.)	refers to female person only
(f sg form)	word takes endings of a feminine singular noun
Gen	genitive case
Gpl	genitive plural
Gsg	genitive singular
(I)	imperfective aspect
indecl.	indeclinable
Instr	instrumental case
(I/P)	one form for both imperfective and perfective aspect
Isg	instrumental singular
[J]	ijekavian word or words
[J] [B/S]	ijekavian words specific to Bosnian and Serbian ijekavian usage
Loc	locative case
m	masculine
(m.)	refers to male person only
(m., general)	refers either to male person or to general category
n	neuter
n.	noun [English glossary only]
Npl	nominative plural
Nsg	nominative singular
num.	number (word class)
(P)	perfective aspect
part.	particle
pl	plural
(pl form)	word exists only in plural form
prep.	preposition
pron.	pronoun
pron.adj.	pronominal adjective
quest.	question word
[S]	Serbian usage
sg	singular
vb.	verb [English glossary only]
Voc	vocative case
vulg.	vulgar
3rd sg	third person singular form

SYMBOLS

✿	grammar section
⊕	geography section
box	information box
☺	aphorisms by D. Radović
📖A	story by D. Albahari
📖B	story by M. Bazdulj
⊶	appendix

A

a *conj.* and, but 1A1

a! *excl.* aha! 2A2

abeceda *f* [B,C,S] [Latin] alphabet 5A2✿

abecedni *adj.* [B,C,S] alphabetical 2A4

administracija *f* [B,S] administration 16A1a

adresa *f* address 16A2a

advokat *m; Gsg* **advokata** [B,S] lawyer 5A3, 11A2✿

aerodrom *m* [B,C,S] airport 📖B.III

aforizam *m; Gsg* **aforizma** aphorism 7☺

afrički *adj.* African

Afrika *f; DLsg* **Africi** Africa

ajvar *m* eggplant and/or red pepper relish

akcenat *m; Gsg* **akcenta** *Gpl* **akcenata** [B,S] accent 📖B.III

akcent *m; Gpl* **akcenata** [C] accent 📖B.III

akcioni *adj.* action 7A3; **akcioni film** action movie

ako *conj.* if 5A2, 13A4✿; **ako nemate ništa protiv** if you have no objections 13A4

akuzativ *m* accusative [case]

Albanac *m; Gsg* **Albanca** Albanian *(m., general)*

Albanija *f* Albania 1🌎

Albanka *f; DLsg* **Albanki** *Gpl* **Albanki** Albanian *(f.)*

alergičan, alergična *adj.* allergic 3A3

ali *conj.* but 1A4

alo *excl.* hello [as telephone greeting] 📖A.VII

aluminijski *adj.* aluminum 19A3b

ama *conj.* but; **ama baš ništa** not a single thing 15A2

ambasada *f* embassy

američki *adj.* American 2A4

Amerika *f; DLsg* **Americi** America 16A1b, 6A2✿

Amerikanac *m; Gsg* **Amerikanca** American *(m., general)* 1A4

Amerikanka *f; DLsg* **Amerikanki** *Gpl* **Amerikanki** American *(f.)* 1A4

amidža *m; Npl* **amidže** [B] [paternal] uncle 5A3, 5A3✿

amidžinica *f* [B] aunt [= paternal uncle's wife] 5A3

angažirati, angažiram, angažiraju (I/P) [B,C] to involve [someone]; **angažirati se, angažiram se, angažiraju se** (I/P) [B,C] to get involved 16A3b

angažovati, angažujem (I/P) [B,S] to involve [someone]; **angažovati se, angažujem se** (I/P) [B,S] to get involved 16A3b

anglistika *f; DLsg* **anglistici** English studies 13B3

anketa *f* survey, questionaire 16A1a

anonimnost *f; Gsg* **anonimnosti** *Isg* **-ošću** *or* **-osti** anonymity 13☺

aorist *m* aorist [verbal tense] 17C1

aplaudirati, aplaudiram, aplaudiraju (I) to applaud

aplauz *m* applause 📖B.VIII

apotekar *m* pharmacist *(m., general)* 11A3, 11A2✿

apotekarica *f* [B,C] pharmacist *(f.)* 11A3, 11A2✿

apotekarka *f; DLsg* **apotekarki** *Gpl* **apotekarki** [B,S] pharmacist *(f.)* 11A3, 11A2✿

april *m; Gsg* **aprila** [B,S] April 6A2, ⌐6A2⌐

apsolvent *m; Gsg* **apsolventa** *Gpl* **apsolvenata** university student having completed coursework but not yet passed all exams required for graduation 6A2

apsolventski *adj.* pertaining to final exam year at university

apstraktan, apstraktna *adj.* abstract 19A1b

Arapin *m; Npl* **Arapi** Arab *(m., general)*

Arapkinja *f* Arab *(f.)*

arheolog *m; Npl* **arheolozi** archaeologist

arhitekt *m; Gpl* **arhitekata** [B,C] architect 11A3, 11A2✿

arhitekta *m; Npl* **arhitekte** *Gpl* **arhitekata** [B,S] architect 11A3, 11A2✿

arhitektura *f* architecture 13B3

atentat *m; Gsg* **atentata** assassination 12A4; **izvršiti atentat na** + *Acc* to assassinate

atmosfera *f* atmosphere 11A2

atraktivan, atraktivna *adj.* attractive 16A3b

Australac *m; Gsg* **Australca** *Gpl* **Australaca** [C] Australian *(m., general)* 1A4

Australijanac *m; Gsg* **Australijanca** [B,S] Australian *(m., general)* 1A4

Australijanka *f; DLsg* **Australijanki** *Gpl* **Australijanki** [B,S] Australian *(f.)* 1A4

Australka *f; DLsg* **Australki** *Gpl* **Australki** [C] Australian *(f.)* 1A4

Austrija *f* Austria 1🌎

Austrijanac *m; Gsg* **Austrijanca** Austrian *(m., general)*

Austrijanka *f; DLsg* **Austrijanki** *Gpl* **Austrijanki** Austrian *(f.)*

austrijski *adj.* Austrian 9A1

Austro-Ugarska *f (adj.form)* Austria-Hungary 18A3

austrougarski *adj.* Austro-Hungarian 18A3

auto *m; Npl* **auti** [B,C] **automobili** [S] car 1A2

autobus *m* bus 7A2

autobuski *adj.* [B,S] bus ⌐9A3⌐, 13A4; **autobuska stanica** bus station

autobusni *adj.* [B,C] bus 9A3 , 13A4
  autobusna stanica bus station
  autobusni kolodvor bus station, bus
  terminal
autor *m* author *(m., general)*
autorica *f* [B,C] author *(f.)* 19A2b
autorka *m* [S] *DLsg* **autorki** *Gpl* **autorki**
  author *(f.)* 19A2b
avgust *m* [B,S] August 6A2
avion *m; Gsg* **aviona** [B,C,S] airplane 7A2
avionski *adj.* air, airmail; **avionsko pismo**
  airmail letter 2A4
azbučni *adj.* alphabetical [Cyrillic] 2A4
azbuka *f; DLsg* **azbuci** [Cyrillic] alphabet
  5A4☼
Azija *f* Asia
azijski *adj.* Asian

B

baba *f* [B,S] grandmother 9A4, 5A3☼
baciti, bacim (P); **bacati** (I) to throw 16A1a
Bačka *f (adj.form)* region of western Vojvodina
badem *m* almond
bajka *f; DLsg* **bajci** *Gpl* **bajka** *or* **bajki** fairy
  tale 📖B.VIII
baka *f; DLsg* **baki** [B,C,S] grandmother 9A4,
  5A3☼
Balkan *m; Gsg* **Balkana** the Balkans
balkanski *adj.* Balkan 8A3
Banat *m; Gsg* **Banata** region of eastern Vojvodina
banka *f; DLsg* **banci** *Gpl* **banaka** bank 5A2
Banja Luka, Banjaluka *f; DLsg* **Banjaluci**
  Banja Luka 4🌍
bara *f* marshland 16A3b
barem *adv.* at least 16A1a
baš *adv.* precisely 9A3; **ama baš ništa** not a
  single thing 15A2; **baš mi je drago!** I am
  truly delighted! 6A3; **baš sam zaboravna!**
  I really am forgetful! 📖A.V
bašta *f* [B,S] garden 16A3b
baština *f* legacy, heritage 16A2b
baviti se (I) + *Instr* to do, to occupy oneself
  with 11A3, 9A2☼
bazen *m; Gsg* **bazena** swimming pool
Beč *m; Gsg* **Beča** Vienna 4A1
bedan, bedna *adj.* [E] poor
bedem *m* rampart 19A3a
beg *m; Npl* **bezi, begovi** [E] flight, escape
  20.VII
begunac *m; Gsg* **begunca** [E] fugitive 18A3
beležnica *f* [S] notebook 1A2
benzin *m; Gsg* **benzina** gasoline, petrol 5A2
beo, bela; beli *adj.* [E] white 2A3, 2A3☼;
  beli dan broad daylight 19A3a; **beli luk**
  garlic

Beograd *m* Belgrade *see map*
Beograđanin *m; Npl* **Beograđani** resident of
  Belgrade *(m., general)* 16A3a
Beograđanka *f; DLsg* **Beograđanki** *Gpl*
  Beograđanki resident of Belgrade *(f.)*
beogradski *adj.* Belgrade 6A2
berberin *m; Npl* **berberi** [S] barber 11A4☼
bes *m; Npl* **besovi** [E] fury, rage
besediti (I) [E] *(archaic)* to talk 19A3a
besjediti (I) [J] *(archaic)* to talk 19A3a
besplatan, besplatna *adj.* free [of charge]
  16A2b
bespomoćan, bespomoćna *adj.* helpless 14A2
bespoštedan, bespoštedna *adj.* unrelenting
  18A3
besvestan, besvesna *adj.* [E] unconscious
  14A3
besvjestan, besvjesna *adj.* [J] unconscious
  14A3
bez *prep.* + *Gen* without ↦5 4A3
bez obzira na + *Acc* regardless of 9A4
bezdan *m; Gsg* **bezdna** *Isg* **bezdanom** abyss,
  deep, depth 17C1
bezuslovan, bezuslovna *adj.* [B,S]
  unconditional
bezuvjetan, bezuvjetna *adj.* [B,C]
  unconditional
bežati *see under* **pobeći**
bi *[conditional]* auxiliary [you *sg*, he, she]
  would 13A1☼
biber *m* [B,S] pepper [= spice]
biblioteka *f; DLsg* **biblioteci** [B,S] library
  7A4
bicikl *m; Gpl* **bicikla** *or* **bicikala** bicycle 7A2,
  7A2☼
bih *[conditional]* auxiliary 1. [I] would; 2. yes
  please 13B2☼
bih, bi, bi, bismo, biste bi *[conditional]*
  auxiliaries 13A2☼, 13A3☼
bijedan, bijedna *adj.* [J] poor
bijeg *m; Nsg* **bijezi** *or* **bjegovi** [J] flight, escape
  20.VII
bijel, bijela; bijeli *adj.* [J] white 2A3; **bijeli
  dan** broad daylight 19A3a; **bijeli luk** [J]
  [B/S] garlic
bijes *m; Npl* **bjesovi** [J] fury, rage
bila jednom *(f sg)*, **bilo jednom** *(n sg)*, **bio jednom** *(m sg)* once upon a time there was
  10A3, 10A3
bili jednom *(m pl)* once upon a time there were
  10A3, 10A3
bilo ko *pron* [B,S] whoever, anyone at all
  18A3
bilo šta *pron* [B,S] whatever, anything at all ,
  18A3
bilo što *pron* [C] whatever, anything at all

18A3

bilo tko *pron* [C] whoever, anyone at all 18A3

bilježnica *f* [B,C] notebook 1A2

biljka *f; DLsg* **biljci** *Gpl* **biljaka** *or* **biljki** plant 17A2a

biolog *m; Npl* **biolozi** biologist 11A2✿

biologija *f* biology 13B3

bioskop *m* [S] movie theater, cinema 5A2, 5A4✿, 6A1✿

birati, biram, biraju (I) to select 📖A.VIII *see* **sabirati**

bismo [*conditional*] *auxiliary* [we] would 13A1✿

biste [*conditional*] *auxiliary* [you *pl*] would 13A1✿

bitan, bitna *adj.* essential 📖B.VIII

biti (I/P) to be ↩6

clitic **sam, si, je, smo, ste, su** (I) 1A1, 1A1✿, 6A4✿, 10A1✿, 12A1✿, 12A4✿; *full* **jesam, jesi, jest** [B,C] **jeste** [B,S], **jesmo, jeste, jesu** (I) 1A4, 1A4✿; *negated* **nisam, nisi, nije, nismo, niste, nisu** (I) 1A4, 1A4✿; *negated (Montenegrin)* **nijesam, nijesi, nije, nijesmo, nijeste, nijesu** 19A3b

perf. pres. **budem, budeš, bude, budemo, budete, budu** (P) 5A3, 5A3✿, 12A1✿; *past tense* **bio, bilo, bila, bili, bila, bile** 6A2✿, 6A3✿; *aorist* **bih, bi, bi, bismo, biste, biše** 12A4✿, 17A2a

imperfect **bejah, bejaše bejaše, bejasmo, bejaste, bejahu** [E] 12A4✿, 17A2a; **bijah, bijaše, bijaše, bijasmo, bijaste, bijahu** [J] 12A4✿, 17A2a

bivati, bivam, bivaju (I) to be, to become, to occur 18A1a

bivši *adj.* former 12A2✿

bjegunac *m; Gsg* **bjegunca** [J] fugitive 18A3

bježati *see under* **pobjeći**

blag, blaga; blagi *adj.* gentle, mild 📖B.IV; **blago** [**vama**] lucky [you]

blagajna *f; Gpl* **blagajni** [B,C] cash register 2A4

blago *n* treasure 19A3b

blagostanje *n* prosperity

blagovaonica *f* [C] dining room 16A1b

blaži *adj.* gentler, milder *see* **blag**

bled, bleda; bledi *adj.* [E] pale

bleđi *adj.* [E] paler *see* **bled**

blesav *adj.* silly, idiotic, foolish 📖B.VI

blijed, blijeda; blijedi *adj.* [J] pale

blizak, bliska; bliski *adj.* close, near, intimate 18A3

blizina *f* nearness, proximity 20.III

blizu *prep.* + *Gen* near, close to ↩5 4A4

blizu *adv.* close, nearby 4B4

bliže *adv.* closer *see* **blizak, blisko**

bliži *adj.* closer *see* **blizak**

bližiti, bližim (I) to approach, to come near 📖B.IV *see also* **približiti**

bluza *f* blouse 📖A.VIII

bljeđi *adj.* [J] paler *see* **blijed**

boca *f* bottle

boemski *adj.* bohemian 18A3

Bog, bog *m; Gsg* **Boga, boga** *Npl* **bogovi, bozi** God, god 17A3a

bogat *adj.* rich, wealthy 16A2b

bogoslovija *f* theology 13B3

bogzna *(with* **ne***)* not ... anything; **nije bogzna šta** it's not anything much 19A1; **ne izgleda bogzna kako** it doesn't look like much of anything 9☺

boja *f* 1. color 2A3; 2. paint

bojati se, bojim se (I) + *Gen* to fear 7A2, 5A2✿, 9A2✿, 10A3

bok *excl.* [C] 1. hello; 2. goodbye 1A1, 1A1

bol *f; Gsg* **boli** *Isg* **boli** *or* **bolju** pain, [physical] ache 20.IV

bol *m; Gsg* **bola** *Npl* **bolovi** pain, anguish

bolan, bolna *adj.* painful 9A3

bolesnički *adj.* patient-related 20.II

bolestan, bolesna *adj.* sick, ill 10A4

boleti, boli (I) [E] *(3rd person only)* to hurt, to ache 10A4, 10A4✿ *see also* **oboleti** (P)

bolnica *f* hospital 14A3

bolničar *m* nurse *(m., general)* 11A2✿

bolničarka *f; DLsg* **bolničarki** *Gpl* **bolničarki** nurse *(f.)* 11A2✿

bolnički *adj.* hospital 14A3

bolje *adv.* better 6A3, 6A3✿, 11A2✿ *see* **dobro**

boljeti, boli; bolio, boljela (I) [J] *(3rd person only)* to hurt, to ache 10A4 *see also* **oboljeti**

bolji *adj.* better 11A2, 11A1✿ *see* **dobar**

bombon *m; Gsg* **bombona** [B,C] piece of candy 12A2

bombona *f* [B,S] piece of candy 12A2

bono *adv.* painfully [*poetic contraction of* **bolno**] 17A3a

bor *Gsg* **bora** *Npl* **borovi** 1. pine tree; 2. Christmas tree

boravak *m; Gsg* **boravka** *Npl* **boravci** stay 9A1

boravište *n* dwelling place 17A2a

boraviti (I) to stay, to dwell 16A2a

borba *f; Gpl* **borba** *or* **borbi** struggle, fight, battle ↩4

Bosanac *m; Gsg* **Bosanca** Bosnian *(m., gener-*

al) 1A4, 1A4

Bosanka *f; DLsg* **Bosanki** *Gpl* **Bosanki**
   Bosnian *(f.)* 1A4, 6A2🗲, 1A4
bosanski *adj.* Bosnian 2🌐
Bosna i Hercegovina *f* Bosnia and Herzegovina *or* Bosnia-Herzegovina *see map* 1🌐
Bošnjak *m; Gsg* **Bošnjaka** *Npl* **Bošnjaci**
   Bosniak *(m., general)* 1A4
Bošnjakinja *f* Bosniak *(f.)* 1A4
božji *adj.* divine 17C1
br. *abbr.* no., number 12A2
braco *m; Npl* **brace** *colloq.* brother B.VII
braća *Npl (sg form)* brothers 8A2, 8A2🗲 *see*
   brat
braniti, branim (I) to defend
brat *m* 1. brother [B,C,S] 2A3, 6A4🗲;
   2. cousin [B,S] *for pl. see* **braća**
brati, berem (I) to pick, to pluck ↦6
   📖A.I, 10A1🗲 *see* **sabrati**
bratić *m* cousin [C]
brdo *n* hill
brdovit *adj.* hilly
briga *f; DLsg* **brizi** worry, concern 7A1;
   budi bez brige don't worry 7A1
brijač *m; Gsg* **brijača** [B,C] barber 11A3
brijati se, brijem se (I) to shave 9A2, 9A2🗲
brinuti, brinem (I) to worry 13A3 *see* **zabrinuti**
brisati, brišem (I); **izbrisati, izbrišem** (P)
   1. to wipe; 2. to remove; 3. to erase 10A3
brod, *Gsg* **broda** *Npl* **brodovi** boat, ship 7A2
broj *m; Gsg* **broja** *Npl* **brojevi** 1. number
   3A1, 3A1🗲, 3A2🗲; 2. issue [of a
   publication]
brojan, brojna *adj.* numerous 17A4
brz, brza; brzi *adj.* quick, fast 2A2, 2A3🗲,
   11A2🗲
brzina *f* speed, velocity 15A1
brži *adj.* faster 11A2🗲 *see* **brz**
bubreg *m; Npl* **bubrezi** kidney 3A3, 3A3🗲
budala *f* fool
budem *see under* **biti**
budilica *f* [B,C] alarm clock 📖A.V
budilnik *m; Npl* **budilnici** [B,S] alarm clock
   📖A.V
buditi, budim (I); **probuditi, probudim** (P) to
   wake [someone] up 9A2; **buditi se, budim se**
   (I); **probuditi se, probudim se** (P) to wake up
   9A2🗲 *see also* **razbuditi**
budući *adj.* future; **buduće vreme** [E] **buduće vrijeme** [J] future tense 15A2
budući da *conj.* since 12A1, 12A1🗲
budućnost *f; Gsg* **budućnosti** *Isg* -**ošću** *or* -**osti**
   future 7A2
Bugarska *f (adj. form)* Bulgaria 1🌐
buka *f; DLsg* **buci** noise 20.I

buket *m; Gsg* **buketa** bouquet 📖A.IV
buktinja *f* torch 📖A.III

C

car *m; Isg* **carem** *Npl* **carevi** emperor 19A2b
celina *f* [E] [the] whole 19A1b
celokupan, celokupna *adj.* [E] entire 20.V
celovit *adj.* [E] complete, integral 19A1b
cena *f* [E] price, cost 16A2b
centar *m; Gsg* **centra** center 10A1
ceo, cela; celi *adj.* [E] whole 7A4; **ceo dan**
   all day 7A4
cesta *f* [B,C] road 14A2
ciao [C] *adv.* 1. hello; 2. goodbye 1A1,
   1A1
cigareta *f* cigarette 20.V
cijel (also **cio**), **cijela; cijeli** *adj.* [J] whole
   7A4; **cijeli dan** all day 7A4
cijena *f* [J] price, cost 16A2b
ciklus *m* cycle 19A1b
cimer *m* roommate *(m., general)* 12A1
cimerica *f* [B,C] roommate *(f.)* 12A1
cimerka *f; DLsg* **cimerki** *Gpl* **cimerki** [B,S]
   roommate *(f.)* 12A1
cimet *m* cinnamon 20.III
cio (also **cijel**), **cijela; cijeli** *adj.* [J] whole 7A4
cipela *f* shoe 1A2
cjelina *f* [J] [the] whole 19A1b
cjelokupan, cjelokupna *adj.* [J] entire 20.V
cjelovit *adj.* [J] complete, integral 19A1b
crkva *f; Gpl* **crkava** *or* **crkvi** church
crn, crna; crni *adj.* black 2A3, 14A3
Crna Gora *f* Montenegro 1🌐
crneti, crnim (I) [E] to blacken
crneti se, crnim se (I) [E] to look black *or* to
   become black 18A1a
Crnogorac *m; Gsg* **Crnogorca** Montenegrin
   (m., general) 1A4
Crnogorka *f; DLsg* **Crnogorki** *Gpl* **Crnogorki**
   Montenegrin *(f.)* 1A4
crnogorski *adj.* Montenegrin 2🌐
Crnogorsko primorje Montenegrin coast
crnjeti, crnim; crnio, crnjela (I) [J] to blacken
crnjeti se, crnim se; crnio se, crnjela se (I) [J]
   to look black *or* to become black 18A1a
crta *f; Gpl* **crti** 1. line; 2. feature, trait 10A3
crtani *adj.* 1. drawn; 2. animated [film] 7A3
crtanje *n* drawing, sketch 10A3, 10A4🗲
crtati (I); **nacrtati** (P) to draw, to sketch
   18A1b, 10A4🗲
crven, crvena; crveni *adj.* red 2A3, 2A3🗲,
   4A4🗲
crvendać *m* robin
cura *f* girl B.V
cveće *n; coll.* [E] flowers 12A2, 12A2🗲 *for
   sg see* **cvet**

cvet *m; Npl* cvetovi flower 12A2⚙ *see also*
  cveće

cvijeće *n; coll.* [J] flowers 12A2, 12A2⚙ *for
  sg see* cvijet

cvijet *m; Npl* cvjetovi [J] flower 12A2⚙ *see
  also* cvijeće

cvrkutati, cvrkućem (I) to chirp 16A1b

Č

ča *pron. (čakavian dialect)* what

čaj *m; Isg* čajem *Npl* čajevi tea 4A3

čak *adv.* even, as far as 4A2

čarapa *f* stocking, sock

čarobnjak *m; Gsg* čarobnjaka *Npl* čarobnjaci
  magician, wizard 13A3

čaršaf *m* [B] sheet (bedding) 12A1

čaršav *m* [S] sheet (bedding) 12A1

čas *m; Npl* časovi 1. class, lesson [B,S only];
    2. hour, o' clock (24-hour clock, [S only]);
  dvadeset časova 8 p.m. 14A3; 3. moment;
  istog časa that very moment 14A1; u
  zadnji čas at the last moment 16A1a; čas
  ... čas now … now 14A2; 14A1

časopis *m* magazine 2A4

častiti (I/P) to treat, to pay for 15A1

čaša *f* glass, cup 4A3

čašičica *f* small glass, small cup 📖B.VIII

Čeh *m; Npl* Česi Czech *(m., general)*

Čehinja *f* Czech *(f.)*

čega *pron.* what *(Gen)* 4A4, 4A2⚙, 7A1⚙
  see under šta *or* što

čekanje *n* waiting 11A2

čekati (I) to wait 5A2, 5A3⚙, 14A1⚙; jedva
  čekam I can hardly wait 📖A.V *see also*
  dočekati

čelo *n* forehead 18A2a

čemu *pron.* what *(Dat-Loc)* 7A1⚙; je li
  čemu is it worth anything? 14☺ *see under*
  šta *or* što

čest *adj.* often 11A2⚙

čestitati, čestitam, čestitaju (I) + *Dat* to congratulate 12A3

često *adv.* often, frequently 7A1, 10A2⚙

češće *adv.* more often 11A2⚙ *see* često

češći *adj.* more often 11A2⚙ *see* čest

češljati (I); počešljati (P) to brush, comb 9A2,
  9A2⚙

češnjak *m; Npl* češnjaci [C] garlic

četiri *num.* four (4) 5A2, 12A1⚙, 12A2⚙

četrdeset *num.* forty (40) 5A1, 5A1⚙

četiristo *num.* four hundred (400) 12A1⚙

četrnaest *num.* fourteen (14) 5A1, 5A1⚙

četrnaesti *adj.* fourteenth (14th) 14A1

četvero *n* [C] four [mixed gender] 📖B.VI,
  12A2⚙

četverokut *m* [C] quadrangle, rectangle

četvorica *f* four [men] 12A2⚙

četvoro *n* [B,S] four [mixed gender] 📖B.VI,
  12A2⚙

četvorougao *m; Gsg* četvorougla [B,S]
  quadrangle, rectangle

četvrtak *m; Gsg* četvrtka Thursday 2A1;
  četvrtkom on Thursdays 7A2⚙

četvrti *adj.* fourth (4th) 4A1, 6A2⚙, 12A3⚙

četvrt *f; Gsg* četvrti *Isg* četvrti 1. quarter [of
  an hour] [C] 14A2, 12A1⚙; 2. quarter [of a
  city]; 3. quarter [of a loaf of bread]

četvrtina *f* one fourth, a quarter (in mathematics) 12A1⚙

čiji, čije, čija *pron. adj.* whose 3A3, 3A3⚙

čim *conj.* as soon as 13A2

čim prije *adv.* as soon as possible [B,C] 13A2

čim, čime *pron.* what *(Instr)* 7A1⚙, 11A3⚙
  see under šta *or* što

čin *m; Npl* činovi act 📖B.I

činiti, činim (I); učiniti, učinim (P) to make, to
  do 19A3a

činiti se, čini se (I) 6A4; učiniti se, učini se
  (P) *(3rd person only)* 16A2a to seem, to
  appear 10A2⚙, 11A3⚙; čini mi se it
  seems to me, I think 6A4

činovnica *f* clerk *(f.)* 11A2⚙

činovnik *m; Npl* činovnici clerk *(m., general)*
  11A2⚙

činjenica *f* fact

čist *adj.* clean, pure 9A2

čistiti (I); počistiti (P) to clean 15A1

čisto *adv.* purely, simply

čitalac *m; Gsg* čitaoca *Gpl* čitalaca [B,C,S]
  reader [= person who reads]

čitanje *n* reading 📖B.III, 11A4⚙

čitaonica *f* reading room 16A2a

čitatelj *m* [C] reader [= person who reads] *(m.,
  general)*

čitateljica *f* [C] reader [= person who reads]
  (f.)

čitati (I) 2A1, 6A2⚙; pročitati (P) 10A2,
  10A4⚙ to read

čizma *f; Gpl* čizama boot

član *m; Npl* članovi member

članak *m; Gsg* članka article 18A3; novinski
  članak newspaper article 18A3

čokolada *f* chocolate

čovek *m* [E] 1. man; 2. person 1A4, 3A1⚙
  for pl see ljudi

čovjek *m* [J] 1. man; 2. person 1A4, 3A1⚙
  for pl see ljudi

čudan, čudna *adj.* strange, surprising, odd

čuditi se (I) + *Dat* to be amazed (at) 16A1b

čudo *n; Npl* čuda, čudesa miracle, wonder
  16A1a; divna li čuda what a miracle!
  16A1a; gle čuda well what d'ya know!

&B.IV

čuđenje *n* surprise, amazement 20.II

čujan, čujna *adj.* audible &B.VII

čuti, čujem (I/P) to hear 5C1, 7A3☼; **čuti se, čujem se** (I/P) to talk to one another, to be in contact [*as in* **čujemo se** we're in touch] 8A3, 8A3☼ *see* **začuti se**

čuvar *m; Gsg* **čuvara** guard, watchman 20.VII

čuvati, čuvam, čuvaju (I) to keep, to guard 10A4; **očuvati, očuvam, očuvaju** (P) to preserve 19A3b; **čuvati se, čuvam se, čuvaju se** (I) to watch out, to be careful 10A4

čuven, čuvena; čuveni *adj.* famous, renowned 15A1

čvrst *adj.* firm, sturdy 14A1

čvršći *adj.* firmer, sturdier *see* **čvrst**

Ć

ćao *excl.* [S] 1. hello; 2. goodbye 1A1, ⌐1A1⌐

ćaskati (I) to chat &B.V

ćebe *n; Gsg* **ćebeta** [S] blanket 12A1

ćerati (I); **poćerati** (P) to drive away, to chase *(Montenegrin)* ⌐19A3b⌐ *see* **tjerati**

ćerka, DLsg ćerki Gpl ćerki [S] daughter 8A1 *see* **kćerka**

ćevapčići *m (pl form)* grilled minced meat 10A1

ćirilica *f* Cyrillic alphabet

ću, ćeš, će, ćemo, ćete, će 9A1☼ ⌐9B1⌐ *see under* **hteti** [E] **htjeti** [J]

ćuprija *f* [B,S] bridge

ćutati, ćutim (I) [B,S] to be silent 17A3a

D

da yes 1A2

da *conj.* in order to, that, let... 2A1, 2A1☼, 11A4☼, 13A2☼, 13A3☼

da li [B,S] *(opening phrase for question)* 1A2, 1A2☼

dah *m; Npl* **dahovi** breath 20.VIII

daidža *m; Npl* **daidže** [B] maternal uncle 5A3, 5A3☼

daidžinica *f* [B] aunt [= maternal uncle's wife] 5A3

dakle *adv.* consequently, therefore 4A2

daleko *adv.* far 4A4, 4A4☼

Dalmacija *f* the Croatian coast from Zadar to the border with Montenegro 6☉

Dalmatinska zagora *f* mountainous region inland from the Dalmatian coast 6☉

dalmatinski *adj.* Dalmatian 8A3

dalje *adv.* further 7☺; **i tako dalje** *(abbr.* **itd.**) and so forth 16A1a *see* **daleko**

daljina *f* distance 15A1

dan *m; Gsg* **dana** *Npl* **dani** *Gpl* **dana** day ↦4 1A3, 3A2☼; **dan danas** (to) this very day

18A3; **danima** for days; **beli dan** [E] **bijeli dan** [J] broad daylight 19A3a; **narednog dana** [S only] **idućeg dana** [B,C,S] **sledećeg dana** [E] **sljedećeg dana** [J] on the next day

danas *adv.* today 3A1, 10A2☼; **dan danas** (to) this very day 18A3

današnji *adj.* today, today's 17A2b

dar *m; Npl* **darovi** gift &B.III

darovati, darujem (I) to give a gift 20.VIII

daska *f; DLsg* **dasci** *Gpl* **dasaka** board &A.VIII; **daska za peglanje** [B,C,S] **daska za glačanje** [C] ironing board &A.VIII

dati, dam (P) 5A2; **davati, dajem** (I) ↦6 3A1☼, 10A2☼, 12A4☼ to give; **ne da** [mi] **se** [B,C] [I] am not in the mood 9A3, 7A3☼; **ma, daj!** come on, you've got to be kidding 7A3 *see also* **dodati, izdati, predati, prodati, udati se**

dativ *m* dative [case]

datum *m* date 20.VIII

davati *see under* **dati**

davni *adj.* distant [in time] 17A2b

debeo, debela; debeli *adj.* fat 3A3, 2A3☼, 6A2☼, 11A2☼

deblji *adj.* fatter, thicker *see* **debeo**

deca *pl (f sg form)* [E] children 8A2, 8A2☼, 9A2☼ *for sg see* **dete**

decembar *m; Gsg* **decembra** [B,S] December 6A2, ⌐6A2⌐

dečak *m; Gsg* **dečaka** *Npl* **dečaci** [E] boy, young man 17A1a

dečko *m; Npl* **dečki** boy &B.V

ded *m; Npl* **dedovi** [E] grandfather 9A4

deda *m; Npl* **dede** grandpa 8☺

deka *f; DLsg* **deki** [B,C] blanket 12A1

deliti, delim (I); **podeliti, podelim** (P) [E] 1. to share; 2. to divide, to separate 9A3

delo *n* [E] work, act

delovati, delujem (I) [E] to act, to take action 20.VIII

demokratski *adj.* democratic ⌐14B2⌐

deo *m; Gsg* **dela** *Npl* **delovi** [E] part, portion 4☉

deset *num.* ten (10) 5A4, 5A1☼, 12A3☼

desetak *num.* ten or so, about ten 12A1☼

desetero *n* [C] ten (group of mixed gender)

deseti *adj.* tenth (10th) 10A1, 6A2☼

desetorica *f* ten [men]

desetoro *n* [B,S] ten (group of mixed gender)

desiti se (P) &B.VIII; **dešavati se, dešava se, dešavaju se** (I) [B,S] *(3rd sg only)* 17A2b to happen

desni *adj.* right (as opposed to left) 13A4

dešavati se *see under* **desiti se**

dete *n; Gsg* **deteta** [E] child 8A2, 8A2☼

for pl see **dèca**

devedèset *num.* ninety (90) 5A1, 5A1☼

dèvet *num.* nine (9) 5A2, 5A1☼, 12A1☼

dèvetero *n* [C] nine (group of mixed gender)

dèveti *adj.* ninth (9th) 9A1, 6A2☼, 12A3☼

devètnaest *num.* nineteen (19) 5A1, 5A1☼

devètnaesti *adj.* nineteenth (19th) 19A1

devetòrica *f* nine [men]

dèvetoro *n* [B,S] nine (group of mixed gender)

devetstȍ *num.* nine hundred (900) 12A1☼

dèvojka *f; DLsg* **dèvojci** *Gpl* **devòjaka** [E] girl, young woman ☛4 4A1, 5A1☼, 8A1☼

dèžuran, dèžurna *adj.* on duty 20.VII

dìći [dìgnuti], dȉgnem (P); **dìzati, dȉžem** (I) to raise, to lift 14A1

digitàlni *adj.* digital 19A3b

dìgnuti *see under* **dìći**

dijèliti, dijèlim (I); **podijèliti, podìjelim** (P) [J] 1. to share; 2. to divide, to separate 9A3

dijèta *f* diet 20.VI

dijète *n; Gsg* **djèteta** [J] child 8A2, 8A2☼
for pl see **djèca**

dȋm *m; Npl* **dìmovi** smoke 20.II

dìnar *m; Gpl* **dìnara** currency of Yugoslavia; **hrvàtski dìnar** transition currency in Croatia of early '90s 12A2 **srpski dìnar** (*abbr.* RSD) currency of Serbia

dȉo *m; Gsg* **dìjela** *Npl* **djèlovi** [J] part, portion 4☼

diplòmirati, diplòmiram, diplòmiraju (I/P) to graduate (from an institution of higher learning) ☐B.VI

dìrektor *m* [B,C,S] director (*m., general*) 11A2☼

direktòrica *f* [B,C,S] director (*f.*) 11A2☼

disciplìna *f* discipline ☐B.III

dȋsk *m; Npl* **dìskovi** disk 19A3b

dìskretan, dìskretna *adj.* discreet ☐B.VI

diskùsija *f* discussion 19A2b

dȋvan, dȋvna *adj.* marvelous, wonderful 3A2; **dȋvna li čùda** what a miracle! 16A1b

dìzati *see under* **dìći**

djèca *pl (f sg form)* [J] children 8A2, 9A2☼, 6☼ *for sg see* **dijète**

djèčak *m; Gsg* **djèčaka** *Npl* **djèčaci** [J] boy, young man 17A1a

djȅd *m; Npl* **djȅdovi** [J] grandfather 9A4

djèlo *n* [J] work, act

djèlovati, djèlujem (I) [J] to act, to take action 20.VIII

djèvojka *f; DLsg* **djèvojci** *Gpl* **djevòjaka** [J] girl, young woman ☛4 4A1, 8A1☼, 6☼ 19A3b

dlȃn *m; Npl* **dlànovi** palm of the hand 19A1b

dnȇvni *adj.* daily 12A1; **dnȇvna sòba** living room 16A1a

dnȍ *n; Gsg* **dnȁ** bottom 14A1

dȍ *prep. + Gen* to, next to, by, up to ☛5 4A4, 4A4☼

dȍba *n; indecl.* time, season, times 17A3b

dòbar, dòbra; dòbri *adj.* 1. good; 2. fine ☛4 1A3, 5A1☼, 6A1☼, 8A1☼, 10A2☼, 11A1☼; **dòbro jùtro** good morning 2A4; **dòbar dȃn** hello 1A3, 2A4, 13A1; **dòbro vèče** [B,S] **dòbra vèčer** [C] good evening 3A2 *see also* **bòlji**

dòbiti, dòbijem (P) 11A2; **dobívati, dobívam, dobívaju** (I) [B,C,S] **dobìjati, dobìjam** (I) [B,S] to receive, to get, to obtain 12A1☼

dòbro *adv.* well 2A3 *see also* **dòbar**

dòbro *n; Gpl* **dòbara** 1. good, wellbeing; 2. property

dòbro dòšao, dòbro dòšla, dòbro dòšli *excl.* welcome! 13A1, 13A1☼

dobrodòšao, dobrodòšla *adj.* welcome 13A1☼

dočárati, dòčaram, dočáraju (P); **dočáravati, dòčaravam, dočáravaju** (I) to conjure up 17A3b

dòčekati (P) to greet, to welcome [someone arriving] 5A3, 5A3☼ *see* **čèkati**

dòći, dȍđem; dòšao, dòšla (P); **dòlaziti** (I) to come, to arrive ☛6 5A2, 5A2☼, 10A2☼, B.VIII; **ne dòlazi u òbzir** out of the question 5A4, 7A3☼, 10A1☼ *see* **ìći**

dòdatan, dòdatna *adj.* additional 16A3b

dòdati (P) ☐B.II; **dodávati, dòdajem** (I) ☐A.III to add *see* **dàti**

dodávati *see under* **dòdati**

dòdirnuti, dȍdirnem (P); **dodírivati, dodìrujem** (I) to touch 20.II

dòduše *adv.* 1. truly, indeed; 2. although 11A2

dògađaj *m* event 16A3b

dògađati se *see under* **dogòditi se**

dogòdine *adv.* next year 16A2a

dogòditi se, dògodi se (P) 12A4, 9A2☼; **dògađati se, dògađa se, dògađaju se** (I) [B,C,S] 20.VI (*3rd person only*) to happen

dògovor *m* agreement ☐B.VII

dogovòriti se, dogòvorim se (P); **dogovárati se, dogòvaram se, dogováraju se** (I) to agree upon (*often used with* **òko** + *Gen*) 11A2, 14A1☼

dòhvatiti (P) to grab hold of 19A3a

dòista *adv.* truly 16A2b

dòjam *m; Gsg* **dòjma** *Npl* **dòjmovi** [B,C] impression 16A3

dȍk *conj.* while 4☼; **dȍk ne** until 10A3, 6A2☼

dòktor *m* [B,C,S] doctor (*m., general*) 11A2☼

doktorica *f* [B,C,S]   doctor *(f.)*   11A2✿

doktorka *f; DLsg* **doktorki** *Gpl* **doktorki** [S]
doctor *(f.)*   11A2✿

dokumentarac *m; Gsg* **dokumentarca**   documentary film   7A3

dolazak *m; Gsg* **dolaska**   arrival   14A4

dolaziti   *see under* **doći**

dole *adv.* [E]   below, down

doliti, dolijem (P)   14A1; **dolivati, dolivam,
dolivaju** (I) [E] *or* **dolijevati, dolijevam,
dolijevaju** (I) [J]   to add by pouring

dolje *adv.* [J]   below, down

dom *m; Gsg* **doma** *Npl* **domovi**   1. home;
2. dormitory;   **doma** *adv.* [C]   1. [toward]
home;   2. at home   9A2

domaći *adj.*   domestic   1A4;   **domaća zadaća**
[B,C] **domaći zadatak** [S]   homework   1A4

domaćica *f*   housekeeper (female)   11A2✿

domovina *f*   homeland   17A1a

doneti, donesem (P)   13A2, 10A1✿; **donositi**
(I) [E]   to bring   *see* **nositi**

donijeti, donesem; donio, donijela (P)   13A2,
10A1✿; **donositi** (I) [J]   to bring   *see* **nositi**

dopadati se   *see under* **dopasti se**

dopasti se, dopadnem se; dopao se, dopala se
(P) 📖B.IV; **dopadati se** (I) + *Dat* [B,S]   to
be pleasing to   16A1a, 6A4✿

dopirati   *see* **dopreti**

dopreti, doprem; dopro, doprla (P); **dopirati,
dopirem** (I) [E]   to reach, to penetrate, to get
through to   20.I

doprijeti, doprem; dopro, doprla (P); **dopirati,
dopirem** (I) [J]   to reach, to penetrate, to get
through to   20.I

dopustiti, dopustim (P)   16A2a; **dopuštati, do-
puštam, dopuštaju** (I)   📖B.III   to permit
see **pustiti**

dopuštati,   *see under* **dopustiti**

doručak *m; Gsg* **doručka**   breakfast   7A1

doručkovati, doručkujem (I/P)   to eat breakfast   7A1

dosadan, dosadna *adj.*   1. boring, dull;   2. annoying   5A1, 6A3✿

dosadašnji *adj.*   former, previous   16A2b

dosaditi, dosadim (P)   📖B.V; **dosađivati,
dosađujem** (I) to bore [someone];   **dosaditi
se, dosadim se** (P); **dosađivati se, dosađujem
se** (I)   to be bored

doseći [dosegnuti], dosegnem (P) 20.III; **dosezati, dosežem** (I)   to reach [up to something]

dosegnuti   *see under* **doseći**

doseliti se, doselim se (P)   16A3b; **doseljavati
se, doseljavam se, doseljavaju se** (I)   to
move to

dospeti, dospem (P)   16A1a; **dospevati,
dospevam, dospevaju** (I) [E]   to arrive at

dospjeti, dospijem; dospio, dospjela (P)
16A1a; **dospijevati, dospijevam, dospij-
evaju** (I) [J]   1. to arrive at;   2. to mature

dosta *adv.*   1. enough, enough of;   2. rather
10A4

dostojanstvo *n*   dignity   20.I

dovesti, dovedem; doveo, dovela (P)   20.III;
dovoditi, dovodim (I)   to bring, to lead to, to
conduct   *see* **voditi**

dovesti, dovezem; dovezao, dovezla (P);
dovoziti, dovozim (I)   to bring by vehicle
10A1✿   *see* **voditi**

doviđenja *excl.*   goodbye   2A4

dovoljan, dovoljna *adj.*   sufficient, enough
11A4

dozivati, dozivam, dozivaju (I)   to call out to
19A3a

dozvoliti, dozvolim (P): **dozvoljavati, dozvolj-
avam, dozvoljavaju** (I)   to allow   16A3b

doživeti, doživim (P): **doživljavati, doživljavam, doživljavaju** (I) [E]   to experience
📖B.IV

doživjeti, doživim; doživio, doživjela (P): **doživljavati, doživljavam doživljavaju** (I) [J]
to experience   📖B.IV

doživljaj *m*   experience

doživljavati   *see under* **doživeti** *or* **doživjeti**

drag *adj.*   dear   2A2;   **baš mi je drago!**   I am
truly delighted!   6A3;   **drage volje**   gladly
16A3b;   **drago kamenje**   precious stones
12A2

dramski *adj.*   dramatic;   **dramske umetnosti**
[E] **dramske umjetnosti** [J]   dramatic arts
13B3

dres *m; Npl* **dresovi**   sports jersey   📖B.I

drhtati, dršćem (I)   to tremble, to shiver
17A3a

drška *f; DLsg* **dršci** [B,S]   handle   14A1

drug *m; Npl* **drugovi**   1. friend, pal, schoolmate, companion *(m., general)* [B,S only]
1A4, 3A2✿;   2. comrade *(m., general)*

drugarica *f* [B,S]   1. friend, pal, schoolmate *(f.)*
[B,S only]   4A2;   2. comrade *(f.)*

drugi *adj.*   1. second (2nd)   2A1, 6A2✿;
2. other, another   5A1   **Drugi svetski rat** [E]
Drugi svjetski rat [J]   Second World War
12A4, 12A3✿;   **jedan drugi**   one another
[*as in* **jedni drugima** to one another]
11A2✿, 15A2✿, ⌐16B1⌐

drugo *adv.*   1. secondly   4A4;   2. other   16A1b;
3. else   13A1

društven *adj.*   social   19A2b;   **društvene
nauke** [B,S] **društvene znanosti** [C]   social
sciences   13B3

društvo *n; Gpl* **društava**   1. society;   2. company of friends   10A1, 10A1✿

družiti se, družim se (I)   to socialize   📖B.IV

drveće *n* (*coll.*)   trees   12A2✿   *for sg see* **drvo**

drven *adj.*   wooden   20.V

drvo *n; Gsg* **drveta** *Npl* **drveta**   tree   12A2✿,
📖A.VI   *see also* **drveće**

drvo *n; Gsg* **drveta** *Npl* **drva**   wood, firewood

drzak, drska *adj.*   insolent   20.IV

držak *m; Gsg* **drška** [C]   handle   14A1

držati, držim (I)   to hold, to keep   ↤6
12A1, 10A1✿   *see also* **izdržati, održati,
sadržati**

država *f*   state   6A1, 6A1✿

državljanin *m; Npl* **državljani**   citizen (m.,
general)

državljanka *f; DLsg* **državljanki** *Gpl*
državljanki   citizen (f.)

dubina *f*   depth   15A1

dublji *adj.*   deeper   *see* **dubok**

dubok *adj.*   deep

dućan *m; Gsg* **dućana** [B,C,S]   store, shop
12A2, ⌐12A2⌐

duet *m; Gsg* **dueta**   duet   15A1

dug, duga; dugi *adj.*   long [in time *or* distance]
3A3, 10A2✿, 11A2✿

duga *f; DLsg* **dugi**   rainbow   📖A.VIII

dugačak, dugačka; dugački *adj.*   long [in dis-
tance]

dugmad *f; Gsg* **dugmadi** [B,S] (*sg form*)
buttons

dugme *n; Gsg* **dugmeta** [B,S]   button   8A2,
8A2✿   *for pl see* **dugmad**

dugo *adv.*   long [in time or distance]

duh *m; Npl* **dusi**   spirit   17C1, 8A1✿

duh *m; Npl* **duhovi**   ghost   17C1

duhovit, duhovita *adj.*   witty   7A3

dulje *adv.*   longer   20.V   *see* **dugo**

dulji *adj.*   longer   *see* **dug**

duša *f*   soul   17A2

duži *adj.*   longer   *see* **dug**

dužina *f*   length

dva *num.* (with *m* or *n* noun)   two (2)   4A3,
4A3✿, 5A1✿, 12A1✿, 12A2✿

dvadeset *num.*   twenty (20)   6A1, 5A1✿,
12A1✿

dvadeseti *adj.*   twentieth (20th)   20A1

dvanaest *num.*   twelve (12)   5A4, 5A1✿,
12A1✿,

dvanaesti *adj.*   twelfth (12th)   12A1, 6A2✿

dve *num.* [E] (with *f* noun)   two (2)   4A3,
4A3✿, 12A1✿

dvesta *num.* [E]   two hundred (200)
12A1✿,12A2✿

dvesto *num.* [E]   two hundred (200)
12A1✿,12A2✿

dvije *num.* [J] (with *f* noun)   two (2)   4A3,
4A3✿, 12A1✿, 12A2✿

dvjesta *num.* [J] [B/S]   two hundred (200)
12A1✿, 12A2✿

dvjesto *num.* [J]   two hundred (200)   12A1✿,
12A2✿

dvoje *n*   two [a couple, mixed gender]   12A2✿

dvojica *f*   two [men]   12A2✿

dvor *m; Gsg* **dvora** *Npl* **dvorovi**   1. courtyard
2. court   📖B.V

dvorana *f*   hall [*e.g.* concert]   16A1a

dvorište *n*   yard   📖A.VI

dvostruk *adj.*   double, twofold   15A1

DŽ

džamija *f*   mosque

džem *m; Gsg* **džema** *Npl* **džemovi**   jam   7A1

džezva *f; Gpl* **džezava** *or* **džezvi**   Turkish
coffeepot   *see photos in Lesson 14*   14A1

džez *m*   jazz

Đ

đak *m; Gsg* **đaka** *Npl* **đaci**   elementary or secondary school student, pupil   5A1, 8A1✿

E

ej! *excl.*   hey!   2A3

egzibicija *f*   show   15A1

ekavica *f*   ekavian   15A1

ekipa *f*   team   16A1a

ekonomija *f*   economics   13B3

elegantan, elegantna *adj.*   elegant   11A1

električar *m*   electrician (m., general)   11A2✿

električarka *f; DLsg* **električarki** *Gpl*
električarki *m*   electrician (f.)   11A2✿

elektrotehnika *f; DLsg* **elektrotehnici**
electrical engineering   13B3

Engleska *f (adj. form)*   England   4A1

engleski *adj.*   English   4A1

Engleskinja *f*   Englishwoman   1A4

Englez *m; Gsg* **Engleza**   English person, Englishman   1A4

eno *part.*   there (pointing)

epoha *f; DLsg* **epohi** *or* **eposi**   age, epoch   6A2,
6A2✿

epski *adj.*   epic   19A3b

esej *m; Gsg* **eseja**   essay   18A3

etnologija *f*   ethnology   16A2b

eto *part.*   look!   📖B.VI

Europa *f* [C]   Europe   4A1

euro *m* [B,C]   1. euro [currency];   2. currency of
Montenegro   ⌐12B5⌐

eventualan, eventualna *adj.*   possible, concei-
vable but uncertain   16A3a

evo *part.*   here (pointing)   4A4, 4A4✿

evro *m* [B,S]   1. euro [currency];   2. currency of
Montenegro   ⌐12B5⌐

Evropa *f* [B,S]   Europe   4A1

F

fabrika *f; DLsg* **fabrici** [B,S]   factory   20.II
fakat *colloq.*   really, indeed   📖B.VII
fakat *m; Gsg* **fakta** *Gpl* **fakata** [B,S]   fact
fakt *m: Gpl* **fakata** [B,C]   fact
fakultet *m; Gsg* **fakulteta**   school or college of a university, faculty [*e.g.* Faculty of Medicine] 5A2, 4A1✿, 6A1✿, ⌐5A2¬
faliti (I)   1. to lack   [*as in* **nešto tu fali**   there's something missing here];   2. to miss + *Dat* [*as in* **fališ mi**   I miss you]
farmaceut *m*   pharmacist   11A3
fašistički *adj.*   fascist   18A3
februar *m* [B,S]   February   6A2, ⌐6A2¬
Federacija Bosne i Hercegovine   the Federation of Bosnia and Herzegovina   *see map* 4🌐
fenirati, feniram, feniraju (I); **isfenirati, isfeniram, isfeniraju** (P)   to blow dry [hair] 📖B.V
festival *m; Gsg* **festivala**   festival   16A1a
figura *f*   figure   19A1b
fildžan *m*   Turkish coffee cup   *see photos in* 14A1
film *m; Npl* **filmovi**   movie, cinema   2A3; **akcioni film**   action movie   7A3; **crtani film** animated film, cartoon   7A3
filmski *adj.*   pertaining to film or movies 📖B.VII
filologija *f* [B,S]   philology   13B3
filozofija *f*   philosophy   13B3
fin *adj.*   nice, fine   2A3, 3A1✿, 6A1✿, 8A1✿
financiranje *n* [C]   financial support   16A2a
finansiranje *n* [B,S]   financial support   16A2a
fizički *adj.*   physical; **fizička kultura** *or* **fiskultura** [B,C,S]   physical education   13B3
fizika *f; DLsg* **fizici**   physics   13B3
folklor *m; Gsg* **folklora**   folklore; **smotra folklora**   folklore festival   16A2a
forma *f; Gpl* **forma, formi**   form, shape   19A3b
formalan, formalna *adj.*   formal   📖B.VIII
formular *m; Gsg* **formulara**   blank, form 16A2a
fotelj *f; Gsg* **fotelja** [B,S]   armchair   📖B.V
fotelja *f* [B,C]   armchair   📖B.V
foto-aparat *m; Gsg* **foto-aparata**   camera 📖A.VI
fotografija *f*   photo   20.V
Francuska *f (adj. form)*   France   4A1
francuski *adj.*   French   2A4
Francuskinja *f*   Frenchwoman   1A4
Francuz *m; Gsg* **Francuza**   1. French person; 2. Frenchman   1A4
fraza *f*   phrase   17A1b
frizerka *f; DLsg* **frizerki** *Gpl* **frizerki** hairdresser *(f.)*   📖B.I

frizerski *adj.*   pertaining to hairdressing   📖B.V
frizura *f*   hairdo   📖B.V
frižider *m; Gsg* **frižidera** [B,C,S]   refrigerator
fudbal *m* [B,S]   soccer   📖A.I
fudbaler *m; Gsg* **fudbalera** [B,S]   soccer player 📖B.IV
fudbalski *adj.* [B,S]   soccer; **fudbalski klub** soccer team   📖B.I
funkcija *f*   function
funkcionirati, funkcioniram, funkcioniraju (I/P) [C]   to function   19A1b
funkcionisati, funkcionišem (I/P) [B,S]   to function   19A1b
furati se, furam se, furaju se (I) *colloq.* [B,C]   1. to drive;   2. to go after   📖B.V

G

ga *pron. (clitic)   (Acc-Gen)*   1. him;   2. it   2A1, 6A3✿, 6A4✿, 10A1✿   *see under* **on**
gaće *f (pl form)*   men's underpants
gaćice *f (pl form)*   women's underpants
galama *f*   ruckus, hubbub   20.VII
galeb *m; Npl* **galebi** *or* **galebovi**   sea gull
gasiti, gasim (I); **ugasiti, ugasim** (P)   to put out, to extinguish   20.V
gavran *m; Npl* **gavrani** *or* **gavranovi**   raven
gde *adv.* [E]   where   4A2, 5A1✿, 9A2✿, ⌐7A4¬ **gde god**   wherever   18A3
gdje *adv.* [J]   where   4A2, 5A1✿, 9A2✿ ⌐7A4¬ ⌐6🌐¬; **gdje god**   wherever   18A3, **đe** where *(Montenegrin)*   19A3a, ⌐19A3a¬ ⌐19A3b¬
genitiv *m*   genitive [case]
geografija *f*   geography   13B3
geografski *adj.*   geographical   [B,C,S] 1🌐
germanistika *f; DLsg* **germanistici**   study of Germanic languages   13B3
germanski *adj.*   Germanic   B.II
gimnazija *f*   secondary school   📖B.I
gimnazijalac *m; Gsg* **gimnazijalca**   secondary school student *(m., general)*   📖B.I
gimnazijalka *f; DLsg* **gimnazijalki** *Gpl* **gimnazijalki**   secondary school student *(f.)*
gitara *f*   guitar
gladak, glatka *adj.*   smooth
gladan, gladna; gladni *adj.*   hungry   4A3
glađi *adj.*   smoother   *see* **gladak**
glagol *m*   verb   17A1b
glas *m; Npl* **glasovi**   1. voice   19A2b;   2. vote; 3. word, news   19A3a;   **u jedan glas** [speaking] as one   📖B.IV
glasan, glasna *adj.*   loud   📖B.IV
glasovir *m* [C]   piano
glava *f; Asg* **glavu** *DLsg* **glavi** *Npl* **glave** *Gpl* **glava**   head   10A4
glavobolja *n.*   headache

glavni *adj.* main, principal; **glavni grad** capital [city] 2🌐

glazba *f; Gpl* **glazbi** [C] music 7A4

glazbalo *n* [C] musical instrument 19A3b

glazbeni *adj.* [C] musical 16A3b

glazbenica *f* [C] musician *(f.)* 11A2✿

glazbenik *m; Npl* **glazbenici** [C] musician *(m., general)* 11A2✿

gle! *excl.* look!; **gle čuda** well, what d'ya know! 📖B.IV

gledalac *m; Gsg* **gledaoca** *Gpl* **gledalaca** [B,C,S] spectator, audience member 15A1

gledatelj *m* [C] spectator, audience member *(m., general)* 15A1

gledateljica *f* [C] spectator, audience member *(f.)* 15A1

gledati (I) to look at, to watch ↦6 2A2; **pogledati** (P) to glance at 20.V; **ugledati** (P) to catch sight of 20.VIII; **gle!** *excl.* look!; **gle čuda** well, what d'ya know! 📖B.IV *see also* **odgledati, izgledati**

gluh, gluha; gluhi *adj.* [B,C] deaf 18A1a

glumac *m; Gsg* **glumca** actor 11A2✿

glumica *f* actress 11A2✿

glumiti, glumim (I) 1. to act [a role] 📖B.IV 2. to feign [B,C,S]

glup, glupa, glupi *adj.* stupid 2A2, 11A2✿

glupača *f* stupid female 📖B.V

gluplji *adj.* stupider 8☺, 11A2✿ *see* **glup**

glupost *f; Gsg* **gluposti** *Isg* **-ošću** *or* **-osti** stupidity 13☺

gluši *adj.* [B,C] deafer *see* **gluh**

gluv, gluva; gluvi *adj.* [S] deaf 18A1a

gluvlji *adj.* [S] deafer *see* **gluv**

gnezdo *n Gpl* **gnezda** [E] nest ↦4 5A1

gnijezdo *n; Gpl* **gnijezda** [J] nest ↦4 5A1

go, gola; goli *adj.* [B,S] naked 18A1a

-god *adv.* -ever [*as in* **kad god** whatever 13A3✿, 18A3 ; **kako god**, however, etc.]

godina *f* year 6A2, 12A3✿; **godinama** for years 7A2, 7A2✿; **godinu dana** [for] a year 6A2, 6A2✿, 9A1✿; **nepunih 15 godina** not quite 15 years old 20.II

godišnji *adj.* annual 12A1

godište *n* year of birth 12A3, 12A3✿

goditi (I) to please, to gratify 20.III

gol, gola *adj.* [B,C] naked 18A1a

golem, golema *adj.* enormous 19A3a

golub *m; Npl* **golubi** *or* **golubovi** dove, pigeon

gora *f* wooded mountain or hill

gord, gorda; gordi *adj.* proud 18A1a

gore *adv.* above, up

gore *adv.* worse 11A1, 11A1✿ *see* **loše**

gori *adj.* worse 11A2, 11A1✿ *see* **loš**

goreti, gorim (I) [E] to burn

gorjeti, gorim; gorio, gorjela (I) [J] to burn

gornji *adj.* upper 17A4

gorski *adj.* hilly, mountainous 18A1a

gospoda *pl (f sg form)* gentlemen 8A2 *for sg see* **gospodin**

gospodar *m; Gsg* **gospodara** 1. master, lord; 2. owner 📖A.V

gospodarstvo *n* [B,C] economy

gospodin *m* gentleman, Mr., sir 2A2 *for pl see* **gospoda**

gospođa *f* married woman, Mrs., Ms., ma'am, lady 2A2

gospođica *f* unmarried woman, Ms., Miss 16A2b

gost *m; Gsg* **gosta** *Gpl* **gostiju** *(m., general)*; guest 13A1; **u gostima** visiting, being a guest 17A4

gostionica *f* inn, tavern, small restaurant 14A2

gostovati, gostujem (I) to be a guest 16A2a

gošća *f* guest *(f.)*

gotov *adj.* finished, done

gotovo *adv.* 1. that's that! 11A1, 4A1✿ 2. almost 20.IV

govno *n; Gpl* **govana** 1. excrement; 2. *vulg.* shit

govoriti, govorim (I) to speak 6A4 *see also* **izgovoriti, odgovoriti, nagovoriti, progovoriti, razgovoriti**

grad *m; Npl* **gradovi** city ↦4 3A3, 3A1✿, 4A1✿, 5A1✿, 6A1✿, 7A1✿, 8A1✿; **plan grada** map of town 11A3; **glavni grad** capital [city] 2🌐

gradić *m; Gsg* **gradića** small town 3A3

gradski *adj.* city, urban 13A4

građanin *m; Npl* **građani** 1. citydweller, resident of a city; 2. citizen *(m., general)*

građanka *f* 1. citydweller, resident of a city; 2. citizen *(f.)*

grah *m* [B,C] beans

gramatički *adj.* grammar, grammatical 17A2b

gramatika *f; DLsg* **gramatici** grammar 2A4

grana *f; Asg* **granu** *Npl* **grane** *Gpl* **grana** branch 18A1a *see also* **granje**

granje *n; coll.* branches 12A2✿ *for sg see* **grana**

granica *f* border 3🌐

granuti, grane (P) *(3rd person only)* to burst forth 14A2

Grčka *f; adj. form* Greece 4A1

greška *f; Gpl* **grešaka** mistake, error 📖B.III

grip *n.* [S] flu, influenza

gripa *n.* [B,C] flu, influenza

Grk *m; Npl* **Grci** Greek person *(m., general)*

Grkinja *f* Greek person *(f.)*

grliti (I); **zagrliti** (P) to embrace 16A1b

grlo *n* throat 18A3

grom *m; Gsg* **groma** *Npl* **gromovi** thunder,

lightning

grozan, grozna *adj.* terrible, horrible 3A1

groznica *f* fever

grub, gruba; grubi *adj.* rough

grublji *adj.* rougher see grub

grudnjak *m; Npl* grudnjaci bra, brassiere

grupa *f* group 16A3b

grupirati, grupiram, grupiraju (I/P) [B,C] to group 19A2b

grupisati, grupišem (I/P) [B,S] to group 19A2b

gubitak *m; Gsg* gubitka loss 20.II

gubiti (I); izgubiti, izgubim (P) to lose 9A3; izgubiti glavu to panic, to lose one's composure 10A2

guma *f* 1. rubber; 2. eraser 10A3

gumb *m; Npl* gumbi [C] button 📖A.VIII

guska *f; Gpl* guski *or* gusaka goose

gusle *f; Gpl* gusala *(pl form)* traditional one-stringed instrument that accompanies the singing of epic songs *see photos in* 19A3b

gust, gusta; gusti *adj.* thick, dense 14A4

gušći *adj.* thicker, denser *see* gust

gužva *f; Gpl* gužvi [B,C,S] 1. crowd; 2. *colloq.* trouble 📖B.IV

H

hajde *excl.* come on! 7A3

hajduk *n; Gsg* hajduka *Npl* hajduci brigand 19A3a

haljina *f* dress 11A1

hauba *f* 1. salon hairdryer 📖B.V; 2. hood (Am.), bonnet (Br.) [of car]

hemičar *m* [B,S] chemist *(m., general)* 11A2✿

hemičarka *f; DLsg* hemičarki *Gpl* hemičarki [B,S] chemist *(f.)* 11A2✿

hemija *f* [B,S] chemistry 13B3

hemijski *adj.* [B,S] chemical; hemijska olovka ballpoint pen 2A4

herceg *m; Npl* hercezi duke ⟦ 17C5 ⟧

hiljada *f* [B,C,S] thousand 12A1, 12A1✿; hiljadu one thousand (1,000) 12A1, 12A1✿ ⟦ 12A2 ⟧

hiniti, hinim (I) [B,C] to feign 20.V

historija *f* [B] history 13B3, ⟦ 17A1b ⟧

hit *m; Npl* hitovi popular song

hitan, hitna *adj.* urgent, emergency 14A1; hitna kola ambulance 14A3; hitna pomoć emergency response, first aid, 911 14A3

hlače *f (pl form)* [B,C] pants, trousers 11A1

hladan, hladna; hladni *adj.* cold 4A3

hladnjak *m; Npl* hladnjaci [C] refrigerator

hleb *m; Npl* hlebovi [E] 1. bread; 2. loaf of bread 4A3

hljeb *m; Npl* hljebovi [J] 1. bread [J] [B/S]

only]; 2. loaf of bread 4A3

hodati, hodam, hodaju (I) 1. to walk; 2. to go out together 7A2

hodnik *m; Npl* hodnici hallway, corridor 13A1

hostel *m* hostel 16A2a

hotel *m; Gsg* hotela; *Gpl* hotela hotel 14A2

hrabar, hrabra; hrabri *adj.* brave

hrabrost *f; Gsg* hrabrosti *Isg* -ošću *or* -osti courage, bravery 📖B.VI

hrana *f* food 6A4

hraniti, hranim (I); othraniti, othranim (P) to raise, to nurture 20.IV

hrast *m; Gsg* hrasta *Npl* hrastovi oak tree

hrenovka *f; DLsg* hrenovci *Gpl* hrenovki hot dog, frankfurter

hrid *f; Gsg* hridi *Gpl* hridi cliff 17A3a

hrišćanin *m; Npl* hrišćani [B,S] Christian *(m., general)*

hrišćanka *f: DLsg* hrišćanki *Gpl* hrišćanki [B,S] Christian *(f.)*

hrišćanski *adj.* [B,S] Christian 19A3b

hrišćanstvo *n* [B,S] Christianity

hronika *f; DLsg* hronici [B,S] chronicle 11A3, ⟦ 14A3 ⟧

Hrvat *m; Gsg* Hrvata Croat *(m., general)* 1A4

Hrvatica *f* Croat *(f.)* 1A4

Hrvatska *f (adj. form)* Croatia 1❸

hrvatski *adj.* Croatian 2❸

hteti (I) [E] want, will ↦6

(full forms) hoću, hoćeš, hoće, hoćemo, hoćete, hoće [also future auxiliary] 5A2, 5A2✿, 9A2✿;

(clitics) ću, ćeš, će, ćemo, ćete, će [future auxiliary only] 9A1, 9A1✿, 9A2✿;

(negated) don't want, won't neću, nećeš, neće, nećemo, nećete, neće [B,S] ne ću, ne ćeš, ne će, ne ćemo, ne ćete, ne će [C] [also future auxiliary] 9A2, 5A2✿, 9A2✿, ⟦ 13B1 ⟧

(past tense) hteo, htela 10A3, 10A1✿ hoćeš-nećeš like it or not 9A3

htjeti (I) [J] want, will ↦6

(full forms) hoću, hoćeš, hoće, hoćemo, hoćete, hoće [also future auxiliary] 5A2, 5A2✿, 9A2✿;

(clitics) ću, ćeš, će, ćemo, ćete, će [future auxiliary only] 9A1✿, 9A2✿;

(negated) don't want, won't neću, nećeš, neće, nećemo, nećete, neće [B,S] ne ću, ne ćeš, ne će, ne ćemo, ne ćete, ne će [C] [also future auxiliary] 5A2✿, ⟦ 13B1 ⟧; *(past tense)* htio, htjela 10A1✿ hoćeš-nećeš like it or not 9A3

hvala *f* thanks 2A4, ⟦ 13B1 ⟧; hvala lijepa [C] hvala lepo [S] hvala lijepo [J] [B/S] thank you very much 2A4; **hvala na pitanju** thanks for asking

hvaliti, hvalim (I) to praise *see also* **pohvaliti, zahvaliti se**

hvatati (I); **uhvatiti** (P) to catch

I

i *conj.* and 1A1; **i tako dalje** and so forth 16A1a; **i ... i** both ... and 10A4

iako *conj.* although 16A2b

ičega *pron. (Gen)* anything *see under* **išta**

ići, idem; išao, išla (I) to go 5A1, 5A2✿, 7A2✿, 7A3✿, 9A1✿, 9A2✿; **ići u podstanare** to become a tenant, to rent 9A3; **ići svojim putem** to go one's own way 12A2; **ići** [nekome] **izvrsno** to go very well [for someone] 📖B.II *see also* **doći, izaći, izići, naći, naći se, naići, obići, otići, poći, preći, prići, proći, razići se, ući, zaći**

ideja *f* idea 3A3

identificirati, identificiram, identificiraju (I/P) [B,C] to identify 19A2b

identifikovati, identifikujem (I/P) [B,S] to identify 19A2b

idući *adj.* next, coming 5A3, 12A1✿; **idućeg dana** [B,C,S] on the next day

igde *adv.* [E] anywhere

igdje *adv.* [J] anywhere

igla *f; Gpl* **igala** *or* **igli** needle 📖A.VIII

igra *f; Gpl* **igara** 1. game; 2. dance [B,S only] 15A1

igrač *m; Gsg* **igrača** 1. player *(m., general)*; 2. dancer *(m., general)* [B,S only] 11A2✿

igračica *f* 1. player *(f.)*; 2. dancer *(f.)* [B,S only] 11A2✿

igračka *f; DLsg* **igrački** *Gsg* **igračaka** *or* **igrački** toy 16A1b

igralište *n* playground 📖B.IV

igrati, igram, igraju (I) 1. to play [a game] 5C1, 5A2✿, 10A1✿; 2. to dance [B,S only] 15A1; **igrati se, igram se, igraju se** (I) to play 16A1b *see also* **odigrati**

ih *pron. (clitic) (Acc-Gen)* them 2A1, 2A1✿, 6A3✿ *see under* **oni**

ijekavica *f* ijekavian 15A1

ikad, ikada *adv.* ever 📖B.IV

iko *pron.* [B,S] anyone *(Gen)* **ikoga** *(Dat-Loc)* **ikom, ikome** *(Instr)* **ikim**

ili *conj.* or 1A3; **ili ... ili** either ... or

im *pron. (clitic) (Dat-Loc-Inst)* them 6A3, 6A3✿ *see under* **oni**

imam *m; Gsg* **imama** imam (Muslim cleric)

imati (I) to have 2A1; **ima** there is, there are 5A2, 10A1✿; **imati pravo** to be right 7A2 *see also* **nemati**

ime *n; Gsg* **imena** *Npl* **imena** *Gpl* **imena** name

↪4   1A2, 3A2✿

imenica *f* noun 17A1b

imperfekt *m* imperfect [tense] 17C1

inače *adv.* otherwise, aside from that 19A2b

informacija *f (often pl)* **informacije** information 16A2a

informatika *f; DLsg* **informatici** information science 13B3

inostranstvo *n; Gpl* **inostranstava** [B,S] foreign lands; **u inostranstvu** abroad 8A3

inozemstvo *n; Gpl* **inozemstava** [C] foreign lands; **u inozemstvu** abroad 8A3

insistiranje *n* insistence 13☺

instanca *f; Gpl* **instanci** institution, level 16A2a

inteligentan, inteligentna *adj.* intelligent 11A3✿

instrument *m; Gpl* **instrumenata** [B,C,S] 1. musical instrument; 19A3b 2. tool

instrumental *m* instrumental [case]

intenzivan, intenzivna *adj.* intensive 16A3b

interesantan, interesantna *adj.* interesting 16A3a

interesiranje *n* [C] interest 19A3b

interesirati, interesiram, interesiraju (I) [B,C] to interest 16A1a

interesovanje *n* [B,S] interest 19A3b

interesovati, interesujem (I) [B,S] to interest 16A1a

internet *m* internet 8A3

inženjer *m; Gsg* **inženjera** engineer 11A3

ionako *adv.* 1. although; 2. anyhow 📖B.III

ipak *adv.* nonetheless, nevertheless, yet 13A3

isfenirati *see* **fenirati**

iskapiti, iskapim (P) to drain to the last drop 📖B.VIII

iskati, ištem (I) to seek 17A3a

iskaz *m* statement 19A1b

iskaznica *f* membership card 16A2a

isključiti, isključim (P); **isključivati, isključujem** (I) 1. turn off; 2. exclude

iskoristiti (P) 15A1; **iskorištavati, iskorištavam, iskorištavaju** (I) to use *see also* **koristiti**

iskren *adj.* sincere 📖B.VIII

ispasti, ispadnem; ispao, ispala (P); **ispadati** (I) 1. to turn out, to end up 12A1; 2. to drop or fall out of *see also* **pasti**

ispadati *see under* **ispasti**

ispit *f* exam 6A2

ispitati, ispitam, ispitaju (P); **ispitivati, ispitujem** (I) 1. to question, to examine; 2. to interrogate 20.VII *see also* **pitati**

ispitivanje *n* [B,S] examination [e.g. medical], testing 20.I

403

ispitni *adj.* exam 9A1

isplatiti se, isplati se (P) *(3rd sg only)* to be worthwhile 14A2 2. *see* platiti

isplatiti se, isplatim se (P) to pay off *see* platiti

ispod *prep.* + *Gen* under, beneath ⊢5 8A4, 8A4✿

ispred *prep.* + *Gen* in front of ⊢5 8A4, 8A4✿

ispričati, ispričam, ispričaju (P) to tell everything 16A1b *see* pričati

isprva *adv.* at first 18A3

istaći [istaknuti], istaknem (P); isticati, ističem (I) to emphasize, to remark 📖B.III

istaknuti *see under* istaći

istarski *adj.* Istrian 8A3

isti *adj.* same 9A2; istog časa *or* istog trena that very moment 14A1

isticati *see under* istaći

istina *f* truth 10A3

istinski *adj.* authentic, true 20.IV

istočni *adj.* eastern

istok *m* east 6⊕

istorija *f* [S] history 13B3, ⌐17A1b¬

istovremen *adj.* simultaneous 15A1

istražiti, istražim (P) 16A2b; istraživati, istražujem (I) 15A2 to research *see* tražiti

istraživački *adj.* research 16A2

istraživanje *n* research 16A2

istraživati *see under* istražiti

iščitati (P) to read out to the end 20.VIII *see* čitati

iščekivanje *n* anticipation 📖B.VI

išta *pron.* anything [at all] *(Gen)* ičeg, ičega *(Dat-Loc)* ičem, ičemu *(Instr)* ičim 7A1, 9A3✿

Italija *f* Italy 1⊕

italijanski *adj.* [B,S] Italian 📖B.II

itd. *(abbr. for* i tako dalje) etc.

itekako *adv.* definitely 13A4

itko *pron.* [C] anyone *(Gen)* ikoga *(Dat-Loc)* ikom, ikome *(Instr)* ikim

iz *prep.* + *Gen* 1. from; 2. out of ⊢5 4A1, 4A2✿

iza *prep.* + *Gen* 1. behind; 2. after ⊢5 8A4, 8A4✿

izaći, izađem; izašao, izašla (P) [B,C,S] 10A1; izlaziti (I) to go out 20.VI; izaći na piće [B,C,S] to go out for a drink 📖B.VII *see* ići

izbivanje *n* time spent away 18A3

izbrisati, izbrišem *see* brisati

izdaleka *adv.* from afar 14A4

izdanje *n* [B,C,S] edition, publication 20.V

izdati (P); izdavati, izdajem (I) 1. to publish 16A2; 2. to betray *see* dati

izdavati *see under* izdati

izdržati, izdržim (P) 20.V; izdržavati, izdržavam, izdržavaju (I) 1. to endure; 2. to support; 3. to survive *see* držati

izgled *m* appearance 📖B.V; izgledi prospects 20.IV

izgledati, izgledam, izgledaju (I) to appear, to seem 9A2 *see* gledati

izgovor *m* 1. pronunciation 📖B.III; 2. excuse

izgovoriti, izgovorim (P) 19A2a; izgovarati, izgovaram, izgovaraju (I) to pronounce *see also* govoriti

izgubiti *see under* gubiti

izići, iziđem; izišao, izišla (P) [B,C only] 10A1; izlaziti (I) to go out 20.V; izići na piće [B,C only] to go out for a drink 📖B.VII *see* ići

izjadati se (P) to complain, to pour out one's sorrows 15A1

izjava *f* statement 14A3

izjednačiti se, izjednačim se (P); izjednačivati se, izjednačujem se (I) to become equal 17A2a

izjednačivati se *see* izjednačiti se

izlazak *m; Gsg* izlaska *Npl* izlasci 1. exit 20.III; 2. going out 5A4

izlaziti *see under* izaći *or* izići

izlet *m* excursion 14A4

izlog *m; Npl* izlozi store window, display case 12A2

između *prep.* + *Gen* between, among ⊢5 4A4, 8A4✿

izmenjati, izmenjam, izmenjaju (P); izmenjivati, izmenjujem (I) [E] to alternate, to exchange 20.II

izmenjivati *see* izmenjati

izmešati *see under* mešati

izmet *m* excrement

izmiješati *see under* miješati

izmisliti (P) 20.VIII; izmišljati, izmišljam (I) to fabricate, to think up *see* misliti

izmijenjati, izmijenjam (P); izmjenjivati, izmjenjujem (I) [J] to alternate, to exchange 20.II

izmjenjivati *see* izmijenjati

iznad *prep.* + *Gen* over, above ⊢5 8A4, 8A4✿

iznajmiti, iznajmim (P) 9A3, ⌐9A3¬; iznajmljivati, iznajmljujem (I) 16A2b to rent [to]

iznajmljivati *see under* iznajmiti

iznenaditi, iznenadim (P) 20.IV; iznenađivati, iznenađujem (I) 📖B.III to surprise

iznenađenje *n* surprise 📖B.V

iznenađivati *see under* iznenaditi

iznervirati se, iznerviram se, izneviraju se (P); to get irritated, to get angry 11☺

see **nerviriti se**

izneti, iznesem (P) [E] to carry out, to bring out 19A3 *see also* **nositi**

iznijeti, iznesem (P) [J] to carry out, to bring out 19A3a *see also* **nositi**

izniman, iznimna adj. [C] exceptional 16A2b

izravan, izravna adj. [C] direct, immediate 16A2b

izraz m expression 15A2

izraziti, izrazim (P) 19A1b; **izražavati, izražavam, izražavaju** (I) to express

izreći, izrečem, izreku [izreknem]; izrekao, izrekla (P) 19A2b; **izricati, izričem** (I) to pronounce, to declare

izricati *see under* **izreći**

izučavati, izučavam [I] to make a study of 19A3b

izum m invention

izumjeti, izumijem; izumio, izumjela (P) [J] to invent 15A1, 15A1✿

izuzetan, izuzetna adj. [B,C,S] exceptional 16A2b

izuzeti, izuzmem (P) 20.VI; **izuzimati** (I) to exempt *see* **uzeti**

izvesti, izvedem; izveo, izvela (P); **izvoditi, izvodim** (I) to perform 15A1 *see* **voditi**

izveštaj m [E] report 14A2

izvideti, izvidim (P) [E] to scout 19A3a *see* **videti**

izvidjeti, izvidim; izvidio, izvidjela (P) [J] to scout 19A3a *see* **vidjeti**

izvijati, izvijam (I) to soar 19A3a

izvikati se, izvičem se (P) to yell at length 20.VII *see* **vikati**

izviniti, izvinim (P) [B,S] to excuse; **izvini** *(sg)*, **izvinite** *(pl)* sorry! 2A1, 2A4✿

izvinjavati se, izvinjavam se, izvinjavaju se (I) [B,S] to apologize 2A1

izvješće n [C] report 14A2

izvještaj m [J] [B/S] report 14A2

izvoditi *see under* **izvesti**

izvoli *(sg)* **izvolite** *(pl, polite)* (P) 1. here you are; 2. may I help you; 3. please 2A4

izvor m source 16A2a

izvorni adj. original, authentic 16A2a

izvrstan, izvrsna adj. excellent, outstanding 10A1; **ići [nekome] izvrsno** to go very well [for someone] 📖B.II

izvršiti, izvršim (P) 12A3; **izvršavati, izvršavam, izvršavaju** (I) to perform, to carry out, to execute; **izvršiti atentat (na)** + Acc to assassinate 12A4

izvući, izvučem, izvuku (P); **izvlačiti, izvlačim** (I) to pull out, to extricate 20.V, 11A1✿; **izvući se, izvučem se, izvuku se** (P) 20.II; **izvlačiti se, izvlačim se** (I) to extricate

oneself, to wiggle out *see* **vući**

J

ja pron. I ↦4 1A1, 2A1✿, 2A2✿ *(Acc-Gsg)* **mene** 2A2✿, 7A1✿, **me** 2A1✿, 7A1✿ *(Dat)* **meni, mi** 6A3✿ *(Loc)* **meni** 6A3✿ *(Instr)* **mnom** 7A1✿ *for pl see* **mi**

jablan m; Npl **jablani** or **jablanovi** poplar 18A1a

jabuka f; DLsg **jabuci** apple 4A3, 14A1✿

jači adj. stronger 11A2✿ *see* **jak**

Jadransko more Adriatic Sea 1⊘

jagoda f strawberry 5A1

jaje n; Gsg **jajeta** Npl **jaja** egg ↦4

jaje na oko egg sunnyside up 7A1, 8A2✿

jak, jaka; jaki adj. strong 14A2, 11A2✿

jako adv. very 3A1

januar m [B,S] January 6A2, ⸢6A2⸣

jao excl. 1. oh, no! 2. ouch 9A2, ⸢9A3⸣

Japan n; Gsg **Japana** m Japan 6A4

jasan, jasna adj. 1. clear; 2. transparent 9A4

jasen m; Npl **jaseni** or **jasenovi** European ash [tree]

jastreb m; Npl **jastrebi** or **jastrebovi** hawk

jastuk m; Npl **jastuci** pillow 12A1

javiti se, javim se (P); **javljati se, javljam se, javljaju se** (I) + Dat to get in contact [e.g. call, write, send email or SMS] 8A3, 8A3✿, 9A2✿

javljanje n contact, [instance of] communication 16A3b

javljati se *see under* **javiti se**

javnost f; Npl **javnosti** Isg -ošću or -osti [the] general public 14A3

javor m; Npl **javori** or **javorovi** maple tree

je is 1A2, 6A4✿, 10A1✿, 10A2✿ *see under* **biti**

je pron. (clitic) (Acc-Gen) 1. her; 2. it 2A1, 6A3✿ *see under* **ona**

jecati (I) to sob 17A3a

jedan, jedna num (adj. form) one (1) 3A1, 12A1✿, 12A2✿; **jedan po jedan** one by one 15A2; **jednom** once 10A3; **odjednom** suddenly 14A4; **nijednom** never 14A2; **jedan drugi** one another [as in **jedni drugima** to each other] 11A2✿, 15A2✿, ⸢16B1⸣; **jedno drugo** one another (mixed genders) [as in **jedno drugome** to each other] ⸢16B1⸣; **s jedne strane ... s druge strane** on the one hand ... on the other hand 8A4✿

jedan, jedna adj. one, a; pl. **jedni** some 3A1, 3A1✿, 4A3✿, 5A1✿

jedànaest *num.* eleven (11) 5A2, 5A1✿

jedànaesti *adj.* eleventh (11th) 11A1, 6A2✿

jedànput *adv.* once 10A1

jèdini *adj.* one and only, sole 16A2a

jèdino *adv.* 1. solely; 2. only 14☺

jedinstven *adj.* 1. single; 2. unique 19A3b;
    3. uniform; 4. only; 5. united

jèdni *pl. adj.* *see* jèdan *adj.*

jèdno *adv.* approximately 16A1a [*as in*
    jèdno desètak roughly ten]

jednòdušan, jednòdušna *adj.* unanimous
    15A1

jednòličan, jednòlična *adj.* monotonous 20.II

jednòm *adv.* once *see* jèdan

jednòmesečni *adj.* [E] one-month 16A2b

jednòmjesečni *adj.* [J] one-month 16A2b

jednòstavan, jednòstavna *adj.* simple

jednòžičan, jednòžična *adj.* single-stringed
    19A3b

jèdva *adv.* barely 📖B.VI; jèdva čèkam I
    can hardly wait 📖A.V

jeftin *adj.* cheap, inexpensive

je l'da *part.* isn't that so? ⌞9A3⌟

je li *part.* *(opening phrase for question)*
    [B,C] ⌞9A3⌟

jelo *n* dish [on menu] 6A4

jèlovnik *m; Npl* jèlovnici 1. menu 6A4;
    2. food plan

je l'te *part.* isn't that so? ⌞9A3⌟

jer *conj.* because 4A2

jèsam (I) [I] am *see* biti

jèsen *f; Isg* jèseni *Npl* jèseni autumn 3A2; na
    jèsen in the autumn 9A3; jèsenas this
    fall, the coming fall, last fall

jèsenski *adj.* [C] autumnal 14A4

jèsenji *adj.* [B,S] autumnal 14A4

jèsi [you] are *see* biti

jèsmo [we] are *see* biti

jèst [is] *see* biti

jest [C] [s/he, it] is *(emphatic)*

jèste [you] are *see* biti

jèste [B,S] [s/he, it] is *(emphatic)*

jèsti, jèdēm; jèo, jèla (I) to eat; pòjesti,
    pòjedēm; pòjeo, pòjela (P) to eat up ↦6
    5A1, 5A4, 4A4✿, 5A4✿, 6A2✿, 9A1✿,
    9A2✿, 10A1✿, 10A2✿, 11A1✿, 14A1✿

jèsu (I) they [are] *see* biti

Jèvrej *or* Jèvrejin *m; Npl* Jèvreji [B,S] Jew
    (m., general)

Jèvrejka *f; DLsg* Jèvrejki [B,S] Jew *(f.)*

jèvrejski *adj.* [B,S] Jewish

jèzero *n* lake 16A3b

jèzički *adj.* [B,S] language, language-related
    7A4✿

jèzični *adj.* [C] language, language-related
    7A4✿

jèzik *m; Npl* jèzici *Gpl* jèzika 1. language;
    2. tongue 9A1; strani jèzik foreign
    language 📖B.I

jezikoslòvlje [C] linguistics 13B3

jogurt *n* yogurt

joj *pron. clitic (Dat-Loc)* 1. her; 2. it 6A3,
    6A3✿ *see under* òna

joj! *excl.* 1. oops! 2. ouch!

jorgòvan *m* lilac

jȍš *adv.* 1. still; 2. yet; 3. more 4A3

ju *pron. (clitic) (Acc)* 1. her; 2. it 2A1✿,
    10A1✿ *see under* òna

jùče *adv.* [B,S] yesterday 6A3

jùčer *adv.* [C] yesterday 6A3

jùčerašnji *adj.* yesterday's 20.VIII

jùha *f; DLsg* jùhi [C] soup 11A2

jug *m* south

Jugoslàvija *f* Yugoslavia 17A4✿

jul *or* jùli *m; Gsg* jùla [B,S] July 6A2
    ⌞6A2⌟

jun *or* jùni *m; Gsg* jùna [B,S] June 6A2
    ⌞6A2⌟

junàčki *adj.* heroic 19A3b

jùnak *m; Gsg* junàka *Npl* junàci hero ↦4

jùtro *n; Gpl* jùtārā morning 2A4

jùtros *adv.* this morning 3A1

júžni *adj.* southern 4A1; Júžna Amèrika
    DLsg Júžnoj Amèrici South America 4A1

južnoslàvenski *adj.* [C] South Slavic 19A3b,
    ⌞9A1⌟

južnoslàvistika *f; DLsg* južnoslàvistici South
    Slavic studies 13B3

južnoslòvenski *adj.* [B,S] South Slavic
    19A3b, ⌞9A1⌟

K

k, ka *prep. + Dat* toward; to [B,C,S] ↦5
    7A3, 7A3✿,

kàd, kàda *adv.* when 5A4, 9A2✿, 13A1✿;
    kàko kàda it all depends on when 11A3

kàhva *f* [B] coffee ⌞14A1⌟

kàfa *f* [B,S] coffee 4A3, ⌞10A1⌟, ⌞14A1⌟

kafàna *f* [B,S] café 5A4, 6A1✿

kàfić *m; Gsg* kafìća café 12A2

kaj *pron. (kajkavian dialect)* what ⌞B.VII⌟

kàjgana *f* scrambled eggs 7A1

kàkav, kàkvo, kàkva *pron. adj.* what kind of
    ↦4 3A3, 3A3✿

kàko *adv.* how 1A1; kàko da ne of course,
    definitely 5A4; kàko kàda it all depends
    on when 11A3; kàko se kàže how do you
    say 1A3, 9A2✿; kàko ... tàko as ... so
    18A3; kàko za kòga a matter of taste 5A3

Kalifòrnija *f* California 4A1

kàmen *m; Npl* kàmenovi *or* kàmeni stone

17A2a   *see also* **kàmenje**

kàmenje *coll.*   stones   12A2, 12A2☼; **drȁgo kàmenje** precious stones   12A2 *for sg see* **kàmen**

kamìlica *f*   1. chamomile flower;   2. chamomile tea   📖A.II

kȁmo *adv.* [C]   where to   5A1, 5A1☼, ⸢7.A4⸣

Kanàđanin *m; Npl* **Kanàđani**   Canadian resident, Canadian man   1A4

Kanàđanka *f; DLsg* **Kanàđanki** *Gpl* **Kanàđanki**   Canadian woman   1A4

kancelàrija *f* [B,C,S]   office   6A1, 6A1☼

kȁnjon *m*   1. river gorge;   2. canyon   16A3b

kao *adv.*   like, as   9A2, 4A1☼; **kao što** *conj.* as   4A1☼; **kao da** *conj.*   as if   📖A.III; **k'o** *contraction of* **kao**   17A2a

kapa *f*   cap   15A1

kȁpati (I)   to drip   14☺

kapìrati, kàpiram (I); **ukapìrati, ukàpiram** (P)   *colloq.*   to understand, to catch on

kàput *m; Gsg* **kapùta**   coat   7A3

karàkter *m*   character   19A1b

kárta *f; Gpl* **karáta**   1. ticket   📖A.V;   2. map   13A4

kȁrtica *f*   postcard

kȁsa *f* [S]   cash register   2A4

kȁsan, kȁsna; kȁsni *adj.*   late   6A2

kȁsapin *m; Npl* **kȁsapi** [S]   butcher   11A2☼

kàšičica *f* [S]   little spoon   14A1

kàšika *f; DLsg* **kàšici** [B,S]   spoon   14A1

kàšikica *f* [B]   little spoon   14A1

kat *m; Npl* **katovi** [B,C]   floor, story   6A1

kȁtedra *f; Gpl* **katèdara** *or* **kȁtedri**   1. lectern, rostrum   8A4;   2. university department   16A2b

katòlički *adj.*   Catholic

katòlik *m; Npl* **katòlici**   Catholic *(m., general)*

katolìkinja *f* [S] Catholic *(f.)*

katòlkinja *f* [B,C] Catholic *(f.)*

kȁva *f* [C]   coffee   4A3, ⸢10A1⸣

kavàna *f* [C]   café   5A4, 6A1☼

kàzališni *adj.* [C]   theater, theatrical   16A3a

kàzalište *n* [C]   theater   5A2, 5A4☼, 6A1☼

kàzati, kȁžem (I/P)   to say, to tell   5A1, 4A1☼, ⸢B.VII⸣;   **kȁže se**   it's said   1A3, 1A1☼, 9A2☼

kazìvati, kàzujem (I)   to narrate, to relate   ↪6   10A1☼

kázniti (P)   18A3; **kažnjávati, kažnjávam, kažnjávaju** (I)   to punish

kćȅrka *f; DLsg* **kćȅrki** *Gpl* **kćȅrki** [B,C]   daughter   8A1

kći *f; Asg* **kćer** *Gsg* **kćeri** *Isg* **kćerju** *or* **kćeri** *Gpl* **kćeri** [B,C,S]   daughter   ↪4   8A1

keks *m; Npl* **keksi**   cookie, biscuit   4A3

kelner *m* [B,S]   waiter   11A2☼

kelnerica *f* [B,S]   waitress   11A2☼

kèmičar *m* [C]   chemist *(m., general)*   11A2☼

kèmičarka *f; DLsg* **kèmičarki** *Gpl* **kèmičarki** [C] chemist *(f.)*   11A2☼

kèmija *f* [C]   chemistry   13B3

kèmijski *adj.* [C]   chemical;   **kèmijska òlovka** ballpoint pen   2A4

kèsten *m; Nsg* **kèsteni** *or* **kestènovi**   1. chestnut tree;   1. chestnut nut;   **kèsten pìre**   chestnut purée   *see also* **kèstenje**

kèstenje *coll.*   chestnuts   *for sg see* **kèsten**

kìla *f* [C]   kilogram   12A2

kilo *n* [B,S]   kilogram   12A2

kilòmetar *m; Gsg* **kilòmetra**   kilometer   7A2

kim *or* **kíme** *pron. (Instr)*   whom   7A1, 7A1☼   *see under* **ko, tko**

kímnuti, kímnem (P)   20.V; **kímati** (I)   to nod   *see also* **klímnuti**

kineziològija *f* [C]   physical education   13B3

Kína *f*   China   9A1

kìneski *adj.*   Chinese   9A1

Kìneskinja *f*   Chinese [person] *(f.)*

Kìnez *n; Gsg* **Kinèza**   Chinese [person] *(m., general)*

kìno *n* [B,C]   movie, cinema   5A2, 5A4☼, 6A1☼;   **kìno-dvorana**   movie theater   16A1a

kiosk *m; Npl* **kiosci**   newspaper stand, kiosk   13A4

kìpar *m; Gsg* **kipàra** [B,C]   sculptor   11A2☼

kiparica *f* [B,C]   sculptor *(f.)*   11A2☼

kìrija *f* [B,S]   rent   9A3

kìseo, kìsela *adj.*   sour   6A4;   **kìselo mléko** [E] **kìselo mlijèko** [J]   yogurt-like beverage   7A1

kȉša *f*   rain   14A2

kišòbran *m*   umbrella

kítiti (I); **nàkititi** (P)   to decorate   19A3a

klàvir *m; Gsg* **klavìra** [B,C,S]   piano

klèčati, klèčim (I); **klèknuti, klèknem** (P)   to kneel   17A3a

klìmati   *see under* **klímnuti**

klímnuti, klímnem (P); **klímati** (I)   1. to wobble;   2. to nod;   **klímati / klímnuti glávom** to nod   📖B.I   *see also* **kímnuti**

klub *m*   team;   **fudbalski klub** [B,S] **nogòmetni klub** [B,C]   soccer team   📖B.I

klúpa *f*   bench   📖A.III

ključ *m; Npl* **ključevi**   key   1A2

kneginja *f*   princess, duchess

knez *m; Npl* **knezovi** *or* **kneževi**   prince, duke

knjiga *f; DLsg* **knjizi**   1. book   ↪4   1A2, 4A1☼, 6A2☼;   2. epistle, letter *(archaic, folklore)*   19A3a

književni *adj.*   literary   16A2b

književnost *f; Gsg* **književnosti** *Isg* **-ošću** *or* **-osti**   literature   13B3 knjižnica *f* [C] library 7A4

ko *pron.* [B,S] who ↦4   1A1, 1A1✿,
   2A2✿, 6A2✿, 7A1✿;
   (Acc-Gen) koga 2A2, 2A2✿
   (Dat) komu 6A2✿, komu ↦4
   (Loc) kom, kome 6A2✿; kom ↦4
   (Instr) kim, kime 8A4, 7A1✿

k'o *see* kao

kobasica *f* sausage 7A1

kod *prep.* + *Gen* 1. with, at the home of, at, by
   ↦5   4A2; 2. to the home of [B,S only];
   kod kuće at home 5C1

koga *pron. (Acc-Gen)* whom 2A2, 2A2✿,
   6A2✿, 7A1✿; kako za koga a matter of
   taste 5A3; bilo koga whomever, no matter
   who ¦ 18A3 ¦ *see under* ko *or* tko

kogod *pron.* [B,S] someone or other 16A2a

koješta *adv.* nonsense

koji, koje, koja *pron. adj.* which ↦5   3A3,
   3A3✿, 12A1✿, 13A1✿; kojim putem
   [B,C,S] which way ¦ 7A4 ¦ koja
   slučajnost what a coincidence! ⌨B.VII ;
   kojim slučajem by some chance ⌨B.V

kokoš *f; Isg* kokošju *or* kokoši *Gpl* kokošiju *or*
   kokoši [B,C,S] chicken

kokoška *f; DLsg* kokoški *Gpl* kokošaka *or*
   kokoški [B,S] chicken

kola *n (pl form)* car 7A2; kolima by car
   7A2

kolač *m; Gsg* kolača cake 13A1

koledž *m* college 6A2

kolega *m; DLsg* kolegi *Npl* kolege colleague
   (m., general) 9A4

kolegica *f* [B,C] colleague *(f.)* 13A4

koleginica *f* [B,S] colleague *(f.)* 13A4

koleno *n* [E] 1. knee 10A4; 2. generation
   19A3b

koliko *adv.* how much, how many 5A1,
   4A4✿; koliko god however much
   ¦ 18A3 ¦

kolodvor *m* [C] 1. railway station 5A3, 6A1✿,
   ¦ 9A3 ¦; 2. bus station, bus terminal ¦ 9A3 ¦

kolovoz *m* [C] August 6A2, ¦ 6A2 ¦

koljeno *n* [J] 1. knee 10A4; 2. generation
   19A3b

kome *pron. (Dat-Loc)* whom 6A2✿, 7A1✿
   see under ko *or* tko

komu *pron. (Dat)* whom ↦4
   see under ko *or* tko

komad *m; Gsg* komada [B,C,S] piece 4A3

komarac *m; Gsg* komarca mosquito

komentar *m; Gsg* komentara commentary
   ⌨B.III

komotan, komotna *adj.* comfortable 16A1a

kompjuter *m* [B,S] computer 7A4

kompjutor *m* [C] computer 7A4

kompletan, kompletna *adj.* complete ⌨B.III

kompozitor *m; Gsg* kompozitora [B,S] composer *(m., general)* 11A2✿

kompozitorka *f; DLsg* kompozitorki *Gpl*
   kompozitorki [B,S] composer *(f.)* 11A2✿

komšija *m; Npl* komšije [B,S] neighbor *(m.,*
   general) 6A4

komšinica *f* [B,S] neighbor *(f.)* 6A4

komunikacija *f* communication ⌨B.VIII

komunist *m* [C] communist 18A3

komunista *m; Npl* komuniste [B,S]
   communist 18A3

konac *m; Gsg* konca 1. thread ⌨A.VIII;
   2. end [C only] 16A2a

konačan, konačna *adj.* final 14A4

konačno *adv.* finally 14A4

koncert *m; Gpl* koncerata concert 6A2✿

konobar *m* [B,C,S] waiter 11A2✿

konobarica *f* waitress 11A2✿

kontakt *m; Gpl* kontakata contact ⌨B.IV

kontrolni *adj.* control [*as in* kontrolni zadatak
   "test"; often used alone in the meaning "test"]
   10A2

konverzacijski *adj.* [B,C] conversation, conversational 16A3b

konverzacioni *adj.* [B,S] conversation, conversational 16A3b

konvertabilna marka *f* convertible mark,
   (abbr. KM), currency of Bosnia and
   Herzegovina

konj *m; Gsg* konja *Npl* konji horse ↦4

kora *f* bark [*e.g.* on a tree] 19A1b

korak *m; Npl* koraci step, pace 16A1a

koren *m; Npl* koreni [E] root 19A1b *see also*
   korenje

korenje *n; coll.* [E] roots *for sg see* koren

korijen *m; Npl* korijeni [J] root 19A1b *see*
   also korijenje

korijenje *n; coll.* [J] roots *for sg see* korijen

koristan, korisna *adj.* useful, beneficial
   16A3b

koristiti (I) to use 17A4 *see also* iskoristiti

koriti (I) to scold ⌨B.III

kos *m; Npl* kosovi blackbird

kosa *f* hair 10A4

Kosovo *n* Kosovo 1⊕ , ¦ 1⊕ ¦

kosovski *adj.* Kosovo 8A3

kost *f; Gsg* kosti *Isg* košću *or* kosti bone 7A1,
   7A1✿

kostur *m* skeleton 17A3a

koš *m; Npl* koševi 1. basket [*e.g.* wastebasket,
   in basketball, etc.]

košarka *f; DLsg* košarci *Gpl* košarki
   basketball [= game]

košarkaški *adj.* basketball 12A2

koštati (I) to cost 16A3a

košulja *f* shirt 11A1

kraći *adj.* shorter 11A2🗫 *see* **kratak**

kraj *m; Gsg* **kraja** *Npl* **krajevi** 1. end 7A4; 2. region 14A2

kraj *prep. + Gen* beside, next to, at the side of 13A4

kralj *m; Gsg* **kralja** *Npl* **kraljevi** king 13A3

kraljica *f* queen

kraljević *m* prince 📖B.VIII

kratak, kratka *adj.* short, brief 3A3, 5A1🗫, 11A2🗫

kratko *adv.* briefly

krcat *adj.* packed, crowded 16A1a

kreker *m* cracker 4A3

krenuti, krenem (P) to go, set out ↦6; **kretati, krećem** (I) to get moving 9A2, 10A1🗫

kretati *see under* **krenuti**

krevet *m* bed 12A1

kritika *f; DLsg* **kritici** 1. criticism; 2. literary review 18A3

kriv, kriva; krivi *adj.* 1. guilty 20.VI; 2. wrong 18A2b; 3. curved

krivac *m; Gsg* **krivca** culprit 20.II

krivlji *adj.* 1. more curved 2. more wrong *see* **kriv**

krivnja *f* guilt 20.VII

krompir *m; Gsg* **krompira** [B,S] potato; **krompir pire** mashed potatoes

kronika *f DLsg* **kronici** [C] chronicle 11A3, 14A3

krošnja *f; Gpl* **krošanja** *or* **krošnji** treetop 📖A.III

krov *m; Gsg* **krova** *Npl* **krovovi** roof

kroz (also **kroza** 16A2a) *prep. + Acc* through ↦5 3A2

krpa *f; Gpl* **krpa** 1. dishtowel; 2. rag 📖A.VI

krš *m* karst, barren landscape 17A3a

kršćanin *m; Npl* **kršćani** [C] Christian *(m., general)*

kršćanka *f; DLsg* **kršćanki** *Gpl* **kršćanki** [C] Christian *(f.)*

kršćanski *adj.* [C] Christian 19A3b

kršćanstvo *n* [C] Christianity

kršiti, kršim (I) to violate *or* to break [*e.g.* the law] 19A2b

krući *adj.* more rigid *see* **krut**

krug *m; Npl* **krugovi** circle

kruh *m; Npl* **kruhovi** [B,C] bread 4A3

krumpir *m; Gsg* **krumpira** [C] potato; **pire krumpir** mashed potatoes

kruška *f; DLsg* **krušci** *Gpl* **krušaka** pear 4A3

krut, kruta; kruti *adj.* stiff, unbending.

kružiti, kružim (I) to circle 6A1 *see also* **zaokružiti**

krv *f; Gsg* **krvi** *Isg* **krvlju** *or* **krvi** blood

kucanje knocking 📖B.VIII

kucati *see* **kucnuti**

kucnuti, kucnem (P); **kucati** (I) to knock

kuća *f* house 5A1; **kod kuće** [B,C,S] at home 5C1; **kući** [B,C,S] [toward] home 9A2

kućica *f* little house 18A1a

kućni *adj.* home, domestic; **kućna nega** [E] **kućna njega** [J] home care 20.I

kud, kuda *adv.* [B,C,S] where to 5A1, 5A1🗫, 7.A4

kuhar *m* [B,C] cook *(m., general)* 11A2, 11A2🗫

kuharica *f* [B,C] cook *(f.)* 11A2🗫

kuhati (I); **skuhati** (P) [B,C] 1. to cook 6A4; 2. to boil 14A1

kuhinja *f* kitchen 16A1b

kukati (I) to moan, to keen 19A3a

kukavica *f* 1. cuckoo bird; 2. coward 19A3a

kukavičluk *m* cowardice

kukuruz *m* corn

kula *f* tower 19A3a

kultura *f* culture 18A3; **fizička kultura** *or* **fiskultura** [B,C,S] physical education 13B3

kulturan, kulturna *adj.* cultural 19A3b

kum *m; Gsg* **kuma** *Npl* **kumovi** 1. godfather; 2. best man at wedding 📖B.VIII, B.VIII

kuma *f* 1. godmother; 2. maid or matron of honor at wedding 📖B.VIII, B.VIII

kumče *n* infant being baptised B.VIII

kuna *f* currency of Croatia 12A2

kupalište *n* swimming place, beach 16A3b

kupaonica *f* [C] bathroom 16A1b

kupati, kupam, kupaju (I) to bathe [someone or something]; **kupati se, kupam se, kupaju se** (I) 1. to go swimming; 2. to bathe 16A3a

kupatilo *n* [B,S] bathroom 16A1b

kupiti, kupim (P) to buy; **kupovati, kupujem** (I) to buy ↦6 2A3, 2A3🗫, 7A3🗫, 10A1🗫

kupovati *see under* **kupiti**

kupovina *f* shopping 12A2

kupus *m* [B,C,S] cabbage

kurs *m; Npl* **kursevi** [B,S] course [*e.g.* language] 16A2b

kut *m; Npl* **kutovi** [C] angle

kuvar *f* [S] cook *(m., general)* 11A2, 11A2🗫

kuvarica *f* [S] cook *(f.)* 11A2🗫

kuvati (I); **skuvati** (P) [S] 1. to cook 6A4; 2. to boil 14A1

kužiti, kužim (I); **skužiti, skužim** (P) [B,C] *colloq.* to understand, to catch on

kvadrat *m; Gsg* **kvadrata** [geometric] square; **na kvadrat** squared (mathematics)

kvar *m; Npl* **kvarovi** damage; **u kvaru** out

of order

kvàriti, kvàrim (I); **pòkvariti, pòkvarim** (P)
to ruin, to spoil 📖B.VII

L

laboràtorij *m* [C]   laboratory;   **jèzični laboràtorij** language laboratory 7A4, 7A4✿

laboràtorija [B,S]   laboratory;   **jèzička laboràtorija** language laboratory 7A4, 7A4✿

làgan *adj.*   light (in weight) 19A3a

làgati, làžem (I) 19A2a; **slàgati, slàžem** (P) to
lie, to tell a falsehood

lahak, làhka; làhki *adj.* [B]   1. light [= not
heavy] 2A2, ⌐2A2 ¬; 2. easy

lak, làka; làki *adj.* [B,C,S]   1. light [= not
heavy]   2A2, ⌐2A2 ¬; 2. easy; **làku nòć**
good night (*Asg in* **žèlim ti** [or **vam**] **làku
nòć**) 3A2, ⌐3A2 ¬

lak *m; Npl* **làkovi** lacquer, varnish

làkat *m; Gsg* **làkta** *Npl* **làktovi** elbow 10A4

làkši *adj.* easier, lighter 11A2✿ *see* **lak**

làla *f* [S] tulip 📖A.IV

làmpa *f; Gpl* **làmpi** lamp 8A4

lastàvica *f* swallow [= bird] 19A3a

latinoamèrički *adj.* Latin American 📖B.I

lav *m; Npl* **làvovi** lion 8A1

làž *f; Gsg* **làži** *Isg* **làžju** *or* **làži** lie, falsehood
10A3

làžan, làžna *adj.* lying, false 19A2a

làžljiv *adj.* fake, deceptive 17A1a

lèbdeti, lèbdim (I) [E] to float 20.II

lèbdjeti, lèbdim; lèbdio, lèbdjela (I) [J]   to
float 20.II

lèći, lègnem; lègao, lègla (P) to lie down
11A4✿

lèd *m; Gsg* **lèda** ice 4A3

lèđa *n (pl form)* back [= body part] 10A4

lèkar *m; Gsg* **lekàra** [E] doctor *(m., general)*
11A2✿

lèkarka *f; Gpl* **lèkarki** [E] doctor *(f.)* 5A3,
11A2✿

lèkcija *f* lesson 1A1

lènj, lènja *adj.* [S] lazy 16A1a; **nè budi lènj**
[S] not being lazy, being alert 16A1a

lèp, lèpa; lèpi *adj.* [E] beautiful, nice 2A2,
5A1✿, 8A1✿, 11A2✿; **lèpo** nicely, fine;
hvala lèpo thanks so much 2A4

lepòtica *f* [E] a beauty 17A1a

lèpši *adj.* nicer, more beautiful 11A2✿ *see*
lep

lèptir *m* butterfly; **lèptir màšna** bow tie

lèšinar *f* vulture 20.V

lètenje *n* flying 15A1

lèteti (I) to fly; **polèteti** (P) [E] to take off, to
fly off 15A1

lètjeti, lètim; lètio, lètjela (I) to fly; **polètjeti,**

polètim; polètio, polètjela (P) [J]   to take
off, to fly off 15A1

lètnji *adj.* [E] summer 6A2

lèto *n* [E] summer 9A1; **lèti** *adv.* in summer;
lètos *adv.* this summer; **na lèto** in the
summer

lèvi *adj.* [E] left [= not right] 13A4

lèžaj *m* bed 20.IV

lèžati, lèžim (I) to be lying down 11A4,
11A4✿

li *question particle* 1A2, 9A2✿, 10A2✿

lìce *n* 1. face; 2. person [B,S] 9A2

licèmerje *n* [E] hypocrisy

licèmjerje *n* [J] hypocrisy

lìčan, lìčna *adj.* [B,S] personal

lìčiti, lìčim (na) + *Acc* (I) [B,S]   to resemble
20.VI

lìčnost *f; Gsg* **lìčnosti** *Isg* **-ošću** *or* **-osti**
personality 18A3

liječnica *f* [J] [C]   doctor *(f.)* 5A3, 11A2✿

lijèčnik *m; Npl* **lijèčnici** [J] [C]   doctor *(m.,
general)* 11A2✿

lìjen *adj.* [J] [B,C] lazy 16A1a; **nè budi lìjen**
[B,C]   not being lazy, being alert 16A1a

lìjep, lìjepa; lìjepi *adj.* [J] beautiful, nice 2A2;
lìjepo nicely, fine; **hvala lìjepo** [J] [B/S]
hvala lìjepa [J] [C]   thanks so much 2A4

lìjevi *adj.* [J] left [= not right] 13A4

lìk *m; Npl* **lìkovi** character, figure 10A3

lìmun *m* lemon 7A1

limunàda *f* 1. lemonade 4A3; 2. sentimental
film or television show [B,S only] 7A3

lingvìstika *f; DLsg* **lingvìstici** linguistics 13B3

lìpanj *m; Gsg* **lìpnja** [C] June 6A2, ⌐6A2 ¬

lìrski *adj.* lyrical 19A2b

lìsje *see* **lìšće**

lìst *m; Npl* **lìstovi** leaf [of tree] *see also* **lìšće**

lìst *m; Npl* **lìstovi** leaf [= sheet of paper]

lìsta *f* list 16A3b

lìstopad *m* [C] October 6A2

lìšće *n; coll.* leaves 11A2✿; **lìsje** *(archaic)*
18A1a *for sg see* **list**

lìti, lìjem (I) to pour 14☺ *see also* **òdliti,
prèliti**

lokàcija *f* location 6A1

lòkal *m; Gsg* **lokàla** bar, neighborhood hangout
12A2

Lòndon *m; Gsg* **Lòndona** London 4A1,
4A1✿

lòpov *m; Gsg* **lòpova** thief, robber, rascal
11A2✿

lòpta *f; Gpl* **lòpti** ball 5C1

lòš, lòša; lòši *adj.* [B,C,S] bad ↦4
2A2, ⌐2A2 ¬; 3A1✿, 11A1✿

lòše *adv.* badly 3A1

lùd, lùda *adj.* mad, crazy; **on je lùd za tòbom**

he's crazy about you 📖B.V

luđi *adj.* crazier *see* **lud**

luk *n; Npl* **lukovi** onion; **mladi luk** spring onion, scallion; **beli luk** [E] **bijeli luk** [J] [B/S] garlic

luka *f; DLsg* **luci** port; **zračna luka** [C] airport 📖B.III

lukav *adj.* clever, sly 20.V

lupiti se (P); **lupati se, lupam se, lupaju se** (I) to strike oneself, to hit oneself [*e.g.* on the forehead] 📖A.V *see* **zalupiti**

lutka *f; Gpl* **lutaka** *or* **lutki** doll 9A2✿

LJ

ljekar *m; Gsg* **ljekara** [J] [B/S] doctor *(m., general)* 11A2✿

ljekarka *f; DLsg* **ljekarki** *Gpl* **ljekarki** [J] [B/S] doctor *(f.)* 5A3, 11A2✿

ljepotica *f* [J] a beauty 17A1a

ljepši *adj.* nicer, more beautiful 11A2✿ *see* **lijep**

ljetni *adj.* [J] summer 6A2

ljeto *n* [J] summer 9A1; **ljeti** *adv.* in summer; **ljetos** *adv.* this summer; **na ljeto** in the summer

ljubak, ljupka *adj.* cute 15A1

ljubav *f; Gsg* **ljubavi** *Isg* **ljubavlju** *or* **ljubavi** *Voc* **ljubavi** love ↪4 3A2, 3A2✿, 4A1✿, 8A1✿

ljubavni *adj.* love, amorous, romantic 18A2b

ljubazan, ljubazna *adj.* kind, friendly, thoughtful 13A1

ljubić *m* [B,C] romantic comedy 7A3

ljubičast *adj.* violet, purple

ljubimac *m; Gsg* **ljubimca** favorite 15A1

ljubiti, ljubim (I); **poljubiti, poljubim** (P) 1. to kiss; 2. to love 📖B.VIII

ljući *adj.* 1. angrier 2. spicier *see* **ljut**

ljudi *m (pl only) Acc* **ljude** *Gen* **ljudi** 1. people; 2. men 3A1, 3A1✿, 3A2✿ *for sg see* **čovek** [E] **čovjek** [J]

ljudski *adj.* human 18A1; **ljudska prava** human rights

ljut, ljuta; ljuti *adj.* 1. angry 10A3; 2. spicy 6A4

ljutit *adj.* angry

ljutiti, ljutim (I); **naljutiti, naljutim** (P) to anger

ljutiti se, ljutim se [**na** + *Acc*] (I) 📖B.VIII to be angry [at] *see* **naljutiti se**

M

ma *conj.* but 7A3; **ma nemoj** you don't say 7A3; **ma šta** [B,S] **ma što** [C] no matter what 20.VI; **ma, daj!** come on, you've got to be kidding 7A3

mačka *f; DLsg* **mački** *Gpl* **mačaka** *or* **mački** cat 1A2, 14A1✿

mada *conj.* although 16A3b

Mađarska *f (adj. form)* Hungary 1✪, ⌜6✪⌝

magarac *m; Gsg* **magarca** donkey

magistarski *adj.* master's; **magistarski rad** master's thesis 16A2a

magla *f* fog, mist 14A4

mahnuti, mahnem (P) 20.VIII; **mahati, mašem** (I) to wave

maj *m* [B,S] May 6A2, ⌜6A2⌝

majka *f; DLsg* **majci** *Gpl* **majka** *or* **majki** mother 2A3, 5A1✿, 9A2✿

majmun *m* monkey 2A3

makar *adv.* at least

makar *conj.* even if, although 13A2

Makedonac *m; Gsg* **Makedonca** Macedonian *(m., general)*

Makedonija *f* Macedonia 1✪

Makedonka *f; DLsg* **Makedonki** *Gpl* **Makedonki** Macedonian *(f.)*

malen, malena; maleni *adj.* small, little 20.V

mali *adj.* small, little 2A2, 2A3✿, 8A1✿, 11A1✿, 11A2✿; **mala matura** elementary school graduation

mali *m; adj. form* little boy ⌞B.VIII⌟

mala *f; adj. form* little girl

malo *adv.* a little, somewhat 5A1

maloletan, maloletna *adj.* [E] underage, juvenile 📖B.VIII

maloljetan, maloljetna *adj.* [J] underage, juvenile 📖B.VIII

mama *f* mama, Mom 9A4

mamin *adj.* mama's ↪4

manastir *m* [Orthodox] monastery 16A3b

manje *adv.* less 11A2, 11A2✿; **manje više** more or less *see* **malo**

manji *adj.* 1. smaller; 2. less 11A2 *see* **mali**

manjkati (I/P) to lack, to be short of

maramica *f* handkerchief 📖A.VII

marka *f; DLsg* **marki**; *Gpl* **maraka** 1. stamp 2A4; 2. former currency of Germany; **konvertabilna marka** *f* convertible mark, (*abbr.* KM), currency of Bosnia and Herzegovina

mart *m* [B,S] March 6A2, ⌜6A2⌝

maslac *m; Gsg* **maslaca** [B,C,S] butter 7A1

mašinstvo *n* [B,S] mechanical engineering 13B3

mašna *f; Gpl* **mašni** bow; **leptir mašna** bow tie

matematičar *m* mathematician 11A3

matematika *f; DLsg* **matematici** mathematics 3A2

materijal *m; Gsg* **materijala** 1. material; 2. documents 13A3 materijalan, materijalna *adj.* material 20.VI

matičar *m* justice of the peace; registrar
📖B.VIII

matura *f* secondary school graduation, 📖B.IV;
mala matura elementary school graduation

me *pron. (clitic)*
(Acc-Gen) me 2A1, 2A1☼, 6A3☼
see under ja

meč *m; Npl* mečevi match, [soccer] game
12A2

med *m; Gsg* meda honey 7A1; medeni
mesec [E] medeni mjesec [J] honeymoon
📖B.VIII

medicina *f* medicine 13B3

medicinska sestra nurse *(f.)* 11A2☼

medved *m* [E] bear 2A3

medvjed *m* [J] bear 2A3

među *prep. + Instr* among, between 8A4☼

međusoban, međusobna *adj.* mutual 📖B.IV

međutim *adv.* however 12A2

mehaničar *m* [B,C] mechanic 11A2☼

mek *adj.* soft 19A3a, 11A2☼

meksički *adj.* Mexican 📖B.II

Meksikanac *m; Gsg* Meksikanca Mexican
(m., general)

Meksikanka *f; DLsg* Meksikanki *Gpl*
Meksikanki Mexican *(f.)*

mekši *adj.* softer 11A2☼ *see* mek

mene *pron. (Acc-Gen)* me 2A1, 2A2☼, 6A3☼,
7A1☼ *see under* ja

meni *pron. (Dat-Loc)* me 6A3, 6A3☼, 7A1☼
see under ja

menjati, menjam, menjaju (I); promeniti, pro-
menim (P) [E] to change 20.II

mera *f* [E] measurement, measure

mesar *m; Gsg* mesara [B,C,S] butcher
11A2☼

mesec *m; Gpl* meseci [E] 1. month 6A2,
6A2 ; 2. moon 6A1; mesec dana [for]
a month 9A1, 6A2☼; mesecima for
months; medeni mesec 📖B.VIII

meso *n* meat 6A4

mesto *n* [E] 1. place, spot 10☺; town, settled
area 14A2; radno mesto job, place of employment 11A4

mešati, mešam, mešaju (I); izmešati, izmešam,
izmešaju (P) [E] to stir up, to mix 14A1

metar, metra *m* meter 📖B.I

metrički *adj.* metric, metrical 19A3b

mi *pron.* we ↦4 1A3, 2A1☼, 6A3☼,
6A4☼, 7A1☼
(Acc-Gen) nas 2A2☼, nas 2A2☼
(Dat) nama, nam, nam 6A3☼
(Loc) nama, nam 6A3☼
(Instr) nama 7A1☼
for sg see ja

mi *pron. (clitic) (Dat)* me 6A3, 6A3☼,
6A4☼, 7A1☼, 7A3☼, 11A2☼
see under ja

mijenjati, mijenjam, mijenjaju (I); promijeniti, promijenim (P) [J] to change 20.II

miješati, miješam, miješaju (I); izmiješati, iz-
miješam, izmiješaju (P) [J] to stir up, to mix
14A1

milijarda *num; Gpl* milijardi billion;
milijardu one billion

milijun *num; Gsg* milijuna [B,C] million
(1,000,000) 17A2a, 12A1☼

milion *num; Gsg* miliona [B,S] million
(1,000,000) 17A2a, 12A1☼

milosrdan, milosrdna *adj.* merciful 19A2a

milosrđe *n* mercy 19A2a

milost *f; Gsg* milosti *Isg* -ošću or -osti mercy
10A3

mineralni *adj.* mineral; mineralna voda
mineral water, sparkling water 4A3

ministar *m; Gsg* ministra government minister
(m., general) 11A2☼

ministrica *f* [C] government minister *(f.)*
11A2☼

minut *m; Gsg* minuta [B,S] minute 9A4

minuta *f* [C] minute 9A4

mio, mila *adj.* pleasant, nice, dear, charming

mir *m* [B,C,S] peace, tranquility 7A3; pusti
me na miru leave me be, leave me alone
7A3

miran, mirna *adj.* peaceful, calm, quiet 8A2

miris *m* smell, fragrance 20.II

mirisati, miriše (I) *(3rd person only)* to smell
fragrantly

misao *f; Gsg* misli *Isg* mišlju *or* misli thought
↦4 18A2

misaon *adj.* thought-related, contemplative,
thoughtful 15A1

misliti (I); pomisliti (P) 1. to think 3A1,
10A4☼; misliti na (I) + *Acc* to think of
3A1; 2. to mean [*as in* mislim ... I mean ...
📖B.IV] *see* izmisliti, razmisliti, smisliti,
zamisliti

miš *m; Npl* miševi mouse 8A1; slepi miš [E]
slijepi miš [J] bat

mišljenje *n* opinion 10A4, 10A4☼; po mom
mišljenju in my opinion 10A4

mjera *f* [J] measurement, measure

mjesec *m; Gpl* mjeseci [J] 1. month 6A2;
2. moon 6A1, 6A2 ; mjesec dana [for] a
month 9A1; medeni mjesec [J]
honeymoon 📖B.VIII; mjesecima for
months;

mjesto *n* [J] 1. place, spot 10☺; town, settled
area 14A2; radno mjesto job, place of employment 11A4

mlad, mlàda; mlàdi *adj.* young 7A2, 5A1✿, 11A2✿; **mlàda** *f; adj. form* bride 📖B.VIII

mlàdić *m; Gsg* **mlàdića** boy, young man 8A1

mladost *f; Gsg* **mladosti** *Isg* -ošću *or* -osti youth

mladòženja *m; Npl* **mladòženje** bridegroom 📖B.VIII

mlàđi *adj.* younger 11A2✿ *see* **mlad**

mlèko *n* [E] milk 4A3; **kiselo mlèko** yogurt-like beverage 7A1

mleti, meljem (I); **sàmleti, sàmeljem** (P) [E] to grind 14A1

mlijèko *n* [J] milk 4A3; **kiselo mlijèko** yogurt-like beverage 7A1

mljeti; meljem (I); **sàmljeti, sàmeljem** (P) [J] to grind 14A1

mnogi *adj.* 1. many; 2. many a 6A4

mnogo *adv.* many, much, a lot 5A1, 10A2✿, 11A2✿

mnom *pron.* me (Instr) 7A1, 7A1✿ *see under* **ja**

mnoštvo *n; Gpl* **mnoštava** multitude 20.VII

množiti (I) to multiply 12A1, 12A1✿

mobitel *m* cellular phone

moćan, moćna *adj.* powerful 19A2b

moć *f; Gsg* **moći** *Isg* **moći** *or* **moću** power, might

moći (I) to be able to 2A4, 2A4✿, 10A1✿, 10A2✿, ⌊13B1⌋; **mogu, možeš, može, možemo, možete, mogu; mogao, mogla; može** *3rd sg* sure! OK 2A1

moderan, moderna *adj.* 1. modern; 2. pertaining to the period that spans the early and mid-20th century 18A3

moguće *adv.* possible 11A3

mogući *adj.* possible 12A1✿

mogućnost *f; Gsg* **mogućnosti** *Isg* -ošću *or* -osti possibility 16A1a

moj, moje, moja *pron. adj.* my, mine ↪4 1A2, 6A4✿

mokar, mokra *adj.* wet 18A1a

mòkraća *f* urine

molba *f; Gpl* **molbi** request, application, petition 16A2a

mòliti, molim (I) to pray, to plead 17A3a

molim please 2A4

molim? yes? 2A1

molim! 1. you're welcome [in response to 'thank you'] 2A4; 2. that's OK, think nothing of it [in response to an apology]

mòliti, molim (I) 2A4; **zamòliti, zamolim** (P) 13A1 to ask for, to request

mòmak *m; Gsg* **mòmka** *Npl* **mòmci** *Gpl* **momaka** young man, lad 4A1, 5A1✿, 8A1✿

momčad *f; Gsg* **momčadi** *Isg* **momčadi** team 12A2✿

momče *n* lad, boy 12A2✿

mòmenat *m; Gsg* **mòmenta** *Gpl* **momenata** [B,S] moment 3A2, 5A4✿, 6A1✿

mòment *m; Gpl* **mòmenata** [B,C] moment 3A2

momentàlno *adv.* [B,S] at the moment 16A2a

monàrhija *f* monarchy 18A3

monoton *adj.* monotonous 18A1a

mòrati, moram, mòraju (I) must, to be obliged, to have to 2A1, 7A2✿, 13A1✿

more *n* sea 1☉; **polarno more** Arctic (or Antarctic) Ocean 15A1, 7A1✿

mòriti (P) to torment, to trouble 15A1

Moskva *f* Moscow 4A1

most *m; Npl* **mòstovi** [B,C,S] bridge

motocikl *m; Gpl* **motocikala** motorcycle 7A2

mòtriti (I) to observe 18A1a

mozàik *m* mosaic 20.II

možda *adv.* perhaps, maybe 9A3

može *unchanging form* sure! OK 2A1 *see under* **moći**

mračan, mračna; mrački *adj.* dark, gloomy 18A1a

mrak *m* darkness 14A2

mrav *m; Npl* **mravi** *Gpl* **mravi** *or* **mrava** ant

mrèti, mrem (P) [E] (archaic) to die 18A1a *see* **umreti**

mrijèti; mrem (P) [J] (archaic) to die 18A1a *see* **umrijeti**

mrk *adj.* gloomy 18A1a

mrkva *f; Gpl* **mrkvi** [B,C] carrot

mrtav, mrtva; mrtvi *adj.* dead

mržnja *f* hatred

mu *pron. (clitic) (Dat)* 1. him; 2. it 6A3, 6A3✿, 6A4✿, 10A2✿ *see under* **on**

mučan, mučna; mučni *adj.* agonizing 20.VI

mučiti torment, torture

mučiti se 1. struggle; 2. have trouble

mudar, mudra; mudri *adj.* wise 8A1, ⌊8A1⌋

muha *f; DLsg* **muhi** [C] fly [= insect]

muk *m* silence

muka *f; DLsg* **muci** 1. torment, torture; 2. nausea

muslìman *m; Gpl* **muslimana** adherent of Islam (m., general)

Muslìman *m; Gpl* **Muslimana** member of former Yugoslav ethnic group now known as Bosniaks (m., general)

muslìmanka *f; DLsg* **muslìmanki** *Gpl* **muslìmanki** adherent of Islam (f.)

Muslìmanka *f; DLsg* **Muslìmanki** *Gpl* **Muslìmanki** member of former Yugoslav ethnic group now known as Bosniaks (f.)

muslìmanski *adj.* Muslim 19A3b

muškȁrac *m; Gsg* muškȁrca   man   3A1

muški *adj.*   male, masculine   10A3

muštȅrija *m or f*   customer, client   13A2

mȕva *f; DLsg* mȕvi [B,S]   fly [= insect]

mȕzej *m; Gsg* mȕzeja   museum   5A4

muzȉčar *m* [B,C,S]   musician *(m., general)*   11A2☼

muzȉčarka *f DLsg* mȕzičarki *Gpl* mȕzičarkī [B,S]   musician *(f.)*   11A2☼

muzȉčkī *adj.* [B,C,S]   musical   16A3b

mȕzika *f; DLsg* mȕzici [B,C,S]   music   7A4

mȗž *m; Isg* mȗžem *Npl* mȕževi   husband   ↤4   7A2, 7A1☼

N

na *prep. + Loc*   on, at   ↤5   6A1, 6A1☼

na *prep. + Acc*   to, onto   ↤5   5A1, 5A2☼, 9A1☼, ⸢3A3⸣; bez obzira na + *Acc*   regardless   9A4;   izȁći na pȉće   go out for a drink   📖B.VII;   lȉčiti na   to resemble   📖A.III;   na jȅsen   in the autumn   9A3;   na lȅto [E] na ljȅto [J]   in the summer;   na prolȅće [E]   na prȍljeće [J]   in the spring;   na zȉmu   in the winter;   na tȁj nȁčin   (in) that way   10A4;   na žȁlost   unfortunately   12A3;   na prȉmer [E] na prȉmjer [J]   for example   11A3;   mȉsliti na + *Acc*   to think of   3A1;   padȁ [mi] na pȁmet   it occurs [to me]   11A4;   pȁziti na + *Acc*   to watch out for, to care for   📖B.VIII

nȁbaviti (P)   16A1a; nȁbavljati (I)   to obtain, to procure

nacionȃlnī *adj.*   national   16A2a

nȁcrtati   *see under* crtati

nȁčin *m*   way, manner   10A4;   na tȁj nȁčin   (in) that way   10A4

nȃći, nȃđem; nȁšao, nȁšla (P)   12A2, 9A2☼, 10A1☼; nȁlaziti (I)   to find

nȃći se, nȃđem se; nȁšao se, nȁšla se (P)   1. to meet [with];   2. to find oneself   10A1;   nȁlaziti se (I)   *see* ȉći

nad *prep. + Instr*   over, above   ↤5   8A1, 7A2☼, 8A4☼

nad *prep. + Acc*   [moving to a position] over, above   ↤5

nȁda *f*   hope   16A3a

nȁdati se, nȁdam se, nȁdaju se (I)   to hope   14A2

nȁdimak *m; Gsg* nȁdimka   nickname   18A3

nadovȅzati, nadovȅžem (P); nadovezȋvati, nadovezȕjem (I)   to add on   📖B.VIII   *see also* vȅzati

nadvlȃdati, nadvlȃdam, nadvlȃdaju (P); nadvlađȋvati, nadvlађȕjem (I)   to overcome   20.III   *see also* vlȃdati

nadvojvoda *m; Npl* nadvojvode   archduke   12A4

nadžȉveti, nadžȉvim (P) [E]   to outlive   18A3   *see* žȉveti

nadžȉvjeti, nadžȉvīm; nadžȉvio, nadžȉvjela (P)   [J]   to outlive   18A3   *see* žȉvjeti

nȁgao, nȁgla *adj.*   sudden, abrupt   20.VI

nagovárati nagovȃram, nagovȃraju (I)   to urge   *see also* nagovóriti

nagovȅstiti, nagovȅstīm (P)   16A3b; nagovešt-ávati, nagovéštavam, nagovéštavaju (I) [E]   to hint, to alert

nagovijȅstiti, nagovijȇstīm (P)   16A3b; nago-vještávati, nagovjȇštavam, nagovjȇštavaju (I) [J]   to hint, to alert

nagovóriti, nagovórim (P)   20.VI   to convince   *see also* nagovárati

nȁgrada *f*   prize   📖B.II;   nagrȁdnā ȉgra   competition for a prize   📖B.II

nȃći, nȃđem; nȁišao (na) (P)   14A2; nailȁziti (na) (I)   to happen upon   *see* ȉći

nailȁziti   *see under* nȃći

nȁime *adv.*   namely   15A1

nȁjaviti, nȁjavīm (P)   📖B.V; nàjavljȋvati, nàjavljȕjem (I)   to announce

nȁjbolje *adv.*   best, the best   5C1, 11A1☼

najȅžiti se, najȇžīm se (P)   to get goose bumps   20.VIII

nȁjpre *adv.*[E]   first of all   16A2a

nȁjprije *adv.* [J]   first of all   16A2a

nȁjviše *adv.*   most, the most   11A1

nȁjzad *adv.*   finally, at the end   5C1

nȁkititi   *see under* kititi

naklȁda *f* [C]   edition, publication   20.V

nakon *prep. + Gen*   after   ↤5   12A2, 11A1☼; nakon toga što *conj.*   after   13A4☼

nȁlaz *m*   finding, result   20.III

nȁlaziti   *see under* nȃći

nȁlaziti se (I)   to be located   6A1, 9A2☼, 15A1☼   *see under* nȃći se

nȁlet *m*   gust [*e.g.* of wind]   14A2

nȁliti, nȁlijem; nȁlio, nȁlila (P)   11A1☼; nalȋvati (I)   to pour

naljútiti, naljútim (P)   to anger   *see* ljútiti

naljútiti se, naljútim se [na + *Acc*] (P)   to get angry [at]   *see* ljútiti se

nam *pron. (clitic) (Dat)*   us   6A3, 6A3☼, 7A1☼   *see under* mi

nama *pron. (Dat-Loc)*   us   6A3; *(Instr)* us   7A1, 6A3☼, 7A1☼, 7A3☼   *see under* mi

namerávati, namȇravam, namȇravaju (I) [E]   to intend   11A3

namèštaj *m* [E]   furniture   12A1

namjerávati, namjȇravam, namjȇravaju (I) [J]   to intend   11A3

namjèštaj *m* [J]   furniture   12A1

napȁmet *adv.*   by heart   10A3

nȁpasti, nȁpadnem; nȁpao, nȁpala (P)   12A4;

nàpadati (I) to attack
napìsati *see under* **pìsati**
napòkon *adv.* finally 10A2
napòlje *adv.* [B,S] out, outside
napòlju *adv.* [B,S] outside 5A4, 5A4✿
nàporan, nàporna *adj.* strenuous, hard 12A2
naposlètku *adv.* [E] finally 16A2b
naposljètku *adv.* [J] finally 16A2b
napràviti *see under* **pràviti**
nàpredak *m; Gsg* **nàpretka** progress ⌸B.III
nàprotiv *adv.* on the contrary 20.III
napùniti *see under* **pùniti**
napùstiti, nàpustim (P) 15A1; **napùštati, nà-puštam, napùštaju** (I) 18A3 1. to abandon, to give up; 2. to leave *see* **pùstiti**
napùštati *see under* **napùstiti**
nàranča *f; Gpl* **nàranči** [C] orange [= fruit] 4A3
nàrančast *adj.* [C] orange [= color]
nàrandža *f; Gpl* **nàrandži** [B,S] orange [= fruit] 4A3
nàrandžast *adj.* [B,S] orange [= color]
nàravno *adv.* of course 7A1
nàredan, nàredna *adj.* [B,S] next, following; **nàrednog dàna** on the next day
nàročito *adv.* especially 10A4
nàrod *m* [one's] people, folk 17A2a, ⫶17A2a⫶
nàrodni *adj.* 1. national 7☺; 2. of the people, folk 19A3b; **nàrodna prìča** folktale ⌸B.VIII
narogùšen *adj.* bristling 10A3
narùčiti, nàručim (P); **narùčivati, narùčujem** (I) to order 10A1
nàrudžba *f; Gpl* **nàrudžbi** *or* **nàrudžaba** order [e.g. from a catalogue]
nas *pron. (clitic) (Acc-Gen)* us 2A1, 6A3✿, 7A1✿ *see under* **mi**
nas *pron. (Acc-Gen)* us 2A1, 6A3✿, 7A1✿ *see under* **mi**
nàsilan, nàsilna *adj.* violent 20.VII
nàsilje *n* violence
nàslednik *m; Npl* **nàslednici** [E] heir 20.IV
nàsledstvo *n* [E] legacy, heritage 20.V
naslòniti (P); **nàslanjati** (I) to lean, to rest 20.III
nàslov *m* title 17A3b
nàsljednik *m; Npl* **nàsljednici** [J] heir 20.IV
nàsljedstvo *n* [J] legacy, heritage 20.V
nasmèjati se, nàsmejem se (P) [E] to laugh a lot 20.VI *see also* **smèjati se**
nasmìjati se, nàsmijem se (P) [J] to laugh a lot 20.VI *see also* **smìjati se**
nàstanak *m; Gsg* **nàstanka** origin 17A4
nàstaviti (P) 14A2; **nàstavljati** (I) ⌸A.III to continue
nàstavljati *see under* **nàstaviti**

nàstavnica *f* teacher *(f.)* 11A2✿
nàstavnik *m; Npl* **nàstavnici** teacher *(m., general)* 11A2✿
nàsuprot *prep. + Dat.* opposite, across from ↦5 8A4
naš, naše, naša *poss. pron.* our, ours ↦4 1A2
nàterati (P) [E] to force ⌸B.III
nàtjerati (P) [J] to force ⌸B.III
nàtkasna *f; Gpl* **nàtkasni** [B,S] bedside table, nightstand 12A1
nàtrag *adv.* back 14A2
naùčiti, naùčim (P) to learn 10A2, 9A2✿, 10A2✿, *see also* **ùčiti**
nàučnik *m; Npl* **nàučnici** [B,S] scientist, scholar 11A2✿
nàuka *f; DLsg* **nàuci** [B,S] science, learning 11A3; **polìtičke nàuke** [B,S] political science 13B3; **prìrodne nàuke** [B,S] natural sciences 13B3
nàveče *adv.* [B] in the evening 5A4
nàvečer *adv.* [C] in the evening 5A4
nàvesti, navèdem; nàveo, nàvela (P); **navòditi, navòdim** (I) 1. to state, to cite, to quote 20.VIII; 2. to lead, to induce ⌸B.III *see* **vòditi**
navìjati, nàvijam, navìjaju (I) to root, to cheer ⌸B.II
navràtiti, nàvratim (P); **navràćati** (I) to drop in, to stop in 12A2
nàzreti, nàzrem (P) 19A2a; **nàzirati** (I) to catch sight of
nàzvati, nàzovem (P) 17C1, 12A4✿; **nàzivati, nàzivam, nàzivaju** (I) 19A1b to call *see* **zvàti**
nàžalost *or* **na žàlost** unfortunately 12A3
ne *part.* no 1A2, 2A1✿, 3A2✿, 5A4✿; not 2A1
nebo *n; Npl* **neba** *or* **nebèsa** 1. sky 6A1, 6A1✿; 2. heaven 17A2a
nećak *m; Npl* **nećaci** nephew 20.II
nećaka *f; DLsg* **nećaki** [S] niece
nećàkinja *f* [B,C] niece
nèću, nèćeš, nèće, nèćemo, nèćete, nèće [B,S] *see under* **htèti** *or* **htjèti**
nè ću, nè ćeš, nè će, nè ćemo, nè ćete, nè će [C] *see under* **htèti** *or* **htjèti**
nèdelja *f* [E] 1. Sunday 2A1; 2. week 5A3, 5A3✿, 5A4✿; **nèdeljom** on Sundays 7A2
nèdeljni *adj.* [E] weekly 16A3a
nèdjelja *f* [J] 1. Sunday 2A1; 2. week [J] [B/S only] 5A3, 5A3✿, 5A4✿; **nèdjeljom** on Sundays 7A2
nèdjeljni *adj.* [J] [B/S] weekly 16A3a
nedòstajati, nedòstajem (I) + *Dat* to miss [as in **oni nam nedòstaju** we miss them]

nedostatak *m; Gsg* **nedostatka** *Npl* **nedostaci** *Gpl* **nedostataka**   lack, insufficiency

nedvosmislen *adj.*   unambiguous   20.VIII

negacija *f*   negation   17C1

negde *adv.* [E]   somewhere   9A3✿

negdje *adv.* [J]   somewhere   9A3✿

nega *f; DLsg* **nezi** [E]   care;   **kućna nega** home care   20.I

nego *conj.*   1. but, rather   2A1;   2. than   11A2, 11A2✿, 13A4✿;   **pre nego što** [E] **prije nego što** [J] *conj.*   before   20.V

nego šta *excl.* [B,S]   of course!   11A4

nego što *excl.* [C]   of course!   11A4

negoli *conj.*   than;   **prije negoli** *conj.*   before 20.V

neimenovan *adj.*   unnamed   19A2b

neizmeran, neizmerna *adj.* [E]   immeasurable 20.VIII

neizmjeran, neizmjerna *adj.* [J]   immeasurable 20.VIII

neizvesnost *f; Gsg* **neizvesnosti** *Isg* **-ošću** *or* **-osti** [E]   uncertainty   11A4

neizvjesnost *f; Gsg* **neizvjesnosti** *Isg* **-ošću** *or* **-osti** [J]   uncertainty   11A4

nejestiv *adj.*   inedible   20.I

neka, nek   let *(used with 3rd person verbs)* [*as in* **neka pišu** let them write]   7A3, 7A3✿

nekada *adv.*   1. once [in the past]   16A1b; 2. sometimes

nekakav, nekakvo, nekakva *pron. adj.*   some kind of   16A1a

nekako *adv.*   somehow   ▢B.II

neki, neko, neka *pron. adj.*   some, any, a certain   ↦4   3A3;   **nekih pedesetak** fifty-some, fifty-odd, roughly fifty   13A3;   **u neku ruku**   in a sense, in a way   7A2

neko *pron.* [B,S]   someone   ↦4   9A3, 9A3✿
   (Acc-Gen) **nekog, nekoga**
   (Dat-Loc) **nekom, nekome**
   (Instr) **nekim**

nekolicina *f*   several, a few [seen as a unit] 19A2b

nekoliko *adv.*   several, a few   6☉

nema *unchanging form*   there is/are none   4A2, 4A2✿, 10A1✿

Nemac *m; Gsg* **Nemca** [E]   German *(m., general)*

Nemačka *f; adj. form*   Germany   4A1

nemački *adj.* [E]   German   2A4

nemati, nemam, nemaju (I)   not to have   2A1, 4A1✿, 5A2✿;   **ako nemate ništa protiv** (I) if you have no objections   13A4;   **nemam pojma**   I have no idea   13A3

Nemica *f* [E]   German *(f.)*

nemir *m*   restlessness, agitation   18A1a

nemiran, nemirna *adj.*   restless   8A2

nemoj   don't!   7A2, 7A2✿;   **ma nemoj!**   you don't say!   7A3;   **nemojte** don't!   7A2✿; **nemojmo** let's not   7A3

nena *f* [B]   grandmother   5A3✿, 8☉

neobičan, neobična *adj.*   unusual   15A1

neovisnost *f; Gsg* **neovisnosti** *Isg* **-ošću** *or* **-osti** [C]   non-dependency

neozbiljan, neozbiljna *adj.*   1. not serious; 2. frivolous, silly   3A3

neposredan, neposredna *adj.* [B,C,S]   direct, immediate   16A2b

neprijatan, neprijatna *adj.* [B,S]   unpleasant 9A2

nepristojan, nepristojna *adj.*   impolite

nervirati se, nerviram se, nerviraju se (I)   to be irritated, to be angry   11☉
   see **iznerviriti se**

neskroman, neskromna *adj.*   immodest   13☉

nesreća *f*   1. unhappiness;   2. accident   7A2; **prometna nesreća** [C only]   **saobraćajna nesreća** [B,S]   traffic accident

nestanak *m; Gsg* **nestanka**   disappearance 17A4

nestati, nestanem (P)   14A4;   **nestajati, nestajem** (I)   19A1a   to disappear   *see* **stati**

nestrpljenje *n*   impatience   8A2

nešto *pron.*   something   4A3, 9A3✿
   (Gen) **nečeg[a]**
   (Dat-Loc) **nečem[u]**
   (Instr) **nečim**

nešto *adv.*   somewhat   ▢B.V

nesvršen *adj.*   1. imperfective;   2. incomplete; **nesvršen vid**   imperfective aspect

netaktičan, netaktična *adj.*   tactless   20.IV

netko *pron.* [C]   someone   ↦4   9A3, 9A3✿
   (Acc-Gen) **nekog, nekoga**
   (Dat-Loc) **nekom, nekome**
   (Instr) **nekim**

netremice *adv.*   without blinking   ▢B.VII

neugodan, neugodna *adj.* [B,C]   uncomfortable 9A2

neuredan, neuredna *adj.*   messy, untidy   9A2

neutralan, neutralna *adj.*   neutral

neuverljiv *adj.* [E]   unconvincing   20.I

neuvjerljiv *adj.* [J]   unconvincing   20.I

nevešt *adj.* [E]   1. awkward, clumsy;   2. unwitting   ▢B.IV

nevješt *adj.* [J]   1. awkward, clumsy;   2. unwitting   ▢B.IV

nevoljan, nevoljna *adj.*   listless   9☉

nevolja *f*   trouble   19A3a

nevreme *n; Gsg* **nevremena** *Npl* **nevremena** *Gpl* **nevremena** [E]   foul weather, storm 14A2

nevrijeme *n; Gsg* **nevremena** *Npl* **nevremena**

Gpl **nevreme̦na** [J]   foul weather, storm 14A2

New York *m* [B,C]   New York   4A1

Neza̦visna̦ Država Hr̦vatska̦ [**NDH**] Independent State of Croatia (1941-1944)   18A3

neza̦visnost *f; Gsg* **neza̦visnosti** *Isg* **-ošću** or **-osti**   independence   12A4, 12A4✿

ne̦zgodan, ne̦zgodna *adj.*   awkward   📖B.II

nezna̦nje *n*   ignorance   11☺

nežan, nežna *adj.* [E]   tender, gentle   19A1a

ni *part.*   not, neither, either   7A1;   **ni ... ni** neither ... nor...   11A3, 5A4✿;   **ni... ni ... ni** not ... or ... or   7A1;   **ni toli̦ko**   not even that much   📖A.VII

ni̦čiji, ni̦čija *pron.adj.*   no one's;   **ni̦čija̦ ze̦mlja** no man's land   16A1a

nigde *adv.* [E]   nowhere   9A3✿

nigdje *adv.* [J]   nowhere   9A3✿

nije̦dan, nije̦dna *adj.*   not a single one   15A2

nije̦dno̦m *adv.*   not once, never   14A2   *see* **jedno̦m**

Nije̦mac *m; Gsg* **Nije̦mca** [J]   German *(m., general)*

nikad, nikada̦ *adv.*   never   7A1;   **nikad se ne̦ zna̦**   you never know, one never knows   11A4

niko *pron.* [B,S]   no one   9A3, 5A4✿, 9A3✿
  (Acc-Gen) **nikog, nikoga**
  (Dat-Loc) **nikom, nikome**
  (Instr) **niki̦m**

ni̦sam, ni̦si, ni̦je, ni̦smo, ni̦ste, ni̦su   *see under* **biti**

ništa *pron.*   nothing   ↦4   4A3, 5A4✿, 9A3✿
  (Gen) **ni̦čeg, ni̦čega**
  (Dat-Loc) **ni̦čem, ni̦čemu**
  (Instr) **ni̦či̦m**
  ako ne̦mate ništa protiv   if you have no objections   13A4;   **ama baš ništa**   not a single thing   15A2;   **ništa za̦ to̦**   it doesn't matter, it's nothing   12A3

niti *conj.*   neither   5C1;   **niti ... niti**   neither ... nor   5C1, 5A4✿

nitko *pron.* [C]   no one   9A3, 5A4✿, 9A3✿
  (Acc-Gen) **nikog, nikoga**
  (Dat-Loc) **nikom, nikome**
  (Instr) **niki̦m**

ni̦vo *m; Gsg* **nivo̦a** [B,C,S]   1. level;   2. plane 19A1b

nizak, ni̦ska; niski̦ *adj.*   1. low, short [in stature]   2A2, 11A2✿;   2. base, mean

nizvodno *adv.*   downstream   20.VIII

niži̦ *adj.*   lower, shorter   11A2✿   *see* **nizak**

no *conj.*   be that as it may, but, anyway   15A1

no̦ć *f; Gsg* **noći̦** *Isg* **no̦ći** or **no̦ću**   night   ↦4 3A2;   **la̦ku no̦ć** good night   3A2   *see also* **no̦ćas, sino̦ć**

no̦ćas   1. tonight, this very night;   2. last night 13A3

noćni̦ *adj.*   night, nocturnal;   **noćni̦ orma̦rić** [B,C]   bedside table, nightstand   12A1

no̦ga *f; Asg* **nogu** *DLsg* **nozi** *Gpl* **nogu**   1. leg;   2. foot   10A3, 10A4 ;   **s nogu** while standing   12A2

nogome̦t *m* [B,C]   soccer   📖A.I

nogometa̦š *m; Gsg* **nogometa̦ša** [B,C]   soccer player   📖B.IV

nogometni̦ *adj.* [B,C]   soccer;   **nogometni̦ klub** soccer team   📖B.I

no̦s *m; Gsg* **nosa** *Npl* **nosovi**   nose   10A4

nositi, nosi̦m (I)   to carry   ↦6   5C1, 7A2✿, 7A3✿, 10A4✿   *see also* **izne̦ti** [E] **iznije̦ti** [J],   **odne̦ti** [E] **odnije̦ti** [J],   **pone̦ti** [E] **ponije̦ti** [J],   **prene̦ti** [E] **prenije̦ti** [J],   **pridone̦ti** [E] **pridonije̦ti** [J],   **prine̦ti** [E] **prinije̦ti** [J],   **une̦ti** [E] **unije̦ti** [J]

nov, nova; novi̦ *adj.*   new   4A1, 4A1✿;   **Novi̦ za̦vet** [E] **Novi̦ za̦vjet** [J]   New Testament

no̦vac *m; Gsg* **no̦vca**   money   5A2

no̦ve̦mbar *m; Gsg* **no̦ve̦mbra** [B,S]   November 6A2, 6A2

novina̦r *m*   journalist *(m., general)*   11A2✿

novina̦rka *f; DLsg* **novina̦rki** *Gpl* **novina̦rki** journalist *(f.)*

novine *f (pl form)*   newspaper   3A3

novinski̦ *adj.*   pertaining to news;   **novinski̦ čla̦nak**   newspaper article   18A3

no̦ž *m; Gsg* **no̦ža** *Isg* **no̦žem** *Npl* **no̦ževi**   knife

nožni̦ *adj.*   leg, foot;   **nožni̦ palac**   big toe 10A4

npr. *abbr. for*   **na pri̦mer** [E] **na pri̦mjer** [J] 11A3

nuditi (I); **po̦nuditi** (P)   13A1   to offer

nula *num.*   zero

nužan, nužna *adj.*   necessary   20.III

NJ

nje̦ *pron. (Gen)*   1. her;   2. it   6A3✿
  see under **ona**

njega *f; DLsg* **njezi** [J]   care;   **kućna̦ njega** home care   20.I

njega *pron. (Acc-Gen)*   1. him;   2. it   2A2, 6A3✿   *see under* **on, ono**

njegov, njegovo, njegova *pron. adj.*   1. his;   2. its   ↦4   1A2, 2A3✿, 4A2✿

Nje̦mačka̦ *f* [J]   Germany   4A1

nje̦mački̦ *adj.* [J]   German   4A4

Nje̦mica *f* [J]   German *(f.)*

njemu *pron. (Dat-Loc)*   1. him;   2. it   6A3, 6A3✿   *see under* **on, ono**

nje̦n, nje̦no, nje̦na *pron. adj.* [B,C,S]   1. her, hers;   2. its   1A2, 2A2 , 4A2✿

nje̦zin, nje̦zino, nje̦zina *pron. adj.* [C]   1. her,

hers; 2. its 1A2, 2A2 , 4A2☼

nježan, nježna *adj.* [J] tender, gentle 19A1a

njih *pron.* *(Acc-Gen)* them 2A2, 6A3☼ *see under* **oni, ona, one**

njihov, njihovo, njihova *pron. adj.* their, theirs 1A2, 3A1☼, 4A2☼

njim *or* **njime** *pron.* *(Instr)* 1. him; 2. it 7A1☼ *see under* **on, ono**

njima *pron.* *(Dat-Loc-Instr)* them 6A3☼ *see under* **oni**

njiva *f* plowed field 18A1a

njoj *pron.* *(Dat-Loc)* 1. her; 2. it 6A3 *see under* **ona**

njom *pron.* *(Instr)* 1. her; 2. it 7A1, 6A3☼ *see under* **ona**

nju *pron.* *(Acc)* 1. her; 2. it 2A2, 6A3☼ *see under* **ona**

Njujork *m* [B,S] New York 4A1

O

o *prep.* + *Loc* about, concerning ↦5 6A2; **o čemu se radi?** what's it about? 6A2

oba *num.* (with *m* or *n noun*) both 4A4, 4A3☼

obala *f* shore, coast 6☺

obalni *adj.* shore, coastal 16A2a

obasjati (P); **obasjavati, obasjavam, obasjavaju** (I) to cast light on, to illuminate 20.V

obavestiti, obavestim (P); **obaveštavati, obaveštavam, obaveštavaju** (I) [E] to inform 14A3

obaveza *f* [B,C,S] obligation 12A3

obavijestiti, obavijestim (P); **obavještavati, obavještavam, obavještavaju** (I) [J] to inform 14A3

obe *num.* (with *f* noun) [E] both 4A4, 4A3☼

obećanje *n* promise

obećati (P); **obećavati, obećavam, obećavaju** (I) to promise 11☺

obezbediti, obezbedim (P) 16A1b; **obezbeđivati, obezbeđujem** (I) [E] to secure, to provide

obezbijediti, obezbijedim (P) 16A1b; **obezbjeđivati, obezbjeđujem** (I) [J] [B/S] to secure, to provide

običaj *m* custom 12A3; **po običaju** as usual B.VI

običan, obična *adj.* ordinary 2A4

obići, obiđem; obišao, obišla (P) 20.IV; **obilaziti** (I) 16A3a 1. to go from place to place, to tour; 2. to stop in for a visit 16A3a *see* **ići**

obigrati (P) 1. to ride around or fly around; 2. to evade 19A3a *see* **igrati**

obijanje *n* break-in, burglary 20.VII

obilaziti *see under* **obići**

obilaženje *n* tour 16A3b

obitelj *f; Gsg* **obitelji** *Isg* **obitelju** *or* **obitelji** [C]

family 9A1

obiteljski *adj.* [C] family, familial 12A3

objasniti, objasnim (P); **objašnjavati, objašnjavam, objašnjavaju** (I) to explain 10A3, 10A4☼

objašnjenje *n* explanation 20.VIII, 10A4☼

objaviti, objavim (P); **objavljivati, objavljujem** (I) 1. to declare, to announce B.I; 2. to publish 17A4

objavljivanje *n* declaration, publication 18A3

objavljivati *see under* **objaviti**

obje *num. (with f noun)* [J] both 4A4, 4A3☼

objektivan, objektivna *adj.* objective 13☺

oblak *m; Npl* **oblaci** cloud 10A3

oblik *m; Npl* **oblici** shape, form 15A2; **obličje** *n; archaic* shape, form 17C1

obližnji *adj.* nearby, proximate 12A2

obnavljati *see under* **obnoviti**

obnoviti, obnovim (P) 15A1; **obnavljati, obnavljam, obnavljaju** (I) 16A3a to renew

oboleti, obolim (P) 18A3; **obolevati, obolevam, obolevaju** (I) [E] to fall ill *see* **boleti**

oboljeti, obolim 18A3; **obolio, oboljela** (P); **obolijevati, obolijevam, obolijevaju** (I) [J] to fall ill *see* **boljeti**

obraćati se *see under* **obratiti se**

obraditi, obradim (P) 13A3; **obrađivati, obrađujem** (I) to process, to go through *see* **raditi**

obradovati, obradujem (P) to delight 16A1b; **obradovati se, obradujem se** (P) + *Dat* to be overjoyed [at] *see also* **radovati**

obrana *f* [C] defense

obratiti se, obratim se (P) 16A2a; **obraćati se** (I) + *Dat* 16A3a to address, to turn to

obrazina *f* mask 19A2a

obrok *m; Npl* **obroci** meal (breakfast, lunch, dinner)

obrva *f* eyebrow 10A4

obući, obučem (P); **oblačiti, oblačim** (I) to put on [clothes] A.VIII; **obući se, obučem se** (P) **oblačiti se, oblačim se** (I) to get dressed 9A2☼

obveza *f* [C] obligation 12A3

obzir *m* regards, consideration 16A2a; **bez obzira na** + *Acc* regardless (of) 9A4; **ne dolazi u obzir** out of the question 5A4; **obzirom** *or* **s obzirom na** + *Acc* regarding, in view of 16A2a

ocena *f* [E] grade, evaluation

oceniti, ocenim (P); **ocenjivati, ocenjujem** (I) [E] to evaluate, to assess, to grade 10A3

ocenjivati *see under* **oceniti**

ocijeniti, ocijenim (P); **ocjenjivati, ocjenjujem** (I) [J] to evaluate, to assess, to grade 10A3

ocjena *f* [J] grade, evaluation

ocjenjivati *see under* ocijeniti

očaj *m* despair 20.III

očajan, očajna *adj.* miserable, despairing 14A2

očekivati, očekujem (I) to expect 14A4

očigledno *adv.* obviously

očit *adj.* obvious 📖B.V

očuvati *see under* čuvati

od *prep.* + *Gen* from, away from, of ↩5 4A3, 4A4✿, 9A3✿, 11A2✿

odakle *adv.* from where 4A1, 4A1✿

odati (P); odavati, odajem (I) 1. to disclose, show; 2. to betray 20.I

odavde *adv.* from here 13A4

odavno *adv.* long ago, a long time 16A1

odbrana *f* [B,S] defense

odeća *f* [E] clothing 20.VII

odeljenje *n* [S] hospital ward, department, section

odenuti, odenem (P); odevati, odevam, odevaju(I) [E] to don, to put on 📖B.I

odenuti se, odenem se (P); odevati se, odevam se, odevaju se (I) [E] to be dressed, to wear

odevati *see under* odenuti

odevati se *see under* odenuti se

odgledati (P) to watch a series [*e.g.* of films] 16A1a *see* gledati

odgojiti, odgojim (P) 20.VI; odgajati, odgajam, odgajaju (I) to raise, to bring up

odgovarajući *adj.* corresponding 16A2a, 12A1✿

odgovarati *see under* odgovoriti

odgovor *m* answer, response 2A1

odgovoriti, odgovorim (P) 16A2a; odgovarati, odgovaram, odgovaraju (I) 5A1 1. to answer, to respond, 10A2✿, 12A1✿; 2. + *Dat* to suit, to be convenient, to correspond to 6A4✿, 9A3✿

odigrati (P); odigravati, odigravam, odigravaju (I) to play 9☺ *see* igrati

odijevati *see under* odjenuti

odijevati se *see under* odjenuti se

odjeća *f* [J] clothing 20.VII

odjel *m; Gsg* odjela [B,C] hospital ward, department

odjednom *adv.* suddenly 14A4 *see* jednom

odjenuti, odjenem (P); odijevati, odijevam, odijevaju (I) [J] to don, to put on 📖B.I

odjenuti se, odjenem se (P); odijevati se, odijevam se, odijevaju se (I) [J] to be dressed, to wear

odlaziti *see under* otići

odleitati *see under* odleteti

odleteti, odletim (P) 15A1; odletati, odlećem (I) [E] 📖A.III to fly off *see* leteti

odletjeti, odletim; odletio, odletjela (P) 15A1;

odlijetati, odlijećem (I) [J] 📖A.III to fly off *see* letjeti

odličan, odlična *adj.* excellent

odlično *adv.* excellent 2A4

odlijetati *see under* odletjeti

odlika *f; DLsg* odlici 1. feature, characteristic; 2. excellent grade [in school] 17A3b

odliti, odlijem (P) 14A1; odlijevati, odlijevam, odlijevaju (I) [J] odlivati, odlivam, odlivaju (I) [E] pour off *see* liti

odlučiti, odlučim (P) 12A3; odlučivati, odlučujem (I) to decide

odmah *adv.* immediately 5A2

odmahnuti, odmahnem (P); odmahivati, odmahujem (I) to dismiss with a wave of the hand 20.VI

odmor *m* 1. rest; 2. vacation; 3. school recess 5C1, 6A1✿

odnekud *adv.* from somewhere 📖B.III

odneti, odnesem (P); odnositi, odnosim (I) [E] to carry away 7A3, 7A3✿, 10A4✿ *see* nositi

odnijeti, odnesem; odnio, odnijela (P); odnositi, odnosim (I) [J] to carry away 7A3, 7A3✿, 10A4✿ *see* nositi

odnos *m* relationship 11A4

odnosno *adv.* that is, i.e., and, or rather, in regard to, in reference to, in other words, versus, as to, respectively, relatively, regarding, concerning, accordingly 12A1, 12A1

odobriti, odobrim (P) 16A1a; odobravati, odobravam, odobravaju (I) to approve

odrediti, odredim (P) 18A1b; određivati, određujem (I) to determine, to set

određen *adj.* determined, definite, specific, certain 19A1b

održati, održim (P) 📖B.VI, 11A1✿; održavati, održavam, održavaju (I) 16A3b 1. to hold 2. to maintain, to sustain *see* držati

održavati *see under* održati

odsek *m; Npl* odseci [E] university department 16A1a

odseliti se, odselim se (P) 18A3; odseljavati se, odseljavam se, odseljavaju se (I) to move away *see* seliti se

odsesti, odsednem (P); odsedati, odsedam, odsedaju (I) [E] to stay as a guest 16A1a

odsjek *m; Npl* odsjeci [J] university department 16A1a

odsjesti, odsjednem (P); odsjedati, odsjedam, odsjedaju (I) [J] to stay as a guest 16A1a

odvažiti se, odvažim se (P) to muster courage 16A3a

odvesti, odvedem; odveo, odvela (P); odvoditi, odvodim (I) to lead, to take 10A4, 7A3✿, 10A4✿ *see* voditi

òdvesti, odvèzēm; òdvezao, òdvezla (P);
   odvòziti, òdvozīm (I) to drive or take (by
   vehicle) 7A3☼, 10A4☼, 11A1☼ *see*
   vòziti
òdvjetnīk *m; Npl* òdvjetnīci [B,C] lawyer
   5A3, 11A2☼
odvrátiti, òdvratīm (P) 20.VII; òdvraćati (I)
   to retort, to deflect
odžíveti, òdživīm (P) [E] to live out one's life
   20.II *see* žíveti
odžívjeti, òdživīm; òdživio, òdživjela (P) [J]
   to live out one's life 20.II *see* žívjeti
oglèdalo *n* [B,C,S] mirror 9A2
okániti se, òkanīm se (P) to avoid, to shun
   📖B.IV
oko *n; Npl* òči *(pl forms f) Gpl* òčiju eye
   10A3, 10A4☼; jàje na oko egg sunnyside
   up 7A1
oko *prep. + Gen* around ↦5 5⊕
òkolina *f* environment, surroundings 16A3a
òkolnōst *f; Gsg* òkolnosti *Isg* -ošću *or* -osti
   circumstance; stìcajem [B,S] stjècajem [C]
   òkolnosti as things turned out
okrénuti, òkrenēm (P) 20.VIII; okrétati,
   òkrećēm (I) to turn, to turn over *see*
   krénuti
òktobar *m; Gsg* òktobra [B,S] October 6A2,
   6A2
okupátor *m; Gsg* okupátora occupying forces
   18A3
òkupiti (P); òkupljati, òkupljām, òkupljajū (I)
   to gather, to assemble 14A4,; òkupiti se (P);
   òkupljati se, òkupljām se, òkupljajū se (I)
   to gather around 18A3, 14A1☼
òkupljati *see under* òkupiti
òkupljati se *see under* òkupiti
òkvirnī *adj.* approximate, in outline form
   16A2a
Olimpijáda *f* Olympic Games 16A1b
òlovka *f; DLsg* òlovci *Gpl* òlovākā *or* òlovkī
   pencil 1A2; hèmījska òlovka [B,S]
   kèmījska òlovka [C] ballpoint pen 2A4,
   7A4

òlovan, òlovna *adj.* lead, leaden 18A1a
òlovo *n* lead [= metal]
olúja *f* storm 14A2
òmladina *f* young people 16A1b
òmlet *m* omelet 7A1
òn *m; pron.* 1. he; 2. it ↦4 1A2, 2A1☼,
   7A1☼
   (Acc-Gen) njèga 2A2☼, ga 2A1, 2A1☼
   (Dat) njèmu, mu 6A3☼
   (Loc) njèmu 6A3☼
   (Instr) njím, njíme 7A1☼
   for pl see òni
òna *f; pron.* 1. she; 2. it ↦4 1A2,

2A1☼, 6A3☼, 7A1☼
   (Acc) njū 2A2, 2A2☼, je 2A1, 2A1☼,
      ju 2A1☼, 10A1☼
   (Gen) njē, je 6A3☼
   (Dat) njōj, jōj 6A3☼
   (Loc) njōj 6A3☼
   (Instr) njōm, njōme 7A1☼
   for pl see òni
òna *n; pron.* they ↦4 1A4, 2A2☼, 6A3☼,
   7A1☼ *for other forms see* òni
ònaj, òno, òna *pron. adj.* 1. that; 2. that one
   ↦4 2A2
ònakav, ònakvo, ònakva *pron. adj.* that kind
   of
ònamo *adv.* 1. there; 2. in that direction 20.VI
ònda *adv.* 1. then; 2. thereupon 3A2
ònde *adv.* [E] there 14A2
òndje *adv.* [J] there 14A2
òne *f; pron.* they ↦4 1A4, 2A2☼, 6A3☼,
   7A1☼ *for other forms see* òni
òni *m; pron.* they ↦4 1A4, 2A2☼, 6A3☼,
   7A1☼
   (Acc-Gen) njīh, ih 2A2☼, 6A3☼, 7A1☼
   (Dat-Loc-Instr) njīm, njīma, im 6A3☼
   7A1☼
òno *n; pron.* it ↦4 1A2, 2A1☼, 2A2☼,
   6A3☼, 7A1☼ *for other forms see* òn
ònuda *adv.* that way, in that direction
òpćī *adj.* [B,C] general
òpasan, òpasna *adj.* dangerous 7A2
operácija *f* operation 20.IV
operírati, operírām, operírajū (I/P) [C] to
   operate 20.V
operísati, operíšēm (I/P) [B,S] to operate
   20.V
òpet *adv.* again 10A2
opísati, òpišēm (P); opisívati, opisújēm (I) to
   describe 10A3 *see* písati
oponášati, oponášām, oponášajū (I) to imitate
   📖B.VIII
opòravak *m; Gsg* opòravka convalescence,
   recovery 20.I
opòraviti se (P) 20.VI; opòravljati se (I) to
   recover
òporuka *f; DLsg* òporuci [B,C] testament, will
   20.IV
opráštati *see under* opròstiti
òprati *see under* práti
oprávdati (P) 20.II; oprávdavati, oprav-
   dávām, oprávdavajū (I) to justify
opredéliti se, òpredelīm se (P) 16A3b; opre-
   déljivati se, opredéljujēm se (I) [E] to opt
   [for]
opredijèliti se, òpredijelīm se (P) 16A3b;
   opredjèljivati se, opredjèljujēm se (I) [J]
   to opt [for]

oprema *f* equipment 14A1

oprostiti, òprostīm (P); **opraštati, òpraštām, òpraštajū** (I) to forgive 2A1; **oprosti, oprostite** [C] sorry! 2A1, 2A4⚙

opraštati se, òpraštām se, òpraštajū se (I) to bid farewell 20.VI

òpsednuti, òpsednēm; òpsednuo (P): **opsèdati, opsèdām** (I) [E] 1. to besiege; 2. to obsess 11A1⚙

òpsjednuti, òpsjednēm; òpsjednuo (P): **opsjèdati, opsjèdām** (I) [J] 1. to besiege; 2. to obsess 11A1⚙

òpšti *adj.* [B,S] general

opteretiti (P) 16A3a; **opterèćivati, opterèćujēm** (I) to burden

optìmīzam *m;* *Gsg* **optìmīzma** optimism 20.VI

optùžiti, òptužīm (P) 20.VII; **optužìvati, optužùjēm** (I) to accuse 20.II

optužìvati *see under* **optùžiti**

opùstiti, òpustīm (P) 📖B.II; **opùštati, òpuštām, òpuštajū** (I) to cause to relax

opùstiti se, òpustīm se (P); **opùštati se, òpuštām se, òpuštajū se** (I) to relax *see* **pustiti**

òrah *m;* *Npl* **òrasi** walnut, nut 4A3, 3A3⚙

organizácija *f* organization

organizìrati, organìzīram, organìzīrajū (I/P) [B,C] to organize 16A3b, 11A1⚙

organizòvati, organìzujēm (I/P) [B,S] to organize 16A3b, 11A1⚙

òrao *m;* *Gsg* **órla** *Npl* **órlovi** eagle

òrmān *m;* *Gsg* **ormána** [B,S] cupboard, built-in closet

òrmār *m;* *Gsg* **ormára** [B,C] cupboard, built-in closet

òrmarić *m* [B,C] small cupboard or storage unit 20.VII; **nòćni òrmarić** nightstand, bed table 12A1

òsam *num.* eight (8) 5A1, 5A1⚙

osamdèset *num.* eighty (80) 5A1, 5A1⚙

osàmnaest *num.* eighteen (18) 5A1, 5A1⚙

osàmnaestī *adj.* eighteenth (18th) 18A1

osàmstō *num.* eight hundred (800) 12A1⚙

osèćaj *m* [E] feeling, sentiment 19A3b

osèćati *see under* **osètiti**

osèćati se *see under* **osètiti se**

osètiti (P); **osèćati** (I) [E] to feel [= sense of touch]

osètiti se (P) 15A1; **osèćati se** (I) [E] to feel [= emotion] 10A3, 10A2⚙

òsetljiv *adj.* [E] sensitive

osigurati (P); **osigurávati, osigurávam, osigurávajū** (I) 1. to secure, to provide [C only] 16A1b; 2. to insure

òsim *prep.* + *Gen* [B,C,S] except, besides 8A3;

òsim toga besides, furthermore 8A3

osjèćaj *m* [J] feeling, sentiment 19A3b

osjèćati *see under* **osjètiti**

osjèćati se *see under* **osjètiti se**

osjètiti (P); **osjèćati** (I) [J] to feel [= sense of touch]

osjètiti se (P) 15A1; **osjèćati se** (I) [J] to feel [= emotion] 10A3, 10A2⚙

òsjetljiv *adj.* [J] sensitive

osmànskī *adj.* Ottoman 19A3b

òsmeh *m;* *Npl* **osmesi** [E] smile 20.III

osmèhnuti se, òsmehnēm se (P) 📖B.I; **osmèhivati se, osmèhujēm se** (I) [E] to flash a smile

òsmero *n* [C] eight (group of mixed gender)

òsmī *adj.* eighth (8th) 8A1, 6A2⚙, 12A1⚙, 12A3⚙

òsmijeh *m;* *Npl* **osmijesi** [J] smile 20.III

osmìna *f.* one-eighth 12A1⚙

osmjèhnuti se, òsmjehnēm se (P) 📖B.I; **osmjèhivati se, osmjèhujēm se** (I) [J] to flash a smile

osmogòdišnjī *adj.* eight-year 20.III

osmòrica *f* eight [men]

òsmoro *n* [B,S] eight (group of mixed gender)

òsnōv *m* [B,S] 1. basis 16A3b; 2. foundation 📖B.III

osnòva *f* [B,C,S] 1. basis 16A3b; 2. foundation 📖B.III

osnóvnī *adj.* basic 10A3

òsoba *f* person 3A1, 3A1⚙

òsoban, òsobna *adj.* [B,C] personal

òsoblje *n* personnel, staff 11A4

Osòvina *f* Axis [WW II alliance] 12A4

òstajati *see under* **òstati**

òstalī *adj.* remaining, other 13A3

òstareo, òstarela *adj.* [E] elderly, aged 19A3a

òstario, òstarjela *adj.* [J] elderly, aged 19A3a

òstati, òstanēm (P) 9A2; **òstajati, òstajēm** (I) to remain, to stay 14A1, 10A2⚙, ⌐17A2a⌐ *see* **stati**

òstava *f* storage room, closet 16A1b

òstaviti (P) 14A1; **òstavljati** (I) 17A1a to leave [behind]

òstrvo *n* [B,S] island 15A1, 6A1⚙

osvèžiti (P); **osvežávati, osvežávam, osvežávajū** (I) [E] to refresh; **osvèžiti se, òsvežīm se** (P) 📖B.IV; **osvežávati se, osvežávam se, osvežávajū se** (I) to freshen up, to refresh oneself

osvjèžiti (P); **osvježávati, osvježávam, osvježávajū** (I) [J] to refresh; **osvjèžiti se, òsvježīm se** (P) 📖B.IV; **osvježávati se, osvježávam se, osvežávajū se** (I) to freshen up, to refresh oneself

òšišati *see* **šìšati**

oštar, oštra *adj.* sharp 10A3

otac *m; Gsg* oca *Npl* očevi father 2A3, 2A3✿, 3A2✿

otadžbina *f* [B,S] fatherland, homeland

oteti, otmem (P); otimati, otimam (I) 1. to grab 2. to abduct

oteti se, otmem se (P); otimati se, otimam se (I) to escape 20.II

othraniti *see under* hraniti

oticati, otičem (I) [B,S] to drain, to flow away 7☺

otići, odem; otišao, otišla (P); odlaziti (I) to leave, to depart 10A2, 10A2✿, 12A4✿ *see* ići

otjecati, otječem (I) [B,C] to drain, to flow away; otjecati pored to flow around 7☺

otkad, otkada *conj.* ever since

otkriti, otkrijem (P) 20.VI; otkrivati, otkrivam, otkrivaju (I) to discover

otkud *adv.* from where; otkud ti to where'd you get that idea 📖B.VII

otok *m; Npl* otoci [B,C] island 15A1, 6A1✿

otprilike *adv.* approximately 12A1

otpustiti, otpustim (P) 20.I; otpuštati, otpuštam, otpuštaju (I) to release, to fire [from a job] *see* pustiti

otputovati, otputujem (P) to go off on a trip 16A3b *see also* putovati

otvoren *adj.* open 16A3b; na otvorenom outdoors [*e.g.* on an outdoor stage] 16A3b

otvoriti, otvorim (P) 12A2; otvarati, otvaram, otvaraju (I) to open 19A3b

ovaj, ovo, ova *pron. adj.* this, this one ↦4 1A2, 3A2✿

ovaj *excl.* umm, uh... ⟦9A3⟧

ovakav, ovakvo, ovakva *pron. adj.* this kind of 2A4

ovako *adv.* in this way, like this 13A3

ovamo *adv.* 1. in this direction; 2. here 7A3, ⟦7.A4⟧

ovde *adv.* [E] here 2A3

ovdje *adv.* [J] here 2A3

ovisan, ovisna *adj.* [C] 1. depending, dependent 16A3b; 2. addicted

ovo je this is 1A2

ovoliko *adv.* this much

ovuda *adv.* this way, here, in this direction ⟦7.A4⟧ 📖B.VII

ozariti, ozarim (P) to illuminate, to glow 18A2a

ozbiljan, ozbiljna *adj.* serious 3A3

označiti, označim (P) 17A1b; označavati, označavam, označavaju (I) to mark, to designate

označivač *m; Gsg* označivača marker 20.V

oženiti *see under* ženiti

oženiti se *see under* ženiti se

ožujak *m; Gsg* ožujka [C] March 6A2, ⟦6A2⟧

P

pa *conj.* and, and also 7A2

pacijent *m* patient 20.I

pad *n; Npl* padovi fall, drop

padaline *f (pl form)* [C] precipitation 14A2

padati *see under* pasti

padavine *f (pl form)* [B,S] precipitation 14A2

padež *m* case [grammar]

pahuljice *f (pl form)* flakes 7A1

pak *conj.* and, rather, on the other hand 5A3

palac *m; Gsg* palca thumb 10A4; nožni palac big toe 10A4

pametan, pametna *adj.* intelligent, smart 11A2

pamćenje *n* memory

pamtiti (I) to remember; zapamtiti (P) 1. to remember; 2. to memorize 16A1b

pantalone *f (pl form)* [S] pants, trousers 11A1

papagaj *m* [B,S] 1. parrot; 2. parakeet

papar *m; Gsg* papra [C] pepper [= spice]

pepeo *m; Gsg* pepela ash

papiga *f; DLsg* papigi [B,C] 1. parrot; 2. parakeet 6A2, 6A2✿

papir *m; Gsg* papira paper 1A2

papirnica *f* stationery store 2A4

paprika *f; DLsg* paprici pepper [= vegetable] 7A1

par *m* pair 14A3

paradajz *m* [B,C,S] tomato 7A1, 5A4✿

parče *m; Gsg* parčeta [B,S] piece 4A3

pare *f (pl form)* money, change 5A2

Pariz *m; Gsg* Pariza Paris 4A1

park *m; Gpl* paraka park 📖A.III

parkiranje *n* parking 10☺

parkirati, parkiram, parkiraju (I); uparkirati, uparkiram, uparkiraju (P) to park 12A2

partner *m; Gsg* partnera partner 13A3

pas *m; Gsg* psa *Gpl* pasa dog 1A2, 2A3✿, 3A2✿

pasoš *m* [B,S] passport 4☻

pasti, padnem; pao, pala (P); padati (I) to fall 10A2, 10A1✿, 10A2✿; pada [mi] na pamet it occurs [to me] 11A4 *see also* dopasti se, ispasti, napasti

pasulj *m; Gsg* pasulja [S] beans

patka *f; Gpl* pataka duck

paviljon *m; Gsg* paviljona wing, pavilion 12A1

paziti (I) to watch out, to be careful 📖B.VIII *see also* upaziti

pažljiv *adj.* careful 14A1

pažnja *f* attention 20.III

pecanje *n* fishing 20.II

pecivo *n* bread roll 5A1

pedagogija *f* teacher training 13B3

pedeset *num.* fifty (50) 5A1, 5A1✿, 12A1✿

pedesetak *num.* about fifty 13A3

peglanje *n* ironing; daska za peglanje [B,C,S] daska za glačanje [C] ironing board 🕮A.VIII

pekar *m* baker 11A2✿

pena *f* [E] foam 14A1

period *m* period, time 17A4

pero *n* pen, fountain pen 2A1

pesma *f; Gpl* pesama [E] 1. song 5C1; 2. poem 10A3

pesnički *adj.* [E] poetic 19A1b

pesnik *m; Npl* pesnici [E] poet *(m., general)* 11A2✿

pesnikinja *f* [E] poet *(f.)* 11A2✿

pešak *m; Gsg* pešaka *Npl* pešaci [E] pedestrian 5A2

peške *adv.* [S] on foot 5A2

pet *num.* five (5) 5A1, 5A1✿, 12A1✿, 12A2✿

petak *m; Gsg* petka Friday 2A1; petkom on Fridays 7A2

petero *n.* [C] five (group of mixed gender) 12A1✿

peti *adj.* fifth (5th) 5A1, 6A2✿, 12A3✿

petnaest *num.* fifteen (15) 5A1, 5A1✿, 14A2✿

petnaestak *num.* fifteen or so 12A1✿

petnaesti *adj.* fifteenth (15th) 15A1

petorica *f* five [men] 12A2✿

petoro *n.* [B,S] five (group of mixed gender) 12A1✿

petsto *num.* five hundred (500) 12A1✿

pevač *m; Gsg* pevača [E] singer

pevati (I) [E] 1. to sing 5C1; 2. to compose verse 19A3b *see also* spevati

piće *n* drink 🕮B.VII; jelo i piće food and drink; izići na piće [B,C only] izaći na piće to go out for a drink 🕮B.VII

pijaca *f* [B,S] marketplace 🕮A.I

piletina *f* chicken [meat]

pingvin *m; Gsg* pingvina penguin 15A1

pingvinski *adj.* penguin 15A1

pire *m; Gsg* pirea purée; kesten pire chestnut purée; krompir pire [B,S] pire krumpir [C] mashed potatoes

pirinač *m* [B,S] rice

pisac *m; Gsg* pisca writer *(m., general)* 5A3

pisaći *adj.* writing 12A1; pisaći sto [B,S] pisaći stol [C] desk 12A1

pisanje *n* writing 10A4, 10A4✿

pisar *m; Gsg* pisara clerk 11A2✿

pisati, pišem (I) ↵6 2A1, 2A1✿, 7A4✿, 10A1✿, 10A2✿, 10A4✿; napisati, napišem

(P) 11A1✿ to write *see also* opisati, potpisati, upisati

pismen *adj.* literate, able to write 6A2

pismo *n; Gpl* pisama letter ↵4 1A2; avionsko pismo airmail letter 2A4, 5A1✿

pita *f* pie

pitanje *n* 1. question 1A2, 3A1✿, 3A2✿; 2. issue 1🕭

pitati, pitam, pitaju (I) to ask 3A1; upitati, upitam, upitaju (P) to inquire 🕮B.I *see also* zapitati, raspitati se

piti, pijem (I) to drink ↵6 5A1; popiti, popijem (P) to drink up 5A4, 5A4✿, 10A1✿, 11A1✿

piva *n* [C] beer

pivo *n* [B,C,S] beer 4A3

pjena *f* [J] foam 14A1

pjesma *f; Gpl* pjesama [J] 1. song 5C1; 2. poem 10A3

pjesnički *adj.* [J] poetic 19A1b

pjesnik *m; Npl* pjesnici [J] poet *(m., general)* 11A2✿

pjesnikinja *f* [J] poet *(f.)* 11A2✿

pješak *m; Gsg* pješaka *Npl* pješaci [J] pedestrian 5A2

pješice *adv.* [B,C] on foot 5A2

pješke *adv.* [J] [B/S] on foot 5A2

pjevač *m; Gsg* pjevača [J] singer

pjevati (I) [J] 1. to sing 5C1; 2. to compose verse 19A3b *see also* spjevati

plaća *f* [B,C] salary 18A3

plafon *m; Gsg* plafona [B,S] ceiling 8A4

plafonski *adj.* [B,S] ceiling 8A4

plahta *f; Gpl* plahti [C] sheet (bedding) 12A1

plakati, plačem (I) to cry 18A2a

plan *m; Npl* planovi plan, map 16A1a; plan grada map of town 11A3

planet *m; Gsg* planeta [C] planet 6A1

planeta [B,S] planet 6A1

planina *f* mountain 16A3b

planirati, planiram, planiraju (I) to plan 16A1b

plašiti (I), uplašiti (P) to frighten; plašiti se 10A3 ↕, uplašiti se + *Gen* (I) to be frightened 11☺

plata *f* [B,S] salary 18A3

platiti, platim (P); plaćati, plaćam, plaćaju (I) to pay 2A4

plav, plava; plavi *adj.* 1. blue 2A3; 2. blond

plavuša *f* blonde 🕮B.I

plaža *f* beach 16A3a

ples *m; Npl* plesovi [B,C] dance 15A1

plesač *m; Gsg* plesača [B,C] dancer *(m., general)* 11A2✿

plesačica *f* [B,C] dancer *(f.)* 11A2✿

plesati, plešem (I) [B,C] to dance 15A1,

15A1✿

pliĉi *adj.* shallower *see* **plitak**

plin *m; Npl* **plinovi** 1. natural gas *(usually sg)*; 2. digestive gas *(usually pl)*

plitak, plitka; plitki *adj.* shallow

plivati (I) to swim 18A1a

ploča *f* blackboard [C] 4A4; gramophone record, memorial plaque [B,C,S]

pločnik *m; Npl* **pločnici** [C] sidewalk 14A3

pljeskati, plješćem (I) to applaud ⬚B.VIII

pljuštati, pluštim (I) to rain cats and dogs, to pour down rain 14☺

po *prep. + Acc* for ↦5; **ići po njih** to fetch them, to get them 9A4

po *prep.* each, per [*as in* **kupili su po jedan sladoled** they each bought one ice cream; they bought one ice cream per person] 5A1, 5A1✿

po *prep. + Loc* ↦5; 1. according to 6A2; 2. on ⬚A.V.; 3. around 12A1; 4. of 20.III; 5. at, upon ⬚B.VII; 6. per 12A1; **po mom mišljenju** in my opinion 10A4; **po običaju** according to custom ⬚B.VI; **po prilici** approximately 12A1; **po čelu** on the forehead ⬚A.V.; **po gradu** all around town 20.VII; **po završetku** at the end ⬚B.VII; **po cimetu** of cinnamon 20.III; **po sobi** per room 12A1; **jedan po jedan** one by one 15A2

po *num.* half *see under* **polovica** [B,C] *or* **polovina** [B,S]

pobeći, pobegnem (P); **bežati, bežim** (I) [E] to flee, to run away 18A3

pobjeći, pobjegnem (P); **bježati, bježim** (I) [J] to flee, to run away 18A3, ⁝B.VIII⁝

počešljati *see under* **češljati**

početak *m; Gsg* **početka** *Npl* **počeci** beginning 7A4

početi, počnem (P) 13A2; **počinjati, počinjem** (I) 6A2 to begin, to start

početni *adj.* initial 16A3b

počinjati *see under* **početi**

počinuti, počinem (P) *(archaic)* to rest 19A1b

počistiti *see under* **čistiti**

poći, pođem; pošao, pošla (P) 9A4; **polaziti** (I) to go, to set out 9A2; **poći** [nekome] **za rukom** to able to do 18A3 *see* **ići**

poćutati, poćutam (P) [B,S] to fall silent briefly 20.IV

pod *prep. + Instr* under ↦5 8A1, 8A4✿

pod *prep. + Acc* [moving to a position] under ↦5

pod *m; Gsg* **poda** floor 6A1

podatak *m; Gsg* **podatka** *Npl* **podaci** *Gpl* **podataka** datum, data 16A3b

podcrtati (P); **podcrtavati, podcrtavam,**

podcrtavaju (I) [C] underline 18A1b

podeliti *see under* **deliti**

podići [**podignuti**], **podignem** (P) 15A1; **podizati, podižem** (I) ⬚A.VI to lift up, to raise

podijeliti *see under* **dijeliti**

podizati *see under* **podići** [**podignuti**]

podnaslov *m* subheading 19A2b

podne *n; Gsg* **podneva** *or* **podne** (*i.e.* indecl.) noon 10A1; **pre podne** [E] **prije podne** [J] [in the] morning, late morning 10A1

Podravina *f* Drava river valley

Podrinje *n* Drina river valley

područje *n* area, region 6🌑

podstaći, podstaknem; podstakao, podstakla (P) 19A3b; **podsticati, podstičem** (I) to encourage

podstanar *m* tenant, subletter 9A3; **ići u podstanare** to become a tenant, to rent 9A3

podučavati *see under* **podučiti**

podučiti (P); **podučavati, podučavam, podučavaju** (I) to tutor 18A3

Podunavlje *n* Danube river valley

poduzeće *n* [B,C] business, company 11A4

poduzeti, poduzmem (P) 16A1a; **poduzimati, poduzimam, poduzimaju** (I) [B,C] to undertake *see* **uzeti**

podvući, podvučem, podvuku (P) 18A1b; **podvlačiti, podvlačim** (I) [B,S] to underline *see* **vući**

poetski *adj.* poetic 19A1b

poezija *f* poetry 3A2, 3A2✿

pogačica *f* bread roll 9☺

pogađati, pogađam, pogađaju (I) 1. to make a guess ⬚B.VII; 2. to shoot at; 3. to attempt to hit [a target] *see* **pogoditi**

poginuti, poginem (P) to be killed, to perish 14A3

poglavlje *n* chapter 10A2

pogled *m* 1. gaze 10A3; 2. **pogled (na)** view (of)

pogledati (P) 20.V; **pogledati, pogledam, pogledaju** (I) to glance at, to take a look 2A4; **pogledati se** (P); **pogledati se, pogledam se, pogledaju se** (I) to look at oneself [*e.g.* in the mirror] 9A2 *see* **gledati**

pogoditi, pogodim (P) 1. to figure out, to get the answer; 2. to hit [a target]

pogreška *f; DLsg* **pogrešci** *or* **pogreški** *Gpl* **pogrešaka** mistake ⬚B.III

pohađati, pohađam, pohađaju (I) to attend [classes, school] 16A2b

pohvaliti, pohvalim (P) to praise *see also* **hvaliti**

pohvaliti se, pohvalim se (P) to boast 15A1

pojam *m; Gsg* **pojma** *Npl* **pojmovi** concept, notion, idea 13A3; **nemam pojma** I have no idea 13A3

pojava *f* 1. appearance; 2. phenomenon
18A1b

pojaviti se, pojavim se (P) 13A3; **pojavljivati
se, pojavljujem se** (I) to appear

pojedinac *m; Gsg* **pojedinca** individual
19A2b

pojedinačan, pojedinačna *adj.* individual
16A3b

pojedini *adj.* some, several, certain

pojedinost *f; Gsg* **pojedinosti** *Isg* **-ošću** or **-osti**
detail 📖B.VI

pojesti *see under* **jesti**

pokazati, pokažem (P) 20.VI, 9A2✿;
pokazivati, pokazujem (I) 📖A.IV to show,
to demonstrate

pokazivati *see under* **pokazati**

poklanjati *see under* **pokloniti**

pokloniti, poklonim (P) 12A2; **poklanjati** (I)
📖B.VIII 1. to give a gift; 2. to bow

pokrenuti, pokrenem (P) 16A2a; **pokretati,
pokrećem** (I) to set in motion

pokret *m* movement

pokrivač *m; Gsg* **pokrivača** [C] blanket 12A1

pokušati (P) 11A1; **pokušavati, pokušavam,
pokušavaju** (I) 📖B.V to try, to attempt

pokvariti *see under* **kvariti**

pola half 14A2, 14A2✿

polagati *see under* **položiti**

polako *adv.* slowly, take it easy 13A3

polaran, polarna *adj.* polar 15A1; **polarno
more** Arctic (or Antarctic) Ocean 15A1

polaziti *see under* **poći**

polaznica *f* one who attends a school or a
course *(f.)* 📖B.IV

polaznik *m; Npl* **polaznici** one who attends a
school or course *(m., general)* 16A2b

poleteti *see under* **leteti**

poletjeti *see under* **letjeti**

polica *f* shelf 📖A.VI

policija *f* police 14A3

policijski *adj.* police 14A3; **policijska
stanica** [B,C,S] **policijska postaja** [C]
police station ⌐9A3⌐

poliglot *m* [C] polyglot, person who speaks
many languages 📖B.III

poliglota *m; Npl* **poliglote** [B,S] polyglot,
person who speaks many languages 📖B.III

politički *adj.* political; **političke nauke** [B,S],
političke znanosti [C] political science
13B3

politika *f; DLsg* **politici** 1. politics 📖B.V;
2. policy

polovica *f* [B,C] half 12A1, 12A1✿ *see
under* **po** *or* **pola**

polovina *f* [B,S] half 12A1, 12A1✿ *see*

under **po** *or* **pola**

položiti, položim (P); **polagati, polažem** (I)
put 10A2✿; **polagati ispit** to take/write an
exam 6A2; **položiti ispit** (P) to pass an
exam 6A2, 6A2✿

poluostrvo *n* [B,S] peninsula 6🌐

poluotok *m; Npl* **poluotoci** [B,C] peninsula
6🌐

polje *n* field ↦4 19A1b

poljoprivreda *f* agriculture 13B3

poljoprivrednik *m; Npl* **poljoprivrednici** farmer, person employed in agriculture 11A2✿

poljubac *m; Gsg* **poljupca** kiss 20.III

poljubiti *see also* **ljubiti**

pomagati *see under* **pomoći**

pomenuti, pomenem (P); **pominjati, pominjem**
(I) [B,S] to mention 16A1b

pomfrit *m* French fried potatoes

pomilovanje *n* clemency, pardon 19A2a

pomirljiv *adj.* conciliatory 20.IV

pomoć *f; Gsg* **pomoći,** *Isg* **pomoću** help, aid
14A3; **hitna pomoć** emergency response,
first aid, 911 14A3; **prva pomoć** first aid

pomoći, pomognem; pomogao, pomogla (P);
pomagati, pomažem (I) + *Dat* to help
10A4, 10A1✿, 14A2✿

pomorandža *f; Gpl* **pomorandži** [S] orange
[= fruit] 4A3

Pomoravlje *n* Morava river valley

ponajviše *adv.* most of all 15A1

ponaosob *adv.* individually 15A2

ponašati se, ponašam se, ponašaju se (I) to
behave 18A2b

ponedeljak *m; Gsg* **ponedeljka** [E] Monday
2A1; **ponedeljkom** on Mondays 7A2

ponedjeljak *m; Gsg* **ponedjeljka** [J] Monday
2A1; **ponedjeljkom** on Mondays 7A2

ponekad *adv.* sometimes 7A1

poneti, ponesem (P) [E] to take 16A1a *see*
nositi

ponijeti (P), **ponesem; ponio, ponijela** [J] to
take 16A1a *see* **nositi**

poništiti (P) 13A4; **poništavati, poništavam,
poništavaju** (I) to stamp, to void

poniziti, ponizim (P) 19A2a; **ponižavati,
ponižavam, ponižavaju** (I) to humiliate

ponoć *f; Gsg* **ponoći,** *Isg* **ponoću** or **ponoći**
midnight

ponosan, ponosna *adj.* proud 16A1a

ponovno *adv.* [C] again 9☺, 14A1

ponovo *adv.* [B,C,S] again 9☺, 14A1

ponuditi *see under* **nuditi**

pop *m; Gsg* **popa** *Npl* **popovi** [Orthodox] priest
11A2✿

popeti se, popnem se (P) to rise, to climb up
14A1

pòpis *m* list [C]; **pòpis stanovnȋštva** [B,C,S] **pòpis pučȃnstva** [C] census

pòpiti *see under* **piti**

popȍdne *n; Gsg* **popȍdneva** *or* **popȍdne** (*i.e. indecl.*) noon 5A4 *see* **pȍdne**

popȍdne *adv.* in the afternoon 10A1

pòpraviti (P) 13A2; **pòpravljati** (I) to repair

pòpričati (P) to chat for awhile 📖B.VI *see under* **prȋčati**

popríličan, poprílična *adj.* considerable 16A2b

pòpušiti (P) to have a smoke 20.V *see* **pušiti**

pòput *prep. + Gen* similar to, like 19A1b

porazgovárati, porazgovȃram, porazgovȃraju (P) to converse briefly, chat 16A2b *see* **razgovárati**

porcelȁnski *adj.* [S] porcelain 12A2

porculȁnski *adj.* [B,C] porcelain 12A2

pòreći, pòrečem, pòreku [**pòreknem**]; **pòrekao, pòrekla** (P); **poricati, pòričem** (I) to deny 📖B.V

pòred *prep. + Gen* 1. next to, along ↦5 4A4

pòredati *see* **rȅdati**

pòređati *see* **rȅđati**

poréđenje *n* [B,S] comparison 11A2

pòreklo *n* [E] origin 16A3a

poricati *see* **pòreći**

porijȅklo *n* [J] origin 16A3a

pòrodica *f* [B,S] family 9A1

pòrodični *adj.* [B,S] family, familial 12A3

pòruka *f; DLsg* **pòruci** message 15A2; **SMS pòruka** text message

pòsao *m; Gsg* **pòsla** *Npl* **pòslovi** *or* **pòsli** job, employment ↦4 5A3; [**imȁti**] **pùne rȗke pòsla** to be very busy, to have one's hands full 9A2

Pòsavina *f* Sava river valley 6🌐

pòseban, pòsebna *adj.* special 7A4

posedòvati, posèdujem (I) [E] to possess 19A2b

posȅta *f* [E] visit 16A3b

posètilac *m; Gsg* **posètioca** [E] visitor (*m., general*) 15A1

posètiti (P) 16A2a; **posèćivati, posèćujem** (I) [E] to visit

posjedòvati, posjèdujem (I) [J] to possess 19A2b

posjet *m* [B,C] visit 16A3b

posjèta *f* [J] [B/S] visit 16A3b

posjètilac *m; Gsg* **posjètioca** [J] [B/S] visitor (*m., general*) 15A1

posjètitelj *m* [C] visitor (*m., general*)

posjètiteljica *f* [C] visitor (*f.*) 20.III

posjètiti (P) 16A2a; **posjèćivati, posjèćujem** (I) [J] to visit

poslàstica *f* [B,S] dessert 11A2

pòslati *see under* **slati**

pòsle *prep. + Gen* [E] after ↦5 5A2

pòsle *adv.* [E] later, afterwards 📖A.V

pòsledica *f* [E] consequence 19A3b

pòslednji *adj.* [E] final, last 14A1

poslepȍdne *n; Gsg* **poslepȍdneva** *or* **poslepȍdne** (*i.e. indecl.*) [E] afternoon

pòslije *prep. + Gen* [J] after ↦5 5A2

pòslije *adv.* [J] later, afterwards 📖A.V

poslijedȋplomski [C] graduate [Am.] post-graduate [Br.]; **poslijedȋplomski stȕdij** [C] graduate [Am.] postgraduate [Br.] study 16A2a

poslijepȍdne *n; Gsg* **poslijepȍdneva** *or* **poslijepȍdne** (*i.e. indecl.*) [J] afternoon

pòslovan, pòslovna *adj.* business, commercial 13A3

poslúžiti, poslúžim (P); poslúživati, poslúžujem (I) to serve 13A1 *see under* **slúžiti**

pòsljedica *f* [J] consequence 19A3b

pòsljednji *adj.* [J] final, last 14A1

posmátrati, posmȃtram, posmȃtraju (I) [B,S] to observe 14☺

pòspan *adj.* sleepy, drowsy

pòsmrtan, pòsmrtna *adj.* posthumous 17A4

pòstaja *f* [C] station 20.VIII; **policȋjska pòstaja** police station; **rȁdio pòstaja** radio station 9A3

pòstajati *see under* **pòstati**

pòstati, pòstanem [P] 18A3; **pòstajati, postòjim** [I] to become, to exist *see* **stati**

pòstaviti (P) 15A2, 11A1⚙; **pòstavljati** (I) 16A1a to put, to pose, to place; **pòstaviti / pòstavljati pȉtanje** pose a question

postdȋplomski [B,C,S] graduate [Am.] post-graduate [Br.] study; **postdȋplomski stȕdij** [B,C,S] graduate [Am.] postgraduate [Br.] study 16A2a

pòstelja *f* bed 19A3a

pòsteljina *f* bedding 12A1

pòstepen *adj.* gradual 19A3b

pòstići [**pòstignuti**], **pòstignem; pòstigao, pòstigla** (P); **pòstizati, pòstižem** (I) to accomplish 13☺

pòstignuti *see under* **pòstići**

pòstojanje *n* existence 17A4

pòstojeći *adj.* existing 19A1b

posúditi, posúdim (P) 16A1a; **posúđivati, posúđujem** (I) to borrow

pòsuđe *n; coll.* [B,C] dishes 12A2

pòsve *adv.* completely 14A4

posvéta *f* dedication 20.VIII

posvétiti, posvétim (P) 16A2a; **posvéćivati, posvéćujem** (I) to dedicate; **posvétiti se, posvétim se** (P) 18A3; **posvéćivati se,**

posvećujem se (I)   to dedicate oneself

posvojan, posvojna *adj.* [C]   possessive;
posvojna zamenica [E] **posvojna zamjenica**
[J]   possessive pronoun

pošiljac *n; Npl* **pošiljoci** [B,S]   sender

pošiljilac *n; Npl* **pošiljioci** [B,C]   sender

pošten *adj.*   fair, honest, honorable   7☺, 20.IV

poštovan *adj.*   respected, esteemed   16A2a

poštovanje *n*   respect, esteem   16A2a

poštovati, poštujem (I)   to respect, to honor   12A3

pošutjeti, pošutim; pošutio, pošutjela (P) [C]
to fall silent   20.IV   *see* **šutjeti**

Potisje *n*   Tisa river valley

potiti (I) *(archaic)*   to perspire   18A2a

potkošulja *f*   undershirt

potom *adv.*   then, later   12A2

potpis *m*   signature   20.VIII

potpisati, potpišem (P)   20.V; **potpisivati, pot-
pisujem** (I)   to sign   *see* **pisati**

potpredsednik *m; Npl* **potpredsednici**   vice
president

potpredsjednik *m; Npl* **potpredsjednici**   vice
president

potpun *adj.*   complete, full, total

potpuno *adv.*   totally

potraga *f; DLsg* **potrazi**   search   19A2b

potreba *f*   need   19A2b

potreban, potrebna *adj.*   necessary   11A2

potrošiti   *see under* **trošiti**

potruditi se   *see under* **truditi se**

potvrda *f*   confirmation, certificate   16A2b

potvrdan, potvrdna *adj.*   affirmative   📖B.VI

poumreti, poumrem; poumro, poumrla (P) [E]
to die off [one by one]   17A2a, ¦ 17A2a ¦
see **umreti**

poumrijeti; poumrem, poumro, poumrla (P)
[J]   to die off [one by one]   17A2a,
¦ 17A2a ¦   *see* **umrijeti**

povezan *adj.*   connected, interconnected   📖B.IV

povezati, povežem (P)   📖B.IV; **povezivati,
povezujem** (I)   to connect   16A1b

povijest *f; Gsg* **povijesti** *Isg* **poviješću, povijesti**
[C]   history   13B3, ¦ 17A1b ¦

povod *m*   reason, occasion   📖B.I

povratak *m; Gsg* **povratka**   return   14A4

povratan, povratna *adj.*   1. reflexive; 2. re-
current;   **povratna zamenica** [E] **povratna
zamjenica** [J] reflexive pronoun *(e.g.* **sebe***)*

povremeno *adv.*   occasionally, now and then
8A3

povrnuti, povrnem (P) *(archaic)*   to return
19A3a

površina *f*   surface

pozdrav *f*   greeting   6A3

pozdraviti (P)   📖A.VII; **pozdravljati** (I)   6A3

to greet, to send greetings

pozdraviti se (P)   12A1; **pozdravljati se** (I)
6A3   to greet one another

pozdravljati   *see under* **pozdraviti**

poznat *adj.*   famous   18A3; familiar   📖B.I

poznati (P)   10A2, 10A2✿; **poznavati,
poznajem** (I)   3A1, 3A1✿, 10A1✿, 10A2✿
to be familiar with   *see* **znati**

pozorišni *adj.* [B,S]   theater, theatrical   16A3a

pozorište *n* [B,S]   theater   5A2, 5A4✿, 6A1✿

pozvati, pozovem (P); **pozivati, pozivam,
pozivaju** (I)   1. to invite; 2. to call   13A1;
pozvati u goste to invite for a visit   13A1
see **zvati**

poželeti   *see under* **želeti**

poželjeti   *see under* **željeti**

požuriti se   *see under* **žuriti se**

prag *m; Npl* **pragovi**   threshold   19A1a

prasnuti, prasnem (P)   📖B.IV; **praskati** (I)   to
burst out, to flare up

prati, perem (I); **oprati, operem** (P)   to wash
9A2, 9A2✿

pratiti (I)   12A2; **ispratiti** (P)   to follow, to
accompany

pratilac *m; Gsg* **pratioca** *Gpl* **pratilaca**   person
serving as an escort   ↪4

pratnja *f*   escort, accompaniment   20.VII

pravda *f; Gpl* **pravdi**   justice   19A2b

pravedan *adj.*   just, righteous

pravi *adj.*   real, true   3A2

pravilo *n*   rule   20.II

praviti (I); **napraviti** (P)   to make   20.III

praviti se (I) [B,C,S]   1. to pretend, to feign
📖B.IV, 20.IV

pravo *n*   1. law [= discipline]   13B3; 2. right
[= that which is just];   **imati pravo**   7A2
biti u pravu   📖B.V   to be right;   **ljudska
prava**   human rights

pravo *adv.*   1. right, correct   7A2; 2. straight
ahead [B,S]   13A4

pravoslavac *n; Gsg* **pravoslavca**   Orthodox
Christian *(general)*

pravoslavan, pravoslavna *adj.*   Orthodox
Christian

prazan, prazna *adj.*   empty   13A1

pre *prep. + Gen* [E]   before   ↪5   5A2,
13A4✿;   **pre podne** *adv.* [E]   late morning
10A1

pre *adv.* [E]   earlier, before   13A2

prebaciti, prebacim (P); **prebacivati, prebac-
ujem** (I)   to pass on, to transfer   20.VII

prebacivati   *see under* **prebaciti**

preći, pređem; prešao, prešla (P); **prelaziti** (I)
[B,C,S]   to go across   19A1a   *see* **ići**

preći *adj.*   more sudden, more short-tempered
see **prek** [E] **prijek** [J]

427

pred *prep. + Instr* in front of, before ↦5
7A2, 7A2✿, 8A4✿

pred *prep + Acc* [moving to] in front of 📖B.I

predak *m; Gsg* **pretka** *Npl* **preci** ancestor
16A3b

predati (P); **predavati, predajem** (I) to submit, to hand in 16A2a; **predati se** (P): **predavati se, predajem se** (I) to surrender, to
give oneself up *see* **dati**

predavanje *n* lecture 6A2, 6A2✿

predavati, predajem (I only) to teach, to
lecture 16A3a

predavati *see under* **predati**

predjelo *n* appetizer 11A2

predlog *m; Npl* **predlozi** [E] 1. proposal
20.IV; 2. preposition 17A1b

predložiti, predložim (P); **predlagati, predlaž-
em** (I) to propose 20.IV

predmet *m* 1. object, thing; 2. subject, topic

predrasuda *f* prejudice 📖B.IV

predsednica *f* [E] president *(f.)* 11A2✿

predsednik *m; Npl* **predsednici** [E] president
(m., general) 11A2✿

predsjednica *f* [J] president *(f.)* 11A2✿

predsjednik *m; Npl* **predsjednici** [J] president
(m., general) 11A2✿

predsoblje *n* front hall 16A1b

predstava *f* performance 5A4

predstaviti (P) 19A3b; **predstavljati** (I)
19A2b to present

predstavljati *see under* **predstaviti**

predstojnik *m; Npl* **predstojnici** head; **predstojnik odelenje** [S] **odjela** [B,C] department head 20.VII

preduzeće *n* [B,S] business, company 11A4

preduzeti, preduzmem (P) 16A1a; **preduzimati, preduzimam, preduzimaju** (I) [B,S]
to undertake *see* **uzeti**

predvideti, predvidim (P) 📖B.III; **predviđati,
predviđam, predviđaju** (I) [E] to foresee, to
predict

predvidjeti, predvidim; predvidio, predvidjela
(P) 📖B.III; **predviđati, predviđam,
predviđaju** (I) [J] to foresee, to predict

pregled *m* 1. inspection, overview; 2. medical
examination 20.IV

pregledati (P), **pregledati, pregledam,
pregledaju** (I) to inspect, to examine, to
check 11A1✿

prek, preka; preki *adj.* sudden, short-tempered

prekinuti, prekinem (P) 20.II; **prekidati, pre-
kidam, prekidaju** (I) to interrupt

prekjuče *adv.* [B,S] the day before yesterday

prekjučer *adv.* [C] the day before yesterday

preko *prep.* across ↦5 9A1

preksutra *adv.* day after tomorrow

prekosutra *adv.* day after tomorrow 20.IV

prekratak, prekratka *adj.* too short 📖B.III

prelaz *n* [B,C,S] 1. transition; 2. crosswalk

prelep *adj.* [E] so lovely, exquisite 📖B.IV

prelijep *adj.* [J] so lovely, exquisite 📖B.IV

preliti, prelijem (P) 14A1; **prelijevati, pre-
lijevam, prelijevaju** (I) [J] *or* **prelivati, pre-
livam, prelivaju** (I) [E] to pour over *see* **liti**

prema *prep. + Dat* toward, toward, according
to ↦5 11A4

premda *conj.* although 20.V

premestiti (P) 📖B.V; **premeštati, premeštam,
premeštaju** (I) [E] to shift position, to move

premjestiti (P) 📖B.V; **premještati, premješ-
tam, premještaju** (I) [J] to shift position, to
move

preneti, prenesem (P); **prenositi, prenosim** (I)
[E] to transmit 19A3b, 10A4✿ *see* **nositi**

prenijeti, prenesem; prenio, prenijela (P); **prenositi, prenosim** (I) [J] to transmit 19A3b,
10A4✿ *see* **nositi**

prenoćiti, prenoćim (P) to spend the night
19A1a

prenositi *see under* **preneti** [E] **prenijeti** [J]

preobraženje *n* 1. transfiguration *(relig.)*;
2. transformation 17A4

prepisati, prepišem (P) 20.IV; **prepisivati,
prepisujem** (I) 1. to copy over; 2. to sign
over

preporučiti, preporučim (P); **preporučivati,
preporučujem** (I) to recommend 13A1

prepoznati (P); **prepoznavati, prepoznajem** (I)
to recognize 20.III

prepoznavati *see* **prepoznati**

prepričati, prepričam (P) 15A2; **prepričavati,
prepričavam, prepričavaju** (I) to narrate, to
retell *see* **pričati**

preraditi, preradim (P) 15A2; **prerađivati,
prerađujem** (I) to rework, to redo *see*
raditi

prerasti, prerastem; prerastao, prerasla (P)
to outgrow 18A3 *see* **rasti**

preseliti se *see under* **seliti se**

prespavati, prespavam, prespavaju (P) to
sleep over 14A2

presrećan, presrećna *adj.* [S] overjoyed 10☺

presretan, presretna *adj.* [B,C] overjoyed
10☺

prestajati *see under* **prestati**

prestajati, prestojim (P) to continue standing,
to stay on one's feet 14☺

prestati, prestanem (P) 14☺; **prestajati, pre-
stajem** (I) 📖A.VI to stop, to cease *see*
stati

prestonica *f* [S] throne 16A3

presuda *f* verdict, sentence 19A2a

presudan, presudna *adj.* decisive 19A3b

pretežak, preteška *adj.* too difficult, too heavy 15A2

pretpostaviti (P); pretpostavljati (I) to assume, to presume.

pretraga *f; DLsg* pretrazi [B,C] medical test 20.I

pretvarati *see under* pretvoriti

pretvarati se *see under* pretvoriti se

pretvoriti (P); pretvarati, pretvaram, pretvaraju (I) to transform 14A2

pretvoriti se (P): pretvarati se, pretvaram se, pretvaraju se (I) to pretend 15A1

preuraniti (P) to act prematurely 16A2a

prevaliti, prevalim (P) to cover, to pass 20.I

prevara *f* [E] deception

prevariti (P) to deceive, to trick 15A1

prevesti, prevedem; preveo, prevela (P) 10A4✿; prevoditi, prevodim (I) 18A3 to translate *see* voditi

prevesti, prevezem; prevezao, prevezla (P) 10A4✿; prevoziti, prevozim (I) to transport *see* voziti

previše *adv.* too much 📖B.III

prevod *m* [B,C,S] a [written or spoken] translation 18A3

prevodilac *m; Gsg* prevodioca [B,S] translator *(general)* 5A3

prevoditelj *m* [C] translator *(m., general)* 5A3

prevoditeljica *f* [C] translator *(f.)*

prevoditi *see under* prevesti

prevođenje *n* translation [= discipline] 18A3

prevoz *m* [B,C,S] transportation

prezime *n; Gsg* prezimena *Npl* prezimena *Gpl* prezimena last name, surname

preživeti, preživim (P); preživljavati, preživljavam, preživljavaju (I) [E] to survive 14A3 *see* živeti

preživjeti, preživim; preživio, preživjela (P); preživljavati, preživljavam, preživljavaju (I) [J] to survive 14A3 *see* živjeti

pri *prep. + Dat.* near, by, with, at ↦5

pribaviti (P); pribavljati (I) to get hold of 16A2a

približiti se, približim se (P) 16A3b; približavati se, približavam se, približavaju se (I) to approach

pribor *m* equipment; pribor za pecanje fishing gear 20.V

priča *f* story 5A1

pričati, pričam, pričaju (I) to talk, to tell a story 12A2 *see also* ispričati, popričati, prepričati, zapričati se

prići, priđem; prišao, prišla (P); prilaziti (I) to approach, to come over to 20.IV *see* ići

pridev *m* [E] adjective 17A1b

pridjev *m* [J] adjective 17A1b

pridoneti, pridonesem (P) [E] 16A2b; pridonositi, pridonosim (I) to contribute *see* nositi

pridonijeti, pridonesem; pridonio, pridonijela (P) [J] 16A2b; pridonositi, pridonosim (I) to contribute *see* nositi

prihvatiti (P) 16A1a; prihvaćati [C] prihvatati [B,S] (I) to accept

prijatan, prijatna *adj.* pleasant, comfortable 11A2

prijatelj *m; Gpl* prijatelja 1. pal, schoolmate [B,C only]; 2. lifelong or family friend 1A4, 1A4✿, 8A1✿

prijateljica *f* [B,C,S] friend *(f)* 4A2

prijateljstvo *n; Gpl* prijateljstava friendship 📖B.IV

prijati (I) to suit 13A1; to mi prija that suits me 13A1

prijaviti, prijavim (P); prijavljivati, prijavljujem (I) to report 14A3

prije *prep. + Gen* [J] before ↦5 5A2; prije podne *adv.* [J] late morning 10A1, 13A4✿; prije nego što *conj* before; prije negoli *conj.* before 20.V

prije *adv.* [J] earlier, before 13A2

prijeći, prijeđem; prešao, prešla [C] (P); prelaziti (I) to go across, to traverse 19A1a

prijedlog *m; Npl* prijedlozi [J] 1. proposal 20.IV; 2. preposition 17A1

prijek *adj.* [J] sudden, short-tempered

prijelaz *n* [C] 1. transition; 2. crosswalk

prijestolnica *f* [B,C] throne 16A3b

prijevara *f* [J] deception

prijevod *m* [C] a [written or spoken] translation 18A3

prijevoz *m* [C] transportation

priključiti se, priključim se (P) 16A2b; priključivati se, priključujem se (I) to join in

prikupiti (P) 19A3b; prikupljati, prikupljam, prikupljaju (I) to bring together

priličan, prilična *adj.* considerable 20.IV

prilika *f; DLsg* prilici opportunity 16A1a; po prilici approximately 12A1

prilog *m; Npl* prilozi 1. adverb 17A1b; 2. side dish 11A2

primaći [primaknuti], primaknem; primakao, primakla (P) 14A1; primicati, primičem (I) 1. to bring closer, to move [something] closer; 2. to approach

primaknuti *see under* primaći

primati *see under* primiti

primer *m* [E] example 17C1; na primer for example *(abbr.* npr.) 11A3

primerak *m; Gsg* primerka *Npl* primerci [E] 1. copy; 2. exemplar 13A3 primetiti, primetim (P) 14A4; primećivati, primećujem (I) [E] to notice

primijetiti, primijetim (P) 14A4; primjećivati, primjećujem (I) [J] to notice

primiti, primim (P); primati, primam, primaju (I) to receive 18A3

primjer m [J] example 17C1; na primjer for example (abbr. npr.) 11A3

primjerak m; Gsg primjerka Npl primjerci [J] 1. copy; 2. exemplar 13A3

primorje n coastal area

Primorje n Croatian coast from Rijeka to Zadar 6☺

primorski adj. coastal 16A3b

princeza f [fairy tale] princess 📖B.VIII

prineti, prinesem (P) [E] 20.V; prinositi, prinosim (I) to bring up to see nositi

prinijeti, prinesem; prinio, prinijela (P) [J] 20.V; prinositi, prinosim (I) to bring up to see nositi

prinositi see under prineti or prinijeti

priprema f preparation 14A1

pripremiti, pripremim (P) 13A3; pripremati, pripremam, pripremaju (I) to prepare

priredba f; Gpl priredaba performance 16A3b

priroda f nature 18A2b

prirodan, prirodna adj. natural; prirodne nauke [B,S] natural sciences 13B3; prirodne znanosti [C] natural sciences 13B3

priručnik m; Npl priručnici handbook, manual 📖B.III

pristupačan, pristupačna adj. accessible, affordable 16A2b

prisvojan, prisvojna adj. [B,S] possessive 17A2b; prisvojna zamenica [E] prisvojna zamjenica [J] possessive pronoun

prišiti, prišijem (P); prišivati, prišivam, prišivaju (I) to sew on 📖A.VIII

pritom adv. in so doing 15A1

privatan, privatna adj. private; privatna soba rented room 16A2a

priviknuti se, priviknem se (P) to get used to 20.II

privlačiti see under privući

privreda f [B,S] economy

privući, privučem, privuku (P); privlačiti, privlačim (I) to attract 📖B.V see vući

prizemlje n ground floor 6A1, 6A1

priznati (P) 📖B.II; priznavati, priznajem (I) 📖B.IV to admit, to confess see znati

priznavati see under priznati

prizor m scene 18A1b

prljav adj. dirty, filthy 9A2

problem m; Gsg problema problem 5A2

probuditi see under buditi

pročitati see under čitati

proći, prođem; prošao, prošla (P) 13A4; prolaziti (I) to pass 📖B.VII see ići

prodati (P) 20.II; prodavati, prodajem (I) 9☺ to sell

prodavač m; Gsg prodavača salesperson (m., general)

prodavačica f saleswoman 📖A.IV

prodavaonica f [B,C] store, shop 12A2

prodavati see under prodati

prodavnica f [B,S] store, shop 12A2

proderati se, proderem se (P) to shout out 📖B.VIII

prodreti, prodrem; prodro, prodrla (P) 20.I; prodirati, prodirem (I) [E] to penetrate

prodrijeti, prodrem; prodro, prodrla (P) 20.I; prodirati, prodirem (I) [J] to penetrate 20.I

profesor f professor, teacher (m., general) 1A4

profesorica f [B,C] professor, teacher (f.) 1A4

profesorka f; DLsg profesorki Gpl profesorki [S] professor, teacher (f.) 1A4

profesorski adj. professorial 8A4

proglasiti, proglasim (P) 12A4; proglašavati, proglašavam, proglašavaju (I) to proclaim

progoniti, progonim (P); proganjati, proganjam, proganjaju (I) to persecute 18A3

progovoriti, progovorim (P) 20.IV; progovarati, progovaram, progovaraju (I) to speak out

prohladan, prohladna adj. chilly, cool 17A3a

prohujao, prohujala adj. swept away 📖A.VII

proizvod m product

proizvesti, proizvedem, proizveo (P), proizvoditi, proizvodim (I) to produce, to manufacture see voditi

proizvodnja f production

projekat m; Gsg projekta Gpl projekata project [B,S] 16A1a

projekt m; Gpl projekata project [B,C] 16A1a

prokockati (P) to gamble away, to fritter away 7A2

prolaziti see under proći

prolaznik m; Npl prolaznici passerby 14A3

proleće n [E] spring; na proleće in the spring 9A1

prolećni adj. [E] spring 15A1

prolepšati se (P); prolepšavati, prolepšavam, prolepšavaju (I) [E] to become prettier or nicer 14A2

proletos adv. this spring, the coming spring, last spring

proljeće n [J] spring; na proljeće in the spring 9A1

proljećni *adj.* [J] [B/S] spring 15A1

proljepšati se (P); **proljepšavati, proljepšavam, proljepšavaju** (I) [J] to become prettier or nicer 14A2

proljetni *adj.* [C] spring 15A1

proljetos this spring, the coming spring, last spring

promatrati, promatram, promatraju (I) [C] to observe 14☺

promena *f* [E] change

promeniti *see under* **menjati**

prometan, prometna *adj.* [C] traffic 7A2; **prometna nesreća** traffic accident

promijeniti *see under* **mijenjati**

promjena *f* [J] change

pronaći, pronađem; pronašao, pronašla (P); **pronalaziti** (I) 1. to find 14A3, 11A1☢, 14A1☢; 2. to invent [B,S only] 15A1

pronalazak, *Npl* **pronalasci** 1. discovery; 2. invention

proparati, proparam, proparaju (P) 1. to rip; 2. to interrupt 🕮B.VIII

propeler *m; Gsg* **propelera** propeller 15A1

propustiti, propustim (P) 12A3; **propuštati, propuštam, propuštaju** (I) to miss [an opportunity] *see* **pustiti**

proputovati, proputujem (P) to travel through 16A2a *see* **putovati**

proraditi, proradim (P) 15A1, 15A1☢; **prorađivati, prorađujem** (I) to start working *see* **raditi**

prosečan, prosečna *adj.* [E] average 12A1

prosinac *m; Gsg* **prosinca** [C] December 6A2, ⸢6A2⸥

prosječan, prosječna *adj.* [J] average 12A1

proslava *n* celebration 12A3

proslaviti *see* **slaviti**

prost *adj.* simple 16A1b

prostor *m* space, room, area 11A2

prostorija *f* premises, room, area 6A1

prošetati *see under* **šetati**

proširiti, proširim (P); **proširivati, proširujem** (I) to expand 🕮B.III

prošli *adj.* past 10A2; **prošlo vreme** [E] **vrijeme** [J] past tense 17C1

prošlost *f; Gsg* **prošlosti** *Isg* -ošću *or* -osti past 17A2b

protagonist *m* [B,C] protagonist 18A2b

protagonista *m; Npl* **protagoniste** [B,S] protagonist 18A2b

proteći, proteknem, proteku; protekao, protekla (P); **proticati, protičem** (I) [B,S], **protjecati, protječem** (I) [B,C] 1. to pass [*e.g.* time]; 2. to flow through 7☺ *see* **teći**

protekli *adj.* last [period of time], past 20.II

proticati *see* **proteći**

protiv *prep.* + *Gen* against 13A4; **ako nemate ništa protiv** if you have no objections 13A4

protjecati *see* **proteći**

protrnuti, protrnem (P) to go numb 20.VIII

provesti, provedem; proveo, provela (P); **provoditi, provodim** (I) 1. to lead through 2. to carry out 16A2a; 3. to spend [a period of time]; **provesti se, provedem se** (P) to spend one's time 9A2 *see* **voditi**

proziran, prozirna *adj.* transparent 20.I

prozor *m* window 3A2, 6A1☢

prozvati, prozovem (P) 1. to give someone a nickname; 2. to call, to dub 🕮B.I *see* **zvati**

prst *m; Npl* **prsti,** *Gpl* **prstiju** 1. finger; 2. toe 10A4

prsten *m; Npl* **prstenovi** ring 🕮A.V

pružiti (P) 12A2; **pružati, pružam, pružaju** (I) to offer, to extend; **pružiti ruku** to extend a hand 12A2

prvi *adj.* first (1st) 1A1, 6A2☢; **Prvi svetski rat** [E] **Prvi svjetski rat** [J] First World War 12A4, 12A3☢; **prva pomoć** first aid

prvo *adv.* first, firstly 4A4

prvobitan, prvobitna *adj.* original, primary 19A1b

psihologija *f* psychology 13B3

ptica *f* bird 5A1; **'tica** *colloq.* bird 17A2a

ptičiji *adj.* [B,S] bird, bird's 5C1

ptičji *adj.* [C] bird, bird's 5C1

publika *f; DLsg* **publici** 1. the public; 2. audience

pučina *f* open sea 17A3a

puk *m* [C] the folk, the people 17A2a

pučanstvo *n; Gpl* **pučanstava** or **pučanstva** [C] population; **popis pučanstva** census

pun, puna; puni *adj.* full 4A3; [**imati**] **pune ruke posla** to be busy, to have one's hands full 9A2

puniti (I); **napuniti** (P) 1. to fill; 2. to complete (a year of age) 12A3

puno *adv.* a lot, much 5A1

pust, pusta; pusti *adj.* barren, empty 17C1

pustiti, pustim (P) 7A3; **puštati, puštam, puštaju** (I) 10A2☢ to release, to let go; **pusti me na miru** leave me be, leave me alone 7A3 *see also* **dopustiti, napustiti, opustiti, otpustiti, propustiti, spustiti**

pušač *m; Gsg* **pušača** smoker 12A2

pušenje *n* smoking 20.V

pušiti (I) to smoke 12A2 *see also* **popušiti**

puštanje *n* release 20.VIII

puštati *see under* **pustiti**

put *m; Gsg* **puta** *Isg* **putem** [B,C,S] **putom** [C] *Npl* **putevi** [B,C,S] **putovi** [B,C] 1. road, path, way ↦4 14A2; 2. journey, trip,

way 7A2; ìći svòjim pùtem *or* pùtom to
go one's own way 12A2; kòjim pùtem *or*
pùtom which way ⸠7.A4⸠; srèćan pùt
[B,S] sretan pùt [B,C] bon voyage 12A3

pùt *m* time, instance [*as in* tri pùta thrice,
three times] 10A1

putalj *m (archaic)* steed 19A3a

pùtem *prep.* + *Gen* by means of 16A2a

pùter *m* [B,S] butter 7A1

putòvati, pùtujem (I) to travel 4⟳ *see also*
otputòvati, proputòvati

putòvanje *n* journey, travels 14A2

putòvnica *f* [C] passport 4⟳

R

ràbin *m; Gsg* rabìna rabbi

ràbiti, rȁbim (I) [C] to use

ràčunati (I) to calculate; ràčunati (na) + *Acc*
to count (on) ▢B.II

rȁd *m; Npl* ràdovi 1. work 16A3b; 2. work
[= piece of writing] 16A2a

ràdi *prep.* + *Gen* for the sake of, because of
7A2; rèda radi for the sake of appearances,
as one ought 14A2

rȁdije *see* rado

ràdio *m* ràdio stànica [B,C,S] ràdio
pòstaja [C] radio station ⸠9A3⸠

ráditi, rȁdim (I) 1. to work 11A3, 9A2✿;
2. to do 2A1; o čèmu se radi? what's it
about? 6A2; rȁdi se o ... it is a matter of
... 6A2 *see also* proràditi, uràditi

ràdnica *f* worker, employee *(f.)* 11A2✿

rȁdnik *m; Npl* rȁdnici worker, employee *(m.,
general)* 11A2✿

ràdni *adj.* work 11A4; rȁdno mèsto [E]
rȁdno mjèsto [J] job, place of employment
11A4

ràdnja *f; Gpl* rȁdnji 1. store, shop [B,C,S]
12A2, ⸠12A2⸠; 2. plot, storyline, action
17A3b

rȁdo *adv.* gladly 13A1; rȁdije 1. rather,
2. more gladly; 3. preferably 19A2a

ràdost *f; Gsg* ràdosti Isg* -ošću *or* -osti joy
↦4 3A2

ràdostan, ràdosna *adj.* joyous 15A1

ràdovati, ràdujem (I) to gladden ▢B.III;
ràdovati se, ràdujem se (I) + *Dat* to be glad
14A4 *see also* obradòvati

ràđanje *n* birth, birthing ▢B.VIII

rája *f* [B] *colloq.* crowd, people ▢B.VII

rajčìca *f* [C] tomato 7A1, 5A4✿

rȁk *m; Npl* rȁkovi 1. cancer 18A3; 2. crab

rȁme *n; Gsg* ramèna Npl* ramèna Gpl* ramèna
shoulder 10A4

ràna *f* wound 18A1a

rániti (P); rànjavati, rànjavam, rànjavaju (I)
to wound 20.V

ràno *adv.* early 7A4, 9A4✿, 10A2✿

rashláditi se, rashládim se (P); rashlađìvati se,
rashlađujem se (I) to cool off 16A3b

ràspeti, ràspnem (P); rȁspinjati (I) to crucify
17A3a

raspítati se, raspítam se, raspítaju se (P)
▢B.III; raspitìvati se, raspìtujem se (I)
20.III to ask around, to inquire

raspitìvati se *see under* raspítati se

raspolòženje *n* mood

ràsprava *f* discussion 11A1

ràstajati se *see under* rȁstati se

rȁstanak *m; Gsg* ràstanka parting, farewell
▢B.IV

rȁstati se, rȁstanem se (P); ràstajati se, ràstaj-
em se (I) to part ways 14A2 *see* stȁti

rásti, rástem; rástao, rásla to grow 16A1b
see also prèrasti

rastúžiti se, rastúžim se (P) 15A1; rastužìvati
se, rastužujem se (I) to become sad

ràširiti *see under* šìriti

ràširiti se *see under* šìriti se

rȁt *m; Npl* ràtovi war 12A4, 12A1✿; Prvi
svetski rȁt [E] Prvi svjetski rȁt [J] First
World War 12A4; Drugi svetski rȁt [E]
Drugi svjetski rȁt [J] Second World War
12A4

ràvan, ràvna *adj.* 1. straight; 2. even; 3. flat
13A4

rávnatelj *m* [C] director *(m., general)* 11A2✿

ravnàteljica *f* [C] director *(f.)* 11A2✿

rávno *adv.* [B,C] straight ahead 13A4

ravnòteža *f* balance 19A2b

razbúditi, razbúdim (P); razbuđìvati, razbuđ-
ujem (I) to perk up, to stir 10A4 *see* búditi

rȁzdoblje *n* period [of time] 16A2b

razglèdnica *f* postcard 2A4

razgovárati, razgòvaram, razgòvaraju (I) to
converse 12A2 *see* porazgovárati

rȁzgovor *m* conversation 12A2

ràzgovoran, ràzgovorna *adj.* conversational

ràzići se, ràziđem se; ràzišao se, ràzišla se (P)
14A2; razìlaziti se (I) to disperse *see* ìći

ràzina *f* [C] 1. level; 2. plane 19A1b

razjásniti, razjásnim (P); razjašnjávati, raz-
jašnjávam, razjašnjávaju (I) to clarify
10A4

ràzličit *adj.* different, distinct 11A2

rázlika *f; DLsg* rázlici difference 16A1b

razlikòvati, razlìkujem (I) to distinguish
18A2b

rázlog *m; Npl* rázlozi reason 8☺

razmìsliti (P) 10A3; razmìšljati, razmìšljam,
razmìšljaju (I) 8A3 to think, to consider
see mísliti

razmišljati *see under* **razmisliti**

razni *adj. (pl form)* various 11A3

razočarati, razočaram, razočaraju (P); **razočaravati, razočaravam, razočaravaju** (I) to disappoint

razočarati se, razočaram se, razočaraju se (P) 20.V ; **razočaravati se, razočaravam se, razočaravaju se** (I) to be disappointed

razotkriti, razotkrijem (P); **razotkrivati, razotkrivam, razotkrivaju** (I) to find out, to discover 17A3b; **razotkriti se, razotkrijem se** (P) to disclose oneself 20.IV

razred *m* 1. class, grade (year in school); 2. school homeroom 5C1

razum *m* reason, intellect

razumeti, razumem, razumeju (I/P) [E] to understand 7A3, 7A3✿

razumevanje *n* [E] understanding 11A4

razumijevanje *n* [J] understanding 11A4

razumjeti, razumijem, razumiju; razumio, razumjela (I/P) [J] to understand 7A3, 7A3✿

razvedriti se, razvedrim se (P) 14A2; **razvedravati se, razvedravam se, razvedravaju se** (I) to clear up [of weather, facial expression, emotion]

razveseliti (P) 15A1; **razveseljavati, razveseljavam, razveseljavaju** (I) to cheer up, to make happy

razvoj *m* development

rđav *adj.* 1. bad [S only] 2A2, 2A2 ; 2. rusty

recept *m; Gpl* **recepata** 1. recipe 14A1; 2. medical prescription

reč *f; DLsg* **reči** *Isg* **reču** *or* **reči** *Gpl* **reči** [E] word 3A2, 6A1✿, 7A1✿

rečenica *f* sentence 15A2

rečni *adj.* [E] river 20.V

rečnik *m; Npl* **rečnici** [E] 1. dictionary, glossary; 2. vocabulary 2A1

reći [**reknem**]; **rekao, rekla** (P) to say [*present tense seldom used*] 7A3, 7A3✿, 12A2✿, 12A4✿

red *m; Npl* **redovi** 1. order; 2. line, queue 11A4; 3. schedule; **reda radi** for the sake of appearances, as one ought 14A2; **red vožnje** train or bus schedule B.III; **u redu** OK, fine 13A2

redak, retka; retki *adj.* [E] rare

redati, redam, redaju (I); **poredati, poredam, poredaju** (P) [B,C] to line up 14A1

redovan, redovna *adj.* [B,C,S] regular 16A3b

redovit *adj.* [B,C] regular 16A3b

rеđati, rеđam, rеđaju (P); **porеđati, porеđam, porеđaju** (P) [B,S] to line up 14A1

rеđi *adj.* [E] rarer *see* **redak**

referada *f* [C] university registrar 16A2a

reka *f; DLsg* **reci** [E] river 3⊕

remek-delo *n* [E] masterpiece 19A2b

remek-djelo *n* [J] masterpiece 19A2b

rep *m; Npl* **repovi** tail A.VI

replika *f; DLsg* **replici** reply, rejoinder B.I

Republika Srpska *f; DLsg* **Republici Srpskoj** Republic of Srpska *see map* 4⊕

reputacija *f* reputation 13A3

restoran *m; Gsg* **restorana** restaurant 10A1

rešavati *see under* **rešiti**

rešiti, rešim (P) to solve, to resolve 11A1; **rešavati, rešavam, rešavaju** (I) [E] 1. to address [a problem], to grapple with [a problem] 12☺

rezervirati, rezerviram, rezerviraju (I/P) [B,C] to reserve 16A1a

rezervisati, rezervišem (I/P) [B,S] to reserve 16A1a

režije *f (pl form)* [C] utility bills 9A3

režiser *m; Gsg* **režisera** [film] director 15A1

riba *f* fish 6A4

ribar *m* [professional] fisherman

ribarski *adj.* fishing; **ribarska kućica** fishing hut 20.VIII

ribič *m; Gsg* **ribiča** [recreational] fisherman 20.V; **ribički štap** fishing pole 20.VIII

riječ *f; DLsg* **riječi** *Isg* **riječju** *or* **riječi**; *Gpl* **riječi** [J] word 3A2, 6A1✿, 7A1✿

riječni *adj.* [J] river 20.V

rijedak, rijetka; rijetki *adj.* [J] rare

rijeka *f; DLsg* **rijeci** [J] river 3⊕

riješiti, riješim (P) to solve, to resolve 11A1; **rješavati, rješavam, rješavaju** (I) [J] to address [a problem], to grapple with [a problem] 12☺

Rim *m; Gsg* **Rima** Rome 12A3

riskantan, riskantna *adj.* risky 20.IV

ritam *m; Gsg* **ritma** rhythm 20.II

riža *f* [B,C] rice

rječnik *m; Npl* **rječnici** [J] 1. dictionary, glossary; 2. vocabulary 2A1

rjeđi *adj.* [J] rarer *see* **rijedak**

rješavati *see under* **riješiti**

roba *f* merchandise

rod *m; Npl* **rodovi** gender; **muški rod** masculine gender; **srednji rod** neuter gender; **ženski rod** feminine gender

rodbina *f* relatives, kin 17A2a

roditelj *m* parent 4A1

roditi (P) 14A1✿; **rađati, rađam, rađaju** (I) to bear, to bring forth [a child, fruit]; **roditi se** (P) 14A3, 9☺; **rađati se, rađam se, rađaju se** (I) to be born

rodom *adv.* by birth 18A3

rođak *m; Npl* **rođaci** relative (*m., general*)

8A3

rođaka *see under* **rođakinja**

rođakinja *f* relative *(f.)*

rođaka *f; DLsg* **rođaki** relative *(f.)* [less commonly used] 15A1

rođendan *m* birthday 12A3

rođeni *adj. (pl form)* close family 16A1b

rok *m; Npl* **rokovi** period, deadline 9A1

roman *m; Gsg* **romana** novel 2A1

romanistika *f; DLsg* **romanistici** study of the Romance languages 13B3

rositi (I) to drizzle 14☺

roštilj *m* grill 11A2

rub *m; Npl* **rubovi** edge 20.IV

ručak *m; Gsg* **ručka** *Npl* **ručkovi** 1. main meal of the day; 2. lunch 5A2, 6A1✿, ⟦ 5A2 ⟧

ručati, ručam (I/P) to dine, to have lunch 7A3✿

rugati se, rugam se, rugaju se (I) to mock 📖B.V

rujan *m; Gsg* **rujna** [C] September 6A2, ⟦ 6A2 ⟧

ruka *f; Asg* **ruku** *DLsg* **ruci** *NApl* **ruke** *Gpl* **ruku** 1. arm; 2. hand ↪4 9A2, 6A2✿, ⟦ 10A4 ⟧; [**imati**] **pune ruke posla** to be busy, to have one's hands full 9A2 **poći** [**nekome**] **za rukom** to be able to do 18A3; **u neku ruku** in a sense, in a way 7A2

rumen, rumena; rumeni *adj.* ruddy, glowing red 17A3a

Rumunija *f* [B,S] Romania 1☞

Rumunjska *f (adj. form)* [C] Romania 1☞

Rus *m; Npl* **Rusi** Russian *(m., general)*

ruski *adj.* Russian 4A4

Ruskinja *f* Russian *(f.)*

ruža *f* rose 📖A.IV

ružan, ružna *adj.* ugly 2A2

S

s, sa *prep. + Gen* from, down from, off ↪5 4A4, 4A4✿, 8A4✿; **s nogu** while standing 12A2

s, sa *prep. + Instr* with ↪5 7A1, 7A1✿, 9A3✿

s, sa *prep. + Acc (archaic)* over to; **s onu stranu** on that other side 17A2a

sabrati, saberem (P) 20.V, 11A1✿; **sabirati** (I) to collect *see* **brati**

sačekati (P) 📖B.V; **sačekivati, sačekujem** (I) to wait a bit *see* **čekati**

SAD *m; Gsg* **SAD-a** *DLsg* **SAD-u** USA [= **Sjedinjene američke države**], United States of America] 4A1, 4A1✿

sad, sada *adv.* now 6A3

sadašnji *adj.* current, present 17C1; **sadašnje vreme** [E] **sadašnje vrijeme** [J]

present tense 17C1

sadržati, sadržim (P) 19A1b; **sadržavati, sadržavam, sadržavaju** (I) to contain *see* **držati**

sag *m; Npl* **sagovi** [C] rug 8A4

sagnuti, sagnem (P); **saginjati, saginjem** (I) to bend; **sagnuti se, sagnem se** (P); **saginjati se, saginjem se** (I) to bend over 20.VIII

sakriti, sakrijem (P) 20.VI; **sakrivati, sakrivam, sakrivaju** (I) to hide, to conceal *see also* **skriti**

sakupiti (P); **sakupljati, sakupljam, sakupljaju** (I) [B,S] to collect, to amass 19A3b *see also* **skupiti**

salata *f* 1. salad 11A2; 2. lettuce

salon *m; Gsg* **salona** salon; **frizerski salon** hairdresser's, hairdressing salon 📖B.V

sam *verbal clitic* [I] am 1A1, 6A4✿ *see under* **biti**

sam, samo, sama; sami *pron. adj.* alone, by oneself; **na samome danu** on the very day 6A3, 6A3✿

samleti *see under* **mleti**

samljeti *see under* **mljeti**

samo *adv.* only 3A3, 6A4✿

samac *m; Gsg* **samca** 1. loner; 2. bachelor 18A1a

samoća *f* solitude, loneliness 18A2a

samoposluga *f; DLsg* **samoposluzi** [B,C] self-service grocery store 📖A.II

samostalnost *f; Isg* **-ošću** *or* **-osti** independence 12A4✿

samostan *m* [Catholic] monastery 16A3b

samousluga *f; DLsg* **samousluzi** [S] self-service grocery store 📖A.II, ⟦ 12A2 ⟧

samrt *f; Gsg* **samrti** deathbed 18A3

san *m; Gsg* **sna** *Npl* **snovi** 1. dream; 2. sleep 17A3a

Sandžak *m* region in southwestern Serbia

sanjati, sanjam (I) to dream 9A1

saobraćajni *adj.* [B,S] traffic 7A2; **saobraćajna nesreća** [B,S] traffic accident

sapatnik *m; Npl* **sapatnici** [B,S] fellow sufferer 20.V

sapun *m; Gsg* **sapuna** soap

sapunica *f* 1. soap suds; 2. soap opera 📖B.II

saradnja *f* [B,S] cooperation 18A3

Sarajevo *n* Sarajevo *see map*

Sarajka *f; DLsg* **Sarajki** *Gpl* **Sarajki** resident of Sarajevo *(f.)*

Sarajlija *m; Npl* **Sarajlije** resident of Sarajevo *(m., general)*

sarajevski *adj.* pertaining to Sarajevo 6A2

sastanak *m; Gsg* **sastanka** *Npl* **sastanci** meeting 13A3

sastav *m* composition 📖B.II

sastaviti (P) 19A3b; **sastavljati** (I) to assemble

sastojak *m; Gsg* **sastojka** *Npl* **sastojci** ingredient 14A1

sastojati se, sastojim se [iz] (I) to consist [of] 4🌀

sasvim *adv.* completely 11A2

sat *m; Npl* **sati** *Gpl* **sati** hour, o'clock 5A2; **sat vremena** for an hour 6A3, 6A2🌼; **satima** for hours 📖A.III

sat *m; Npl* **satovi** 1. clock 8A4; 2. class, lesson [C only] 7A4

sav *m; pron. adj.* all ↦4 3A3, 3A3🌼, 15A2🌼
  singular forms
    (Gen) **sveg, svega** 15A2
    (Dat-Loc) **svem, svemu** 15A2
    (Instr) **svim, svima**
  plural forms (Nom) **svi**
    (Acc) **sve** 6A2
    (Gen) **svih** 15A1 *or* **sviju**
    (Dat-Loc-Instr) **svim, svima**
  see also **sav, sva, sve, svi**

savet *m* [E] advice, counsel 16A3a

savetovati, savetujem (I); **posavetovati, posavetujem** (P) [E] to advise

savetovati se, savetujem se (I); **posavetovati se, posavetujem se** (P) [E] to take advice 11A4

savez *m* [E] union 12A4

savjet *m* [J] advice, counsel 16A3a

savjetovati, savjetujem (I); **posavjetovati, posavjetujem** (P) [J] to advise 11A4

savjetovati se, savjetujem se (I); **posavjetovati se, posavjetujem se** (P) [J] to take advice 11A4

savladati, savladam, savladaju (P) 📖B.VIII; **savladavati, savladavam, savladavaju** (I) to gain control over

savremen *adj.* [B,S] contemporary, modern

savršen *adj.* perfect 9A3

saznati (P) 14A2, ¦ 17A2a ¦; **saznavati, saznajem** (I) 19A3b to find out, to learn, to glean *see* **znati**

scena *f* theater stage, scene

se *verbal clitic* [e.g. **ticati se**] 5A2, 1A2🌼, 6A2🌼, 6A3🌼, 9A2🌼, 10A1🌼, 10A2🌼, 14A1🌼, 14A2🌼

se *reflexive clitic (Acc-Gen)* self *see under* **sebe**

sebe *pron.* self ↦4;
    (Acc-Gen) **sebe** 7A1, 6A3🌼, 7A1🌼
    Dat-Loc **sebi, si** [C only] 6A3, 6A3🌼
    (Instr) **sobom** 7A1, 7A1🌼

sebi *pron. (Dat-Loc)* self 6A3, 6A3🌼 *see under* **sebe**

sebičan, sebična *adj.* selfish 13A2

sećati se *see under* **setiti se**

sedam *num.* seven (7) 5A1, 5A1🌼, 12A1🌼

sedamdeset *num.* seventy (70) 5A1, 5A1🌼

sedamnaest *num.* seventeen (17) 5A1, 5A1🌼, 12A1🌼

sedamnaesti *adj.* seventeenth (17th) 17A1

sedamsto *num.* seven hundred (700) 12A1🌼

sedati [E] *see under* **sesti**

sedeti, sedim (I) [S] to sit, to be sitting 6A3, 11A4🌼

sedmero *n* [C] seven (group of mixed gender) 12A2🌼

sedmi *adj.* seventh (7th) 7A1, 6A2🌼, 12A3🌼

sedmica *f* [B,S] week 5A3, 5A3🌼, 5A4🌼

sedmični *adj.* [B,S] week 16A3a

sedmorica *f* seven [men] 12A2🌼

sedmoro *n* [B,S] seven (group of mixed gender) 12A2🌼

seka *f; DLsg* **seki** little sister, sis

sekunda *f; Gsg* **sekundi** second [unit of time] 14A1

seliti, selim (I) 1. to move; 2. to migrate 18A3

seliti se, selim se (I); **preseliti se, preselim se** (P) to move [to a new place] 18A3

selo *n; Npl* **sela** village ↦4 3A3, 4A1🌼, 6A1🌼, 7A1🌼, 8A1🌼

sem *prep.* + *Gen* [S] except, besides

semestar *m; Gsg* **semestra** semester 6A2

sena *f* [E] shadow 18A1a

seoba *f* migration 17A2a

septembar *m; Gsg* **septembra** [B,S] September 6A2, ¦ 6A2 ¦

serija *f* [TV] series 📖B.II

sesti, sednem; seo, sela (P); **sedati** (I) [E] to sit down 11A4, 11A4🌼

sestra *f; Gpl* **sestara** 1. sister [B,C,S] 3A1, 3A1🌼, 5A1🌼, 6A3🌼; 2. cousin [B,S] 2A3; **medicinska sestra** nurse 11A3

sestrica *f* little sister, small sister 16A1b

sestrična *f* cousin [C]

setiti se (P) 12A3; **sećati se** (I) [E] 11A3 to remember

sever *m* [E] north 6A1🌼

severni *adj.* [E] north; **Severna Amerika** *DLsg* **Severnoj Americi** [E] North America 4A1

sezona *f* season 16A3b

shodan, shodna *adj.* [C] fitting, appropriate; **shodno** + *Dat* in accordance with 18A3

shvaćati *see under* **shvatiti**

shvatiti (P) 14A4, 15A1🌼; **shvaćati** (I) 20.V to understand, to grasp

si *verbal clitic* [you] are *(informal)* 1A1 *see under* **biti**

si *reflexive clitic (Dat)* [C] self 9A2 *see under*

sebe

sići, siđem; sišao, sišla (P)   13A4; **silaziti** (I)   to descend, to get off, to get down from, to alight *see* **ići**

siguran, sigurna *adj.*   safe, sure, certain   14A1✿°

sigurno *adv.*   certainly   3A3

siječanj *m; Gsg* **siječnja** [C]   January   6A2, 6A2✿°

sila *f*   force, power

silan, silna *adj.*   powerful, forceful   📖B.V

sin *m; Npl* **sinovi**   son   8A1

sinoć *adv.*   last night   14A3

sinovac *m; Gsg* **sinovca**   nephew (son of brother)

sinovica *f*   niece (daughter of brother)

sipati (I/P)   1. to serve a beverage, to pour [B,S]   13A1, 14A1✿°;   2. to pour or scatter a granular substance [*e.g.* salt, sand] [B,C,S]

sir *m; Npl* **sirevi**   cheese   4A3

siromašan, siromašna *adj.*   poor

sistem *m; Gsg* **sistema** [B,C,S]   system   6A1;   **sunčev sistem** [B,S]   solar system   6A1

sitan, sitna *adj.*   tiny, fine   14A1

situacija *f*   situation   14A2

siv, siva; sivi *adj.*   gray   8A1, ⌐8A1⌐

sjajan, sjajna *adj.*   1. marvelous;   2. shiny   16A3a

sjećati se *see under* **sjetiti se**

sjediniti, sjedinim (P); **sjedinjivati, sjedinjujem** (I)   to unite   12A4

sjedinjen   united   12A4;   **Sjedinjene Američke Države** (*abbr.* SAD)   United States of America

sjedati [J] *see under* **sjesti**

sjediti (I) [B,C]   to sit, to be sitting   6A3, 11A4✿°

sjena *f* [J]   shadow   18A1a

sjesti, sjednem; sjeo, sjela (P); **sjedati** (I) [J]   to sit down   11A4, 11A4✿°

sjetiti se (P)   12A3; **sjećati se** (I) [J]   11A3   to remember

sjever *m* [J]   north   6A1✿°

sjeverni *adj.* [J]   northern; **Sjeverna Amerika** *DLsg* **Sjevernoj Americi** [J]   North America   4A1

skladatelj *m* [C]   composer (*m., general*)   11A3, 11A2✿°

skladateljica *f* [C]   composer (*f.*)   11A3, 11A2✿°

skloniti, sklonim (P)   13A2; **sklanjati** (I)   to put away

skloniti se, sklonim se (P); **sklanjati se** (I)   to take shelter   14A2

skočiti, skočim (P): **skakati, skačem** (I)   to jump   19A3a

skoknuti, skoknem (P)   to hop, to pop in   16A1a

skorašnji *adj.*   1. recent;   2. forthcoming, imminent   20.III

skoro *adv.*   nearly, almost   B.V

skrb *f; Gsg* **skrbi** *Isg* **skrbi** [C]   care, welfare   3A2

skrenuti, skrenem (P)   13A4; **skretati, skrećem** (I)   to turn, to divert

skriti, skrijem (P); **skrivati, skrivam, skrivaju** (I)   to hide, to conceal   18A1a   *see also* **sakriti**

skrivati *see under* **skriti**

skroman, skromna *adj.*   modest, humble   20.VIII

skrovit *adj.*   secretive, mysterious   20.VIII

skuhati *see under* **kuhati**

skup *m; Npl* **skupovi**   meeting, gathering

skup, skupa; skupi *adj.*   expensive   7A2

skupa *adv.* [C]   together   10A4

skupiti (P)   📖B.VI; **skupljati, skupljam, skupljaju** (I) [B,C,S]   to gather, to collect   📖A.I   *see* **sakupiti**

skupiti se (P)   1. to gather as a group   📖B.VI   2. to curl up   20.V

skupljati *see under* **skupiti**

skuvati *see under* **kuvati**

slab *adj.*   weak, feeble   5A1

slabo *adv.*   poorly, weakly   6A3

slabost *f; Gsg* **slabosti** *Isg* **-ošću** or **-osti**   weakness   19A2a

sladak, slatka; slatki *adj.*   sweet   1A3

sladoled *m*   ice cream

slađi *adj.*   sweeter   *see* **sladak**

slagati 1 *see under* **lagati**

slagati 2 *see under* **složiti**

slan, slana; slani *adj.*   salty   6A4

slastica *f* [B,C]   dessert   11A2

slati, šaljem (I)   6A3, 11A1✿°, 14A2✿°; **poslati, pošaljem** (P)   📖B.II   to send

slatkiš *m; Gsg* **slatkiša**   a sweet, a piece of candy   4A3

Slaven *m; Gsg* **Slavena** [B,S]   Slav   19A3b

slavenski *adj.* [B,C]   Slavic   9A1, ⌐9A1⌐

slavist *m* [B,C]   Slavist, Slavicist

slavista *m Npl* **slaviste** [B,S]   Slavist, Slavicist

slavistika *f; DLsg* **slavistici**   Slavic studies   13B3

slaviti (I)   12A3; **proslaviti** (P)   to celebrate   18A3

Slavonija *f*   Slavonia   6🌐

slavonski *adj.*   Slavonian   8A3

slavuj *m; Gsg* **slavuja**   nightingale   19A1a

sleći [slegnuti] (P); **slegati, sležem** (I) [E]   **slijegati, sliježem** (I) [J] **[ramenima]**   to shrug [shoulders]   9☺

sleći se [slegnuti se], slegnem se; slegao se, slegla se (P) to settle, to form sediment 14A1

sledeći adj. [E] next, the following 13A2, 12A1✿

slegati see under sleći se

slep, slepa; slepi adj. [E] blind 18A1a

sličan, slična adj. similar 11A2

sličiti, sličim (na) + Acc (I) [B,C] to resemble 20.VI

slijegati see under sleći se

slijep, slijepa; slijepi adj. [J] blind 18A1a; slepi miš [E] slijepi miš [J] bat

slika f; DLsg slici image, picture, painting 6A3

slikar m painter (m., general) 11A2✿

slikarica f [C] painter (f.) 11A2✿

slikarka f; DLsg slikarki; slikarki [B,S] painter (f.) 11A2✿

slikati, slikam (I) to paint, to make a picture of 📖A.VI

sloboda f freedom, liberty 19A2b

slobodan, slobodna adj. free 16A2b

slon m; Npl slonovi elephant

Sloven m; Gsg Slovena [B,S] Slav 19A3b

Slovenac m; Gsg Slovenca Slovenian (m., general)

slovenački adj. [B,S] Slovenian 6🌀, ⌐9A1¬

Slovenija f Slovenia 1🌀

Slovenka f; DLsg Slovenki Gpl Slovenki Slovenian (f.)

slovenski adj. [B,S] Slavic 9A1, ⌐9A1¬

slovenski adj. [C] Slovenian 6🌀, ⌐9A1¬

složen adj. complex 19A1b

složiti, složim (P); slagati, slažem (I) to arrange 20.II

složiti se, složim se (P); slagati se, slažem se (I) to agree with 10A4

slučaj m; Npl slučajevi 1. case, instance; kojim slučajem by some chance 📖B.V 2. event 14A3

slučajan, slučajna adj. random, chance, accidental 14A3

slučajnost f; Gsg slučajnosti Isg -ošću or -osti coincidence 📖B.VII; koja slučajnost what a coincidence 📖B.VII

sluga m, f; DLsg sluzi or slugi Npl sluge Gpl slugu or sluga servant 7A3

slušalica f [telephone] receiver 📖A.VII

slušati (I) 1. to listen to 7A3; 2. to obey; 3. to attend a university course 6A2, 6A2✿

slutiti, slutim (I) 1. to sense dimly; 2. to suspect 18A1a

služba f service; služba za zapošljavanje employment service 11A4

službeni adj. official, business; službeni put business trip 14A2

služiti, služim (I) 10A2; poslužiti, poslužim (P) 13A1 to serve

sljedeći adj. [J] next, the following 13A2, 12A1✿

smatrati, smatram, smatraju (I) consider 11A1, 11A3✿

smeđ adj. brown

smeh m; Gsg smeha Npl smehovi [E] laughter 19A1a

smejati se, smejem se (I) [E] to laugh 20.III see also nasmejati se

smena f [E] 1. work shift; 2. replacement 6A1✿

smestiti (P) 17A3b; smeštati, smeštam, smeštaju (I) [E] 1. to situate; 2. to accommodate

smešan, smešna; smešni adj. [E] funny, humorous

smešiti se, smešim se (I) [E] to smile 📖A.III

smeškati se [E] to grin 📖B.V

smeštaj m [E] accommodation 16A2a

smetati, smetam, smetaju (I) + Dat to bother 11A4

smeten, smetena adj. confused 📖B.VI

smeti, smem (P) [E] 1. to dare; 2. may; 3. to be allowed 12A3, 10A1✿, 12A3✿

smijati se, smijem se (I) [J] to laugh 20.III see also nasmijati se

smijeh m; Gsg smijeha Npl smjehovi [J] laughter 19A1a

smjena f [J] 1. work shift; 2. replacement 6A1✿

smjestiti (P) 17A3b; smještati, smještam, smještaju (I) [J] 1. to situate; 2. to accommodate

smiješan, smiješna; smiješni adj. [J] funny, humorous

smiješiti se, smiješim se (I) [J] to smile 📖A.III

smiraj m [C] tranquility 20.II

smisao m; Gsg smisla sense, meaning 16A3a

smisliti (P) 16A1a; smišljati, smišljam, smišljaju (I) to come up with, to devise see misliti

smješkati se (I) [J] to grin 📖B.V

smještaj m [J] accommodation 16A2a

smjeti, smijem (I) [J] 1. to dare; 2. may; 3. to be allowed 12A3, 10A1✿, 12A3✿

smo verbal clitic [we] are 1A1 see under biti

smokva f; Gpl smokava or smokvi fig 5A1

smotra f; Gpl smotri review, survey 16A2a; smotra folklora folklore festival 16A2a

smrt f; Gsg smrti Isg smrću death 17A2a

snaga f; DLsg snazi power, force 12A4, 6A4✿

snažan, snažna adj. powerful 15A1

sneg m; Npl snegovi [E] snow 14A2

snijeg *m; Npl* snjegovi [J] snow 14A2

snimiti, snimim (P) 19A3b; snimati, snimam, snimaju (I) to record [on tape or on film]

snivati, snivam, snivaju (I) to dream 18A1a

so *f; Gsg* soli *Isg* solju *or* soli [B,S] salt

soba *f* room 6A1; dnevna soba living room 16A1b; spavaća soba bedroom 16A1b

sobni *adj.* room 8A4

sobom *pron. (Instr)* self 7A1✿ *see under* sebe

socijalan, socijalna *adj.* social; socijalna pomoć [B,S] socijalna skrb [C] welfare 3A2

sok *m; Gsg* soka *Npl* sokovi juice 4A3, 4A3✿

sol *f; Gsg* soli *Isg* solju *or* soli [C] salt

sonet *m; Gsg* soneta sonnet 18A3

sopstven *adj.* [B,S] own 15A2

spajalica *f* paper clip

spajati *see under* spojiti

spasiti, spasim (P); spašavati, spašavam, spašavaju (I) [C] to save, to rescue 13☺

spasti, spasem (P); spasavati, spasavam, spasavaju (I) [B,S] to save, to rescue 13☺

spavanje *n* sleep 7A3

spavati, spavam, spavaju (I) to sleep 7A3, 7A3✿

specifičan, specifična *adj.* specific ⌸B.IV

specijalitet *m; Gsg* specijaliteta specialty 11A2

spetljati se (P) ⌸B.VI; spetljavati se, spetljavam se, spetljavaju se (I) to bumble

spevati (P) [E] to compose verse or a song 19A3b

spisak *m; Gsg* spiska *Npl* spiskovi [B,C,S] list

spisateljica *f* writer (f.) 11A2✿

spjevati (P) [J] to compose verse or a song 19A3b

spojiti, spojim (P) ⌸B.VIII; spajati, spajam, spajaju (I) 18A3 to connect, to bind together

spomenik *m; Npl* spomenici monument 16A3b

spomenuti, spomenem (P) [B,C] 16A1b; spominjati, spominjem (I) ⌸B.VII to mention

spominjati *see under* spomenuti

sport *m; Npl* sportovi [B,S] sports 16A1b

sposobnost *f; Gsg* sposobnosti *Isg* -ošću *or* -osti capability, competence 10A3

spoznati (P) 20.III; spoznavati, spoznajem (I) to realize, to comprehend, to recognize [the truth] *see* znati

sprat *m; Npl* spratovi [B,S] floor, story 6A1

spreman, spremna *adj.* prepared, ready 15A1

spremanje *n* 1. preparation, readying; 2. housekeeping 15A1

spremati *see under* spremiti

spremiti, spremim (P); spremati, spremam,

spremaju (I) to prepare 7A1

sprovesti, sprovedem; sproveo, sprovela (P) 16A1a; sprovoditi, sprovodim (I) to carry out, to realize, to put into effect *see* voditi

spustiti, spustim (P) 13A2; spuštati, spuštam, spuštaju (I) to lower, to put down ⌸A.VII *see* pustiti

spuštati *see under* spustiti

Srbija *f* Serbia 1➊

Srbin *m; Npl* Srbi Serb (m., general) ↦4 1A4

srce *n; Gpl* srca *or* srdaca heart 15A1

srdačan, srdačna *adj.* heartfelt, warm 16A2b

srebro *n* silver

sreća *f* 1. happiness; 2. fortune, luck 8A3; srećom luckily, fortunately 14A3

srećan, srećna *adj.* [B,S] 1. happy; 2. fortunate, lucky 2A2; srećan put [B,S] bon voyage 12A3

sreda *f; Asg* sredu [E] Wednesday 2A1; sredom on Wednesdays 7A2✿

sredina *f* middle, mean 7A4

srednji *adj.* middle

srednjevekovni *adj.* [E] Middle Ages, medieval 16A3b

srednjevjekovni *adj.* [J] [B/S] Middle Ages, medieval 16A3b

srednjovjekovni *adj.* [C] Middle Ages, medieval 16A3b

sredstvo *n; Gpl* sredstava apparatus, tool; sredstva means, funds

Srem *m* [E] region of western Vojvodina and eastern Slavonia

sresti, sretnem (P); sretati, srećem (I) to meet; ⌸B.IV *see also* susresti

sretan, sretna *adj.* [B,C] 1. happy; 2. fortunate, lucky 2A2; sretan put [B,C] bon voyage 12A3

sretati *see under* sresti

srijeda *f; Asg* srijedu [J] Wednesday 2A1; srijedom on Wednesdays 7A2✿

Srijem *m* [J] region of eastern Slavonia and western Vojvodina

srknuti, srknem (P); srkati, srčem (I) to sip 14A1

sročiti (P) to formulate, to compose 16A1a

srpanj *m; Gsg* srpnja [C] July 6A2, ⌐6A2⌐

Srpkinja *f* Serb (f.) 1A4

srpski *adj.* Serbian 2➊

stajati, stojim (I) 1. to stand 6A1, 11A4✿, 12A4✿ stajati u redu to stand in line 11A4; 2. + *Dat* to suit, to fit

stajalište *n* tram or bus stop

staklo *n; Gpl* stakala glass (material)

stalan *adj.* permanent, constant; oni se stalno svađaju they're always fighting 15A2✿

stalo [**mu je**] **do** + *Gen*   it mattered to [him] 18A1b   *see also* **stati**

stan *m; Npl* **stanovi**   apartment, flat   7A4

stanarina *f*   rent   9A3

stanica *f*   1. station   5A3, 6A1✿, 9A3 ;   2. [bus *or* tram] stop   13A4;   **policijska stanica** [B,S]   police station   9A3 ;   **autobusna** [C] **autobuska** [B,S] **stanica**   bus station   9A3 ;   **radio stanica** [B,S]   radio station   9A3 ;   **železnička stanica** [E] **željeznička stanica** [J] [B/S]   train station   5A3, 9A3   *see also* **kolodvor**

stanovanje *n*   living, residing   9A3

stanovati, stanujem (I)   to reside, to live at   9A1

stanovnik *m; Npl* **stanovnici**   inhabitant, resident

stanovništvo *n; Gpl* **stanovništava, stanovništva** [B,C,S]   population;   **popis stanovništva**   census

stanje *n*   condition   14A3

star, stara; stari *adj.*   1. old   6A3, 11A1✿;   2. *colloq. (long form only)*   male or female parent   9A4, 9A4 ;   **Stari zavet** [E] **Stari zavjet** [J]   Old Testament   17C1

starost *f; DLsg* **starosti** *Isg* **-ošću** *or* **-osti**   1. age;   2. old age

stati, stanem (P); **stajati, stajem** (I)   1. to stand up, to get up   6A1, 11A4✿, 14A2✿;   2. to stop   11A3;   3. to start [doing something]   15A2   *see also* **stalo** [**mu je**], **nestati, ostati, postati, prestati, rastati**

staviti (P)   6A3, 10A1✿; **stavljati** (I)   6A4   to put

stavljati   *see under* **staviti**

ste *verbal clitic*   1. [you] are *(plural)*;   2. you are *(formal)*   1A1, 1A1✿   *see under* **biti**

stećak *m; Npl* **stećci**   Bosnian medieval tombstone   17A4

steći, steknem; stekao, stekla (P) **sticati, stičem** [B,C,S], **stjecati, stječem** [C] (I)   to acquire, to get   📖B.VIII

stepen *m; Gpl* **stepena** *or* **stepeni** [B,S]   1. degree [of temperature];   2. step;   3. stage   16A3a

sticaj *m* [B,S]   concurrence, coincidence;   **sticajem okolnosti**   as it turned out

sticati   *see under* **steći**

stići [**stignuti**], **stignem; stigao, stigla** (P)   ↪6   9A4; **stizati, stižem** (I)   14A4   1. to arrive;   2. to catch up with;   3. to get around to   10☺

stignuti   *see under* **stići**

stih *m; Npl* **stihovi**   verse   17A1b

stil *m; Npl* **stilovi**   style   20.V

stilski *adj.*   stylistic   19A1b

stipendija *f*   scholarship, stipend   16A1a

stipendiranje *n*   financing, funding   16A1a

stišati (P)   14A4, 14A1✿; **stišavati, stišavam, stišavaju** (I)   to quiet down

stizati   *see under* **stići**

stjecaj *m* [C]   concurrence, coincidence;   **stjecajem okolnosti**   as it turned out

stjecati   *see under* **steći**

sto *num.*   hundred (100)   6A1, 5A1✿, 12A1✿

sto *m; Gsg* **stola** *Npl* **stolovi** [B,S]   table   6A1;   **pisaći sto**   desk   12A1

stol *m; Gsg* **stola** *Npl* **stolovi** [C]   table   6A1;   **pisaći stol**   desk   12A1

stolar *m* [B,C]   carpenter   11A2✿

stolica *f*   chair   4A4

stoljeće *n* [B,C]   century   17A2a

stomak *m; Gsg* **stomaka** [S]   stomach, gut, abdomen   10A4, 10A4

stomatologija *f*   dentistry   13B3

stopalo *n*   foot   10A4, 10A4

stotina *f*   hundred;   **stotinu**   one hundred   12A1, 12A2, 12A2

stotinjak *m*   a hundred or so   12A1✿

strah *m; Npl* **strahovi**   fear   10A3;   **strah** [**ga**] **je**   [he] is afraid   10A3, 10A3

stran, strana; strani *adj.*   foreign   16A1a;   **strani jezik**   foreign language   📖B.I

strana *f*   1. side   8A4;   **s jedne strane ... s druge strane**   on the one hand ... on the other hand   8A4✿;   2. slope   18A1a;   3. page;   **s onu stranu**   over to that other side   17A2a

stranac *m; Gsg* **stranca**   foreigner *(m., general)*   16A2b

stranica *f*   page   13A3;   **web stranica**   web page

strankinja *f*   foreigner *(f.)*

strastan, strasna *adj.*   passionate   18A2a

strašan, strašna *adj.*   terrible, awful   8A1

strašno *adv.*   terribly   3A1

strela *f* [E]   arrow   19A3a

strepeti, strepim (I) [B,S]   to live in fear   📖B.V

strepiti, strepim (I) [B,C]   to live in fear   📖B.V

stric *m; Npl* **stričevi** [B,C,S]   paternal uncle   5A3, 5A3✿

strijela *f* [J]   arrow   19A3a

strina *f* [B,C,S]   aunt   5A3

strofa *f*   stanza   17A1b

strog *adj.*   strict   6A3

strojar *m* [C]   mechanic   11A2✿

strojarstvo *n* [C]   mechanical engineering   13B3

strop *m; Npl* **stropovi** [C]   ceiling   8A4

strog *adj.*   strict   6A3

stropni *adj.* [C] ceiling 8A4

stroži *adj.* stricter *see* **strog**

strpljenje *n* patience 8A1

strpljiv *adj.* patient 8A1

stručnjak *m; Npl* **stručnjaci** expert 16A2

struja *f* 1. current; 2. electricity

struka *f; DLsg* **struci** profession, occupation 11A3

studeni *m; Gsg* **studenog** [C] November 6A2, 6A2

student *m; Gpl* **studenata** university student, *(m., general)* 1A1, 3A1✿

studentica *f* [B,C] university student *(f.)* 1A4

studentkinja *f* [B,S] university student *(f.)* 1A4

studentski *adj.* student; **studentski dom** student dormitory 7A4

studij *m* study [of a discipline], studies 16A1b

studijski *adj.* study-related 9A1

studirati, studiram, studiraju (I) to study, to be a university student 6A2

stupanj *m; Gsg* **stupnja** *Npl* **stupnjevi** [C] degree [of temperature] 16A3a

stupiti, stupim (P) 1. to step; 2. to begin 16A2a; **stupiti u vezu** to get in touch 16A2a

stvar *f; Gsg* **stvari** *Isg* **stvarju** *or* **stvari** thing ↦4 3A3, 3A2✿, 8A1✿

stvarati *see under* **stvoriti**

stvarno *adv.* really, truly 2A2

stvarnost *f; Gsg* **stvarnosti** *Isg* **-ošću** *or* **-osti** reality

stvor *m; Gsg* **stvora** creature 📖B.VI

stvoriti, stvorim (P) 17A4; **stvarati, stvaram, stvaraju** (I) 3⟲ to create

su *verbal clitic* [they] are 1A4 *see under* **biti**

subota *f* Saturday 2A1; **subotom** on Saturdays 7A2✿

sud *m; Gsg* **suda** *Npl* **sudovi** court of law 6A1✿

sud *m; Npl* **sudovi** [B,S] dish [e.g. plate, bowl] 12A2

sudac *m; Gsg* **suca** *Npl* **suci** [C] judge 5A3

sudariti se (P) 📖B.V; **sudarati se** (I) to collide

sudija *m; Npl* **sudije** [B,S] judge 5A3

suditi, sudim (I) to judge 20.VI

sudjelovati, sudjelujem [B,C] to participate 16A1a

suđen *adj.* destined 20.VI

suh, suha; suhi *adj.* [B,C] dry 18A1a

sukobiti se (P) 18A3; **sukobljavati se, sukobljavam se, sukobljavaju se** (I) to clash

sumnjati, sumnjam, sumnjaju (I); **posumnjati, posumnjam, posumnjaju** (P) to doubt 10A3

sunce *n* sun 6A1; **sunčev sistem** [B,S] **sunčev sustav** [C] solar system 6A1

supa *f* [B,S] soup 11A2

suparnik *m; Npl* **suparnici** rival 18A3

suparništvo *n* rivalry 18A3

supatnik *m; Npl* **supatnici** [C] fellow sufferer 20.V

super *adv.* terrific 3A1

suprug *m; Npl* **supruzi** spouse *(m.)* 7A2

supruga *f; DLsg* **supruzi** spouse *(f.)* 7A2

suptilan, suptilna *adj.* subtle 20.V

sur, sura; suri *adj. (archaic)* gray 17A3a

suradnja *f* [C] cooperation 18A3

susjed *m* [B,C] neighbor *(m.)* 6A4

susjeda *f* [B,C] neighbor *(f.)* 6A4

susresti, susretnem (P) 20.IV; **susretati, susrećem** (I) 📖B.V to meet with *see* **sresti**

susretati *see under* **susresti**

sustav *m* [C] system; **sunčev sustav** [C] solar system 6A1

suton *m* dusk 18A1a

sutra *adv.* tomorrow 2A1; **sjutra** tomorrow *(Montenegrin)* 19A3b

sutradan *adv.* the next day 14A2

suv, suva; suvi *adj.* [S] dry 18A1a

suviše *adv.* too much, excessively 16A3a

suvremen *adj.* [C] contemporary, modern

suši *adj.* drier *see* **suh** [B,C] **suv** [S]

suza *f* tear (from crying)

sva *f: pron. adj.* all ↦4 3A3, 3A3✿, 15A2✿;

  singular forms
    (Acc) **svu**
    (Dat-Loc) **svoj** 15A2
    (Instr) **svom**
  plural forms
    (Nom) **sve**
    (Acc) **sve** 6A2
    (Gen) **svih** 15A1 *or* **sviju**
    (Dat-Loc-Instr) **svim, svima** 15A2
    see also **sav, sve, svi**

svadba *f; Gpl* **svadaba** *or* **svadbi** wedding 📖B.VIII

svaditi se (P); **svađati se** (I) to quarrel, to fight 15A2✿

svađati se (I) *see under* **svaditi se**

svakako *adv.* certainly 2A4

svaki *adj.* every; **svaki dan** every day 6A4

svako *pron.; Gsg* **svakoga** [B,S] everyone

svakodnevan, svakodnevna *adj.* everyday 📖B.III

svakidašnjica *f* everyday life, the commonplace 20.III

svašta *pron.; Gsg* **svačega** *DLsg* **svačemu** *Isg* **svačim** 1. all sorts of things 9A3✿; 2. nonsense svatko *pron.*; *Gsg* svakoga [C]   everyone

sve *n; pron.*   everything   ↦4   2A3, 3A3,
  3A3✿, 14A2✿, 15A2✿
  (Gen) sveg, svèga
  (Dat-Loc) svem, svèmu
  (Instr) svȉm, svȉma
  plural forms
  (Nom) sva
  (Acc) sva
  (Gen) svȉh *or* svȉju
  (Dat-Loc-Instr) svȉm, svȉma
  see also sav, sve, svi;

sve bolje   better and better   15A1✿
sve *f; pl pron. adj.   see under* sva
svéća *f* [E]   candle
svéćenīk *m; Npl* svéćenīci [B,C]   [Catholic]
  priest, minister   11A2✿
svedòčiti, svèdočīm (I) [E]   to testify   📖B.VIII
svèdok *m; Gsg* svedòka [E]   witness   20.IV
sveg, svèga   *see under* sav, sve
svejèdno *adv.*   all the same   7A4;   svejèdno mi
  je   it doesn't matter to me, I don't care   7A4
svèmīr *m* [B,C,S]   universe   6A1, 6A1✿
svem, svèmu   *see under* sav, sve
svèska *f; DLsg* svesci *Gpl* svezâka *or* sveskī
  [B,S] 1. notebook 1A2; 2. volume [= book]
  [B,S]
svȇst *f; Gsg* svȅsti *Isg* svéšću *or* svȅsti [E]
  1. consciousness; 2. conscience
svȅstan, svȅsna *adj.* [E]   aware, conscious
  📖B.IV
svèštenīk *m; Npl* svèštenīci [B,S]   [Catholic]
  priest, minister   11A2✿
svȇt *m; Npl* svȅtovi [E]   world   17A2a
svȇt, svéta; svȇti *adj.*   holy, sacred;   Svéto pìsmo   Holy Scripture, the Bible   17C2
svètiljka *f; DLsg* svètiljci *Gpl* svètiljkâ *or*
  svètiljākā [E]   lamp   20.V
svȅtlo *n; Gpl* svètālā [E]   light [= source of
  light]   8A4
svètlōst *f; Gsg* svètlosti *Isg* -ošću *or* -osti [E]
  light (radiated light)   17C1
svȅtskī *adj.* [E]   world   12A4;   Prvi svȅtskī rat
  First World War   12A4;   Drugi svȅtskī rat
  Second World War   12A4
sveučìlišnī *adj.* [C]   university   16A2a
sveučìlište *n* [C]   university   6A2, 6A1✿,
  5A2
svéza *f* [C]   connection   13A2;   u svezi [C]   in
  connection [with]   13A2
svȇž *adj.* [E]   1. fresh   7A1;   2. cool;   svȅžī sir
  cottage cheese   7A1
svȋ *m; pl pron.*   everyone   ↦4   12A2, 3A3✿,
  6A1✿, 14A2✿, 15A2✿;
  plural forms
  (Nom) svi

(Acc) sve   6A2
(Gen) svȋh   15A1 *or* svȉju
(Dat-Loc-Instr) svȉm, svȉma
see also sav, sve, svi

svȋbanj *m; Gsg* svȋbnja [C]   May   6A2, 6A2✿
svȉčice *f (pl form) (archaic)*   undergarment
  19A3a
svȉdeti se (P)   10A2;   svȉđati se, svȉđām se,
  svȉđajū se (I) [E]   6A4, 6A4✿, 10A2✿   to be
  pleasing to;   svȉđa mi se   I like   6A4, 641✿
svidjeti se, svidīm se; svidio se, svidjela se (P)
  10A2;   svȉđati se, svȉđām se, svȉđajū se (I) [J]
  [B,C,S]   6A4, 6A4✿, 10A2✿   to be pleasing
  to;   svȉđa mi se   I like   6A4, 6A4✿,
svȉđati se   *see* svideti se [E]   svidjeti se [J]
svȋjest *f; Gsg* svijesti *Isg* svijéšću *or* svijesti [J]
  1. consciousness; 2. conscience
svȋjet *m; Npl* svjetovi [J]   world   17A2a
svȉnja *f*   pig, swine
svinjètina *f*   pork
svìrati, svȉrām, svȉrajū (I)   to play [an instru-
  ment]   18A3
svjéća *f* [J]   candle
svjedòčiti, svjèdočīm (I) [J]   to testify   📖B.VIII
svjèdok *m; Gsg* svjedòka [J]   witness   20.IV
svjèstan, svjèsna [J]   conscious, aware   📖B.IV
svjètiljka *f; DLsg* svjètiljci *Gpl* svjètiljkâ *or*
  svjètiljākā [J]   lamp   20.V
svjȅtlo *n; Gpl* svjètālā [J]   light [= source of
  light]   8A4
svjètlōst *f; Gsg* svjètlosti *Isg* -ošću *or* -osti [J]
  light (radiated light)   17C1
svjȅtskī *adj.* [J]   world   12A4;   Prvi svjȅtskī
  rat   First World War   12A4;   Drugi svjȅtskī
  rat   Second World War   12A4
svjȇž *adj.* [J]   1. fresh;   2. cool   7A1;   svjȅžī
  sir   cottage cheese   7A1
svȍg *m,n; Gsg*   one's own   *see under* svoj
svój, svòje, svòja *pron. adj.*   one's own   5A3,
  5A3✿
svȏj *f; DLsg*   all   *see under* sva
svojèvrstan, svojèvrsna *adj.*   [one] of a kind
  20.I
svȍm *m,n; DLsg*   one's own   *see under* svoj
svȏm *f; Isg*   all   *see under* sva
svrátiti, svrátim (P)   14A2, 12A4✿;   svráćati,
  svráćām, svráćajū (I)   to stop by   *see* vrátiti
svrha *f; DLsg* svrsi   purpose   6A2, 6A2✿
svršávati   *see under* svršiti
svršen *adj.* 1. perfective; 2. completed;
  svršen vȋd   perfective aspect
svŕšiti, svŕšīm (P)   15A1, 15A1✿;   svršávati,
  svršávām, svršávajū (I)   17A2a   to end, to
  finish
svúda *adv.*   in every direction, everywhere

Š

šah *m* chess 9A2✿

šaka *f; DLsg* šaci 1. hand; 2. fist 10A4, 10A4

šalica *f* [B,C] [coffee, tea] cup 14A1

šaliti se (I) to joke ⌨B.III

šaljiv *adj.* jocular, joking 15A1

Šangaj *m* Shanghai 9A1

šank *m; Npl* šankovi bar 12A2; pušiti za šankom to smoke at the bar 12A2

šansa *f; Gpl* šansi chance ⌨B.VI

šapat *m* whisper; šaptom or šapatom in a whisper 20.VI

šapnuti, šapnem (P); šaptati, šapćem (I) to whisper 18A1a

šaptati *see under* šapnuti

šaren, šarena *adj.* colorful 5A1

šargarepa *f* [S] carrot

šator *m* tent 19A1b

šećer *m* sugar 7A1

šef *m; Npl* šefovi boss *(m., general)* 11A2✿

šefica *f* boss *(f.)* 11A2✿

šeretski jocular, joking ⌨B.IV

šešir *m; Gsg* šešira hat 11A1

šesnaest *num.* sixteen (16) 5A1, 5A1✿

šesnaesti *adj.* sixteenth (16th) 16A1

šest *num.* six (6) 5A2, 5A1✿

šestero *n* [C] six (group of mixed gender) 12A2✿

šesti *adj.* sixth (6th) 6A1, 6A2✿, 12A3✿

šestorica *f* six [men] 12A2✿

šestoro *n* [B,S] six (group of mixed gender) 12A2✿

šeststo *num.* six hundred (600) 12A1✿

šetati, šetam, šetaju (I) ⌨B.IV; prošetati, prošetam, prošetaju (P) 20.V to walk, to stroll

šetnja *f; Gpl* šetnji walk, stroll 12A2

šezdeset *num.* sixty (60) 5A1, 5A1✿

širi *adj.* wider, broader *see* širok

širiti, širim (I); raširiti, raširim (P) to spread [something] out 16A1b; širiti se, širim se (I); raširiti se, raširim se (P) to spread 16A1b

širok, široka; široki *adj.* wide, broad 14A3

širom *adv.* throughout, across 16A3b

šišanje *n* haircut

šišati, šišam, šišaju (I); ošišati, ošišam, ošišaju (P) to give a haircut

šišati se, šišam se, šišaju se (I), ošišati se, ošišam se, ošišaju se (P) to get a haircut ⌨B.IV

šišmiš *m* [B,C,S] bat [mammal]

škola *f* school 5C1, 6A1✿; osnovna škola elementary school; srednja škola secondary school

školski *adj.* school, scholastic; školska godina school year 6A2

školj *m* small island, atoll 17A3a

škrt *adj.* 1. meager; 2. miserly 20.II

šlag *m* whipped cream

šljiva *f* plum 4A3

šolja [B,S] [coffee, tea] cup 14A1

Španac *m; Gsg* Španca [B,S] Spaniard *(m., general)*

Španija *f* [B,S] Spain 4A1

Špankinja *f* [S] Spaniard *(f.)*

španski *adj.* [B,S] Spanish ⌨B.I

Španjolac *m; Gsg* Španjolca [C] Spaniard *(m., general)*

Španjolka *m;* Španjolka *f; DLsg* Španjolki *Gpl* Španjolki [B,C] Spaniard *(f.)*

Španjolska *f (adj. form)* [B,C] Spain 4A1

španjolski *adj.* [B,C] Spanish ⌨B.I

šporet *m* [B,S] stove 14A1

šport *m; Npl* športovi [C] sport, sports 16A1b

šta *pron.* [B,S] what ↦4 1A2, 4A2✿, 6A2✿, 7A1✿, 9A2✿, 9A3✿; *(Gen)* čega *(Dat-Loc)* čemu *(Instr)* čim, čime ma šta no matter what 20.VI; bilo šta *pron* whatever, anything at all 18A3

štampa *f; Gpl* štampi [B,S] the press

štampati (I) [B,S] to print 20.V

štap *m; Npl* štapovi 1. rod; 2. walking cane 20.VIII; ribički štap fishing rod 20.VIII

štednjak *m* [B,C] stove 14A1

šteta *f* 1. a shame, too bad; 2. damage 13A3

što *pron.* [C] what ↦4 1A2, 4A2✿, 6A2✿, 7A1✿, 9A2✿, 9A3✿; *(Gen)* čega *(Dat-Loc)* čemu *(Instr)* čim, čime ma što no matter what 20.VI; bilo što *pron* whatever, anything at all 18A3

što *conj.* [B,C,S] that 12A3, 9A3✿, 12A3✿, 13A4✿; što se mene tiče as far as I am concerned 5A2; što pre [E] prije [J] as soon as possible 13A2

što *quest.* why [= zašto] ⌨B.V

štrudla *f* strudel 20.III

šuma *f* forest 20.VIII

Šumadija *f* region of central Serbia

šumarstvo *n* forestry 13B3

šunka *f; Gpl* šunki ham ⌨A.II

šuteti, šutim (I) [E] to be silent, to shut up ⌨B.IV *see also* pošuteti, zašuteti

šutjeti, šutim; šutio, šutjela (I) [B,C] to be silent, to shut up ⌨B.IV *see also* pošutjeti, zašutjeti

Švedska *f (adj. form)* Sweden ⌨B.II

švedski *adj.* Swedish ⌨B.II

T

ta *f. pron. adj.* this, that ↦4 1A2

(Acc sg) **tu**

(Gen sg) **te**

(Dat-Loc sg) **toj**

(Instr sg) **tom**

see also **taj** *(m)*, **to** *(n)*

tabla *f; Gpl* **tabli** [B,S] blackboard 4A4

tačan, tačna *adj.* [B,S] accurate, precise 6A1

tačka *f; Gpl* **tačaka** [B,S] 1. point; 2. period [Am.], full stop [Brit.] [punctuation mark]; 3. [performance] number 15A1

tada *adv.* then, at that time 14A1

taj, to, ta *pron. adj.* this, that ↪4 1A2

taj *m. pron. adj.* this, that 1A2

(Acc-Gen) **tog, toga**

(Dat-Loc) **tom, tome**

(Instr) **tim, time** *see also* **ta** (f), **to** (n)

tajanstven *adj.* mysterious ▣B.V

tajna *f; Gpl* **tajni** *or* **tajna** secret

takav, takvo, takva *pron. adj.* that sort of 16A3b

tako *adv.* so, thus, such 3A1; **kako ... tako** both ... and 18A3 **tako je** right! 4A2; **i tako dalje** (*abbr.* **itd.**) and so forth, etcetera 16A1a; **tako-tako** so-so 3A1

takođe *adv.* [B,S] also 4A1

također *adv.* [B,C] also 4A1

taksi *m; Gsg* **taksija** taxi 11A3

taksiranje *n* taxidriving 11A3

taksist *m* [C] taxi driver 11A3

taksista *m; Npl* **taksiste** [B,S] taxi driver 11A3

talas *m* [B,S] wave 15A1

talijanski *adj.* [B,C] Italian ▣B.II

talog *m; Npl* **talozi** dregs, sediment 14A1

tama *f* darkness 17A4

taman, tamna; tamni *adj.* dark 18A1a

tamnica *f* dungeon 19A3a

tamo *adv.* there 1A2, 9A2✿

tanak, tanka *adj.* slender, thin 3A3, 11A2✿

tanji *adj.* thinner, more slender *see* **tanak**

tanjir *m; Gsg* **tanjira** [B,S] plate ▣A.VI

tanjur *m; Gsg* **tanjura** [C] plate ▣A.VI

tata *m; Npl* **tate** Dad 9A4

te *conj.* and thus, then 4⦿

te *pron. clitic* you 2A1✿ *see under* **ti**

tebe *pron.* you 6A3✿, 7A1✿ *see under* **ti**

tebi *pron.* you 6A3✿, 7A1✿, *see under* **ti**

teča *m; Npl* **teče** [S] aunt's husband 5A3

tečaj *m; Npl* **tečajevi** *or* **tečaji** [B,C,S] course [*e.g.* language] 16A2b

teći, tečem, teku; tekao, tekla (I) to flow ↪6 3⦿,11A2✿ *see also* **proteći**

tek *adv.* just, only 6A2

teka *f; DLsg* **teci** [B] school notebook 1A2

tekst *m* text 17A4; **gornji tekst** the preceding text

tele *n; Gsg* **teleta** calf 8A2, 8A2✿

telefon *m; Gsg* **telefona** telephone 8A3

telefonirati, telefoniram, telefoniraju (I/P) to phone ▣A.VII

telefonski *adj.* telephone 16A2b

televizija *f* television [= programming] 3A3, ⸣12A2⸠

televizijski *adj.* pertaining to television ▣B.II

televizor *m* television [= set] ⸣12A2⸠

telo *n; Npl* **tela, telesa** body

tema *f* theme, topic 16A2a

temelj *m* foundation 16A2a

temperatura *f* 1. temperature 16A3a; 2. fever

teologija *f* theology 13B3

tepih *m; Npl* **tepisi** [B,S] rug 8A4

terati (I); **poterati** (P) [E] to drive away, to chase ⸣19A3b⸠

terenski *adj.* field [*e.g.* field work] 16A2a

teret *m* load, burden 16A1a

teretana *f* gym, weight-lifting facility ▣A.V

tesan, tesna; tesni *adj.* [E] tight, close

tesar *m* [B,S] carpenter 11A2✿

testo *n* [E] dough, batter

testenine *f (pl form)* [E] pasta

tešnji *adj.* [E] tighter, closer *see* **tesan**

tetak *m; Gsg* **tetka** *Npl* **tetci** [B,C,S] aunt's husband 5A3

tetka *f; Gpl* **tetaka** [B,C,S] aunt [= mother's sister or father's sister] ↪4 5A3

tetreb *m* [E] grouse; **k'o tetreb se zaljubiti** to fall head over heels in love ▣B.VII

tetrijeb *m* [J] grouse; **k'o tetrijeb se zaljubiti** to fall head over heels in love ▣B.VII

težak, teška *adj.* 1. difficult 6A3; 2. heavy 3A3, 11A2✿, ⸣16A2⸠

teži *adj* 1. heavier 2. more difficult 11A2✿ *see* **težak**

ti *pron.* you (*informal*) ↪4 1A1, 2A1✿, 2A2✿, 7A1✿

(Acc-Gen) **tebe, te**

(Dat) **tebi, ti**

(Instr) **tobom**

for pl see **vi**

ti *pron. clitic* you 6A4✿ *see* **ti**

'tica *colloq.* bird 17A2a *see* **ptica**

ticati se, tiče se (I) + *Gen* (*3rd person only*) to concern, to have to do with; **što se mene tiče** as far as I am concerned 5A2, 5A2✿, 6A4✿

tih, tiha; tihi *adj.* quiet 20.VI, 11A2✿

tijek *m; Npl* **tijekovi** [C] flow, current, course ▣B.IV; **u tijeku** [C] underway, in the course of ▣B.IV

tijekom *prep.* + *Gen* [C] during 16A2a

tijelo *n; Npl* **tijela** *or* **tjelesa** body

tijesan, tijesna; tijesni *adj.* [J] tight, close

tijesto *n* [J] dough, batter

tip *m; Npl* **tipovi**   type, kind   16A3b

tisak *m; Gsg* **tiska** [C]   the press

tiskati (I) [C]   to print   20.V

tisuća *f* [B,C]   thousand   12A1, 12A1✿;
  tisuću   one thousand (1,000)   12A1, 12A1✿,
  ⌐ 12A2 ⌐

tiši *adj.*   quieter   11A2✿   *see* **tih**

tišina *f*   silence   15A2

t.j. *abbr.*   (**to jest**) i.e., that is

tjedan *m; Gsg* **tjedna** [C]   week   5A3, 5A3✿

tjedni *adj.* [C]   weekly   16A3a

tjerati (I); **potjerati** (P) [E]   to drive away, to
  chase; **ćerati** (I); **poćerati** (P) to drive away,
  to chase *(Montenegrin)* ⌐ 19A3b ⌐

tjestenine *f (pl form)* [J]   pasta

tješnji *adj.* [J]   tighter, closer   *see* **tijesan**

tko *pron.* [C] who ↦4   1A1, 1A1✿,
  2A2✿, 6A2✿, 7A1✿, 9A3✿
  (Acc-Gen) **koga** 2A2✿
  (Dat) **komu** 6A2✿
  (Loc) **kom, kome** 6A2✿
  (Instr) **kim, kime** 7A1✿

tkogod *pron* [C]   someone or other   16A2a

to *n: pron.adj.*   this, that   1A2, 9A3✿
  (Acc-Gen) **tog, toga**
  (Dat-Loc) **tom, tome**; **tim, time**
  (Instr sg)   *see also* **ta, taj**

tobom *pron.*   you   7A1✿   *see under* **ti**

točan, točna *adj.* [C]   accurate, precise   6A1

točiti (I) [C]   to serve a beverage, to pour   13A1

točka *f; Gpl* **točaka** [C]   1. point;   2. period
  [Am.], full stop [Brit.] (punctuation mark);
  3. [performance] number   15A1

tok *m; Gsg* **toka** [B,S]   flow, current, course
  ⌐B.IV

tokom *prep. + Gen* [B,S]   during   16A2a

toliko *adv.*   so many; so much   16A1a

tonuti (I); **utonuti, utonem** (P)   to sink   18A1a

topao, topla; topli *adj.*   warm   4A3

toplota *f*   warmth   16A3b

toranj *m; Gsg* **tornja**   tower   18A1a

torba *f; Gpl* **torbi**   1. bag, sack   6A1;   2. purse

tost *m; Npl* **tostovi**   [grilled] bread   7A1;
  grilled cheese sandwich

tradicija *f*   tradition   16A2a

tradicionalan, tradicionalna *adj.*   traditional
  19A3b

trag *m; Npl* **tragovi**   trace, track   20.VII

trajan, trajna *adj.*   enduring, lasting,
  permanent

trajanje *n*   duration   16A3a

trajati, trajem (I)   to last, to endure   6A2

trajekt *m; Gpl* **trajekata**   ferry   7A2

tramvaj *m*   tram   7A2

travanj *m; Gsg* **travnja** [C]   April   6A2, ⌐ 6A2 ⌐

travnički *adj.*   of or related to Travnik [town in

Bosnia]   11A3

tražiti, tražim (I)   to seek, to look for   3A1
  see **istražiti**

trbuh *m; Npl* **trbusi**   1. belly [B,C,S];   2. stomach [C]   10A4, ⌐ 10A4 ⌐

trčati, trčim (I)   to run   ⌐A.V

trebati (I)   1. to need [*as in* **trebam auto** [B,C
  only] *or* + *Dat* **treba mi auto**   I need the
  car] 11A2;   2. ought, must, need *(*11A4,
  11A2✿, 11A4✿, 12A3✿, 13A3✿, 14A1✿

treći *adj.*   third (3rd)   3A1, 6A2✿, 12A1✿,
  12A3✿;   **treća godina**   junior year [in
  secondary school or at the university]   16A1a

trećina *f*   one third (1/3)   12A1, 12A1✿

tren *m* [B,C,S]   moment;   **istog trena**   that
  very moment   14A1

trenutačno *adv.* [C]   at the moment   16A2a

trenutak *m; Gsg* **trenutka** *Npl* **trenuci** [B,C,S]
  moment   3A2, 5A4✿, 6A1✿

tresti, tresem; tresao, tresla (I)   to shake ↦6
  10A1✿

trg *m; Npl* **trgovi**   town square   13A4

trgovina *f* [B,C,S]   shop, store   12A2, ⌐ 12A2 ⌐

tri *num.*   three (3)   4A2, 4A3✿, 12A2✿

trideset *num.*   thirty (30)   5A1, 5A1✿, 12A1✿,
  14A1✿

triler *m*   thriller   7A3

trinaest *num.*   thirteen (13)   5A1

trinaesti *adj.*   thirteenth (13th)   13A1

trista *num.* [B,S]   three hundred (300)   12A1✿

tristo *num.* [B,C,S]   three hundred (300)
  12A1✿

trnuti, trnem (I); **utrnuti, utrnem** (P)   to extinguish, to go out   17A3a

troje *n*   three, threesome (group of mixed
  gender)   12A1✿

trojica *f*   three [men]   12A1✿

trokut *m* [B,C]   triangle

trosed *m* [E]   sofa with place for three people to
  sit   20.I

trosjed *m* [J]   sofa with place for three people to
  sit   20.I

trošak *m; Npl* **troškovi**   expense(s)   9A3

trošan, trošna *adj.*   run-down, worn   20.VIII

trošiti (I); **potrošiti, potrošim** (P)   to spend,
  to waste   20.IV

trotoar *m; Gsg* **trotoara** [B,S]   sidewalk
  14A3

trougao *m; Gsg* **trougla** [B,S]   triangle

trpezarija *f* [B,S]   dining room   16A1b

trud *m; Npl* **trudovi**   1. effort   16A2a;   2. labor
  pain

trudna *adj. f*   pregnant   ⌐B.II

truditi se, trudim se (I); **potruditi se, potrudim
  se** (P)   to make an effort   16A1a

tržnica *f* [B,C]   marketplace   ⌐A.I

tu *adv.* here 4A2

tući, tučem; tukao, tukla (I) to spank, to beat 8☺

tuda *adv.* that way, this way, in that/this direction

tuga *f; DLsg* **tuzi** sorrow 15A1

tugovati, tugujem (I) to grieve 15A1, 15A1✿

tulipan *m* [B,C] tulip 📖A.IV

tumač *m; Gsg* **tumača** interpreter 19A2b

tup, tupa; tupi *adj.* dull, blunt

tuplji *adj.* duller, blunter *see* **tup**

Turčin *m; Npl* **Turci** *Apl* **Turke** *Gpl* **Turaka** Turk *(m., general)* ↦4

turistički *adj.* tourist; **turistička agencija** tourist agency 16A2a

Turkinja *f* Turk *(f.)*

turski *adj.* 1. Turkish; 2. Ottoman

tužan, tužna; tužni *adj.* sad 2A2

tvoj, tvoje, tvoja *pron. adj.* your, yours [informal] 1A2

tvornica *f* [B,C] factory 20.II

tvrd, tvrda; tvrdi *adj.* hard [= not soft]

tvrditi, tvrdim (I) to claim 📖B.III *see also* **utvrditi**

tvrđava *f* fortress 16A3b

tvrđi *adj.* harder, more solid *see* **tvrd**

U

u *prep. + Loc* in ↦5 6A1

u *prep. + Acc* into, to ↦5 5A1 on (for days of the week) 2A1, 2A3✿, 5A2✿, 6A1✿; at (telling time) 5A2✿; **u subotu** on Saturday 2A1; **zaljubiti se u** to fall in love with

u *prep. + Gen* belonging to, near 15A1; **u Charliea** Charlie's 15A1

ubediti, ubedim (P) to convince 📖B.VI; **ubeđivati, ubeđujem** (I) [E] to try to persuade

ubijediti, ubijedim (P) to convince 📖B.VI; **ubjeđivati, ubjeđujem** (I) [J] [B/S] to try to persuade

ubiti, ubijem (P) 19A3a; **ubijati, ubijam, ubijaju** (I) to kill

ubog *adj.* miserable, poor 17A3a

ubrzo *adv.* quickly 18A3

ubuduće *adv.* in the future 11A3

učenica *m* pupil; elementary- *or* secondary-school student *(f)*

učenik *m; Npl* **učenici** pupil; elementary- *or* secondary-school student *(m., general)* 14A4

učenjak *m; Npl* **učenjaci** [B,C] scientist, scholar 11A2✿

učenje *n* study 11A4, 10A4✿

učestvovati, učestvujem (I) [B,S] to participate 16A1a

učiniti *see* **činiti se**

učitelj *m* teacher *(m., general)* 5A1, 11A2✿

učiteljica *f* teacher *(f.)* ↦4 8A1✿,11A2✿

učiti (I) to study 2A1, 2A1✿, 9A1✿, 9A4✿, 10A2✿, 10A4✿ *see also* **naučiti**

učlaniti, učlanim (P) 16A2b; **učlanjivati, učlanjujem** (I) to become a member, to join up

ući, uđem; ušao, ušla (P) 12A2, 12A4✿; **ulaziti** (I) 📖B.V, 13A4✿ to enter, to go in *see* **ići**

udati se (P); **udavati se, udajem se** (I) to get married [said of a woman] *(often used with* **za** *+ Acc)* 📖B.II *see* **dati**

udoban, udobna *adj.* comfortable 11A2

udžbenik *m; Npl* **udžbenici** textbook 1A2, 3A3✿

ugao *m; Gsg* **ugla** *Npl* **uglovi** 1. angle [B,S]; 2. corner [B,C,S]

ugasiti *see* **gasiti**

uglavnom *adv.* mainly, chiefly, for the most part 16A1b

ugledati (P) to catch sight of 20.VIII *see* **gledati**

ugodan, ugodna *adj.* pleasant, comfortable 7A2

ugostiti, ugostim (P) 16A1b; **ugošćavati, ugošćavam, ugošćavaju** [B,S] **ugošćivati, ugošćujem** [C] (I) to host

uho *n; Npl* **uši,** *Gpl* **ušiju** *(pl forms f)* [B,C,S] ear 10A3, 10A3✿

uhvatiti (P); **uhvaćati** (I) to take hold of 14A1

ujak *m; Npl* **ujaci** [B,C,S] maternal uncle 5A3, 5A3✿

ujedinjen *adj.* united; **Ujedinjene Nacije** [B,S] **Ujedinjeni Narodi** [B,C] United Nations 📖B.II

ujna *f* [B,C,S] aunt [maternal uncle's wife] 5A3

ujutro *adv.* [B,C] in the morning 7A4

ujutru *adv.* [B,S] in the morning 7A4

ukazati, ukažem (P); **ukazivati, ukazujem** (I) to point out 20.VIII

uključiti, uključim (P) 16A1b; **uključivati, uključujem** (I) 4☞,10A2✿ to include

uključivati *see under* **uključiti**

ukoliko *adv.* inasmuch 19A3b

ukrasiti, ukrasim (P); **ukrašavati, ukrašavam, ukrašavaju** to decorate, to adorn

ukusan, ukusna *adj.* tasty 7A1

ulaziti *see under* **ući**

ulaznica *f* ticket 16A1a

ulica *f* 1. street 12A2; 2. city block 13A4

uloga *f; DLsg* **ulozi** role

uložen *adj.* invested 16A2a

um *m; Npl* **umovi** mind, reason, intellect

uman, umna *adj.* wise 📖B.III

umeren *adj.* [E] moderate 16A3a

umesto *prep. + Gen* [E] instead of 10A3

umeti, umem (I) [E] to know how to ↦6

umetnica *f* [E] artist *(f.)* 11A2☼

umetnički *adj.* [E] artistic 19A3b

umetnik *m: Npl* umetnici [E] artist *(m., general)* 11A2☼

umetnost *f; Gsg* umetnosti *Isg* -ošću *or* -osti [E] art 13B3; **dramske umetnosti** dramatic arts 13B3; **likovna umetnost** fine arts 13B3

umetnuti, umetnem (P) 20.V; umetati, umećem (I) to insert

umirati *see under* umreti [E] umrijeti [J]

umiriti, umirim (P) 20.I; umirivati, umirujem (I) to soothe, to calm

umiti se, umijem se (P); umivati se, umivam se, umivaju se (I) to wash one's face 9A2, 9A2☼

umivati se *see under* umiti se

umjeren *adj.* [J] moderate 16A3a

umjeti, umijem (I) [J] to know how to ↦6

umjesto *prep. + Gen* [J] instead of 10A3

umjetnica *f* [J] artist *(f.)* 11A2☼

umjetnički *adj.* [J] artistic 19A3b

umjetnik *m; Npl* umjetnici [J] artist *(m., general)* 11A2☼

umjetnost *f; Gsg* umjetnosti *Isg* -ošću *or* -osti [J] art 13B3; **dramske umjetnosti** dramatic arts 13B3; **likovna umjetnost** fine arts 13B3

umoran, umorna *adj.* tired 10A4

umoriti se, umorim se (P) 📖B.IV; umarati se, umaram se, umaraju se to get tired

umotati (P) 📖A.IV; umotavati, umotavam, umotavaju (I) to wrap up

umreti, umrem; umro, umrla (P) to die 17A1a, 10A1☼; umirati, umirem (I) [E] to be dying 18A1b *see* poumreti, zaumreti

umrijeti, umrem; umro, umrla (P) to die 17A1a, 10A1☼; umirati, umirem (I) [J] to be dying 18A1b *see* poumrijeti, zaumrijeti

unajmiti, unajmim (P); unajmljivati, unajmljujem (I) to rent [from] 9A3, ⌐9A3⌐

unapred *adv.* [E] in advance 12A3

unaprijed *adv.* [J] in advance 12A3

unesrećiti (P) 19A2a; unesrećavati, unesrećavam, unesrećavaju [B,S] *or* unesrećivati, unesrećujem [C] (I) to make unhappy

uneti, unesem (P); unositi, unosim (I) [E] to enter, to put in 15A2 *see* nositi

univerzitet *m; Gsg* univerziteta [B,S] university 6A2, 6A1☼, ⌐5A2⌐

univerzitetski *adj.* [B,S] university 16A2a

unijeti, unesem; unio, unijela (P); unositi,

unosim (I) [J] to enter, to put in 15A2 *see* nositi

unositi *see under* uneti [E] unijeti [J]

unučad *f* coll. grandchildren 12A2☼ *for sg see* unuče

unuče *n; Gsg* unučeta grandchild 12A2☼

unuk *m; Npl* unuci grandson, grandchild 8☺, 12A2☼

unuka *f; DLsg* unuci granddaughter

unutar *prep. + Gen* [B,S] within, inside of

unutar *prep. + Gen* [C] within, inside of

unutra *adv.* inside 19A3b

uobičajen *adj.* customary, prevailing 16A3a

uoči *prep. + Gen* on the eve of, just before 18A3

uopće *adv.* [B,C] in general, at all 10A1

uopšte *adv.* [B,S] in general, at all 10A1

uostalom *adv.* after all 16A2a

uparkirati *see under* parkirati

upaziti (P) to notice 19A3a *see* paziti

upečatljiv *adj.* striking, impressive 19A1b

upisati, upišem (P) 20.VIII; upisivati, upisujem (I) write in, inscribe *see* pisati

upitan *adj.* quizzical, questioning 9☺

upitati *see under* pitati

uporaba *f* [C] use

uporediti, uporedim (P); uporeðivati, uporeðujem (I) [B,S] to compare 11A2

upotreba *f* use 📖B.III

upotrebiti, upotrebim (P); upotrebljavati, upotrebljavam, upotrebljavaju (I) [E] to use 18A1b

upotrijebiti, upotrijebim (P); upotrebljavati, upotrebljavam, upotrebljavaju (I) [J] to use 18A1b

upotrebljavati *see* upotrebiti [E] *or* upotrijebiti [J]

upoznati (P) 16A1a; upoznavati, upoznajem (I) to get to know

upoznati se (P) 📖B.I; upoznavati se, upoznajem se (I) 📖B.II to get acquainted

uprava *f* administration 14A3

upravitelj *m* [C] manager *(m., general)* 11A2☼

upraviteljica *f* [C] manager *(f.)* 11A2☼

upravnica *f* [B,C,S] manager *(f.)* 11A2☼

upravnik *m; Npl* upravnici [B,C,S] manager *(m., general)* 11A2☼

upravo *adv.* 1. just, right now 6A3; 2. precisely

uprkos *prep. + Dat* despite, in spite of 16A3b

uputiti, uputim (P) 16A2a; upućivati, upućujem (I) to direct [to], to guide, to instruct

uputstvo *n; Gpl* uputstava instructions 13A4

uraditi, uradim (P) 1. to do; 2. to write [homework] [B,S only] 15A2 *see* raditi

uraniti (P) to get up early 19A3a

ured *m* [C] office 6A1, 6A1✿

uredan, uredna *adj.* orderly, tidy 9A2

urediti, uredim (P); **uređivati, uređujem** (I) to arrange 12A1

urediti se, uredim se (P); **uređivati se, uređujem se** (I) to get dressed up 📖B.VI

uručiti, uručim (P) 📖B.VI; **uručivati, uručujem** (I) to hand to

usavršiti, usavršim (P) 16A3a; **usavršavati, usavršavam, usavršavaju** (I) to improve, to perfect

uskoro *adv.* 1. soon 📖A.V; 2. soon thereafter 14A4

uskrsnuće *n* resurrection 17A2a

uslov *m* [B,S] condition 14A2

usmen *adj.* oral, verbal 6A2

usnuti, usnem (P) to fall asleep 20.V

uspaničiti se (P) to panic 20.VII

uspešan, uspešna [E] successful 📖B.VI

uspeti, uspem (P) 10A2; **uspevati, uspevam, uspevaju** (I) [E] to succeed 18A3

uspevati *see under* **uspeti**

uspijevati *see under* **uspjeti**

uspješan, uspješna *adj.* [J] successful 📖B.VI

uspjeti, uspijem; uspio, uspjela (P) 10A2; **uspijevati, uspijevam, uspijevaju** (I) [J] 18A3 to succeed

usporedba *f; Gpl* **usporedaba** *or* **usporedbi** [C] comparison 11A2

usporediti, usporedim (P) **uspoređivati, uspoređujem** (I) [C] to compare 11A2

usred *prep. + Gen* in the middle of 6A1

ustajati *see under* **ustati**

ustati, ustanem (P) 📖B.VIII; **ustajati, ustajem** (I) 📖A.V to stand up, to rise, to get up in the morning

ušće *n* 1. mouth of a river; 2. confluence of rivers 3✪, 7✪

utakmica *f* sports competition, game 12A2

uticati, utičem (I) [B,S] 1. to influence 17A3b; 2. to flow into

utihnuti, utihnem (P) to become quiet 📖B.VIII

utisak *m; Gsg* **utiska** *Npl* **utisci** [B,S] impression 16A3a

utjecati, utječem (I) [B,C] 1. to influence 17A3b; 2. to flow into

utonuti *see* **tonuti**

utorak *m; Gsg* **utorka** Tuesday 2A1; **utorkom** on Tuesdays 7A2, 7A2✿

utvrditi, utvrdim (P); **utvrđivati, utvrđujem** (I) to establish, to confirm 14A3 *see also* **tvrditi**

uveče *adv.* [S] in the evening 5A4

uvek *adv.* [E] always 6A4

uveravati, uveravam, uveravaju (I) [E] 1. to try to persuade; 2. to assure 16A3b *see* **uveriti**

uveriti (P) [E] to persuade, to convince

uvijek *adv.* [J] always 6A4

uvjeravati, ujveravam, uvjeravaju (I) [J] 1. to try to persuade; 2. to assure 16A3b *see* **uveriti**

uvjeriti (P) [J] to persuade, to convince

uvjet *m* [B,C] condition 14A2

uvlačiti *see* **uvući**

uvo *n; Npl* **uši** *Gpl* **ušiju** *(pl forms f.)* [S] ear 10A3, 10A4✿

uvrediti, uvredim (P) 19A2a; **vrediti, vredam, vredaju** (I) [E] to insult

uvrijediti, uvrijedim (P) 19A2a; **vrijeđati, vrijeđam, vrijeđaju** (I) [J] to insult

uvući, uvučem, uvuku (P) 20.VIII; **uvlačiti, uvlačim** (I) 📖A.VIII to pull in, to draw in *see* **vući**

uz *prep. + Acc* along ↦5 3✪; up 20.II

uzak, uska *adj.* narrow, tight

uzalud *adv.* in vain 15A1

uzbudljiv *adj.* exciting

uzbuđenje *n* excitement 15A2

uzdah *m; Npl* **uzdasi** sigh 17A3a

uzdignuće *n* ascension 17A2a

uzeti, uzmem (P) ↦6 5A2, 4A4✿, 7A2✿, 10A1✿; **uzimati** (I) 5A1 to take *see also* **izuzeti, poduzeti, preduzeti**

uzimati *see under* **uzeti**

uzlet *m* upward flight, ascent 17A2a

uzviknuti, uzviknem (P) 📖B.IV; **uzvikati, uzvičem** (I) to shout out

uzvodno *adv.* upstream 20.V

uži *adj.* narrower, tighter *see* **uzak**

uživati, uživam, uživaju (I) to enjoy, to enjoy oneself 12A2

V

v. *abbr. for* **vidi** *or* **vidite** 15A1

vajar *m* [B,S] sculptor *(m., general)* 11A2✿

vajarka *f; DLsg* **vajarki** *Gpl* **vajarki** [B,S] sculptor *(f.)* 11A2✿

vakat *n; Gsg* **vakta** [B] age, time 19A3a

val *m; Npl* **valovi** [B,C] wave 15A1

valjati (I) *(3rd person only)* ought, should 12A3, 12A3✿

valjati (I) be of value, be worth 12A3✿

valjda *adv.* probably 20.VI

vam, vama *pron.* 1. you *(sg. formal)*; 2. you *(pl.)* 6A3✿, 7A1✿ *see under* **vi**

van *adv.* [B,C] out, outside

vani *adv.* [B,C] outside 5A4, 5A4✿

vanjski *adj.* external

varati (I) to cheat 14B2

vas *pron. clitic* 1. you *(sg. formal)* 2. you *(pl.)*

6A3✿, 7A1✿ *see under* **vi**

vas *pron.* 1. you *(sg. formal)* 2. you *(pl.)*
6A3✿, 7A1✿ *see under* **vi**

vasiona *f* [B,S] universe 6A1, 6A1✿

vaš, vaše, vaša *pron. adj.* your, yours 1A2

Vašington *m* [S] Washington

vatra *f; Gpl* **vatri** 1. fire; 2. stove burner
14A1

vazduh *m* [B,S] air 15A1

važan, važna *adj.* important 11A1, 11A1✿

važnost *f; Gsg* **važnosti** *Isg* **-ošću** *or* **-osti**
importance

ve-ce *see* **W.C.**

večan, večna *adj.* [E] eternal 17A2a

veče *n; Gsg* **večera** [B,S] evening 3A2,
⟨ 17A1b ⟩

večer *f; Gsg* **večeri** *Isg* **večeri** *or* **večerju** [C]
evening 3A2, ⟨ 17A1b ⟩

večera *f* dinner 5A2, ⟨ 5A2 ⟩

večeras *adv.* this evening 3A1

večerati (I/P) to dine, to eat supper 10A1

večnost *f; Gsg* **večnosti** *Isg* **-ošću** *or* **-osti** [E]
eternity 17A2a

već *adv.* 1. already 6A3; 2. but, rather 3A2;
to već da that's much better 13A1

veći *adj.* bigger 11A2, 11A1✿ *see* **velik**

većina *f* majority 16A1a

vegetarijanski *adj.* vegetarian 11A2

veđa *f* [E] eyelid 18A2a

vek *m; Npl* **vekovi** [E] 1. century; 2. epoch,
age 17A2a

veleposlanstvo *n; Gpl* **veleposlanstava** *or*
veleposlanstva [C] embassy

velik, velika; veliki *adj.* 1. big, large 2A2,
3A1✿, 4A4✿, 5A1✿, 6A1✿; 2. great,
grand, majestic 3A2

veljača *f* [C] February 6A2, ⟨ 6A2 ⟩

venčanje *n* [E] marriage ceremony 📖A.IV

venčati se (I/P) [E] to get married 📖B.VII

veoma *adv* very 20.III

vera *f* [E] faith, belief 17A2a, ⟨ 17A2a ⟩

verovatan, verovatna *adj.* [E] probable 10A2

verovati, verujem (I); **poverovati, poverujem**
(P) [E] to believe 10A4

verzija *f* version 10A3

veseliti se (I) to be glad 20.III

veselje *n* merriment 15A1

veseo, vesela *adj.* cheerful 8A1

vest *f; Lsg* **vesti** *Isg* **vešću** *or* **vesti** [E] an item
of news; **vesti** *(pl form)* the news 14A2

vetar *m; Gsg* **vetra** *Npl* **vetrovi** [E] wind
14A2

veterinar *m; Gsg* **veterinara** veterinarian
11A2✿

veverica *f* [E] squirrel 📖A.VI

veza *f* connection 13A2; **u vezi** [B,S] in

connection [with] 13A2

vezati, vežem (I) 1. to bind, to connect
📖B.IV; 2. to embroider

veznik *m; Npl* **veznici** conjunction (in
grammar) 17A1

vežba *f; Gpl* **vežbi** [E] exercise 1A4

vežbati (I) [E] to exercise, to practice 2A1

vi *pron.* 1. you *(sg. formal)*; 2. you *(pl.)* ↦4
1A3, 1A1✿, 2A1✿, 6A3✿, 7A1✿, ⟨ 16A2a ⟩
(Acc-Gen) **vas, vas** 2A2
(Dat) **vama, vam** 6A3
(Instr) **vama** 7A1

vid *m; Npl* **vidovi** (grammatical) aspect

videlo *n* [E] *(archaic)* heavenly body 17C1

videoteka *f; DLsg* **videoteci** video and DVD
rental store 16A1a

videti, vidim (I/P) [E] to see ↦6 2A2,
7A3✿, 10A1✿, 11A1✿ **vidimo se!** see you!
2A1, 8A3✿ *see also* **izvideti**

vidjelo *n* [J] *(archaic)* heavenly body 17C1

vidjeti, vidim; vidio, vidjela (I/P) [J] to see
↦6 2A2, 7A3✿, 10A1✿, 11A1✿; **vidimo
se!** see you! 2A1, 8A3✿, **viđeti** to see
(Montenegrin) 19A3a, ⟨ 19A3a ⟩
see also **izvidjeti**

viđati, viđam (I) to see frequently 📖B.VII

viđenje *n* vision 16A3b

vihor *m* gale-strength wind 📖A.VII

vijek *m; Npl* **vjekovi** [J] 1. century [J] [B/S];
2. epoch [J] 17A2a

vijest *f; Gsg* **vijesti** *Isg* **viješću, vijesti** [J] an
item of news; **vijesti** *(pl form)* the news
14A2

vikati, vičem (I) to shout 20.VII *see also* **izvikati, uzvikati**

vikend *m* weekend 5A4, 5A4✿

vilen *adj.* wild, fiery 19A3a

vino *n* wine 4A3

vinograd *m* vineyard 20.II

vinuti se, vinem se (P) to soar 15A1, 15A2✿

violončelo *n* cello 18A3

viršla *f* hot dog, frankfurter

visina *n* height ⟨ 10A3 ⟩

visok, visoka; visoki *adj.* tall, high 2A2,
3A1✿, 11A1✿, 11A2✿

više *adv.* 1. more 3A3, 11A2✿; 2. a lot [of]
6☺; **više voleti, više volim** (I) [E] **više
voljeti, više volim** (I) [J] to prefer 3A3

viši *adj.* 1. taller; 2. higher 11A1✿

vječan, vječna *adj.* [J] eternal 17A2a

vječnost *f; Gsg* **vječnosti** *Isg* **-ošću** *or* **-osti** [J]
eternity 17A2a

vjeđa *f* [J] eyelid 18A2a

vjenčanje *n* [J] marriage ceremony 📖A.IV

vjenčati se (I/P) [J] to get married 📖B.VII

vjera *f* [J] faith, belief 17A2a, ⟨ 17A2a ⟩

vjerojatan, **vjerojatna** *adj.* [J] [C]   probable 10A2

vjerovatan, **vjerovatna** *adj.* [J] [B/S]   probable 10A2

vjerovati, **vjerujem** (I); **povjerovati**, **povjerujem** (P) [J]   to believe 10A4, 17A2a

vjetar *m; Gsg* **vjetra** *Npl* **vjetrovi** [J]   wind 14A2

vjeverica *f* [J]   squirrel ⌂A.VI

vježba *f; Gpl* **vježbi** [J]   exercise 1A4

vježbati (I) [J]   to exercise, to practice 2A1

vlada *f*   government 18A3

vladati, **vladam**, **vladaju** (I)   to rule, to govern

vladavina *f*   governmental rule 19A3b

vlak *m; Npl* **vlakovi** [C]   train 7A2 5A4✿

vlast *f; Gsg* **vlasti** *Isg* **vlašću** *or* **vlasti** authority, power 18A3

vlastit *adj.* [B,C]   [one's] own 15A2

vlažan, **vlažna** *adj.*   moist, damp 20.VIII

voće *n; coll.*   fruit 4A3

voda *f*   water 4A3

vodeći *adj.*   leading 18A3, 12A1✿

voditi, **vodim** (I)   1. to lead 5C1, 7A2✿, 7A3✿, 10A4✿, 10A1 ; 2. to register 18A3 *see also* **dovesti**, **izvesti**, **navesti**, **odvesti**, **prevesti**, **provesti**, **sprovesti**

vođa *m; Npl* **vođe**   leader

vojni *adj.*   military 18A3

vojnik *m; Gsg* **vojnika** *Npl* **vojnici**   soldier 11A2✿, 12A1✿

vojska *f; DLsg* **vojsci**   army 18A3

Vojvodina *f*   area in northern Serbia 1☾

vojvođanski *adj.*   Vojvodina, Vojvodinian 8A3

vokabular *m; Gsg* **vokabulara**   vocabulary ⌂B.III

vokativ *m*   vocative case

voleti, **volim** [E]   to love 2A3, 6A4✿, 9A4✿; **više voleti**   to prefer 3A3

volja *f*   will 16A3b; **drage volje**   gladly 16A3b

voljeti, **volim**; **volio**, **voljela** (I) [J]   to love 2A3, 6A4✿, 9A4✿; **više voljeti**   to prefer 3A3

voz *m; Npl* **vozovi** [B,S]   train 7A2, 5A4✿

vozač *m; Gsg* **vozača**   driver 7A2

vozački *adj.*   driver's, driving-related; **vozačka dozvola**   driver's license 11A2✿,

vozdra *colloq. from* **zdravo**   greetings ⌂B.VII, B.VII

voziti, **vozim** (I)   to drive 7A2, 7A2✿, 7A3✿, 10A4✿; **voziti se**, **vozim se** (I)   to ride, to go by vehicle 7A2

vožnja *f*   ride 7A2; **red vožnje**   train or bus schedule ⌂B.III

vrabac *m; Gsg* **vrapca**   sparrow ⌂A.III

vraćati se   *see under* **vratiti se**

vrana *f*   crow 18A1a

vrat *m; Npl* **vratovi**   neck 10A4

vrata *n (pl form)*   door 6A1, 6A1✿

vratiti se, **vratim se** (P)   9A2, 9A2✿; **vraćati se** (I)   14A2   to return   *see also* **navratiti**, **svratiti**

vrba *f; Gpl* **vrbi**   willow 18A1a

vredan, **vredna**; **vredni** *adj.* [E]   1. valuable; 2. diligent 8A1

vredeti, **vredim** (I) [E]   to be of value

vrednost *f; Gsg* **vrednosti** *Isg* **-ošću** *or* **-osti** [E]   value 13☺

vređati   *see under* **uvrediti**

vreme *n; Gsg* **vremena**; *Npl* **vremena** [E]   1. time; 2. weather; 3. grammatical tense 5A2; **buduće vreme**   future tense 15A2; **nevreme**   foul weather, storm 14A2; **prošlo vreme**   past tense 17C1; **za vreme** + *Gen*   during 5C1

vremenski *adj.*   time *or* weather, time-related, weather-related; **vremenska prognoza**   weather forecast 14A2

vreo, **vrela** *adj.*   hot 14A1

vreva *f*   bustle 20.I

vrh *m; Npl* **vrhovi**   top, summit 14A1

vrh *prep.* + *Gen*   at the top [of] 17A3a

vrijedan, **vrijedna**; **vrijedni** *adj.* [J]   1. valuable; 2. diligent, hardworking 8A1

vrijediti (I) [J]   to be of value

vrijednost *f; Gsg* **vrijednosti** *Isg* **-ošću** *or* **-osti** [J]   value 13☺

vrijeđati   *see under* **uvrijediti**

vrijeme *n; Gsg* **vremena**; *Npl* **vremena** [J]   1. time; 2. weather; 3. grammatical tense 5A2; **buduće vrijeme**   future tense 15A2; **nevrijeme**   foul weather, storm 14A2; **prošlo vrijeme**   past tense 17C1; **za vrijeme** + *Gen*   during 5C1

vrlo *adv.*   very 3A1

vrsta *f; Gpl* **vrsta** *or* **vrsti**   type, kind, sort 6A4

vršnjak *m; Gsg* **vršnjaka** *Npl* **vršnjaci**   person/man of same age

vršnjakinja *f*   woman of same age 20.II

vrt *m; Npl* **vrtovi** [B,C only]   garden 16A3b; **zoološki vrt** *m*   zoo 15A1

vruć, **vruća**; **vrući** *adj.*   hot

vruće *adv.*   hot

vrućina *f*   heat 16A3a

vrućica *f*   fever

vući, **vučem**, **vuku**; **vukao**, **vukla** (I)   to pull, to drag   *see also* **izvući**, **izvući se**, **podvući**, **privući**, **uvući**

vuk *m; Npl* **vuci** *or* **vukovi**   wolf

W

Washington *m* [B,C]   Washington

W.C. *m; Gsg* **W.C.-a**   *(pronounced* **ve-ce** *Gsg* **ve-cea***)* toilet   16A1b

Z

za *prep. + Acc*   for   ↦5   2A3, 2A3✿, 7A2✿; **za razliku od**   unlike   17A4;   **za uzvrat**   in return   15A1

za *prep + Instr*   after, following, by, behind   ↦5   15A1;   **za stolom**   at the table;   **pušiti za šankom**   to smoke at the bar   12A2

zaboravan, zaboravna *adj.*   forgetful   📖A.V

zaboraviti (P); **zaboravljati, zaboravljam, zaboravljaju** (I)   to forget   10A4

zabrana *f*   ban, prohibition   18A3

zabrinuti, zabrinem (P)   20.VIII; **zabrinjavati, zabrinjavam, zabrinjavaju** (I)   to worry, to cause concern   *see* **brinuti**

zabrinutost *f; Gsg* **zabrinutosti** *Isg* -ošću *or* -osti   concern, anxiety   14A4

začuti se, začujem se (P)   to be heard suddenly   19A3a   *see* **čuti se**

zaći, zađem; zašao, zašla (P); **zalaziti** (I)   to go behind, to set [of sun and moon]   16A3b   *see* **ići**

zaćutati, zaćutam (P) [B,S]   to fall suddenly silent   20.IV

zadaća *f* [B,C]   task, assignment;   **domaća zadaća**   homework   1A4

zadatak *m; Npl* **zadaci**   task, assignment;   **domaći zadatak** [S only]   homework assignment   1A4   ↦4

zadiviti, zadivim (P)   15A1; **zadivljavati, zadivljavam, zadivljavaju** [B,S] **zadivljivati, zadivljujem** [C] (I)   to thrill

zadivljen *adj.*   admiring   15A1

zadnji *adj.*   1. last;   2. furthest back   16A1a; **u zadnji čas**   at the last minute   16A1a

zadovoljan, zadovoljna *adj.*   satisfied   11A3

zagrabiti (P)   to scoop up   14A1

zagrebački *adj.*   pertaining to Zagreb   6A2

Zagrepčanin *m; Npl* **Zagrepčani**   resident of Zagreb *(m., general)*

Zagrepčanka *f; DLsg* **Zagrepčanki** *Gpl* **Zagrepčanki**   resident of Zagreb *(f.)*

zagrljaj *m*   embrace   20.I

zagrliti   *see* **grliti**

zahod *m*   separate room for toilet   16A1b

zahvalan, zahvalna *adj.*   grateful   13A4

zahvaliti, zahvalim (P)   20.III; **zahvaljivati, zahvaljujem** (I) [B,C,S]   16A2a   to thank

zahvaliti se, zahvalim se (P)   20.III; **zahvaljivati se, zahvaljujem se** (I) [B,S]   16A2a   to thank

zahvaljivati se   *see under* **zahvaliti se**

zainteresiranost *f; Gsg* **zainteresiranosti** *Isg* -ošću *or* -osti   interest, concern   20.IV

zainteresovan *adj.*   interested   16A1a

zainteresovanost *f; Gsg* **zainteresovanosti** *Isg* -ošću *or* -osti   interest, concern   20.IV

zaista *excl.*   indeed   2A2

zajednica *f*   community   14B2

zajednički *adj.*   shared, common   12A1

zajedno *adv.* [B,C,S]   together   2A1

zakasniti, zakasnim (P)   14A4; **zakašnjavati, zakašnjavam, zakašnjavaju** (I)   to be late

zakašnjenje *n*   delay   14A4

zakazati, zakažem (P)   📖B.VI; **zakazivati, zakazujem** (I)   to set a time for, to make an appointment

zaključak *m; Gsg* **zaključka**   conclusion   17A2b

zaključati (P)   20.VIII; **zaključavati, zaključavam, zaključavaju** (I)   to lock

zaključiti, zaključim (P); **zaključivati, zaključujem** (I)   to conclude   10A3

zakon *m*   law   19A2b

zakonik *m; Npl* **zakonici**   code of law   19A2b, 19A2b

zakonodavac *m; Gsg* **zakonodavca**   lawmaker   19A2b

zakonodavni *adj.*   legislative

zakonski *adj.*   legal   20.IV

zakukati (P)   1. to burst into wails;   2. to coo like a cuckoo bird   19A3a

zalazak *m; Gsg* **zalaska** *Npl* **zalasci**   setting; **zalazak sunca**   sunset

zaljubiti se, zaljubim se (P)   📖B.VII; **zaljubljivati se, zaljubljujem se** (I)   to fall in love *(often used with* **u** *+ Acc)*;   **k'o tetreb** [E] **tetrijeb** [J] **se zaljubiti**   to fall head over heels in love   📖B.VII

zalupiti (P)   to slam   *see* **lupiti se**   17A1a

zamenica *f* [E]   pronoun   17A1b

zameriti se + *Dat* (P) [E] to offend   18A3

zamirati   *see* **zamreti, zamrijeti**

zamirisati, zamiriše (na + *Acc*) (P) *(3rd person only)*   to start smelling of   20.III

zamisao *f; Gsg* **zamisli** *Isg* **zamišlju** *or* **zamisli**   conception, plan   19A1b

zamisliti, zamislim (P)   18A1b; **zamišljati, zamišljam, zamišljaju** (I)   to imagine   *see* **misliti**

zamišljen *adj.*   lost in thought   📖B.IV

zamjenica *f* [J]   pronoun   17A1b

zamjeriti se + *Dat* (P) [J] to offend   18A3

zamoliti   *see under* **moliti**

zamreti, zamrem; zamro, zamrla (P); **zamirati, zamirem** (I) [E]   to die down, to subside   16A3b   *see* **umreti**

zamrijeti, zamrem; zamro, zamrla (P); **zamirati, zamirem** (I) [J]   to die down, to subside

16A3b *see* **umrijeti**

zanimanje *n* 1. occupation; 2. interest 16A3b

zanimati, zanimam, zanimaju (I) to interest [*as in* **zanima me gramatika** grammar interests me] 16A2a; **zanimati se, zanimam se, zanimaju se** (I) to be interested [in] 16A2a

zanimljiv *adj.* interesting 5A3, 11A1✿

zao, zla *adj.* evil 5A1

zaokružiti, zaokružim (P) 17A1b; **zaokruživati, zaokružujem** (I) to draw a circle around *see* **kružiti**

zapad *m* west 6⊕

zapadni *adj.* western

zapamtiti *see* **pamtiti**

zapanjiti, zapanjim (P); **zapanjivati, zapanjujem** (I) to astonish 20.IV

zapitati, zapitam, zapitaju (P) to ask, to inquire 20.VI *see* **pitati**

započeti, započnem (P); **započinjati, započinjem** (I) to start in 20.IV *see* **početi**

zapošljavanje *n* employment 11A4; **služba za zapošljavanje** employment service 11A4

zapravo *adv.* actually 10A3

zapričati se, zapričam se, zapričaju se (P) to start in on a conversation, to get talking ⊞B.IV *see* **pričati**

zar *part.* really? 6B7; **zar ne?** isn't that so?; **zar ne možemo?** can't we? 5A4, 5A4✿

zaraditi, zaradim (P); **zarađivati, zarađujem** (I) to earn 11A3

zarađivati *see under* **zaraditi**

zarumeniti se, zarumenim se (P) to blush ⊞B.IV

zasladiti, zasladim (P); **zaslađivati, zaslađujem** (I) to sweeten 14A1

zastor *m* [C] curtain 20.I

zašto *quest.* why 2A3

zašutjeti, zašutim; zašutio, zašutjela (P) [C] to fall silent 20.V *see* **šutjeti**

zašutjeti *see under* **šutjeti**

zatim *adv.* thereafter, then 12A2

zato *adv.* for that reason ⊞B.IV

zato što *conj.* because 2A3

zatvor *m* prison 20.VII

zatvoriti, zatvorim (P); **zatvarati, zatvaram, zatvaraju** (I) to close 12A2

zauvek *adv.* [E] forever, once and for all 17A2a

zauvijek *adv.* [J] forever, once and for all 17A2a

zauzet *adj.* busy 11A1✿

zauzeti, zauzmem (P); **zauzimati** (I) to occupy, to take, to seize 11A1✿

zaverenički *adj.* [E] conspiratorial ⊞B.VI

zavesa *f* [E] curtain 20.I

zavet *m* [E] testament, oath; **Stari zavet** Old Testament 17C1; **Novi zavjet** New Testament

zavist *f; Gsg* **zavisti** *Isg* **zavišću** *or* **zavisti** envy 20.III

zavisan, zavisna *adj.* [B,S] dependent [on] 16A3b

zavjerenički *adj.* [J] conspiratorial ⊞B.VI

zavjesa *f* [J] [B,C,S] curtain 20.I

zavjet *m* [J] testament, oath; **Stari zavjet** Old Testament 17C1; **Novi zavjet** New Testament

završavati se *see under* **završiti**

završetak *m; Gsg* **završetka** *Npl* **završeci** end 20.VIII

završiti, završim (P); **završavati, završavam, završavaju** (I) to finish 11A1; **završavati se, završavam se, završavaju se** (I) to end 6A2

završni *adj.* final ⊞B.I

zbilja *adv.* really, truly 10A3

zbirka *f; DLsg* **zbirci** collection 17A4

zbog *prep.* + *Gen* because of, due to ↦5 10A3, 13A3✿

zbogom *m, excl.* farewell 20.VIII

zboriti (I) to speak *(Montenegrin)* 19A3b

zbuniti, zbunim (P) ⊞B.VII; **zbunjivati, zbunjujem** (I) to confuse

zderati, zderem (P) to tear off 19A2a

zdrav *adj.* healthy 10A4

zdravica *f* toast [with drink] ⊞B.VIII, B.VIII

zdravlje *n* health 7A2

zdravo *excl.* [B,S] 1. hello; 2. goodbye 1A1, 1A1, B.VII

zebra *f; Gpl* **zebara** *or* **zebri** 1. zebra [= animal]; 2. crosswalk

zec *m; Npl* **zečevi** rabbit

zelen, zelena; zeleni *adj.* green 4A4

zelje *n* cabbage [C]

zeman *n; Gsg* **zemana** *archaic* time 19A3a

zemlja *f* 1. Earth (earth) 6A1; 2. soil; 3. land, country 5⊕, 6A1✿, 7A1✿; **ničija zemlja** no man's land 16A1

zemljopisni *adj.* [C] geographical 1⊕

zezati (I) to tease ⊞B.IV

zgrada *f* building 6A1

zid *m; Npl* **zidovi** wall 4A4

zima *f* winter 9A1; **zimi** in winter; **na zimu** in the winter

zimski *adj.* winter 6A2

zimus *adv.* this winter

zlato *n* gold 19A3a

zlo *n; Gpl* **zala** evil

zmija *f* snake 5A1

značaj *m* significance, meaning

značenje *n* meaning

značiti, znači (I) *(3rd person only)* to mean 6A2

znak *m; Npl* **znaci** *or* **znakovi** sign, mark 17A1b

znamenitost *f; Gsg* **znamenitosti** *Isg* -ošću *or* -osti place of interest 16A3b

znanost *f; Gsg* **znanosti** *Isg* -ošću *or* -osti [C] science, scholarship 11A3; **političke znanosti** [C] political science 13B3; **prirodne znanosti** [C] natural sciences 3B3

znanstvenik *m; Npl* **znanstvenici** [C] scientist, scholar 11A2✿

znanje *n* knowledge 11A4

znatan, znatna *adj.* considerable 14A2

znati, znam (I) to know 4A2, 14B2 ; **nikad se ne zna** one never knows 11A4, 14A1✿ *see also* **poznati, priznati, saznati, spoznati, upoznati**

zoološki *adj.* zoological; **zoološki vrt** zoo 15A1

zov *m; Gsg* **zova** call 15A1

zračni *adj.* [C] air; **zračna luka** [C] airport 📖B.III

zrak *m* [B,C] air 15A1

zrak *m; Npl* **zraci** [B,S] ray [of light] 17A3a

zraka *f; DLsg* **zraci** [C] ray [of light] 17A3a

zrakoplov *m* [C] airplane 7A2

zrcalo *n* [C] mirror 9A2

zreo, zrela *adj.* mature 20.II

zub *m; Npl* **zubi** tooth 9A2

zubar *m* dentist (m., general) 11A2✿

zubarica *f* [B,C] dentist (f.) 11A2✿

zubarka *f; DLsg* **zubarki** *Gpl* **zubarki** [S] dentist (f.) 11A2✿

zublja *f* torch 18A2a

zvanje *n* vocation 11A4

zvati, zovem (I) 1. to call [a name]; 2. to call [by phone]; 3. to invite 10A1 ; **zvati se, zovem se** (I) to be called 1A1, 1A1✿ *see also* **nazvati, pozvati, prozvati**

zver *f; Gsg* **zveri** *Isg* **zveri** [E] beast 17A1a

zvezda *f; Gpl* **zvezda** [E] star 6A1

zvijer *f; Gsg* **zvijeri** *Isg* **zvijeri** [J] beast 17A1a

zvijezda *f; Gpl* **zvijezda** [J] star 6A1

zviždati, zviždim (I) to whistle 5C1

zvoniti, zvonim (I) to ring 📖A.V

zvono *n* bell 17A3a

zvuk *m; Npl* **zvuci** *or* **zvukovi** sound 14A4

Ž

žaliti (I) to feel sorry 📖A.III

žalost *f; Gsg* **žalosti** *Isg* -ošću *or* -osti sorrow, grief 12A3; **nažalost, na žalost** unfortunately 12A3

žalostan, žalosna *adj.* sorrowful 10☺

žao *adv.* sad, sorry [*as in* **žao mi je** I'm sorry] 12A3

žariti, žarim (I) to burn 18A2a

žedan, žedna; žedni *adj.* thirsty 4A3

želeti; želim (I) 2A1; **poželeti, poželim** (P) [E] to wish, to want, to desire 15A1, 4A3✿, 9A2✿, 13A1✿, 15A1✿

železnički *adj.* [E] railway; **železnička stanica** railway station 5A3, 9A3

želudac *m; Gsg* **želuca** *Npl* **želuci** stomach 10A4, 10A4

želja *f* desire 14A1

željeti, želim; želio, željela (I) 2A1; **poželjeti, poželim; poželio, poželjela** (P) [J] to wish, to want, to desire 15A1, 4A3✿, 9A2✿, 13A1✿, 15A1✿

željeznički *adj.* [J] railway; **željeznička stanica** [B/S] railway station 5A3, 9A3

žena *f* 1. woman; 2. wife 1A3, 3A2✿, 8A1✿

ženiti, ženim (I); **oženiti, oženim** (P) to marry, to marry off 20.II

ženiti se, ženim se (I); **oženiti se, oženim se** (P) to get married [said of a man] (often + *Instr*)

ženski *adj.* 1. feminine 2. female 3. women's 10A3; **ženska frizerka** women's hairdresser 📖B.IV

žešći *adj.* more severe, more violent *see* **žestok**

žestok *adj.* harsh, fierce

Židov *m* [C] Jew (m., general)

Židovka *f; DLsg* **Židovki** *Gpl* **Židovki** [C] Jew (f.)

židovski *adj.* [C] Jewish

živ, živa; živi *adj.* 1. alive 2. lively 16A1b

živela! *or* **živeo!** *or* **živeli!** *or* **živele!** [E] cheers! long live! 📖B.VIII

živeti, živim (I) [E] to live 5A3 *see also* **doživeti, nadživeti, odživeti, preživeti**

živjela! *or* **živio!** *or* **živjeli!** *or* **živjele!** [J] cheers! long live! 📖B.VIII

živjeti, živim; živio, živjela (I) [J] to live 5A3 *see also* **doživjeti, nadživjeti, odživjeti, preživjeti**

življi *adj.* livelier, more animated *see* **živ**

život *m; Gsg* **života** life 6A2

životinja *f* animal 5C1

žlica *f* [C] spoon 14A1

žličica *f* [C] small spoon 14A1

žudnja *f* longing, strong desire 20.VI

žurba *f; Gpl* **žurbi** hurry, rush 16A3b

žuriti, žurim (I) to hurry; **požuriti, požurim** (P) to hasten, to rush 7A3

žuriti se, žurim se (I) to hurry 7A2; **požuriti se, požurim se** (P) to hasten, to rush

žut, žuta; žuti *adj.* yellow 2A3

❧English-BCS Glossary

A

a lot puno, mnogo 5A1⚙

abandon *vb.*
  napustiti (P) 15A1; napuštati (I) 18A3

about *prep.* o ↦5 6A2

above *adv.* gore

above *prep.* iznad ↦5 8A4⚙ 8A4, nad
  ↦5 8A1, 7A2⚙, 8A4⚙

abroad *n.*
  u inostranstvu [B,S] u inozemstvu [B,C]
  8A3

abrupt *adj.* nagao 20.VI

abstract *adj.* apstraktan 19A1b

abyss *n.* bezdan 17C1

accent *n.* akcenat [B,S] akcent [B,C] 📖B.III

accept *vb.*
  prihvatiti (P) 16A1a; prihvaćati [C] (I)
  prihvatiti (P) 16A1a; prihvatati [B,S] (I)

accessible *adj.* pristupačan 16A2b

accident *n.* nesreća 7A2

accommodate *vb.*
  smestiti (P); smeštati (I) [E]
  smjestiti (P); smještati (I) [J] 17A3b

accommodation *n.* smeštaj [E] smještaj [J]
  16A2a

accompaniment *n.* pratnja 20.VII

accompany *vb.*
  pratiti (I) 12A2; ispratiti (P)

accomplish *vb.*
  postići [postignuti] (P); postizati (I) 13☺

according to *prep.* po ↦5 6A2, prema
  ↦5 11A4

accurate *adj.* tačan [B,S] točan [C] 6A1

accusative (case) *n.* akuzativ

accuse *vb.*
  optužiti (P) 20.VII; optuživati (I) 20.II

ache *n.* bol 20.IV

acquire *vb.*
  steći (P) 📖B.VIII
  sticati (I) [E] stjecati (I) [J]

across *prep.* preko ↦5 8A4
  across from nasuprot ↦5 8A4

act (= take action) *vb.*
  delovati (I) [E]
  djelovati (I) [J] 20.VII

act (a role) *vb.* glumiti (I) 📖B.IV

act *n.* čin 📖B.I

action *adj.* akcioni
  action movie akcioni film 7A3

actor *n.* glumac 11A2⚙

actress *n.* glumica 11A2⚙

actually *adv.* zapravo 10A3

add *vb.*
  dodati (P) 📖B.II; dodavati (I) 📖A.III

add on *vb.*
  nadovezati (P); nadovezivati (I) 📖B.VIII

add liquid (= top off) *vb.*
  doliti (P) 14A1; dolivati (I)

additional *adj.* dodatan 16A3b

address *n.* adresa 16A2a

address (= speak to) *vb.*
  obratiti se (P) 16A2a; obraćati se (I) 16A3a

adjective *n.* pridev [E] pridjev [J] 17A1b

administration *n.* uprava 14A3, administracija 16A1a

admire *vb.*
  zadiviti se (P) 15A1; zadivljavati se (I) [C]
  zadiviti se (P) 15A1; zadivljivati se (I) [B,S]

admiring *adj.* zadivljen 15A1

admit (= confess) *vb.*
  priznati (P) 📖B.II; 15A1 priznavati (I)
  📖B.IV

Adriatic Sea *n.* Jadransko more 1🌍

adverb *n.* prilog 17A1b

advice *n.*
  savet [E] savjet [J] 16A3a

advise *vb.*
  savetovati (I); posavetovati (P) [E]
  savjetovati (I); posavjetovati (P) [J]
  get advice
    savetovati se (I) 11A4; posavetovati se
    (P) [E]
    savjetovati se (I) 11A4; posavjetovati se
    (P) [J]

affirmative *adj.* potvrdan 📖B.VI

afraid (as in "be afraid of") *see* **fear**

Africa *n.* Afrika

African *adj.* afrički

after *prep.* nakon 12A2, za 2A3, posle [E]
  poslije [J] 5A2

after *conj.* nakon toga što posle [E] poslije [J]
  toga što 13A4⚙

after all *adv.* uostalom ↦5 16A2a

afternoon *n.* popodne 5A4, poslepodne [E]
  poslijepodne [J]
  in the afternoon popodne 10A1

afterwards *adv.* potom 12A2, zatim 12A2,
  posle [E] poslije [J] 📖A.V

again *adv.* opet 10A2, ponovno [C] ponovo
  [B,S] 14A1, 9☺

against *prep.* protiv 13A4

age (= era) *n.* epoha 6A2

age (= number of years) *n.* starost

age-mate *n.*
  vršnjak *(m., general)* vršnjakinja *(f.)* 20.II

agonizing *adj.* mučan 20.VI

agree upon *vb.*
  dogovoriti se (P) 11A2; dogovarati se (I)

agree with *vb.*
  složiti se (P); slagati se (I) 10A4

agreement *n.* dogovor 📖B.VII

agriculture *n.* poljoprivreda 13B3

aha! *excl.* a! 2A2

air *n.* vazduh [B,S] zrak [B,C] 15A1

air *adj.* vazdušni [B,S] zračni [C]

airmail *adj.* avionski 2A4

airmail letter *n.* avionsko pismo 2A4

airplane *n.* avion [B,C,S] zrakoplov [C] 7A2

airport *n.* aerodrom [B,C,S] zračna luka [C]
  📖B.III

alarm clock
  budilica [C] budilnik [B,S] 📖A.V

Albania *n.* Albanija 1🌎

Albanian *n.*
  Albanac *(m., general)* Albanka *(f.)*

alive *adj.* živ 16A1b

all *adj.* sav ↦4   2A3, 3A4✿, 15A2✿, svi
  ↦4 12A2, 15A2✿, sva ↦4   3A3,
  3A3✿, 15A2✿
    all around *prep.* po 20.VII
    all day ceo dan [E] cijeli dan [J] 7A4
    all the more sve više 7☺, 15A1✿
    all the same svejedno 7A4

allergic *adj.* alergičan 3A3

allow *vb.*
  dopustiti (P) 16A2a; dopuštati (I) 📖B.III
  dozvoliti (P) 16A3b; dozvoljavati (I)
  pustiti (P) 10A2✿; puštati (I) 10A2✿

almond *n.* badem

almost *adj.* skoro 📖B.V gotovo 20.IV

along, alongside *prep.* uz ↦5   3🌎

alphabet *n.* (Latin) abeceda, (Cyrillic) azbuka
  5A4✿

alphabetical *adj.* (Latin) abecedni, (Cyrillic)
  azbučni 2A4

already *adv.* već 3A2, 6A2✿

also *adv.* takođe [B,S] također [B,C] 4A1

alternate *vb.*
  izmenjati (P); izmenjivati (I) [E] 20.II
  izmijenjati (P); izmjenjivati (I) [J] 20.II

although *conj.* doduše 11A2, ionako 📖B.III,
  premda 20.V, iako 16A2b, mada 16A3b,
  makar 13A2

aluminum *adj.* aluminijski 19A3b

always *adv.* uvek [E] uvijek [J] 6A4

am *vb.*
  (clitic) sam 1A1, 1A1✿, 6A2✿
  (full) jesam 1A4
  see under **be**

amass *vb.*
  skupiti (P) 📖B.VI; skupljati (I) [B,C,S]

📖A.I sakupiti (P); sakupljati (I) [B,S]
  19A3b

amaze *vb.* čuditi (I)
  be amazed *vb.* čuditi se (I) 16A1b

amazement *n.* čuđenje 20.II

ambulance *n.* hitna kola 14A3

America *n.* Amerika 16A1b

American *adj.* američki 2A4

American *n.*
  Amerikanac *(m., general)* Amerikanka *(f.)*
  1A4

amidst *prep.* usred 6A1

among *prep.* između ↦5   4A4, među
  📖B.IV, 8A4✿

ancestor *n.* predak 16A3b

and *conj.* i 1A1, a 1A1, te 4🌎, pak 5A3
  pa 7A2
    and so forth i tako dalje *(abbr.* itd.) 16A1b

anger *vb.* ljutiti (I); naljutiti (P)
    be/get angry
    ljutiti se (I); naljutiti se (P) 📖B.VIII

angle *n.* kut [C] ugao [B ,S]

angry *adj.* ljut 10A3

animal *n.* životinja 5C1

announce *vb.*
  najaviti (P); najavljivati (I) 📖B.V

annual *adj.* godišnji 12A1

anonymity *n.* anonimnost 13☺

another *adj.* drugi 5A1, **one another, each
  other** jedan drugi 11A2✿, 15A2✿, ¦ 16B1 ¦

answer *n.* odgovor 2A1, 6A4✿

answer *vb.*
  odgovoriti (P) 16A2a, 10A2✿; odgovarati
  (I) 5A1, 10A2✿

ant *n.* mrav

anticipation *n.* iščekivanje 📖B.VI

anyhow *adv.* ionako 📖B.III

anyone *pron.* iko [B,S] itko [C], bilo ko [B,S]
  bilo tko [C] ¦ 18A3 ¦
    not anyone niko [B,S] nitko [C]

anything *pron.* išta 7A1, 7A1✿, bilo šta
  [B,S] bilo što [C] ¦ 18A3 ¦
    not anything ništa 4A3

anywhere *adv.* igde [E] igdje [J], bilo gde [E]
  bilo gdje [J] ¦ 18A3 ¦

apartment *n.* stan 7A4

apartment building *n.* stambena zgrada

aphorism *n.* aforizam 7☺

apiece po ↦5   5A1✿

apologize *vb.*
  izviniti se (P) [B,S] 2A1
  ispričati se (P) [C] 2A1

appeal to *vb.*
  dopasti se (P) 📖B.IV; dopadati se (I) [B,S]
  16A1a
  svideti se (P) 10A2; sviđati se (I) 6A4

svidjeti se (P) 10A2; sviđati se (I) [J]
[B,C,S] 6A4
see also **like, please**
appear (= seem) *vb.* izgledati (I) 9A2
appear (= come to light) *vb.*
pojaviti se (P) 13A3; pojavljivati se (I)
appearance (= outward look) *n.* izgled B.V
appearance (= act of appearing) *n.* pojava
18A1b
appetizer *n.* predjelo 11A2
applaud *vb.*
pljeskati (I) B.VIII
aplaudirati (I)
applause *n.*
aplauz B.VIII, pljesak
apple *n.* jabuka 4A3
approach (= draw near) *vb.*
približiti se (P) 16A3b; približavati se (I)
approach (= come toward) *vb.*
prići (P); prilaziti (I) 20.IV
approve *vb.*
odobriti (P) 16A1a; odobravati (I)
approximate *adj.* okvirni 16A2a
approximately *adv.* otprilike 12A1, po prilici
12A1, jedno 16A1a
April *n.* april [B,S] travanj [C] 6A2
Arab *n.* Arapin *(m., general)* Arapkinja *(f.)*
archaeologist *n.* arheolog
archduke *n.* nadvojvoda 12A4
architect *n.* arhitekt [B,C] arhitekta [B,S]
11A2✿
architecture *n.* arhitektura 13B3, 5A2
are *vb.* 1A1✿
(clitic) si, smo, ste, su
(full) jesi, jesmo, jeste, jesu
see under **be**
arm *n.* ruka ↦4   9A2, 10A4✿ , 10A4
armchair *n.* fotelj [B,S] fotelja [B,C] B.V
army *n.* vojska 18A3
around *prep.* oko ↦5   6A1, po ↦5
20.VII
arrange *vb.*
složiti (P); slagati (I) 20.II
urediti (P) 12A1; uređivati (I)
arrival *n.* dolazak 14A4
arrive *vb.*
stići [stignuti] (P) ↦6   9A4; stizati (I)
14A4, 10A2✿
arrive at *vb.*
dospeti (P) 16A1a; dospevati (I) [E]
dospjeti (P) 16A1a; dospijevati (I) [J]
arrow *n.* strela [E] strijela [J] 19A3a
art *n.* umetnost [E] umjetnost [J] 13B3
artist *n.*
umetnik [E] umjetnik [J] *(m., general)*
umetnica [E] umjetnica [J] *(f.)* 11A2✿

artistic *adj.* umetnički [E] umjetnički [J]
19A3b
as *conj.* kao 9A2, 4A1✿
as if *conj.* kao da A.III
as soon as *conj.* čim 13A2, 12A3✿
as soon as possible što pre [E] što prije [J]
13A2
as usual po običaju B.VI
ascension *n.* uzdignuće 17A2a
ascent *n.* uzlet 17A2a
ash (= burnt ember) *n.* pepeo
ash (= tree) *n.* jasen
Asia *n.* Azija
Asian *adj.* azijski
ask *vb.* pitati (I) 3A1; upitati (P) B.I
ask [someone] to do *vb.*
moliti (I) 2A4; zamoliti (P)
aspect (grammar) *n.* vid
imperfective aspect nesvršen vid
perfective aspect svršen vid
assassinate *vb.* izvršiti atentat (na) 12A4
assassination *n.* atentat 12A4
assemble (= come together) *vb.*
okupiti (P); okupljati (I) 14A4
assemble (= put together) *vb.*
sastaviti (P) 19A3b; sastavljati (I)
assignment *n.* zadaća [B,C] 1A4 zadatak
[B,C,S] ↦4   1A4
assume *vb.* pretpostaviti (P) pretpostavljati (I)
astonish *vb.*
zapanjiti (P); zapanjivati (I) 20.IV
at *prep.* na ↦5   6A1, 6A1✿, u ↦5
6A1, 6A1✿, kod ↦5   4A2, 4A2✿, po
↦5   B.VI, pri ↦5
at the home of kod ↦5   4A2
at the side of kraj ↦5   13A4
at first isprva 18A3
at least makar 13A2, barem 11A3,
najmanje 11A2✿
at the moment momentalno [B,C,S]
trenutačno [C] 16A2a
atmosphere *n.* atmosfera 11A2
atoll *n.* školj 17A3a
atop *prep.* vrh 17A3a
attack *vb.*
napasti (P) 12A4; napadati (I)
attend (classes, school) *vb.* pohađati (I) 16A2b
attention *n.* pažnja 20.III
attorney *n.* advokat [B,S] odvjetnik [B,C]
5A3
attract *vb.*
privući (P); privlačiti (I) B.V
attractive *adj.* atraktivan 16A3b
audible *adj.* čujan B.VII
August *n.* avgust [B,S] kolovoz [C] 6A2
aunt (mother or father's sister) *n.* tetka ↦4

5A3, 5A3

aunt (father's brother's wife) *n.* amidžinica [B] strina [B,C,S] 5A3, 5A3

aunt (mother's brother's wife) *n.* daidžinica [B] ujna [B,C,S] 5A3, 5A3

Australian *n.* Australac [C] Australijanac [B,S] *(m., general)* Australijanka [B,S] Australka [C] *(f.)* 1A4

Austria *n.* Austrija 1😊

Austrian *adj.* austrijski 9A1

Austro-Hungarian *adj.* austrougarski 18A3

Austria-Hungary *n.* Austro-Ugarska 18A3

author *n.* autor *(m., general)* autorica [B,C,S] autorka [S] *(f.)* 19A2b

authority *n.* vlast 18A3

autumn *n.* jesen 3A2

in the autumn na jesen 9A3

autumnal *adj.* jesenski [C] jesenji [B,S] 14A4

average *adj.* prosečan [E] prosječan [J] 12A1

avoid *vb.* okaniti se (P) 📖B.IV

awaken *vb.*
 buditi (I); probuditi (P) 9A2
 see also **wake up**

aware *adj.* svestan [E] svjestan [J] 📖B.IV

away from od ↦5

awful *adv.* grozno 3A1

awkward *adj.* nezgodan 📖B.II

Axis (powers) *n.* Osovina 12A4

B

bachelor *n.* samac 18A1a

back *adv.* natrag 14A2

back (= body part) *n.* leđa 10A4

bad *adj.* loš [B,C,S] ↦4 2A2, 2A2, 3A1😊, 11A1😊, rđav [S] 2A2, 2A2

badly *adv.* loše [B,C,S] 3A1😊, rđavo [S]

bag *n.* torba 6A1

baker *n.* pekar 11A2😊

balance *n.* ravnoteža 19A2b

Balkans *n.* Balkan

Balkan *adj.* balkanski 8A3

ball *n.* lopta 5C1

ban *n.* zabrana 18A3

bank *n.* banka 5A2

bar (= tavern) *n.* lokal 12A2

bar (= counter) *n.* šank 12A2

barber *n.* berberin [S] brijač [B,C] 11A2😊

barely *adv.* jedva 📖B.VI

bark (of a tree) *n.* kora 19A1b

barren *adj.* pust 17C1

basic *adj.* osnovni 10A3

basis *n.* osnov [B,S] osnova [B,C,S] 16A3b

basketball (= game) *n.* košarka

basketball *adj.* košarkaški 12A2

bat (mammal) *n.* slepi miš [E] slijepi miš [J],

šišmiš [B,C,S]

bathroom *n.* kupaonica [C] kupatilo [B,S] 16A1b

be *vb.* biti (I/P) ↦6 1A1😊, 1A2😊, 5A3😊
 clitics: sam, si, je, smo, ste, su (I) 1A1
 full: jesam, jesi, jest [B,C] jeste [B,S], jesmo, jeste, jesu (I) 1A4
 negated: nisam, nisi, nije, nismo, niste, nisu (I) 1A4
 negated (Montenegrin) nijesam, nijesi, nije, nijesmo, nijeste, nijesu 19A3b
 past tense: bio, bilo, bila, bili, bila, bile 6A2
 aorist bih, bi, bi, bismo, biste, biše 12A4😊, 17A2a
 imperfect bejah, bejaše bejaše, bejasmo, bejaste, bejahu [E] 12A4😊, 17A2a, bijah, bijaše bijaše, bijasmo, bijaste, bijahu [J] 12A4😊, 17A2a

be *vb.* ↦6 5A3, 12A3😊
 budem, budeš, bude, budemo, budete, budu (P)

be *vb.* bivati (I) 18A1a

be able *vb.* moći, umeti [E] umjeti [J] ↦6
 see also **know how**

be in touch *vb.* čuti se (I/P) 8A3, javiti se (P); javljati se (I) 8A3

beach *n.* plaža 16A3a

beans *n.* grah [B,C] pasulj [S]

bear *n.* medved [E] medvjed [J] 2A3

beast *n.* zver [E] zvijer [J] 17A1a

beat (= strike *or* win) *vb.* tući (I) 8😊

beautiful *adj.* lep [E] lijep [J] 2A2

beautiful girl *or* **woman** *n.* lepotica [E] ljepotica [J] 17A1a

because *conj.* jer 4A2, zato što 2A3, zbog toga što ↦5 10A3, 13A4😊
 because of *prep.* zbog 10A3, 13A4😊, radi 7A2

become *vb.*
 postati (P) 18A3; postajati (I)

bed *n.* krevet 12A1, ležaj 20.IV, postelja 19A3a

bedding *n.* posteljina 12A1

bedroom *n.* spavaća soba 16A1b

bedside table *see under* **nightstand**

beef *n.* govedina

beer *n.* pivo 4A3

before (= earlier) *adv.* pre [E] prije [J] ↦5 13A2, 13A4😊, pred 7A2, 7A2😊, 8A4😊

before *prep.* pre [E] prije [J] 5A2, pred ↦5 7A2, 7A2😊, 8A4😊

before (= on the eve of) *prep.* uoči 18A3

before *conj.* pre nego što [E] prije nego što [J] 13A4😊 prije negoli 20.V

begin *vb.*
 početi (P) 13A2; počinjati (I) 6A2

beginning *n.* počẹtak 7A4
behave *vb.* ponašati se (I) 18A2b
behind *prep.* iza ↦5   8A4, za ↦5
   15A1, 7A2✿, 8A4✿
Belgrade *n.* Beograd 7☺, 9☺, 14☺ *see map*
Belgrade resident Beograđanin *(m., general)*
   16A3a Beograđanka *(f.)*
Belgrade *adj.* beogradskị 6A2
believe *vb.*
   verovati (I); poverovati (P) [E] 10A4,
   ⌞17A2b⌟
   vjerovati (I); povjerovati (P) [J] 10A4,
   ⌞17A2b⌟
bell *n.* zvono 17A3a
belly *n.*
   trbuh [B,C] stomak [B,S] 10A4, ⌞10A4⌟
below *adv.*
   dole [E] dolje [J]
bench *n.* klụpa 📖A.III
bend over *vb.*
   sagnuti se (P); saginjati se (I) 20.VIII
beneath *prep.* ispod ↦5 8A4
beside *prep.* pored ↦5, kraj 13A4
besides *prep.* osim 8A3
besiege *vb.* opsednuti [E] opsjednuti [J] (P)
   11A1✿
best *adj.* najboljị 11A1✿
best *adv.* najbolje 5C1
best man *n.* kụm 📖B.VIII
betray *vb.*
   izdati (P); izdavati (I)
   odati (P); odavati (I) 20.I
better *adj.* bolji 11A2, 11A1✿
better *adv.* bolje 6A3, 6A3✿
   better and better sve bolje 15A1✿
between *prep.* između ↦5   4A4, među
   📖B.IV, 8A4✿
Bible *n.* Svẹto pịsmo 17C2, Bịblija
bicycle *n.* bicịkl 7A2, 7A2✿
big *adj.* vẹlik 2A2, 3A1✿, 4A4✿, 5A1✿,
   6A1✿, 11A1✿
bigger *adj.* vẹćị 11A1✿
billion *num.* milịjarda
bind *vb.* vẹzati (I) 📖B.IV
biologist *n.* biọlog 11A2✿
biology *n.* biọlogija 13B3
bird *n.* ptịca 5A1
bird (= bird's) *adj.* ptičịjị [B,S] ptičjị [C]
   5C1
birth (= process) *n.* rạđanje 📖B.VIII
birth (= fact) *n.* rọđenje
   by birth rodom 18A3a
birth year gọdište 12A3
birthday *n.* rọđendạn 12A3
black *adj.* crn 2A3
blackbird *n.* kọs

blackboard *n.* ploča *or* škọlskạ ploča [C]
   tạbla *or* škọlskạ tạbla [B,S] 4A4
blacken *vb.*
   crneti (I) [E]
   crnjeti (I) [J]
   turn black *vb.*
   crneti se (I) [E] 18A1a
   crnjeti se (I) [J] 18A1a
blanket *n.* ćebe [S] deka [B] pokrivač [C]
   12A1
blind *adj.* slẹp [E] slijẹp [J] 18A1a
blond *adj.* plạv
blonde (girl, woman) *n.* plạvuša 📖B.I
blood *n.* krv
blouse *n.* blụza 📖A.VIII
blow dry (hair) *vb.*
   isfenịrati (P); fenịrati (I) 📖B.V
blue *adj.* plạv 2A3
blush *vb.* zarumẹniti se (P) 📖B.IV
board (= piece of wood) *n.* dạska 📖A.VIII
boast *vb.* pohvạliti se (P) 15A1
boat *n.* brọd 7A2
body *n.* tẹlo [E] tijẹlo [J]
bohemian *adj.* boẹmskị 18A3
boil *vb.*
   kụhati (I) 6A4; skụhati (P) [B,C] 14A1
   kụvati (I) 6A4; skụvati (P) [S] 14A1
bon voyage
   srẹćan pụt [B,S] srẹtan pụt [B,C] 12A3
bone *n.* kọst 7A1
book *n.* knjịga ↦4   1A2
boot *n.* čịzma
border *n.* grạnica 3⊕
bore (someone) *vb.*
   dosạditi (P); dosạđịvati (I) 📖B.V
   be bored
   dosạditi se (P); dosạđịvati se (I)
boring *adj.* dọsadan 5A1, 6A2✿
born, be *vb.*
   rọditi se (P) 14A3; rạđati se (I)
borrow *vb.*
   posụditi (P) 16A1a; posụđịvati (I)
Bosnia and Herzegovina *n.*
   Bosna i Hercegovina 1⊕
Bosniak *n.*
   Bošnjạk *(m., general)* Bošnjakinja *(f.)* ⌞1A4⌟
Bosnian *adj.* bọsanskị 2⊕
Bosnian *n.* Bọsanac *(m., general)* Bọsanka *(f.)*
   1A4, ⌞1A4⌟
boss *n.* šef *(m., general)* šẹfica *(f.)* 11A2✿
both oba, obe [E] obje [J] 4A4, 4A2✿
bother *vb.* smẹtati (I) 11A4
bottle *n.* bọca
bottom *n.* dnọ 14A1
bouquet *n.* bụkẹt 📖A.IV
bow *vb.*

pokloniti (P); poklanjati (I)

bow (= knot with loops) *n.* mašna

bow tie *n.* leptir mašna

boy *n.* momak 4A1, dečak [E] dječak [J]
17A1a

boy *n.* (= young man) *n.* momak 4A1, 5A1✿,
8A1✿, mladić 8A1, momče 12A2✿

boy *n.* (= little boy) dečko 📖B.V, mali
B.VIII

bra *n.* grudnjak

branch *n.* grana 18A1a
branches *n. coll.* granje 12A2✿

brave *adj.* hrabar

bread *n.* hleb [E] hljeb [J] [B/S] kruh [B,C]
4A3

bread roll *n.* pecivo 5A1, pogačica 9☺

breakfast *n.* doručak 7A1

breath *n.* dah 20.VIII

briefly *adv.* kratko

bride *n.* mlada 📖B.VIII

bridegroom *n.* mladoženja 📖B.VIII

bridge *n.* most [B,C,S], ćuprija [B,S]

brigand *n.* hajduk 19A3a

bring *vb.*
doneti (P) 13A2; donositi (I) [E] 11A1✿
donijeti (P) 13A2; donositi (I) [J] 11A1✿

bring (by vehicle) *vb.*
dovesti (P); dovoditi (I) 20.III, 10A1✿

bristling *adj.* narogušen 10A3

brother *n.* brat 2A3, *pl* braća 8A2, 6A4✿,
8A2✿, braco *colloq.* B.VII

brown *adj.* smeđ

brush (*e.g.* hair) *vb.*
češljati (I); počešljati (P) 9A2

building *n.* zgrada 6A1

Bulgaria *n.* Bugarska 1🌐

bumble *vb.*
spetljati se (P); spetljavati se (I) 📖B.VI

burden *n.* teret 16A1a

burden *vb.*
opteretiti (P) 16A3b; opterećivati (I)

burglary *n.* obijanje 20.VII

burn *vb.* žariti (I) 18A2a,
goreti (I) [E]; gorjeti (I) [J]

burner (on stove) *n.* vatra 14A1

burst forth *vb.* granuti (P) 14A2

burst out *vb.*
prasnuti (P); praskati (I) 📖B.IV

bus *n.* autobus 7A2

bus *adj.*
autobuski [B,S] autobusni [C] 13A4, 9A3

business *adj.* poslovan 13A3

business trip *n.* službeni put 14A2

bustle *n.* vreva 20.I

busy *adj.* zauzet 11A1✿

but *conj.* ali 1A4, a 1A1, ma 7A3, no

15A1, nego 2A1, već 3A2

butcher *n.* kasapin [S] mesar [B,C,S]
11A2✿

butter *n.* maslac [B,C,S] puter [B,S] 7A1

butterfly *n.* leptir

button *n.* dugme [B,S] gumb [C] 📖A.VIII,
8A2✿

buy *vb.* kupiti (P); kupovati (I) ↦6 2A3,
2A3✿

by (= by means of) *use instrumental case* 7A2

by *prep.* kod ↦5 4A2✿, od ↦5 4A3,
4A4✿, 9A3✿, 11A2✿, do ↦5 4A4,
4A4✿, pri ↦5

by birth rodom 18A3a

by means of *adv.* putem 16A2a

by oneself sam 6A3, 6A3✿

C

cabbage *n.* kupus [B,C,S] zelje [C]

café *n.* kafić 12A2, kafana [B,S] kavana [C]
5A4

cake *n.* kolač 13A1

calculate *vb.* računati (I) 📖B.II

calf (= small cow) *n.* tele 8A2, 8A2✿

California *n.* Kalifornija 4A1

call *n.* zov 15A1

call (= give a name *or* by phone) *vb.*
zvati (I) 1A1, 1A1✿
nazvati (P) 17C1; nazivati (I) 19A1b,
pozvati (P) 13A1; pozivati (I)
be called *vb.* zvati se 1A1
my name is ... zovem se ... 1A1

calm *adj.* miran 8A2

camera *n.* foto-aparat 📖A.VI

can *vb.* moći (I) 2A4, 2A4✿, 10A2✿
see also **be able**

Canadian *n.* Kanađanin *(m., general)*
Kanađanka *(f.)* 1A4

cancel (= void) *vb.*
poništiti (P) 13A4; poništavati (I)

cancer *n.* rak 18A3

candy *n.* slatkiš 4A3,
bombon [B,C] bombona [B,S] 12A2

cap *n.* kapa 15A1

capability *n.* sposobnost 10A3

capital (of a country) *n.* glavni grad 2🌐

car *n.* auto 1A2, kola 7A2, 7A2✿
by car kolima 7A2

care *n.* nega [E] njega [J]
home care kućna nega [B,S] kućna
njega [C] 20.I

careful *adj.* pažljiv 14A1

carpenter *n.* stolar [B,C] tesar [B,S] 11A2✿

carrot *n.* mrkva [B,C] šargarepa [S]

carry *vb.* nositi (I) ↦5 5C1, 10A4✿

carry away *vb.*

òdnèti (P); odnòsiti (I) [E] 7A3
òdnijeti (P); odnòsiti (I) [J] 7A3
ìznèti (P) 19A3a; iznòsiti (I) [E]
ìznijeti (P) 19A3a; iznòsiti (I) [J]
carry out (= complete) *vb.*
   izvřšiti (P) 12A4; izvršávati (I)
   sprovèsti (P) 16A1a; sprovòditi (I)
   provèsti (P) 16A2a; provòditi (I)
cartoon *n.* crtàni film 7A3
case (= instance) *n.* slùčaj 14A3
case (grammatical) *n.* padež
cash register *n.* blàgajna [B,C] kàsa [S] 2A4
cat *n.* mačka 1A2
   tomcat *n.* mačak
catch *vb.* hvàtati (I) ùhvatiti (P)
catch sight of *vb.* ùgledati (P) 20.VIII,
   nàzreti (P) 19A2a; nàzirati (I)
catch up with *vb.* stići ↪6 9A4
Catholic *n.* katòlik (*m., general*) katolìkinja
   [S] katòlkinja [B,C] *(f.)*
Catholic church *n.* katòlička crkva
ceiling *n.* plàfon [B,S] strop [C] 8A4
ceiling *adj.* plàfonski [B,S] stropni [C] 8A4
celebrate *vb.*
   slàviti (I) 12A3; pròslaviti (P) 18A3
cello *n.* violončèlo 18A3
census *n.* pòpis stanovnìštva [B,S] pòpis
   pučànstva [C]
center *n.* centar 10A1
century *n.* stòljeće [B,C] 17A2a, vèk [E]
   vìjek [J] [B/S]
certain *adj.* sìguran 14A1✿
certainly *adv.* sìgurno 3A3, svàkako 2A4
chair *n.* stòlica 4A4
chamomile (flower *or* tea) *n.* kamìlica 📖A.II
chance (= opportunity) *n.* šansa 📖B.VI
change *n.* promèna [E] promjèna [J]
change *vb.*
   mènjati (I); promèniti (P) [E] 20.II
   mijènjati (I); promijèniti (P) [J] 20.II
chapter *n.* pòglavlje 10A2
character (*e.g.* in a narrative) *n.* lik 10A3,
   karàkter 19A1b
character (= nature) *n.* karàkter 19A1b
chat *vb.* popríčati (P) 📖B.VI, ćàskati (I)
   B.V, porazgovárati (P) 16A2b
cheat *vb.* vàrati (I) 14B2
cheer [someone] up *vb.*
   razvesèliti (P) 15A1; razveseljávati (I)
cheerful *adj.* vèseo 8A1
cheers! *excl.*
   žìveo! žìvela! žìveli! žìvele! [E] 📖B.VIII
   žìvio! žìvjela! žìvjeli! žìvjele! [J] 📖B.VIII
cheese *n.* sir 4A3
chemical *adj.* hèmijski [B,S] kèmijski [C]
   2A4

chemist *n.* hemìčar [B,S] kemìčar [C] (*m.,*
   general) hemìčarka [B,S] kemìčarka [C] *(f.)*
   11A2✿
chemistry *n.* hèmija [B,S] kèmija [C] 13B3
chess *n.* šah 9A2✿
chicken (= animal) *n.* kòkoš [B,C,S] kokòška
   [B,S]
chicken (= meat) *n.* pìletina
child *n.*
   dète [E] dijète [J] 8A2, 8A2✿
children *n.*
   dèca [E] djèca [J] 8A2, 8A2✿, 9A2✿
chilly *vb.* prohlàdan 17A3a
China *n.* Kìna
Chinese *adj.* kìneski 9A1
chirp *vb.* cvrkùtati (I) 16A1b
chocolate *n.* čokolàda
choose (= select) *vb.* bìrati (I) 📖A.VIII
   opredèliti (P) [E] 16A3b
   opredijèliti (P) [J] 16A3b
Christian *n.* hrìšćanin [B,S] kršćanin [C] (*m.,*
   general) hrìšćanka [B,S] kršćanka [C] *(f.)*
Christian *adj.*
   hrìšćanski [B,S] kršćanski [C] 19A3b
Christianity *n.*
   hrišćanstvo [B,S] kršćanstvo [C]
chronicle *n.*
   hrònika [B,S] krònika [C] 11A3
church *n.* crkva
cigarette *n.* cigarèta 20.V
cinammon *n.* cìmet 20.III
cinema *n.* bìoskop [S] kìno [B,C] 5A2,
   5A4✿, kìno-dvorana 16A1a
circle *n.* krug
circle *vb.*
   krùžiti (I) 6A1; zaokrùžiti (P) 6A1
circumstance *n.* okòlnost
citizen *n.* građanin (*m., general*) građànka *(f.),*
   državljanin (*m., general*) državljànka *(f.)*
city *n.* grad ↪4 3A3
city *adj.* gràdski 13A4
city block *n.* ùlica 13A4
city map *n.* plan gràda 11A3
claim *vb.* tvŕditi (I) 📖B.III
clarify *vb.*
   razjàsniti (P); razjašnjávati (I) 10A4
clash *vb.*
   sùkobiti se (P) 18A3; sukobljávati se (I)
class (*e.g.* in school) *n.* ràzred 5C1
class (= lesson) *n.* čas [B,S] sàt [C] 7A4
clean *vb.*
   čìstiti (I); pòčistiti (P) 15A1
clean *adj.* čist 9A2
clear *adj.* jasan 9A4
clear up (of weather, facial expression) *vb.*
   razvèdriti se (P); razvedrávati se (I) 14A2

clemency *n.* pomilovanje 19A2a

clerk *n.* činovnik, pisar *(m., general)*
  činovnica *(f.)* 11A2☼

cliff *n.* hrid 17A3a

climb up *vb.* popeti se (P) 14A1

clock *n.* sat 8A4

close *vb.*
  zatvoriti (P); zatvarati (I) 12A2

close *adj.* blizak 18A3

closer *adj.* bliži

closer *adv.* bliže

close to blizu ⊷5 4A4

closet (built-in) *n.* orman [B,S] ormar [B,C]

clothing *n.* odeća [E] odjeća [J] 20.VII

cloud *n.* oblak 10A3

clumsy *adj.* nevešt [E] nevješt [J] ⊞B.IV

coast *n.* obala 6⊕

coastal *adj.* obalni 16A2, primorski 16A3b

coastal area *n.* primorje 6⊕

coat *n.* kaput 7A3

coffee *n.* kafa [B,S] kahva [B] kava [C] 4A3,
  ⸤10A1⸥ 14A1

coffee cup (Turkish) *n.* fildžan 14A1

coffeepot (Turkish) *n.* džezva 14A1

coincidence *n.* slučajnost ⊞B.VII

cold *adj.* hladan 4A3

colleague
  kolega *(m., general)* 9A4, kolegica [B,C]
  koleginica [B,S] *(f.)* 13A4

collect *vb.*
  prikupiti (P) 19A3b; prikupljati (I)
  sabrati (P); sabirati (I) 20.V
  sakupiti (P); sakupljati (I) [B,S] 19A3b
  skupiti (P) ⊞B.VI; skupljati (I) [B,C,S]
  ⊞A.I

collection *n.* zbirka 17A4

college *n.* koledž 6A2

collide *vb.*
  sudariti se (P); sudarati se (I) ⊞B.V

color *n.* boja 2A3

colorful *adj.* šaren 5A1

comb *vb.* češljati (I); počešljati (P) 9A2

come *vb.*
  doći (P) ⊷6; dolaziti (I) 5A2, 5A2☼,
  10A2☼

come back *vb.* vraćati se (I) 14A2; vratiti se
  (P) 9A2, 10A1☼

come close *vb.* bližiti (I) ⊞B.IV

come on! *excl.* hajde 7A3

come upon *vb.*
  naići na (P) 14A2; nailaziti na (I)

comfortable *adj.* komotan 16A1a, udoban
  11A2, ugodan 7A2, 11A2☼

comma *n.* zarez

commentary *n.* komentar ⊞B.III

commercial *adj.* poslovan 13A3

communication *n.* komunikacija ⊞B.VIII

communist *n.* komunist [C] komunista [B,S]
  18A3

community *n.* zajednica ⸤14B2⸥

company (= business) *n.* poduzeće [B,C]
  preduzeće [B,S] 11A4

company (= friends) *n.* društvo 10A1

compare *vb.*
  uporediti (P) 11A2; uporedivati (I) [B,S]
  usporediti (P) 11A2; uspoređivati (I) [C]

comparison *n.* poređenje [B,S] usporedba [C]
  11A2

complain *vb.*
  jadati se (I); izjadati se (P) 15A1

complete *adj.* celovit [E] cjelovit [J] 19A1b,
  kompletan ⊞B.III, potpun

completely *adv.* posve 14A4, sasvim 11A2,
  potpuno

complex *adj.* složen 19A1b

compose (= formulate) *vb.* sročiti (P) 16A1a

compose (*e.g.* verse or song) *vb.*
  spevati (P) [E] 19A3b
  spjevati (P) [J] 19A3b

composer *n.* kompozitor [B,S] skladatelj [C]
  (m., general) kompozitorka [B,S]
  skladateljica [C] *(f.)* 11A2☼

composition *n.* sastav ⊞B.II

computer *n.*
  kompjuter [B,S] kompjutor [C] 7A4

comrade *n.*
  drug *(m., general)* drugarica *(f.)* 1A4

concept (= notion) *n.* pojam 13A3
  I have no idea nemam pojma 13A3

concept (= plan) *n.* zamisao 19A1b

concern *n.* zabrinutost 14A4

concern *vb.* ticati se (I) 5A2, 5A2☼, 6A3☼

concerning o ⊷5, 6A2

concert *n.* koncert 6A2☼

conciliatory *adj.* pomirljiv 20.IV

conclude *vb.*
  zaključiti (P); zaključivati (I) 10A3

conclusion *n.* zaključak 17A2b

condition (= situation) *n.* stanje 14A3

condition (= prerequisite) *n.*
  uslov [B,S] uvjet [B,C] 14A2

confirmation *n.* potvrda 16A2b

confluence *n.* ušće 3⊕

confuse *vb.*
  zbuniti (P); zbunjivati (I) ⊞B.VII

confused *adj.* smeten ⊞B.VI

congratulate *vb.* čestitati (I) 12A3

conjunction (grammar) *n.* veznik 17A1b

conjure up *vb.*
  dočarati (P); dočaravati (I) 17A3b

connect *vb.*
  povezati (P) ⊞B.IV; povezivati (I) 16A1b

spojiti (P) 📖B.VIII; spajati (I) 18A3
connected *adj.* povezan 📖B.IV
connection *n.* sveza [C] veza [B,C,S] 13A2
conscience *n.* svest [E] svijest [J]
conscious *adj.* svestan [E] svjestan [J] 📖B.IV
consider (= think, deliberate) *vb.*
    razmisliti (P) 10A3; razmišljati (I) 8A3
consider (= regard to be) *vb.* smatrati (I)
    11A3✿
considerable *adj.* popriličan 16A2b, priličan
    20.IV, znatan 14A2
consideration *n.* obzir 16A2a
consist (of) *vb.* sastojati se (iz) (I) 4✪
conspiratorial *adj.*
    zaverenički [E] zavjerenički [J] 📖B.VI
contact *n.* javljanje 16A3b, kontakt 📖B.IV
contact *vb.*
    javiti se (P); javljati se (I) 8A3
contain *vb.*
    sadržati (P) 19A1b; sadržavati (I)
contemporary *adj.*
    savremen [B,S] suvremen [C]
contest *n.* nagradna igra 📖B.II
continue *vb.*
    nastaviti (P) 14A2; nastavljati (I) 📖A.III
contribute *vb.*
    pridoneti (P) 16A2b; pridonositi (I) [E]
    pridonijeti (P) 16A2b; pridonositi (I) [J]
convalescence *n.* oporavak 20.I
conversation *n.* razgovor 12A2
conversational *adj.* konverzacijski [B,C]
    konverzacioni [B,S] 16A3b, razgovorni
converse *vb.* razgovarati (I) 12A2
converse briefly *vb.* porazgovarati (I) 16A2b
convince *vb.*
    ubediti (P) 📖B.VI; ubeđivati (I) [E]
    ubijediti (P) 📖B.VI; ubjeđivati (I) [J] [B/S]
    uveriti (P); uveravati (I) [E] 16A3b
    uvjeriti (P); uvjeravati (I) [J] 16A3b
cook *n.* kuhar [B,C] kuvar [S] *(m., general)*
    kuharica [B,C] kuvarica [S] *(f.)* 11A2✿
cook *vb.*
    kuhati (I) 6A4; skuhati (P) [B,C] 14A1
    kuvati (I) 6A4; skuvati (P) [S] 14A1
cookie *n.* keks 4A3
cool *adj.* prohladan 17A3a, svež [E] svjež [J]
cool off *vb.*
    rashladiti (P) 16A3b; rashlađivati (I)
cooperation *n.*
    saradnja [B,S] suradnja [C] 18A3
copy (= edition) *n.*
    primerak [E] primjerak [J] 13A3
copy *vb.*
    prepisati (P); prepisivati (I) 20.IV
corn *n.* kukuruz
corner *n.* ugao

corresponding *adj.* odgovarajući 16A2a,
    12A1✿
corridor *n.* hodnik 13A1
cost *vb.* koštati (I) 16A3a
country *n.* zemlja 6A1
couple (= pair of men) *n.* dvojica 12A2
couple (= pair of mixed gender) *n.* dvoje
    12A2
courage *n.* hrabrost 📖B.VI
    muster courage *vb.* odvažiti se (P) 16A3a
course (*e.g.* language) *n.*
    tečaj [B,C,S] kurs [B,S] 16A2b
course (= flow) *n.*
    tijek [C] tok [B,S] 📖B.IV
court (of law) *n.* sud 6A1✿, **in court** na sudu
    6A1✿
court (royal) *n.* dvor 📖B.V
court (= courtyard) *n.* dvor
cousin *n.* brat, [B,S] bratić [C], sestra [B,S]
    sestrična [C]
cowardice *n.* kukavičluk
crab *n.* rak
cracker *n.* kreker 4A3
crazier *adj.* luđi
crazy *adj.* lud 📖B.V
create *vb.*
    stvoriti (P) 17A4; stvarati (I) 3✪
creature *n.* stvor 📖B.VI
crew *n.* ekipa 16A1a
criticism *n.* kritika 18A3
Croat *n.*
    Hrvat *(m., general)* Hrvatica *(f.)* 1A4
Croatia *n.* Hrvatska 1✪
Croatian *adj.* hrvatski 2✪
cross *vb.*
    preći (P); prelaziti (I) [B,C,S] 19A1a
    prijeći (P); prelaziti (I) [C] 19A1a
crosswalk *n.* prelaz [B,C,S] prijelaz [C],
    zebra
crow *n.* vrana 18A1a
crowd (= a large amount of people) *n.* gužva
    [B,C,S] 📖B.IV
crowd (= friends to hang out with) *n.* društvo
    10A1, 10A1✿, raja [B] 📖B.VII
crowded *adj.* krcat 16A1a
crucify *vb.*
    raspeti (P) 17A3a; raspinjati (I)
cry *vb.* (= weep) plakati (I) 18A2a
cuckoo *n.* kukavica
culprit *n.* krivac 20.II
cultural *adj.* kulturan 19A3b
culture *n.* kultura 18A3
cup *n.*
    šalica [B,C] šolja [B,S] 14A1
cupboard *n.*
    orman [B,S] ormar [B,C]

curl up *vb.* skupiti se (P) 20.V

currency *n.* euro [B,C] evro [B,S] *(Europe)* 12B5 , evro *(Montenegrin)*, konvertabilna marka *(Bosnian)*, kuna *(Croatian)* 12A2☼, srpski dinar *(Serbian)*

curtain *n.* zastor [C], zavesa [E] zavjesa [J] [B,C,S] 20.I

curved *adj.* kriv

custom *n.* običaj 12A3

customary *adj.* uobičajen 16A3a

customer *n.* mušterija 13A2

cute *adj.* ljubak 15A1

cycle *n.* ciklus 19A1b

Cyrillic *n.* ćirilica

Czech *n.* Čeh *(m., general)* Čehinja *(f.)*

D

Dad *n.* tata 9A4

daily *adj.* dnevni 12A1

Dalmatia *n.* Dalmacija *see map* 6☺

Dalmatian *adj.* dalmatinski 8A3

damage *n.* šteta 13A3, kvar

damp *adj.* vlažan 20.VIII

dance *n.*
igra [B,S] ples [B,C] 15A1, 15A1☼

dance *vb.*
igrati (I) [B,S] 15A1
plesati (I) [B,C] 15A1

dancer *n.* igrač [B,S] plesač [B,C] *(m., general)* igračica [B,S] plesačica [B,C] *(f.)* 11A2☼

dangerous *adj.* opasan 7A2

Danube *n.* Dunav 7☺

dare *vb.*
smeti (I) [E] 12A3, 12A3☼
smjeti (I) [J] 12A3, 12A3☼

dark *adj.* mračan 18A1a, taman 18A1a

darkness *n.* mrak 14A2, tama 17A4

date *(e.g. on calendar) n.* datum 20.VIII

dative *(case) n.* dativ

datum, data *n.* podatak 16A3

daughter *n.* ćerka [S] kćerka [B,C] 8A1, kći [B,C,S] ↦4 8A1

day *n.* dan ↦4 1A3
day after tomorrow prekosutra 20.IV
day before yesterday prekjuče [B,S] prekjučer [C] 5A2
for days danima
on the next day idućeg dana [B,C,S] narednog dana [S] sledećeg dana [E] sljedećeg dana [J]
(to) this very day dan danas 18A3
all day ceo dan [E] cijeli dan [J] 7A4

dead *adj.* mrtav

deadline *n.* rok 9A1

deaf *adj.* gluh [B,C] gluv [S] 18A1a

deafer *adj.* gluši [B,C] gluvlji [S] 18A1a

dear *adj.* drag 2A2, mio

Dear *adj.* (opening to letter) poštovani 19A2

death *n.* smrt 17A2a

deathbed *n.* samrt 18A3

deceive *vb.* prevariti (P) 15A1

December *n.*
decembar [B,S] prosinac [C] 6A2

decide *vb.* odlučiti (P) 12A3; odlučivati (I)

decisive *adj.* presudan 19A3b

decorate *vb.*
kititi (I); nakititi (P) 19A3a, ukrasiti (P); ukrašavati (I)

dedicate *vb.*
posvetiti (P); posvećivati (I) 16A2a

dedication *n.* posveta 20.VIII

defense *n.* obrana [C] odbrana [B,S]

defend *vb.* braniti (I)

definitely *adv.* itekako 13A4

degree (= gradation) *n.* stepen [B,S] stupanj [C] 16A3a

delay *n.* zakašnjenje 14A4

delight *vb.*
radovati (I); obradovati (P) 16A1b, razveseliti 15A1

dentist *n.*
zubar *(m., general)* zubarica *(f.)* 11A2☼

dentistry *n.* stomatologija 13B3

deny *vb.* poricati (I) 📖B.V; poreći (P)

department (in university) *n.* fakultet 5A2, 5A2 , katedra 16A2b, odsek [E] odsjek [J] 16A1a

dependent (on) *adj.* zavisan (od) [B,S] ovisan (o) 16A3b

depth *n.* dubina 15A1

descend *vb.* sići (P) 13A4; silaziti (I)

describe *vb.* opisati (P); opisivati (I) 10A3

designate *vb.*
označiti (P); označavati (I) 17A1b

desire *n.* želja 14A1

desk *n.* pisaći sto [B,S] pisaći stol [C]

despair *n.* očaj 20.III

despairing *adj.* očajan 14A2

despite *prep.* uprkos 16A3b

dessert *n.* poslastica [B,S] slastica [C] 11A2

destined *adj.* suđen 20.VI

detail *n.* pojedinost 📖B.VI

determine *vb.*
odrediti (P) 18A1b; određivati (I)

development *n.* razvoj

devise *vb.*
smisliti (P) 16A1a; smišljati (I)

dictionary *n.* rečnik [E] rječnik [J] 2A1

die *vb.*
umreti (P) [E] 17A1a
umrijeti (P) [J] 17A1a

be dying *vb.* umirati (I) 18A1b
diet *n.* dijeta 20.VI
difference *n.* razlika 16A1b
different *adj.* različit 11A2
difficult *adj.* težak 2A2
digital *adj.* digitalni 19A3b
dignity *n.* dostojanstvo 20.I
diligent *adj.* vredan [E] vrijedan [J] 8A1
dining room *n.*
  blagovaonica [C] trpezarija [B,S] 16A1b
dinner (= midday meal) *n.* ručak 5A2
dinner (= evening meal) *n.* večera 5A2
direct (= give directions) *vb.*
  uputiti (P) 16A2a; upućivati (I)
direct *adj.*
    izravan [C] neposredan [B,C,S] 16A2b
director (of an enterprise) *n.* direktor [B,C,S]
  ravnatelj [C] *(m., general)* direktorica
  [B,C,S] ravnateljica [C] *(f.)* 11A2✿
director (of a film or theater) *n.* režiser 15A1
dirty *adj.* prljav 9A2
disappear *vb.*
  nestati (P) 14A4; nestajati (I) 19A1a
disappearance *n.* nestanak 17A4
disappoint *vb.*
    razočarati (P); razočaravati (I)
  be disappointed *vb.*
    razočarati se (P); razočaravati se (I) 20.V
discipline *n.* disciplina 📖B.III
disclose *vb.*
  razotkriti (P) 17A3b; razotkrivati (I)
discover *vb.*
  otkriti (P) 20.VI; otkrivati (I)
  pronaći (P) 14A3; pronalaziti (I), 11A1✿
discreet *adj.* diskretan 📖B.VI
discussion *n.* diskusija 19A2b, rasprava
  11A1
dish (*e.g.* plate, bowl) *n.* sud 12A2
  dishes *n.* posuđe [B,C] sudovi [S] 12A2
dish (on a menu) *n.* jelo 6A4
  side dish *n.* prilog
dishtowel *n.* krpa 📖A.VI
disk *n.* disk 19A3b
dismiss (with the wave of a hand) *vb.*
  odmahnuti (P); odmahivati (I) 20.VI
disperse *vb.*
  razići se (P) 14A2; razilaziti se (I)
display window *n.* izlog 12A2
distance *n.* daljina 15A1
distant (in time) *adj.* davni 17A2b
distinguish *vb.* razlikovati (I) 18A2b
divine *adj.* božji 17C1
do (= accomplish) *vb.*
  raditi (I) 2A1
  učiniti (P) 19A3a
  izvršiti (P) 12A4

praviti (P) 20.III
do (= be engaged in) *vb.*
  baviti se (I) 11A3, 11A3✿
  zanimati se (I) 16A2b
  raditi (I) 2A1 9A2✿, 10A2✿
doctor *n.*
  lekar [E] ljekar [J] [B/S] liječnik [C]
    (m., general) 11A2✿
  lekarka [E] ljekarka [J] [B/S] 5A3
  liječnica [C]
  doktor [B,C,S] *(m.,general)* 11A3
  doktorica [B,C] doktorka [S] 11A3 *(f.)*
documentary film dokumentarac 7A3
dog *n.* pas 1A2
doll *n.* lutka 9A2✿
domestic *adj.* domaći 1A4, kućni 20.I
don (= put on) *vb.*
  odenuti se (P); odevati se (I) [E] 📖B.I
  odenuti se (P); odijevati se (I) [J] 📖B.I
donkey *n.* magarac
don't nemoj 7A2, 7A2✿
door *n.* vrata 6A1, 6A1✿
dormitory *n.* studentski dom 7A4
double *adj.* dvostruk 15A1
doubt *vb.*
  sumnjati (I); posumnjati (P) 10A3
dough *n.* testo [E] tijesto [J]
dove *n.* golub
downstream *adv.* nizvodno 20.VIII
down *adv.* dole [E] dolje [J]
down from *prep.* s, sa ⤳5
drag *vb.* vući (I)
dramatic *adj.* dramski 13B3
dramatic arts dramske umetnosti [E] dramske
  umjetnosti [J] 13B3
draw *vb.*
  crtati (I); nacrtati (P) 18A1b
draw in *v.* uvući (P); uvlačiti (I) 📖A.VIII
drawing *n.* crtanje 10A3, 10A4✿, 11A3✿
draw out *vb.* izvući (P) 20.V, 11A1✿;
  izvlačiti (I)
dream *n.* san 17A3a
dream *vb.*
  sanjati (I) 9A1, snivati (I) 18A1a
dress *n.* haljina 11A1
dress *vb.*
  obući (P); oblačiti (I) 📖A.VIII 9A2✿
  get dressed *vb.*
  obući se (P); oblačiti se (I)
drier *adj.* suši
drink *vb.* piti (I) ⤳4 5A1, 2A1✿, 5A4✿
  drink to the last drop *vb.* iskapiti (P)
  📖B.VIII, popiti (P) 5A4, 5A4✿, 11A1✿
drink *n.* piće 📖B.VII, 10A1
drink to the last drop *vb.*
drip *vb.* kapati (I) 14☺

drive (a vehicle) *vb.* voziti (I) 7A2, 7A2✿
drive (= not walk) *vb.* voziti se (I) 7A2
drive away *vb.* odvesti (P); odvoziti (I)
   7A3✿, 10A4✿, 11A1✿
driver *n.* vozač 7A2, 11A2✿
driver's license *n.* vozačka dozvola 11A3
drizzle *vb.* rositi (I) 14☺
drop in *vb.*
   navratiti (P) 12A2; navraćati (I)
dry *adj.* suh [B,C] suv [S] 18A1a
duck *n.* patka
due to zbog ↪5 10A3, 13A3✿
duet *n.* duet 15A1
duke *n.* herceg ⌐18C5⌐
duration *n.* trajanje 16A3a
during *prep.* tijekom [C] tokom [B,S] 16A2a,
   za vreme [E] za vrijeme [J] 5C1
dusk *n.* suton 18A1a
dwelling place *n.* boravište 17A2a

E

each (*e.g.* they each bought an ice cream kupili
   su po jedan sladoled) po ↪5 5A1, 5A1✿
each other *use "se" with verb* 15A2✿, jedan
   drugi 11A2✿, 15A2✿, ⌐16B1⌐
eagle *n.* orao
ear *n.* uho [B,C,S] uvo [S] 10A3, 10A4✿
early *adv.* rano 7A4, 9A2✿
earn *vb.*
   zaraditi (P); zarađivati (I) 11A3
earth *n.* zemlja 6A1
east *n.* istok 6🌐
east (= eastern) *adj.* istočni
easy *adj.*
   lak [B,C,S] lahak [B] 2A2, ⌐2A2⌐, 11A1✿
eat *vb* ↪6.
   jesti (I) 5A1; pojesti (P) 5A4, 5A4✿,
   6A2✿, 9A2✿, 10A2✿, 11A1✿
     eat breakfast doručkovati (I/P) 7A1
     eat lunch, dine ručati 7A3✿
     eat supper večerati (I/P) 10A1
economics *n.* ekonomija 13B3
economy *n.* privreda [B,S] gospodarstvo [B,C]
edge *n.* rub 20.IV
edition *n.* izdanje [B,C,S] naklada [C] 20.V
effort *n.* trud 16A2a
egg *n.* jaje ↪4 7A1, 8A2✿
   egg sunnyside up jaje na oko 7A1
   scrambled eggs kajgana 7A1
eight (8) *num.* osam 12A1✿
eight hundred (800) *num.* osamsto 12A1✿
eight-year *adj.* osmogodišnji 20.III
eighteen (18) *num.* osamnaest 5A1, 12A1✿
eighteenth (18th) *adj.* osamnaesti 18A1
eighth (8th) *adj.* osmi 8A1, 6A2✿, 12A1✿
eighth (1/8) *n.* osmina 12A1✿

eighty (80) *num.* osamdeset 5A1
either ... or *conj.* ili ... ili 1A3
   not either *conj.* ni 7A1
ekavian *n.* ekavica 15A1
elbow *n.* lakat 10A4
electrician *n.* električar *(m., general)* električarka *(f.)* 11A2✿
elegant *adj.* elegantan 11A1
elephant *n.* slon
eleven (11) *num.* jedanaest 5A2, 12A1✿
eleventh *adj.* jedanaesti 11A1, 6A2✿
else *adv.* drugo 13A1
embassy *n.* ambasada [B,S] veleposlanstvo [C]
embrace *vb.* grliti (I); zagrliti (P) 16A1b
emperor *n.* car 19A2b
emphasize *vb.*
   istaći [istaknuti] (P); isticati (I) 📖B.III
employee *n.* radnik *(m., general)* 11A3 radnica *(f.)*
employment *n.* zapošljavanje 11A4
   employment service *n.* služba za
     zapošljavanje 11A4
empty *adj.* prazan 13A1
encourage *vb.*
   podstaći [podstaknuti] (P) 19A3b
   podsticati (I)
end *n.* kraj [B,C,S] 7A4, završetak [B,C,S]
   20.VIII, konac [B,C] 16A2a
end *vb.* završiti se (P); završavati se (I) 6A2
endure *vb.* izdržati (P); izdržavati (I) 20.V
engineer *n.* inženjer 11A3
engineering, electrical *n.* elektrotehnika
   13B3, ⌐5A2⌐
engineering, mechanical *n.* mašinstvo [B,S]
   strojarstvo [C] 13B3
England *n.* Engleska 4A1
English *adj.* engleski 4A1
English studies *n.* anglistika 13B3
Englishman *n.* Englez 1A4
Englishwoman *n.* Engleskinja 1A4
enjoy *vb.* uživati (I) 12A2
enough *adv.* dosta 10A4
enormous *adj.* golem 19A3a
enter *vb.*
   ući (P) 12A2; ulaziti (I) 📖B.V, 15A2✿
enter (into a document, book) *vb.*
   uneti (P); unositi (I) [E] 15A2
   unijeti (P); unositi (I) [J] 15A2
entire *adj.* celokupan [E] cjelokupan [J] 20.V
envelope *n.* koverta [B,S] kuverta [C], koverat
   [B,S], omotnica [C]
environment *n.* okolina 16A3a
envy *n.* zavist 20.III
epic *adj.* epski 19A3b
epoch *n.* doba 17A3b, epoha 6A2,
   vek [E] vijek [J] 19A3b

equate *vb.*
  izjedn<u>a</u>čiti (P); izjednač<u>i</u>vati (I)
  be equal *vb.*
  izjedn<u>a</u>čiti se (P); izjednač<u>i</u>vati se (I)
  17A2a
equipment *n.* oprema 14A1, pr<u>i</u>bor 20.V
erase *vb.* brisati (I); <u>i</u>zbrisati (P) 10A3
eraser *n.* g<u>u</u>ma 10A3
error *n.* greška 📖B.III
escape *n.* b<u>e</u>g [E] bij<u>e</u>g [J] 20.VI
escort (= action or followers) *n.* pr<u>a</u>tnja 20.VII
escort (= individual) *n.* pratilac ↦4
especially *adv.* n<u>a</u>ročito 10A4
essay *n.* es<u>e</u>j 18A3
essential *adj.* bitan 📖B.VIII
establish *vb.* utvr<u>d</u>iti (P) 14A3; utvrđ<u>i</u>vati (I)
esteem *n.* poštov<u>a</u>nje 16A2a
esteemed *adj.* poštov<u>a</u>n 16A2a
etc. *abbr.* itd. 16A1a
eternal *adj.* večan [E] vječan [J] 17A2a
eternity *n.* večn<u>o</u>st [E] vječn<u>o</u>st [J] 17A2a
ethnology *n.* etnol<u>o</u>gija 16A2b
euro (currency) *n.* euro [B,C] evro [B.S]
Europe *n.* Eur<u>o</u>pa [B,C] Evr<u>o</u>pa [B,S] 4A1
evaluate *vb.*
  oc<u>e</u>niti (P); ocenj<u>i</u>vati (I) [E] 10A3
  ocij<u>e</u>niti (P); ocjenj<u>i</u>vati (I) [J] 10A3
even *adj.* r<u>a</u>van 13A4
even *adv.* čak 4A2
evening *n.* več<u>e</u> [B,S] več<u>e</u>r [C] 3A2
  in the evening naveč<u>e</u> [B] naveč<u>e</u>r [C]
  uveč<u>e</u> [S] 5A4
  this evening več<u>e</u>ras 3A1
event *n.* dog<u>a</u>đaj 16A3b
-ever *adv.* -god ¦ 18A3a ¦
ever *adv.* ikada 📖B.IV
  not ever *adv.* nikada
ever since *conj.* <u>o</u>tkada 📖B.VIII
every *adj.* svak<u>i</u> 6A4
everyday *adj.* svakodn<u>e</u>van 📖B.III
everyday life *n.* svak<u>i</u>dašnjica 20.III
everyone *n.* svi 12A2, 15A2⚙
everything *n.* sve 2A3, 15A2⚙
evil *adj.* zao 5A1
evil *n.* zlo
exam, examination (= test in school) *n.* <u>i</u>spit
  6A2, ¦ 10A2 ¦
exam, examination (medical) *n.* pr<u>e</u>gled 20.IV
exam *adj.* <u>i</u>spitni 9A1
examine (= test, interrogate) *vb.* isp<u>i</u>tati (P);
  ispit<u>i</u>vati (I) 20.VII
examine(= evaluate, esp. medically) *vb.*
  pr<u>e</u>gledati (P); pregl<u>e</u>dati (I) 11A1⚙
example *n.* pr<u>i</u>mer [E] pr<u>i</u>mjer [J] 17C1
excellent *adj.* izvrstan 10A1, odl<u>i</u>čan
excellent *adv.* odl<u>i</u>čno 2A4, <u>i</u>zvrsno 📖B.II

except *prep.* osim [B,C,S] 8A3 sem [S]
exceptional *adj.*
  izn<u>i</u>man [C] izuz<u>e</u>tan [B,C,S] 16A2b
excessively *adv.* suviše 16A3a
excitement *n.* uzbuđ<u>e</u>nje 15A2
exciting *adj.* uzbudljiv
exclamation point *n.* <u>u</u>skličnik [B,C] uzvićnik
  [B,S]
exclude *vb.*
  izuz<u>e</u>ti (P); izuz<u>i</u>mati (I) 20.VI
excrement *n.* g<u>o</u>vno (*vulg.*), <u>i</u>zmet
excursion *n.* <u>i</u>zlet 14A4
excuse me izv<u>i</u>ni, izv<u>i</u>nite [B,S] opr<u>o</u>sti,
  opr<u>o</u>stite [C] 2A1⚙
exempt *vb.*
  izuz<u>e</u>ti (P); izuz<u>i</u>mati (I) 20.VI
exercise *n.* vežba [E] vježba [J] 1A4
exercise *vb.*
  vežbati (I) [E] 2A1
  vježbati (I) [J] 2A1
exist *vb.* p<u>o</u>stati (P) 18A3; p<u>o</u>stajati (I)
existence *n.* p<u>o</u>stojanje 17A4
existing *adj.* p<u>o</u>stoj<u>e</u>ći 19A1b
exit (= way out) *n.* <u>i</u>zlaz
exit (= departure) *n.* <u>i</u>zlazak 20.III
expand *vb.*
  pr<u>o</u>širiti (P); prošir<u>i</u>vati (I) 📖B.III
expect *vb.* oček<u>i</u>vati (I) 14A4
expectation *n.* oček<u>i</u>vanje
expense(s) *n.* trošak 9A3
expensive *adj.* sk<u>u</u>p 7A2
experience *vb.*
  dož<u>i</u>veti (P); doživlj<u>a</u>vati (I) [E] 📖B.IV
  dož<u>i</u>vjeti (P); doživlj<u>a</u>vati (I) [J] 📖B.IV
expert *n.* stručnjak 16A2a
explain *vb.*
  objasniti (P) 10A3; objašnj<u>a</u>vati (I) 10A4⚙
explanation *n.* objašnj<u>e</u>nje 20.VIII, 10A4⚙
explore (= investigate) *vb.*
  istr<u>a</u>žiti (P) 16A2b; istraž<u>i</u>vati (I) 15A2
express *vb.*
  izr<u>a</u>ziti (P) 19A1b; izraž<u>a</u>vati (I)
expression *n.* izr<u>a</u>z 15A2
exquisite *adj.* prel<u>e</u>p [E] prelij<u>e</u>p [J] 📖B.IV
extend (= offer) *vb.*
  pr<u>u</u>žiti (P) 12A2; pr<u>u</u>žati (I)
extend (= make longer) *vb.*
  prod<u>u</u>žiti (P); produž<u>a</u>vati (I)
external *adj.* vanjsk<u>i</u>
extinguish *vb.*
  g<u>a</u>siti (I); ug<u>a</u>siti (P) 20.V
  trnuti (I); utrnuti (P) 17A3a
extricate (oneself) *vb.*
  <u>i</u>zvući se (P); izvl<u>a</u>čiti se (I) 20.II
eye *n.* oko 10A3, 10A4⚙
eyebrow *n.* obrva 10A4

eyelid *n.* veđa [E] vjeđa [J] 18A2a

F

fabricate *vb.* izmisliti (P); izmišljati (I) 20.VIII
face *n.* lice 9A2
fact *n.* činjenica [B,C,S], fakt [C] fakat [B,S]
factory *n.* fabrika [B,S] tvornica [B,C] 20.II
fairy tale *n.* bajka 📖B.VIII
faith *n.* vera [E] vjera [J] 17A2a
fake *adj.* lažljiv 17A1a
fall *vb.*
    pasti (P); padati (I) 10A2, 10A1☼, 10A2☼
fall (= autumn) *n.* jesen 3A2
    in the fall na jesen 9A3
fall (= abrupt descent) *n.* pad
fall asleep *vb.* usnuti (P) 20.V
fall ill *vb.*
    oboleti (P); obolevati (I) [E] 18A3
    oboljeti (P); obolijevati (I) [J] 18A3
fall in love *vb.*
    zaljubiti se (P); zaljubljivati se (I) 📖B.VII
false *adj.* lažan 19A2a
falsehood *n.* laž 10A3
family *n.* familija [B,C,S] obitelj [C]
    porodica [B,S] 9A1
familial *adj.*
    obiteljski [C] porodični [B,S] 12A3
famous *adj.* čuven 15A1, poznat 18A3
far *adv.* daleko 4A4
farewell *n.* zbogom 20.VIII
farmer *n.* poljoprivrednik 11A2☼
fascist *adj.* fašistički 18A3
fast *adj.* brz 2A2, 11A1☼
faster *adj.* brži 11A2☼
fat *adj.* debeo 3A3, 2A3☼, 11A2☼
father *n.* otac 2A3, 2A3☼, 9A4
fatter *adj.* deblji 11A2☼
favorite *n.* ljubimac 15A1
favorite *adj.* najdraži
fear *n.* strah 10A3
    (he) is afraid *vb.* strah (ga) je
        10A3, 10A2☼
fear *vb.*
    plašiti se (I); uplašiti se (P) 11☺, 10A3
    bojati se (I) 7A2, 5A2☼, 9A2☼, 10A3
    live in fear strepiti (I) [B,C] strepeti [S]
    📖B.V
feature *n.* crta 10A3, odlika 17A3b
February *n.* februar [B,S] veljača [C] 6A2
Federation of Bosnia and Herzegovina *n.*
    Federacija Bosne i Hercegovine *see map* 4✪
feel (= sense) *vb.*
    osetiti (P) 15A1; osećati (I) [E]
    osjetiti (P) 15A1; osjećati (I) [J]
feel (= experience emotion) *vb.*
    osetiti se (P); osećati se (I) [E]

    10A3, 10A2☼
    osjetiti se (P) ; osjećati se (I) [J]
    10A3, 10A2☼
feeling *n.* osećaj [E] osjećaj [J] 19A3b
feign *vb.*
    hiniti (I) [C] 20.V
    praviti se (I) [B,C,S] 20.V
    glumiti (I) 📖B.V
fellow sufferer *n.*
    sapatnik [B,S] supatnik [C] 20.V
female *adj.* ženski 10A3
feminine *adj.* ženski 10A3
    feminine gender *n.* ženski rod
ferry *n.* trajekt
festival *n.* festival 16A1a
    folklore festival smotra folkora 16A2a
fever *n.* groznica, temperatura, vrućica
few *n.* nekolicina 19A2b
few *adv.* malo 5A1
field *n.* polje ↦4 19A1b
    plowed field *n.* njiva 18A1a
field work *n.* terenski rad 16A2a
fifteen (15) *num.* petnaest 5A1, 12A1☼
fifteen (approx.) *num.* petnaestak 12A1☼
fifth (5th) *adj.* peti 5A1, 6A2☼
fifty (50) *num.* pedeset 5A1, 12A1☼
fig *n.* smokva 5A1
fight *vb.* svaditi se (P); svađati se (I) 15A2☼
figure *n.* figura 19A1b, lik 10A3
fill *vb.* puniti (I); napuniti (P) 12A3
final *adj.* konačan 14A4, završni 📖B.I,
    poslednji [E] posljednji [J] 14A1
finally *adv.* konačno 14A4, najzad 5C1,
    napokon 10A2, naposletku [E] naposljetku
    [J] 16A2b
financial support
    financiranje [C] finansiranje [B,S] 16A2a
find *vb.*
    naći (P) 12A2; nalaziti (I)
find out *vb.*
    saznati (P) 14A2; saznavati (I)
finding (= result) *n.* nalaz 20.III
fine (= good) *adv.*
    fino 2A3, lepo [E] lijepo [J] 2A4
    I'm fine dobro mi je 10A2☼
fine (= OK) *adv.* u redu 13A2
    that's fine može 2A4☼
fine arts *n.* likovna umetnost [E] likovna
    umjetnost [J] 13B3
finger *n.* prst 10A4
finish *vb.*
    završiti (P); završavati (I) 11A1
    svršiti (P) 15A1; svršavati (I) 17A2a
finished *adj.* gotov
fire *n.* vatra 14A1
fire (from a job) *vb.*

otpustiti (P); otpuštati (I)   20.I
firm *adj.* čvrst   14A1
firmer *adj.* čvršći
first (1st) *adj.* prvi   1A1, 6A2✿°, 12A4✿°
first, firstly *adv.* prvo   4A4
first of all *adv.* najpre [E] najprije [J]   16A2a
first aid *n.* hitna pomoć   14A3, prva pomoć
fish *n.* riba   6A4
fisherman (professional) *n.* ribar
fisherman (recreational) *n.* ribič   20.V
fishing *n.* pecanje   20.II
fishing *adj.* ribarski   20.VIII
fishing gear *n.* pribor za pecanje   20.V
fishing hut *n.* ribarska kućica   20.VIII
fishing pole *n.* ribički štap   20.VIII
fist *n.* šaka   10A4
fitting *adj.* shodan   18A3
five (5) *num.* pet   5A1, 5A1✿°, 12A1✿°
five (group of men) *num.* petorica   12A2✿°
five (group of mixed company) *num.* petero [C]
   petoro [B,S]   12A2✿°
five hundred (500) *num.* petsto   12A1✿°
flakes *n.* pahuljice   7A1
flee *vb.*
   pobeći (P); bežati (I) [E]   18A3, ▢B.VIII
   pobjeći (P); bježati (I) [J]   18A3, ▢B.VIII
float (in the air) *vb.*
   lebdeti (I) [E]   20.II
   lebdjeti (I) [J]   20.II
floor (= surface on which one stands) *n.*
   pod   6A1
floor (story of a building) *n.*
   kat [C] sprat [B,S]   6A1, ⌐6A1¬
   ground floor *n.* prizemlje   6A1, ⌐6A1¬
flow *vb.* teći (I)   ⊷6   3☻
flow through *vb.* proticati (I)   7☺
flow out *vb.* oticati (I)   7☺
flower *n.* cvet [E] cvijet [J]
   flowers *n.* cveće [E] cvijeće [J] *(coll.)*
   12A2, 12A2✿°
flu *n.* grip [S] gripa [B,C]
fly *n.* muha [C] muva [B,S]
fly *vb.*
   leteti (I); poleteti (P) [E]   15A1
   letjeti (I); poletjeti (P) [J]   15A1
fly off *vb.*
   odleteti (P)   15A1; odletati (I) [E]   ▢A.III
   odletjeti (P)   15A1; odlijetati (I) [J]   ▢A.III
flying *n.* letenje   15A1
foam *n.* pena [E] pjena [J]   14A1
fog *n.* magla   14A4
folk *n.* narod [B,C,S]   17A2a puk [C]   17A2a
folk *adj.* narodni [B,C,S]   19A3b pučki [C]
folklore *n.* folklor   16A2a
   folklore festival *n.* smotra folkora   16A2a
folktale *n.* narodna priča   ▢B.VIII

following *adj.* za + *Inst*   ⊷5   15A1
food *n.* hrana   6A4
fool *n.* budala
foolish *adj.* blesav   ▢B.VI
foot *n.* noga   10A3, stopalo   10A4, 10A4✿°
   on foot *adv.* pješice [C]   5A2, peške [E]
   pješke [J] [B/S]   5A2
for *prep.* za   ⊷5   2A3, po   9A4
   for the sake of radi   ⊷5   14A2
   for example na primer [E] na primjer [J]
   11A3
   for that reason zato   ▢B.IV
force *n.* sila, snaga   12A4
force *vb.*
   naterati (P) [E]   ▢B.III
   natjerati (P) [J]   ▢B.III
forehead *vb.* čelo   18A2a
foreign *adj.* stran   16A1a
foreign lands *n.* inostranstvo [B,S] inozemstvo
   [C]   8A3
foreign language *n.* strani jezik   ▢B.I
foreigner *n.* stranac   16A2b
forest *n.* šuma   20.VIII
forestry *n.* šumarstvo   13B3
forever *adv.* zauvek [E] zauvijek [J]   17A2a
forget *vb.*
   zaboraviti (P); zaboravljati (I)   10A4
forgetful *adj.* zaboravan   ▢A.V
forgive *vb.*
   oprostiti (P)   2A1; praštati (I)   20.VI
fork *n.* vilica [C] viljuška [B,S]
formal *adj.* formalan   ▢B.VIII
form (*e.g.* application) *n.* formular   16A2a
form *n.* oblik   15A2
former *adj.* bivši   12A2✿°
formulate *vb.* sročiti (P)   16A1a
fortress *n.* tvrđava   16A3b
fortunate *adj.* srećan [S] sretan [B,C]   2A2
fortunately *adv.* srećom   14A3
fortune *n.* sreća   8A3
forty (40) *num.* četrdeset   5A1
foundation *n.* temelj   16A2a, osnov [B,S]
   osnova [B,C,S]   ▢B.VIII
four (4) *num.* četiri   5A2, 4A2✿°, 12A1✿°
four (group of men) *num.* četvorica   12A2✿°
four (group of mixed company) četvero [C]
   četvoro [B,S] *num.*   12A2✿°, ▢B.IV
four hundred (400) *num.* četiristo   12A1✿°
fourteen (14) *num.* četrnaest   5A1, 12A1✿°
fourteenth (14th) *adj.* četrnaesti   14A1
fourth (4th) *adj.* četvrti   4A1, 6A2✿°, 12A3✿°
fragrance *n.* miris   20.II
France *n.* Francuska   4A1
free (= unbound) *adj.* slobodan   16A2b
free (= gratis) *adj.* besplatan   16A2b
freedom *n.* sloboda   19A2b

French *adj.* fràncu̯ski̯ 2A4, 9A2✿°
Frenchwoman *n.* Francu̯skinja 1A4
Frenchman *n.* Fràncu̯z 1A4
frequently *adv.* če̯sto 7A1
fresh *adj.* svež [E] svjež [J] 7A1
freshen up (= refresh oneself) *vb.*
    osve̯žiti se (P); osve̯ža̯vati se (I) [E] 📖B.IV
    osvje̯žiti se (P); osvje̯ža̯vati se (I) [J] 📖B.IV
freshman *n.* student prve̯ godine̯
Friday *n.* pe̯tak 2A1
    on Fridays pe̯tkom 7A2✿°
friend *n.* dru̯g [B,S] prijatelj [B,C,S] *(m., general)* 1A4, 1A4✿°, drugarica [B,S] prijate̯ljica [B,C,S] *(f.)* 4A2
friendship *n.* prijate̯ljstvo 📖B.IV
frighten *vb.*
    plàšiti (I); u̯plàšiti (P) 11☺
    be frightened
    plàšiti se (I); u̯plàšiti se (P) ⌐ 10A3 ¬, 11☺
frivolous *adj.* neozbi̯ljan 3A3
from *prep.* iz ↦5   4A1, 4A4✿°, od ↦5 4A3, s, sa 4A4
from afar *adv.* izdale̯ka 14A4
from here oda̯vde 13A4
front hall *n.* pre̯dso̯blje 16A1b
fruit, fruits *n.* vo̯će 4A3
fugitive *n.* begu̯nac [E] bjegu̯nac [J] 18A3
full *adj.* pùn 4A3
function *n.* fùnkcija
function *vb.*
    funkcioni̯rati (I/P) [C] 19A1b
    funkcionisati (I/P) [B,S] 19A1b
funding *n.* stipendi̯ranje 16A1a
funny (= humorous) *adj.* sme̯šan [E] smije̯šan [J]
funny (= peculiar) *adj.* čùdan
furniture *n.* name̯štaj [E] namje̯štaj [J] 12A1
further *adv.* da̯lje̯ 7☺
furthermore *adv.* osim to̯ga 8A3
fury *n.* be̯s [E] bije̯s [J]
future *n.* budu̯ćno̯st 7A2
future tense *n.* bùdu̯će vre̯me [E] bùdu̯će vrije̯me [J] 15A2

G
gamble away *vb.* pròkockati (P) 7A2
game (= amusement) *n.* ìgra [B,C,S]
game (= sports competition) *n.* ùtakmica 12A2
garden *n.* ba̯šta [B,S] vr̀t [B,C] 16A3b
garlic *n.* be̯li̯ luk [E] bije̯li̯ lu̯k [J] [B/S] če̯šnja̯k [C]
gas (= gasoline) be̯nzi̯n 5A2
gas (= natural) *n.* plin
gas (= stomach) plinovi
gather *vb..*

prìkupiti (P) 19A3b; prìku̯pljati (I)
sàbrati (P); sàbirati (I) 20.V
sàkupiti (P); saku̯pljati (I) [B,S] 19A3b, 11A1✿°
skùpiti (P) 📖B.VI; sku̯pljati (I) [B,C,S] 📖A.I
gather together (a group of people) *vb.*
    òkupiti (P); oku̯pljati 14A1✿°
gathering *n.* skup
gaze *n.* pògle̯d 10A3
gaze *vb.* motriti (I) 18A1a
gender *n.* ro̯d
general *adj.* o̯pći [B,C] o̯pšti [S]
    in general uo̯pće [B,C] uo̯pšte [B,S] 10A1
generation *n.* naràštaj [C] pokolje̯nje [B,S], ko̯leno [E] ko̯ljeno [J] 19A3b
genitive (case) *adj.* geniti̯v
gentle *adj.* bla̯g 📖B.IV
gentleman *n.* gospòdin 2A2
    gentlemen *n.* gospòda 8A2, 8A2✿°
geographical *adj.* geo̯gra̯fski̯ [B,C,S] zemljopi̯sni̯ [C] 1⊕
geography *n.* geo̯gra̯fija 13B3
German *n.* Ne̯mac [E] Nje̯mac [J] *(m., general)* Ne̯mica [E] Nje̯mica [J]
German *adj.* nema̯čki̯ [E] njema̯čki̯ [J] 2A4
Germanic language studies germanìstika 13B3
Germany *n.* Ne̯ma̯čka [E] Nje̯ma̯čka [J] 4A1
get down from *vb.*
    si̯ći (P) 13A4; si̯laziti (I)
get dressed up *vb.* ure̯diti se (P); ure̯đi̯vati se (I) 📖B.VI
get in touch *vb.* stùpiti u vezu 16A2a
get irritated *vb.* iznervi̯rati se (P) 11☺
get married (said of a man) *vb.*
    žèniti se (I); ože̯niti se (P)
get married (said of a woman) *vb.*
    ùdati se (P); uda̯vati se (I) 📖B.II
get to know [someone] *vb.*
    upòznati (P) 16A1a; upozna̯vati (I)
get to know [one another] *vb.*
    upòznati se (P) 📖B.I; upozna̯vati se (I) 📖B.II
get used to *vb.*
    priviknuti se (P); privika̯vati se (I) 20.II
ghost *n.* duh
gift *n.* da̯r 📖B.III, poklon
girl (= teens to early twenties) *n.* de̯vo̯jka [E] djevo̯jka [J] ↦4, cura 📖B.V
girl (= little girl) *n.* ma̯la, devo̯jčica [E] djevo̯jčica [J]
give *vb.*
    dati (P) 5A2; da̯vati (I) ↦6   3A1✿°, 6A3✿°, 10A2✿°
give (*e.g.* a gift) *vb.* darovati (I) 20.VIII, pokloniti (P) 12A2; poklanjati (I) 📖B.VIII

gladden *vb.* veseliti se (I),
  radovati (I) ⊞B.III; obradovati (P)
  be glad *vb.* veseliti se (I) 20.III,
    radovati se (I) ⊞B.III; obradovati se (P)
    14A4
gladly *adv.* drage volje 16A3b, rado 13A1
glance at *vb.*
  pogledati (P) 20.V; pogledati (I) 2A4
glass (for drinking) *n.* čaša 4A3
  small glass *n.* čašičica ⊞B.VIII
glass (material) staklo
gloomy *adj.* mrk 18A1a
glossary *n.* rečnik [E] rječnik [J] 2A1
glow *vb.* ozariti (P) 18A2a
go *vb.* ići (I) 5A1, 5A2☼, 7A3☼
go numb *vb.* protrnuti (P) 20.VIII
go out *vb.*
  izaći (P) 10A1; izlaziti (I) 20.VI
  izići (P) [B,C] 10A1; izlaziti (I) 20.VI
  go out for a drink *vb.*
    izaći na piće [B,C,S]
    izići na piće [B,C] ⊞B.VII
God, god *n.* Bog, bog 17A3a
godfather *n.* kum ⌐B.VIII¬
godmother *n.* kuma ⌐B.VIII¬
gold *n.* zlato 19A3a
good *adj.* dobar ↦4 1A3, 11A1☼
  good morning dobro jutro 2A4
  good night laku noć 3A2
goodbye *adv* doviđenja [B,C,S] 2A4, bok!
  [C] ciao [B,C] ćao! [B,S] 1A1, zdravo
  [B,C,S] 1A1
  say goodbye opraštati se (I) 20.VI
goodbye (final) *n.* zbogom [B,C,S] 20.VIII
govern *vb.* vladati (I)
government minister *n.* ministar [B,C,S] *(m.,*
  general) ministrica [C] *(f.)* 11A2☼
government *n.* vlada 18A3
grab *vb.* dohvatiti (P) 19A3a,
  uhvatiti (P) 14A1; uhvaćati (I)
grade (= year of schooling) *n.* razred 5C1
grade (= evaluation) *n.*
  ocena [E] ocjena [J] ⌐10A2¬
gradual *adj.* postepen 19A3a
graduate (with B.A. or higher) *vb.* diplomirati
  (I/P) ⊞B.VI
graduate study *n.*
  poslijediplomski studij [C] postdiplomski
    studij [B,C,S] 16A2a
graduation (secondary school) *n.*
  matura ⊞B.IV
  elementary school graduation
    mala matura
grammar *n.* gramatika 2A4
grammar *adj.* gramatički 17A2b
grandchild *n.* unuče 12A2☼

grandchildren *n.* unučad 12A2☼
granddaughter *n.* unuka
grandfather *n.* deda [B,S] 8☺ ded [E] djed
  [J] [C] 9A4
grandmother *n.* baka [B,C,S], baba [B,S]
  9A4, 5A3☼, nena [B] 5A3☼
grandson *n.* unuk 8☺▱ 12A2☼
grasp *vb.* shvatiti (P) 14A4; shvaćati (I) 20.V
grateful *adj.* zahvalan 13A4
gratify *vb.* goditi (I) 20.III
gray *n.* siv 8A1, 8A1☼
great! *excl.* super! 3A1
great (= vast, majestic) *adj.* velik 3A2
Greece *n.* Grčka 4A1
Greek *adj.* grčki
Greek *n.* Grk *(m., general)* Grkinja *(f.)*
green *adj.* zelen 4A4
greet (= say hello) *vb.*
  pozdraviti (P) ⊞A.VII; pozdravljati (I) 6A3
greet (one another) *vb.* pozdraviti se (P) 12A1;
  pozdravljati se (I) 6A3
greet (upon arrival) *vb.* dočekati (P) 5A3
greeting *n.* pozdrav 6A3
grieve *vb.* tugovati (I) 15A1, 15A1☼
grill *n.* roštilj 11A2
grin *vb.*
  smeškati se (I) [E] ⊞B.V
  smješkati se (I) [J] ⊞B.V
grind *vb.*
  mleti (I); samleti (P) [E] 14A1
  mljeti (I); samljeti (P) [J] 14A1
group *n.* grupa 16A3b
group *vb.*
  grupirati (I/P) [C] 19A2b
  grupisati (I/P) [B,S] 19A2b
grouse (bird) *n.* tetreb [E] tetrijeb [J] ⊞B.VII
grow *vb.* rasti 16A1b
guess *vb.*
  pogoditi (P); pogađati (I) ⊞B.VII
guest *n.* gost *(m., general)* 13A1 gošća *(f)*
guilt *n.* krivnja 20.VII
guilty *adj.* kriv 20.VI
guitar *n.* gitara
gust (of wind) *n.* nalet 14A2
gym *n.* teretana ⊞A.V

H
hair *n.* kosa 10A4
haircut *n.* šišanje
  get a haircut *vb.*
    šišati se (I); ošišati se (P) ⊞B.IV
hairdo *n.* frizura ⊞B.V
hairdresser *n.* frizerka ⊞B.I
hairdryer (in a salon) *n.* hauba ⊞B.V
half *n.* po, pola 14A2, polovica [B,C]
  polovina [B,S] 12A1, 12A1☼

hall *n.* (*e.g.* for a concert) dvorana 16A1a
hallway *n.* hodnik 13A1
ham *n.* šunka 📖A.II
hand *n.* ruka ↦4   9A2, šaka 10A4,
  10A4☼, ¦10A4¦
  on the one hand s jedne strane 8A4☼
  on the other hand s druge strane
hand to *vb.*
  uručiti (P); uručivati (I) 📖B.VI
handball *n.* rukomet
handbook *n.* priručnik 📖B.III
handkerchief *n.* maramica 📖A.VII
handle *n.* drška [B,S] držak [C] 14A1
happen *vb.*
  dogoditi se (P) 12A4, 9A2☼; događati se (I)
    [B,C,S] 20.VI
  desiti se (P) 📖B.VIII; dešavati se (I)
    [B,S] 17A2b
happen upon *vb.*
  naići na (P) 14A2; nailaziti na (I)
happiness *n.* sreća 8A3
happy *adj.* srećan [B,S] sretan [B,C] 2A2
hard (= not soft) *adj.* tvrd 11A2☼
harder (= firmer) *adj.* tvrđi
harder (= more difficult) *adj.* teži 11A2☼
harsh *adj.* žestok
harsher *adj.* žešći
hat *n.* šešir 11A1
hatred *n.* mržnja
have *vb.* imati (I) 2A1, 2A1☼
  not have *vb.* nemati (I) 2A1, 2A1☼
have to *vb.* morati 2A1, 13A2☼
hawk *n.* jastreb
he *pron.* on ↦4   1A2, 1A2☼
  see also **him**
head (= body part) *n.* glava 10A4, 10A4☼
head (administrator) *n.* predstojnik 20.VII,
    šef 11A3
headache *n.* glavobolja
health *n.* zdravlje 7A2
healthy *adj.* zdrav 10A4
hear *vb.* čuti (I/P) 5C1, 7A3☼
heart *n.* srce 15A1
  by heart napamet 10A3
heartfelt *adj.* srdačan 16A2b
heat *n.* vrućina 16A3a
heaven *n.* nebo 17A2a
heavy *adj.* težak 2A2
heavier *adj.* teži 11A2☼
height *n.* visina ¦10A3¦
heir *n.* naslednik [E] nasljednik [J] 20.IV
hello (general greeting) dobar dan [B,C,S]
    1A3, zdravo [B,C,S], bok! [C], ciao [B,C],
    ćao! [B,S] 1A1
hello (on telephone) *excl.* alo 📖A.VII
help *n.* pomoć 14A3

help *vb.*
  pomoći (P) 10A1☼; pomagati (I) 10A4,
    15A2☼
helpless *adj.* bespomoćan 14A2
her *pron.* ↦4   2A2☼, 6A3☼, 7A1☼
  (*clitic*) je 2A1, 2A2☼, ju 2A2☼, joj
  (*full*) nju 2A2, nje, njoj, njom
  see also **she**
here (location) *adv.*
  tu 4A2, ovde [E] ovdje [J] 2A3
here (= to here) *adv.* ovamo 7A3, ¦7.A4¦
here (= from here) *adv.* odavde 13A4
here (pointing) evo 4A4
here you are! izvoli! *or* izvolite! 2A4
heritage *n.* baština 16A2b
hero *n.* junak ↦4
heroic *adj.* junački 19A3b
hers, her *adj.* njen [B,C,S] njezin [C] 1A2,
    4A2☼, ¦2.A2¦, svoj 5A3, 5A3☼
hey! *excl.* ej! 2A3
hi *excl. see under* **hello**
hide *vb.*
  sakriti (P); sakrivati (I) 20.VI
  skriti (P); skrivati (I) 18A1a
high *adj.* visok
high school *n.* gimnazija 📖B.II
high school student *n.* gimnazijalac (*m.,*
    general) gimnazijalka (*f.*) 📖B.I
higher *adj.* viši 11A1☼
hill *n.* brdo, gora
hill (wooded) *n.* gora
hilly *adj.* brdovit, gorski 18A1a
him *pron.* ↦4   2A2☼, 6A3☼, 7A1☼
  (*clitic*) ga 2A1, 9A2☼ mu
  (*full*) njega 2A2, njemu, njim
  see also **he**
hint *vb.*
  nagovestiti (P) 16A3b; nagoveštavati (I) [E]
  nagovijestiti (P) 16A3b; nagoveštavati (I) [J]
his *adj.* njegov ↦4   1A2, 2A3☼, 4A2☼,
  svoj 5A3,
    5A3☼
history *n.*
  historija [B] istorija [S] povijest [C] 13B3,
  ¦17A1b¦
hit *n.* hit song, popular song
hold *vb.* držati (I) ↦6   12A1
hold (an event) *vb.*
  održati (P) 📖B.VI, 11A1☼; održavati (I)
    16A3b
holy *adj.* svet 17C1
home (= at home) *adv.*
  doma [C] 20.I kod kuće [B,C,S] 5C1
home (= to home) *adv.* doma [C] kući [B,C,S]
    9A2
homeland *n.* domovina 17A1a

homework *n.* domaća zadaća [B,C] domaći zadatak [S] 1A4

honest *adj.* pošten 20.IV

honey *n.* med 7A1

honeymoon *n.* medeni mesec [E] medeni mjesec [J] 📖B.VIII

honor *vb.* poštovati 12A2

honorable *adj.* pošten 20.IV, 7☺

hope *n.* nada 16A3a

hope *vb.* nadati se (I) 14A2

horse *n.* konj ↪4

hospital *n.* bolnica 14A3

hospital *adj.* bolnički 14A3

host *vb.* ugostiti (P) 16A1b

hostel *n.* hostel 16A2a

hot *adj.* vreo 14A1, vruć

hot water *n.* topla voda

hot dog hrenovka [C] viršla [B,S]

hotel *n.* hotel 14A2

hour *n.* čas [S] sat [B,C,S] 5A2, 5A1✿, 5A2✿, 6A2✿

for an hour sat vremena 6A3, 6A2✿

for hours satima 📖A.III

house *n.* kuća 5A1

little house *n.* kućica 18A1a

housekeeper (female) *n.* domaćica 11A2✿

how *adv.* kako 1A1

how are you? kako si? kako ste?

how many koliko 5A1

how much koliko 5A1

how old are you koliko imaš godina *or* koliko imate godina; koliko ti je / vam je godina

however *adv.* međutim 12A2

hubbub *n.* galama 20.VII

human *adj.* ljudski 18A1a

humanities *n.* humanitarne nauke [B,S] humanitarne znanosti [C]

humble *adj.* skroman 20.VIII

humiliate *vb.* poniziti (P) 19A2a; ponižavati (I)

hundred (100) *num.* sto 6A1, 12A1✿

Hungary *n.* Mađarska *see map* 1🌐

hungry *adj.* gladan 4A3

hurry *n.* žurba 16A3b

hurry *vb.* žuriti (I) 7A2; požuriti se (P) 7A3

hurt *vb.*
boleti (I) [E] 10A4, 10A4✿
boljeti (I) [J] 10A4, 10A4✿

husband *n.* muž ↪4 7A2, ⌐5A3¬

hypocrisy *n.*
licemerje [E] licemjerje [J]

I

I *pron.* ja ↪4 1A1

I'm fine dobro sam 3A1✿

see also **me**

ice *n.* led 4A3

ice cream *n.* sladoled

idea *n.* ideja 3A3

identify *vb.*
identificirati (I/P) [B,C] 19A2b
identifikovati (I/P) [B,S] 19A2b

if *conj.* ako 5A2, 12A3✿

ignorance *n.* neznanje 11☺

ijekavian *n.* ijekavica 15A1

illuminate *vb.* obasjavati (I) 20.V

image *n.* slika 6A3

imagine *vb.* zamisliti (P) 18A1b; zamišljati (I)

imam *n.* imam

imitate *vb.* oponašati (I) 📖B.VIII

immeasurable *adj.*
neizmeran [E] neizmjeran [J] 20.VIII

immediate *adj.*
izravan [C] neposredan [B,C,S] 16A2b

immediately *adv.* odmah 5A2

imminent *adj.* skorašnji 20.III

immodest *adj.* neskroman 13☺

impatience *n.* nestrpljenje 8A2

imperfective (grammar) *adj.* nesvršen
imperfective aspect (grammar) nesvršen vid

impolite *adj.* nepristojan

importance *n.* važnost

important *adj.* važan 11A1, 11A1✿

impression *n.*
dojam [B,C] utisak [B,S] 16A3b

improve *vb.*
usavršiti (P) 16A3a; usavršavati (I)

in *prep.* na ↪5 6A1, 6A1✿, u 6A1, 6A1✿

in so doing pritom 15A1

in the future ubuduće 11A3

in advance unapred [E] unaprijed [J] 12A3

in front of *prep.* ispred ↪5 8A4, pred 7A2

in vain uzalud

inasmuch as *adv.* ukoliko 19A3b

include *vb.*
uključiti (P) 10A2✿
uključivati (I) 4🌐, 10A2✿

indeed *excl.* zaista 2A2

independence (of a country) *n.* nezavisnost [B,C,S] 12A4 samostalnost [C] ⌐12A4¬

independence (of a person) *n.* samostalnost [B,C,S] ⌐12A4¬

independent *adj.* nezavisan, samostalan

Independent State of Croatia *hist.*
Nezavisna Država Hrvatska (NDH) 18A3

individual *n.* pojedinac 19A2b

individual *adj.* pojedinačan 16A3b

individually *adv.* ponaosob 15A2

induce *vb.* navesti (P); navoditi (I) 📖B.III

inedible *adj.* nejestiv 20.I

influence *vb.*
    ùticati (I) [B,S] 17A3b
    ùtjecati (I) [B,C] 17A3b
influenza *n.* grip [S] gripa [B,C]
inform *vb.*
    obavèstiti (P); obaveštàvati (I) [E] 14A3
    obavijèstiti (P); obaveštàvati (I) [J] 14A3
information *n.* informàcija, informàcije *often used in pl* 16A2b
information science *n.* informàtika 13B3
ingredient *n.* sàstojak 14A1
inhabitant *n.* stanovnìk
initial (= first in sequence) *adj.* pòčetni 16A3b
initial (= original) *adj.* prvòbitan 19A1b
inquire *vb.*
    raspìtati se (P) 📖B.III;
    raspitìvati se (I) 20.III
    zapìtati (P) 20.VI; zapitìvati (I)
inscribe *vb.* upìsati (P); upisìvati (I) 20.VIII
insert *vb.* ùmetnuti (P); ùmetati (I) 20.V
inside of unùtar [B,S] ùnutar [C]
inside *adv.* unùtra 19A3b
insistence *n.* insìstiranje 13☺
insolent *adj.* drzak 20.IV
instance *n.* pùt 10A1
instant *n.*
    trenùtak [B,C,S] mòmenat [B,S] 5A4✿
instantly *adv.* trenutàčno [B,C]
    momentàlno [B,C,S] 16A2a
instead of ùmesto [E] ùmjesto [J] 10A3
instrumental (case) *n.* instrumentàl
insult *vb.*
    uvrèditi (P) 19A2a; vrèđati (I) [E]
    uvrijèditi (P) 19A2a; vrèđati (I) [J]
insure *vb.* osigùrati (P)
intelligent *adj.*
    pametan 11A2, inteligèntan 11A3✿
intend *vb.*
    nameràvati (I) [E] 11A3
    namjeràvati (I) [J] 11A3
intensive *adj.* intenzìvan 16A3b
interconnected *adj.* pòvezan 📖B.IV
interest *n.* zainteresìranost 20.IV,
    interesòvanje [B,S] 19A3b, zanìmanje [B,C,S] 16A3b
interest *vb.* zanìmati (I) [B,C,S] 16A2a,
    interesìrati (I/P) [B,C] 16A1a
    interesòvati (I/P) [B,S] 16A1a
  be interested *vb.* zanìmati se (I) 16A2b
interested *adj.* zainteresìran [B,C] zàinteresovan [B,S] 16A1a
interesting *adj.*
    interesàntan 16A3a,
    zanìmljiv 5A3, 11A1✿
internet *n.* ìnternet 8A3

interpreter *n.* tùmač 19A2b
interrogate *vb.*
    ispìtati (P); ispitìvati (I) 20.VII
interrupt *vb.*
    prèkinuti (P); prekìdati (I) 20.II
intimate *adj.* blizak 18A3
into *prep.* u ↪5   5A1, 6A1✿
invent *vb.*
    izùmjeti (P) 15A1, 15A1✿
    prònaći (P) 15A1; pronàlaziti (I)
invested *adj.* ùložen 16A2a
invite *vb.* zvati (I) 📖B.I,
    pòzvati (P) 13A1; pozìvati (I)
involve *vb.*
    angažìrati (I/P) [B,C]
    angažòvati (I/P) [B,S]
  to get involved
    angažìrati se (I/P) [B,C] 16A3a
    angažòvati se (I/P) [B,S] 16A3a
ironing board *n.* dàska za glàčanje [C] dàska za pèglanje [B,S] 📖A.VIII
irritate *vb.* nervìrati (I)
  be irritated *vb.* nervìrati se (I) 11☺
is *vb.* je, jest, jeste 1A1✿
  see under **be**
island *n.* ostrvo [B,S] òtok [B,C] 15A1,
    6A1✿
isn't it, aren't they, etc. zar ne 5A4
issue (= topic) *n.* pìtanje 1➐
issue (of a publication) *n.* broj
Istria *n.* Ìstra *see map on page* 96
Istrian *adj.* ìstarski 8A3
it *pron. (subj.)* ȍno, ȍn, ȍna ↪4
    1A2, 1A2✿, 4A4✿;
    (obj. clitic) ga, je 2A1, mu, joj 6A3;
    (obj. full) njega, nju 2A2; njèmu, njōj
      6A3; njim, njōm 7A1
its *adj.* njègov, njȅn [B,S] njȅzin [C], svȍj
Italian *adj.* italìjanski [B,S] talìjanski [B,C]
    📖B.II
Italy *n.* Itàlija 1➐

J

jam *n.* džem 7A1
January *n.* jànuar [B,S] sìječanj [C] 6A2
Japan *n.* Jàpan 6A4
jazz *n.* džez
Jew *n.* Jèvrej *or* Jèvrejin [B,S] Žȉdov [C]
    (m., general) Jèvrejka [B,S] Žȉdovka [C] *(f.)*
Jewish *adj.* jèvrejski [B,S] žȉdovski [C]
job *n.* pòsao ↪4   5A3
jocular *adj.* šèretski 📖B.IV
join (a library, club, etc.) *vb.*
    učlàniti se (P); učlanjìvati se (I) 16A2b
join in *vb.*
    priključìti se (P); priključìvati se (I) 16A2b

joke *vb.* šaliti se (I) 📖B.III
joking *adj.* šaljiv 15A1
journalist *n.*
    novinar *(m., general)* novinarka *(f.)* 11A3
journey *n.* put ↦4 7A2, putovanje 14A2
joy *n.* radost ↦4 3A2
joyous *adj.* radostan 15A1
judge *n.* sudac [C] sudija [B,S] 5A3
judge *vb.* suditi (I) 20.VI
juice *n.* sok 4A3
July *n.* jul *or* juli [B,S] srpanj [C] 6A2
jump *vb.* skočiti (P) 16A1b; skakati (I)
June *n.* jun *or* juni [B,S] lipanj [C] 6A2
junior *n.* student treće godine
junior year (in secondary school or at the
    university) treća godina 16A1a
just *adj.* pravedan
just (= just now) *adv.* upravo 6A3
justice (= rightness, fairness) *n.*
    pravda 19A2b
justice of the peace matičar 📖B.VIII
justify *vb.*
    opravdati (P); opravdavati (I) 20.II
juvenile (= under age) *adj.* maloletan [E]
    maloljetan [J] 📖B.VIII

K

karst *n.* krš 17A3a
keep (= preserve) *vb.*
    čuvati (I); očuvati (P) 10A4
keep (= maintain) *vb.* držati ↦6
key *n.* ključ 1A2
kidney *n.* bubreg 3A4
kill *vb.* ubiti (P) 19A3a; ubijati (I)
kilogram *n.* kilo [B,C,S] kila [C] 12A2
kilometer *n.* kilometar 7A2
kin *n.* rodbina 17A2a
kind *adj.* ljubazan 13A1
king *n.* kralj 13A3
kiss *n.* poljubac 20.III
kiss *vb.* ljubiti (I); poljubiti (P) 📖B.VIII
kitchen *n.* kuhinja 16A1b
knee *n.* koleno [E] koljeno [J] 10A4
kneel *vb.* klečati (I); kleknuti (P) 17A3a
knife *n.* nož
knock *vb.* kucati (I); kucnuti (P)
knocking *n.* kucanje 📖B.VIII
know (= have knowledge of) *vb.*
    znati (I) 4A2, ⸤14B2⸥
know (= be acquainted with) *vb.*
    poznati (P) 10A2;
    poznavati (I) 3A1, 3A1✿, 10A2✿
know how umeti [E] umjeti [J] ↦6 *see also*
    be able
knowledge *n.* znanje 11A4
Kosovo *n.* Kosovo *see map* 1✿, ⸤1✿⸥

Kosovo *adj.* kosovski 8A3

L

lack *n.* nedostatak
lack *vb.* manjkati (I/P), faliti (I)
lady *n.* gospođa 2A2
lake *n.* jezero 16A3b
lamp *n.* lampa 8A4, svetiljka [E] svjetiljka
    [J] 20.V
language *n.* jezik 9A1 [*see also adjective*
    forms for names of individual languages]
language *adj.* jezički [B,S] jezični [B,C]
    language laboratory jezička laboratorija
    [B,S] jezični laboratorij [C] 7A4
large *adj.* velik 2A2
larger *adj.* veći 11A1, 11A1✿
last (= furthest back) *adj.* zadnji 16A1a
last (= in a sequence) *adj.* poslednji [E]
    posljednji [J] 14A1
last night *adv.* sinoć 14A3
last *vb.* trajati (I) 6A2
late *adj.* kasan 6A2, 7A2✿, 9A2✿
late *adv.* kasno 6A2
    late, be *vb.*
    zakasniti (P) 14A4; zakašnjavati (I)
later *adv.* posle [E] poslije [J] 📖A.V,
    kasnije 📖A.V, potom 12A2, zatim
    12A2
Latin American *adj.* latinoamerički 📖B.I
laugh *vb.*
    smejati se (I) 20.III; nasmejati se (P) [E]
    20.VI
    smijati se (I) 20.III; nasmijati se (P) [J]
    20.VI
laughter *n.* smeh [E] smijeh [J] 19A1a
law (= regulation) *n.* zakon 19A2b
law (= discipline) *n.* pravo 13B3
law code *n.* zakonik 19A2b
law school *n.* pravni fakultet
lawmaker *n.* zakonodavac 19A2b
lawyer *n.*
    advokat [B,S] odvjetnik [B,C] 5A3, 11A2✿
lazy *adj.* lenj [S] lijen ⸤[B,C]⸥ 16A1a
lead (metal) *n.* olovo ⸤7A4⸥
lead (metal) *adj.* olovni 18A1a
lead *vb.* voditi (I) 5C1
lead away *vb.* odvesti (P); odvoditi (I) 10A4
leader *n.* vođa
leading *adj.* vodeći 18A3,
leaf (of paper) *n.* list
leaf (on a tree) *n.* list
    leaves *n. coll.* lišće 12A2✿
lean *vb.*
    nasloniti (P); naslanjati (I) 20.III
learn *vb.* naučiti (P) 10A2, 9A2✿, 10A2✿
learning *n.* učenje 11A4, 10A4✿

473
English-BCS Glossary

leave (= depart) *vb.* òtići (P); òdlaziti (I)
  10A2, 10A2☼, 12A4☼

leave (= leave behind) *vb.*
  òstaviti (P) 14A1; òstavljati (I) 17A1a

lectern *n.* kàtedra 8A4

lecture *n.* predávanje 6A2

lecture *vb.* predávati (I) 16A3a

left (= not right) *adj.* lȅvi [E] lijȅvi [J] 13A4

leg *n.* nòga 10A3, 10A4☼

legacy *n.* baština 16A2b, nàsledstvo [E]
  nàsljedstvo [J] 20.V

legal *adj.* zàkonskī 20.IV

legislative *adj.* zakonodávnī

lemon *n.* limùn 7A1

lemonade *n.* limunàda 4A3

less *adv.* mànjē 11A2

lesson *n.* lȅkcija 1A1, čàs [B,S] sȁt [C] 7A4

let neka (+ *present tense verb*) 7A3, 7A3☼

let's hajde 7A3, da (+ *present tense verb*)
  13A2☼

let's not nèmojmo 7A3

letter *n.* pìsmo ↦4 1A2, 6A3☼

lettuce *n.* salàta 11A2

level *n.* nìvo [B,S] razìna [C] 19A3b

library *n.* bibliotèka [B,S] knjȉžnica [C] 7A4

lie (= tell falsehood) *vb.*
  làgati (I); slàgati (P) 19A2a

lie (= be lying down) *vb.*
  lèžati (I) 11A4, 11A4☼

lie down *vb.* lèći (P) 11A4☼

life *n.* žìvot 6A2

lift *vb.* pòdići [pòdignuti] (P) 15A1;
  pòdizati (I) 📖A.VI

light (= radiance) *n.* svètlo [E] svjètlo [J]
  8A4 svetlòst [E] svjetlòst [J] 17C1

light (= not heavy) *adj.* làgan 19A3a, lȁk
  [B,C,S] làhak [B] 2A2, ⌐2A2 ̣

like *prep.* kao 9A2, 4A1☼, poput 19A1b

like this *adv.* ovàko 13A3

like (= appeal to) *vb.*
  svìdeti se (P); svìđati se (I) [E] 6A4, 6A4☼
  svìdjeti se (P); svìđati se (I) [J]
    [B,C,S] 6A4, 6A4☼
  dòpasti se (P) 📖B.IV; dopádati se (I) [B,S]
    16A1a
  see also **appeal to, please, love**

lilac *n.* jorgòvan

line (a drawing) *n.* crta 10A3

line (= queue) *n.* rȅd 11A4

line up *vb.*
  rèdati (I); porèdati (P) [B,C] 14A1
  rèđati (I); porèđati (P) [B,S] 14A1

linguistics *n.* lingvìstika [B,C,S] 13B3,
  jezikoslòvlje [C] 13B3

lion *n.* lav 8A1

list *n.* spìsak [B,C,S] pòpis [C], lista 16A3b

listen *vb.* slušati (I) 6A2, 6A2☼

listless *adj.* nevòljan 9☺

literary *adj.* književnī 16A2b

literate *adj.* písmen 6A2

literature *n.* književnōst 13B3

little *adj.* màlī 2A2, 2A3☼, 8A1☼, 11A1☼,
  11A2☼

little *adv.* malo 5A1, 5A1☼

little sister *n.* sȅstrica 16A1b, sȅka

live *vb.*
  žíveti (I) [E] 5A3, 10A2☼
  žívjeti (I) [J] 5A3, 10A2☼

living room *n.* dnȅvnā soba 16A1b

location *n.* mesto [E] mjesto [J] 10☺
  lokàcija 6A2

be located *vb.* nàći se (P); nàlaziti se (I)
  6A1, 9A2☼, 15A1☼

locative (case) *n.* lokatìv`

lock *vb.* zaključati (P); zaključávati (I) 20.VIII

loneliness *n.* samòća 18A2a

loner *n.* sàmac 18A1a

long (in distance or time) *adj.* dȕg 3A3,
  11A1☼

long (in distance) *adj.* dùgačak

long ago *adv.* odávno 16A1b

longer *adv.* dužī 11A2☼, dulje 20.V

longing *n.* žùdnja 20.VI

look *vb.* glȅdati ↦6 2A2; pòglēdati 20.V

look! *excl.* glȅ! 📖B.IV, eto! 📖B.VI

look at oneself (*e.g.* in the mirror) *vb.*
  pòglēdati se (P); pòglēdati se (I) 9A2

look for *vb.* tràžiti (I) 3A1, ìskati 17A3a

lord *n.* gospòdar 📖A.V

lose *vb.* gùbiti (I) 9A3; izgùbiti (P) 10A2

loss *n.* gùbitak 20.II

loud *adj.* glȁsan 📖B.IV

love *n.* ljùbav ↦4 3A2, 6A4☼, 9A2☼

love *vb.*
  vòleti (I) [E] 2A3
  vòljeti (I) [J] 2A3

low *adj.* nìzak 2A2, 11A2☼

lower *vb.* spùstiti (P); spùštati (I) 📖A.VII

lower *adj.* nìžī 11A2☼

lucky *adv.* srèćan [B,S] srȅtan [B,C] 2A2
  lucky you blȃgo vama

lunch *n.* rùčak 5A2

lyrical *adj.* lìrskī 19A2b

M

Macedonia *n.* Makedònija 1☚

Macedonian *n.* Makedònac (*m., general*)
  Makedònka (*f.*)

magazine *n.* čàsopis 2A4

magician *n.* čàrobnjāk 13A3

maid of honor *n.* kùma 📖B.VIII

main *adj.* glávnī 2☚

mainly *adv.* uglavnom 16A1b

maintain *vb.*
  održati (P) 📖B.VI; održavati (I) 16A3b

majority *n.* većina 16A1a

make *vb.*
  činiti (I); učiniti (P) 19A3a
  praviti (I); napraviti (P) 20.III
  proizvesti (P); proizvoditi (I)

make an effort *vb.*
  truditi se (I); potruditi se (P) 16A1a

make unhappy *vb.*
  unesrećiti (P) 19A2a; unesrećavati (I) [B,S]
  unesrećiti (P) 19A2a; unesrećivati (I) [B,C]

male *adj.* muški 10A3

man (= person) *n.* čovek [E] čovjek [J] 1A4
  pl ljudi 3A1

man (= male person) *n.* muškarac 3A1
  young man *n.* momak 4A1

manager *n.* upravitelj [C] upravnik [B,C,S]
  (m., general) upraviteljica [C] upravnica
  [B,C,S] *(f.)* 11A2✿

many *adj.* mnogi 6A4

many *adv.* mnogo 5A1, 5A1✿, 10A2✿, puno
  5A1

map *n.* karta, plan 16A1a
  map of town plan grada 16A1a

maple *n.* javor

March *n.* mart [B,S] ožujak [C] 6A2, 12A3✿

mark *n.* znak 17A1b

marker *n.* označivač 20.V

marketplace *n.* pijaca [B,S] tržnica [B,C]
  📖A.I

marry *vb.* ženiti (I); oženiti (P) 20.II

marry (in ceremony) *vb.*
  venčati (I/P) [E] vjenčati (I/P) [J]
  get married *vb.*
    venčati se (I/P) [E] 📖B.VII
    vjenčati se (I/P) [J] 📖B.VII

marshland *n.* bara 16A3b

marvelous *adj.* divan 3A2, sjajan 16A3a

masculine *adj.* muški 10A3
  masculine gender *n.* muški rod

mashed potatoes pire krompir [B,S] krumpir
  pire [C]

mask *n.* obrazina 19A2a

master (= gain control over) *vb.*
  savladati (P) B.VIII; savladavati (I)

master's thesis *adj.* magistarski rad 16A2a

masterpiece *n.* remek-delo [E] remek-djelo [J]
  19A2b

match (in sports) *n.* meč 12A2

material *n.* materijal 13A3

material *adj.* materijalan 20.VI

mathematician *n.* matematičar 11A3

mathematics *n.* matematika 3A2

matron of honor kuma 📖B.VIII

mature *adj.* zreo 20.II

May *n.* maj [B,S] svibanj [C] 6A2

may I help you? izvoli, izvolite 2A1✿

may (be allowed) *vb.*
  smeti (I) [E] 12A3, 12A3✿
  smjeti (I) [J] 12A3, 12A3✿

may (be able) *vb.* moći 2A4, 7A2✿

maybe *adv.* možda 9A3

me *pron.* ↪4
  (clitic) me 2A1, mi 6A3;
  (full) mene 2A2, meni 6A3, mnom 7A1
  see also **I**

meal (*e.g.* breakfast, lunch or dinner) *n.* obrok
  10A1

mean *vb.* značiti (I) 6A2, misliti 📖B.IV

meaning *n.* smisao 16A3a, značenje

means *n.* sredstva

measure *vb.* meriti [E] mjeriti [J]

measurement *n.* mera [E] mjera [J]

meat *n.* meso 6A4, 2A1✿, 9A2✿

mechanic *n.* mehaničar [B,C,S] strojar [C]
  11A2✿

medical school *n.* medicinski fakultet

medicine *n.* medicina 13B3

medieval *adj.* srednjevekovni [E] srednj-
  vjekovni [J] [B/S] srednjovjekovni [C]
  16A3b

meet (= encounter) *vb.*
  sresti (P); sretati (I) 📖B.IV
  susresti (P) 20.IV; susretati (I) 📖B.V

meet (*e.g.* at the station) *vb.* dočekati (P)
  5A3✿

meeting (for business) *n.* sastanak 13A3

meeting (political, etc.) *n.* skup

member *n.* član

membership card *n.* iskaznica 16A2a

memorize *vb.*
  zapamtiti (P) 16A1b,
  naučiti napamet (P) 10A3; učiti napamet (I)

memory *n.* pamćenje

men (= male persons) *n.* muškarci 3A1

men (= people) *n.* ljudi 3A1, 3A1✿, 3A2✿

mention *vb.*
  pomenuti (P) 16A1b; pominjati (I) [B,S]
  📖B.VII
  spomenuti (P) 16A1b; spominjati (I) [B,C]
  📖B.VII

menu *n.* jelovnik 6A4

merchandise *n.* roba

merciful *adj.* milosrdan 19A2a

mercy *n.* milosrđe 19A2a, milost 10A3

merriment *n.* veselje 15A1

message *n.* poruka 15A2, 15A2✿

meter *n.* metar 📖B.I

metric *adj.* metrički 19A3b

Mexican *n.* Meksikanac *(m., general)*,

Meksikanka *(f.)*
Mexican *adj.* meksički 📖B.II
middle *n.* sredina 7A4
   in the middle of *prep.* usred 6A1
midnight *n.* ponoć
might *n.* sila, moć, snaga 12A4, 6A4✿
migration *n.* seoba 17A2a
mild *adj.* blag 📖B.IV
milder *adj.* blaži
military *adj.* vojni 18A3
milk *n.* mleko [E] mlijeko [J] 4A3
million *num.* milijun [B,C] milion [B,S]
   17A2a, 12A1✿
mind (= intellect) *n.* um
mine *adj.* moj 1A2
mineral *adj.* mineralni 4A3
   mineral water *n.* mineralna voda 4A3
minute *n.* minut [B,S] minuta [C] 9A4
miracle *n.* čudo 16A1a
mirror *n.* ogledalo [B,C,S] zrcalo [C] 9A2
miserable *adj.* očajan 14A2
miserly *adj.* škrt 20.II
miss *vb.* nedostajati (I/P) 18A3, ⸬18A3⸬
   we miss them oni nam nedostaju
miss *(e.g.* an opportunity) *vb.*
   propustiti (P); propuštati (I) 12A3
Miss gospođica 16A2b
mistake *n.* pogreška, greška 📖B.III
mix *vb.*
   mešati (I); izmešati (P) [E] 14A1
   miješati (I); izmiješati (P) [J] 14A1
mock *vb.* rugati se (I) 📖B.V
moderate *adj.* umeren [E] umjeren [J] 16A3a
modern *adj.* savremen [B,S] suvremen [C],
   moderan 18A3
Mom *n.* mama 9A4
moment *n.* čas [B,C,S] 14A1, tren [B,C,S]
   14A1, trenutak [B,C,S] 3A2, 5A4✿,
   moment [B,C] momenat [B,S] 3A2
   at the moment momentalno [B,C,S]
     trenutačno [C] 16A2a
   at the last moment zadnji čas, u zadnji čas
     16A1a
monarchy *n.* monarhija 18A3
monastery *n.* manastir (Orthodox), samostan
   (Catholic) 16A3b
Monday *n.* ponedeljak [E] ponedjeljak [J]
   2A1
   on Mondays ponedeljkom [E] ponedjeljkom
     [J] 7A2✿
money *n.* novac 5A2, pare 5A2
monkey *n.* majmun 2A3
monotonous *adj.* jednoličan 20.II, monoton
   18A1a
Montenegrin *n.* Crnogorac *(m., general)*
   Crnogorka *(f.)* 1A4

Montenegrin *adj.* crnogorski 2⟳
Montenegrin coast *n.* Crnogorsko primorje
Montenegro *n.* Crna Gora 1⟳
month *n.* mesec [E] mjesec [J] 6A2, 6A2✿
   (for) a month mesec dana [E] mjesec dana
     [J] 9A1, 6A2✿
monument *n.* spomenik 16A3b
mood *n.* raspoloženje
moon *n.* mesec [E] mjesec [J] 6A1
more *adv.* više 3A3, još 4A3
   more and more sve više 7☺, 15A1✿
morning *n.* jutro 2A4, pre podne [E] prije
   podne [J] 10A1
   this morning jutros 3A1
   in the morning
     ujutro [B,C] ujutru [B,S] 7A4
Moscow *n.* Moskva 4A1
mosaic *n.* mozaik 20.II
mosque *n.* džamija
most *adv.* najviše 11A1, 11A2✿
   most of all *adv.* ponajviše 15A1
mother *n.* majka 2A3, 5A1✿, 9A2✿, ⸬9A4⸬
motorcycle *n.* motocikl 7A2
mountain *n.* planina 16A3b
mouse *n.* miš 8A1
move (= get going) *vb.*
   krenuti (P) ↪6 ; kretati (I) 9A2
move (= change residence) *vb.*
   seliti (se) (I); preseliti se (P) 18A3
move (= bring closer) *vb.*
   primaći [primaknuti] (P) 14A1; primicati (I)
move (= move to, resettle) *vb.*
   doseliti se (P) 16A3a; doseljavati se (I)
move (= shift position) *vb.*
   premestiti (P); premeštati (I) [E] 📖B.V
   premjestiti (P); premještati (I) [J] 📖B.V
move away *vb.* odseliti se (P) 18A3
movie *n.* film 2A3, ⸬10A1⸬
movie theater *n.* bioskop [S] kino [B,C] 5A2;
   kino-dvorana 16A1a
Mr. gospodin 2A2 *abbr.* g.
Mrs. gospođa 2A2 *abbr.* gđa
Ms. gospođa 2A2 *abbr.* gđa, gospođica
   16A2b
much *adv.* mnogo [B,C,S] puno [B,C,S] 5A1,
   5A1✿
   too much previše 📖B.III
multiply *vb.* množiti (I) 12A1
multitude *n.* mnoštvo 20.VII
museum *n.* muzej 5A4
music *n.* muzika [B,C,S] glazba [C] 7A4
musical *adj.* muzički [B,C,S] glazbeni [C]
   16A3b
musical instrument *n.* instrument [B,C,S]
   glazbalo [C] 19A3b
musician *n.* muzičar [B,C,S] glazbenik [C]

(m., general) mùzičārka [B,C,S] glàzbenīca
[C] (f.) 11A2☼

Muslim n. (ethnic category in former Yugoslavia) Muslìmān (m, general) Muslìmānka (f.)

Muslim n. (= adherent of Islam) muslìmān (m,
general) muslìmānka (f.)

Muslim adj. muslìmānskī 19A3b

must vb. mòrati (I) 2A1

  mustn't   use negated form of mòći 7A2☼

mutual adj. mèđusoban 📖B.IV

my adj. mòj ↦4   1A2, 5A3☼

mysterious adj. tàjanstven 📖B.V

N

naked adj. go [B,S] gȍl [C] 18A1a

name n. ȉme ↦4   1A2, 8A2☼

namely adv. nàime 15A1

narrow adj. ȕzak

narrower adj. ȕžī

national (e.g. national park) adj. nacionàlnī
16A2a

national (= of the people, the nation) adj.
nàrodnī 7☺, 📖B.IV

natural adj. prìrodan

  natural sciences n. prìrodnē nàuke [B,S]
  prìrodnē znanosti [C] 13B3

nature n. prìroda 18A2b

nausea n. mȕka

near adv. blìzu ↦5   4B4

near prep. blìzu 4A4, pri

nearby (= adjacent) adj. oblìžnjī 12A2

nearly adv. skòro 13A3

nearness n. blìzina 20.III

necessary adj. pòtreban 11A2, nȕžan 20.III

neck n. vrȁt 10A4

need n. pòtreba 19A2b

need vb. trèbati (I) 11A2, 11A2☼, 11A4☼,
12A3☼

needle n. ȉgla 📖A.VIII

negation n. negàcija 17C1

neighbor n.

  kòmšija [B,S] sùsjed [B,C] (m. general)
  kòmšinica [B,S] sùsjeda [B,C] (f.) 6A4

neither... nor conj.

  nȉti ... nȉti 5C1, nȉ ... nȉ 5A4☼

nephew n. nèćāk 20.II, sìnovac

nest n. gnézdo [E] gnijézdo [J] ↦4   5A1

neuter gender n. srédnjī rȍd

neutral adj. nèutralan

never adv. nȉkada 7A1, nijèdnōm 14A2

nevertheless adv. ȉpak 13A3

new adj. nȍv 4A1

New York n. New York [B,C] Njujork [S]
4A1

news n. vȅsti [E] vijèsti [J] 14A2, glȃs
19A3a

newspaper n. nòvine 3A3

newspaper adj. nòvīnskī 18A3

  newspaper article nòvīnskī člának

newsstand n. kiòsk 13A4

next (= coming) adj. ȉdūćī 5A3, 12A1☼

next (= subsequent) adj. slèdēćī [E] sljèdēćī
[J] 13A2, 12A1☼

next day n. sùtrādān 14A2

next to prep. do ↦5   4A4, 4A4☼   kràj
13A4, pòred 4A4

next year ȉdūćē gòdine, dogòdine 16A2a

nice adj. fȋn 2A3, 3A1☼, 6A1☼, 8A1☼, lép
[E] lijèp [J] 2A2

nicer adj. lèpšī [E] ljèpšī [J] 11A2☼

nickname n. nàdimak 18A3

nickname (= to give a nickname) vb.
prozvàti (P); prozívati (I)

niece n. nèćaka [S] nèćakinja [B,C], sìnovica

night n. nȏć ↦4   3A2

  tonight (= this evening) adv. vèčeras 3A1

  tonight (= this very night) adv. nòćas 13A3

  last night adv. sìnoć 14A3, nòćas 13A3

  good night excl. lȁku nȏć 3A2

nightingale n. slàvuj 19A1a

nightstand n. nàtkasna [B,S] nòćnī ormàrić
[B,C] 12A1

nine (9) num. dèvet 5A2 12A1☼

nine hundred (900) num. devetstȍ 12A1☼

nineteen (19) num. devètnaēst 5A1, 12A1☼

nineteenth (19th) adj. devètnaēstī 19A1

ninety (19) num. devedèset 5A1

ninth (9th) adj. dèvetī 9A1, 6A2☼

no nȅ 1A2, 1A2☼, 9A2☼

no man's land nȉčija zèmlja 16A1

no one nȉko [B,S] nȉtko [C] 9A3, 9A3☼

no one's adj. nȉčijī 16A1

nobody n. nȉko [B,S] nȉtko [C] 9A3☼

nocturnal adj. nòćnī 12A1

nod vb.

  kȋmnuti (P); kȋmati (I) 20.V

  klȋmnuti (P); klȋmati (I) 📖B.I

noise n. bȕka 20.I

nominative (case) n. nominàtīv

noon n. pȍdne 10A1

nonsense n. svàšta, kòješta

north n. sȅver [E] sjȅver [J]

north adj. sȅvernī [E] sjȅvernī [J] 4A1

  North America n. Sȅvernā Amèrika [E]
  Sjȅvernā Amèrika [J] 4A1

nose n. nȍs 10A4

not nȅ 2A1

  not anything nȉšta 4A3

  not either nȉ 7A1

  not have vb. nèmati (I) 2A1

notebook n. svèska [B,S] tȅka [B,C] 1A2,
bèležnica [S] bìlježnica [B,C] 1A2

nothing *pron.* ništa ↪4   4A3, 5A4✿,
7A1✿, 9A3✿

notice *vb.*
  primetiti (P) 14A4; primećivati (I) [E]
  primijetiti (P) 14A4; primjećivati (I) [J]

noun *n.* imenica 17A1b

novel *n.* roman 2A1

November *n.*
  novembar [B,S] studeni [C] 6A2

now *adv.* sad, sada 6A3, 9A2✿

nowhere *adv.* nigde [E] nigdje [J]

number (= integer) *n.* broj 3A1, № *abbr.*
  br. 12A2

number (= performance) *n.* točka [C] tačka
  [B,S] 15A1

numerous *adj.* brojan 2A2

nurse *n.* bolničar *(m., general)* bolničarka,
  medicinska sestra *(f.)* 11A2✿

O

o'clock sat [B,C,S] 5A2 čas [S] 14A3
  two o'clock dva sata [B,C,S]
  14.00 hours četrnaest sati [B,C,S] četrnaest
    časova [S]

O.K. u redu 13A2, dobro 2A3

oak *n.* hrast

oath *n.* zavet [E] zavjet [J]

obey *vb.* slušati (I) 6A2

objective *adj.* objektivan 13☺

obligation *n.* obaveza [B,C,S] obveza [C]
  12A3

observe (= watch) *vb.*
  posmatrati [B,S] promatrati [B,C] (I) 14☺

obtain *vb.*
  nabaviti (P) 16A1a; nabavljati (I)
  pribaviti (P); pribavljati (I) 16A2a

obviously *adv.* očito ▢B.V

occasion *n.* povod ▢B.I

occasionally *adv.* povremeno 8A3

occupation *n.* zanimanje 16A3b

occupy *vb.* zauzeti (P); zauzimati (I)

occupying forces *n.* okupator 18A3

October *n.*
  listopad [C] oktobar [B,S] 6A2

of *prep.* od ↪5 4A3, po 20.III

of course *adv.* naravno 7A1, svakako 2A4,
  kako da ne 5A4, nego šta [B,S] nego što
  [B,C] 11A4

off of *prep.* s, sa ↪5 4A4

offend *vb.*
  zameriti se (P) [E] 18A3
  zamjeriti se (P) [J] 18A3

offer *vb.*
  nuditi (I) 16A1b; ponuditi (P) 13A1

office *n.* kancelarija [B,C,S] ured [B,C] 6A1

official *adj.* službeni 14A2

often *adv.* često 7A1, 11A1✿
  more often češće 11A2✿

oh, no! *excl.* jao 9A2

old *adj.* star 6A3, 11A1✿
  Old Testament *n.* Stari zavet [E] Stari
    zavjet [J] 17C1
  oldsters starci ⌐9A4¬

Olympic Games *n.* Olimpijada 16A1b

omelet *n.* omlet 7A1

on *prep.* na ↪5 6A1, u ↪5 2A1,
  po ↪5 A.V.

on duty *adj.* dežuran 20.VII

on foot *adv.* pješice [C] 5A2, peške [E]
  pješke [J] [B,S] 5A2

on the contrary naprotiv 20.III

on the one hand s jedne strane 8A4✿

on the other hand s druge strane

once (= one time) *adv.* jedanput 10A1
  not once nijednom 14A2
  more than once ne jednom

once (= in the past) nekada 16A1b, jednom
  10A3
  once upon a time there was bio / bilo / bila
    jednom 10A3, ⌐10A3¬
  ....there were bili jednom *(m pl)* 10A3,
    ⌐10A3¬

one (1) jedan 3A1, 3A1✿, 4A3✿, 5A1✿,
  12A1✿

one (impersonal subject of sentence) *see*
  14A1✿

one another *n.* jedan drugi 11A2✿, 15A2✿,
  ⌐16B1¬

one by one *n.* jedan po jedan 15A2

one day jednog dana, jednoga dana 15A1✿

one-month *adj.* jednomesečni [E]
  jednomjesečni [J] 16A2b

one's own *adj.* svoj 5A3, 5A3✿
  see also **her/hers, his, their/theirs**

oneself *pron.* sebe, sebi, sobom ↪4
  6A2✿

onion *n.* luk
  spring onion mladi luk

only *adj.* jedini 16A2a, jedinstven 19A3b

only (= nothing else) *adv.* samo 3A3, 6A2✿

only (= just now) *adj.* tek 6A2

onto *prep.* na ↪5 6A1✿

oops! *excl.* joj! ↪5 ⌐9A4¬

open *vb.* otvoriti (P); otvarati (I) 12A2

open *adj.* otvoren 16A3a
  open sea pučina 17A3a

operate *vb.*
  operirati (I/P) [B,C] 20.V
  operisati (I/P) [B,S] 20.V

operation *n.* operacija 20.IV

opinion *n.* mišljenje 10A4, 10A4✿

opportunity *n.* prilika 16A1a

opposite (= across from) *prep.* nasuprot ↦5 8A4

optimism *n.* optimizam 20.VI

or *conj.* ili 1A3

  either ... or *conj.* ili ... ili 1A3

oral *adj.* usmen 6A2

orange (= fruit) *n.* naranča [C] narandža [B,S] pomorandža [S] 4A3

orange (= color) *adj.* narančast [C] narandžast [B,S]

order (= arrangement) *n.* red

order (= request for delivery) *n.* narudžba

order (= arrange, put in order) *vb.* urediti (P); uređivati (I) 12A1

order (= send for something) *vb.* naručiti (P); naručivati (I) 10A1

ordinary *adj.* običan 2A4

organize *vb.* urediti 12A1, 11A1✿ organizirati (I/P) [B,C] 16A3b organizovati (I/P) [B,S] 16A3b

origin (= emergence, genesis) *n.* nastanak 17A4, postanak

origin (= roots) *n.* poreklo [E] porijeklo [J] 16A3a

original *adj.* izvorni 16A2a

Orthodox church *n.* pravoslavna crkva

other *adj.* drugi 2A1, 16A1b

otherwise *adv.* inače 19A2b

Ottoman *adj.* osmanski 19A3b

ouch! *excl.* jao! 9A2, ⸤9A4⸥

ought *vb.* trebalo bi 13A4, valja (I) 12A3

our, ours *adj.* naš ↦5 1A2

out, outside *adv.* napolje [B,S] van [B,C]

out of *prep.* iz ↦5 4A1, 4A2✿

outgrow *vb.* prerasti (P) 18A3

outlive *vb.* nadživeti (P) [E] 18A3 nadživjeti (P) [J] 18A3

outside *adv.* napolju [B,S] vani [B,C] 5A4

over (= above) *prep.* ↦5 nad 8A1, 7A2✿, 8A4✿, iznad 8A4, 8A4✿

over (crossing a boundary) *prep.* preko ↦5 8A3

overcome *vb.* nadvladati (P); nadvlađivati (I) 20.III

overjoyed *adj.* presrećan [B,S] presretan [B,C] 10☺

own *adj.* sopstven [B,S] vlastit [B,C] 15A2

  one's own *adj.* svoj 5A3

P

page *n.* stranica 13A3

pain *n.* bol 20.IV, muka

painful *adj.* bolan ⸤9A3⸥

paint *n.* boja

paint (as artist) *vb.* slikati (I) 📖A.VI

painter (artist) *n.* slikar *(m., general)* slikarica [C] slikarka [B,S] *(f.)* 11A2✿

pair *n.* par 14A3

pal *n.* drug [B,S] prijatelj [B,C] 1A4

pale *adj.* bled [E] blijed [J]

paler *adj.* bleđi [E] bljeđi [J]

palm (of hand) *n.* dlan 19A1b

panic *vb.* uspaničiti se (P) 20.VII

pants (= trousers) *n.* hlače [B,C] pantalone [S] 11A1

paper clip *n.* spajalica

paper *n.* papir 1A2

parakeet *n.* papagaj [B,S] papiga [B,C] 6A2

parent *n.* roditelj 4A1, ⸤9A4⸥

Paris *n.* Pariz 4A1

park *n.* park 📖A.III

park *vb.* parkirati (I); uparkirati (P) 12A2

parking *n.* parkiranje 10☺

parrot *n.* papagaj [B,S] papiga [B,C] 6A2

part (= portion) *n.* deo [E] dio [J] 4☻

part (= role) *n.* uloga

part ways *vb.* rastati se (P); rastajati se (I) 14A2

participate *vb.* sudjelovati [B,C] učestvovati [B,S] 16A1a

parting (= separation) *n.* rastanak 📖B.IV

partner *n.* partner 13A3

pass (= pass by) *vb.* proći (P) 13A4; prolaziti (I) 📖B.VII

pass (of time) *vb.* proteći (P); proticati (I) 7☺

pass (*e.g.* exam) *vb.* položiti (P) 6A2, 10A2✿

passerby *n.* prolaznik 14A3

passionate *adj.* strastan 18A2a

passport *n.* pasoš [B,S] putovnica [C] 4☻

past *n.* prošlost 17A2b

past (= in the past) *adj.* prošli 10A2

  past tense *n.* prošlo vreme [E] prošlo vrijeme [J] 17C1

past (referring to recently concluded period) *adj.* protekli 20.II

pasta *n.* testenina [E] tjestenina [J]

patience *n.* strpljenje 8A1

patient *n.* pacijent 20.I

patient *adj.* strpljiv 8A1

pay (money) *vb.* platiti (P); plaćati (I) 2A4

  it pays to... isplati se (I) 14A2

peace *n.* mir 7A3

pear *n.* kruška 4A3

peanut *n.* kikiriki

peanut butter maslac od kikirikija [C] puter od kikirikija [B,S]

pedestrian *n.* pešak [E] pješak [J] [B/S] 5A2

pen *n.* pero 2A1

  ballpoint pen hemijska olovka [B,S] kemijska olovka [C] 2A4, ⸤7A4⸥

fountain pen pèro 2A1

pencil *n.* (obična) olovka 1A2, `7A4`

penetrate *vb.*
  prodreti (P); prodirati (I) [E] 20.I
  prodrijeti (P); prodirati (I) [J] 20.I

penguin *n.* pingvin 15A1

penguin *adj.* pingvinski 15A1

peninsula *n.*
  poluostrvo [B,S] poluotok [B,C] 6⊙

people (= persons) *n.* ljudi 3A1, 3A1✿

people (= national group) *n. sg* narod [B,C,S]
  17A2a puk [C] 17A2a

pepper (= vegetable) *n.* paprika 7A1

pepper (= spice) *n.* biber [B,S] papar [B,C]

per *prep* po
  three apples per person tri jabuke po osobi

perfect *adj.* savršen 9A3

perfective (grammar) *adj.* svršen
  perfective aspect (grammar) *n.* svršen vid

perfect *vb.*
  usavršiti (P); usavršavati (I) 16A3a

perform (= carry out) *vb.*
  izvršiti (P) 12A4; izvršavati (I)

perform (*e.g.* a number) *vb.*
  izvesti (P); izvoditi (I) 15A1

performance *n.*
  predstava 5A4, priredba 16A3b

period (of time) *n.*
  razdoblje 16A2b, period 17A4

period (in punctuation) *n.*
  tačka [B,S] točka [C]

perish (= get killed) *vb.* poginuti (P) 14A3

permanent *adj.* trajan

permit *vb.*
  dopustiti (P) 16A2a; dopuštati (I) 📖B.III
  dozvoliti (P) 16A3b; dozvoljavati (I)

persecute *vb.*
  progoniti (P) 18A3; proganjati (I)

person (= man [*generic*]) *n.* čovek [E] čovjek
  [J] 1A4, 3A1✿, *pl* ljudi 3A1, 3A1✿

person (= individual) *n.* osoba [B,C,S] 3A1,
  3A1✿ lice [B,S]

personal *adj.* ličan [B,S] osoban [B,C]

personality *n.* ličnost 18A3

personnel *n.* osoblje 11A4

persuade *vb.*
  uveriti (P); uveravati (I) [E] 16A3b
  uvjeriti (P); uvjeravati (I) [J] 16A3b

pharmacist *n.* apotekar, farmaceut *(m.,*
  general) apotekarica [BC] apotekarka [B,S]
  (f.) 11A2✿

phenomenon *n.* pojava 18A1b

philology *n.* filologija 13B3

philosophy *n.* filozofija 13B3

phone *n.* telefon 8A3✿
  cellular phone mobitel

phone *vb.* telefonirati (I/P) 📖A.VII

photo *n.* fotografija 20.V

phrase *n.* fraza 17A1b

physical *adj.* fizički 13B3

physical education *n.* fizička kultura [B,C,S]
  kineziologija [C] 13B3, fiskultura

physics *n.* fizika 13B3

piano *n.* glasovir [C] klavir [B,C,S]

pick *vb.* brati ↤6 A.I

picture *n.* slika 6A3

pie *n.* pita

piece *n.* komad [B,C,S] 4A3 parče [B,S] 4A3

pigeon *n.* golub

pillow *n.* jastuk 12A1

pine *n.* bor

place *n.* mesto [E] mjesto [J] 10☺, 11A2✿

place *vb.* postaviti (P) 15A2, 11A1✿;
  postavljati (I)

place of interest *n.* znamenitost 16A3b

plan *vb.* planirati (I) 16A1b

planet *n.* planet [C] planeta [B,S] 6A1

plant *n.* biljka 17A2a

plate *n.* tanjir [B,S] tanjur [C] 📖A.VI

play (= have fun) *vb.* igrati se (I) 16A1b,
  8A2✿, 9A2✿

play (a game) *vb.* igrati (I) 5C1

play (an instrument) *vb.* svirati (I) 18A3

player (of a game) *n.*
  igrač *(m., general)* igračica *(f.)*

playground *n.* igralište 📖B.IV

pleasant *adj.* prijatan 11A2, ugodan 7A2

please *vb.* prijati (I) 13A1,
  svideti se (P) 10A2, 10A2✿; sviđati se (I)
  [E] 6A4, 10A2✿
  svidjeti se (P) 10A2, 10A2✿; sviđati se (I)
  [J] [B,C,S] 6A4, 10A2✿
  dopasti se (P) 📖B.IV; dopadati se (I) [B,S]
  16A1a

please molim te, molim vas 2A4

plot (of a narrative) *n.* radnja 17A3b

pluck *vb.* brati (I) ↤6 📖A.I

plum *n.* šljiva 4A3

poem *n.* pesma [E] pjesma [J] 10A3

poet *n.* pesnik [E] pjesnik [J] *(m., general)*
  pesnikinja [E] pjesnikinja [J] *(f.)* 11A2✿

poetic *adj.* poetski 19A1b, pesnički [E]
  pjesnički [J] 19A1b

poetry *n.* poezija 3A2

point (= dot) *n.* tačka [B,S] točka [C]

point out *vb.*
  ukazati (P); ukazivati (I) 20.VIII

police *n.* policija 14A3

police *adj.* policijski 14A3, `9A3`

policy *n.* politika 📖B.V

political *adj.* politički 13B3
  political science političke nauke [B,S]

políticke znanosti [C] 13B3, 5A2

politics *n.* polìtika 📖B.V

poor *adj.* siròmašan, bȅdan [E] bijȅdan [J],
  ȕbog *(archaic)* 17A3a

poorly (said of health) *adv.* slabo 6A3

poplar *n.* jablȁn 18A1a

porcelain *adj.*
  porcèlanskī [S] porcùlanskī [B,C] 12A2

pork *n.* svìnjetina

port (= harbor) *n.* lȕka

pose (*e.g.* a question) *vb.*
  pòstaviti (P) 15A2; pòstavljati (I) 16A1b

possess *vb.* ȉmati 2A1
  pòsedovati (I) [E] 19A2b
  pòsjedovati (I) [J] 19A2b

possessive *adj.* (grammar) pòsvojan [C]
  prȉsvojan [B,S]

possibility *n.* mogúćnōst 16A1a

possible *adj.* eventuàlan 16A3a, mогȕć
  12A1✿

possible *adv.* mогȕće 11A3

postcard *n.* kàrtica
  picture postcard *n.* rȁzglednica 2A4

posthumous *adj.* pòsmrtan 17A4

potato *n.* kròmpīr [B,S] krùmpīr [C]
  mashed potatoes *n.* pìre kròmpīr [B,S]
    krùmpīr pìre [C]
  French fries *n.* pòmfrit

pour *vb.* lȉti (I); nàliti (P) 14☺, 11A1✿

pour (= serve a beverage) *vb.*
  sìpati (I/P) [B,S] tòčiti (I) [B,C,S] 13A1

pour off *vb.*
  òdliti (P) 14A1; odlȉvati (I) [E]
  òdliti (P) 14A1; odlijȅvati (I) [J]

pour over *vb.*
  prèliti (P) 14A1; prelȉvati (I) [E]
  prèliti (P) 14A1; prelijȅvati (I) [J]

pour out one's troubles *vb.*
  ìzjadati se (P) 15A1

power *n.* snȁga 12A4, sìla

powerful *adj.* mòćan 19A2b, sȉlan B.V,
  snàžan 15A1

practice *vb.*
  vèžbati (I) [E] 2A1
  vjèžbati (I) [J] 2A1

praise *n.* hvàliti (I)

pray *vb.* mòliti (I) 17A3a

precious stones *n.* drȁgo kàmēnje 12A2

precipitation *n.*
  padaline [C] padavine [B,S] 14A2

precise *adj.* tàčan [B,S] tòčan [C] 6A1

precisely *adv.* baš 9A3, tàčno [B,S] tòčno
  [C] 6A1

predict *vb.*
  prèdvideti (P); predvȉđati (I) [E] 📖B.III
  prèdvidjeti (P); predvȉđati (I) [J] 📖B.III

prefer *vb.*
  vȉše vòleti [E] vȉše vòljeti (I) [J] 3A3

pregnant *adj.* trȕdna 📖B.II

prejudice *n.* predrȁsuda 📖B.IV

premises *n.* prostòrija 6A1

preparation *n.*
  prìprema 14A1, sprȅmanje 15A1

prepare (something) *vb.*
  priprèmiti (P) 13A3; priprèmati (I)
  sprèmiti (P); sprèmati (I) 7A1

prepare (= get ready) *vb.*
  priprèmiti se (P) 13A3; priprèmati se (I)
  sprèmiti se (P); sprèmati se (I) 7A1

preposition *n.*
  prȅdlog [E] prijèdlog [J] 17A1b

present *adj.* sàdašnjī 17C1

present *vb.* prȅdstaviti (P) 19A3b; prȅd-
  stavljati (I) 19A2b

present tense sàdašnje vrȅme [E] sàdašnje
  vrijȅme [J] 17C1

preserve *vb.* čùvati (I); òčuvati (P) 10A4

president *n.*
  prȅdsednīk (*m., general*) prȅdsednica (*f.*) [E]
  prȅdsjednīk [J] (*m., general*) prȅdsjednica (*f.*)
  [J] 11A2✿

press (= printing activity) *n.* štàmpa [B,S]
  tȉsak [B,C] 14C4

presume *vb.* pretpòstaviti (P); pretpòstavljati
  (I)

pretend *vb.*
  pretvòriti se (P); pretvárati se (I) 15A1

pretend to be *vb.* prȁviti se [B,C,S] 📖B.IV

previous *adj.* dòsadašnjī 16A2b

price *n.* cèna [E] cijèna [J] 16A2b

priest (Catholic) *n.*
  svéćenīk [B,C] svéštenīk [B,S] 11A2✿

priest (Orthodox) *n.* pop 11A2✿

prince *n.* knȅz
  fairytale prince *n.* kràljević 📖B.VIII

princess *n.* knèginja
  fairytale princess princèza 📖B.VIII

print *vb.*
  štàmpati (I) [B,S] 20.V
  tìskati (I) [C] 20.V

prison *n.* zàtvor 20.VII

private *adj.* privátan 16A2a

prize *n.* nàgrada 📖B.II

probable *adj.* vèrovatan [E] vjerojatan [J] [C]
  vjȅrovatan [J] [B/S] 10A2

probably *adv.* vàljda 20.VI, vèrovatno [E]
  vjerojatno [J] [C] vjȅrovatno [J] [B/S] 10A2

problem *n.* pròblem 5A2

proclaim *vb.*
  proglásiti (P); proglàšavati (I) 12A4

produce *vb.* pròizvesti (P); pròizvoditi (I)

product *n.* pròizvod

production *n.* proizvodnja
profession *n.* struka 11A3, profesija
professor *n.* profesor *(m., general)* 1A4
 profesorica [B,C] profesorka [S] *(f.)* 1A4
professorial *adj.* profesorski 8A4
progress *n.* napredak ⬜B.III
project *n.* projekat [B,S] projekt [B,C] 16A1a
promise *vb.* obećati (P); obećavati (I) 11☺
promise *n.* obećanje
pronoun *n.* zamenica [E] zamjenica [J]
 17A1b
pronounce *(e.g. sounds) vb.*
 izgovoriti (P) 19A2a; izgovarati (I)
pronounce *(e.g. judgement) vb.*
 izreći (P); izricati (I) 19A2b
pronunciation *n.* izgovor ⬜B.III
propeller *n.* propeler 15A1
proposal *n.* predlog [E] prijedlog [J] 20.IV
propose *vb.* predložiti (P); predlagati (I) 20.IV
protagonist *n.* protagonist [B,C] protagonista
 [B,S] 18A2b
proud *adj.* ponosan 16A1b, gord 18A1a
provide *vb.*
 obezbediti (P) 16A1b; obezbeđivati (I) [E]
 obezbijediti (P) 16A1b; obezbjeđivati (I) [J]
 [B/S]
 osigurati (P); osiguravati (I) [C] 16A1b
psychology *n.* psihologija 13B3
public (= audience) *n.* publika
 the general public javnost 14A3
publication (= activity) *n.* objavljivanje 18A3
publish *vb.*
 izdati (P); izdavati (I) 16A2a
 objaviti (P); objavljivati (I) 17A4
pull *vb.* vući (I)
pull in *vb.*
 uvući (P); uvlačiti (I) 20.VIII
pull out *vb.*
 izvući (P); izvlačiti (I) 20.V
punish *vb.*
 kazniti (P) 18A3; kažnjavati (I)
pupil *n.* đak 5A1, učenik *(m., general)* 14A4
 učenica *(f.)*
purely *adv.* čisto
purple *adj.* ljubičast
purpose *n.* svrha 6A2
put *vb.*
 staviti (P) 6A3; stavljati (I) 6A4
 postaviti (P) 15A2; postavljati (I) 16A1a
 položiti (P); polagati (I) 6A2
put away *vb.*
 skloniti (P); sklanjati (I) 13A2
put down *vb.*
 spustiti (P); spuštati (I) 13A2

Q

quadrangle *n.*
 četverokut [B,C] četvorougao [B,S]
quarrel *vb.* svaditi se (P); svađati se (I)
 15A2✿☞
quarter (in mathematics) *n.*
 četvrt, četvrtina 12A1, 12A1✿☞
quarter (= of an city) *n.* četvrt
queen *n.* kraljica
question *n.* pitanje 1A2, 3A1✿☞, 3A2✿☞
question *vb.* ispitati (P); ispitivati (I) 20.VII
question mark *n.* upitnik
queue *n.* red 11A4
quick *adj.* brz 2A2, 3A2✿☞
quicker *adj.* brži 11A2✿☞
quickly *adv.* brzo 2A2 ubrzo 18A3
quiet *adj.* tih 20.VI, 11A2✿☞
quieter *adj.* tiši 11A2✿☞
quiet down *vb.* utihnuti (P) ⬜B.VIII,
 stišati [se] (P) 14A4; stišavati [se] (I)
quizzical *adj.* upitan 9☺
quote *vb.* navesti (P); navoditi (I) 20.VIII

R

rabbit *n.* zec
radio *n.* radio 9A3
 radio station radio stanica [B,C,S] radio
 postaja [C] 9A3
rag *n.* krpa ⬜A.VI
rage *n.* bes [E] bijes [J]
railway *adj.* železnički [E] željeznički [J]
railway station *n.* kolodvor [C] železnička
 stanica [E] željeznička stanica [J] [B/S] 5A3,
 9A3
rain *n.* kiša 14A2
rainbow *n.* duga ⬜A.VIII
raise (= rear) *vb.*
 odgojiti (P); odgajati (I) 20.VI
 hraniti (I); othraniti (P) 20.IV
raise (= lift) *vb.*
 dići [dignuti] (P); dizati (I) 14A1
random *adj.* slučajan 14A3
rare *adj.* redak [E] rijedak [J]
rarer *adj.* ređi [E] rjeđi [J]
rather (= that is) *conj.* nego 2A1, odnosno
 12A1, pak 5A3, već 3A2
rather (= quite) *conj.* dosta 10A4
rather (= preferably) *conj.* radije 19A2a
raven *n.* gavran
ray (of light) *n.* zrak [B,S] zraka [C] 17A3a
reach (= get through to) *vb.* dopirati (I) 20.I
 dopreti (P)
reach (= achieve) *vb.*
 doseći [dosegnuti] (P); dosezati (I) 20.III
reach (an age) *vb.* napuniti (P)
read *vb.* čitati (I) 2A1; pročitati (P) 10A2
reader *n.* čitatelj *(m., general)* čitateljica *(f.)*

[C], čìtalac [B,C,S]

reading *n.* čìtanje 📖B.III, 10A4✿

reading room *n.* čìtaonica 16A2a

ready *adj.* spreman 15A1

real *adj.* pravi 3A2, stvarni

reality (in the material world) *n.* stvarnost

reality (as an abstraction) *n.* zbìlja

realize *vb.*
  shvatiti (P) 14A4; shvaćati (I) 20.V
  15A1✿
  saznati (P) ¦ 17A2a ¦
  spoznati (P); spoznavati (I) 20.III

really *adv.* doista 16A2a, stvarno 2A2, zaista
  2A2, zbilja 10A3

rear *adj.* zadnji 16A1a

reason (= motivation) *n.* razlog 8☺
  for that reason zato 📖B.IV

reason (= intellect) *n.* razum

receive *vb.*
  primiti (P); primati (I) 18A3
  dobiti (P) 11A2; dobijati (I) [B,S]
  dobiti (P) 11A2; dobivati (I) [B,C]

recipe *n.* recept 14A1

recognize *vb.*
  prepoznati (P); prepoznavati (I) 20.III

recommend *vb.*
  preporučiti (P) 13A1; preporučivati (I)

record (= make a recording) *vb.*
  snimiti (P) 19A3b; snimati (I)

recover (= get better) *vb.*
  oporaviti se (P); oporavljati se 20.VI

red *adj.* crven 2A3, 2A3✿, 4A4✿

reflexive *adj.* povratan

refresh *vb.*
  osvežiti (P); osvežavati (I) [E] 📖B.IV
  osvježiti (P); osvježavati (I) [J] 📖B.IV

refrigerator *n.* frižider [B,C,S] hladnjak [C]

regardless of bez obzira na 9A4

region *n.* kraj 14A2, područje 6🌍

registrar (university) *n.* referada 16A2b

regular *adj.* redovan [B,C,S] redovit [B,C]
  16A3b

relationship *n.* odnos 11A4

relative (= kin) *n.* rođak 8A3 *(m., general)*
  rođaka 15A1, rođakinja *(f.)*

relax *vb.*
  opustiti se (P); opuštati se (I)

release *vb.*
  pustiti (P) 7A3; puštati (I)

remain *vb.*
  ostati (P) 9A2; ostajati (I) 14A1, ¦ 17A2b ¦

remaining *adj.* ostali 13A3

remember *vb.*
  setiti se (P) 12A3; sećati se (I) [E] 11A3
  sjetiti se (P) 12A3; sjećati se (I) [J] 11A3

renew *vb.*

obnoviti (P) 15A1; obnavljati (I) 16A3a

rent (something) *vb.* iznajmiti (P) 9A3,
  ¦ 9A3 ¦ iznajmljivati (I) 16A2b

rent (from someone) *vb.*
  unajmiti (P) ¦ 9A3 ¦ unajmljivati (I) [C]
  16A2b

rent *n.* kirija [B,S] stanarina [B,C,S] 9A3

rented room *n.* privatna soba

repair *vb.*
  popraviti (P) 13A2; popravljati (I)

reply *n.* odgovor 2A1 replika 📖B.I

report *n.* izvješće [C], izveštaj [E] izvještaj
  [J] [B/S] 14A2

report *vb.*
  prijaviti (P); prijavljivati (I) 14A3

Republic of Srpska *n.* Republika Srpska *see*
  map 4🌍

reputation *n.* reputacija 13A3, ugled

request *n.* molba 16A2a

request *vb.* moliti (I) 2A4; zamoliti (P) 13A1

rescue *vb.*
  spasti (P) 13☺
  spasavati (I) [B,S] spašavati (I) [C]

research *n.* istraživanje 16A2a

research *vb.*
  istražiti (P) 16A2b; istraživati (I) 15A2

research *adj.* istraživački 16A2a

resemble *vb.*
  ličiti (na) (I) [B,S] 📖A.III
  sličiti (na) (I) [B,C] 📖A.III

reserve *vb.*
  rezervirati (I/P) [B,C] 16A1a
  rezervisati (I/P) [B,S] 16A1a

reside *vb.* stanovati (I) 9A1

resident *n.* stanovnik

respect *n.* poštovanje 16A2a

respect *vb.* poštovati (I) 12A3

respected *adj.* poštovan 16A2a

respectively *adv.* odnosno 12A1

respond *vb.*
  odgovoriti (P) 10A2; odgovarati (I) 5A1

resurrection *n.* uskrsnuće 17A2a

rest *n.* odmor 5C1

restaurant *n.* restoran 10A1

restless *adj.* nemiran 8A2

restlessness *n.* nemir 18A1a

retell *vb.* prepričati (P) 15A2; prepričavati (I)

return *n.* povratak 14A4

return *vb.* vratiti se (P) 9A2; vraćati se (I)
  14A2, 9A2✿

rework *vb.* preraditi (P) 15A2; prerađivati (I)

rhythm *n.* ritam 20.II

rich *adj.* bogat 16A2b

ride (in a vehicle) *n.* vožnja 7A2

ride (as a passenger or on a bicycle) *vb.* voziti
  se (I) 7A2, 7A2✿

right (= not left) *adj.* desni 13A4
right (= correct) *adj.*
  tačan [B,S] točan [B,C] 6A1
  be right *vb.* imati pravo 7A2, biti u pravu
    ⏛B.V
right (= just or legal claim) *n.* pravo 7A2
  human rights ljudska prava
right! *excl.* tako je! 4A2
ring (on finger) *n.* prsten ⏛A.V
ring *vb.* zvoniti (I) ⏛A.V
rise (= to get up) *vb.*
  ustati (P) ⏛B.VIII; ustajati (I) ⏛A.V
rise early *vb.* uraniti (P) 19A3a
risky *adj.* riskantan 20.IV
rival *n.* suparnik 18A3
rivalry *n.* suparništvo 18A3
river *n.* reka [E] rijeka [J] 3☻
river *adj.* rečni [E] riječni [J] 20.V
rice *n.* riža [B,C] pirinač [S]
road *n.* put [B,C,S] ↦4 cesta [B,C] 14A3
robber *n.* lopov
robin *n.* crvendač
Romance languages, study of
  romanistika 13B3
Romania *n.* Rumunija [B,S]
  Rumunjska [C] 1☻
Rome *n.* Rim 12A3
roof *n.* krov
room *n.* soba 6A1
room *adj.* sobni 8A4
roommate *n.* cimer *(m., general)* cimerica [C]
  cimerka [B,S] *(f.)* 12A1
root *n.* koren [E] korijen [J] 19A1b
root for *vb.* navijati (I) ⏛B.II
roots *n. coll.* korenje [E] korijenje [J]
rose *n.* ruža ⏛A.IV
rough *adj.* grub
rougher *adj.* grublji
ruddy *adj.* rumen 17A3a
rug *n.* sag [C] tepih [B,S] 8A4
ruin *vb.* kvariti (I); pokvariti (P) ⏛B.VII
rule (= regulation) *n.* pravilo 20.II
rule (= reign) *n.* vladavina 19A3b
run *vb.* trčati (I) ⏛A.V
run-down *adj.* trošan 20.VIII
Russian *adj.* ruski 4A4
Russian *n.* Rus *(m., general)* Ruskinja *(f.)*
rusty *adj.* rđav

S
sacred *adj.* svet 17C1
sad *adj.* tužan 2A2
sadden *vb.*
  rastužiti se (P) 15A1; rastuživati se (I)
safe *adj.* siguran 14A1✿
salad *n.* salata 11A2

salary *n.* plaća [B,C] plata [B,S] 18A3
salesperson *n.* prodavač *(m., general)*
  prodavačica *(f.)* ⏛A.IV
salon *n.* salon ⏛B.V
salt *n.* so [B,S] sol [C]
salty *adj.* slan 6A4
same *adj.* isti 9A2
Sarajevan *adj.* sarajevski 6A2
Sarajevo *n.* Sarajevo 12A4✿
Sarajevo resident Sarajlija *(m., general)*
  Sarajka *(f.)*
satisfied *adj.* zadovoljan 11A3
Saturday *n.* subota 2A1, 2A1✿
  on Saturdays subotom 7A2✿
sausage *n.* kobasica 7A1
save (= rescue) *vb.*
  spasti (P) 13☺
  spasavati (I) [B,S] spašavati (I) [C]
say *vb.* kazati (I/P) 5A1 reći (P) 7A3,
  7A3✿,12A2✿, 13A2✿
  it's said kaže se 1A3, 9A2✿
scene *n.* prizor 18A1b
schedule *n.* raspored, red
  train or bus schedule red vožnje ⏛B.III
schedule (*e.g.* an appointment) *vb.*
  zakazati (P); zakazivati (I) ⏛B.VI
scholar *n.* naučnik [B,S] znanstvenik [C]
  učenjak [B,C] 11A2✿
scholarship (= scholarly work) *n.* nauka [B,S]
  znanost [C] 11A3
scholarship (= financial aid) *n.*
  stipendija 16A1a
school (= educational institution) *n.*
  škola 5C1
school (= university subdivision) *n.* fakultet
  ⸝5A2⸜
school *adj.* školski 6A2
science *n.* nauka [B,S] znanost [C] 11A3
  information science informatika 13B3
  political science
    političke nauke [B,S]
    političke znanosti [C] 13B3
  social sciences
    društvene nauke [B,S]
    društvene znanosti [C] 13B3
  natural sciences *n.*
    prirodne nauke [B,S]
    prirodne znanosti [C] 13B3
scientist *n.*
  naučnik [B,S] znanstvenik [C] učenjak
  [B,C] 11A2✿
scold *vb.* koriti (I) ⏛B.III
scoop up *vb.* zagrabiti (P) 14A1
sculptor *n.* kipar [B,C] vajar [B,S] *(m.,*
  general) kiparica [B,C] vajarka [B,S] *(f.)*
  11A2✿

sea *n.* more 1🌑

  open sea pučina 17A3a

sea gull *n.* galeb

sea *adj.* morski

search *n.* potraga 19A2b

search *vb.* tražiti (I) 3A1, iskati (I) 17A3a

season *n.*

  godišnje doba 17A3b, sezona 16A3b

second (= unit of time) *n.* sekunda 14A1

second (2nd) *adj.* drugi 2A1, 6A2✿

secondly *adv.* drugo 4A4

secret *n.* tajna

secretive *adj.* skrovit 20.VIII

secure *vb.*

  obezbediti (P) 16A1b; obezbeđivati (I) [E]

  obezbijediti (P) 16A1b; obezbjeđivati (I) [J]
  [B/S]

  osigurati (P); osiguravati (I) [C] 16A1b

secure *adj.* siguran 14A1✿

sediment *n.* talog 14A1

see *vb.* videti (I/P) [E] vidjeti (I/P) [J] ↪6
  2A2, 7A3✿, 11A1✿

  see frequently *vb.* viđati (I) 📖B.VII

  see you! vidimo se! 2A1

seek *vb.* tražiti (I) 3A1, iskati (I) 17A3a

seem *vb.* izgledati 9A2

  činiti se (I) 6A4; učiniti se (P) 16A2a

  it seems to me

  čini mi se 6A4, izgleda mi 9A2

select *vb.* birati (I) 📖A.VIII

selfish *adj.* sebičan 13A2

sell *vb.* prodati (P) 20.II; prodavati (I) 9☺

semester *n.* semestar 6A2

send *vb.* slati (I) 6A3; poslati (P) 📖B.II,
  11A1✿, 15A2✿

senior *n.* student četvrte godine

sense (= meaning) *n.* smisao 16A3a

sense (= suspect) *vb.* slutiti (I) 18A1a

sensitive *adj.* osetljiv [E] osjetljiv [J]

sentence (grammar) *n.* rečenica 15A2

separate *vb.*

  deliti (I); podeliti (P) [E]

  dijeliti (I); podijeliti (P) [J]

September *n.* rujan [C] septembar [B,S] 6A2

Serb *n.* Srbin *(m., general)* Srpkinja *(f.)* ↪4
  1A4

Serbia *n.* Srbija 1🌑

Serbian *adj.* srpski 2🌑

series (TV) *n.* serija 📖B.II

serious *adj.* ozbiljan 3A3

servant *n.* sluga 7A3

serve *vb.* služiti (I)

  poslužiti (P) 13A1; posluživati (I)

service *n.* služba

  employment service *n.*

  služba za zapošljavanje 11A4

set (of sun or moon) *vb.*

  zaći (P); zalaziti (I) 16A3b

set in motion *vb.*

  pokrenuti (P); pokretati (I) 16A2a

set out *vb.* krenuti (P) ↪6; kretati (I) 9A2
  poći (P) 9A4; polaziti (I) 9A2

settle (of sediment) *vb.*

  sleći se [slegnuti se] (P) 14A1

seven (7) *num.* sedam 12A1✿

seven (group of men) *num.* sedmorica 12A2✿

seven (group of mixed company) *num.* sedmero
  [C] sedmoro [B,S] 12A2✿

seven hundred (700) *num.* sedamsto 12A1✿

seventeen (17) *num.* sedamnaest 5A1, 12A1✿

seventeenth (17th) *adj.* sedamnaesti 17A1

seventh (7th) *adj.* sedmi 7A1, 6A2✿

seventy (70) *num.* sedamdeset 5A1

several *adj.* nekoliko 6🌑

sew *vb.* šiti (P); šivati (I)

  sew on *vb.* prišiti (P); prišivati (I) 📖A.VIII

shadow *n.* sena [E] sjena [J] 18A1a

shake *vb.* tresti (I) ↪6 10A1

shallow *adj.* plitak

shallower *adj.* plići

Shanghai *n.* Šangaj 9A1

shape *n.* oblik 15A2, forma 19A3b

share *vb.*

  deliti (I); podeliti (P) [E] 9A3

  dijeliti (I); podijeliti (P) [J] 9A3

shared *adj.* zajednički 12A1

sharp *adj.* oštar 10A3

she *pron.* ona ↪4 1A2, 1A2✿

  see also **her**

sheet (= bedding) *n.*

  čaršaf [B] čaršav [S] plahta [C] 12A1

shelf *n.* polica 📖A.VI

shirt *n.* košulja 11A1

shit *n.* *(vulg.)* govno

shoe *n.* cipela 1A2

shoot (= hit target) *vb.*

  pogađati (I); pogoditi (P) 📖B.VII

shop *n.* ⸢12A2⸥ dućan [B,C,S] 12A2, prodavaonica [C], prodavnica [B,S], radnja
  [B,C,S] 12A2, samoposluga [B,C] 📖A.II,
  samousluga [S] 📖A.II, trgovina [B,C,S]
  12A2

shopping *n.* kupovina 12A2

short (in length) *adj.* kratak 3A3, 11A2✿

short (in stature) *adj.* nizak 2A2

shorter (in length) *adj.* kraći 11A2✿

shorter (in stature) *adj.* niži 11A2✿

should treba 12A3✿

shoulder *n.* rame 10A4

shout *vb.* vikati (I) 20.VII

  shout at length *vb.*

  izvikati se (P); izvikivati se (I) 20.VII

shout out *vb.* prodèrati se (P) 📖B.VIII, uzvȉknuti (P); uzvȋkati (I) 📖B.IV

show *vb.* pokázati (P) 20.VI, 9A2✿; pokazívati (I) 📖A.IV

sick *adj.* bolèstan 10A4

side *n.* strána 8A4, 8A4✿

side dish *n.* prȉlog 11A2

sidewalk *n.* pločnȉk [C] trotoȁr [B,S] 14A3

sigh *n.* ùzdah 17A3a

sign *n.* znȁk 17A1b

sign (one's name) *vb.* potpísati (P); potpisívati (I) 20.V

sign over *vb.* prèpisati (P) 20.IV

signature *n.* pòtpis 20.VIII

significance *n.* znàčaj

silence *n.* tišìna 15A2

silent *adj.* tȉh 20.VI

  be silent *vb.*
    ćútati (I) [B,S] 17A3a
    šútjeti (I) [J] [B,C] 📖B.IV

  fall silent *vb.*
    zaćútati (P) [E] 20.V
    zašútjeti (P) [J] 20.V

silly *adj.* blèsav 📖B.VI, neòzbiljan 3A3

silver *n.* srèbro

similar *adj.*
    slȉčan 11A2, pòput (prep.) 19A1b

simple *adj.* pròst 16A1b, jednòstavan

simultaneous *adj.* istòvremen 15A1

since (= inasmuch as) *conj.* budúći da 12A1, 12A1✿

since (= ever since) *conj.* òtkada 📖B.VIII

sincere *adj.* ìskren 📖B.VIII

sing *vb.*
    pèvati (I) [E] 5C1
    pjèvati (I) [J] 5C1

singer *n.* pèvač [E] pjèvač [J] 19A3b

single *adj.* jèdan jèdini, jèdinstven

sink *vb.* utònuti (P) 18A1a

sip *vb.* sȑknuti (P) 14A1; sȑkati (I)

sister *n.* sèstra 2A3, 5A1✿, 6A2✿

sit (= be sitting) *vb.*
    sèdeti (I) [E] 6A3, 11A4✿, 15A2✿
    sjèditi (I) [J] 6A3, 11A4✿, 15A2✿

sit (= to take a seat) *vb.*
    sèsti (P) [E] 11A4, 11A4✿
    sjèsti (P) [J] 11A4, 11A4✿

situate *vb.*
    smèstiti (P) 17A3b; smèštati (I) [E]
    smjèstiti (P) 17A3b; smjèštati (I) [J]

situation *n.* stànje 14A3, situácija 14A2

six (6) *num.* šèst 5A2, 12A1✿

six (group of men) *num.* šestòrica 12A2✿

six (group of mixed company) *num.* šèstero [C] šèstoro [B,S] 12A2✿

six hundred (600) *num.* šèststo 12A1✿

sixteen (16) *num.* šèsnaest 5A1, 12A1✿

sixteenth (16th) *adj.* šesnàesti 16A1

sixth (6th) *adj.* šèsti 6A1, 6A2✿

sixty (60) *num.* šezdèset 5A1

skeleton *n.* kòstur 17A3a

sketch *n.* crtánje 10A3

sky *n.* nèbo 6A1

slam *vb.* zàlupiti (P) 17A1a

Slav *n.* Slàven [B,S] Slòven [B,S] 19A3b

Slavic *adj.* slàvenski [B,C] slòvenski [B,S] 9A1, 9A1

Slavic studies slavìstika 13B3

Slavicist *n.* slàvist [B,C] slàvista [B,S]

Slavonia *n.* Slavònija 6🌐

Slavonian *adj.* slàvonski 8A3

sleep *n.* sȁn 17A3a, spávanje 7A3

sleep *vb.* spávati (I) 7A3

sleep over *vb.* prespávati (P) 14A2

sleepy *adj.* pòspan

  I feel sleepy spáva mi se 7A3✿

slender *adj.* tànak 3A3

slenderer *adj.* tànji

Slovene *n.* Slovènac (m., general) Slovènka (f.)

Slovenia *n.* Slovènija 1🌐

Slovenian *adj.* slòvenački [B,S] slòvenski [C] 6🌐

slowly *adv.* pòlako 13A3

sly *adj.* lùkav 20.V

small *adj.* màli 2A2, 11A1✿, màlen 20.V

smaller *adj.* mànji 11A2, 11A1✿

smell *n.* mìris 20.II

smile *n.* òsmeh [E] òsmijeh [J] 20.III

smile *vb.*
    smèšiti se (I) [E] 📖A.III
    smjèšiti se (I) [J] 📖A.III

  flash a smile *vb.*
    òsmehnuti se (P) [E] 📖B.I
    òsmjehnuti se (P) [J] 📖B.I

smoke *n.* dìm 20.II

smoke *vb.*
    pùšiti (I) 12A2; pòpušiti (P) 20.V

smoker *n.* pùšač 12A2

smoking *n.* pùšenje 20.V

smooth *adj.* glàdak

smoother *adj.* glàđi

snake *n.* zmìja 5A1

snow *n.* snȇg [E] snijȇg [J] 14A2

so (= in such a manner) *adv.* tàko 3A1

  so-so tàko-tàko 3A1

so (= then, thus) *conj.* pà 7A2

so many *adv.* tòliko 16A1a

so much *adv.* tòliko 16A1a

soap *n.* sàpun

soap opera sapùnica 📖B.II

soar *vb.* vȉnuti se (P) 15A1

sob *vb.* jecati (I) 17A3a
soccer *n.* fudbal [B,S] nogomet [C] 📖A.I
soccer *adj.*
    fudbalski [B,S] nogometni [B,C] 📖B.I
  soccer player
    fudbaler [B,S] nogometaš [B,C] 📖B.IV
  soccer team
    fudbalski klub [B,S] nogometni klub [B,C]
    📖B.I
social *adj.* društven 19A2b
  social sciences društvene nauke [B,S]
    društvene znanosti [C] 13B3
socialize *vb.* družiti se (I) 📖B.IV
society *n.* društvo
sock *n.* čarapa
sofa *n.* kauč
  three-seater sofa trosed [E] trosjed [J] 20.I
soft *adj.* mek 19A3a, 11A2☿
softer *adj.* mekši 11A2☿
soil *n.* zemlja 5☉
solar system *n.* sunčev sistem [B,S] sunčev
  sustav [C] 6A1
soldier *n.* vojnik 11A2☿, 11A3☿
sole *adj.* jedini 16A2a, 14☺
solely *adv.* jedino
solitude *n.* samoća 18A2a
solve *vb.*
  rešiti (P) 11A1; rešavati (I) [E]
  riješiti (P) 11A1; rješavati (I) [J]
some *adj.* jedni *(pl only)* 3A1, 3A1☿,
  neki 3A3, nekakav 16A1a, pojedini
somebody *n.* neko [B,S] netko [C] 9A3☿
somehow *adv.* nekako 📖B.II
someone *n.* neko [B,S] netko [C] ↦4
  9A3, kogod [B,S] tkogod [C] 16A1b
something *n.* nešto 4A3, 7A1☿, 9A2☿,
  9A3☿
sometimes *adv.* ponekad 7A1, katkada,
  nekad
somewhat *adv.* nešto 📖B.V
somewhere *adv.* negde [E] negdje [J]
  from somewhere odnekud 📖B.III
son *n.* sin 8A1
song *n.* pesma [E] pjesma [J] 5C1
sonnet *n.* sonet 18A3
soon *adj.* skoro 13A3, uskoro 14A4
soothe *vb.* umiriti (P); umirivati (I) 20.I
sophomore *n.* student druge godine
sorrow *n.* tuga 15A1, žalost
sorrowful *adj.* žalostan 10☺
sorry! oprosti oprostite [C] izvini izvinite
  [B,S] 2A1
  feel sorry for *vb.* žaliti (I) 📖A.III
  I'm sorry žao mi je 12A3
sort *n.* vrsta 6A4
soul *n.* duša 17A2a

sound *n.* zvuk 14A4
soup *n.* juha [B,C] supa [B,S] 11A2
sour *adj.* kiseo 6A4
source *n.* izvor 16A2a
south *n.* jug
southern *adj.* južni 4A1
South America *n.* Južna Amerika 4A1
South Slavic *adj.*
  južnoslavenski [C] južnoslovenski [B,S]
  19A3b
  South Slavic studies *n.*
    južnoslavistika 13B3
space (= room) *n.*
  prostor 11A2, prostorija 6A1
space (= cosmos) *n.*
  svemir [B,C,S] 6A1 vasiona [B,S] 6A1
Spain *n.* Španija [B,S] Španjolska [B,C] 4A1
Spaniard *n.*
  Španac (*m., general*) Špankinja (*f.*) [B,S]
  Španjolac (*m., general*) Španjolka (*f.*) [C]
Spanish *adj.* španski [B,S] španjolski [B,C]
  📖B.I
spank *vb.* tući (I) 8☺
sparrow *n.* vrabac 📖A.III
speak *vb.* govoriti (I) 6A4
speak out *vb.*
  progovoriti (P); progovarati (I) 20.IV
special *adj.* poseban 7A4, svojevrstan 20.I
specialty *n.* specijalitet 11A2
specific *adj.* poseban 7A4, specifičan
  📖B.IV, određen 19A1b
spectator *n.* gledalac [B,C,S] 15A1, gledatelj
  [C] (*m., general*) gledateljica [C] (*f.*)
speed *n.* brzina 15A1
spend (money) *vb.*
  trošiti (I); potrošiti (P) 20.IV
spend (time) *vb.*
  provesti (P); provoditi (I) 16A2a
  provesti se (P); provoditi se (I) 9A2
spend the night *vb.* prenoćiti (P) 19A1a
spicier *adj.* ljući
spicy *adj.* ljut 6A4
spider *n.* pauk
spirit *n.* duh 17C1
spoil *vb.* pokvariti (P) 📖B.VII
spoon *n.* kašika [B,S] žlica [C] 14A1
  little spoon *n.*
    kašičica [S] kašikica [B] žličica [C] 14A1
sports *n.* sport [B,S] šport [C] 16A1b
sports jersey *n.* dres 📖B.I
spouse *n.* suprug (*m.*) supruga (*f.*) 7A2
spread *vb.*
  širiti (se) (I); raširiti (se) (P) 16A1b
spring (= season) *n.* proleće [E] proljeće [J]
  in the spring *adv.*
    na proleće [E] na proljeće [J] 9A1

spring *adj.* prolećni [E] proljećni [J] [B/S]
proljetni [B,C] 15A1
   spring cleaning *n.* prolećno spremanje [S]
proljećno spremanje [J] [B/S] proljetno
spremanje [B,C] 15A1
square (in city) *n.* trg
square (in math) *n.* kvadrat
squared (in math) *adv.* na kvadrat
squirrel *n.* veverica [E] vjeverica [J] 📖A.VI
stage *n.* scena
stamp (postage) *n.* marka 2A4
stamp *vb.* (*e.g.* a ticket)
poništiti (P) 13A4; poništavati (I)
stand *vb.* stajati (I) 6A1, 11A4☼
   stand in line stajati u redu 11A4
   keep standing prestajati (P) 14☺
stand up *vb.* stati (P) 11A4, 11A4☼
stanza *n.* strofa 17A1b
star *n.* zvezda [E] zvijezda [J] 6A1
start *vb.* početi (P) 13A2; počinjati (I) 6A2
start out *vb.*
krenuti (P); kretati (I) 9A2
poći (P); polaziti (I) 9A4
state *n.* država 6A1
state (= claim) *vb.* tvrditi (I) 📖B.III
state (= say) *vb.* kazati (I/P) 5A1, 4A1☼,
B.VII ; reći 7A3, 7A3☼, 12A2☼, 12A4☼
statement *n.* iskaz 19A1b, izjava 14A3
station (*e.g.* train, bus) *n.* kolodvor [C] stanica
[B,C,S] 13A4, 5A4☼, 9A3 postaja [C]
20.VIII 9A3 *see also* **bus station, railway
station**
stationery store *n.* papirnica 2A4
stay (= remain) *vb.*
ostati (P) 9A2; ostajati (I) 10A2, 10A2☼
stay (= be a guest) *vb.*
odsesti (P) 16A1a; odsedati (I) [E]
odsjesti (P) 16A1a; odsjedati (I) [J]
stay (= dwell) *vb.* boraviti (I) 16A2a
stay *n.* boravak 9A1
step *n.* korak 16A1a
step *vb.* stupiti (P) 16A2a
stiff *adj.* krut
stiffer *adj.* krući
still *adv.* još 4A3
stir up *vb.*
izmešati (P) [E] 14A1
izmiješati (P) [J] 14A1
stocking *n.* čarapa
stomach (= general abdominal area) *n.*
stomak [B,S] trbuh [B,C] 10A4
stomach (= digestive organ) *n.*
želudac [B,C,S] 10A4
stone *n.* kamen 17A2a
   stones *n.* kamenje (*coll.*) 12A2, 12A2☼
stop by *vb.*

svratiti (P) 14A2; svraćati (I)
stop (= cease doing something) *vb.*
prestati (P) 14☺; prestajati (I) 📖A.VI
stop (= stand still) *vb.* stati (P) 11A2, 15A2☼
stop (bus or tram) *n.* stajalište
stop! *excl.* stani! 15A2☼
storage area (= closet, pantry) *n.* ostava
16A1b
store *n.* dućan [B,C,S] 12A2, radnja [B,C,S]
12A2, prodavaonica [B,C] trgovina [B,C]
12A2 12A2
   self-service grocery store *n.*
samoposluga [B,C] samousluga [S]
📖A.II, 12A2
   store window *n.* izlog
storm *n.* oluja 14A2, vihor 📖A.VII,
nevreme [E] nevrijeme [J]
story *n.* priča 5A1
stove *n.* šporet [B,S] štednjak [B,C] 14A1
straight *adj.* ravan [B,C] pravo [B,S] 13A4
strange *adj.* neobičan 15A1 čudan
strawberry *n.* jagoda 5A1
stream *n.* potok
street *n.* ulica 12A2
strenuous *adj.* naporan 12A2
strict *adj.* strog 6A3
strike *vb.* lupiti (P); lupati (I)
striking *adj.* upečatljiv 19A1b
stroll *n.* šetnja 12A2
stroll *vb.*
prošetati (P) 20.V; šetati (I) 📖B.IV
strong *adj.* jak 14A2, 11A2☼
stronger *adj.* jakši 11A2☼
strudel *n.* štrudla 20.III
struggle *n.* borba ↪4
struggle *vb.* mučiti se
student (elementary or secondary) *n.* đak 5A1,
učenik *(m, general)* 14A4 učenica *(f.)*
student (university) *n.*
student *(m., general)* 1A1, 1A4☼, 10A2
studentica [B,C] studentkinja [B,S] *(f.)* 1A4,
1A4☼
student *adj.* studentski 7A4
study (= completed project) *n.* rad 16A2a,
referat
study, studies (activity, discipline) *n.* studij
[B,C] studije [S] 16A1b, učenje 11A4
study *vb.*
studirati (I) 6A2, učiti (I) 2A1, 2A1☼,
9A2☼, 10A2☼
study *adj.* studijski 9A1
stupid *adj.* glup 2A2, 11A1☼
stupider *adj.* gluplji 11A2☼
stupidity *n.* glupost 13☺
style *n.* stil 20.V
stylistic *adj.* stilski 19A1b

subheading *n.* podnaslov 19A2b
subletter *n.* podstanar 9A3
submit *vb.* (*e.g.* an application)
  predati (P); predavati (I) 16A2a
subside *vb.*
  zamreti (P); zamirati (I) [E] 16A3b
  zamrijeti (P); zamirati (I) [J] 16A3b
subtle *adj.* suptilan 20.V
succeed *vb.*
  uspeti (P) 10A2; uspevati (I) [E] 18A3
  uspjeti (P) 10A2; uspijevati (I) [J] 18A3
successful *adj.*
  uspešan [E] uspješan [J] 📖B.VI
such (a) *adj.* takav 16A3b, ovakav 2A4,
  onakav
suddenly *adv.* odjednom 14A4
sufficient *adj.* dovoljan 11A4
sugar *n.* šećer 7A1
suit (= be agreeable) *vb.* prijati (I) 13A1
suit (= be appropriate) *vb.*
  odgovoriti (P) 10A2; odgovarati (I) 5A1,
  9A3✿
summer *n.* leto [E] ljeto [J] 9A1
  in the summer leti [E] ljeti [J]
  this summer letos [E] ljetos [J]
summer *adj.* letnji [E] ljetni [J] 6A2
summit *n.* vrh 14A1
sun *n.* sunce 6A1
  sunrise *n.* izlazak sunca
  sunset *n.* zalazak sunca
Sunday *n.* nedelja [E] nedjelja [J] 2A1
  on Sundays nedeljom [E] nedjeljom [J]
  7A2
support *vb.* izdržati (P); izdržavati (I) 20.V
sure! *excl.* može 2A1
surface *n.* površina
surprise *n.* iznenađenje 📖B.V
surprise *vb.*
  iznenaditi (P) 20.I; iznenađivati (I) 📖B.III
surrender *vb.* predati se (P); predavati se (I)
survey *n.* anketa 16A1a
survive *vb.*
  preživeti (P); preživljavati (I) [E] 14A3
  preživjeti (P); preživljavati (I) [J] 14A3
swallow (= bird) *n.* lastavica 19A3a
Sweden *n.* Švedska 📖B.II
Swedish *adj.* švedski 📖B.II
sweet *adj.* sladak 1A3
sweeten *vb.* zasladiti (P) 14A1; zaslađivati (I)
sweeter *adj.* slađi
swim *vb.* plivati (I) 18A1a, kupati se 16A3a
swimming *n.* plivanje
  swimming beach kupalište 16A3b
  swimming pool bazen
system *n.* sistem [B,C,S] sustav [C] 6A1
T

table *n.* sto [B,S] stol [C] 6A1, 7A2✿
tactless *adj.* netaktičan 20.IV
tail *n.* rep 📖A.VI
take (in hand) *vb.*
  uzeti (P) ↦6 5A2; uzimati (I) 5A1
take (somewhere) *vb.*
  poneti (P) [E] 16A1a
  ponijeti (P) [J] 16A1a
take (a university course) *vb.* slušati (I) 6A2
take (an exam) *vb.* polagati (I) 6A2, 6A2✿,
  10A2✿
take (somewhere on foot) *vb.* odvesti (P);
  odvoditi (I) 10A4✿
take (somewhere by vehicle) *vb.* odvesti (P)
  10A4č odvoziti (I) 10A4✿
take (= lead) *vb.* voditi (I) 5C1
take away *vb.*
  odneti (P); odnositi (I) [E] 7A3
  odnijeti (P); odnositi (I) [J] 7A3
take off (= commence flight) *vb.*
  poleteti (P) [E] 15A1
  poletjeti (P) [J] 15A1
take shelter *vb.*
  skloniti se (P) 14A2; sklanjati se (I)
talk *vb.* govoriti (I) 6A4, pričati (I) 12A2
tall *adj.* visok 2A2, 3A1✿, 11A1✿, 11A2✿
taller *adj.* viši 11A1✿
task *n.*
  zadaća [B,C] zadatak [B,C,S] ↦4 1A4
tasty *adj.* ukusan 7A1
tavern *n.* gostionica 14A2
taxi driver *n.* taksist [C] taksista [B,S] 11A3
  taxi driving (occupation) taksiranje 11A3
taxi *n.* taksi 11A3
tea *n.* čaj 4A3
teach *vb.* predavati (I) 16A3a
teacher *n.*
  nastavnik *(m., general)* nastavnica *(f.)* 11A3,
  učitelj 5A1 *(m., general)* učiteljica *(f.)* ↦4
  11A2✿
teacher training *n.* pedagogija 13B3
team (sports) *n.* klub 📖B.I, momčad
  12A2✿
team (work project) *n.* ekipa 16A1a
tear (= teardrop) *n.* suza
tear off *vb.* zderati (P) 19A2a
tease *vb.* zezati (I) 📖B.IV
telephone *n.* telefon 8A3
  telephone receiver *n.* slušalica 📖A.VII
telephone *adj.* telefonski 16A2b
television (= programming) *n.* televizija 3A3,
  ¦ 12A2 ¦
television (= set) *n.* televizor ¦ 12A2 ¦
television *adj.* televizijski 📖B.II
tell *vb.* pričati (I) 12A2, kazati (I/P),
  kazivati (I) ↦6 10A1✿

tell (all) *vb.* ispričati (P) 16A1b
temperature *n.* temperatura 16A3a
temple *n.* hram
ten (10) *num.* deset 5A4, 12A1☼
ten (approx.) *num.* desetak 12A1☼
tenant *n.* podstanar 9A3
tender *adj.* nežan [E] nježan [J] 19A1a
tense (grammar) *n.* vreme [E] vrijeme [J] 5A2
  present tense sadašnje vreme [E] sadašnje
  vrijeme [J] 17C1
  future tense buduće vreme [E] buduće
  vrijeme [J] 15A2
  past tense prošlo vreme [E] prošlo vrijeme
  [J] 17C1
tent *n.* šator 19A1b
tenth *adj.* (10th) deseti 10A2, 6A2☼
terrible *adj.* grozan 3A1, strašan 8A1
terribly *adv.* strašno 3A1
terrific *adj.* super 3A1
test (examination) *n.*
  ispit 6A2, kontrolni zadatak 10A2
test (medical) pretraga [B,C] ispitivanje [B,S]
  20.I
testament (= will) *n.*
  oporuka [B,C] testament [B,S] 20.IV
testament (= Biblical) *n.*
  zavet [E] zavjet [J] 17C1
  Old Testament
  Stari zavet [E] Stari zavjet [J] 17C1
  New Testament
  Novi zavet [E] Novi zavjet [J]
testify *vb.*
  svedočiti (I) [E] 📖B.VIII
  svjedočiti (I) [J] 📖B.VIII
text *n.* tekst 17A4
text message *n.* SMS poruka
than *conj.* nego 2A1, 11A2☼, negoli 20.V
thank *vb.* zahvaliti (P) 20.III; zahvaljivati (I)
  [B,C,S] 16A2a
  zahvaliti se (P) 20.III; zahvaljivati se (I)
  [B,S] 16A2a
thanks *n.* hvala 2A4
  thank you very much hvala lepo [E] hvala
  lijepo [J] [B/S] hvala lijepa [J] [C] 2A4
  thanks for asking hvala na pitanju 📖B.I
that *adj.* taj ↦4 1A2, onaj 2A2, 2A2☼,
  3A1☼
that *conj.* da 1A2, 13A2☼, što 12A3,
  12A3☼
that (= which) *conj.* koji 3A3, 12A3☼
that way (= by that path) onuda, tuda
that way (= in that manner) tako 3A1,
  na taj način 10A4
that is odnosno 12A1, t.j.
that's that! gotovo je! 11A1, tako je! 4A2
theater *n.*

theater *adj.*
  kazališni [C] pozorišni [B,S] 16A3a
their, theirs *adj.* njihov 1A2, 3A1☼, 4A2☼
  svoj 5A3, 5A3☼
them *pron.*
  (clitic) ih 2A1, im 6A3
  (full) njih 2A2,, njim njima 6A3
  see also **they**
theme *n.* tema 16A2a
then (= next) *adv.* potom 12A2, zatim 12A2,
  dakle 4A2, te 4☺, onda 3A2
then (= at that point) *adv.*
  onda 3A2, tada 14A1
theology *n.* bogoslovija, teologija 13B3
there (place) *adv.* tamo 1A2, 9A2☼,
  onde [E] ondje [J] 14A2
there (= to there) *adv.* onamo 20.VI, tamo
there (pointing) *adv.* eno 4A4, 4A4☼
thereafter *adv.* onda 3A2, zatim 12A2
therefore *adv.*
  dakle 4A2, shodno tome 18A3
they *pron.* oni, ona, one ↦4
  1A4, 1A2☼ *see also* **them**
thick *adj.* gust 14A4
thicker *adj.* gušći
thief *n.* lopov 11A2☼
thin (*e.g.* ice, nerves, etc.) *adj.*
  tanak 3A3, 11A2☼
thing *n.* stvar ↦4 3A3
think *vb.* misliti (I); pomisliti (P) 3A1, razmišljati (I) razmisliti (P) 8A3, 10A3, 7A2☼
thinner *adj.* tanji 11A2☼
third (1/3) *n.* trećina 12A1, 12A1☼
third (3rd) *adj.* treći 3A1, 6A2☼, 12A1☼
thirsty *adj.* žedan 4A3
thirteen (13) *num.* trinaest 5A1, 12A1☼
thirteenth (13th) *adj.* trinaesti 13A1
thirty (30) *num.* trideset 5A1, 12A1☼
this *adj.* ovaj 1A2, taj ↦4 1A2,
  1A3☼, 2A2☼, 3A1☼
this is ovo je 1A2
this kind *adj.* ovakav 2A4
this way (= in this manner) *adv.*
  ovako 13A3, na taj način 10A4
this way (= by this route) *adv.* ovuda ⌐7.A4 ̣
  📖B.VII
thought *n.* misao ↦4 18A2a
  lost in thought zamišljen 📖B.IV
thought *adj.* misaon 15A1
thoughtful *adj.* zamišljen
thousand *num.*
  hiljada [B,C,S] tisuća [C] 12A1, 12A1☼
  one thousand hiljadu [B,C,S] tisuću [C]
  12A1, 12A1☼
thread *n.* konac 📖A.VIII

three (3) *num.* tri̱ 4A2, 4A2✿, 12A1✿
three (a mixed company) *num.* troje 12A2✿
three (a group of men) *num.* trojica 12A2✿
three hundred *num.* (300) tristo [B,C,S]
    trista [B,S] 12A1✿
threshold *n.* prag 19A1a
thrill *vb.*
    zadi̱viti (P) 15A1; zadivlja̱vati (I) [C]
    zadi̱viti (P) 15A1; zadivlji̱vati (I) [B,S]
thriller *n.* triler 7A3
throat *n.* grlo 18A3
throne *n.*
    pre̱sto̱nica [S] prije̱sto̱lnica [B,C] 16A3b
through *prep.* kroz ↦5 3A2, kroza 16A2a
throughout *prep.* širom 16A3b
throw *vb.* ba̱citi (P); ba̱cati (I) 16A1a
thumb *n.* palac 10A4
thunder *n.* thunder
Thursday *n.* četvṟtak 2A1, 2A1✿
    on Thursdays četvṟtkom 7A2✿
ticket (train, bus, etc.) *n.* ka̱rta 📖A.V
ticket (concert, theater, sports event, etc.) *n.*
    u̱laznica 16A1a
tidy *adj.* u̱redan 9A2
tight *adj.* te̱san [E] tije̱san [J]
tighter *adj.* te̱šnji̱ [E] tje̱šnji̱ [J]
time (point in time or duration) *n.* vre̱me [E]
    vrije̱me [J] 5A2, do̱ba 17A3b
time (instance) *n.* pu̱t 10A1
    three times tri̱ pu̱ta
tiny *adj.* si̱tan 14A1
tire *vb.* umo̱riti se (P); uma̱rati se (I) 📖B.IV
tired *adj.* umo̱ran 10A4
title *n.* na̱slov 17A3b
to *prep.* na 5A2, k, ka 7A3, 7A3✿, u 5A1,
    do 4A4✿, kod [B,S] ↦4
toast (= grilled bread) *n.* tost 7A1
toast (to someone's health) *n.* zdra̱vica
    📖B.VIII
today *adv.* da̱nas 3A1
today's *adj.* da̱našnji̱ 17A2b
toe *n.* prst 10A4
    big toe no̱žni̱ palac 10A4
together *adv.*
    skupa [C] 10A4, zajedno [B,C,S] 2A1
toilet *n.*
    W.C. [B,C,S] 16A1b, za̱hod [B,C] 16A1b
tomato *n.*
    paradajz [B,C,S] ra̱jčica [C] 7A1 5A4✿
tomorrow *adj.* su̱tra 2A1
    day after tomorrow *adv.* preko̱sutra 20.IV
tongue *n.* je̱zik 9A1
tonight *adv.* ve̱čeras 3A1, no̱ćas 13A3
too bad! *excl.* šteta! 13A3
too much *adv.* previše 📖B.III
tooth *n.* zu̱b 9A2, 9A2✿

top *n.* vrh 14A1
topic *n.* te̱ma 16A2a
torch *n.* bu̱ktinja 📖A.III, zublja 18A2a
torment *vb.* mo̱riti 15A1, mu̱čiti
torture *vb.* mu̱čiti
touch *vb.*
    dodi̱rnuti (P); dodi̱rivati (I) 20.II
    be in touch *vb.* ču̱ti se (I/P) 8A3, 8A3✿
        ja̱viti se (P); ja̱vljati se (I) 8A3, 8A3✿
tour *n.* obi̱lažen̲je 16A3b
tour *vb.* obi̱ći (P) 20.IV; obi̱laziti (I) 16A3a
tourist *adj.* turisti̱čki̱ 16A2a
tourist agency *n.* turisti̱čka age̱ncija 16A2a
toward *prep.* prema 11A4, k, ka 7A3
tower *n.* to̱ranj 18A1a, ku̱la 19A3a
town *n.* grad 3A3, varoš [S], mesto [E]
    mjesto [J] 14A2
    small town *n.* gra̱dić 3A3
town square *n.* trg 13A4
toy *n.* i̱gračka 16A1b
trace *n.* tra̱g 20.VII
tradition *n.* tra̱di̱cija 16A2a
traditional *adj.* tradicio̱nalan 19A3b
traffic *adj.* pro̱metan [C] saobra̱ćajni̱ [B,S]
    7A2
traffic accident *n.* pro̱metna̱ ne̱sreća [C]
    saobra̱ćajna̱ ne̱sreća [B,S]
train *n.* vla̱k [C] vo̱z [B,S] 7A2, 5A4✿
trait *n.* crta 10A3
tram *n.* tramva̱j 7A2, 7A2✿
tranquility *n.*
    mi̱r [B,C,S] 7A3 smiraj [C] 20.II
transfiguration *n.* preobra̱žen̲je 17A4
transform *vb.*
    pretvo̱riti (P); pretva̱rati (I) 14A2
transformation *n.* preobra̱žen̲je 17A4
translate *vb.* preve̱sti (P) 15A2; prevo̱diti (I)
    18A3, 10A4✿
translation (activity) *n.* prevo̱đen̲je 18A3
translation (end result) *n.*
    pre̱vod [B,C,S], prije̱vod [C] 18A3
translator *n.* prevo̱dilac [B,S] prevo̱ditelj [C]
    (m., general) 5A3 prevo̱diteljica *(f.)*
transmit *vb.*
    pre̱neti (P); preno̱siti (I) [E] 19A3b, 10A4✿
    pre̱nijeti (P); preno̱siti (I) [J] 19A3b, 10A4✿
transparent *adj.* prozi̱ran 20.I
transpire *vb.* ispasti (P); ispadati (I) 12A1
transport *vb.*
    preve̱sti (P); prevo̱ziti (I) 10A4✿
transportation *n.* pre̱voz [B,C,S], prije̱voz [C]
travel *vb.* puto̱vati (I) 4☀;
    travel through *vb.* proputo̱vati (P) 16A2a
traverse *vb.*
    pre̱ći (P); pre̱laziti (I) [B,C,S] 19A1a
    prije̱ći (P); pre̱laziti (I) [C] 19A1a

treasure *n.* blago 19A3b
treat (*e.g.* to a drink) *vb.* častiti (I/P) 15A1
tree *n.* drvo 📖A.VI
   trees *n.* drveće 12A2✿
treetop *n.* krošnja 📖A.III
tremble *vb.* drhtati (I) 17A3a
triangle *n.* trokut [B,C] trougao [B,S]
trouble *n.* nevolja 19A3a, muka
true *adj.* istinski 20.IV
truly *adv.* doista [B,C,S] 16A2b, fakat [B,C]
  📖B.VII, stvarno [B,C,S] 2A2, zaista
  [B,C,S] 2A2
truth *n.* istina 10A3, zbilja
try *vb.*
  pokušati (P) 11A1; pokušavati (I) 📖B.V
Tuesday *n.* utorak 2A1,
  on Tuesdays utorkom 7A2✿
tulip *n.* lala [S] tulipan [B,C] 📖A.IV
Turk *n.* Turčin *(m., general)* Turkinja *(f.)* ↦4
Turkish *adj.* turski
  Turkish coffee cup *n.* fildžan 14A1
  Turkish coffeepot džezva 14A1
turn *vb.* skrenuti (P) 13A4; skretati (I)
turn around *vb.*
  okrenuti (P); okretati (I) 20.VIII
turn away *vb.*
  odvratiti (P); odvraćati (I) 20.VII
turn on (a device) *vb.*
  uključiti (P); uključivati (I) 16A1b
turn off (a device) *vb.*
  isključiti (P); isključivati (I)
tutor *vb.* poučavati (I) 18A3
twelfth (12th) *adj.* dvanaesti 12A1, 6A2✿
twelve (12) *num.* dvanaest 5A4, 12A1✿
twentieth (20th) *adj.* dvadeseti 20A1
twenty (20) *num.* dvadeset 6A1, 12A1✿
two *num.* (2) dva, dve [E] dvije [J] 4A3,
  4A2✿, 12A1✿
two (pair of males) *num.* dvojica 12A2✿
two (pair, mixed gender) *num.* dvoje 12A2✿
two hundred *num.* (200) dvesto [E] dvjesto [J]
  [B,C,S] dvesta [S] dvjesta [B, S] 12A1✿
type *n.* tip 16A3b

U

ugly *adj.* ružan 2A2
umm (= hesitation sound) ovaj ⌐9A4⌐
umbrella *n.* kišobran
unambiguous *adj.* nedvosmislen 20.VIII
unanimous *adj.* jednodušan 15A1
unblinkingly *adv.* netremice 📖B.VII
uncertainty *n.*
  neizvesnost [E] neizvjesnost [J] 11A4
uncle (= mother's brother) *n.* daidža [B] ujak
  [B,C,S] 5A3, 5A3✿, ⌐5A3⌐
uncle (= father's brother) *n.* amidža [B] stric

[B,C,S] 5A3, 5A3✿, ⌐5A3⌐
uncle (= husband of mother's or father's sister)
  teča [B,S] tetak [B,C,S] 5A3, 5A3✿, ⌐5A3⌐
uncomfortable *adj.* neugodan [B,C] 9A2
unconditional *adj.*
  bezuslovan [B,S] bezuvjetan [B,C]
unconscious *adj.*
  besvestan [E] besvjestan [J] 14A3
unconvincing *adj.*
  neuverljiv [E] neuvjerljiv [J] 20.I
under *prep.* pod ↦5 8A1, 8A4, 8A4✿
underline *vb.*
  podcrtati (P) 18A1b; podcrtavati (I) [C]
  podvući (P) 18A1b; podvlačiti (I) [B,S]
underpants (men's) *n.* gaće
underpants (women's) *n.* gaćice
undershirt *n.* potkošulja
understand (= comprehend) *vb.* razumeti (I/P)
  [E] 7A3, 7A3✿ razumjeti (I/P) [J] 7A3,
  7A3✿
understand (= grasp) *vb.* shvatiti (P) 14A4,
  15A1✿; shvaćati (I)
understand (= get [*colloq.*]) *vb.* **kapirati** (I);
  ukapirati (P) **kužiti** (I); **skužiti** (P)
understanding *n.*
  razumevanje [E] razumijevanje [J] 11A4
undertake *vb.*
  poduzeti (P) 16A1a; poduzimati (I) [B,C]
  preduzeti (P) 16A1a; preduzimati (I) [B,S]
underway *adv.*
  u tijeku [C] u toku [B,S] 📖B.IV
unfortunately *adv.* na žalost, nažalost 12A3
uniform *adj.* jedinstven
union *n.* savez 12A4
unique *adj.* jedinstven 19A3b
unite *vb.* sjediniti (P) 12A4; sjedinjivati (I)
united (= functioning as one) *adj.*
  sjedinjen 12A4
united (= brought together) *adj.*
  ujedinjen 📖B.II
United Nations Ujedinjene Nacije [S]
  Ujedinjeni Narodi [B,C] 📖B.II
United States of America Sjedinjene Američke
  Države 4A1
universe *n.* svemir [B,C,S] vasiona [B,S] 6A1
university *n.* sveučilište [C] univerzitet [B,S]
  6A2, ⌐5A2⌐, ⌐10A2⌐
university *adj.*
  sveučilišni [C] univerzitetski [B,S]
  university department katedra 16A2b,
  odsek [E] odsjek [J] 16A1a
  university school fakultet 5A2, ⌐5A2⌐
unnamed *adj.* neimenovan 19A2b
unpleasant *adj.* neprijatan [B,S] 9A2
unrelenting *adj.* bespoštedan 18A3
untidy *adj.* neuredan 9A2

until *conj.* dok ne *(+ perfective verb)* 10A3
unusual *adj.* neobičan 15A1
up *adv.* gore
up *prep.* uz 20.II
up to *prep.* do ↦5   4A4✿
upper *adj.* gornji 17A4
upstream *adv.* uzvodno 20.V
urban *adj.* gradski 13A4
urge *vb.*
　nagovoriti (P); nagovarati (I) 20.VI
urgent *adj.* hitan 14A1
urine *n.* mokraća
us *pron.*
　(clitic) nas 2A1, nam 6A3
　(full) nas 2A2, nam, nama 6A3
　see also **we**
USA *abbr.* SAD 4A1, 4A1✿
use *n.* uporaba [C] upotreba [B,C,S]   📖B.III
use *vb.* koristiti (I) 17A4, rabiti (I) [C],
　iskoristiti (P) 15A1; iskorištavati (I),
　upotrebiti (P); upotrebljavati (I) [E] 17A1b
　upotrijebiti (P); upotrebljavati (I) [J] 17A1b
useful *adj.* koristan 16A3b
utility bills kirija [B,S] režije [C] 9A3

V

vacation *n.* odmor
valuable *adj.* vredan [E] vrijedan [J] 8A1
value *n.* vrednost [E] vrijednost [J] 13☺
　be of value *vb.*
　vredeti (I) [E] vrijediti (I) [E], valjati (I)
　12A3✿
various *adj.* razni 11A3
vegetables *n.* povrće
vegetarian *adj.* vegetarijanski 11A2
verb *n.* glagol 17A1b
verb, verbal *adj.* glagolski
verdict *n.* presuda 19A2a
verse *n.* stih 17A1b
version *n.* verzija 10A3
very *adv.* vrlo 3A1, jako 3A1, veoma
　20.III
veterinarian *n.* veterinar 11A2✿
via *adv.* preko 8A3, putem
vice president *n.*
　potpredsednik [E] potpredsjednik [J]
video cassette *n.* video 16A1a
video store *n.* videoteka 16A1a
Vienna *n.* Beč 4A1
village *n.* selo ↦4   3A3, 6A1✿
vineyard *n.* vinograd 20.II
violate *(e.g. the law)* *vb.* kršiti (I) 19A2b
violence *n.* nasilje
violent *adj.* nasilan 20.VII
violet *adj.* ljubičast
vision *n.* viđenje 16A3b

visit *n.* poseta [S] posjet [B,C] 16A3b
visit *vb.* obići (P) 20.IV; obilaziti (I) 16A3b,
　odsesti (P); odsedati (I) [E] 16A1a,
　odsjesti (P); odsjedati (I) [J] 16A1a,
　posetiti (P) [E] posjetiti (P) [J] 16A2a,
　gostovati (I)
　be visiting *vb.*
　　biti u gostima 17A4
visitor *n.*
　posetilac [E] posjetilac [J] [B/S] 15A1
　posjetitelj [C] *(m., general)* posjetit-
　eljica [C] *(f.)* 20.III
vocabulary *n.*
　vokabular, leksik [C] leksika [B,S]
vocation *n.* zvanje 11A4
vocative (case) *n.* vokativ
voice *n.* glas 19A2b
Vojvodina *n.* area in northern Serbia 1⦿
Vojvodinian *adj.* vojvođanski 8A3
volleyball *n.* odbojka
vote *n.* glas
vote *v.*
　glasati (I) [B,S]
　glasovati (I) [C]
vulture *n.* lešinar 20.V

W

wait *vb.* čekati (I) 5A2, 5A3✿
wait a bit *vb.*
　sačekati (P); sačekivati (I)   📖B.V
waiter *n.*
　kelner [B,S] konobar [B,C,S] 11A2✿
waitress *n.*
　kelnerica [B,S] konobarica [B,C,S] 11A2✿
wake up *vb.*
　buditi se (I); probuditi se (P) 9A2✿
wake up fully *vb.*
　razbuditi (P); razbuđivati (I) 10A4
waken (someone) *vb.* buditi (I); probuditi (P)
walk *n.* hodati (I) 7A2
wall *n.* zid 4A4
walnut *n.* orah 4A3
want (= desire something) *vb.*
　želeti (I) [E] 2A1, 9A2✿
　željeti (I) [J] 2A1, 9A2✿
want (= require, need, lack, desire, etc.) *vb.*
　infinitive: hteti [E] htjeti [J] ↦6
　　5A2, 5A2✿
　present tense (affirmative): hoću, hoćeš,
　　hoće, hoćemo, hoćete, hoće 5A2
　present tense (negated) neću, nećeš, neće,
　　nećemo, nećete, neće 9A2, 9A2✿
war *n.* rat 12A4
　First World War Prvi svetski rat [E] Prvi
　svjetski rat [J] 12A4, 12A1✿
　Second World War Drugi svetski rat [E]

Drugi svjetski rat [J]   12A4, 12A1☼

ward *n.*
ȍdelenje [E] ȍdjeljenje [J]
ȍdjel *or* ȍdio [C]   20.VII

warm *adj.* topao 4A3

warmth *n.* toplȍta 16A3b

was *vb.* bȉo je, bȉlo je, bȉla je
see under **be**

wash *vb.* prati (I); ȍprati (P) 9A2

wash (someone) *vb.* kȕpati

wash (one's) face *vb.*
ùmiti se (P); umȉvati se (I) 9A2

wastebasket *n.* koš

watch (= observe) *vb.*
glȅdati (I) ↪6   2A2,
posmȁtrati (I) [B,S] 14☺
promȁtrati (I) [B,C] 14☺

watch (= take care) *vb.* pȁziti (I)   📖B.VIII
watch out! *excl.* čȕvaj se! 10A4

watchman *n.* čȕvar 20.VII

water *n.* vȍda 4A3

wave *n.* vȁl [B,C] tȁlas [B,S] 15A1

wave *vb.* mȁhnuti (P); mȁhati (I) 20.VIII

way (= road) *n.* pȕt [B,C,S] ↪6
cèsta [B,C] 14A3

way (= manner) *n.* nȁčin 10A4
(in) that way na tȁj nȁčin 10A4

we *pron.* mȋ ↪4   1A3 *see also* **us**

weak *adj.* slab 5A1

weakness *n.* slabȍst 19A2a

weather *n.* vrȅme [E] vrijème [J] 5A2
weather forecast
vrȅmenska prognȍza 14A2

wedding (= celebration) *n.* svȁdba   📖B.VIII

wedding (= ceremony) *n.*
vènčanje [E] vjènčanje [J]   📖A.IV

Wednesday *n.* srȅda [E] srijèda [J] 2A1
on Wednesdays
srȅdom [E] srijèdom [J] 5A3☼

week *n.* sèdmica [B,S] tjȅdan [C] 5A3,
2A3☼, 5A3☼ nèdelja [E] nèdjelja [J] [B/S]
5A3, 2A3☼, 5A3☼

weekend *n.* vȉkend 5A4, 5A3☼

weekly *adj.*
sȅdmični [B,S] tjȅdni [C] 16A3a
nèdeljni [E] nèdjeljni [J][B/S] 16A3a

welcome *vb.* dȍčekati (P) 5A3

welcome *adj.* dobrodòšao 13A1☼

welcome! (said on someone's arrival) *excl.*
dobro dòšao! dobro dòšla! dobro dòšli!
13A1, 13A1☼

you're welcome (in response to "thank you")
mȍlim lȅpo [E] mȍlim lijȅpo [J] 2A4

welfare *n.*
drùštvena brȉga [B,S] socìjalna skrb [C]

well *adv.* dòbro 2A3

were *vb.* bȉli su bȉla su bȉle su
see under **be**

west *n.* zȁpad 6🌐

western *adj.* zȁpadni

wet *n.* mòkar 18A1a

what *pron.* štȁ [B,S] štȍ [C]   ↪4
1A2, 1A1☼, 6A2☼, 9A3☼, 12A1☼

whatever *adv.* štȍgod, bȉlo štȁ [B,S] bȉlo štȍ
[C]   ⸤18A3⸥

what kind of *adj.* kȁkav 3A3, 3A4☼

when *adj.* kȁd, kàda 5A4, 12A3☼

whenever *adv.* kȁdgod, bȉlo kȁd   ⸤18A3⸥

where (question about location)
gde [E] gdje [J] 4A2, 4A2☼

where (question about destination) kàmo [C]
5A1, kud, kùda [B,C,S] 5A1, gde [E] gdje
[J] [B/S] 5A1   ⸤7.A4⸥

where (question about origin)
òdakle 4A1, 4A1☼

where are you going?
kàmo idȅš? *or* kàmo idȅte [C]
kùda idȅš? *or* kùda idȅte? [B,C,S]
gde idȅš? *or* gde idȅte [E] gdje idȅš? *or* gdje
idȅte [J] [B/S]

wherever *adv.* gde gȍd [E] gdje gȍd [J],
bȉlo gde [E] bȉlo gdje [J] 18A3, ⸤18A3⸥

which *adj.* kòji 3A3, 3A4☼, 12A1☼, 13A4☼

which way? kàmo [C] kòjim pùtem [B,C,S]
kòjim pùtom [C]   ⸤7.A4⸥

while *conj.* dȍk *(+imperfective verb)* 4🌐

whipped cream *n.* šlag

whisper *vb.* šȁpnuti (P); šȁptati (I) 18A1a

whisper *n.* šȁpat
in a whisper šȁpatom, šȁptom 20.VI

whistle *vb.* zvíždati (I) 5C1

white *adj.* beo [E] bijel [J] 2A3, 2A3☼

who *pron.* ko [B,S] tko [C] 1A1, 1A1☼,
2A2☼, 6A2☼, 12A1☼,

who *conj.* kòji 13A4☼

whole *n.* cèlina [E] cjèlina [J] 19A1b

whole *adj.* ceo, cèli [E] cio, cijȇli [J] 7A4

whom *pron.*
kòga, kòme, kòmu, kȋm 2A2, 12A1☼

whose *adj.* čìji 3A3, 3A4☼

why *adv.* zȁšto 2A3, štȍ 📖B.V

wife *n.* žèna 1A3, ⸤5A3⸥

will *n.* vòlja 16A3b

will (= future tense) *vb.* ↪6   9A1☼
(clitic) ću, ćeš, će, ćemo, ćete, će 9A1, 9B1
(full) hòću, hòćeš, hòće, hòćemo, hòćete,
hòće 5A2
(negated) nèću, nèćeš, nèće, nèćemo, nèćete,
nèće 9A2

willow *n.* vŕba 18A1a

wind *n.* vȅtar [E] vjȅtar [J] 14A2

gale-strength wind vihor 📖A.VII

window *n.* prozor 3A2

  window display izlog

wine *n.* vino 4A3

wing (of bird, plane, building) *n.* krilo

wing (of dormitory) *n.* paviljon 12A1

winter *n.* zima 9A1

  in the winter zimi

  this winter zimus

winter *adj.* zimski 6A2

wipe *vb.* brisati (I); izbrisati (P) 10A3

wise *adj.* mudar 8A1, uman 📖B.III, 8A1

wish *vb.*

  želeti (I) 2A1; poželeti (P) [E] 15A1, 4A3✿,
  9A2✿, 13A1✿, 15A1✿

  željeti (I) 2A1; poželjeti (P) [J] 15A1,
  4A3✿, 9A2✿, 13A1✿, 15A1✿

with *prep.* s, sa ↦5 7A1, 7A4✿, kod
  4A2, pri

within *prep.* unutar [B,S] unutar [C]

without *prep.* bez ↦5 4A3

witness *n.* svedok [E] svjedok [J] 20.IV

witty *adj.* duhovit 7A3

wizard *n.* čarobnjak 13A3

wolf *n.* vuk

woman *n.* žena 1A2, 3A2✿, 8A1✿

  young woman devojka [E] djevojka [J] ↦4

women's *adj.* ženski 10.A3, 📖B.IV

wood *n.* drvo 📖A.VI

wooden *adj.* drven 20.V

won't *vb,*

  neću, nećeš, neće, nećemo, nećete, neće
  [B,C,S]

  ne ću, ne ćeš, ne će, ne ćemo, ne ćete, ne će
  [C] 9A2, 9A2✿

word *n.* reč [E] riječ [J] 3A2, 6A1✿, 7A1✿

work (= activity) *n.* rad 16A3b

work (= job) *n.* posao 6A3, 7A2✿, radno
  mesto [E] radno mjesto [J] 11A4

work (= creative achievement) *n.* delo [E]
  djelo [J]

work (= project) *n.* rad 16A2a

work *vb.* raditi (I) 2A1

  start working *vb.*

  proraditi (P); prorađivati (I) 15A1, 15A1✿

work *adj.* radni 11A4

  workplace *n.*

  radno mesto [E] radno mjesto [J] 11A4

work out (= solve) *vb.*

  obraditi (P) 13A3; obrađivati (I)

worker *n.*

  radnik *(m., general)* radnica *(f.)* 11A2✿

world *n.* svet [E] svijet [J] 17A2a

world *adj.* svetski [E] svjetski [J] 12A4

worry *n.* briga 7A1

  don't worry budi bez brige 7A1

worry *vb.* brinuti (I) 13A3,
  zabrinuti (P); zabrinjavati (I) 20.VIII

worse *adj.* gori 11A1✿

worse *adv.* gore

be worth *vb.* valja 12A3✿

would you like... ? želiš li ..., želite li ... [B,C]
  da li želiš ..., da li želite ... [B,S]

would bih, bi, bi, biste, bismo, bi 13A1✿,
  13A2✿

wound *n.* rana 18A1a

wound *vb.* raniti (P); ranjavati (I) 20.V

wrap up (*e.g.* a package) *vb.*
  umotati (P); umotavati 📖A.IV

write *vb.* pisati (I) ↦6 2A1, 2A1✿;
  napisati (P) 10A2, 6A3✿, 11A1✿

write in *vb.* upisati (P); upisivati (I) 20.VIII

writer *n.* pisac 5A3 *(m., general)*
  spisateljica *(f.)* 11A2✿

writing *n.* pisanje 10A4✿

wrong *adj.* kriv 18A2b

Y

yard *n.* dvorište 📖A.VI

year *n.* godina *(abbr. g.)* 6A2, 12A3✿,
  12A4✿

  1924 g. in the year 1924

  for years godinama 7A2, 7A2✿

  (for) a year godinu dana 6A2

  year of birth godište 12A3, 12A3✿

yell at length *vb.* izvikati se (P); izvikivati se
  (I) 20.VII

yellow *adj.* žut 2A3

yes da ↦4 1A2, 1A2✿, 9A2✿

  yes? molim? 2A1

yesterday *adv.*

  juče [B,S] jučer [C] 6A3

  the day before yesterday

  prekjuče [B,S] prekjučer [C]

yesterday's *adj.* jučerašnji 20.VIII

yet *adv.* još 4A3

you (= sg, informal) *pron.*

  (subj.) ti 1A1, 1A1✿

  (obj. clitic) te 2A1, ti 6A3

  (obj. full) tebe 2A2, tebi 6A3, tobom 7A1

you (= pl or sg.polite) *pron.*

  (subj.) vi 1A3

  (obj. clitic) vas 2A1, vam 6A3

  (obj. full) vas 2A2, vam, vama 6A3

you (impersonal subject of sentence)
  see 14A1✿

you're welcome molim! 2A4

young *adj.* mlad 7A2, 5A1✿, 11A2✿

younger *adj.* mlađi 11A2✿

your, yours *adj.*

  (sg, familiar) tvoj 1A2

  (pl, polite) vaš 1A2

youth (= abstract idea) *n.*   mlad<u>o</u>st
youth (= the younger generation) *n.*   òmladina
  16A1b
Yugoslavia *n.*   Jug<u>ò</u>sl<u>a</u>vija   17A4

Z
Zagreb *n.*   Z<u>à</u>greb
Zagreb resident *n.*
  Z<u>à</u>grepčanin *(m., general)*
  Z<u>à</u>grepč<u>a</u>nka *(f.)*
Zagreb *adj.*   z<u>à</u>grebačk<u>i</u>   6A2
zebra *n.*   zèbra
zero *n.*   nula
zoo *n.*   z<u>ò</u>ološk<u>i</u> vrt   15A1

ꙅ Sources of illustrations

Index

baviti se (usage with instrumental) 167
Bazdulj, Muharem 62, 347-357
Bećković, Matija 295
Beograde, dobro jutro (by Dušan Radović) 111, 232
"Bio jednom jedan lav" – Dušan Radović 149
biti
    as past tense auxiliary 82, 143
    bilo (indefinite) 283
    budem form 68
    full paradigm 339
    in passive sentences 219
    present tense long form 7
    present tense short form 2
    use in phrase 'once upon a time' 148
Body-ache sentences 152
Body-part names 152
bojati se (usage with genitive) 66, 147
bok 1
bolan, bona 133
Bosnia
    cultural traditions 269, 270
    history 276
    map 61
Bosnian
    alphabet use in 1
    accusative pronouns in 21
    aorist use in 189
    form of in this book 69
    ijekavian in 21
    infinitive meaning, expression of 21, 69, 101, 134
    introductions 198
    longer adjectives in 54
    question formation in 3
    slang (syllable switching) 355
    spelling of foreign names in 5, 47, 192
    spelling rules shared with C 128
    spelling rules shared with S 130
    use of *trebati* in 164, 170
    vocabulary shared with C (but not S) 7, 70, 103, 128, 164-165, 184
    vocabulary shared with S (but not C) 2, 7, 23, 38, 64, 70, 82, 103, 104, 105, 132, 164-165, 179, 184, 185
    vocabulary specific to 23, 68, 70, 133, 216, 263
Bosnian, Croatian, Serbian Grammar xii, xiii, 1, 359
Bošnjak vs. *Bosanac* 7
brati
    full paradigm (type 10) 339
bre 133
budem 68
    with exact future 187
Capitalization, see **Spelling**

Car Dušan 291, 292
Cases of nouns 20
ciao 1
Clitics
    and word order 21, 86, 128, 130, 145
    clitic forms of *biti* 2, 143, 198
    clitic forms of *hteti* [E] *htjeti* [J] 128
    object pronouns 21, 22, 85
Code of Laws – Emperor Dušan 291, 292
Collective nouns 185
Comparison
    of adjectives 160-161, 163-164
    of adverbs 164
    superlatives (with *naj-*) 160-161, 163-164
    usage (comparison 'than') 164
    used with *sve* 235
Conditional mood 198, 203
    conditional in toned-down statements 201
    conditional of politeness 198
    conditional of purpose 203
    conditional sentences ('if A then B') 203
    conjunctions (*ako, kad, da*) 203
Conjugation
    general 1, 21, 54
    predicting conjugational forms 142
    specific types 25, 27, 37, 54
    sample paradigms 333-339
Conjunctions
    ako 203, 206
    and aspect meaning 83
    and question words 48
    compound conjunctions 206
    da 21, 201, 203, 206
    kad 206
    kao što 48
    koji (relative conjunction) 180, 206
    meaning 'before' and 'after' 206
    meaning 'than' 164
    nego 164, 206
    ni ... ni 70
    što 187, 206
    što in 'what' clauses 132
    vs. prepositions 206
Consonant shifts
    see also under **Softening of consonants**
    caused by fleeting vowels (assimilation) 23
Counting form 52, 179, 185
Counting on fingers 64
Crna hronika [B,S] *Crna kronika* [C] 223, 231
Croatia
    literary traditions 110, 285
    map 96
Croatian
    accusative pronouns in 21
    adjectives, form and usage of 25, 50, 54
    alphabet use in 1

Croatia 96
  Montenegro 78
  rivers 46
  Serbia 78
gledati
  full paradigm (type 1) 333
Glossaries
  Abbreviations and symbols used in the
    glossaries 389
  BCS-English 391-452
  English-BCS 453-496
  How to use the BCS glossary 385-387
  How to use the English glossary 388
-god (particle) 283
Gospođica (by Ivo Andrić) 167
Grades (marks in school) 145
Grammar terms (BCS forms of) 262, 266, 268
Guide for Teachers xiii
Guide for Students xii
hajde 103
historija vs. *istorija, povijest* 263
hteti [E] *htjeti* [J] 66
  as future auxiliary 128
  full paradigms 338
  meaning 'want' 66, 130
  negated forms 66, 130
Ijekavian xvii, 21
  and past tense forms 143
  and the number 'two' 52
  in Montenegrin 139, 296
  in Serbian 21, 139
  spelling of *-dj-* 96
  words ending in *-o* 25
ima and *nema* 66, 143
Imperative 103
  forms and usage 103
  in politeness formulas 27
  meaning expressed by infinitive 218
  negative imperative 101
Imperfect tense 189, 265
Imperfective *see under* Aspect
Impersonal sentences 219
  relation to passive 219
  past tense of 219
Inclinational *see under se-*verbs
Indefinite articles in English
  and short adjectives 37
Indirect discourse 201
Infinitives
  and formation of passive participles 160
  and formation of past tense 82, 143
  and the future tense 128, 134
  endings 21
  optionally expressed as *da* + present tense 21,
    69, 134
  role in determining verb type 142

used in giving instructions 218
  variant spellings of in future tense 128
Instrumental case 98, 101
  consonant softening in 98, 114
  expressing means of communication 117
  in adverbial expressions 101
  of pronouns 98
  plural forms 114
  singular forms 98
  used to express means 105
  with a second object 167
  with *baviti se* 167
  with *činiti* 167
  with prepositions 99, 101, 118, 331
  with *smatrati* 167
Interrogative, see **Pronouns, Pronominal**
  adjectives, Questions
Introducing oneself 198
Invitations and paying 142
Irregular plurals
  body part names 152
  plural form / singular meaning 80
  singular form / plural meaning 115
istorija vs. *historija, povijest* 263
išta 98
'It is ...' sentences 54
iznajmiti vs. *unajmiti* 132
jao 133
javiti se 117
je (**3rd sg of** *biti*) 143
  and *ju* 21, 143
  and word order 86, 143, 145
jedan 37
jedan drugi 164, 237
je li, jel', jel'da, jel'te 133
jesti 54
  full paradigm (type 13) 337
"Jesenje veče" – A. G. Matoš 277
joj (exclamation) 133
ju (alternate fem.sg. accusative)
  existence of 21
  usage in past tense 143
Judita (by Marko Marulić) 285
kad 203, 206
kahva vs. *kafa* 216
Karadžić, Vuk Stefanović 295
kazivati
  full paradigm (type 8b) 335
Kinship terms 68
Ključ / Key to A exercises 367-382
ko vs. *tko* 2, 83
koji (usage in relative clauses) 180, 206
  paradigmatic forms 326
kolodvor 132
Kora (by Vasko Popa) 288, 299
Kosovo, boundaries of 12